TRAUMA NURSING CORE COURSE

PROVIDER MANUAL
SEVENTH EDITION

Emergency Nurses Association
Des Plaines, IL

ENA®
EMERGENCY NURSES ASSOCIATION
SAFE PRACTICE, SAFE CARE

Foreword

This 7th Edition of TNCC was a monumental undertaking, but a labor of love, guided by the vision of making a difference in the lives of others. Saving lives and improving the quality of care for trauma patients was our ultimate mission and goal.

My sincere thanks for a job well done goes out to the outstanding TNCC 7th Edition workgroup, authors, peer reviewers, pilot course team, and ENA staff, who were involved in bringing this project to its culmination.

We thank the thousands of TNCC course directors and instructors who will teach this revision, as well as all of the nurses who will dedicate time from their busy lives to take this course and improve their trauma knowledge and skills.

With my deepest gratitude,

Diane Gurney

Diane Gurney, MS, RN, CEN, FAEN
TNCC Revision Work Group Chairperson and Lead Editor

Dedication

The 7th Edition of TNCC is dedicated to nurses who care for injured patients, anywhere and everywhere. You all hold our profound respect.

Table of Contents

Table of Contents

Chapters

Acknowledgements

The Emergency Nurses Association would like to extend its appreciation to the TNCC Seventh Edition Revision Work Team for the development and implementation of the Trauma Nursing Core Course (TNCC).

TNCC Seventh Edition Revision Work Team

Lead Editor
Diane Gurney, MS, RN, CEN, FAEN
Hyannis, MA

Work Team Members
Jami Blackwell, BSN, RN, CEN
Trauma Program Manager
Cox Health
Springfield, MO

Joseph S. Blansfield, MS, RN, ANP-BC
Trauma and Acute Care Surgery Program Manager
Boston Medical Center
Boston, MA

Melanie Crowley, MSN, RN, CEN
Clinical Manager, Trauma Administration
Northridge Hospital Medical Center
Northridge, CA

Dawn McKeown, RN, CEN, CPEN
Trauma Program Manager
LSU Health Shreveport
Shreveport, LA

Course Administration Faculty Liaison
Ray Bennett, BSN, RN, CEN, CFRN, CTRN, NREMT-P
SCTU Coordinator, Mobile Health Services
Robert Wood Johnson University Hospital
New Brunswick, NJ

Board Liaison
Kathleen Carlson, MSN, RN, CEN, FAEN
Hampton, VA

Curriculum Consultant
Vicki Patrick, MS, RN, ACNP-BC, CEN, FAEN
Clinical Instructor/Lead Teacher
University of Texas Arlington College of Nursing
Arlington, TX

ENA Staff Liaisons
Paula M. Karnick PhD, ANP-BC, CPNP
Director, Institute of Emergency Nursing Education

Marlene L. Bokholdt, MS, RN, CPEN
Nursing Education Editor

Renée Herrmann, MA
Copy Editor

Wilson Santiago, MEd
Instructional Designer

Bree Sutherland, CNM
eLearning Manager

ENA Staff Support
Maureen Howard, BS
Member and Course Services, Director

Susan Rajkovich, MBA
Marketing, Director

Lauri Grzelak, BA
Marketing Specialist

Acknowledgements

Contributing Authors

Pamela A. Assid, MSN, RN, NEA-BC, CEN, CNS, CPEN
Clinical Manager, Emergency Department
St. Francis Medical Center
Colorado Springs, CO
Chapter 22

Cynthia Blank-Reid, MSN, RN, CEN
Trauma Clinical Nurse Specialist
Temple University Hospital
Philadelphia, PA
Chapter 20

Marlene L. Bokholdt, MS, RN, CPEN
Nursing Education Editor
Emergency Nurses Association
Des Plaines, IL
Chapters 8, 20

Cynthia M. Bratcher, BSN, RN, CEN
Emergency Department Charge Nurse, Clinical Specialist II
HCA Greenview Regional Hospital
Bowling Green, KY
Chapters 12, 14

Audrey S. Cornell, PhD, RN, CNE
Clinical Associate Professor
Western Kentucky University
Bowling Green, KY
Chapter 8

Cathy Provins-Churbock, PhD, RN, APRN-BC, CCNS, CCRN
Emergency Service Acute Care Nurse Practitioner
Apollo MD/Wellstar Health System
Atlanta, GA
Chapter 15

Melanie Crowley, MSN, RN, CEN
Clinical Manager, Trauma Administration
Northridge Hospital Medical Center
Northridge, CA
Chapter 13

Michael W. Day, MSN, RN, CCRN
Trauma Care Coordinator
Providence Sacred Heart Medical Center & Children's Hospital
Spokane, WA
Chapter 11

Darcy Egging, MS, RN, C-ANP, CEN
Nurse Practitioner
Valley Emergency Care, Inc., & Cadence Delnor Hospital
Geneva, IL
Chapter 10

Robin Goodman, MSN, RN, CPEN
Registered Nurse Lead, Emergency Department
Pediatric Liaison Nurse
Children's Hospital Los Angeles
Los Angeles, CA
Chapter 17

Diane Gurney, MS, RN, CEN, FAEN
Hyannis, MA
Chapters 1, 5, 6, and 21

Mary Margaret Healy, MA, BSN, CEN, CPEN
Nurse Manager, Emergency Department
Lakeview Hospital
Stillwater, MN
Staff Nurse
Regions Hospital
St. Paul, MN
Chapter 21

Susan M. Hohenhaus, LPD, RN, CEN, FAEN
Executive Director, ENA and ENA Foundation
Des Plaines, IL
Chapter 2

Catherine Jagos, MSN-Ed, RN
Education Specialist, Emergency Department, 1B Short Stay Unit
Dignity Health Mercy Gilbert Medical Center
Gilbert, AZ
Chapter 18

B. Alex Markwell, MSN, MHA, MBA, CEN
Education Specialist
Morton Plant Mease Health Care
New Port Richey, FL
Chapter 23

Jill C. McLaughlin, MSN, RN, CEN, CPEN
Staff RN
Orange Regional Medical Center
Middletown, NY
Chapter 9

Jessie M. Moore, MSN, APRN
Program Manager, Metabolic & Bariatric Surgery
Yale New Haven Hospital
New Haven, CT
Chapter 19

Patricia Nierstedt, MS, RN, CEN
Trauma Program Manager
Hackensack University Medical Center
Hackensack, NJ
Chapter 2

Deborah A. Pentecost, MBA, BSN, RN
Trauma Program Manager
South Shore Hospital
Weymouth, MA
Chapter 7

Robin S. Powers-Jarvis, MS, RNC, CCRN, CEN
Staff Nurse/Adult ED
St. Mary's Medical Center
West Palm Beach, FL
Chapter 23

Sean G. Smith, BSN, RN, NREMT-P, FP-C, C-NPT, CCRN-CMC-CSC, CEN, CFRN, CPEN
Clinical Educator/Staff RN
Granville Medical Center
Critical-Care Professionals International
Durham, NC
Project Medishare, Hospital Bernard Mevs
Haiti
Chapter 7

Rebecca A. Steinmann, APN, CCNS, CCRN, CEN, CPEN, FAEN
Clinical Nurse Specialist, Emergency Services
Ann & Robert H. Lurie Children's Hospital of Chicago
Chicago, IL
Chapter 16

Judy Stevenson, MS, RN-BC, CCRN, CEN, CPEN, CSRN
Clinical Instructor, Emergency Department
St. John Medical Center
Tulsa, OK
Chapter 24

Tiffiny Strever, BSN, RN, CEN
Trauma Program Manager
Maricopa Medical Center
Phoenix, AZ
Chapter 3

Arvie M. Webster, MSN, RN, CEN
Trauma Program Manager
University of Arizona Medical Center
Tucson, AZ
Chapter 12

Angela M. Westergard, MSN, MBA, RN, CEN
Patient Care Manager
University of Arizona Health Network
University Campus Emergency Services
Tucson, AZ
Chapter 5

Aaron Wolff, BSN, RN, CEN
President
Vital Operations Consulting
Redding, CA
Chapter 4

Acknowledgements

International Contributing Authors

Australia
Liz Cloughessy, AM, MHM, RN, FAEN
Executive Director
Australian College of Emergency Nursing
Glenwood, NSW, Australia
Chapter 3

Canada
Darcie Goodman, RN, BScN, MPA Candidate 2015
Injury Prevention Program Lead Vancouver Acute
Vancouver Coastal Health Authority
Vancouver, B.C. Canada
Chapter 3

Tracey Taulu, RN BScN CCRN MHS
Director of Operations
University of British Columbia Hospital
Vancouver, British Columbia, Canada
Chapter 3

Heather Wong, RN, CCRN BSN
Trauma Coordinator
Vancouver General Hospital
Vancouver, British Columbia, Canada
Chapter 3

Hong Kong
Peggy Wun Man Lee, RN
Nurse Manager
Hospital Authority
Quarry Bay, Hong Kong
Chapter 3

The Netherlands
Joop Breuer, RN, CEN
Staff Nurse
Leiden University Medical Center
Rijnsburg, Netherlands
Chapter 3

Els Michies, RN
Staff Nurse
MMC Veldhoren
Eindhoven, Netherlands
Chapter 3

South Africa
Col. Theo Ligthelm, RN
Staff Officer Military Health Operations
South African Military Health
Gauteng, South Africa
Chapter 3

Rene Grobler, RN
Trauma Programme Manager
Netcare Milpark Hospital
Southcrest, Alberton, South Africa
Chapter 3

Ltc. Myoung Ran Yoo, RN
Director of Nursing Education Department
Armed Forces Nursing Academy
Daejeon City, South Korea
Chapter 3

Sweden
Agneta Brandt, RN, CRNA, CNE, MSN
Specialist Nurse
Organization Swedish Trauma Association
Stockholm, Sweden
Chapter 3

United Kingdom
Gabrielle Lomas, RN, BSc (Hons)
Matron, Emergency Medicine
Salford Royal Hospital Foundation Trust
Salford, Manchester, UK
Addendum: Chapter 3

Jill Windle, RN, MSc, FRCN
Lecturer Practitioner in Emergency Nursing
Salford Royal Hospital Foundation Trust
Salford, Manchester, UK
Addendum: Chapter 3

Content Reviewers

Joop Breuer, RN, CEN
Committee on Trauma Nursing (Netherlands)
Leiden University Medical Centre Emergency Department
Leiden, The Netherlands

Liz Cloughessy, AM, MHM, RN, FAEN
Executive Director
Australian College of Emergency Nursing Ltd.
Sydney, Australia

Maureen Curtis Cooper, BSN, RN, CEN, CPEN, FAEN
Registered Nurse
Boston Medical Center Pediatric Emergency
Boston, MA

Chris Dellinger, BSN, RN
Director of Trauma Services
Camden Clark Medical Center
Parkersburg, WV

Renee de Prazer, BSc, GradCertClinNurs
Staff Development Educator, Critical Care Division
Royal Perth Hospital
Perth, Australia

Nancy Stephens Donatelli, MS, RN, CEN, NE-BC, FAEN
Project Coordinator
Shenango Presbyterian Senior Care
New Wilmington, PA

Susan Drummond, MSN, RN, C-EFM
Associate in Obstetrics
Vanderbilt University Medical Center
Nashville, TN

Margaret Dymond, BSN, RN
Clinical Nurse Educator
University of Alberta Hospital/Stollery Childrens Hospital
Edmonton, Alberta, Canada

Sheila D. Early, BScN, RN
Coordinator/Instructor, Forensic Health Sciences
British Columbia Institute of Technology
Burnaby, British Columbia, Canada

Faye P. Everson, RN
Clinical Educator
University of Massachusetts Memorial Medical Center
Worcester, MA

Marcia Gamaly, MSN, MHA, RN-BC, CEN
Clinical Nurse Educator
St. Mary Medical Center
Langhorne, PA

Amber Greeno, MSN, APRN, CPN, CPNP-AC
Trauma Program Manager
Monroe Carell Jr. Children's Hospital at Vanderbilt
Nashville, TN

J. Jeffrey Jordan, MS, MBA, RN, CNE, EMT-LP, FAEN
RN to BSN Coordinator/Instructor
East Central University
Ada, OK

Alyssa Kelly, MSN, RN, CEN, CNS
Nursing Education Editor
Emergency Nurses Association
Des Plaines, IL

Marge Letitia, BSN, RN, CEN, EMT-P
Trauma Performance Improvement Nurse
St. Francis Hospital and Medical Center
Hartford, CT

Cindy Lefton, PhD, RN
Clinical Education Specialist, Trauma and Acute Care
Surgery
Barnes-Jewish Hospital
St. Louis, MO

Christopher McKay, RN
Resource Nurse, Emergency Department
Beth Israel Deaconess Hospital
Needham, MA

Monique McLaughlin, MN, NP(F)
Emergency Nurse Practitioner
Vancouver General Hospital Emergency Department
Vancouver, British Columbia, Canada

Acknowledgements

Content Reviewers continued

Benjamin E. Marett, MSN, RN-BC, CEN, CCRN, NE-BC, FAEN
Director of Education
Piedmont Medical Center
Rock Hill, SC

Loretta Martin, MSN, RN, CEN
Clinical Educator
Sentara Norfolk General Hospital
Norfolk, VA

Yvonne Michaud, MSN, RN
Nurse Director, Trauma and Burn Program
Brigham and Women's Hospital
Boston, MA

Lynn D. Mohr, MSN
Women, Children, and Family Nursing Instructor
Program Coordinator, Pediatric/Neonatal Clinical Nurse
Specialist Program
Rush University College of Nursing
Chicago, IL

Annabelle Pearcey, BAppSci (Nursing), RN
Clinical Nurse Specialist, Emergency Department
Armadale-Kelmscott Memorial Hospital
Perth, Western Australia

N. Erin Reeve, BSN, CEN, FCN
Staff Registered Nurse
Winchester Medical Center Emergency Department
Winchester, VA

Terri M. Repasky, MSN, RN, CEN, EMT-P
Clinical Nurse Specialist, Trauma and Emergency Services
Tallahassee Memorial Hospital
Tallahassee, FL

Cheryl Riwitis, MSN, RN, FNP-BC, CEN, CFRN, EMT-B
Critical Care Transport Nurse
Life Line 2-Muncie
Muncie, IN

Christine Russe, MSN, RN, CEN, CPEN
Clinical Education Specialist
Texas Health Presbyterian Hospital Plano
Plano, TX

Carl Schramm, BSN, RN-BC, EMT
Registered Nurse
Huntington Hospital
Huntington, NY
Hazardous Materials Specialist (Retired)
New York City Fire Department
New York, NY

Joan Somes, PhD, RNC, CEN, CPEN, NREMT-P, FAEN
Staff Nurse/Department Educator
St. Joseph's Hospital
St. Paul, MN

Rebecca A. Steinmann, APN, CCNS, CCRN, CEN, CPEN, FAEN
Clinical Nurse Specialist, Emergency Services
Ann & Robert H. Lurie Children's Hospital of Chicago
Chicago, IL

Nancy G. Stevens, DNP, MSN, APRN-BC, CEN, FAEN
Nurse Practitioner, Clinical Educator
Erlanger Health Systems
Chattanooga, TN

Madonna R. Walters, MS, BSN, RN
Trauma Program Manager
Allegiance Health
Jackson, MI

William White, MS, BSN, RN, CFRN
Department Nursing Director
United States Army
Honolulu, HI

Darlene S. Whitlock, RN, APRN, CEN, CPEN, EMT
Independent Consultant, Trauma Program Development
Silver Lake, KS

Mindy B. Yorke, MSN, ARNP, FNP-BC, CEN, CPEN
Staff Nurse, Emergency Department
Wuesthoff Health System Melbourne
Melbourne, FL

A special thanks to those who worked on the previous editions of TNCC.

TNCC Sixth Edition

Beth Broering, MSN, RN, CEN, CCRN
Melody Campbell, MSN, RN, CEN, CCRN, CCNS
Laura Favand, MS, RN, CEN
Andrew Galvain, APRN, BC, CEN
Reneé Holleran, PhD, RN, CEN, CCRN, CFRN, CTRN, FAEN

TNCC Fifth Edition

Liz Cloughessy, AM, MHM, RN, FAEN
Mary E. Fecht Gramley, PhD, RN, CEN
K. Sue Hoyt, MN, RN, CEN
Barbara Bennett Jacobs, MPH, MS, RN
Louise LeBlanc, BSCN, RN, ENC(c)
Ginger Morse, MN, RN, CCRN, CEN, CS, PhDc
Vicki Patrick, MS, RN, ACNP-BC, CS, CEN
Jill Windle, BA, RN

TNCC Fourth Edition

Barbara Bennett Jacobs, MPH, MS, RN
Pam Baker, BSN, RN, CEN, CCRN
Peggy Hollingsworth-Fridlund, BSN, RN
Ginger Morse, MN, RN, CEN, CCRN
Vicki Patrick, MS, RN, CEN
Mark Parshall, MSN, RN, CS, CEN
Jean Proehl, MN, RN, CEN, CCRN

TNCC Third Edition

LTC Ruth Rea, PhD, RN, CEN
Karen Kernan Bryant, MSN, RN, CEN
Sharon Gavin Fought, PhD, RN
Jane Goldsworth, BSN, RN, CEN
Mary Martha Hall, MSN, RN, CEN
K. Sue Hoyt, MN, RN, CEN
Barbara Bennett Jacobs, MPH, RN
Linda Larson, MS, RN, ENP, CEN
Marguerite Littleton, RN, DNSc
Lynne Nemeth, MS, RN, CEN
Cecelia Irene Paige, MSN, RN, CEN
Vicki Patrick, MS, RN, CEN
Jacqueline Rhoads, PhD, RN, CEN, CCRN
Judy Selfridge, MSN, RN, CEN
Jill Schoerger Walsh, MS, RN

TNCC First and Second Editions

Ruth Rea, MS, RN, CEN
Sharon Gavin Fought, PhD, RN
Mary Martha Hall, MSN, RN, CEN
Linda Larson, MS, RN, ENP, CEN
Marguerite Littleton, RN, DNSc
Lynne Nemeth, MS, RN, CEN
Cecelia Irene Paige, MSN, RN, CEN
Judy Selfridge, MSN, RN, CEN

Chapter 1 • Trauma Nursing and the Trauma Nursing Core Course

Diane Gurney, MS, RN, CEN, FAEN

Objectives

Upon completion of this chapter, the learner will be able to:

1. Define trauma nursing.

2. Discuss the philosophy of trauma nursing.

3. Describe the purpose of the Trauma Nursing Core Course.

Preface

It is **strongly** suggested that the learner read the following textbook before attending the Trauma Nursing Core Course (TNCC). The nursing process serves as the foundation for the construction and comprehension of the format for TNCC, and the nursing process approach is used to direct the care of the trauma patient.

Introduction

Trauma remains a major cause of death for people ages 1 to 44 years.[1] The development of trauma centers, the implementation of integrated trauma systems, and the systematic and standardized approach to care have been instrumental in saving lives and improving outcomes for those affected by trauma.[2] Trauma nurses are essential in order to meet the complex needs of the trauma patient and to deliver care to produce the best possible outcomes. Excellence in trauma nursing care can contribute to optimal patient outcomes and the prevention of complications, long-term consequences, or death.

Trauma Nursing

Trauma nursing occurs wherever nurses care for injured patients. It takes place throughout the continuum of care from the prehospital environment through the resuscitation, surgery, recovery, rehabilitation, and return to the community. Trauma nursing includes advocating for patient care—including local and national legislature—providing prevention education, and conducting research to further practice. Trauma nursing occurs in nursing schools, prehospital settings, trauma centers, rural hospitals, clinics, homes, and military environments.

The practice of trauma nursing employs a standardized, systematic approach to care. It involves core knowledge derived both from scientific sources and personal experience. Trauma nursing is care-specific and is not dependent on specialized care environments.

The Discipline of Trauma Nursing

Nursing is a body of knowledge based in science and philosophy. It is a professional discipline in that it involves the element of clinical practice. It is a science based on evidence and research, and trauma nurses base much of their practice on this science and technology. The trauma nurse gains the appropriate knowledge base and assessment skills to recognize the trauma patient and predict injury patterns and severity. The trauma nurse uses critical application skills to manage unique patient situations and the moral agency to advocate for excellence in patient care, even in the face of cultural and administrative obstacles.[3,4]

The Wolf Model is a useful framework examining the components of the nurse and the environment in which one practices. The model is an open environmental model comprised of three elements that inform and influence each other (Fig. 1-1):

- The core elements are specific to each nurse, including:

  ○ A solid knowledge base

  ○ Critical application (the ability to recognize a problem by critical cues, integrate findings, and recognize resources)

  ○ Moral agency (the deliberate and persistent search for information to determine the presence or absence of critical cues in the face of environmental challenge; action for the good of the patient in light of the problem)

- The immediate elements include unit culture, nurse–provider relationships, and the environment in which the nurse practices. Communication and relationships between nurses and providers were found to influence

Figure 1-1. The Wolf Model

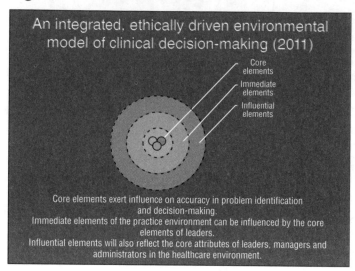

An integrated, ethically driven environmental model of clinical decision-making (2011)

Core elements
Immediate elements
Influential elements

Core elements exert influence on accuracy in problem identification and decision-making.
Immediate elements of the practice environment can be influenced by the core elements of leaders.
Influential elements will also reflect the core attributes of leaders, managers and administrators in the healthcare environment.

With permission from Emergency Nurses Association.

the accuracy of clinical decision making, in that accuracy, to some extent, depended on the provider.[3,4] Another component of clinical judgment was the ability of the nurse to clearly identify problems and their ramifications, and to correctly articulate these in a way to which providers could respond.

- Influential elements encompass the institutional and general healthcare environment with regard to nurse autonomy, support for education, and standards of practice

In terms of trauma nursing, the nurse who is well-trained in trauma nursing skills and assessment may make the correct decisions about the patient; the nurse also functions in an environment, which must foster a teamwork-oriented approach and be supportive of nursing judgment and action for the good of each patient. Environments in which nursing skills are not respected or where there is problematic nurse–provider communication do not allow for a complete expression of nursing clinical judgment and may contribute to less effective patient care.

Therefore, it is important for the trauma nurse to have adequate education in the assessment and care of the trauma patient and also skills-based training in communication and teamwork. The environment in which the nurse practices must support advocacy, respect, and care for the good of the patient.

The Philosophy of Trauma Nursing

After analyzing the impact of traumatic injury nationally and internationally, as well as the potential for positive contributions by professional nurses in the care of the trauma patient, the Emergency Nurses Association (ENA) developed the following belief statements:

- The optimal care of the trauma patient is best accomplished within a framework in which all members of the trauma team use a systematic, standardized approach

- Emergency nurses are essential members of the trauma team. Morbidity and mortality of trauma patients can be significantly reduced by educating nurses to competently provide care to trauma patients.

- ENA and its constituents have the responsibility to facilitate trauma-related continuing education opportunities for nurses who provide care to trauma patients

- ENA supports injury prevention and control that is collaborative, identifies specific problems within specific populations, utilizes databases, and addresses the three approaches to prevention (engineering/technology, enforcement/legislation, and education/behavioral)

Trauma Nursing Core Course

History

Formulation of those belief statements, together with an identified need for trauma nursing education, led ENA to develop TNCC as a method for identifying a standardized body of trauma nursing based on current knowledge. In 1986, the first course was held in Hawaii to train providers and instructors, and a year later, over 3,000 nurses across the United States (U.S.) completed the provider course. In 1991, the first international courses began when ENA collaborated with nurses from the United Kingdom (UK), and the following year, TNCC was introduced to Australia and Canada.[5] By 1994, 915 provider courses were held across the world in the U.S., Canada, the UK, Australia, and New Zealand. Interest in TNCC continues to grow. TNCC is currently taught in 13 countries with 49,675 nurses attending provider courses in 2012.

Purpose

The purpose of TNCC is to teach registered nurses (RNs) core-level knowledge and psychomotor skills, which are defined as central or key elements of the multidimensional processes involved in the initial assessment and management of injured patients. TNCC also provides a foundation for integrated communication and collaboration in trauma teamwork. The trauma nursing process (TNP) skill station was created to develop and reinforce a systematic and standardized approach for the assessment and interventions of the trauma patient, helping nurses to build a firm foundation and refine skills in trauma nursing. The intent of TNCC is to help the nurse develop a rapid and accurate approach to caring for the trauma patient and ultimately contribute to a decrease in the morbidity and mortality associated with trauma.

Course Description

TNCC consists of lectures, hands-on psychomotor skill stations, and interactive online learning. TNCC is based on the nursing process, which is emphasized through the components of the course. Although many of the trauma care principles are basic in theory, rationale for standard concepts is presented, and underlying critical thinking is included. The chapter content is organized in a consistent format for ease of learning, and redundancy across chapters has been reduced in order to focus on the unique aspects of each system or population. Lectures highlight critical concepts presented in the chapters to reinforce learning of these concepts and the nursing process.

The psychomotor skill stations integrate cognitive knowledge with skill practice in simulated patient situations. Each teaching station scenario highlights a selected patient population experiencing different mechanisms of injury (MOI). This illustrates and emphasizes chapter content for the demonstration of assessment skills and applicable injury management.

Teaching psychomotor skill stations include:
- The TNP
- Airway and ventilation
- Trauma care considerations

New to this edition, interactive online learning reinforces chapter content with case studies and learning activities designed to enhance the learner's knowledge of care principles presented within chapters.

Evaluation of learners consists of a written 50-question multiple choice examination and successful completion of the psychomotor testing station. Only the TNP station is tested; however, skills and knowledge from the other skill stations are incorporated into aspects of the evaluations. These evaluations are designed to assess acquisition of cognitive knowledge, essential psychomotor skills, and critical thinking.

To successfully complete TNCC, the learner must achieve a minimum of 80% on the written examination, actively participate in all psychomotor teaching stations, and

demonstrate all of the critical criteria and a minimum of 70% of all the steps in the psychomotor testing station. Verification status is awarded for a period of four years.

Course Learners

Any nurse involved in the care of trauma patients may benefit from this course. It is expected that the course learner possess a generic nursing knowledge, has an understanding of emergency care terminology and is familiar with standard emergency equipment. The curriculum is designed for new trauma nurse learners to acquire essential knowledge and skills. Post-course mentoring and support will be essential to further develop and master trauma nursing expertise. Experienced trauma nurses will update their learning to validate and improve established practice.

TNCC is officially intended for RNs. Other healthcare providers may attend the course at the discretion of the TNCC course director; however, only RNs (or equivalent as defined in each country) are eligible for verification.

TNCC Provider Manual

The TNCC Provider Manual is designed to serve as a foundation and supplement the lectures, psychomotor skill stations, and interactive online learning. The chapters have been developed in a consistent format:

- **Chapter Objectives:** These provide an emphasis on the most important concepts to guide the learner

- **Anatomy and Physiology Review:** Many chapters give a brief overview of anatomy and physiology for the convenience of the learner. This material will not be covered in the lectures nor tested directly, but as foundational content, it may be the basis for some test questions and skill evaluation steps.

- **Pathophysiology as a Basis for Assessment Findings:** Pathophysiologic concepts are related to the body's response and associated assessment findings

- **Selected Injuries:** The most life-threatening and the most frequently occurring injuries associated with the particular system are presented

- **Nursing Care of the Patient:** The organization of nursing care is based on the nursing process principles of assessment, analysis, planning, implementation, evaluation, and ongoing assessment. For consistency of practice and collaborative teamwork, the initial assessment mnemonic is presented within the overarching concept of process points related to the Advanced Trauma Life Support (ATLS) structure.[6] These process points include:

- Preparation and Triage
- Primary Survey (A,B,C,D,E)
- Resuscitation Adjuncts to the Primary Survey (F,G)
- Reevaluation for Transfer to a Trauma Center
- Secondary Survey (H,I)
- Reevaluation Adjuncts to the Secondary Survey
- Reevaluation and Post Resuscitation Care
- Definitive Care or Transport

- **Emerging Trends:** New to this edition, this section presents evidence-based information and/or research on concepts or approaches to practice that may or may not be yet considered or accepted as standard of practice
- **Summary and References:** Each chapter closes with chapter highlights and a section of current references

The provider manual also include a template for the psychomotor skill teaching station to help learners prepare for these sessions.

Summary

Trauma continues to be a major threat to the health and socioeconomic well-being of individuals, communities, and countries around the world. A coordinated, collaborative, and systematic approach to the initial assessment and management of trauma is essential to ensure optimal outcomes and minimize morbidity and mortality.

ENA believes that the knowledge and skills presented in TNCC will assist professional nurses to systematically assess the trauma patient, to rapidly intervene and/or assist with interventions, and to function within the context of a trauma team. Ongoing commitment and efforts to improve injury surveillance, research, trauma systems development, and governmental support for trauma care and injury prevention remain a top priority.

References

1. Centers for Disease Control and Prevention. (2012, February 9). *Trauma care.* Retrieved from http://www.cdc.gov/TraumaCare/

2. Ciesla, D. J., Tepas, J. J., Pracht, E. E., Langland-Orban, B., Cha, J. Y., & Flint, L. M. (2013). Fifteen-year trauma system performance analysis demonstrates optimal coverage for most severely injured patients and identifies a vulnerable population. *Journal of the American College of Surgeons, 216*(4), 687–695.

3. Wolf, L. (2012). An integrated, ethically driven environmental model of clinical decision-making in emergency settings. *International Journal of Nursing Knowledge, 24*(1), 49–53.

4. Wolf, L. (2010). Assigning acuity: An ethnographic exploration of clinical decision-making by emergency nurses at initial patient presentation. *Advanced Emergency Nursing Journal, 32*(3), 1–13.

5. Emergency Nurses Association. (1995). Accomplishments. In *Silver threads, golden memories*: ENA 25th anniversary celebration handbook (pp. 15–21). Des Plaines, IL: Author.

6. American College of Surgeons. (2012). Initial assessment and management. In *Advanced trauma life support student course manual* (9th ed., pp. 3–21). Chicago, IL: Author.

Chapter 2 • Teamwork and Trauma Care

Susan M. Hohenhaus, LPD, RN, CEN, FAEN
Patricia Nierstedt, MS, RN, CEN

Objectives

Upon completion of this chapter, the learner will be able to:

1. Discuss the benefits of team structure and teamwork in trauma care.

2. Identify the essential components of a trauma team.

3. Discuss the elements of teamwork that mitigate patient harm in the delivery of trauma care.

Introduction

A systematic, organized approach is used by all members of the trauma team to provide optimal care for the trauma patient.[1] The primary and secondary surveys assure a consistent approach and direct the priorities and course of management.[1] Trauma nurses are essential to meet the complex needs of the trauma patient and deliver care to produce an optimal outcome. Excellence in trauma nursing care contributes to optimal patient outcomes and the prevention of complications, long-term consequences, or death. Although the trauma nurse has many responsibilities, care coordination, clear communication, and systematic, timely assessments are paramount. Regardless of the geographic setting—remote, rural, urban, or suburban—whether a trauma designation exists in a hospital, or if trauma care is delivered in an alternative setting, the trauma nurse is a core team member, responsible for the coordination of trauma care.

Trauma Team Structure and Roles

Clear roles and responsibilities are key to the safe and effective delivery of trauma care. A team is defined as a set of individuals who are cognizant of one another, interact with each other, and have a shared sense of each other as a group. Effective teams are group-driven. Trauma resuscitation has been referred to as a team sport—one that requires all team members to perform together for successful results.[2] High-performing teams hold shared mental models, optimize resources, have strong team leadership, engage in a regular discipline of feedback, develop a strong sense of collective trust and confidence, create mechanisms to cooperate and coordinate, and manage and optimize performance outcomes.[3]

Barriers to team performance have been identified and should be considered when creating team-focused policies and procedures for trauma care. These barriers include lack of role clarity, relying on conventional thinking, varying communication styles, distractions, conflict, hierarchy, fatigue, and workload.[4] Consistent application of teamwork principles helps to reduce errors, improve patient outcomes, and increase patient and staff satisfaction.[4]

Members of the trauma team vary by clinical setting and resources. However, there are team elements that are critical to every successful trauma event, regardless of location or time of the event. These trauma roles and responsibilities include:

- **The patient:** The trauma nurse's highest priority is to ensure the patient remains the focus of the provision of trauma care. This may seem simplistic; however, the highly technical nature of trauma care often eclipses the simple human connection with the patient and family. Involving and communicating with the patient and family is a key role of the trauma nurse.

- **The team leader:** There are two types of leaders: (1) those who are designated or are assigned by title and role, and (2) those who are situational or have the skills to effectively manage the situation

  ○ Effective team leaders:

    ◆ Organize the team

    ◆ Articulate clear goals

    ◆ Make decisions through collective input of other team members

    ◆ Empower members to speak up and ask questions

    ◆ Model teamwork behaviors

- The team leader may be a physician, an advanced practice nurse (APN), or a nurse. The important thing to remember is that the team leader is responsible for maintaining situational awareness, clearly communicating to the team, and encouraging mutual support. Nursing science and art make the trauma nurse ideally suited to lead the core patient care team, coordinating the care of both the patient and the team.

- **Core team:** This group of care providers works interdependently to manage a trauma patient from assessment to disposition.[4] Roles and responsibilities for technical skills such as airway management, vascular access attainment, transport, and documentation vary by clinical setting. Clear policies and procedures specific to the resources available should be in place and consistently applied.

- **Contingency and support services:** These team members provide support to the core team to facilitate optimal trauma patient care. The contingency team comes together to solve a specific problem. A contingency team might include an airway team (anesthesia, respiratory therapist, paramedic) or a trauma code team, which practices following a standardized response to designated categories of patient injury. Members of the trauma support team might include a house supervisor, pharmacist, radiology professional, and/or chaplain.

Effective team members are dynamic, interdependent and adaptive, moving toward the common goal of optimal trauma care. Each team member plays an important role and has responsibilities that compliment and support the other members of the team, including the patient and family.

Specific Trauma Nurse Roles and Responsibilities

During the delivery of trauma care, team members respond to provide specific expertise to the process with a common goal for achieving the best possible outcome for a patient. A physician or APN is typically in charge of managing the clinical care of the patient, while the trauma nurse has responsibility for managing the team and coordinating necessary resources. It is also the trauma nurse's responsibility to ensure continuity of care throughout the initial phase of care until admission, discharge, or transfer. The trauma nurse role provides consistency. Additional responsibilities include ensuring that serial assessments are performed, analyzed, and documented, and reporting trends and changes in the patient's condition. Trauma nurse characteristics include the ability to:

- Anticipate and determine priorities
- Function in a complex, unpredictable, and uncontrolled situation
- Carry on a brief but intense nurse–patient interaction
- Delegate and coordinate trauma team roles and responsibilities
- Formulate efficient and effective decisions based on limited information
- Remain focused in an organized fashion
- Communicate effectively

Communication

Communication, cooperation, and coordination are the foundations of successful teamwork in a trauma patient event. Crucial communication situations include:

- Prehospital
  - Established triage and treatment protocols as well as transfer agreements in advance allowing for smooth transitions
  - Standardized patient notification to the receiving facility
  - Update on patient including change in condition on arrival
- Trauma team
  - Communication about pertinent findings during assessment to guide treatment and provide timely interventions for the patient's optimal outcome
  - Communication between the team leader and other team members regarding the patient's injuries, plan of care, and progress through the system
  - Communication among team members to relay important information and findings
- Trauma nurse
  - Responsible for the flow of communication with:
    - The other trauma team members
    - Various other care providers across the continuum
      - Radiology and laboratory personnel
      - Intensive care nursing
      - Surgery suite personnel
      - The receiving hospital if the patient is to be transferred
    - The family or other support as identified to promote family-centered care
    - The patient to include advanced directives and/or full patient participation when possible

Communication Tools

Effective team performance includes the consistent application of standardized, evidence-based communication tools. Many of these tools can be found in the Team Strategies and Tools to Enhance Performance and Patient Safety (TeamSTEPPS™) curriculum. These include briefs, huddles, and debriefs.[4]

Brief

A brief is a planned teamwork event designed to form the team, designate team roles and responsibilities, establish climate and goals, and engage the team in short and long-term planning.[4] Ideally this is done at the beginning of a traditional clinical event such as the start of the shift. Briefs should also occur at designated times throughout the shift in order to maintain situational awareness. Due to the unpredictable nature of trauma events, a daily briefing helps the team to plan for the arrival of an unannounced trauma patient. Use of a standardized briefing checklist is helpful. Some hospitals use a whiteboard to facilitate the brief; others have incorporated the brief electronically.

Elements of the brief checklist may include:
- Introductions
- Staff availability
- Work load and organizational/community situation
- Available resources

Table 2-1. Strategies for Effective Communication

Strategy	Components	Purpose
SBAR	• S: Situation • B: Background • A: Assessment • R: Recommendation	To provide a framework for communication among members of the healthcare team
DESC	• D: Describe the specific situation or behavior • E: Express your concerns or how the situation makes you feel • S: Suggest alternatives and seek agreement • C: State consequences in terms of impact on performance goals	Used in conflict management • Paraphrasing the other person's comments is an important technique that should be done throughout the DESC script • Following discussion of consequences, team members should work towards consensus
CUS	• C: I am Concerned • U: I am Uncomfortable • S: This is a Safety issue/ I am Stressed	Used to "stop the line" if a team member senses or discovers an essential safety breach
Callout and Check Back	• Sender initiates the critical message • Receiver accepts the message and provides feedback • Sender double-checks to ensure that the message was received	Used to ensure closed-loop communication and information given by the sender was understood as intended by the receiver

Data from Agency for Healthcare Research and Quality.[4]

Huddle

Another component of teamwork communication is a huddle.[3] A huddle is ideally convened prior to the trauma patient's arrival for the purpose of solving a problem and to regain situational awareness. The huddle checklist helps the team leader to communicate critical issues and emerging events, anticipate outcomes and likely contingencies, assign resources, and express concerns.[4] It is important to identify and widely communicate huddle triggers so that anyone who recognizes a potential critical event has the ability to call a huddle.

During a huddle, information is shared openly in a nonjudgmental environment. Recommendations presented are referred by the trauma nurse to the appropriate services, requesting a timely follow-up and loop closure. This nurse-led, multidisciplinary debriefing team reviews the event with an emphasis on communication and enhancement of a teamwork environment.

Debrief

A debrief is where learning occurs. The purpose of a debrief is process improvement. A debrief can be a quick, informal information exchange or feedback session that should occur after an event and is designed to improve teamwork skills. A debrief checklist can be quite simple:

- What went well?

- What might be done differently next time?

- Does anything need to be fixed right away and who needs to know?

When the review process is interdisciplinary and extends to all members of the team, there is an increased opportunity for future success. The debriefing can be conducted in a matter of minutes and should be standardized to the clinical setting. In one hospital setting, a quick debrief may be held as the patient is being taken to the radiology suite for further studies. In another, it may occur just after the patient is transported to another facility. The timing varies depending on the setting, but the importance of the debrief occurring every time cannot be overstated. If members of the trauma team are not available for the debrief, the team leader assures that the missing team member's feedback and concerns are solicited and included.

Communication before, during and after a trauma event should be brief, clear, concise and timely. Evidence-based standardized communication strategies have been identified.[4] Table 2-1 outlines these strategies.

Performance Improvement and Trauma Care

Performance improvement (PI) is a system of multidisciplinary reviews with a feedback loop for the purpose of identifying areas for improvement and developing a demonstrated action plan.[2] This forms the basis of a strong performance improvement system.[2] Effective communication, teamwork, and collaboration with feedback for improvement are the foundations of organized, timely, safe, and quality care. These components help the team to provide increasingly excellent care.

Summary

Whether a trauma event occurs in a community with a sophisticated multi-resource trauma center or a critical access hospital, an organized team with a systematic approach who practice effective teamwork provides optimal trauma patient care. An effective trauma team has clearly defined roles and responsibilities with an emphasis on efficiency, safety, and performance. The trauma nurse is the coordinating member of the team ensuring there is effective communication and organization among team members.

References

1. Emergency Nurses Association. (2010). *Sheehy's emergency nursing: Principles and practice* (6th ed.). St. Louis, MO: Mosby.

2. American College of Surgeons Committee on Trauma. (2006). *FAQ for resources for the optimal care of the injured patient.* Retrieved from http://www.facs.org/trauma/optimalcare.pdf

3. Salas, E., Burke, C. S., & Stagl, K. C. (2004). Developing teams and team leaders: Strategies and principles. In R. G. Demaree, S. J. Zaccaro, & S. M. Halpin (Eds.), *Leader development for transforming organizations* (pp. 325–358). Mahwah, NJ: Lawrence Erlbaum Associates.

4. Agency for Healthcare Research and Quality. (n.d.). *TeamSTEPPS.* Retrieved from www.ahrq.gov/teamsteppstools/instructor/essentials/pocketguide.htm

Chapter 3 • Epidemiology

Tiffiny Strever, BSN, RN, CEN
International Contributing Authors see page viii

Objectives

Upon completion of this chapter, the learner will be able to:

1. **Define trauma.**

2. **Review multinational epidemiologic characteristics associated with trauma.**

3. **Describe injury prevention program outcome strategies to decrease injuries.**

Introduction

Trauma is injury to living tissue caused by an extrinsic agent.[1] Regardless of the mechanism of injury (MOI), trauma creates stressors that exceed the tissue's or organ's ability to compensate. The field of epidemiology studies factors that determine and influence the frequency and distribution of injury, disease, and other health-related events and their causes in a defined human population.[2] These data are then used to establish prevention programs and to control the incidence and prevalence of these injury and disease factors.

Traumatic events are, in some capacity, preventable. Even after a traumatic event occurs, the injuries themselves may be avoided or the degree of injury can be lessened with safety measures. A traumatic incident may be classified as intentional (assault or suicide) or unintentional (falls or collisions).

Incidence in the United States (U.S.)

Unintentional injury remains the fifth leading cause of death across all ages in the U.S. and the leading cause of death for people ages 1 to 44 years.[3] In 2009, 75% of injury-related deaths were from poisoning, motor vehicle collisions (MVCs), firearms, and falls. Additionally traumatic brain injuries (TBIs) factor into 30.5% of all injury-related deaths annually in the U.S.[4]

Most injuries do not result in death, but do impact the community and entire healthcare system from the prehospital setting to rehabilitation and beyond. In 2009, 33.4% of all emergency department (ED) visits were injury related.[5]

Human Characteristics

Epidemiology is based on the study of factors that influence a particular disease state—in this case the injuries that affect trauma. When looking at traumatic injuries, certain human characteristics link populations to particular mechanisms of injury. These include age, gender, and substance use. This information is important in developing injury prevention programs. Community programs can target those at greatest risk or the most influential factor.

Age

Different MOIs are more common in different age groups. For example, falls are the leading cause of injury-related death for individuals over 65 years old.[6] For ages 5 to 24 years, MVCs are the leading causes of death, whereas poisoning is the leading cause of death for ages 25 to 64 years.[6]

Aging significantly impacts injuries and their effects in older patients. Decreases in vision, hearing, and mobility as well as cognitive changes are age-related factors affecting the older adult. Comorbidities, along with these age-related factors, place this population at a higher risk for morbidity and mortality. Older adults are more likely to experience complications from and die as a result of their injuries than are younger patients.[7] Adults who are age 75 years and older experience the highest rates of hospitalization and death related to TBIs.[4] Older adults are also cited as an at-risk group for fire-related injuries.[7] See Chapter 18, Special Populations: The Older Adult Trauma Patient.

Gender

Injury and death rates vary between genders. These are thought to be impacted by cultural norms, occupation, risk-taking activities, and MOI.

In every age group, TBI rates are higher for males than females.[4] The highest rates of TBI-related hospitalizations and deaths occur in males ages 0 to 4 years. Fall data reveal that older men are more likely to die from a fall, but older women are twice as likely to sustain a fracture. When looking specifically at hip fractures, the rate for women is almost three times that of men.[9] Among those who died from unintentional poisoning in 2009, men were nearly twice as likely as woman to die.[8] Men have higher injury rates with spinal cord injuries (SCIs). Women have higher rates of injury and death from interpersonal violence.

Substance Use

Alcohol

Alcohol is both a cause of traumatic injury and a confounding factor when diagnosing and treating injured patients.[14] In 2009, nearly one third of all traffic-related deaths involved alcohol. Alcohol was involved in 48% of the traffic crashes that resulted in pedestrian fatalities and was detected at some level in both drivers and pedestrians.[15] Blood alcohol concentration of greater than 0.08% was present in 6% of both drivers and pedestrians. However, the pedestrian rate of blood alcohol levels greater than 0.08% was two thirds higher than the drivers (35% and 13%, respectively).[15]

Smoking/Tobacco

Smoking affects trauma and traumatic injury in two ways. Smoking is the leading cause of fire-related deaths.[7] In addition, tobacco use contributes to health issues that can increase morbidity and mortality in the trauma patient.

Other Substances

Substances other than alcohol (marijuana and cocaine) are involved in about 18% of motor vehicle driver deaths.[16] Alcohol and these substances are often used simultaneously, adding to the complexity of assessing the person with a traumatic injury. Substance use also contributes to morbidity and mortality and additional health issues, such as pulmonary issues and liver failure.

The risk of substance abuse is not limited to the adult population; one study surveyed youth in the U.S. and revealed that nearly three-quarters of students have consumed alcohol by the end of high school and 39% have done so by eighth grade.[17] Statistics indicate 47% of students have tried an illicit drug by the time they have finished high school.[17] Substance abuse is not a benign condition. It can be life altering, particularly when it results in trauma.

Violence

Homicide, assault, interpersonal violence, and abuse (sexual, physical, and psychological) are just a few types of violence that lead to traumatic injury. Whatever form, violence is a public health issue.

Homicide is one of the top five causes of injury-related death for individuals ages 1 to 44 years, the second leading cause of death for those ages 15 to 24 years, and the third leading cause for ages 1 to 4 and 25 to 34 years.[3]

U.S. Department of Justice figures indicate that, annually, 21.5% of nonfatal assaults against women are perpetrated by intimate partners, whereas this number is only 3.6% in men.[18] Other figures note that one in four women has been the victim of severe physical violence by an intimate partner compared with one in seven men.[19]

In the U.S., it is believed that over 500,000 older adults are abused or neglected each year.[20] In 2010, Child Protective Services estimated that 695,000 children (9.2/1,000) were victims of maltreatment.[13] It is also estimated that there were 1,560 deaths from maltreatment in 2010. See Chapter 20, Special Populations: The Interpersonal Violence Trauma Patient, for more information.

Injury Prevention

Injury prevention is an important step in reducing the financial burden of injury, and financial data have shown that prevention always costs less than treatment. A study by the Centers for Disease Control and Prevention (CDC) of injuries in both Canada and the U.S. shows the following costs:[21]

- $1 spent on smoke alarms saves $69
- $1 spent on bicycle helmets saves $29
- $1 spent on child safety seats saves $32
- $1 spent on road safety improvements saves $3
- $1 spent on injury prevention counseling by pediatricians saves $10
- $1 spent on poison control services saves $7

Injury prevention aims to reduce the number of injury events, whereas injury control considers the number of events and the severity of injuries when they do occur. Injury prevention interventions can be applied to three different phases of the injury event process: primary, secondary, and tertiary. Each phase maintains a separate focus and set of goals, but the ultimate endpoint is injury reduction or elimination:

- Primary: Prevention of the occurrence of the injury
- Secondary: Reduction in the severity of the injury that has occurred
- Tertiary: Improvement of outcomes related to the traumatic injury

Whether a hospital has one program focusing on injury prevention or a department that implements many programs, the process shares common components. Assessment of the problem is the first step in development of any injury prevention program. The following injury prevention model describes the basic principles of injury control:

- Injury incidence is monitored through data collection related to the type of injury, whether the injury is fatal or nonfatal, and the associated cost

- After collecting these data, injury risk factors (social, genetic, and environmental factors) are identified

- Injury risk factors are used to determine where, how, and with whom to intervene

- After interventions are completed, the efforts are evaluated, and any effect on injury incidence is determined[22]

In addition, incorporation of the three E's of injury control is important. They are as follows:

- Engineering: This relates to technological interventions such as, in the case of MVCs, side impact airbags, automated alarms alerting drivers of vehicles in their blind spots, and ignition lock devices for those convicted of driving under the influence (DUI). In playgrounds and sports, this involves surface material under playground equipment and athletic safety gear. Another intervention is improved use of smoke alarms in fire prevention.

- Enforcement and legislation: These include laws at all jurisdictional levels regarding driving while intoxicated, booster seats, primary seatbelt use, and distracted driving. For sports this includes rules regarding illegal hits, examination after impact, and return-to-play requirements after a head injury

- Education: These can be community-based initiatives such as public service announcements for improved seatbelt use, education regarding risks of distracted driving, programs to commit to no texting while driving, and promotions for bicycle helmet giveaways with instructions for proper use

The trauma nurse can have an impact when it comes to the legislative process by advocating for stronger laws and more consistent enforcement. Nurses provide data, expert testimony, and education to legislators, community leaders, and citizens. They can present programs in schools, to parent groups, or in senior centers and educate patients and families every day in their practice environment. There are many programs and information for community education opportunities at little or no cost. Resources for injury prevention are included in Box 3-1.

Box 3-1. Injury Prevention Web Resources for Nurses

Organization	Website
Centers for Disease Control and Prevention	http://www.cdc.gov/injury/ http://www.cdc.gov/HomeandRecreationalSafety/index.html http://www.cdc.gov/ViolencePrevention/index.html http://www.cdc.gov/motorvehiclesafety/index.html http://www.cdc.gov/homeandrecreationalsafety/falls/index.html http://www.healthypeople.gov/
Emergency Nurses Association	http://www.ena.org/practice-research/Practice/Safety/Injury%20Prevention/Pages/Informational.aspx http://www.ena.org/practice-research/Practice/Safety/Injury%20Prevention/Pages/Community.aspx
National Council on Aging	http://www.ncoa.org/improve-health/center-for-healthy-aging/
National Highway Traffic Safety Administration	http://www.nhtsa.gov/ http://www.nhtsa.gov/Driving+Safety http://www.nhtsa.gov/Vehicle+Safety
SafeKids Worldwide	http://www.safekids.org/worldwide/
STOP Sports Injuries	http://www.stopsportsinjuries.org/
U.S. Administration for Children and Families	https://www.childwelfare.gov/systemwide/domviolence/prevention/
World Health Organization	http://www.who.int/violence_injury_prevention/en/

Substance Use Education

Healthcare providers can engage in non-judgmental conversations about substance use. Screening, brief intervention, and referral to treatment (SBIRT) is an effective, evidence-based approach to identifying patients at high risk for complications from substance use. A routine screening identifies at-risk individuals who might benefit from an in-depth evaluation. Personalized feedback and the ability to modify harmful alcohol- or drug-related behaviors are provided through a brief intervention. Appropriate referrals are provided for further evaluation and treatment depending on the individual's substance abuse risk level. Numerous studies illustrate that brief interventions for problems related to alcohol use can decrease future alcohol consumption, injury recurrence, and repeat trauma visits.[23] The goal of SBIRT is to "reduce alcohol use and related injuries, illnesses and death by early identification and intervention for harmful drinking."[23]

Summary

Unintentional injury is a leading cause of death across all age groups in the U.S. For those injuries that do not result in death, the community and healthcare settings feel an impact on the economic and social levels. Human characteristics such as age, gender, race, and substance use play a role in the rate of injury and type of injuries seen in the U.S. population. Taking these into consideration, injury prevention strategies can be used to reduce the incidence of traumatic injury through public awareness and education campaigns. Trauma nurses play a role by providing discharge education, working in their communities, and advocating for legislation that can affect injuries related to trauma.

Epidemiology of Trauma in Selected Countries

Note: Statistics and data were provided by representatives from each of the countries listed below. As data collection processes vary from country to country, information and references were as recent and complete as available at time of publication.

Australia

Introduction

Data collected on injury and traumatic death in Australia are sporadic and currently not well compiled to produce nationally reflective statistics. The development of the National Trauma Registry Consortium of Australia and New Zealand and the newly formed National Trauma Research Institute have yet to deliver combined statistics for epidemiologic report outcomes in Australia. However, the Australian Bureau of Statistics publishes the most recent epidemiologic information on the health status of the Australian population.[24]

Incidence

In 2010, the median age of death from external causes (suicide, transport collisions, falls, and poisonings) was 52.7 years, younger than the median age for all registered deaths of 81.2 years. As with previous years, around two thirds of all deaths from external causes were males. The biggest gap between male and female deaths was in the 20 to 44 year age group with a ratio of 343 male deaths per 100 female deaths.[25]

Trauma results in approximately 10,000 deaths annually in Australia. Nearly 20,000 persons are permanently disabled from trauma.[26] Trauma care costs $3.4 billion annually and is 7% of the total healthcare costs. Due to the loss of economic production, its annual cost to the Australian economy is $18 billion.[26]

Overall, deaths and injury from suicide, transport-related collisions, and work-related incidents have declined.[26] With an aging population, death rates and hospitalization rates from falls in the older adult population have increased significantly.[26]

Suicide

Suicide-related deaths have been declining since 1997. In 2009, 14.1 per 100,000 of total deaths in men were due to suicide, which has declined from 20.3 per 100,000 in 2001. Suicide rates in females are 5.3 per 100,000 deaths.

Suicide rates were highest in older men 85 years and older with 28.2 per 100,000 deaths. This is followed by men ages 35 to 45 years (22.8/100,000) and in all genders ages 45 to 50 years (21.6/100,000). Among women, those ages 45 to 55 years had the highest rates of suicide with 7.2 suicide-related deaths per 100,000 deaths.[27]

Hanging is the most frequent (56.2%) method of suicide in Australia.[28]

Falls

Falls have increased by 28% since 2007 and were the underlying cause of death for more females than males.[29] The death rate from falls has increased by 54% since 2004.[31] Falls accounted for 38% of all hospitalized injuries from 2008 to 2009 and represented the largest group of serious life-threatening injuries.[32] In pediatric patients ages 1 to 14 years, twice as many boys were injured in falls than girls.[30]

Older adults are more at risk from serious injury related to falls. Those over 65 years old represent 51.3% of those seriously injured by falls, and this increases with the over 75 age group.[30] Older women have twice the hospitalization rate following falls as men.[30] The median age of death for falls was 85.9 years. Adults over 70 years old represented 87% of all deaths attributed to falls.[31]

Transport-related Collisions

The majority of trauma deaths (74% in 2007) were associated with motor vehicles driven on public roads.[32] In Australia, 6.05 deaths per 100,000 persons in 2010 were due to MVCs.[32]

Overall deaths have declined 25% from 2002 to 2011.[33] This represents the lowest number of road fatalities in Australia since 1946.[34,35]

Death rates for transport-related collisions in men have declined from 14.8 per 100,000 in 2001 to 9.6 per 100,000 in 2009. Female death rates have declined from 5.7 per 100,000 in 2001 to 3.5 per 100,000 in 2009.[32] The 17 to 25 year old age group still represents the largest group of deaths at 22% but has shown the greatest decline of deaths in age groups since 2002.[36]

The Northern territory has a very high death rate for transport-related collisions of 21.37 per 100,000.[37]

Work-related Injury

From 2009 to 2010, 1.9 deaths per 100,000 people were work related. This rate has gradually declined and is at its lowest since data were recorded. Older workers suffered the highest death rates, and 94% of work-related deaths were in males.[38]

Violence

Violence is increasing within Australia. Approximately 6% of hospitalized injury occurs as a result of an assault at a ratio of 111 per 100,000. Penetrating injuries account for 12.8% of hospitalizations. The most serious assault mechanism in Australia continues to be the use of bodily forces. Head injuries account for almost two thirds of injuries, and males between ages 14 and 35 years old are the most likely victims.[39] In 2010, there were 260 homicides; knives were used in 39% and firearms used in 13% of cases.[39]

Human Characteristics
Age
Children
Injury remains the primary cause of death among children. Data suggest children ages 5 to 14 years are most likely to sustain an injury. From 2004 to 2005, 25% of children ages 0 to 14 years had experienced an injury during a 4-week review period. The most common causes of the injuries included:

- Falls from a low height (≤ 1 m) (43%)
- The child hitting something or being hit by something (14%)
- Bites and stings (13%)

The incidence of preventable injuries was higher among children compared with all other age groups. In 2004, the Australian government named injuries in children as a priority for injury prevention.[40]

Older Adults
Older Australians are injured at a lower rate than other age groups but are more likely to die as a result of their injuries. As noted above, they are at higher risk of death as a result of falls.[26]

Race
Among Aboriginal and Torres Strait Island Australians, suicide was the sixth leading cause of death. When standardized for age, the suicide rate was 2.4 to 2.5 times higher for Aboriginal and Torres Strait Islanders compared with nonindigenous Australians. The age-standardized mortality rate for land-transport collisions was almost three times higher for the Aboriginal and Torres Strait Islander population compared with nonindigenous persons.[41] MVCs involving indigenous Australians are 2.6 times more likely to result in death and 1.3 times likely to result in serious injury when compared with nonindigenous Australians. Alcohol was involved in 24% of motor vehicle deaths.[41] Aboriginal pedestrians are 5.5% more likely to die than the general population.[42]

Alcohol
There is a strong correlation between alcohol and violence in Australia. Deregulation of alcohol licensing in hotels and clubs has led to an expansive late night drinking culture and has increased the risk of associated violence.

Males report twice the rates of alcohol-related violence to police, although it is recognized that only 25% of alcohol-related violence is reported. Often the victim reporting the violence has been drinking alcohol as well. Alcohol was associated with 47% of homicide-related deaths between 2006 and 2009. Alcohol abuse in Australia is linked with family violence and child neglect.[43]

Drowning

The death rate from drowning has increased since 2007 to an average of 1.35 per 100,000 deaths annually. In 2010 to 2011, 315 persons drowned, with a rate of 1.40 per 100,000. However, drowning rates for children under the age of 4 years have decreased.[44]

Prevention
Road Safety Initiatives
Despite an increase in number of motor vehicles, the introduction of road safety initiatives and increased public awareness have contributed to a reduction in road fatalities since the 1970s.

These initiatives include the following:[45]
- Improvements to roads, such as separated dual-lane highways, major road bypassing of towns and suburbs, use of audible edge lining, and removal of roadside hazards
- Changes to vehicles in line with the Australian Design Rules standards, including child-restraint anchorages and seats, head restraints, air bags, and increased impact resistance
- Legislation requiring the compulsory restraint of children in cars
- Legislation requiring the fitting and wearing of seatbelts and motorcycle and bicycle helmets
- Initiatives against drunk driving, such as random breath testing and public education campaigns
- Enhanced police enforcement aided by technology such as red light and speed cameras

Community support organizations have raised awareness and provided assistance to modify public areas to reduce fall risk. Local council playgrounds use safer play equipment, place soft-fall technology under play gym equipment, and govern public facilities with respect to workplace health and safety. Examples of workplace health and safety initiatives include handrails and nonslip flooring.[46-48]

Educational conferences are conducted across Australia and New Zealand in a bid to reduce the mortality and morbidity associated with falls.[49]

Drowning
The Australian Water Safety Council has a goal of reducing the drowning statistic by 50% by the year 2020. The priorities include:[50]

- Differentiating risks at different life stages
- Identifying and targeting high-risk locations
- Reducing the number of deaths from water recreation activities, alcohol and substance use, extreme weather conditions, and in high-risk populations

Swimming lessons have been heavily promoted and modified to include not only swimming technique but also contingency training, such as being able to locate a pool edge and learning how to climb out of a pool. Instances of childhood drowning decreased in the 1990s after legislation to make swimming pool fencing compulsory.

Schools continue to increase awareness of water safety. Community organizations, such as the Royal Surf Life Savers, use school and media campaigns to increase awareness of water safety issues.[44]

Alcohol
Initiatives enacted to reduce the number of alcohol-related injuries include lowering the permissible blood alcohol limit to 0.05%, increasing the amount of random breath testing, and giving heavy penalties reinforced with publicity and information measures aimed at making drunk driving socially unacceptable.

Canada

Introduction
Canadians experience approximately 3.5 million injuries annually, although many incidences go unreported as they may not require treatment by a healthcare professional.[51] Trauma is the leading cause of death among those younger than 45.3 years old. Injuries are also a cause of long-term disability.[51] See "Cost".

In 2009, 6.5% of deaths in Canada were injury related.[52] Between 2009 and 2010 there were 14,481 cases of major traumatic injury with an Injury Severity Score (ISS) greater than 12. Of these major injury cases, 11% died in the emergency department or after hospital admission.[53]

Incidence
In Canada, the leading causes of major injury among all admitted cases from 2009 to 2010 were:[53]
- MVCs—40%
  - MVCs account for 32% of all injury-related deaths. The most frequently injured person in a MVC is the driver (58%), including those on motorcycles, followed by their passengers (21%). Pedestrians account for 14% of those injured. Cyclists made up 4% of transportation-related injuries.

- Unintentional falls—39%
  - Causes of unintentional falls correlated to age and illustrate important focus areas for injury prevention[53]
- Intentional injury (homicide, suicide, assault)—4%
- Other—17%

Human Characteristics

Age

MVCs are the leading cause of injury for all age groups except older adults, in whom unintentional falls are more common. From 2009 to 2010, the mean age for sustaining a major injury (ISS > 12) was 49 years. Leading causes of injury are shown in Fig. 3-1.

Gender

From 2009 to 2010, males accounted for 70% of those sustaining major injuries. The most common injuries were internal organ injuries (81%), followed by musculoskeletal (73%), and superficial injuries (35%). Blunt injury (94%) was the most common cause of injury, followed by penetrating injury (5%) and burn injury (1%). Males (67%) were also more likely than their female counterparts to die as a result of a MVC.[53]

Socioeconomics and the Social Determinants of Injury

Although injury rates have been declining across all income levels, a significant gap still exists between the richest and poorest Canadians. A variety of studies of hospitalizations in 2008 observed decreases in socioeconomic standards (SES) and are associated with increases in fatal and serious injuries. As SES increases, rates of injury decline. The Canadian Institute for Health Information reports that the poorest Canadians experience injury at a rate 1.3 times higher than the wealthiest.[54]

Figure 3-1. Leading Causes of Injury by Age in Canada (2009–2010)

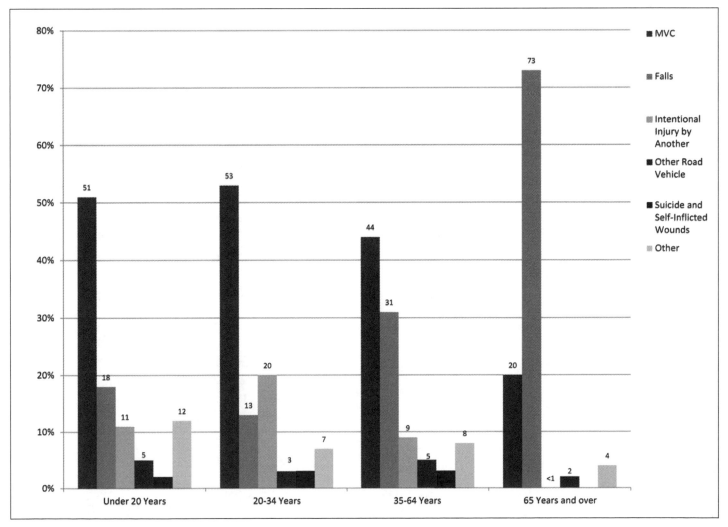

Data from Statistics Canada.[55]

Aboriginal Peoples

The Aboriginal people of Canada continue to experience significantly higher injury rates than non-Aboriginal people. Injury is a leading cause of death for First Nations and Inuit people, with rates 3.5 times the national average. These rates of injury in Aboriginal communities may be due to many complex social and economic determinants of health, such as high rates of poverty, social exclusion, poor housing quality and housing shortages, lower levels of education and employment, and a younger population.[54]

Researchers specifically studying rates of suicide among Aboriginal communities found that rates were lowest in those with certain characteristics relevant to enhancing cultural continuity, such as self-governance, education, health and emergency services, cultural facilities, and land claims resolution.[54]

Intentional Injury

Interpersonal Violence

From 2009 to 2010, 9% of all injures were due to interpersonal violence. Among these, 9% were due to homicides and assault. The most commonly specified means of homicide and assault were bodily force (52%), stab wounds (25%), and gunshot wounds (11%). Interpersonal violence victims were primarily male (90%), and the average age was 31 years. Blunt trauma injuries (66%) were predominantly featured, followed by penetrating trauma at 34%. Where reported, mechanisms of intentional injuries included other causes of blunt injuries (52%), stab wounds (25%), gunshot wounds (11%), other causes (11%), MVCs (< 1%), and falls (< 1%). Most major injury hospitalizations due to interpersonal violence occurred among those ages 20 to 64 years (80%).[56] In addition, the risk of both interpersonal and self-inflicted violence was highest for adolescents from families in receipt of welfare benefits.[54]

Self-directed Violence

Low-income individuals are 3.2 times more likely to die by suicide than individuals of middle-or-high income groups.[54] From 2009 to 2010, 2% of all injuries were from suicide and self-inflicted injury, and self-directed violence represented 4% of all injury deaths. Over 75% of the cases were male, with a mean age of 40 years. Falling from a high place (32%), gunshot wounds (18%), stab wounds (17%), MVCs (5%), and other (28%) were the most common means of self-inflicted injury. Most major injury hospitalizations due to suicide and self-inflicted injury occurred among those ages 20 to 64 years (77%).[53]

Substance Abuse

Alcohol use plays a significant role in trauma. From 2008 to 2009, 15% of those injured above the age of 15 years old had a blood alcohol concentration (BAC) above the Canadian legal limit (0.08%).[53]

Injury cases in which the patient had a measurable BAC were higher across MOIs in those older than age 15 years and accounted for the following:

- Stab wounds (43%)
- Gunshot wounds (28%)
- MVCs (23%)
- Incidents involving pedestrians, cyclists, or other land transport (19%)
- Falls (12%)

Nearly one half (43%) of people who consumed more than eight alcoholic drinks per week admitted to driving after consuming more than two consecutive drinks. Men were three times more likely to report such drinking and driving activities.[53]

Illicit substances and prescription medications are also factors in intentional and unintentional injury. A study of Ontario students found that during the previous year 19.3% of drivers in high school reported driving within an hour of using marijuana. Other studies reported detection of cannabinoids in 13.9% and 19.5% seriously injured and fatally injured drivers, respectively.[55]

The annual proportion of alcohol-related motor vehicle fatalities has not declined significantly since the 1990s, and other causes, such as fatigue and the substance used, are being tracked in these cases. Distracted driving, notably related to the use of cellphones and other interactive electronic devices, is another risk that has emerged in recent decades and disproportionately affects young drivers.[56]

Cost

The Economic Burden of Unintentional Injury in Canada[54] highlights the economic impact of injury to Canadians. Similar studies have since been completed in various Canadian provinces; current data can be found at Injury Surveillance Online through Public Health Agency of Canada.[57] Injury costs about $19.8 billion Canadian. The total cost of injury is separated into direct costs (healthcare costs arising from injuries) and indirect costs (costs related to reduced productivity from hospitalization, disability, and premature death). The direct costs accounted for 54% of total injury costs, and indirect costs accounted for 46%.[51]

Injury Prevention

Canada has moved towards creating a National Strategy for Injury Prevention and developed Parachute – Leaders in Injury Prevention (formerly Thinkfirst, Smartrisk, Safe Communities, and Safe Kids Canada). This group focuses on all ages and intentional and unintentional injuries. Federal and various provincial governments along with Canadian companies have shown support for the organization.

Box 3-2 provides contact information for provincial injury prevention organizations. Box 3-3 describes national injury databases.

Hong Kong

Introduction

No centrally based data collection system exists in Hong Kong to record morbidity and mortality related to trauma. Without a central registry, it is difficult to maintain accurate figures and injury data; however, five trauma centers do collect data. In 2011, 2,924 major trauma cases were recorded by these trauma centers.[58] Among those major trauma cases, 704 required inpatient treatment in intensive care units.[58] The mean of hospitalization length of stay (LOS) is 10 days and the median LOS is four days.[58]

The Hospital Authority Hong Kong aims to assist governmental departments to coordinate trauma prevention programs and to organize a nationwide trauma service development plan.

Incidence

External causes of morbidity and mortality were the sixth leading causes of death in Hong Kong from 2001 to 2011.[59] Following the implementation of public injury prevention education, the number of registered deaths decreased from 27.5 per 100,000 in 2001 to 22.2 per 100,000 in 2011.[59]

In 2011, the three most common MOI were falls within 2 m (30%), MVCs (11%), and falls over 2 m (9%). Blunt trauma (88.1%), burns (6.4%), and penetrating trauma (5.5%) were the most common types of traumatic injury.[58]

Box 3-2. Canadian Provincial Injury Prevention Organizations

Regional Center	Website
British Columbia Injury Research & Prevention Unit, Vancouver, BC	http://www.injuryresearch.bc.ca
The Community Against Preventable Injuries, Vancouver, BC	http://preventable.ca
Alberta Centre for Injury Control and Research, Edmonton, AB	http://acicr.ca
Alberta Health Services, Calgary, AB	http://www.albertahealthservices.ca/injuryprevention.asp
Saskatchewan Prevention Institute, Saskatoon, SK	http://www.preventioninstitute.sk.ca
IMPACT, the Injury Prevention Centre of Children's Hospital, Winnipeg, MB	http://www.hsc.mb.ca
Parachute – Leaders in Injury Prevention, Toronto, ON	http://parachutecanada.org
Quebec WHO Collaborating Center for Safety Promotion and Injury Prevention, Montreal, PQ	https://www.inspq.pc.ca
Child Safety Link, IWK Children's Health Centre, Halifax, NS	http://www.childsafetylink.ca
Nova Scotia Healthy Communities, Halifax, NS	http://www.gov.ns.ca/hpp/cdip/injury_prevention.asp
Atlantic Collaborative on Injury Prevention, Halifax, NS	http://www.acip.ca/

Box 3-3. National Injury Databases

Organization	Website
The Public Health Agency of Canada	http://www.phac-aspc.gc.ca
Canadian Hospitals Injury Reporting and Prevention Program (CHIRPP)	http://www.phac-aspc.gc.ca/injury-bles/chirpp/injrep-rapbles/
National Trauma Registry—the Canadian Institute for Health Information (CIHI)	http://www.cihi.ca/
Statistics Canada	http://www.statcan.gc.ca
Canadian Red Cross	http://www.redcross.ca
The Canadian Agricultural Injury Reporting (CAIR)	http://www.cair-sbac.ca/
Canadian Motor Vehicle Traffic Collision Statistics from Transport Canada	http://www.tc.gc.ca/eng/roadsafety/tp-1317.htm
First Nations and Inuit Health Information System (FNIHIS)	http://www.hc-sc.gc.ca/fniah-spnia/services/home-domicile/index-eng.php

Human Characteristics

Age

In Hong Kong, the median age of patients with traumatic injury is 46 years old.

Gender

Gender differences exist in injury rates, depending on the causes of the traumatic injury.[58] Exposure to the injury-producing event, the amount of risk involved, the occupation, and cultural norms are possible reasons for the gender differences.

From 2010 to 2011, the overall death rate from fall injuries was twice as high for men as women.[60]

Motor Vehicle Collisions

In Hong Kong, the most commonly injured patients in MVCs are pedestrians (339), drivers (147), bicyclists (136), passengers (117), and motorcyclists (113).[60]

In 2011, 26 of 19,803 (0.13%) MVCs were related to alcohol and drug use by the driver.[61]

Acknowledgement

The authors would like to acknowledge the Central Committee (Trauma Service), Hospital Authority Hong Kong.

The Netherlands

Introduction

The Netherlands[62–69] is a densely populated country, with more than 16 million people. All data are collected by the bureau of statistics, which publishes the most recent epidemiologic information on the health status of the Dutch population. Of the 140 hospitals in the Netherlands, 17 do not have an emergency department. Eleven level I hospitals are located in strategic parts of the country. Because of the relatively small distances to hospital care, there are only four trauma helicopters. These are also used for urgent patient care on the islands. In border areas, healthcare providers work with the German and Belgian colleagues and hospitals.

Incidence

In 2011, a total of 5,844 people in the Netherlands died of a non-natural cause, or 35 deaths per 100,000 people. This number has been relatively stable in recent years. Suicide was the leading non-natural cause of death (28.2%), followed by traffic-related incidents (11.2%). Additional causes of death include:

- Falls (2,376)
- Home-related incidents (911)
- Violence (143)
- Drowning (70)
- Firearms (49)

Traffic-related Incidents

The Netherlands has seen a decrease in traffic-related deaths—from around 1,000 in 1990 to 653 in 2011. Introduction of speed limits on highways, tougher enforcement of speed limits, and the increase of traffic (which forces drivers to adapt their speed to the increasing traffic) are a few of the factors contributing to this decrease. While more deaths resulted from MVCs (35.1%), bicycle-versus-vehicle collisions (30.2%) are also a main concern in the Netherlands. Many citizens are frequent bicycle users, not only for recreation, but for commuting to and from school or work. Around 46,000 people visit an emergency department after a fall off a bike every year. Young children and older adults are prone to bicycle-related falls. Decreased reaction time in traffic also plays a factor in injury. During the weekends, the incidence of alcohol- and bicycle-related accidents is much higher.

There are no helmet laws in place in the Netherlands; however, the use of a helmet when riding a bicycle recreationally (speed cycling or mountain biking) is common.

South Africa

Introduction

Trauma in South Africa is referred to as a "malignant epidemic," as around 70,000 South Africans die each year as a result of trauma. Another 3.5 million seek care for injuries. An estimated 9,000 individuals are killed each year on roads, with another 33,000 seriously injured.[70]

Incidence

Injuries are major contributors to Africa's triple burden of disease (death due to injuries, pretransitional cause related to poverty, and the emerging chronic disease burden), road traffic mortality, and homicide (due to interpersonal and collective violence with a rate of 57% which is approximately four times higher than the average rates globally). The World Health Organization (WHO) estimates that injuries will increase to the second major contributor to African mortality by 2020.[71]

Injury Type

The majority of the type of injuries presenting in most of the emergency departments in the Netcare Private Hospital Group were blunt trauma followed by penetrating injuries.[72]

Injury Priority

Most injuries in South Africa are classified as Priority 2. Men are more likely to present as Priority 1 patients compared with women.[72]

Human Characteristics

Age

The second largest number of older adults in Africa lives in South Africa. Despite the impact of the human immuno-deficiency virus/acquired immune deficiency syndrome (HIV/AIDS) epidemic, the number of older adults is expected to grow over the next two decades.

Different mechanisms of injury are more common among the pediatric population. Burns and pedestrian injuries were leading causes of death across all pediatric age groups. Drowning, burns, and MVCs were leading causes of death in children ages 1 to 14 years. Other causes of death included firearms and unspecified traffic-related injuries.[73]

Gender

Of those with traumatic injury, men ages 20 to 45 years were the most commonly admitted to the hospital.[72] Among adults 66 years and older, women were more frequently admitted than men.[72]

One study at a major trauma center in Johannesburg found that men were at higher risk for trauma, particularly over the weekends.[74] Men are also approximately twice as likely to be exposed to all categories of traumatic injury than women.[72]

Alcohol Use

In South Africa, the legal BAC is 0.05%, and 46.5% of all drivers involved in fatal traffic-related injuries were above the legal limit. Around 40% of fatally injured passengers had a positive BAC, roughly 60% of pedestrians and 40% of cyclists.[71,75]

Types of Injuries

Motor Vehicle Collisions

MVCs cost South Africa an estimated ZAR3.9 billion annually.[73] This includes the costs of emergency response, such as ambulances, emergency personnel, and tow trucks.

Rates of road traffic deaths in South Africa are one of the highest in the world.[76] Many factors contribute to this including:[76]

- Aggressive driving
- Misunderstood traffic laws
- Issuing of fraudulent driver's licenses
- Lack of police on the roads
- Alcohol use
- Poor road conditions
- Increasing number of vehicles on the roads
- Lack of suitable road infrastructure to accommodate an increase in traffic density

Additional factors affecting the rate of MVC-related injuries include the lack of mandatory legislation for the use of child restraints in vehicles. However, many children travel by taxi, by bus, and especially in rural areas, on the back of a bakkie (a small truck with open body and low sides) or utility van.[73]

Violence

Table 3-1 describes the types of violent injuries reported to the Netcare Private Hospital Group from 2011 to 2012.[72] Violence related injuries account for 7% of all emergency department visits during the evaluated period.[72] Men were more likely to be victims of violence than women.[72]

Burns

Burns are a leading cause of mortality, injury, disability, and psychosocial trauma in children, especially between ages 1 and 5 years. However, adults ages 20 to 45 years account for 50% of all burn injuries.[72] Burns accounted for 3% of all ED visits from 2011 to 2012.[72] A majority of burn injuries are classified as Priority 2, and men are more likely to have burn injuries than women.[72]

An estimated ZAR262 million is spent annually in South Africa for the care of kerosene (paraffin) stove burns. Indirect costs—lost wages, prolonged care for deformities, emotional trauma, and commitment of family resources—add to the socioeconomic impact of the injuries on patients and their families.[77]

Suicide

At least one suicide is committed every hour in South Africa, with 20 unsuccessful attempts made in this same time frame. Suicide has increased 48% in the past 10 years. The average age is 36 years. One third of all non-fatal attempts were among children.[78]

Table 3-1. Types of Violent Injury in South Africa

Type of Injury	Percentage
Assault	81%
Stabbing	11%
Gunshot wounds	7.5%
Hijacking	0.3%
Human bites	0.2%

Data from Van Niekerk et al.[71]

Patterns of suicidal behavior in South Africa include the following:[78]
- Up to 8,000 South Africans commit suicide annually
- Nearly five times as many men than women commit suicide
- The highest number of fatal suicides occurred in the 15- to 19-year-old age group
- The WHO reports hanging accounted for 36.2% of suicides in South Africa, followed closely by shooting (35%), poisoning (9.8%), gassing (6.5%), and burning (4.1%)

Drowning

Drowning is underreported primarily as no national drowning prevention strategy exists and statistics are not updated and/or accurate. In 2004, children under the age of 15 years accounted for nearly 42% of all fatal drowning cases.

Eighteen percent of the drowning cases occurred in swimming pools in private residences and a further 3% occurred in swimming pools in parks or leisure resorts. Drownings can also occur in pools of water or streams around informal settlements or slums, and the victims are often young children playing in these areas due to a lack of recreational facilities. One study found that 43.6% of drowning cases reported had positive BAC of 0.05% or more.[79]

Injury Prevention

In South Africa, the social and scientific responses to the containment and prevention of injuries remain inadequate. The inadequacy is attributed to the absence of quality data indicative of the precise extent of the problem, inadequate resources, and the unbalanced attention to criminal justice responses.[73]

Several well-established safety intervention practices are in place for the prevention of passenger and cyclist deaths, such as the use of child seats, seatbelts, and cycle helmets. However, no single intervention is completely effective, and prevention should include pedestrian skills programs, parent education, legislation, environmental modifications, and vehicle changes at regional, provincial, and national levels.

Road Safety Changes and Initiatives

The South African Insurance Association (SAIA) recommends the formation of a Coalition on Road Safety, which seeks to achieve a coordinated approach to road safety initiatives at the provincial and national level. Another initiative is the Breathalyzer Test Initiative, sponsored by the SAIA and driven by the Johannesburg Metro Police Department.[76]

The Road Safety Foundation (RSF) is currently leading "A Call for a Decade of Road Safety" in conjunction with the United Nations (UN). The Road Traffic Report by the Road Traffic Management Corporation noted a reduction in the following due to a proactive road traffic management campaign:[80]

- Unroadworthy vehicles (4.64%)
- Number of fatal crashes per 10,000 motorized vehicles (2.51%)
- Number of fatalities per 10,000 motorized vehicles (1.22%)
- Fatal crashes (0.18%)

They reported this was due to an increase in the following:[83]

- Vehicles stopped and screened
- Notices issued
- Vehicles discontinued, suspended, or impounded
- People arrested for road traffic offenses, such as driving under the influence (DUI)

Sweden

Introduction

Sweden is a country of more than 9.5 million people. Population density is highest around the capital, Stockholm, and in southern parts of the country. About 84% of the population lives in towns and other population centers. Average life expectancy is one of the highest in the world: 79.35 years for men and 83.35 years for women.[81]

The Swedish Traffic Accident Data Acquisition (STRADA) program gathers information from the police and hospitals related to road traffic collisions. Statistics from The National Board of Health and Welfare regarding injuries, poisonings, and other external causes is based on a mortality register, patient register and the Injury Data Base in Sweden.[82]

Incidence

Trauma is a serious threat to the well-being of Swedish inhabitants. It is the fourth leading cause of death, behind heart and vascular disease, respiratory organ disease, and cancer. Young healthy persons often are involved in trauma, which causes a loss of their productive years.

According to the Injury Data Base, about 658,000 people in Sweden visited emergency care due to injury in 2010. Men were overrepresented in general, except among older adults, where women were more affected.[82]

In 2011, 16,119 road traffic collisions involving personal injury (including fatal, severe, and slight injuries) were reported by the police. In these incidents, 319 persons were killed, 3,127 were severely injured, and 19,233 were slightly injured. Since 2010, the official statistics on road traffic collisions exclude suicides and other deliberate acts.[83]

Each year, about 100,000 injuries occur due to sports and games and 13% at school or other type of educational environment. Two thirds of these injuries affected boys and men.[84]

Human Characteristics

Age

Most injuries leading to death caused by trauma occur between the ages of 15 and 44 years. Most of the deaths between 16 and 64 years of age are associated with suicide and traffic collisions, whereas falls are more common in older adults.

Gender

For men up to the age of 45 years, trauma is the most common cause of death; in women up to the age of 45 years, it is the second most common cause of death. Men tend to be involved in more MVCs and suicide, whereas women sustain falls more often than men.

Of those killed in road traffic collisions in 2011, about 76% were men. Looking at different groups of road users, men account for most of the motorcycle riders (96%) and moped riders (91%) while the proportion of men is lowest among killed cyclists and pedestrians.[85]

Alcohol

In 2011, 173 drivers of motor vehicles were killed in road traffic collisions. Sixteen percent had a higher BAC than what is legally accepted.[85]

Suicide

Nearly 1 in 500 people take their own life each year in Sweden. The ratio of men to women is 2.6:1. Two to three times as many deaths result from suicide as do MVCs. According to the National Center for Suicide Research and Prevention of Mental Ill Health, suicide occurs more often among adults, especially those ages 45 to 64 years. Statistics show that the amount of suicides among younger people is decreasing in those older than 25 years but is increasing among 15 to 24 year olds.[86]

Violence

Violence leading to death accounts for 100 to 150 deaths annually, and about 2,600 people, mostly men, need hospital care due to violence annually. Studies show that the amount of violence is increasing. Deadly violence often occurs between people with some kind of social connection and the perpetrator often has abuse problems and/or is suffering from mental illness.[86]

Costs

The total societal costs for unintentional injuries is around $9.1 billion each year, and falls and traffic collisions account for nearly 75% of this figure. These costs do not reflect the suffering and impact on health and well-being for affected individuals and families.[85]

Prevention

Sweden is very proactive in injury prevention. In 2005, Sweden enacted a law that made it mandatory for all children younger than 15 years to wear a helmet when on a bicycle. Different studies show that wearing a helmet reduces the risk for concussion by 65% to 85%. Since 1975 the legislation requires all motorcycle and moped riders to wear a helmet.

Safety belts are mandatory in all cars and buses (except local buses in cities). Using a three-point safety belt in a car reduces risk of deadly injuries to front seat passenger and drivers by 65% and with an additional airbag the risk is reduced another 3%. Since 1986, the law states that all passengers must use safety belts in the car and children under 7 years must have special safety arrangements.

In 1997, Swedish Parliament developed "Zero Vision," which aims to eliminate severe injury or death from road traffic collisions. The goal is to minimize mechanical injury to avoid severely harming and deadly injuries. This program places the responsibility on the individual to follow road traffic laws and regulations, such as following speed limits and use of safety devices, to engineering developments, such as creating barriers between traffic lanes, pedestrians, and wild animals.

Addendum

Additional epidemiologic data from the United Kingdom has been added with this printing. Please turn to the Addendum: Chapter 3 Epidemiology on page 361.

References

1. Trauma (n.d.) *Merriam-Webster dictionary online.* Retrieved from http://www.merriam-webster.com/medical/trauma?show=0&t=1358537715

2. Epidemiology. (n.d.). *Merriam-Webster dictionary online.* Retrieved from http://www.merriam-webster.com/medical/epidemiology

3. National Center for Health Statistics. (n.d.). *10 leading causes of death by age group, U.S.–2010.* Retrieved from http://www.cdc.gov/injury/wisqars/pdf/10LCID_All_Deaths_By_Age_Group_2010-a.pdf

4. Centers for Disease Control and Prevention. (2012, March 23). *How many people have TBI?* Retrieved from http://www.cdc.gov/traumaticbraininjury/statistics.html

5. Kochanek, K. D., Xu, J., Murphy, S. L., Minino, A. M., & Kung, H. C. (2011). Deaths: Final data for 2009. *National Vital Statistics Report, 60*(3). Retrieved from http://www.cdc.gov/nchs/data/nvsr/nvsr60/nvsr60_03.pdf

6. National Center for Health Statistics. (n.d.). *10 leading causes of injury deaths by age group highlighting unintentional injury deaths, U.S.–2010.* Retrieved from http://www.cdc.gov/injury/wisqars/pdf/10lcid_unintentional_deaths_2010-a.pdf

7. Centers for Disease Control and Prevention. (2011, October 11). *Fire deaths and injuries: Fact sheet.* Retrieved from http://www.cdc.gov/homeandrecreationalsafety/fire-prevention/fires-factsheet.html

8. Centers for Disease Control and Prevention. (2012, June 29). *Poisoning in the U.S.: Fact sheet.* (2012). Retrieved from http://www.cdc.gov/HomeandRecreationalSafety/Poisoning/poisoning-factsheet.htm

9. Walker, K. M. (2012, December 13). Hip fractures in adults. *UpToDate* Retrieved from http://www.uptodate.com/contents/hip-fractures-in-adults

10. Hoopes, M., Dankovchik, J., & Kukuska, E. (2012). *Northwest American Indian and Alaska native mortality.* Portland, OR: Northwest Tribal EpiCenter.

11. Centers for Disease Control and Prevention. (2012). *Suicide: Facts at a glance.* Retrieved from http://www.cdc.gov/ViolencePrevention/pdf/Suicide_DataSheet-a.pdf

12. Foundation for Spinal Cord Prevention, Care & Cure. (n.d.). *Home page.* Retrieved from http://www.fscip.org

13. Centers for Disease Control and Prevention. (2012). *Child maltreatment: Facts at a glance.* Retrieved from http://www.cdc.gov/violenceprevention/pdf/cm_datasheet2012-a.pdf

14. Hayman, A. V., & Crandall, M. L. (2009). Deadly partners: Interdependence of alcohol and trauma in the clinical setting. *International Journal of Environmental Research and Public Health, 6,* 3097–3104.

15. National Highway Traffic Safety Administration. (2009). *Traffic safety facts 2009 data: Pedestrians.* Retrieved from http://www-nrd.nhtsa.dot.gov/Pubs/811394.pdf

16. Centers for Disease Control and Prevention. (2012, October 2). *Impaired driving: Get the facts.* Retrieved from http://www.cdc.gov/motorvehiclesafety/impaired_driving/impaired-drv_factsheet.html

17. Schweer, L. (2009). Pediatric SBIRT: Understanding the magnitude of the problem. *Journal of Trauma Nursing, 16*(3), 142–147.

18. Pratchett, L. C., Pelcovitz, M. R., & Yehuda, R. (2010). Trauma and violence: Are women the weaker sex? *Psychiatric Clinics of North America, 33,* 465–474.

19. Centers for Disease Control and Prevention. (2012, September 25). *National Intimate Partner and Sexual Violence Survey.* Retrieved from http://www.cdc.gov/violenceprevention/nisvs

20. Centers for Disease Control and Prevention. (2012, June 11). *Elder maltreatment prevention.* Retrieved from http://cdc.gov/features/elderabuse/index.html

21. Centers for Disease Control and Prevention. (2000). *Working to prevent and control injury in the U.S.—Fact book for the year 2000.* Atlanta, GA: Author.

22. Occupational Therapy Association of California. (n.d.). *Models for success.* Retrieved from http://www.eldersafety.org/Models_For_Success/Models_For_Success.html

23. Desy, P., Howard, P. K., Perhats, C. & Li, S. (2010). Alcohol screening, brief intervention, and referral to treatment conducted by emergency nurses: An impact evaluation. *Journal of Emergency Nursing, 36*(6), 538–545.

24. Curtis, K., & Ramsden, C. (2011). *Emergency and trauma care for nurses and paramedics* (2nd ed.). Sydney, Australia: Mosby Elsevier.

25. Australian Bureau of Statistics. (2012, March 20). *Causes of death, Australia, 2010: External causes.* Retrieved from http://www.abs.gov.au/ausstats/abs@.nsf/0/1676C30C00F8776CCA2579C6000F7064

26. National Trauma Research Institute. (2011). *Strategic plan 2011–2014.* Retrieved from http://www.ntri.org.au/images/stories/home/NTRI-STRATEGIC-PLAN-2011-13.pdf

27. Australian Bureau of Statistics. (2012, March 20). *Causes of death, Australia, 2010: Overview.* Retrieved from http://www.abs.gov.au/ausstats/abs@.nsf/Products/7993A7CBAEDFE462CA2579C6001B644A?opendocument

28. Australian Bureau of Statistics. (2011, August 26). *Gender indicators, Australia, Jul 2011: Suicides.* Retrieved from http://www.abs.gov.au/ausstats/abs@.nsf/Lookup/by+Subject/4125.0~Jul+2011~Main+Features~Suicides~3240

29. Australian Bureau of Statistics. (2012, March 20). *Causes of death, Australia 2010: Method of suicide.* Retrieved from http://www.abs.gov.au/ausstats/abs@.nsf/Products/94BBA3060FC0657BCA2579C6001B676E

30. Department of Infrastructure and Transport (2012). *International road safety comparisons 2010.* Retrieved from http://www.bitre.gov.au/publications/2012/files/stats_001.pdf

31. Australia Bureau of Statistics. (2010). *Causes of death.* Retrieved from http://www.ausstats.abs.gov.au/ausstats/subscriber.nsf/0/E39670183DE1B0D9CA2579C6000F7A4E/$File/33030_2010.pdf

32. Department of Infrastructure and Transport. (2012). *Roads deaths Australia: 2011 statistical summary.* Retrieved from http://www.bitre.gov.au/publications/2012/files/RDA_Summary_2011.pdf

33. Minister for Infrastructure and Transport. (2012, January 25). *Australian road deaths continue to fall* [media release]. Retrieved from http://www.minister.infrastructure.gov.au/ck/releases/2012/january/ck001_2012.aspx

34. Australian Bureau of Statistics. (2010, September 15). *Measure of Australia's progress, 2010: Road safety.* Retrieved from http://www.abs.gov.au/ausstats/abs@.nsf/Lookup/by%20Subject/1370.0~2010~Chapter~Road%20safety%20(4.9.2)

35. Australian Bureau of Statistics. (2011, August 26). *Gender indicators, Australia, Jul 2011: Deaths in motor vehicle accidents.* Retrieved from http://www.abs.gov.au/ausstats/abs@.nsf/Lookup/by+Subject/4125.0~Jul+2011~Main+Features~Deaths+in+motor+vehicle+accidents~3250

36. Department of Infrastructure and Transport. (2013, April 16). *Road safety.* Retrieved from http://www.infrastructure.gov.au/roads/safety/index.aspx

37. Safe Work Australia. (2012, March). *Work-related traumatic injury fatalities, Australia 2009–10.* Retrieved from http://www.safeworkaustralia.gov.au/sites/SWA/AboutSafeWorkAustralia/WhatWeDo/Publications/Documents/662/Traumatic%20Injury%20Fatalities%202009-10.pdf

38. McKenna, K., & Harrison, J. E. (2012). *Hospital separations due to injury and poisoning, Australia 2008–09.* Retrieved from http://www.aihw.gov.au/WorkArea/DownloadAsset.aspx?id=10737422891

39. Australian Institute of Criminology. (2012). *Australian crime, Facts and figures 2011.* Retrieved from http://www.aic.gov.au/documents/0/B/6/%7B0B619F44-B18B-47B4-9B59-F87BA643CBAA%7Dfacts11.pdf

40. Australian Bureau of Statistics. (2007, February 15). *Health of children in Australia: A snapshot, 2004–05.* Retrieved from http://www.abs.gov.au/ausstats/abs@.nsf/mf/4829.0.55.001/

41. National Road Safety Council. (2013, February). *Indigenous road safety.* Retrieved from http://www.infrastructure.gov.au/roads/safety/indigenous_road_safety/index.aspx

42. Ferguson, C., & Segre A. (2012). *Aboriginal road trauma: Key informant views of physical and psychological effects.* Retrieved from http://acrs.org.au/wp-content/uploads/36_Ferguson-PR.pdf

43. Australian Government Institute of Criminology, *Key Issues in alcohol related-violence* http://www.aic.gov.au/documents/A/8/C/%7BA8CA2B96-4BE6-4B79-A61D-8408081903BA%7Drip04_001.pdf

44. Royal Life Saving. (2012). *Annual report 2011/2012.* Retrieved from http://www.royallifesaving.com.au//resources/documents/DrowningReport_2011_LR.pdf

45. Department of Infrastructure and Transport. (2013, February). *National road safety strategy, 2011–2020.* Retrieved from http://www.infrastructure.gov.au/roads/safety/national_road_safety_strategy/index.aspx

46. New South Wales Falls Prevention Program. (n.d.). *Fall prevention strategies.* Retrieved from http://fallsnetwork.neura.edu.au/resources/files/cec-falls_strategies.pdf

47. Clinical Excellence Commission. (2012). *Falls prevention program.* Retrieved from http://www.cec.health.nsw.gov.au/programs/falls-prevention

48. Government of Western Australia Department of Health. *Stay on your feet WA.* Retrieved from http://www.health.wa.gov.au/stayonyourfeet/home/

49. Australian & New Zealand Falls Prevention Society. (n.d.). *5th biennial Australian and New Zealand falls prevention conference.* Retrieved from http://www.anzfpsconference.com.au/

50. Australian Water Safety Council. (2012). *Australian water safety strategy 2012–15.* Retrieved from http://www.royallifesaving.com.au/__data/assets/pdf_file/0011/4016/AWSC_Strategy2012_Brochure-Lowres.pdf

51. SmartRisk. (2009). *The economic burden of injury in Canada.* Retrieved from http://www.smartrisk.ca/downloads/burden/Canada2009/EBI-Eng-Final.pdf

52. Statistics Canada. (2012, May 31). *Deaths and mortality rate, by selected grouped causes and sex, Canada, provinces, and territories.* Retrieved from http://www5.statcan.gc.ca/cansim/a26?lang=eng&retrLang=eng&id=1020552&pattern=Deaths+and+mortality+rate+by+selected+grouped+causes+and+sex&tabMode=dataTable&srchLan=-1&p1=1&p2=1

53. Canadian Institute for Health Information. (2012). *National trauma registry 2012 report: Hospitalizations for major injury in Canada, 2009–2010 data.* Toronto, Ontario: Author.

54. Atlantic Collaborative on Injury Prevention. (2011). *Social determinants of injury.* Retrieved from http://hpclearinghouse.net/files/folders/social_determinants_of_health/entry15826.aspx

55. Mann, R. E., Brands, B., Macdonald, S., & Stoduto, G. (2003). *Impacts of cannabis on driving: An analysis of current evidence with an emphasis on Canadian data.* Ottawa, Ontario: Transport Canada.

56. Public Health Agency of Canada. (2012). *Injury in review, 2012 edition: Spotlight on road and transport safety.* Ottawa, Ontario: Surveillance and Epidemiology Division Injury Section.

57. Public Health Agency of Canada. (n.d.). *Injury surveillance on-line.* Retrieved from http://dsol-smed.phac-aspc.gc.ca/dsol-smed/is-sb/index-eng.php

58. Hospital Authority. (2012). *Annual report 2011–2012.* Retrieved from http://www.ha.org.hk/ho/corpcomm/ar201112/html/eng/main.html

59. Centre for Health Protection. (2012, October 18). *Death rates by leading causes of death, 2001– 2011.* Retrieved from http://www.chp.gov.hk/en/data/4/10/27/380.html

60. Hospital Authority. (2011). *Hospital Authority statistical report 2010–2011.* Retrieved from http://www.ha.org.hk/upload/publication_15/411.pdf

61. Transport Department. (2011). *Figure 1.7 road traffic casualties by casualty contributory factor and degree of injury 2011.* Retrieved from http://www.td.gov.hk/filemanager/en/content_4563/f1.7.pdf

62. Lennquist, S. (Ed.). (2007). *Traumatologi.* Solna, Sweden: Liber AB.

63. Ministerie van Volksgezondheid, Welzijn en Sport. (2012, December 13). *Sterfte naar doodsoorzaak: Waaraan overlijden mensen in Nederland?* Retrieved from http://www.nationaalkompas.nl/gezondheid-en-ziekte/sterfte-levensverwachting-en-daly-s/sterfte-naar-doodsoorzaak/waaraan-overlijden-mensen-in-nederland/

64. Ministerie van Verkeer en Waterstaat (2008). *Strategisch Plan Verkeersveiligheid 2008-2020: Van, voor en door iedereen.* The Hague, The Netherlands: Author.

65. Schepers, P. (2008). *De rol van infrastructuur bij enkelvoudige fietsongevallen.* Delft, The Netherlands: Rijkswaterstaat Dienst Verkeer en Scheepvaart.

66. Ormel, W., Klein Wolt, K., & Den Hertog, P. (2008). *Enkelvoudige fietsongevallen; een LIS-vervolgonderzoek.* Amsterdam, The Netherlands: Stichting Consument en Veiligheid.

67. Methorst, R., Van Essen, M., Ormel, W., & Schepers, J.P. (2009). *Letselongevallen van voetgangers en fietsers.* Delft, The Netherlands: Rijkswaterstaat Dienst Verkeer en Scheepvaart.

68. Dutch department of infrastructure and traffic: strategic plan for the improvement of the roadside safety (2008)

69. Centraal Bureau voor de Statistiek. (n.d.). *Home page.* Retrieved from http://www.cbs.nl

70. Lutge, E. E., & Muirhead, D. (2005). The epidemiology and cost of trauma to the orthopaedic department at a secondary-level hospital. *South African Journal of Surgery, 43*(3), 74–77.

71. Van Niekerk, A., Suffla, S. & Seedat, M. (Eds.). (2008). *Crime, violence and injury prevention in South Africa: Data to action.* Tygerberg, South Africa: Medical Research Council – University of South Africa Crime, Violence and Injury Prevention Lead Programme.

72. Medibank Trauma Data Statistics. Netcare Private Hospital Group South Africa. 2011-2012

73. Pongoma, L. (2013, January 6). Festive road carnage costs billions. *The New Age.* Retrieved from http://thenewage.co.za/77001-9-53-Festive_road_carnage_costs_billions

74. Bruce, J. C., Schmollgruber, S., Easles, J., Gassiep, J., & Doubell, V. (2003). Injury surveillance at a level I trauma centre in Johannesburg, South Africa. *Health SA Gesondheid, 8*(3), 3–12.

75. Trauma Society of South Africa. (n.d.). *Alcohol and driving: Arm yourself with the facts (part 2).* Retrieved from http://www.traumasa.co.za/news/alcohol-and-driving-arm-yourself-with-the-facts-part2

76. South African Insurance Association. (n.d.). *Road safety.* Retrieved from http://www.saia.co.za/key-focus-areas/motor/road-safety.html

77. World Health Organization. (2012, May). *Burns: Fact sheet N365.* Retrieved from http://www.who.int/mediacentre/factsheets/fs365/en/index.html

78. Newman, L. (2004, September 13). *SA's shocking suicide statistics.* Retrieved from http://www.iol.co.za/news/south-africa/sa-s-shocking-suicide-statistics-1.221741

79. Sewduth, D. (2007). *The data related to the cases of drowning in South Africa and the implications of this.* Retrieved from http://www.ilsf.org/nl/node/1617

80. Road Traffic Management Corporation. (2010, December 31). *Road traffic report.* Retrieved from http://www.rtmc.co.za/RTMC/Files/Traffic_Reports/Calendar%20Year/December%202010%20Part1.pdf

81. Statistics Sweden. (n.d.). *Home page.* Retrieved from http://www.scb.se

82. National Board of Health and Welfare. (2011). *Hospitalization due to injuries and poisoning in Sweden 2010.* Stockholm, Sweden: Author.

83. Swedish Transport Agency. (2011, February 15). *STRADA–Swedish traffic accident data acquisition.* Retrieved from http://www.transportstyrelsen.se/en/road/STRADA/

84. Swedish Civil Contingencies Agency. *Injuries and injury prevention – an anthology.* Karlstad, Sweden: Author.

85. Swedish Transport Administration. (2012). *Road traffic injuries 2011.* Borlänge, Sweden: Author.

86. Karolinska Institutet. (2010). *Suicide in Stockholm and Sweden 1980–2008.* Stockholm, Sweden: Author.

Chapter 4 • Biomechanics, Kinematics, and Mechanisms of Injury

Aaron Wolff, BSN, RN, CEN

Objectives

Upon completion of this chapter, the learner will be able to:

1. Define biomechanics, kinematics, and mechanisms of injury.

2. Describe different forms of energy transfer related to trauma.

3. Compare the effects of environmental energy transfer on human tissues.

4. Predict potential injuries from specific mechanisms and patterns of injury.

Introduction

The potential for traumatic injury is present whenever energy comes in contact with the human body. Energy from one aspect of the environment may impact a person as heat, motion, electricity, or other forms. When the intensity of that energy exceeds the capacity of tissue to resist change, damage, or trauma ensues. The laws of physics govern this energy transfer, and comprehension of those laws, when combined with knowledge of anatomy and physiology, allow the nurse to better anticipate, recognize, and treat traumatic injury.

Terminology

As terms are applied to a context of traumatic injury study, these terms are often confused or misused (Table 4-1).

- *Kinematics* is the study of energy transfer as it applies to identifying actual or potential injuries[1]
- *Biomechanics* is the general study of forces and their effects on living tissue and the human body[2]

- *Mechanism of injury* (MOI) speaks specifically to how injuries occur as a result of how external energy forces in the environment are transferred to the body[3]

An understanding of these three concepts helps to illustrate that multiple factors—ranging from physiologic to environmental conditions—hold implications for the care of the trauma patient.

Assessment and care of the trauma patient can be enhanced with integrating knowledge of biomechanics, kinematics, and MOIs.

Kinematics: The Physics of Energy Transfer

Energy can be in a state of *potential* meaning "at rest" (a pot of water sitting on the edge of the stove) or *kinetic* meaning "in motion" (the same pot falling to the floor after being knocked off of its resting place). Once an object or mass is in motion, the potential energy becomes kinetic energy.

Table 4-1. Terminology

Term	Definition
Kinematics	The study of energy transfer as it applies to identifying actual or potential injuries
Biomechanics	The general study of forces and their effects
Mechanism of injury	How external energy forces in the environment are transferred to the body

Table 4-2. Newton's Laws of Motion and the Law of Conservation of Energy

Law	Definition
Newton's First Law of Motion	A body at rest will remain at rest, and a body in motion will stay in motion
Newton's Second Law of Motion	Force = Mass × Acceleration
Newton's Third Law of Motion	For every action, there is an equal and opposite reaction
Law of Conservation of Energy	Energy can neither be created nor destroyed, but it can change form

Newton's Laws of Motion (Table 4-2)

Newton's First Law of Motion stated that *a body at rest will remain at rest, and a body in motion will remain in motion unless acted upon by an outside force (energy).* In the case of the pot described on page 25, the force of gravity holds the pot on the flat stovetop until energy is transferred to the pot, such as by a toddler grabbing the handle. Once the pot is in motion, it will sustain its motion until interrupted by another force. As the pot strikes the child in the head, the strength of bone imposes a force of resistance upon impact, thereby changing the directional path of the pot. The stationary head stays in a fixed position until a volume of energy adequate to move the head is transferred to it. This concept of movement–energy transfer–countermovement applies to all mechanical traumas.[1]

Newton's Second Law of Motion states that *the acceleration (a) of a body is parallel and directly proportional to the net force (F) acting on the body, is in the direction of the net force, and is inversely proportional to the mass (m) of the body, or force equals mass multiplied by acceleration ($F = m \times a$).* This law describes how an object's velocity changes when it is subjected to an external force; heavier objects require more force to accelerate (or decelerate) them. In the example of the pot, the pot continues to fall at a steady rate unless it is acted on by an outside force (a hand pushing it out of the way or catching it).[4]

Newton's Third Law of Motion states that *for every action (energy impact), there is an equal and opposite reaction resulting from the transfer of energy.* In the case of the falling pot, that transfer causes a redirection of the pot and movement of the head, as well as energy absorption causing anatomic changes to the tissue that received the energy transfer.

Law of Conservation of Energy (Table 4-2)

The Law of Conservation of Energy stated that *energy can neither be created nor destroyed, but it can change form.* Energy is not created, nor is it destroyed at the site where the pot impacts the head. Instead, energy is transferred from the kinetic (moving) object to the object being impacted.

Energy Forms

Energy exists in many forms and these energy sources include:

- Mechanical (energy transfer from one object to another in the form of motion)
- Thermal (energy transfer of heat in the environment to the host)
- Chemical (heat energy transfer from active chemical substances such as chlorine, drain cleaner, acids, or plants)
- Electrical (energy transfer from light socket, power lines, or lightning)
- Radiant (energy transfer from blast sound waves, radioactivity such as a nuclear facility, or rays of the sun)

Preexisting and concomitant exposure to energy sources can change the intensity and effect of the energy transfer. For example, a chemical exposure to intact skin may yield only a minor irritation unless the exposure is incurred concomitantly with thermal or electrical trauma.

Biomechanics: Energy Forces and Their Effects

The consequences of mechanical energy are directly related to kinetic energy. The amount of energy available for transfer is related to mass and weight. While not synonymous, for the practical purposes of trauma care, weight and speed are reasonable substitutions for mass and velocity. Higher mass and/or higher speed delivers greater energy.

Kinetic Energy = ½ mv²

Kinetic energy (KE) is equal to ½ the mass (m) multiplied by the velocity squared (v²). While mass and velocity contribute to the energy present in a moving object, they do not possess a constant ratio. When mass is doubled, so too is the net energy. However, when velocity is doubled, energy is quadrupled. This principle explains why high-velocity (rifle) gunshot wounds deliver dramatically greater damage than medium-velocity (handgun) wounds even when the handgun projectile is physically larger or heavier. Another example is to compare the energy forces involved when a vehicle traveling 20 mph hits a pedestrian with a vehicle traveling 40 mph that hits a pedestrian. The energy force is quadrupled in the vehicle traveling 40 mph.

External Forces

External energy can be exerted on the body by the following forces:[1]

- Deceleration forces include those applied in falls and collisions where injuries are caused by a sudden stop of the body's motion

- Acceleration forces are not as common as deceleration forces and result from a sudden and rapid onset of motion (a parked car that is hit by a vehicle traveling at a high rate of speed)

- Compression force is an external force applied at time of impact. Examples include:
  - Stationary objects, such as dashboards or steering wheels, that collide with or push up into a person
  - Objects in motion, such as bullets and stabbing instruments, bats and balls, fists and feet, or heavy falling objects
  - Blast forces

Internal Forces

Stress describes the internal force that resists the applied external force. Stress is exerted on the body as tissues and organs change their dimensions. Body tissues respond differently to energy impact, and the capacity to withstand energy transfer is based on the characteristics of each body system. Knowledge of these tissue characteristics, combined with knowledge of biomechanics and MOIs, can improve the understanding of kinematics. Considerations include:[1]

- The strength of bone varies and can be augmented by adjacent muscle systems

- Solid organs tolerate pressure-wave energy better than air-filled organs

- Air-filled organs can often resist shear forces better than solid organs

Figure 4-1. Three Types of Energy Forces

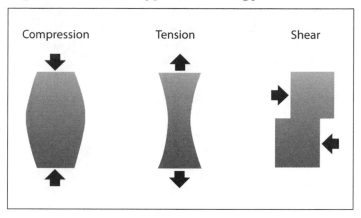

From New South Wales Government Institute of Trauma & Injury Management.[6]

The degree to which tissues resist destruction under circumstances of energy transfer depends on their proximity to the impact and their structural characteristics.

Structural strengths of tissue are described in three ways (Fig. 4-1):[6]

- *Compression* strength refers to the tissue's ability to resist crush force
  - Compression injuries to organs occur when the organs are crushed from surrounding internal organs or structures such as a seatbelt worn up across the abdomen causing compression of the small bowel or a fracture to the lumbar spine

- *Tensile* strength describes the tissue's ability to resist pulling apart when stretched
  - Tendons, ligaments, and muscles can tear when they are overstretched (Achilles tendon)

- *Shear* strength describes the tissue's ability to resist a force applied parallel to the tissue
  - Coup/contrecoup injury, such as a boxer being hit in the head, is an example of this. See Chapter 9, Brain, Cranial, and Maxillofacial Trauma, for additional information

The various strengths of tissue, especially bone, can be augmented or diminished by the pre-event circumstances. The muscle density surrounding bone absorbs energy of compressing and shearing forces. Tensile strength is augmented by the strength of opposing muscles. The tissue most proximal to the point of impact is affected by the maximum amount of energy from the object striking the tissue, or maximal energy. As energy traverses tissue, it is absorbed by cells. As a result of this cellular energy absorption, the net energy available for transfer is attenuated over distance.[7]

To illustrate these terms in relation to the falling pot: If the flat bottom of the pot fell squarely on the top of the toddler's head, the tissue would be strained primarily by the transfer of compressive energy. Soft tissue flattens, and depending on the amount of energy transfer present, tissues may rupture. The microvasculature may rupture resulting in a hematoma, or skin may rupture resulting in laceration, or bone may be crushed resulting in fracture.

If the pot struck the toddler on the side of the head in a glancing manner, the skin may experience tensile or stretching strain more than compression strain. Skin characteristically stretches; however, if the energy transfer is sufficient to exceed skin's tensile strength, a laceration is likely to result.

Types of Injuries

Injuries are caused by the following:
- Blunt trauma
- Penetrating trauma
- Thermal trauma (see Chapter 15, Surface and Burn Trauma, for more information)
- Blast trauma (see Chapter 22, Disaster Management, for more information)

Blunt Trauma

Blunt trauma occurs as a result of several common mechanisms including:
- Falls
- Motor vehicle, motorcycle, or bicycle collisions (this includes separation of riders from vehicles)
- Vehicle-versus-pedestrian collisions
- Assaults

Blunt trauma can result from broad energy impacts across large surface areas and involve energy transfer causing deceleration or acceleration. In addition to the laws of physics mentioned previously, the distance and total surface area over which the energy transfer occurs is significant to injury pattern identification. Greater distance of transfer diminishes deleterious impacts, and the more focused the impact, the greater the damage. The kinematics of such examples can be the result of falls or collisions and include both deceleration and acceleration forces and both can cause tissue damage.

Deceleration Injuries

Deceleration occurs as energy that is dispersed from the moving object. For example, a body sliding across pavement transfers energy to the pavement through friction. The restraint device within a vehicle will dissipate energy as the body impacts it. The overall result is deceleration over distance, and the more distance involved, the better the outcomes for the patient. When assessing the kinematics of trauma, the speed of an impact, whether resulting in deceleration or acceleration, is often of less significance than the distance over which that energy is transferred.

Consider the following examples:
- **Example one:** A motorcyclist is ejected at 100 mph on a racetrack and slides on the pavement for 30 yards, then across a field of loose gravel for another 50 yards before he achieves a state of rest. Potential injuries range from minor abrasions to possible skeletal fractures. The 100 mph kinetic energy is dispersed to thousands of tiny, movable objects over 80 yards of resistance.

- **Example two:** A motorcyclist is ejected at 100 mph on a highway and slides for 30 yards across the pavement before striking a tree. Potential injuries are more likely to be catastrophic and unlikely to be compatible with survival. A portion of the kinetic energy (15 mph) may be dispersed over the first 30 yards, but the remaining kinetic energy (85 mph) is applied to a single stationary object (the tree) over a distance of less than an inch, leading to tremendous energy absorption and injury to the body.

Acceleration Injuries

The same principles used to describe deceleration forces apply to acceleration forces. In example one, as energy is slowly transferred to the stationary pieces of gravel, the gravel accelerates while the body and internal organs continue to travel as a single entity. By comparison, when the body strikes the tree in example two, the exterior surfaces are rapidly decelerating, so relative to their container, the internal organs will continue forward movement before colliding with the internal chest wall and rapidly decelerate. This acceleration can cause organs to shear off from their vascular supply or anatomic points of attachment.

Falls

Injuries resulting from falls involve acceleration/deceleration principles as described above as well as Newton's Laws of Motion.
- Consider the older adult who becomes dizzy and falls from a standing position. The energy transfer begins as the patient begins to fall through the air. When the patient falls to the ground, the impact of the ground or floor causes energy transfer and injuries related to the following:

- The point of impact on the patient's body (head, hip, outstretched arm) determines the major point of energy transfer and underlying injuries or tissues impacted

- The type of surface that is hit (tile floor, grassy yard, carpeted floor) and the extent that surface can absorb the energy affects injuries. Carpet and grass can help to absorb energy, but tile does not.

- The tissue's ability to resist also affects potential injuries. Bone is less flexible than soft tissue. Air-filled organs may rupture; solid organs may fracture.

- If a person is pushed or accidentally knocked down, acceleration increases, causes additional transfer of energy, and results in a greater impact on deceleration

- Consider the construction worker who falls from greater than 20 feet. Increased distance increases acceleration, thereby increasing the energy force, transfer of energy, and impact on deceleration.

- A fall is considered significant in the pediatric patient if the fall is from three times his or her height[11]

Motor Vehicle Impact Sequence

Several impacts occur during the progression of a motor vehicle collision (MVC):[6]

- The first impact occurs when the vehicle hits another object such as a tree. The occupants experience a relative acceleration as the vehicle stops over the distance of the crushing metal, but they have not begun to absorb the energy of the abrupt vehicle stop.

- The second impact occurs when the vehicle occupant collides with the interior of the vehicle, yet the internal organs continue in motion (Fig. 4-2A). After the initial impact, the occupant continues to move in the original direction of travel until they collide with the interior of the vehicle or meet the resistance of a seatbelt or airbag. Keep in mind that the airbag accelerates toward the occupants at the rate produced by the blast of the deployed device.

- The third impact occurs when internal structures collide within the body cavity. The organs meet the resistance of the structures that encapsulate them and/or are torn loose and continue in motion until they meet the resistance of another structure. (Fig. 4-2B).

Predicting the survivability of all of these collisions is based on velocity and stopping distance. When assessing the patient injured in a MVC, the trauma nurse anticipates the potential injuries as a result of the energy transfer during this third impact. The trauma nurse also uses MOI descriptions to anticipate certain injury patterns. See Chapter 5, Initial Assessment, for more information.

Mechanism of Injury and Potential Injury Patterns in MVCs

- In frontal collisions, front seat occupants may experience one of two primary injury patterns:[12]

- A path "up and over" the steering wheel or dashboard occurs when the head and chest lead the way to the front windshield. This is associated most commonly with head, neck, chest, and abdominal injuries.

Figure 4-2A. The Second Collision in a MVC

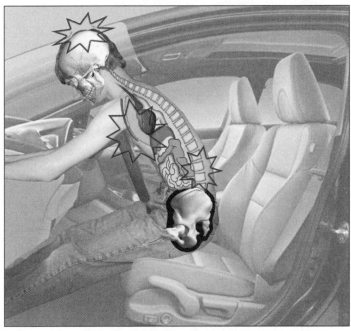

The body continues in motion until it impacts the inside of the vehicle.

Figure 4-2B. The Third Collision in a MVC

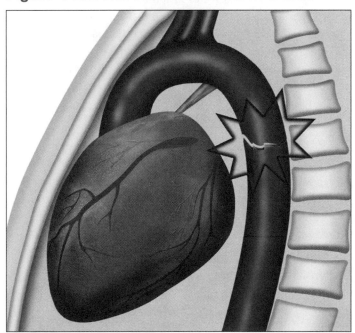

Organs continue in motion and are torn away from their attachment. In this example, the aorta is torn at the ligamentum arteriosum until it impacts inside the thoracic cavity.

- A path "down and under" the steering wheel or dashboard is associated with lower extremity and pelvis fractures (Fig. 4-3)
- The "up and over" path can result when no seatbelt is used while the "down and under" path can result from a seatbelt placed above the pelvis, possibly across the abdomen

- Lateral (T-bone) impacts result in different injury patterns depending on where a person is seated in the vehicle in relation to the location of the impact. The occupant closest to the point of impact is likely to experience a greater number and severity of injuries because he or she may experience impact from the intrusion of vehicular crush as well as impact from the vehicle interior (Fig. 4-4). The occupant opposite of the point of impact is unlikely to have a primary impact with the intruding vehicle as it crushes inward, and the occupant's lateral energy will be partially absorbed over the interior space and resistance provided by the seatbelt. Lateral impacts are associated with shear injuries to the aorta and other organs, fracture of the side clavicle, lateral pelvic and abdominal injuries, and lateral head and neck injury.[13]

- Rotational impacts occur when a vehicle is struck on one corner, causing the rest of the vehicle to move laterally around the pivot point. This results in a combination of frontal and lateral (see above) impacts as the occupants will first travel forward before the interior side of the car impacts their forward-moving bodies.[1,14]

- Rear impacts result in immediate forward acceleration of the vehicle while the occupant compresses into the seat. The person is then launched forward into the steering wheel, dashboard, or whatever lies in front of the occupant, much like in a frontal impact. Injuries include extension and flexion of the neck as well as patterns aligning with frontal impacts because the occupants are propelled forward.[15]

- Rollover crashes result in any of the injury patterns described above, depending on the direction of the crash. Head injuries are of particular concern as the roof intrudes into the passenger compartment or the centrifugal force directs the occupant out of the window.[1]

- Ejection from the vehicle significantly increases the probability of fatal injury[16]

Figure 4-3. The "Down and Under" Path

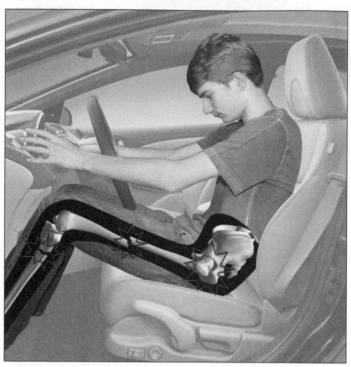

Figure 4-4. Lateral Impact

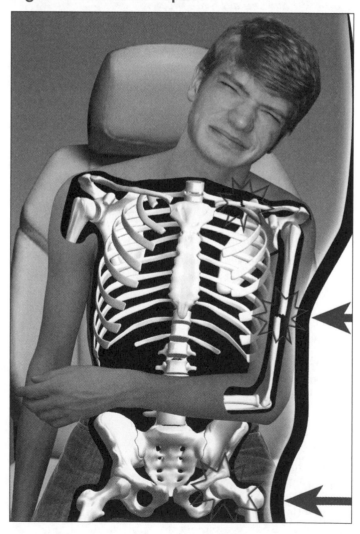

Motorcycle Injuries[1]

The absence of restraint devices and enclosure makes the probability of ejection from the vehicle common in motorcycle collisions. Several MOIs contribute to motorcycle collisions including:[17]

- A low-side crash refers to "laying the bike down" with the tires leading the direction of travel. When the tires are not in contact with the roadway, less speed-reducing friction is present. A motorcycle sliding on its side is not slowing down quickly, so impact speeds can be similar to precrash speeds. In this type of crash, abrasions, shoulder and clavicle injuries, and lateral head and lower extremity injuries are common.

- A high-side crash occurs when a motorcycle begins to crash to the low side but then grabs traction and flips over, catapulting the rider into the air. Injury patterns include all of those common to the low-side crash as well as those associated with the speed and impact of landing.

- Head-on impacts eject the rider forward with the head and torso leading the way. Depending on the motorcycle design and rider positioning, the lower extremities can collide with the handlebars, resulting in femur and pelvis fractures and hip dislocations. The remaining injuries are dependent upon the subsequent collisions but are likely to involve the head, neck, chest, and extremities.

- Lateral or angular impacts initially result in significant lower extremity injuries, but other patterns can be present as well. The angular impact may initially crush the lower extremities but will likely cause the motorcycle to rapidly impact the ground, resulting in upper extremity, lateral head, and neck injuries. A T-bone impact to the motorcyclist may result in a lower extremity crush injury followed by side impact shoulder and head injuries as the rider slams into the hood and windshield of the other vehicle. Then the rider is likely to tumble off of the car and impact the ground.

Vehicle-versus-pedestrian Injuries

When an adult is struck by a vehicle, the injury pattern is similar to a lateral impact on a motorcyclist. Depending on the height of the vehicle, there is crush force from the impacting surface usually to the lower extremity of the adult. In the moment before impact, adults tend to try to escape the impact, commonly leading to lateral or posterior impacts, while children tend to turn toward the vehicle, causing anterior impact.[1] The adult patient is then commonly thrown onto the hood and windshield then slides off of the car to incur yet another collision with the ground (Fig. 4-5). The pediatric patient may also follow this

Figure 4-5. Adult Pedestrian Struck by a Vehicle

sequence but can just as commonly be thrown from the initial impact, colliding with the ground. The Waddell triad is a pattern of injury that suggests that pediatric pedestrians involved in vehicular collisions present with a triad of head, thorax, and lower extremity injuries.[18] In practice, presentation with all three component injuries is uncommon.[19]

Assault

The extent of injuries resulting from assault is dependent on multiple factors, including:

- The amount of force—the larger the mass, the greater the force

- The distance the force travels—force that travels from a distance is dissipated over that distance

- The object used to deliver the force—is it sharp or blunt, large or small?

- The type of tissue receiving the force and the ability to resist or absorb the stress—consider the difference in the tissue affected such as the bony portion of the head versus the abdomen

- The speed or velocity of the force—speed can cause a fourfold increase in force

- The trajectory of the force—consider the difference in a boxer who is struck square in the nose versus the boxer who takes a glancing blow as he moves just enough to "roll" with the punch. The direct blow may result in a fractured nose, but the glancing blow may only result in a bruise or contusion.

- Presence of penetrating trauma

Penetrating Trauma[20]

Injuries as a result of penetrating mechanisms are dependent on several variables, including:

- Point of impact: The injuring potential of a penetrating object is related to the point of impact as well as the speed of impact

  ○ Medium- and high-velocity injuries result from the use of firearms and explosives

- Velocity or speed of impact: The velocity of the penetrating object carries with it significantly different injury potential in each category

  ○ Low-velocity injuries, such as stab wounds, carry the most simple injury patterns of all penetrations. These may involve laceration of external and internal tissue and crushing of focused areas of bone.

- Handguns and shotguns fall into the category of medium velocity while long guns (rifles) are capable of higher velocities.[20] Recalling the formula of kinetic energy, while mass does matter, velocity holds the greatest potential for injury. Both medium- and high-velocity penetrations cause injury through lacerating and crushing tissue in the direct path of the penetrating projectile. However, the higher the velocity, the larger the path of tissue destruction due to other forces.

Cavitation

Cavitation refers to the separation of tissue resulting from a sound and/or hydraulic wave force. The leading side of the projectile pushes a wave of high pressure, while the trailing edge draws a vacuum. The effect is a crushing pressure wave, which creates a temporary cavity, followed by a rapid and violent closing of the cavity that draws first in the direction of the projectile path and then retracts back to the original position.[21] This rapid motion can lead to crushing, tearing, and shearing forces on tissue. The impact of cavitation is dependent on the characteristics of the affected tissue.[22,23] Additional considerations include the following:

- Air-filled organs, such as the lungs or stomach, are elastic, so this tissue tolerates high-velocity cavitation relatively well compared to other tissues[24]

- Solid organs, such as the liver, have a greater propensity to shear or tear under the same forces

- If those same forces are instead released inside the cranium, bone will resist expansion, augmenting soft tissue crushing, until the tensile strength of the bone is exceeded and an explosive release of pressure results[25]

Projectile Considerations

Bullet design affects wounding potential dramatically. The materials that compose the exterior and interior of the bullet as well as its purpose determine how tissue is damaged upon impact:[16]

- Full metal jacket (FMJ) bullets are made of a dense, heavy metal such as lead that is encased completely with a harder metal such as copper. They deform minimally in tissue and often travel in one side and out the other, referred to as "through and through." This design is most commonly found in military and paper target practice applications. When this projectile exits the body, it takes with it all the energy it did not transfer to the tissues.

- Soft nose bullets are common in hunting and are similar to the FMJ except that the tip is not encased in the hard metal. The effect is much like an unsealed envelope, as it tears open easily upon impact. The bullet mushrooms on impact and increases in surface area, allowing increased energy transfer to the target.

- Hollow point bullets include only a partial jacket as well as a cavity tip that facilitates maximal mushroom deformity upon impact. This ensures maximal energy transfer and minimal likelihood of exiting the target or traveling through and through. This design is most commonly used in law enforcement or hunting. While highly effective with direct tissue impact, this design loses significant energy to objects it may strike (layered/bulky clothing or windshields) prior to the target, making it less likely to be lethal outside of a direct impact.

- Frangible bullets are designed to break apart upon impact, thereby dissipating all of their energy in the target while also causing multiple chaotic fragment paths. These designs can be controversial and were developed for close quarters defense and law enforcement use.

The shotgun is unique as it can discharge projectiles of different types and sizes, which will affect the velocity of the projectile.

Projectile Flight Pattern

The flight pattern of a projectile can also affect its wounding potential. The *yaw* of a projectile is its ability to wobble up and down.[26] This produces a waved cavitation pattern (Fig. 4-6) and may also alter the path a projectile takes in the body as it may cause it to tumble upon impact. The tumble results in a larger surface area of the projectile to come into contact with the tissue, leading to increased resistance and thereby allowing the transfer of more energy from the projectile to the tissue.

Figure 4-6. The Effect of Tumble and Yaw on Cavitation

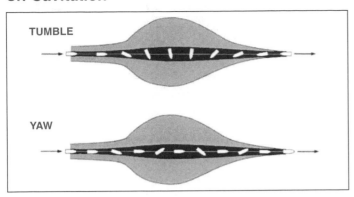

Reprinted from Yee, D. A., & Devitt, J. Hugh. (1999). Mechanisms of injury: Causes of trauma. *Anesthesiology Clinics of North America, 17*(1), 1–16 with permission from Elsevier.

Proximity

All firearms' wounding potential is influenced by proximity. Air and objects absorb energy from the projectile while it is in flight and slows its speed. In very close proximity (< 3 feet), the burning particulate and expanding gases that propel the projectile can cause injury.[27] With more distance comes more friction with the air, which slows the projectile and reduces the potential for injury from this particulate. While handguns have an effective (lethal) range measured in feet or yards, rifles have an effective range of hundreds to thousands of yards.

Thermal Trauma

See Chapter 15, Surface and Burn Trauma, for a discussion of the impacts and injuries associated with thermal trauma.

Blast Trauma[28]

The rapid release of blast energy results in chemical, physical, and possibly radioactive exposures. Blast waves can travel at more than five times the speed of even high-velocity firearms and are described in two components:

- *Overpressure* occurs as the victim is enveloped on all sides with crush forces. Then pressure rapidly returns past the pre-blast ambient pressure, and a momentary vacuum is created.
- *Dynamic pressure* is directional, similar to a gust of wind. This can carry with it fragments and debris at velocities exceeding those in high-velocity firearms. The devastating force of dynamic pressure waves are measured in tens of feet, but the fragments may have ranges of thousands of feet.

Table 4-3 describes mechanisms of blast injury.

The United States (U.S.) Department of Defense classifies blast injuries in five levels:[28]

- Primary blast injuries are found in those closest to the detonation, with enclosed space detonation resulting in the most lethal impacts. Air-filled organs (tympanic membranes, lungs, stomach, and bowel) are most susceptible to rupture with primary blast injuries.
- Secondary injuries include fragment injuries and generally cause the greatest volume of casualties. They can include injuries such as puncture wounds, lacerations, and impaled objects.
- Tertiary injuries include impacts with larger objects propelled by the blast wind resulting in blunt trauma. These cause high energy transfer and can result in pelvic or femur fractures or major thoracic injuries such as aortic and great vessel rupture.
- Quaternary injuries are the result of heat, flame, gas, and smoke. These injuries include external burns and internal burns from inhaled hot gases.
- Quinary injuries are those associated with exposure to hazardous materials from radioactive, biologic, or chemical components of a blast.

It is rare to have victims of only one category of blast injuries. Table 4-4 describes common injuries in explosions. See Chapter 22, Disaster Management, for more information.

Occlusive/Obtrusive Injuries

The definition of injury as it relates to energy transfer has been expanded to include drowning and choking or asphyxiation.[8,9] Conditions that were thought to result from deficiencies in oxygen utilization and gas exchange are now recognized to involve restriction, occlusion, or obstruction of blood flow or altered hemodynamics.[9]

Drowning[10]

- Mechanical energy forces are involved when water enters the lungs and shearing force cause the lungs to expand and bleed
- Dry drowning occurs as a result of a spasm of the larynx when water enters the throat. The person is not necessarily submerged in a body of water. This causes mechanical airway obstruction and altered hemodynamics or blood flow.

Hanging, Strangulation, and Compression Asphyxia[9]

- Mechanical force is required to occlude the airway and cervical blood vessels. Compression energy forces that result from hanging, strangulation, and compression asphyxia can constrict blood flow and oxygen perfusion and cause unconsciousness and death.
- Compression may occur from the effects of chemical substances and can cause edema, restricting or obstructing the airway, oxygenation, and ventilation.

Table 4-3. Mechanisms of Blast Injury

Category	Characteristics	Body Part Affected	Types of Injuries
Primary	Unique to HE, results from the impact of the over-pressurization wave with body surfaces	Gas-filled structures are most susceptible, including the lungs, GI tract, and middle ear	• Blast lung (pulmonary barotrauma) • TM rupture and middle ear damage • Abdominal hemorrhage and perforation • Globe (eye) rupture • Mild TBI (TBI without physical signs of head injury)
Secondary	Results from flying debris and bomb fragments	Any body part may be affected	• Penetrating ballistic (fragmentation) or blunt injuries • Eye penetration (can be occult)
Tertiary	Results from individuals being thrown by the blast wind	Any body part may be affected	• Fracture and traumatic amputation • Closed and open brain injury
Quaternary	• All explosion-related injuries, illnesses, or diseases not due to primary, secondary, or tertiary mechanisms • Includes exacerbation or complications of existing conditions	Any body part may be affected	• Burns (flash, partial, and full thickness) • Crush injuries • Closed and open brain injury • Asthma, COPD, or other breathing problems from dust, smoke, or toxic fumes • Angina • Hyperglycemia, hypertension

Note: COPD indicates chronic obstructive pulmonary disease; GI, gastrointestinal; HE, high-order explosives; TBI, traumatic brain injury; TM, tympanic membrane. *Data from* Centers for Disease Control and Prevention. (2006, June 14). *Explosions and blast injuries: A primer for clinicians.* Retrieved from http://www.bt.cdc.gov/masscasualties/explosions.asp

This can result from aspiration of liquids or inhalation of powder or noxious gas.

The Study of Prevention Countermeasures

The study of injury reduction strategies began in the 1960s, and for years, the main focus was on changing human behavior as a means of preventing injury, primarily in MVCs. The introduction of the Haddon Matrix (Table 4-5) broadened the approach and placed emphasis on countermeasures, which were more effective than changing human behavior.[29] This led to the introduction of passive restraints such as airbags, vehicle design, and road blueprints as opposed to active restraints—such as the conscious act of applying the seatbelt and monetary fines to punish noncompliance with seatbelt laws. However, in most states in the U.S. seatbelt use is now mandatory, carrying a fine for non-compliance. Haddon describes three phases of the injury event: the pre-event, the event, and the post-event. For each phase of the event, countermeasures for prevention can be applied. They include the host (human), the agent (motor vehicle), and the physical environment (socioeconomic environment).[29] While seemingly specific to MVCs, its intended use is for all MOIs.

Motor Vehicle Safety Features

Vehicular safety features can be considered effective because they spread the deceleration force over distance and surface area. Crumple zones are engineered into late-model vehicles to absorb energy as rapid deceleration forces are distributed across feet versus inches of collapsing steel. Seatbelts resist and distribute deceleration force over more body surface area across the chest, pelvis, and shoulders, thereby preventing a more focused impact such as that of the one-inch steering wheel on any single rib. Airbags further absorb energy of

Table 4-4. Overview of Explosive-related Injuries

System	Injury or Condition	
Auditory	• TM rupture • Ossicular disruption	• Cochlear damage • Foreign body
Eye, orbit, face	• Perforated globe • Foreign body	• Air embolism • Fractures
Respiratory	• Blast lung • Hemothorax • Pneumothorax • Pulmonary contusion and hemorrhage	• AV fistulas (source of air embolism) • Airway epithelial damage • Aspiration pneumonitis • Sepsis
Digestive	• Bowel perforation • Hemorrhage • Ruptured liver or spleen	• Sepsis • Mesenteric ischemia from air embolism
Circulatory	• Cardiac contusion • Myocardial infarction from air embolism • Shock	• Vasovagal hypotension • Peripheral vascular injury • Air embolism-induced injury
CNS injury	• Concussion • Closed and open brain injury • Stroke	• Spinal cord injury • Air embolism-induced injury
Renal injury	• Renal contusion • Laceration • Acute renal failure due to rhabdomyolysis	• Hypotension • Hypovolemia
Extremity injury	• Traumatic amputation • Fractures • Crush injuries • Compartment syndrome • Burns	• Cuts • Lacerations • Acute arterial occlusion • Air embolism-induced injury

Note: AV indicates arteriovenous; CNS, central nervous system; TM, tympanic membrane.
Data from Centers for Disease Control and Prevention. (2006, June 14). *Explosions and blast injuries: A primer for clinicians.* Retrieved from http://www.bt.cdc.gov/masscasualties/explosions.asp

Table 4-5. The Haddon Matrix

Phase	Host	Agent	Physical Environment	Socioeconomic Environment
Pre-event	Driver is studying for exams and did not get much sleep	Motor vehicle is old, small and not well designed for crash protection	It is raining	Driver was at a party and had 2–3 drinks
Event	Driver did not see the sign to slow down for a curve ahead	Vehicle tires are worn	The exit ramp roadway slants outward and not inward (centrifugal force)	Occupants are arguing and radio has loud music playing
Post-event	Driver has a history of diabetes	Seats break apart and occupant trapped	Temperature below 38°F (3°C)	People drive by but delay in notifying 9-1-1

Adapted from Williams.[29]

the body parts not fully restrained by the seatbelt. Vehicle interiors are padded for traveling comfort and help to absorb the energy of impact. Despite safety engineering, patterns of injuries remain associated with particular collision types.

Airbag Considerations

While the overall value of the airbag is clear, appropriate fit and use of supportive safety devices is critical. If the driver's arm is across the steering wheel at the time of deployment, forearm fractures may result. Eye injuries can result from airbag deployment and are of particular concern when patients are wearing glasses. The chemicals used to preserve and deploy airbags may cause corneal abrasions and minor skin burns as the bag explodes to rapidly inflate.[30] Despite the risks of relatively minor secondary injury patterns, advances in airbag technology have decreased the mortality and morbidity associated with MVCs.[31]

Summary

The extent of energy transfer defines the boundaries of potential for traumatic injury. This transfer occurs according to known, reliable laws of physics. The human body possesses a variable tolerance for energy absorption. Trauma teams can predict injury patterns and improve the speed and accuracy of injury identification using knowledge of the dynamic interface between energy and the human body.

References

1. National Association of EMTs; American College of Surgeons Committee on Trauma. (2011). Kinematics of trauma. In *Prehospital trauma life support* (7th ed., pp. 44–85). St. Louis, MO: Mosby Jems.

2. *American Heritage medical dictionary*. (2007). Boston, MA: Houghton Mifflin Company.

3. *Mosby's medical dictionary* (9th ed.). (2012). St. Louis, MO: Mosby Elsevier.

4. National Aeronautics and Space Administration. (2010, September 10). *Newton's law of motion*. Retrieved from http://www.grc.nasa.gov/WWW/k-12/airplane/newton.html

5. Energy, sources of. (2011). In *Columbia electronic encyclopedia*. West Sussex, United Kingdom: Columbia University Press. Retrieved from http://www.infoplease.com/encyclopedia/science/energy-sources-of-types-energy.html

6. New South Wales Government Institute of Trauma & Injury Management. (2012, June 29). *Mechanism of injury*. Retrieved from http://itim.nsw.gov.au/wiki/Mechanism_of_injury

7. Potenza, B., & Nolan, J. (2007). Mechanism and epidemiology in trauma. In C. W. Wilson, C. M. Grande, & D. B. Hoyt (Eds.), *Trauma: Emergency resuscitation, perioperative anesthesia, and surgical management* (pp. 25–42). New York, NY: Informa Healthcare.

8. Grossman, D. C. (2000). The history of injury control and the epidemiology of child and adolescent injuries. *The Future of Children, 10*(1), 23–25.

9. Graham, M. A., & Sandomirsky, M. (2011, April 6). *Pathology of asphyxial death*. Retrieved from http://emedicine.medscape.com/article/1988699-overview

10. Claridge, J. (2013, February 18). *Drowning and forensics*. Retrieved from http://www.exploreforensics.co.uk/drowning.htm

11. Denke, N. (2012). Trauma. In Emergency Nurses Association, *Emergency nursing pediatric course* (4th ed., pp. 261–294). Des Plaines, IL: Emergency Nurses Association.

12. Dickinson, E. T. (2010). Mechanisms of injury related to motor vehicle crashes. In R. J. Riviello, *Manual of forensic emergency medicine: A guide for clinicians* (pp. 98–106). Sudbury, MA: Jones & Bartlett.

13. Riley, P. O., Arregui-Dalmases, C., Purtserov, S., Parent, D., Lessley, D. J., Shaw, G., … Yasuki, T. (2012). Kinematics of the unrestrained vehicle occupants in side-impact crashes. *Traffic Injury Prevention, 13*(2), 163–171.

14. Ryb, G. E., Dischinger, P. C., Kufera, J. A., & Burch, C. A. (2007). Delta V, principal direction of force, and restraint use contributions to motor vehicle collision mortality. *Journal of Trauma, 63*(5), 1000–1005.

15. Chen, H. B., Yang, K. H., & Wang, Z. G. (2009). Biomechanics of whiplash injury. *Chinese Journal of Traumatology, 12*(5), 305–314.

16. Naumann, R. B., Dellinger, A. M., Zaloshnja, E., Lawrence, B. A., & Miller, T. R. (2010). Incidence and total lifetime costs of motor vehicle-related fatal and nonfatal injury by road user type, United States, 2005. *Traffic Injury Prevention, 11*, 353–360.

17. Da Corte, J. (2010). *Motorcycle safety and crashes*. New York, NY: Nova Science Publishers.

18. Wadell, J. P., & Drucker, W. R. (1971). Occult injuries in pedestrian accidents. *Journal of Trauma, 11*(10), 844–852.

19. Orsborn, R., Haley, K., Hammond, S., & Falcone, R. E. (1999). Pediatric pedestrian versus motor vehicle patterns of injury: Debunking the myth. *Air Medical Journal, 18*(3), 107–110.

20. Hunt, J. P., Marr, A. B., & Stuke, L. E. (2013). Kinematics. In K. L. Mattox, E. E. Moore, & D. V. Feliciano, *Trauma* (7th ed., pp. 2–17). New York, NY: McGraw-Hill.

21. American College of Surgeons. (2012). *Advanced trauma life support student course manual* (9th ed.). Chicago, IL: Author.

22. Hollerman, J. J., Fackler, M. L., Coldwell, D. M., & Ben-Menachem, Y. (1990). Gunshot wounds: Bullets, ballistics, and mechanisms of injuries. *American Journal of Roentgenology, 155*(4), 685–690.

23. Alexandropoulou, C. A., & Panagiotopoulos, E. (2010). Wound ballistics: Analysis of blunt and penetrating trauma mechanisms. *Health Science Journal, 4*(4), 225–236.

24. Ramasamy A., Hill, A. M., Masourous, S., Gibb, I., Bull, A. M., & Clasper, J. C. (2010). Blast-related fracture patterns: A forensic biomechanical approach. *Journal of the Royal Society Interface, 8*(59), 689–698.

25. Burr, D. B. (2011). Why bones bend but don't break. *Journal of Musculoskeletal & Neuronal Interactions, 11*(4), 270–285.

26. Maiden, N. (2009). Historical overview of wound ballistics research. *Forensic Science, Medicine, and Pathology, 5*(2), 85–89.

27. University of Utah Spencer S. Eccles Health Sciences Library. (n. d.). *Patterns of tissue injury*. Retrieved from http://library.med.utah.edu/WebPath/TUTORIAL/GUNS/GUNINJ.html

28. U. S. Department of Defense. (2006, July 5). *Medical research for prevention, mitigation, and treatment of blast injuries* (Department of Defense directive number 6025.21E). Retrieved from http://www.dtic.mil/whs/directives/corres/pdf/602521p.pdf

29. Williams, A. F. (1999). The Haddon matrix: Its contribution to injury prevention and control. In R. McClure (Ed.), *Third national conference on injury prevention and control*. Retrieved from http://eprints.qut.edu.au/10081/

30. Barnes, S. S., Wong, W., & Affeldt, J. C. (2012). A case of severe airbag related ocular alkali injury. *Hawaii Journal of Medicine and Public Health, 71*(8), 229–231.

31. Glassbrenner, D., & Starnes, M. (2009, December). *Lives saved calculations for seatbelts and frontal air bags*. Washington, DC: National Highway Traffic Safety Administration.

Chapter 5 • Initial Assessment

Diane Gurney, MS, RN, CEN, FAEN

Angela M. Westergard, MSN, MBA, RN, CEN

Objectives

Upon completion of this chapter, the learner will be able to:

1. **Recognize that competence in the initial assessment process is the foundation of trauma nursing practice.**

2. **Demonstrate the components of the initial assessment process.**

3. **Differentiate between the goals of the primary and secondary surveys.**

4. **Determine actual and potential threats to life and limb using the initial assessment process.**

5. **Select interventions to manage life-threatening conditions identified during the initial assessment process.**

Introduction

The approach to trauma patient care requires a process to identify and treat or stabilize life-threatening injuries in an efficient and timely manner. Time is critical, thus an approach that is systematic, yet easy to learn and implement is most effective. This process is labeled *initial assessment*. For clarity and ease of flow, it is divided into the following process points:[1]

- Preparation and triage
- Primary survey (ABCDE) with resuscitation adjuncts (FG)
- Reevaluation (consideration of transfer)
- Secondary survey (HI) with reevaluation adjuncts
- Reevaluation and post resuscitation care
- Definitive care or transfer to an appropriate trauma center

The A–I mnemonic helps the trauma nurse rapidly assess for and intervene in life-threatening injuries and identify all injuries in a systematic manner. The steps of the mnemonic are as follows:

- A–Airway and Alertness with simultaneous cervical spinal stabilization
- B–Breathing and Ventilation
- C–Circulation and Control of hemorrhage
- D–Disability (neurologic status)
- E–Exposure and Environmental control
- F–Full set of vital signs and Family presence
- G–Get resuscitation adjuncts:
  - L–Laboratory studies (arterial blood gases [ABGs]) and obtain a specimen for blood type and crossmatch
  - M–Monitor for continuous cardiac rhythm and rate assessment
  - N–Naso- or orogastric tube consideration
  - O–Oxygenation and ventilation analysis: Pulse oximetry and end-tidal carbon dioxide (ETCO$_2$) monitoring or capnography
  - P–Pain assessment and management
- H–History and Head-to-toe assessment
- I–Inspect posterior surfaces

Preparation and Triage

Preparation

The approach to trauma care typically begins with notification that a trauma patient is arriving in the emergency department (ED). Whether notification is from prehospital providers or the triage nurse, it is the trauma nurse's responsibility to prepare to receive that patient.

Safe Practice, Safe Care

When preparing to receive a trauma patient in the ED, keep the following tenet in mind: Safe practice, safe care. *Safe practice* means taking into consideration the protection of the team, including:

- Observing universal precautions
- Donning personal protective equipment (PPE), such as gown, gloves, mask, and other equipment as necessary, prior to the patient's arrival

Safe practice also includes consideration of any potential patient exposure to hazardous material that may put the trauma team, other patients, and the ED and hospital at risk. Some patients may require decontamination before entering the trauma resuscitation room. See Chapter 22, Disaster Management, for additional information.

Safe care means assuring the patient is getting to the *right* hospital in the *right* amount of time for the *right* care. The trauma triage criteria developed by the American College of Surgeons Committee on Trauma (ACS-COT) serves as the international standard to identify the trauma patient who would benefit from resuscitation and care at *the right trauma facility* with the appropriate resources (Fig. 5-1). Call for trauma team activation as indicated. See Chapter 2, Teamwork and Trauma Care, for additional information.

The *right time* has long been referred to as the "golden hour"; however, patients presenting with some serious injuries will not survive an hour for definitive treatment. Timely, effective, and efficient interventions facilitate improved outcomes for trauma patients.[1] Prehospital providers play a key role in the survival of the trauma patient. Optimal outcomes result when time in the field is minimized with care focused on airway maintenance, control of hemorrhage, and immobilization.[2] Field triage is key to the appropriate use of community resources with the most severely injured patients being transported directly to the highest level of trauma care in the community (Fig. 5-1).[2,3]

The *right resources* to care for the trauma patient are outlined by the ACS-COT and include essential trauma team members available during activation, an appropriate skill mix represented, necessary equipment in the trauma room, available and appropriate surgical care, skilled post resuscitation care, and rehabilitation and support services.[1]

Preparation in the Trauma Room
Mechanism of injury (MOI), estimated blood loss, and key clues found at the scene can help facilitate the initial assessment process and enable the trauma team to anticipate and prepare for interventions likely to be required upon arrival in the trauma room.[4]

The trauma nurse begins by preparing the room to assure resuscitation equipment is readily available and in working order. This should be done on a regular basis as defined by ED policy—effectively at the beginning of the shift and as necessary after each use of the trauma room. Document the prehospital report where it is readily visible for easy review by all trauma team members.

Triage
Triage involves the sorting of patients based on their need for treatment and the resources available to provide that treatment.[1] Triage also pertains to the sorting of patients in the field and is based on MOI (head-on collision, fall from > 20 feet in an adult), physiologic criteria (vital signs), anatomic criteria (flail chest, fractured pelvis), and special considerations (age) (Fig. 5-1).

Whether the patient presents via an ambulance or through the front door, the priorities for the identification of life-threatening injuries are guided by the primary survey (ABCDE).

Primary Survey

Across-the-room Observation
The primary survey begins immediately upon the patient's arrival to the trauma room. Across-the-room observation is completed as the patient is brought into the room. This can allow for a rapid determination of the patient's overall physiologic stability and the identification of any uncontrolled external hemorrhage. While the patient is safely transferred to a trauma stretcher, the team is given an update on the patient's condition from prehospital personnel or accompanying family or friends. During the primary survey, life-threatening conditions are identified and immediately corrected.[1]

For teaching purposes, the information in this chapter is presented sequentially in order of importance. It is recognized that in reality the trauma team will complete the components of assessment and interventions simultaneously. The trauma nurse chooses the appropriate examination elements of inspection, auscultation, and palpation for assessment.

NOTE: Uncontrolled hemorrhage is the major cause of preventable death after injury.[1,5] If uncontrolled external hemorrhage is noted during the preliminary appraisal, in some environments, under some circumstances, the priorities may be re-ordered to <C>ABC. Historically, the standard approach for emergency or trauma care and advanced life support programs has been ABC(D). However, practitioners in the military, through evidence and experience, found that external peripheral hemorrhage is the leading cause of combat casualty death.[6] Hodgetts et al. reported that the United Kingdom's military has now replaced ABC with <C>ABC, where <C> signifies catastrophic hemorrhage.[6] Tactical Combat Casualty Care from the United States (U.S.) Department of Defense teaches the mnemonic MARCH:[7]

- **M**assive hemorrhage—control life-threatening bleeding

- **A**irway—establish and maintain a patent airway

- **R**espiration—decompress suspected tension pneumothorax, seal open chest wounds, and support ventilation and oxygenation as required

Figure 5-1. Guidelines for Field Triage of Injured Patients—United States, 2011

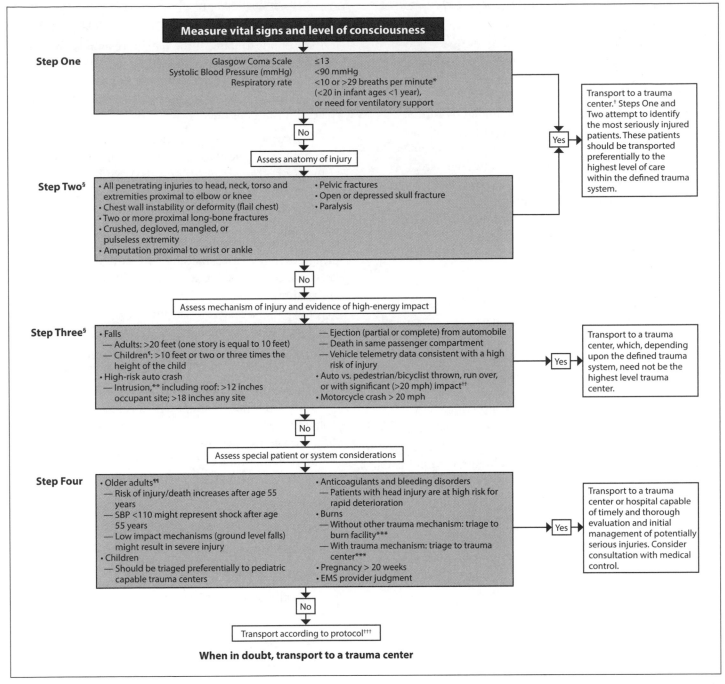

From Sasser et al.[3] Retrieved from http://www.cdc.gov/mmwr/preview/mmwrhtml/rr6101a1.htm

* The upper limit of respiratory rate in infants is >29 breaths per minute to maintain a higher level of overtriage for infants.

† Trauma centers are designated Level I-IV. A Level I center has the greatest amount of resources and personnel for care of the injured patient and provides regional leadership in education, research, and prevention programs. A Level II facility offers similar resources to a Level I facility, possibly differing only in continuous availability of certain subspecialties or sufficient prevention, education, and research activities for Level I designation; Level II facilities are not required to be resident or fellow education centers. A Level III center is capable of assessment, resuscitation, and emergency surgery, with severely injured patients being transferred to a Level I or II facility. A Level IV trauma center is capable of providing 24-hour physician coverage, resuscitation, and stabilization to injured patients before transfer to a facility that provides a higher level of trauma care.

§ Any injury noted in Step Two or mechanism identified in Step Three triggers a "yes" response.

¶ Age <15 years.

** Intrusion refers to interior compartment intrusion, as opposed to deformation which refers to exterior damage.

†† Includes pedestrians or bicyclists thrown or run over by a motor vehicle or those with estimated impact >20 mph with a motor vehicle.

§§ Local or regional protocols should be used to determine the most appropriate level of trauma center within the defined trauma system; need not be the highest-level trauma center.

¶¶ Age >55 years.

*** Patients with both burns and concomitant trauma for whom the burn injury poses the greatest risk for morbidity and mortality should be transferred to a burn center. If the nonburn trauma presents a greater immediate risk, the patient may be stabilized in a trauma center and then transferred to a burn center.

††† Patients who do not meet any of the triage criteria in Steps One through Four should be transported to the most appropriate medical facility as outlined in local EMS protocols.

- **C**irculation—vascular access (intravenous or intraosseous) and administer fluids as required to treat shock

- **H**ead injury/**H**ypothermia—prevent or treat hypotension and hypoxia to prevent worsening of traumatic brain injury and prevent or treat hypothermia

Since civilian trauma care has been guided by military battlefield evidence and practice, present day civilian trauma care guidelines may, under some circumstances, recommend the <C>ABC approach to trauma care. However, the current civilian approach to trauma resuscitation involves multiple trauma team members allowing several priorities to be addressed simultaneously, mitigating the need to reprioritize. The first priority remains to treat the greatest life-threatening condition.[1,7,8]

A–Airway and Alertness
Cervical Spinal Immobilization
A cervical spinal injury (CSI) is suspected in any patient with multisystem trauma, until the patient has a Glasgow Coma Scale (GCS) score of 15 and has been fully evaluated for CSI by an experienced physician or has been cleared of spinal injury via radiography or computed tomography (CT).[9] While in the ED, alignment and protection of the cervical spine can be accomplished by either:

- Manual stabilization: Two hands holding the patient's head and neck in alignment

- Immobilization: A correctly sized, semi-rigid cervical collar securely fastened

The spine board is primarily a transportation device; therefore, remove the patient from the board as soon as spinal cord injury (SCI) has been ruled out.

Take extreme care when removing the helmet from patients who have a potentially unstable CSI. This requires the coordination of two people. One person maintains manual inline stabilization of the head and neck while a second person removes the helmet.[11]

Assessment
The mnemonic AVPU can help the nurse to quickly assess for the patient's level of alertness. Its use at the beginning of the initial assessment can be an important determinant to assist the nurse in selecting the appropriate airway intervention. The components of AVPU are as follows:

- A–Alert. If the patient is alert, he or she will be able to maintain his or her airway once it is clear.

If any of the responses below are elicited at this point, the airway may be compromised:

- V–responds to Verbal stimuli. If the patient needs verbal stimulation to respond, an airway adjunct may be needed to keep the tongue from obstructing the airway.

- P–responds to Pain. If the patient responds only to pain, he or she may not be able to maintain his or her airway, and an airway adjunct may need to be placed while further assessment is made to determine the need for intubation.

- U–Unresponsive. If the patient is unresponsive, announce it loudly to the team and direct someone to *check if the patient is pulseless* while assessing if the cause of the problem is the airway. Consider reprioritizing the assessment priority to <C>ABC.[6,7]

Inspect, Auscultate, and Palpate
During the initial assessment and identified interventions, protect the cervical spine with immobilization or manual stabilization.

- If the patient is alert or responds to verbal stimuli, ask the patient to open his or her mouth

- If the patient is unable to open the mouth, responds only to pain, or is unresponsive, use the jaw-thrust maneuver to open the airway and assess for obstruction. In the patient with suspected CSI, the jaw-thrust procedure is recommended and is performed by two providers: one provides manual stabilization of the cervical spine and the second performs the jaw-thrust procedure.[10]

- Inspect for:
  - The tongue obstructing the airway
  - Loose or missing teeth
  - Foreign objects
  - Blood, vomitus, or secretions
  - Edema
  - Burns or evidence of inhalation injury

- Auscultate or listen for:
  - Obstructive airway sounds such as snoring, gurgling, or stridor

- Palpate for:
  - Possible occlusive maxillofacial bony deformity
  - Subcutaneous emphysema

If the patient has a definitive airway in place, assess for proper placement of the airway device and move to the next step of the primary survey. Proper placement findings include:

- Presence of adequate rise and fall of the chest with assisted ventilation
- Absence of gurgling on auscultation over the epigastrium
- Bilateral breath sounds present on auscultation
- Presence of carbon dioxide (CO_2) verified by a CO_2 detector device or monitor

Interventions

Information below represents the general approach for all trauma patients. See Chapter 6, Airway and Ventilation, for additional information regarding specific airway devices and interventions.

If the airway is patent:

If the patient is awake and has a patent airway, he or she may assume a position that facilitates adequate air exchange.

If the airway is NOT patent:

- Suction the airway.
  - Use care to avoid stimulating the gag reflex
  - If the airway is obstructed by blood, vomitus, or other secretions, use a rigid suction device
  - If a foreign body is noted, remove it carefully with forceps or another appropriate method
- If suctioning does not relieve airway obstruction, the tongue may be the cause of the obstruction. Insert an airway adjunct. See Chapter 6, Airway and Ventilation, for more information.
  - Use the jaw-thrust maneuver to open the airway while maintaining manual stabilization
  - A nasopharyngeal airway can be used in patients who are conscious or unconscious
  - An oropharyngeal airway can be used in patients without a gag reflex
- Consider a definitive airway (endotracheal intubation)
  - A definitive airway is a tracheal tube securely placed in the trachea with the cuff inflated[11]
  - Cuffed tubes are now recommended for use in children under 8 years of age.[12] See Chapter 17, Special Populations: The Pediatric Trauma Patient, for more information.
  - The following conditions or situations require a definitively secured airway:[11]

- Apnea
- GCS score of 8 or less
- Severe maxillofacial fractures
- Evidence of inhalation injury (facial burns)
- Laryngeal or tracheal injury or neck hematoma
- High risk of aspiration and the patient's inability to protect the airway
- Compromised or ineffective ventilation
- Anticipation of deterioration of neurologic status that may result in an inability to maintain or protect the airway

Difficult Airways

Injury or anatomic variations may make it difficult to successfully intubate the patient. In these cases, continue to ventilate the patient with a bag-mask device connected to oxygen at 15L/min until an alternative airway can be established. See Chapter 6, Airway and Ventilation.

B–Breathing and Ventilation
Assessment

To assess breathing, expose the patient's chest and complete the following:

- Inspect for:
  - Spontaneous breathing
  - Symmetrical rise and fall of the chest
  - Depth, pattern, and rate of respirations
  - Signs of respiratory difficulty such as the use of accessory muscle or diaphragmatic breathing
  - Skin color (normal, pale, flushed, cyanotic)
  - Contusions, abrasions, or deformities that may be a sign of underlying injury
  - Open pneumothoraces (sucking chest wounds)
  - Jugular venous distention (JVD) and the position of the trachea (tracheal deviation and JVD are late signs that may indicate a tension pneumothorax)
  - Signs of inhalation injury (singed nasal hairs, carbonaceous sputum)
- Auscultate for:
  - Presence, quality, and equality of breath sounds bilaterally at the second intercostal space midclavicular line and the bases at the fifth intercostal space at the anterior axillary line
- Palpate for:
  - Bony structures and possible rib fractures, which may impact ventilation

- Subcutaneous emphysema, which may be a sign of a pneumothorax
- Soft tissue injury
- Jugular venous pulsations at the suprasternal notch or in the supraclavicular area[14,15]

Intervention

See Chapter 6, Airway and Ventilation, for more information.

If breathing is absent:
- Open the airway using the jaw-thrust maneuver while maintaining manual cervical spinal stabilization
- Insert an oral airway adjunct
- Assist ventilations with a bag-mask device
- Prepare for a definitive airway

If breathing is present:
- Administer oxygen at 15 L/min via a nonrebreather mask with reservoir bag.[4]
  - Inability to maintain adequate oxygenation, causes hypoxemia resulting in anaerobic metabolism and acidosis
  - Trauma patients need early supplemental oxygen; however, recent evidence suggests to closely monitor and titrate oxygen delivery for stabilized trauma patients to avoid the detrimental physiologic effects of hyperoxia.[16–19] See Chapter 6, Airway and Ventilation, for more information.
- Determine if ventilation is effective.
  - An end tidal carbon dioxide ($ETCO_2$) measurement between 35 and 45 mm Hg shows effective ventilation.[11,13] A level above 50 mm Hg signifies depressed ventilation.[20]
  - An oxygen saturation (SpO_2) of 94% or higher is associated with effective ventilation[11,13,18]

If ventilation is ineffective:
- Assist ventilation with a bag-mask device connected to an oxygen source at 15 L/min to administer 10 to 12 breaths per minute or one every 5 to 6 seconds[11,18,21]
- Determine the need for a definitive airway

Identify life-threatening pulmonary injuries. These injuries require rapid identification and immediate intervention before proceeding to the next step in the primary survey.[11] See Chapter 11, Thoracic and Neck Trauma, for more information. Examples of these injuries include:
- Open pneumothorax
- Tension pneumothorax
- Flail chest
- Hemothorax

C–Circulation and Control of Hemorrhage Assessment

The major assessment parameters that produce important information within seconds of a patient's arrival are level of consciousness, skin color, and pulse.[22] Skin color can be assessed using an across-the-room observation as the patient is brought into the trauma room. The use of AVPU can reveal the patient's level of consciousness and help to determine if the initial assessment may proceed as ABC or be reprioritized as <C>ABC to address hemorrhage control.[6,7] The assessment of circulation during the primary survey includes early evaluation of the possibility of hemorrhage in the abdomen and pelvis in any patient who has sustained blunt trauma.[23] In those cases, an emergent abdominal or pelvic assessment may be performed to include a focused assessment with sonography for trauma (FAST) examination or a radiograph of the pelvis.[23]

Inspect for:
- Uncontrolled external bleeding
- Skin color

Auscultate for:
- Muffled heart sounds, which may indicate pericardial tamponade

Palpate for:
- Presence of carotid and/or femoral (central) pulses for rate, rhythm, and strength
- Skin temperature and moisture (cool and diaphoretic or warm and dry)

If pulses are absent:
- Initiate life-supporting measures following the guidelines of the American Heart Association (AHA) for basic life support.[21]
- Assess for signs of uncontrolled internal bleeding.
- Consider and assess for the following:
  - A penetrating wound to the heart
  - Pericardial tamponade
  - Rupture of great vessels
  - Abdominal hemorrhage

Common sites for hemorrhage in the traumatically injured patient are the chest, abdomen, pelvis, long bones, and external bleeding from wounds or amputation. Assessment of the chest, abdomen, and pelvis may be indicated at this time to determine the site of the hemorrhage.[1]

If pulses are present:

- Inspect for:
  - Any external bleeding
  - Skin color
- Palpate for:
  - Central pulses
    - Pulses that are strong, regular, and at a normal rate may indicate normovolemia
    - A rapid, thready pulse may indicate hypovolemia, and an irregular pulse may warn of potential cardiac dysfunction[1]
  - Skin temperature and moisture

If pulses are present, but circulation is ineffective:

- Immediately assess for signs of uncontrolled internal bleeding
- If the patient has ineffective circulation, consider common sites for hemorrhage such as the chest, abdomen, and pelvis[1]

Interventions

Control and treat uncontrolled external bleeding by the following:

- Apply direct pressure over the site
- Elevate a bleeding extremity
- Apply pressure over arterial sites
- Consider a pelvic binder if an unstable pelvic fracture is suspected
- Consider the use of a tourniquet (see Chapter 7, Shock, for more information)
- If the patient has signs of bleeding, without pausing in the primary survey, another team member may obtain a blood pressure for baseline and trending

Cannulate two veins with large-caliber intravenous (IV) catheters:[1,21]

- If unable to gain venous access quickly, consider intraosseous (IO) or central venous access, depending on available resources
- Obtain a blood sample for type and crossmatch
- Initiate infusions of warmed isotonic crystalloid solution
- Use blood administration tubing and normal saline (0.9%) to facilitate the possible need for blood administration
- Consider balanced resuscitation needs (see Chapter 7, Shock for more information)

- Administer blood or blood products as ordered
- Use a rapid infusion device per facility protocol

Intervene in life-threatening situations:

- Prepare and assist with emergency thoracotomy as indicated
- Prepare and assist with pericardial needle aspiration to relieve a cardiac tamponade as indicated
- Be prepared to expedite patient transfer to the operating suite

Volume Resuscitation

The standard approach to treating hypotension in trauma patients has been to infuse large volumes of IV fluids. Recent studies now recommend a different approach and note that an elevated blood pressure may dislodge the body's formation of clots and promote further bleeding.[4] In addition, large volumes of fluid lead to dilutional coagulopathy which worsens metabolic acidosis and may cause hypothermia.[4]

Component therapy is now suggested for fluid resuscitation to replace patient losses, including administering red blood cells, plasma, and platelets. This balanced approach to resuscitation includes massive transfusion so that oxygen delivery is optimized, acidosis is corrected, coagulopathy is prevented, and damage control surgery is performed.[5] See Chapter 7, Shock, for more information.

D–Disability (Neurologic Status)
Assessment

The GCS offers a standardized method for evaluating level of consciousness. It also serves as an excellent communication tool for members of the trauma team to convey objective information. Scores range from 3 (indicating deep unconsciousness) to 15 (indicating a patient who is alert, converses normally, and is able to obey commands).

One limitation of the GCS is that it does not provide for an accurate assessment of patients who are intubated or aphasic and unable to respond to the verbal component.[24] Regardless, it continues to be the clinical standard against which newer scales are compared and it is used widely by emergency and trauma teams, medical and surgical intensive care units, and prehospital providers.[24] Assess the GCS score upon patient arrival and repeat according to policy. Trend analysis of GCS findings is important to detect deteriorating or improving neurologic function. See Chapter 9, Brain, Cranial, and Maxillofacial Trauma, for more information.

Assess pupils for equality, shape, and reactivity (PERRL).

Interventions

- Evaluate for needed computed tomography (CT) of the head. Consider any changes in level of consciousness to be the result of CNS injury until proven otherwise.[24] See Chapter 9, Brain, Cranial, and Maxilofacial Trauma for more information.

- Consider ABGs. A decreased level of consciousness may be an indicator of decreased cerebral perfusion, hypoventilation, or acid-base imbalance.

- Consider bedside glucose, alcohol level, or toxicology screening. Hypoglycemia, along with other conditions, such as the presence of alcohol, may play a role in the patient's neurologic status but need to be excluded as the primary cause.

E–Exposure and Environmental Control
Assessment

- Carefully and completely undress the patient to facilitate a thorough assessment. Use caution as there may be needles, glass shards, weapons, or other sharp items in clothing.

- Inspect for any uncontrolled bleeding and quickly note any obvious injuries

Interventions

- If clothing may be used as evidence, preserve it according to institutional policy. Cut around suspected evidence and place clothing in a paper bag. Maintain the chain of evidence with law enforcement as indicated. Care of the patient always supersedes evidence collection. See Chapter 20, Special Populations: The Interpersonal Violence Trauma Patient, for more information.

- Maintain body temperature by the following:
  ○ Covering the patient with warm blankets
  ○ Keeping the ambient temperature warm
  ○ Administering warmed IV fluids
  ○ Using forced air warmers
  ○ Using radiant warming lights

Hypothermia combined with hypotension and acidosis is a potentially lethal combination in the injured patient.[25] This assessment parameter is intentionally placed in the primary survey in order to assure that aggressive measures are taken to prevent the loss of body heat.

F–Full Set of Vital Signs and Family Presence
Full Set of Vital Signs

To monitor the effectiveness of the resuscitation, obtain and trend vital signs at regular intervals, including blood pressure, pulse, respirations, and temperature.

Family Presence

Facilitate family presence as soon as a member of the trauma team is available to act as liaison to the family. If a social worker or hospital chaplain is a member of the team, they may fill this role. Honesty, sensitivity, and a caring approach are important when interacting with the patient's family and friends as this can be a stressful time. Consider factors such as the patient's age, ethnicity, cultural background, and religion when interacting with the family.

Evidence shows that patients prefer to have family members present during resuscitation.[26] There is also strong evidence supporting that family members wish to be offered the option to be present during invasive procedures and resuscitation of a family member.[23] The Emergency Nurses Association (ENA), along with several other professional organizations, supports the option of family presence during resuscitation.

While some providers may have concerns regarding family presence during resuscitation and invasive procedures, family members should not be viewed as a complication, but rather as an extension of the patient.[27] Being present at the time of a person's death is viewed as a privilege, and trauma teams are encouraged to share this privilege with the patient's family in accordance with the patient's and family's wishes.[27]

G–Get Resuscitation Adjuncts

Consider the mnemonic LMNOP to remember these resuscitation adjuncts:

- L–Laboratory studies arterial blood gases (ABGs) or in some cases, venous blood gases and obtain a specimen for blood type and crossmatch

  ○ Lactic acid is an excellent reflection of tissue perfusion

    ◆ High levels are associated with hypoperfusion[28, 29]

    ◆ A lactic acid level greater than 2 to 4 mmol/L is associated with poor outcomes[29, 30]

  ○ ABGs provide values of oxygen, CO_2 and base excess, which are reflective of endpoint measurements of the effectiveness of cellular perfusion, adequacy of ventilation, and the success of the resuscitation

    ◆ An abnormal base deficit may indicate poor perfusion and tissue hypoxia, which results in the generation of hydrogen ions and metabolic acidosis

- A base deficit of less than –6 is associated with poor outcomes[31]

- M–Monitor cardiac rate and rhythm: Compare the patient's pulse to the monitor rhythm. Dysrhythmias—such as premature ventricular contractions (PVCs), atrial fibrillation, or S-T segment changes—may indicate blunt cardiac trauma.[32] Pulseless electrical activity (PEA) may point to cardiac tamponade, tension pneumothorax, or profound hypovolemia.[33]

- N–Naso- or orogastric tube consideration: The insertion of a gastric tube provides for evacuation of stomach contents and the relief of gastric distention. This may help to optimize inflation of the lungs and prevent vomiting and/or aspiration. If mid-face fractures or head injury are suspected, the oral route is preferred.[13] Maintain cervical spinal immobilization, and ensure that suction equipment is readily available.

- O–Oxygenation and ventilation assessment

  ○ Pulse oximetry detects changes in oxygenation that cannot be readily observed clinically. It is non-invasive and measures the oxygen saturation (SpO_2) of arterial blood or percentage of bound hemoglobin. A pulse oximetry reading of 95% or greater is viewed as convincing evidence that peripheral arterial oxygenation is adequate.[11,13,18] However, accurate readings rely on adequate peripheral perfusion. Oximetry offers a measurement of oxygen saturation and not evidence of ventilation.

  ○ $ETCO_2$ monitoring (or capnography) provides instantaneous information about the ventilation, perfusion, and metabolism of carbon dioxide. Normal values are 35 to 45 mm Hg.[34]

- P–Pain assessment and management

  ○ The assessment and management of severe pain is an important part of the treatment of trauma patients with the goal to give comfort to the patient while avoiding respiratory depression

  ○ Many injuries sustained by the trauma patient may be life-changing for both the patient and family, so it is essential that the trauma team also provide appropriate spiritual and psychosocial support. See Chapter 8, Pain, for additional information.

Reevaluation

Portable Radiograph

A portable anterior-posterior chest radiograph and pelvis radiograph can be obtained at this phase of the resuscitation. These studies are performed in the resuscitation area and may help to identify any suspected and potentially life-threatening injuries such as a pneumothorax or pelvic fracture with uncontrolled internal hemorrhage. Radiographs can also contribute to confirming placement of endotracheal tubes, chest tubes, and gastric tubes.

Consider the Need for Patient Transfer

The trauma team leader gathers essential information during the primary survey and resuscitation phase that may indicate the need to transfer the patient to another facility.[1] The team leader will delegate the initial steps to begin immediate transfer and continue with ongoing evaluation and resuscitation. Follow institutional guidelines for contacting the appropriate facility that has the capability to provide care for the severely injured. See Chapter 23, Transition of Care for the Trauma Patient, for more information.

Secondary Survey

The secondary survey (HI) begins after the completion of the primary survey (ABCDE), after the initiation of resuscitative efforts, once vital functions have been stabilized and after consideration for resuscitation adjuncts (FG).

H–History

The patient's condition is greatly influenced by the MOI. Certain injuries can be predicted based on the direction and amount of energy behind the MOI.[1] See Chapter 4, Biomechanics, Kinematics, and Mechanisms of Injury, for more information. Additional history includes the following:

- Mnemonic MIST prehospital report:

  ○ **M**OI

  ○ **I**njuries sustained

  ○ **S**igns and symptoms (in the field),

  ○ **T**reatment (in the field)—can be used as a guide.

- Patient history: If the patient's family is present, solicit input regarding the traumatic event and the health history. If the patient is responsive, eliciting answers may assist the trauma nurse in evaluating the patient's level of consciousness and help to identify areas of pain and injury. The SAMPLE mnemonic highlights important aspects of patient history:

- ◦ **S**ymptoms associated with the injury
- ◦ **A**llergies and tetanus status
- ◦ **M**edications currently used, including anticoagulant therapy
- ◦ **P**ast medical history (include hospitalizations and/or surgeries)
- ◦ **L**ast oral intake
- ◦ **E**vents and **E**nvironmental factors related to the injury

Comorbid factors are existing conditions that place the patient at greater risk for complications related to the injury. They include the following:[33]

- • Older age: Risk for injury or death increases after age 55
- • Burns: Patients with burns may require early transfer to a burn facility
- • Pregnancy greater than 20 weeks: Obtain an early obstetric consult

H–Head-to-toe Assessment

During this phase, a complete head-to-toe examination is performed and documented. This information is obtained primarily from inspection, auscultation, and palpation. In a noisy trauma room, the use of percussion is difficult to perform and has been replaced in some cases by the use of FAST examinations. Systematically move from the patient's head to the lower extremities and posterior surface following the process outlined below in order to identify all injuries.

General Appearance

Note the position and posture of the patient or the presence of any spontaneous guarding. Observe for stiffness, rigidity, or flaccidity of extremities. Document specific odors, such as alcohol, gasoline, or other chemicals. Specific presentations may alert the trauma team to injuries (shortening and external rotation of a leg might suggest a hip fracture).

Head and Face
- • Soft tissue injuries
- • Inspect for:
  - ◦ lacerations, puncture wounds, abrasions, contusions, edema, ecchymoses, or impaled objects
- • Palpate for:
  - ◦ areas of tenderness, step-offs, and crepitus
- • Bony deformities
  - ◦ Inspect for:

- ◆ Asymmetry of facial expression
- ◆ Any exposed tissue or bone that may suggest disruption of the central nervous system (brain matter)
- ◦ Palpate for:
  - ◆ Depressions
  - ◆ Angulations
  - ◆ Tenderness

Eyes
- • Determine gross visual acuity by holding up fingers and asking the patient to identify how many are being held up. Assess for prescription eyeglasses or contact lenses; remove before edema develops.
- • Inspect for:
  - ◦ Pupils to determine size, equality, shape, and reactivity to light
  - ◦ Muscle function by asking the patient to follow a moving finger in the six cardinal positions

Ears
- • Inspect for:
  - ◦ Unusual drainage, such as blood or clear fluid from the external ear
  - ◦ Do not pack the ear since a cerebrospinal fluid (CSF) leak may be present and packing could increase the intracranial pressure
  - ◦ Test otorrhea for CSF[35–40]
    - ◆ β_2-Transferrin: This test requires fluid to be sent to the laboratory and is considered the gold standard for identifying CSF otorrhea or rhinorrhea
  - ◦ The halo sign and glucose tests can be done rapidly and give a general suspicion of CSF leak. See Chapter 9, Brain, Cranial, and Maxillofacial Trauma, for more information.
  - ◦ Ecchymosis behind the ear (Battle sign; usually a later development)
  - ◦ Ear avulsions or lacerations
    - ◆ Repairs often require the expertise of a plastic surgeon

Nose
- • Inspect for:
  - ◦ Unusual drainage such as blood or clear fluid
    - ◆ Do not pack the nose to stop clear fluid drainage as it may be CSF and packing could increase intracranial pressure
  - ◦ Test rhinorrhea for CSF

- If CSF is suspected, notify the physician and do not insert a nasogastric tube
- Note the position of the nasal septum

Neck and Cervical Spine

Presume that patients with maxillofacial or head trauma may also have an unstable CSI (fracture and or ligament injury). Immobilize the cervical spine until adequate studies have been completed and an injury has been excluded. The absence of neurologic deficit does not exclude CSI.[1,3] See Chapter 13, Spinal Cord and Vertebral Column Trauma, for more information.

- Inspect for:
  - Signs of penetrating or surface trauma, including presence of impaled objects, contusions, edema, or any open wounds
  - The position of the trachea and the appearance of the jugular veins
- Palpate for:
  - Cervical tenderness or deformities
  - Tracheal deviation
  - Subcutaneous emphysema and areas of tenderness

Chest

- Inspect for:
  - Presence of spotaneous breathing
  - Respiratory rate, depth, and degree of effort required, use of accessory or abdominal muscles, and any paradoxical chest movement
  - Anterior and lateral chest walls—including the axillae—for lacerations, puncture wounds, abrasions, contusions, avulsions, ecchymoses, edema, impaled objects, and scars that may indicate previous chest surgery
  - The expansion and excursion of the chest during ventilation
  - Expressions or reactions that indicate the presence of pain with inspiration and expiration (facial grimace)
- Auscultate for:
  - Lung sounds, noting the presence of any adventitious sounds, such as wheezes or crackles
  - Heart sounds for the presence of murmurs, friction rubs, or muffled heart tones
- Palpate for:
  - Signs of subcutaneous emphysema
  - Bony crepitus or deformities (step-offs or areas of tenderness) to the clavicles, sternum, and ribs

Abdomen/Flanks

- Inspect for:
  - Lacerations, puncture wounds, abrasions, contusions, avulsions, ecchymoses, edema, impaled objects, and scars that may indicate previous abdominal surgery
  - Evisceration
  - Distention
- Auscultate for:
  - The presence or absence of bowel sounds
- Palpate for:
  - Rigidity, guarding, masses, and areas of tenderness in all four abdominal quadrants
    - Begin light palpation in an area where the patient has not complained of pain or where there is no obvious injury

Pelvis/Perineum

- Inspect for:
  - Lacerations, puncture wounds, abrasions, contusions, avulsions, ecchymoses, edema, impaled objects, and scars
  - Bony deformities or exposed bone
  - Blood at the urethral meatus (more common in males than females because of the extraperitoneal position of the urethra), vagina, and rectum
  - Priapism
  - Pain and/or the urge, but inability to void
  - Scrotal/labial hematoma
- Palpate for:
  - Instability of the pelvis by applying gentle pressure over the iliac wings downward and medially[23]
  - Instability of the pelvis by placing gentle pressure on the symphysis pubis

Urinary output is a reflection of end-organ perfusion and considered a sensitive indicator of the patient's volume status. Continuous or frequent monitoring is best accomplished with an indwelling urinary catheter. However, it is necessary to assess the patient's condition to determine the need for urinary catheter insertion, taking into account indications and contraindications. Urinary tract infections in the healthcare setting are strongly associated with the presence of an indwelling catheter and alternate methods should be considered before placement.[41]

Valid indications for the insertion of a urinary catheter include:[42]

- Urinary obstruction or retention
- Alteration in blood pressure or volume status
- The need to determine accurate input and output and the patient is unable to use a urinal or bedpan
- Emergency surgery or major trauma
- Urologic procedures or bladder irrigation
- Comfort care for the terminally ill

Insertion of a urinary catheter is contraindicated if urethral transection is suspected. Signs and symptoms of urethral injury include:[1]

- Blood at the urethral meatus
- Perineal ecchymosis
- Scrotal ecchymosis
- High-riding or nonpalpable prostate
- Suspected pelvic fracture

Extremities

When noting extremity assessment, it is important to evaluate the neurovascular status, with circulation, motor function, and sensation.

- Inspect for:
  - Soft tissue injuries
    - Bleeding
    - Presence of lacerations, abrasions, contusions, avulsions, puncture wounds, impaled objects, ecchymoses, edema, deformity, and any open wounds
  - Bony injuries
    - Angulation, deformity, and open wounds with evidence of protruding bone fragments, or edema
  - Previously applied splints for correct placement: Leave in place if correctly applied and neurovascular function is intact
  - Skin color
  - Presence of dialysis catheters, peripherally inserted central catheters (PICCs) or other signs of complex medical history
- Palpate for:
  - Circulation
    - Skin temperature and moisture
    - Pulses
      - Always compare one side with the other and note any differences in the quality of the pulses

- Femoral, popliteal, dorsalis pedis, and posterior tibialis in the lower extremities; the brachial and radial pulses in the upper extremities
  - Bony injury
    - Crepitus
    - Deformity and areas of tenderness
  - Sensation
    - Determine the patient's ability to sense touch in all four extremities
  - Motor function
    - Elicit the presence or absence of spontaneous movement in extremities
    - Determine motor strength and range of motion in all four extremities
    - Test equality of strength in bilateral extremities

I–Inspect Posterior Surfaces

- Maintain cervical spinal protection
- Support extremities with suspected injuries
- Logroll the patient with the assistance from members of the trauma team
  - The team leader is at the head, directing the team to turn together
  - Other team members maintain the torso, hips, and lower extremities
  - This maintains the vertebral column in alignment during the turning process
  - When possible, avoid rolling the patient onto the side of an injured extremity. The patient is logrolled away from the examiner so the back, flanks, buttocks, and thighs can be visually examined.
  - See "Emerging Trends" for more information
- Inspect for:
  - Presence of blood in or around the rectum
  - Lacerations, puncture wounds, abrasions, contusions, avulsions, ecchymoses, edema, impaled objects, and scars
- Palpate for:
  - Deformity and areas of tenderness along the vertebral column, including the costovertebral angles
  - Deformity and areas of tenderness along posterior surfaces to include the flanks
- Perform a rectal examination
  - A digital rectal examination (DRE) is commonly performed by a physician or advanced practice nurse (APN) during the secondary survey; however,

the sensitivity of this test has been called into question.[43] An alternative is to ask the alert patient to squeeze the buttocks to evaluate spinal cord function. Determine the following assessment parameters:

- ♦ Presence or absence of rectal tone
- ♦ Presence of a high-riding prostate gland: This can indicate a significant pelvic fracture[23]

- Promote timely removal of the patient from the spine board if there are no contraindications.

Reevaluation Adjuncts

Upon completion of the secondary survey anticipate orders for additional diagnostic tests and interventions to identify specific injuries. These include (but are not limited to):

- Additional laboratory studies
- Radiologic imaging
  - ○ Radiographs
  - ○ CT scans
  - ○ Magnetic resonance imaging (MRI)
- Wound care
- Application of splints
- Application of traction devices
- Tetanus prophylaxis
- Administration of medications
  - ○ Antibiotics
  - ○ Pain medications
  - ○ Sedation
  - ○ Neuromuscular blocking agents
- Angiography
- Contrast urography and angiography
- Bronchoscopy or esophagoscopy
- Preparation for the operating room
- Preparation for admission or transfer

These procedures may require transportation of the patient out of the ED; therefore, ensure the appropriately trained personnel, necessary medications and resuscitative equipment are available during transport of the patient. Ideally these procedures will not be performed until the patient is hemodynamically stabilized. Injuries identified in the primary and secondary surveys continue to be reassessed along with pain and response to analgesics.

Additional considerations include the following:

- Documentation: Careful and accurate documentation of the assessment, interventions, resuscitation, and the patient's response is an expectation of the trauma nurse

- Family support: The trauma nurse with primary responsibility for the patient can contribute to the ongoing psychosocial support of both patient and family. Collaboration with the family support person that is assigned will assure needs are met and information is shared. Whenever possible, allow the family to stay with the patient and give adequate time for them to have questions answered.

Reevaluation and Post Resuscitation Care

The reevaluation phase of trauma assessment includes the trauma nurse's ongoing reevaluation of the patient's response to the injury and the effectiveness of all of the interventions. Achievement of expected outcomes is evaluated, and the treatment plan is adjusted to enhance patient outcomes.

Post resuscitation care parameters that are continually reevaluated include:

- Components of the primary survey (ABCDE)
- Vital signs
- Pain and response to pain medications and non-pharmacologic interventions
- All identified injuries and the effectiveness of the treatment or interventions

See Chapter 24, Post Resuscitation Care in the Emergency Department, for more information.

Definitive Care or Transport

Definitive care includes the need for specific subspecialty care such as neurosurgery or orthopedics, monitoring and care in an intensive care unit (ICU), or the need for evaluation and operative intervention by a trauma surgeon. The decision to transfer to another facility depends on the patient's injuries, facility resources and pre-established transfer agreements. This decision is a matter of medical judgment, and evidence supports the position that trauma outcomes improve if patients who are critically injured are cared for in trauma centers.[1]

Emerging Trends

As the science and evidence of trauma care continues to evolve, tools to improve patient outcomes continue to be trialed and refined. Evidence is tested and replicated, and new standards of care are transitioned into practice. This section on trauma care considerations explores some of the evidence and the potential significance to trauma patient care. Regarding the initial assessment, the use of computer-aided decision-making and logrolling are discussed.

Computer-aided Decision-making in Trauma Resuscitation

A Level I trauma center in Melbourne, Australia, studied the efficacy of evidence-based trauma management algorithms in the initial 30 minutes of trauma resuscitation. Computer-generated prompts for critical decision-making decisions were created every 72 seconds. A computer-assisted video monitored compliance to the algorithms, and error rates were measured per patient. The researchers found that compliance to protocols increased and that the computer-prompted decision-making decreased morbidity and errors in trauma management.[44]

Logrolling the Patient

Logrolling is the most commonly used maneuver to inspect a patient's posterior surface. However, some have suggested that use of this procedure can cause excess movement in patients with suspected SCI and have recommended discontinuation of its use.[45] At this time, evidence does not fully support this suggestion and the ACS supports the use of logrolling.[1] Research is ongoing.

Summary

The initial assessment approach for injured patients is the essence of trauma nursing care. Initial assessment of the trauma patient is achieved through the use of an organized system of assessment, interventions, evaluation, and definitive care. Essential components include:

- Preparation and triage
- Primary survey (ABCDE) with resuscitation adjuncts (FG)
- Reevaluation (consideration of transfer)
- Secondary survey (HI) with reevaluation adjuncts
- Reevaluation and post resuscitation care
- Definitive care and transfer

By using this approach in the care of the trauma patient, emergency and trauma nurses can be more aware of the body's pathophysiologic response to injury and proactively intervene with lifesaving, goal-directed therapies and current management strategies for optimal outcomes for the trauma patient.

References

1. American College of Surgeons. (2012). Initial assessment and management. In *Advanced trauma life support student course manual* (9th ed., pp. 2–22). Chicago, IL: Author.

2. American College of Surgeons Committee on Trauma. (2010). *Prehospital trauma life support* (7th ed.). Chicago, IL: Author.

3. Sasser, S. M., Hunt, R. C., Faul, M., Sugerman, D., Pearson, W., Dulski, T., … Lerner, E. B.; Centers for Disease Control and Prevention. (2012). Guidelines for clearing the cervical spine in conscious trauma patient for field triage of injured patients: Recommendations of the National Expert Panel on Field Triage, 2011. *MMWR Recommendations and Reports, 61*(RR-1), 1–20.

4. Cole, E. (2009). *Trauma care: Initial assessment and management in the emergency department.* Hoboken, NJ: John Wiley & Sons.

5. Cherkas, D. (2011). Traumatic hemorrhagic shock: Advances in fluid management. *EB Medicine, 13*(11), 1–20.

6. Hodgetts, T. J., Mahoney, P. F., Russell, M. Q., & Byers, M. (2006). ABC to <C>ABC: Redefining the military trauma paradigm. *Emergency Medicine Journal, 23*(10), 745–746.

7. Military Health System. (2012, September). *Tactical combat casualty care.* Retrieved from http://www.health.mil/Education_And_Training/TCCC.aspx

8. Kirkpatrick, A. W., Ball, C. G., D'Amours, S. K., & Zygun, D. (2008). Acute resuscitation of the unstable adult trauma patient: Bedside diagnosis and therapy. *Canadian Journal of Surgery, 5*(1), 57–69.

9. Blackham, J., & Benger, J. (2009). Clearing the cervical spine in conscious trauma patients. *Trauma, 11* (2), 93–109.

10. Berg, M.D., Schexnayder, S. M., Chameides, L., Terry, M., Donoghue, A., Hickey, R. W., … , and Hazinski, M. F. (2010). Part 13: Pediatric basic life support: 2010 American Heart Association guidelines for cardiopulmonary resuscitation and emergency cardiovascular care. Circulation, 122(18), S962–S975.

11. American College of Surgeons. (2012). Airway and ventilatory management. In *Advanced trauma life support student course manual* (9th ed., pp. 30–49). Chicago, IL: Author.

12. Santillanes, G., & Gausche-Hill, M. (2008). Pediatric airway management. *Emergency Clinics of North America, 26*, 961–975.

13. Walls, R. M., & Murphy, M. F. (2012). *Manual of emergency airway management* (4th ed.). Philadelphia, PA: Wolters Kluwer/Lippincott Williams & Wilkins.

14. Lessig, M. L. (2006). The cardiovascular system. In J. G. Alspach (Ed.), *Core curriculum for critical care nursing* (6th ed., pp.185–380). St. Louis, MO: Saunders Elsevier.

15. Wilkinson, J. M. & Treas, L. S. (2011). *Fundamentals of nursing* (2nd ed.). Philadelphia, PA: F. A. Davis Company.

16. Cabello, J. B., Burls, A., Emparanza, J. I., Bayless, S., & Quinn, T. (2010). Oxygen therapy for acute myocardial infarction. *Cochrane Database of Systematic Reviews,* (6), CD007160.

17. Brenner, M., Stein, D., Hu, P., Kufera, J., Wooford, M., & Scalea, T. (2012). Association between early hyperoxia and worse outcomes after traumatic brain injury. *Archives of Surgery, 147*(111), 1042–1946.

18. Peberdy, M. A., Callaway, C. W., Neumar, R. W., Geocadin, R. G., Zimmerman, J. L., Donnino, M., … Kronick, S.L. (2010). Part 9: Post-cardiac arrest care: 2010 American Heart Association Guidelines for Cardiopulmonary Resuscitation and Emergency Cardiovascular Care. *Circulation, 122*(18 Suppl 3), S768–S786.

19. Kilgannon, J. H., Jones, A. E., Shapiro, N. I., Angelos, M. G., Milcarek, B., Hunter, K., … Trzeciak, S. (2010). Association between arterial hyperoxia following resuscitation from cardiac arrest and in-hospital mortality. *Journal of the American Medical Association, 303*(21), 2165–2171.

20. Proehl, J., Arruda, T., Crowley, M., Egging, D., Walker-Cillo, G., Papa, A. M., … Walsh, J. (2009, December). *Clinical practice guideline: The use of capnography during procedural sedation/analgesia in the emergency department.* Retrieved from http://www.ena.org/IENR/CPG/Documents/CapnographyCPG.pdf

21. American Heart Association. (2011). *Basic life support for healthcare providers student manual.* Dallas, TX: Author.

22. Zengerink, I., Brink, P., Laupland, K., Raber, E., Zygun, D., & Kortbeek, J. (2008). Needle thoracostomy in the treatment of a tension pneumothorax in trauma patients: What size needle? *Journal of Trauma, 64*(1), 111–114.

23. American College of Surgeons Committee on Trauma. (2012). Abdominal and pelvic trauma. In *Advanced trauma life support student course manual* (9th ed., pp. 122–140). Chicago, IL: Author

24. Kornbluth, J., & Bhardwaj, A. (2011). Evaluation of coma: A critical appraisal of popular scoring systems. *Neurocritical Care, 14*(1), 134–143.

25. Bergeron, T. (2009). *Trauma triad of death: Hypothermia, acidosis, and coagulopathy.* Retrieved from http://www.aacn.org:88/WD/NTI/NTI2009/nti_cd/data/papers/main/34870.pdf

26. Emergency Nurses Association (2010) *Family presence during invasive procedures and resuscitation in the emergency department* [position statement]. Retrieved from http://www.ena.org/SiteCollectionDocuments/Position%20Statements/FamilyPresence.pdf

27. Wolf, L., Storer, A., Barnason, S., Brim, C., Halpern, J., Leviner, S., … Bradford, J.Y. (2012, December). *Clinical practice guideline: Family presence during invasive procedures and resuscitation.* Retrieved from http://www.ena.org/IENR/CPG/Documents/FamilyPresenceCPG.pdf

28. Nicks, B. A., McGinnis, H. D., Borron, S. W., & Megarbane, B. (2013, March 28). *Acute lactic acidosis.* Retrieved from http://emedicine.medscape.com/article/768159-overview

29. Jeong, J.S., Lee, J.B., Jin, Y.H, Yoon, J., Jun, Y.I., and Park, B. (2012). Initial hyperlactatemia in the ED is associated with poor outcome in patients with ischemic stroke. American Journal of Emergency Medicine, 3, 449-455.

30. Dutton, R. (2008). Pathophysiology of trauma shock. *International TraumaCare, 18*(1), 12–15.

31. Cohen, M. J. (2012). Towards hemostatic resuscitation: The changing understanding of acuter traumatic biology, massive bleeding, and damage-control resuscition. *Surgical Clinics of North America, 92*(4), 877–891.

32. Hossain, M., Ramavath, A., Kulangara, J., & Andrew, J. G. (2010). Current management of isolated sternal fractures in the UK: Time for evidence based practice? A cross-sectional survey and review of literature. *Injury, 41,* 495–498.

33. American College of Surgeons. (2012). Thoracic trauma In *Advanced trauma life support student course manual* (9th ed., pp. 94–112). Chicago, IL: Author.

34. Kraus, B., Silvestri, S., & Falk, J. L. (2012). *Carbon dioxide monitoring (capnography).* Retrieved from http://www.uptodate.com/contents/carbon-dioxide-monitoring-capnography

35. Prosser, J. D., Vender, J. R., & Solares, C. A. (2011). Traumatic cerebrospinal fluid leaks. *Otolaryngology Clinics of North America, 44,* 857–873.

36. Welch, K. C., Caballero, N., & Stankiewicz, J. (2013, April 29). *CSF rhinorrhea.* Retrieved from http://emedicine.medscape.com/article/861126-overview

37. Sunder, R., & Tyler, K. (2013). Basal skull fracture and the halo sign. *Canadian Medical Association Journal, 185*(5), 416.

38. Gibson, A., & Boswell, K. (2011). Facial trauma: Challenges, controversies, and therapeutic options. *Trauma Reports, 12*(2), 1–11.

39. McCudden, C. R., Senior, B. A., Hainsworth, S., Oliveira, W., Silverman, L. M., Bruns, D. E., & Hammett-Stabler, C. A. (2013). Evaluation of high resolution gel β2-transferrin for detection of cerebrospinal fluid leak. *Clinical Chemistry and Laboratory Medicine, 51*(2), 311–315.

40. Sherif, C., DiLeva, A., Gibson, D., Pakrah-Bodingbauer, B., Widhalm, G., Krusche-Mandl, I., … Matula, C. (2012). A management algorithm for cerebrospinal fluid leak associated with anterior skull base fractures: Detailed clinical and radiological follow-up. *Neurosurgical Review, 35*, 227–238.

41. Fakih, M. G., Pena, M. E., Shemes, S., Rey, J., Berriel-Cass, D., Szpunar, S. M., … Saravolatz, L. D. (2010). Effect of establishing guidelines on appropriate urinary catheter placement. *Academic Emergency Medicine, 17,* 337–340.

42. Makic, M. B. F., VonRueden, K. T., Rauen, C., & Chadwick, J. (2011). Evidence-based practice habits: Putting more sacred cows out to pasture. *Critical Care Nurse, 31*(2), 38–61.

43. Hankin, A., & Baren, J. (2009). Should the digital rectal examination be a part of the trauma secondary survey? *Annals of Emergency Medicine, 53*(2), 208–212.

44. Fitzgerald, M., Cameron, P., Mackenzie, C., Farrow, N., Scicuna, P., Gocentas, R., … Rosenfeld, J. V. (2011). Trauma resuscitation errors and computer-assisted decision support. *Archives of Surgery, 146*(2), 218–225. doi:10.1001/archsurg.2010.333

45. Conrad, B. P, Del Rossi, G., Horodyski, M. B., Prasam, M. L., Alemi, Y., & Rechntine, G. R. (2012). Eliminating log rolling as a spine trauma order. *Surgical Neurology International, 3*(Suppl S3), 188–197.

Chapter 6 • Airway and Ventilation

Diane Gurney, MS, RN, CEN, FAEN

Objectives

Upon completion of this chapter, the learner will be able to:

1. Describe pathophysiologic changes as a basis for assessment of the trauma patient with actual or potential airway and ventilation complications.

2. Demonstrate the nursing airway assessment of the trauma patient including key aspects of anatomy and physiology.

3. Plan appropriate interventions for the trauma patient with actual or potential airway and ventilation complications.

4. Evaluate the effectiveness of nursing interventions for the trauma patient with actual or potential airway and ventilation complications.

Preface

Knowledge of normal anatomy and physiology serves as a foundation for understanding anatomic derangements and pathophysiologic processes that may result from trauma. Before reading this chapter, it is strongly suggested that the learner review the following material. This material will not be covered in the lectures nor tested directly, but as foundational content, it may be the basis for some test questions and skill evaluation steps.

Anatomy and Physiology of the Airway

The pulmonary system is a divided into upper and lower airways. The upper airway is composed of the nose, mouth, pharynx, larynx, epiglottis, and trachea (Fig. 6-1), and the lower airway is composed of the bronchi and lungs. The functional unit of the pulmonary system is the alveolus.

Upper Airway[1]

The nose is the primary passageway for air into the lungs and is composed mostly of cartilage. It filters, warms, and moistens inhaled air and provides the sense of smell via the olfactory nerve (CN I). Coarse hairs line the outer nasal passages and filter out dust and other particles. A mucous membrane within the nasal cavity contains small blood vessels and provides warmth and moisture. The blood supply to the nose originates from the internal and external carotid arteries.

The mouth is the secondary passageway for inhaled air (Fig. 6-2). Presence of swelling, blood, foreign objects, or the tongue may compromise upper airway patency and prevent adequate ventilation. Airway obstruction by the tongue is of particular concern in the unconscious patient.

The nasopharynx and oropharynx meet at the base of the skull and extend to the lower border of the cricoid cartilage. The structures within the nasopharynx and oropharynx serve as guides to locate the trachea during the intubation process.

The epiglottis, a cartilaginous structure, lies on the top of the larynx. This structure serves to route air to the lungs and liquids and foods into the esophagus diverting from the larynx during swallowing.

The larynx is a tubular structure composed of cartilage that connects the oropharynx to the trachea. Its primary function is to allow air into the trachea. The larynx is the most heavily innervated sensory structure in the body (Fig. 6-3). The vagus nerve (CN X) serves as the primary parasympathetic nerve. Therefore, stimulation of the larynx during intubation can activate the parasympathetic nervous system, causing bradycardia, bronchial vasoconstriction, and increased intracranial pressure (ICP). This phenomenon is known as the vagal response to laryngoscopy and intubation.[2]

Below the larynx is the cricothyroid membrane (Fig. 6-4), which extends from the upper surface of the cricoid cartilage to the inferior border of the thyroid cartilage (Adam's apple). The cricothyroid membrane is approximately 10 mm in height and 22 mm in width.[2] In women, the neck is relatively smaller and the cricoid cartilage is located slightly higher than in men.

The trachea begins at the inferior border of the cricoid ring and is also innervated by the vagus nerve. It is usually 9 to 15 mm in diameter and 11 to 13 cm in length in the adult patient.[3]

Figure 6-1. Upper Airway Structures

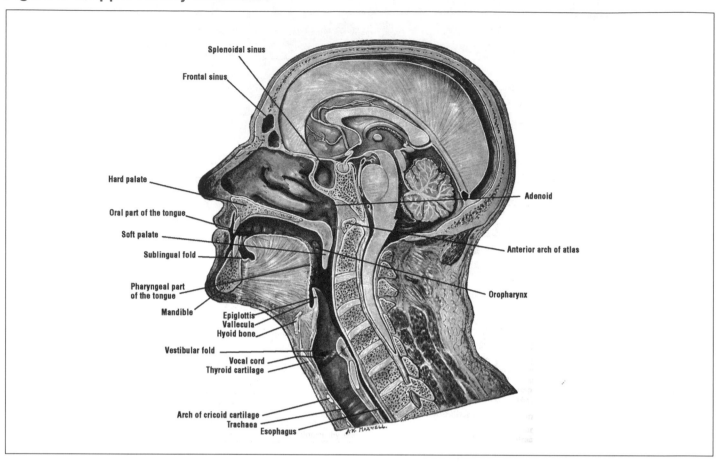

Reprinted from Williams, P. L., & Banniester, L. H. (Eds.). (1999). *Gray's anatomy* (38th ed.). St. Louis, MO: Elsevier Health Sciences.

Figure 6-2. Structures in the Mouth

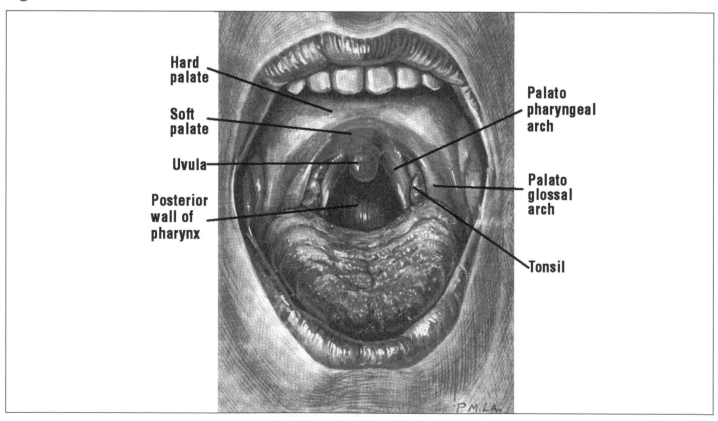

Reprinted from Williams, P. L., & Banniester, L. H. (Eds.). (1999). *Gray's anatomy* (38th ed.). St. Louis, MO: Elsevier Health Sciences.

Figure 6-3. Innervation of the Larynx by the Vagus Nerve

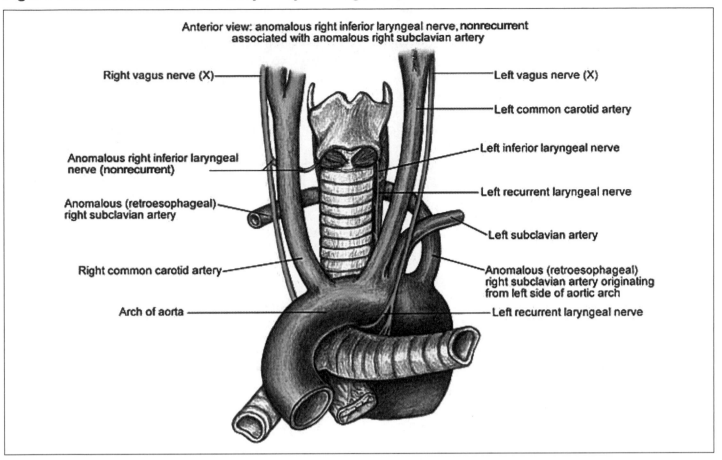

Anterior view: anomalous right inferior laryngeal nerve, nonrecurrent associated with anomalous right subclavian artery

Right vagus nerve (X)

Anomalous right inferior laryngeal nerve (nonrecurrent)

Anomalous (retroesophageal) right subclavian artery

Right common carotid artery

Arch of aorta

Left vagus nerve (X)

Left common carotid artery

Left inferior laryngeal nerve

Left recurrent laryngeal nerve

Left subclavian artery

Anomalous (retroesophageal) right subclavian artery originating from left side of aortic arch

Left recurrent laryngeal nerve

From Yau, A. Y., & Verma, S. P. (2013, February 13). *Laryngeal nerve anatomy.* Retrieved from http://emedicine.medscape.com/article/1923100-overview

Figure 6-4. Anterior Cervical Anatomy of the Larynx and Trachea

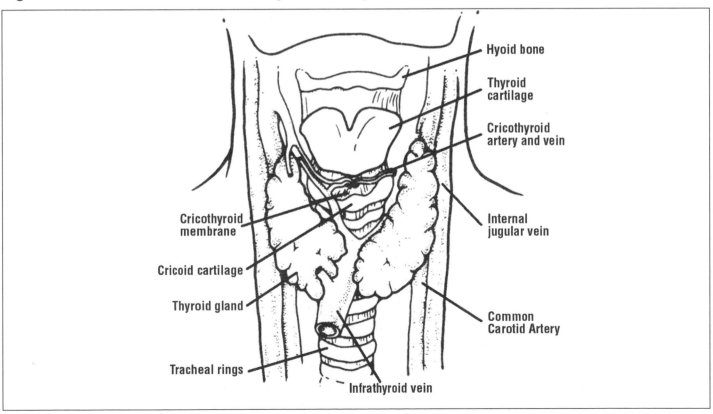

Hyoid bone

Thyroid cartilage

Cricothyroid artery and vein

Internal jugular vein

Common Carotid Artery

Cricothyroid membrane

Cricoid cartilage

Thyroid gland

Tracheal rings

Infrathyroid vein

Reprinted from Roberts, J. R., & Hedges, J. R. (2004). *Clinical procedures in emergency medicine* (4th ed.). St. Louis, MO: Saunders Elsevier.

Lower Airway[1]

The lower airway is located within the thoracic cage and includes the bronchi and the lungs. The bronchi and the bronchioles conduct atmospheric air to the alveoli, where gas exchange takes place.

The mediastinum, the space between the lungs, is bordered anteriorly by the sternum, posteriorly by the 12 thoracic vertebrae, and inferiorly by the diaphragm. Within the mediastinum is the heart, thoracic aorta, vagus nerve, phrenic nerve, inferior and superior vena cava, and other vascular structures (see Chapter 11, Thoracic and Neck Trauma, for more information).[1] The base of each lung rests against the diaphragm; the apex of each lung extends approximately 1.5 inches (4 cm) above where the clavicle meets the sternum.[3]

Physiology

Three processes transfer oxygen from the air to the lungs and bloodstream. They include the following:[4]

- *Ventilation* is the movement of air in and out of the lungs
- *Diffusion* is the passive movement of gases from an area of high concentration to an area of lower concentration
- *Perfusion* is the movement of blood to and from the lungs as a delivery medium of oxygen to the entire body

Ventilation[1,4]

Ventilation, or breathing, begins with inhalation of air through the upper airway. It is a dynamic process. Signals from the brain stem direct the pharyngeal muscles to open the pharynx during inhalation. During inspiration, the diaphragm contracts and flattens increasing the size of the thorax, extending it into the tenth or twelfth intercostal space. During expiration, the diaphragm relaxes and the lungs recoil to decrease the size of the pleural cavity to the fourth intercostal space.

The external intercostal muscles raise the rib cage and increase the anterior-to-posterior diameter of the thoracic cavity, and the lungs expand. Conversely, the anterior-to-posterior diameter decreases as the internal intercostal muscles contract, allowing for the passive exhalation of the lungs. The sternocleidomastoid and scalene muscles, and the accessory muscles of respiration, raise the sternum to the level of the first two ribs. Other accessory muscles used during expiration include the internal intercostals and the abdominals.

Diffusion[1,4]

In diffusion, air that enters the lungs reaches the alveoli, and oxygen enters the bloodstream via the capillaries in the lungs. Carbon dioxide (CO_2) passes from the blood into the alveoli and then is exhaled. This passive process requires no energy or effort from the body.

Perfusion[1,4]

Circulation provides a link between oxygen in the air and oxygen in the cells of the body. During perfusion, blood flows from the heart to the lungs, where it becomes oxygenated, and then is transported to the cells in the rest of the body. This process depends on the adequacy of the following:[1,4]

- Airway patency
- Ventilatory effort
- Gas exchange in the alveoli
- Hemoglobin to carry oxygen
- Blood pressure, a function of both vascular volume and cardiac contractility, in the circulatory system to transport blood to the cells[4]

Introduction

The first priority in managing a trauma patient is to establish an open, protected, unobstructed airway and ensure effective ventilation in order to prevent hypoxemia and its harmful effects. Knowledge of airway and ventilation management can provide the trauma nurse with the understanding and skills to support tissue perfusion, which can prevent cellular destruction, organ failure, and death.[5]

Pathophysiology as a Basis for Assessment Findings

Airway Obstruction

The trauma patient's airway may become obstructed in many ways, including the following:[5]

- The tongue can be a common cause of obstruction in patients who are not alert
- Patients under the influence of substances and alcohol may have an altered level of consciousness and be unable to protect their airways by swallowing or coughing
- Maxillofacial trauma may cause edema, increased secretions, bleeding, or dislodged teeth within the oral cavity
- Vomiting can lead to airway obstruction
- Injury to the neck and larynx may result in disruption to the tracheobronchial tree, causing swelling and hemorrhage

Oxygenation and Ventilation

In order to understand the principles of oxygenation and ventilation it is helpful to define the following terms:

- SaO_2 is the percentage of hemoglobin saturated with oxygen as determined by an arterial blood gas (ABG)

- SpO_2 is a pulse oximetry reading of arterial oxygen saturation (SaO_2) and is measured as a percentage[2,22]

- PaO_2 is the partial pressure of oxygen dissolved in arterial blood and is measured in millimeters of mm/Hg.[1,21] This is a reflection of tissue oxygenation.[23]

- $PaCO_2$ is the partial pressure of carbon dioxide dissolved in the blood and is measured in millimeters of mm/Hg[2,22]

- FiO_2 is the inspired concentration of oxygen measured in fraction, but more commonly it is referred to in clinical practice as a percentage[2]

- Room air is approximately 0.21 FiO_2 (21%)

- Hypoxemia is an oxygen deficiency within arterial blood and is measured by SpO_2, SaO_2, or PaO_2[23,24]

- Hypoxia is a deficiency in oxygen perfusion of the tissues. It is not directly measurable but is considered to be present in decreased PaO_2.[2,18,23,24]

Ineffective Ventilation

Once a patent airway is established and confirmed, the next priority becomes promoting adequate ventilation and supporting oxygenation. Contributing factors to inadequate ventilation and oxygenation include:

- Altered mental status from brain injury, prolonged loss of consciousness (LOC), increased intracranial pressure (ICP), hypoxia, or medication, substance or alcohol use

- Trauma in the high cervical spine with disruption of the sympathetic pathways

- Spinal cord injury (SCI) with possible involvement of the phrenic nerve resulting in hypoventilation

- Blunt thoracic trauma with rib fractures and chest wall instability

- Penetrating thoracic trauma resulting in a hemothorax or a pneumothorax

- Preexisting history of respiratory disease

- Increased age with decreased pulmonary reserve

- Tachypnea as compensation for diminished oxygenation and perfusion

Nursing Care of the Trauma Patient with Airway and Ventilation Problems

Refer to Chapter 5, Initial Assessment for the systematic approach to care of the trauma patient. The following assessment parameters are specific to airway and ventilation.

Preparation
Safe Practice, Safe Care

Airway and ventilation are essential components for an optimal outcome in the trauma patient. Preparation includes proper equipment and education:

- Equipment: Assure availability and working order of appropriate equipment and supplies in various sizes to accommodate all patients. Many emergency departments maintain a cart or box with equipment for effective airway management.

- Education: Trauma education includes a review of airway and ventilation as well as hands-on practice in management of the airway, identification of potential problems, and proficiency with necessary equipment

Triage

The prehospital report may provide clues to the patient's potential risks for airway and ventilation problems including:

- Mechanism of injury (MOI)
- Injuries sustained
  - Facial, neck, or thoracic trauma
  - Inhalation injury and/or thermal or chemical burns
- Signs and symptoms
  - Altered mental status
  - Complaints of dyspnea, dysphagia, or dysphonia
  - Indications of substance use
  - Nausea or vomiting

Primary Survey
A–Airway and Alertness

One of the greatest risks to patient outcomes is the failure of the trauma team to recognize an immediate problem or a change in the patient's condition.[5] Recognition of an airway problem is an essential first step.[5] Once the problem has been identified, lifesaving interventions can be implemented.

Assess for Alertness

Use the AVPU mnemonic to determine the patient's level of alertness.

- A–the patient is alert and responsive
- V–the patient responds to verbal stimulation

Figure 6-5. Jaw-thrust Maneuver

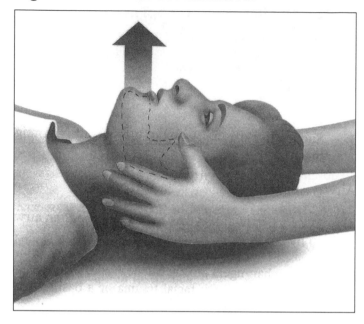

- P–the patient responds only to painful stimulation
- U–the patient is unresponsive

If the patient is not alert, the ability to protect his or her airway may be lost.

Open the Airway

Until injury to the cervical spine has been ruled out, maintain the spine in proper alignment. While maintaining cervical spinal immobilization or manual stabilization, assess for airway patency. This can be accomplished by the following:[2]

- Talk to the patient. Asking for the patient's name, current location ("Do you know where you are?"), and ability to open his or her mouth are simple techniques to determine if a patient is alert.

- If the patient is unable to open his or her mouth, responds only to pain, or is unresponsive, use the jaw-thrust to open the airway and assess for obstruction

  - Jaw-thrust (Fig. 6-5)

    - Stand at the head of the bed, place the index fingers under the angle of the lower jaw on each side, with the thumbs on each cheekbone for stabilization and move the mandible forward and upward[6]

    - In the patient with suspected cervical spinal injury, the jaw-thrust procedure is recommended and may be best performed by two providers; one maintains cervical spinal stabilization and the second performs the jaw-thrust procedure[6]

Once the airway is open, continue with the airway assessment:

- Inspect for:
  - Tongue obstructing the airway
  - Loose or missing teeth
  - Foreign objects
  - Blood, vomitus, or secretions
  - Edema
  - Facial burns or evidence of inhalation injury
- Listen for:
  - Obstructive airway sounds such as snoring, gurgling, or stridor
- Palpate for:
  - Possible occlusive maxillofacial bony deformity or subcutaneous emphysema

If the patient has a definitive airway in place, assess for proper placement with the following:

- Inspect for equal and adequate rise and fall of the chest

- Auscultate for bilateral breath sounds with absence of gurgling over the epigastrium

- Use a CO_2 monitoring device to assess for presence of CO_2 in the exhaled air (see "CO_2 Monitoring" for more information)

Airway Interventions

If the airway is patent:

- An airway that is currently patent is not guaranteed to stay that way

  - Note any potential risks for airway obstruction (injury to the mouth, active bleeding, or blistering of the oral mucosa)

- Continually monitor airway patency while the assessment continues

If the airway is NOT patent:

- Use the jaw-thrust maneuver to open the airway with a second person maintaining manual stabilization[6]

- Suction for blood, vomitus, or secretions using care to not stimulate the gag reflex or vomiting

- Reassess the airway

  - If suctioning does not relieve the airway obstruction, the tongue may be the cause

- Insert an airway adjunct (See "Airway Adjuncts")

  - Oral and nasal airways can be used to support spontaneous ventilation

- Keep in mind that an airway adjunct, when used for airway patency, is a temporary measure, bridging to a definitive airway
- Airway adjuncts facilitate bag-mask ventilations
- Consider need for a definitive airway (See "Definitive Airways")
- Reassess the effectiveness of all interventions

B–Breathing and Ventilation

To assess breathing, expose the patient's chest and complete the following:

- Inspect for:
  - Spontaneous breathing
  - Symmetric and adequate rise and fall of the chest
  - Depth, pattern, and rate of respirations
  - Work of breathing, including:
    - Use of accessory muscles
    - Diaphragmatic or abdominal breathing in adult patients
    - In the pediatric patient, look for:
      - Suprasternal, substernal, or intercostal retractions
      - Nasal flaring, grunting, or head bobbing
    - Skin color
      - Observe for pallor, duskiness, or cyanosis
    - Jugular venous distention (JVD) and position of the trachea
    - Tracheal deviation and JVD are late signs that may indicate a tension pneumothorax
    - Open pneumothoraces (sucking chest wounds)
    - Signs of inhalation injury
      - Singed nasal hairs
      - Blistering of the oral mucosa
      - Facial burns
- Auscultate:
  - Listen to the lungs bilaterally at the second intercostal space midclavicular line and at the fifth intercostal space at the anterior axillary line
  - Diminished or absent breath sounds may be the result of pneumothorax, hemothorax, or airway obstruction, splinting, or inadequate ventilation as a response to pain
- Palpate for:
  - Tenderness and swelling
  - Jugular venous pulsations at the suprasternal notch or in the supraclavicular area[8,9]
  - Bony structures
    - Rib fractures may impact ventilation
    - Bony crepitus may be an indication of fracture
  - Subcutaneous emphysema
    - Subcutaneous air may be a sign of a pneumothorax or pneumomediastinum
  - Soft tissue injury (contusions and lacerations)
- Percuss for:
  - Dullness
    - This suggests a hemothorax: blood or fluid in the pleural space
  - Hyperresonance
    - This suggests a pneumothorax: air in the pleural space

Breathing Interventions

If breathing is present:
- Assess for ventilation effectiveness, including skin color and respiratory effort

If breathing is absent:
- Reassess and open the airway if not already done
- Insert an airway adjunct if not already done
- Use a bag-mask device connected to an oxygen source to administer 10 to 12 normal breaths per minute or one every 5 to 6 seconds[2,5,10]
- Reassess the effectiveness of the interventions
- Prepare for a definitive airway

If ventilation is effective:
Oxygenation in the trauma patient is an essential resuscitative priority.[2,5,10]
- Initially, deliver oxygen with a flow rate of 10 to 15 L/min via a nonrebreather mask with a tight-fitting seal and functional reservoir bag
- To prevent hyperoxia and its deleterious effects, rapid weaning of oxygen (maintaining SpO_2 between 94%–98%) should begin as soon as the patient is stabilized, after completion of the primary survey and immediate life-threats have been managed[2,5,10–13]
- Reassess ventilation effectiveness

If ventilation is ineffective:
- Use a tight-fitting bag-mask device connected to an oxygen source at 15 L/min to administer 10 to 12 normal breaths per minute or one every 5 to 6 seconds[5,10]

- Compress the bag just enough to produce visible chest rise[14]
- Excessive depth of ventilations and rapid rates have been associated with increased intrathoracic pressure and hypotension during cardiopulmonary resuscitation (CPR), causing a decrease in the venous return to the heart and reduced cardiac output[14,15]
- Once the patient is stabilized, support the patient's oxygen saturation level at or above 94% to 98%[2,5,10]

- Anticipate the need for a definitive airway

- Life-threatening injuries require rapid identification and immediate intervention before proceeding to the next step in the primary survey. These include (see Chapter 11, Thoracic and Neck Trauma, for more information):
  - Tension pneumothorax
  - Flail chest
  - Hemothorax
  - Open pneumothorax

- Consider other selected conditions as a source of inadequate ventilations:
  - Preexisting pulmonary disease
  - Circumferential burns to the chest
  - Pain
  - Spinal cord injury that may cause diaphragmatic breathing and inadequate ventilation and/or paralysis of the intercostal muscles
  - Multiple rib fractures
  - Blunt thoracic trauma

Airway Adjuncts
Nasopharyngeal Airway

A nasopharyngeal airway can be used in responsive or unresponsive patients but is contraindicated in patients with facial trauma or a suspected basilar skull fracture. When inserting a nasopharyngeal airway, consider the following:[16]

- Use the largest diameter that can be easily inserted into the patient's naris

- Select the correct length by measuring from the tip of the patient's nose to tip of the earlobe

- Apply a water-soluble lubricant before insertion

- Insertion into the right naris:
  - Insert the nasopharyngeal airway with the bevel facing the nasal septum
  - Direct the airway posteriorly and slightly rotate toward the ear until the flange rests against the naris

- If resistance is met or there is a known septal deviation, polyps, or other similar problem, stop insertion and try the left naris

- Insertion into the left naris:
  - Keep in mind that most available nasal airways are made to insert in the right naris. Therefore, it is necessary to turn the airway upside down to assure the bevel is facing the septum.
  - Direct the airway posteriorly and downward, rotating slightly until the airway is inserted and flange rests against the naris

- Reassess airway patency and determine the need for a definitive airway

- Consider the need for bag-mask ventilation

Oropharyngeal Airway

An oropharyngeal airway is used in the unresponsive patients as a temporary measure to facilitate ventilation with a bag-mask device or spontaneous ventilation until the patient can be intubated. It is important to measure for the correct fit. If the airway adjunct is too large, it may occlude the patient's airway, hinder the use of a face mask, or damage laryngeal structures. If it is too small, it may occlude the airway by pushing the tongue back. A correctly sized airway is one that holds the tongue in the normal anatomic position and follows its natural curvature. When inserting an oropharyngeal airway, consider the following:[16]

- Measure the correct size airway by placing the proximal end of the airway adjunct at the corner of the mouth. If the distal end reaches the tip of the earlobe, it is a correct fit.

- Depress the tongue using a tongue blade and insert the airway toward the back of the mouth, careful not to push the tongue backward, blocking the airway[5]

Definitive Airways

A definitive, protected airway is a tube securely placed in the trachea with the cuff inflated, if applicable.[2,5,17,18] In an emergency or trauma situation there are three indications for definitive airway management:[2]

- Failure to maintain or protect the airway

- Failure to maintain oxygenation or ventilation

- A specific anticipated clinical course

The following conditions or situations are examples of the need for a definitively secured airway:[2,17]

- Apnea
- Glasgow Coma Scale (GCS) score of eight or less
- Severe maxillofacial fractures
- Evidence of inhalation injury (facial burns)

- Laryngeal or tracheal injury or neck hematoma

- High risk of aspiration and inability to protect the airway

- Compromised or ineffective ventilation

- Anticipation of deterioration of neurologic status that may result in an inability to maintain or protect the airway

Types of Definitive Airways

Definitive airways are placed by licensed practitioners with demonstrated competency whose practice standards include the performance of these interventions. Trauma nurses will help prepare the patient and equipment, then monitor and assist during the procedure.

Endotracheal Tubes

- Endotracheal tubes (ETTs) can be inserted via the nasal or oral route

- Nasotracheal intubation (NTI) is performed blindly and requires that the patient is breathing on his or her own. It has a relatively high failure rate and has largely been replaced with alternative techniques. Contraindications for NTI include:[2]

  - A patient who is apneic

  - If there are signs of mid-face fractures (maxillary fractures LeFort II and III) or basilar skull fractures

  - Fractures of the frontal sinus or cribriform plate are considered relative contraindications for a NTI

- NTI is not recommended in the pregnant trauma patient because of the fragility of the nasal mucosa and risk for bleeding

Surgical Airways

When an ETT cannot be placed due to conditions such as a larynx fracture, oropharyngeal edema, or hemorrhage, a surgical airway is considered as an alternative.

A surgical cricothyrotomy is rarely the first choice unless the patient has major trauma to the lower face.[2] In surgical cricothyrotomy, an incision is made through the cricothyroid membrane, and an ETT or tracheostomy tube is inserted.[2] Complications include:[2]

- Hemorrhage
- Pneumomediastinum
- Laceration of the cricoid ring
- Tracheal trauma
- Subglottic stenosis
- Vocal cord damage

Difficult Airways

Prior to any intubation attempt thorough examination of the airway is performed by the person performing the intubation. A difficult airway is described by Hung and Murphy as a concept rather than a definition. This concept includes anticipation of difficult bag-mask technique, difficult laryngoscopy and difficult intubation.[19] This anticipation and identification of a difficult airway may help to avoid a scenario in which the team is unable to intubate and unable to ventilate the patient.[2] Signs of a potentially difficult airway include the presence of any of the following:

- Cervical spine injury or severe arthritis

- Mandibular trauma

- Obesity

- Signs of swelling or inflammation (stridor)

- Signs of inhalation injury

- Anatomic variations (short neck)

An increasing trend in assuring a successful intubation is the usage of a video laryngoscope. This should be performed by an experienced provider after assessment of the airway.

Rapid Sequence Intubation

Rapid sequence intubation (RSI) uses a strong sedative to render the patient unconscious, immediately followed by a neuromuscular blocking agent for motor paralysis to facilitate the insertion of an ETT. The patient will become apneic; however, assited ventilation with a bag-mask device is not recommended due to the risk for aspiration in nonfasting patients. In order to prepare the patient for this apneic phase, preoxygenation is essential.[2,7]

RSI is considered the standard of care in many cases where the risk of difficult intubation is low. Appendix 6-A describes the seven P's involved in RSI.

It is important for the trauma nurse to understand how to optimize the RSI process in order to anticipate the needs of the team. This includes changing the size or style of the laryngoscope blade, and the use of a gum elastic bougie as an ETT introducer, (Fig. 6-6) and external laryngeal manipulation (see "Research in Trauma Care" for more information).

Extraglottic Rescue Airways

Extraglottic airway (EGA) devices can be used for airway management in trauma patients with failed airways and in situations when unsuccessful intubation is anticipated. They are blindly positioned above or posterior to the larynx to facilitate immediate ventilation

Figure 6-6. Gum Elastic Bougie Device

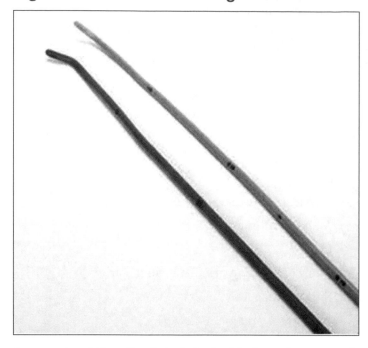

Image courtesy of Airway Cam Technologies, Inc. http://www.airwaycam.com/tube-introducers.html

and oxygenation. EGA devices can be divided into two categories: supraglottic, which are placed above and seal the glottis, and retroglottic, which enter the esophagus and isolate the glottic opening.

Supraglottic Airway

Laryngeal mask airway (LMA) (Fig. 6-7)

- An LMA requires training to ensure proper placement, but has high success rates[2]

- These are used in operating suites and are well tolerated by patients[2]

- An LMA does not provide protection against aspiration and is not recommended in patients who have recently eaten

- An intubating LMA (ILMA) is a specially designed LMA that allows for endotracheal intubation guided through the device[2]

Retroglottic Airways

Multilumen esophageal airway (Fig. 6-8)

- Multilumen esophageal airways are most commonly used in the prehospital environment

- The King LTS-D is a single tube with two lumens. It is a retroglottic device that seals the oropharynx from above and the esophagus from below leaving ventilation outlets that sit in front of the larynx.

  ◦ It is designed with two lumens that allow for ventilation and insertion of a gastric tube for decompression

Figure 6-7. Laryngeal Mask Airway

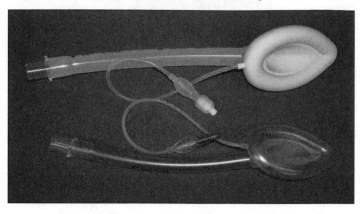

Image courtesy of Legend Medical Devices. http://www.legendmd.com/

  ◦ One access port inflates both the proximal balloon, which seals the oropharynx and the distal balloon, which seals the esophagus

  ◦ The King LT-D does not have the lumen allowing access for gastric tube insertion

- In addition to failed airway or unsuccessful intubation attempts, retroglottic airways may be useful in patients with upper gastrointestinal bleeding, upper airway bleeding, or severe facial burns

- It is only recommended for adults and children taller than 35 inches

Breathing Intervention Reassessment

After intubation, the cuff is inflated and placement is confirmed using the following:

- Attach a CO_2 detection device or monitoring sensor and begin assisted ventilations

- Watch for symmetric rise and fall of the chest *and at the same time,* listen for the presence of gurgling over the epigastrium, which may indicate the tube is in the esophagus

- Listen for the presence of bilateral breath sounds at the midaxillary and midclavicular lines

  ◦ If breath sounds are heard, after 5 to 6 breaths have been delivered, assess for positive indications of exhaled CO_2 from the CO_2 device or monitor

  ◦ If breath sounds are absent, there is no rise and fall of the chest, gurgling is heard at the epigastrium, and there is no evidence of exhaled CO_2 remove the ETT and oxygenate the patient before another attempt

  ◦ If the breath sounds are only heard on the right, the ETT is likely in the right mainstem bronchus and has been inserted too far. It needs to be pulled back until equal breath sounds are heard bilaterally

Figure 6-8. Multilumen Esophageal Airway

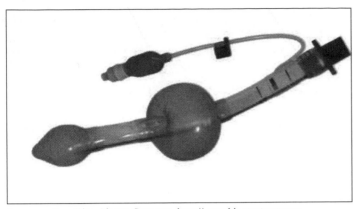

Image courtesy King Airway Systems. http://www.kingsystems.com

- Secure the ETT, note the number at the lip for positioning, and document

- Prepare for mechanical ventilation

- Note the patient's color for improvement; the patient's color is likely to improve once ventilations are assisted and the patient is oxygenated

- Obtain a chest radiograph for verification of ETT depth after the secondary survey

G–Get Resuscitation Adjuncts

Arterial blood gases (ABGs), pulse oximetry, and capnography are resuscitation adjuncts used in conjunction with the primary survey to assess for adequacy of oxygenation and effectiveness of ventilation.

L–Laboratory Studies

- ABGs provide information regarding oxygenation and ventilation with analysis of acid-base balance, lactic acid and base excess

  ∘ Base deficit can serve as an endpoint measurement of the adequacy of cellular perfusion, and predict the success of the resuscitation

  ∘ Because tissue hypoxia associated with poor perfusion results in the production of hydrogen ions and metabolic acidosis, base excess or deficit values can be useful. A base deficit of less than –6 mEq/L is associated with poor outcomes.[20]

- Lactic acid increases as a result of tissue hypoxia. Levels of more than 2 to 4 mmol/L are associated with poor outcomes.[21]

O–Oxygenation and Ventilation
Pulse Oximetry

Pulse oximetry is a non-invasive method of providing oxygenation information and detecting changes in oxygenation that cannot be readily observed with visual assessment.[25] Some circumstances that may lead to unreliable readings include:[26]

- Poor peripheral perfusion caused by vasoconstriction, hypotension, or hypothermia

- A blood pressure cuff inflated above the sensor

- Carbon monoxide (CO) poisoning (carboxyhemoglobin)

- Methemoglobinemia

- Severe dehydration

Pulse oximetry provides evidence of SaO_2 but not PaO_2 as reported in ABG results. The non-linear relationship between the two measurements is reflected in the oxyhemoglobin-dissociation curve.

Oxyhemoglobin-dissociation Curve

The oxyhemoglobin-dissociation curve indicates the correlation of tissue oxygenation (PaO_2) as it saturates the hemoglobin molecule (SO_2). P50 describes the oxygen pressure when the hemoglobin molecule is 50% saturated. Normal P50 is 26.7 mm Hg.[24,26] A shift in the curve notes changes in this relationship:

- *A shift to the right* occurs in an environment of high metabolic demand. Hemoglobin's affinity for oxygen decreases, making it easier to release the bound oxygen to the tissues. A shift to the right occurs in response to the following conditions:[24,26]

  ∘ Increased carbon dioxide (hypercapnia)

  ∘ Increased temperature (hyperthermia)

  ∘ Increased 2,3-diphosphoglycerate levels (a substance in the blood that helps oxygen move from hemoglobin to the tissues).

  ∘ Decreased pH (acidemia)

- *A shift to the left* occurs in an environment of low metabolic demand. Hemoglobin's affinity for oxygen increases, making it harder to release bound oxygen to the tissues. A shift to the left occurs in response to the following conditions:[24,26]

  ∘ Decreased carbon dioxide (hypocapnia)

  ∘ Decreased temperature (hypothermia)

  ∘ Decreased 2,3-diphosphoglycerate levels.

  ∘ Elevated pH (alkalosis)

  ∘ Carbon monoxide and methemoglobinemia

Pulse oximetry alone does not indicate the patient's effectiveness to diffuse oxygen to the cells. The considerations for the trauma nurse are to attempt to maintain normothermia and normocarbia, which decreases the risk of hypothermia, acidosis, or coagulopathy.

Carbon Dioxide Monitoring

CO_2 is the end product of ventilation, a reflection of metabolism and pulmonary function. CO_2 monitors gauge the partial pressure of CO_2, and if the measurement is taken at the end of a breath, it is referred to as $ETCO_2$, which is similar to CO_2 in the alveoli. Presence of exhaled CO_2 can help to confirm ETT position, and ongoing monitoring can provide insight into the effectiveness of mechanical ventilation. These devices provide quantitative or qualitative measurements.[2]

Quantitative

Capnography monitors provide a numeric value, as well as a continuous waveform, indicating real-time measurement and trending over time.[2] Capnometers provide a one-time numeric value of the $ETCO_2$ of each breath without any waveform.[2] They can be useful in obtaining a snapshot measurement for confirmation of ETT placement or after movement or repositioning.

Qualitative

Colorimetric CO_2 detectors provide information about the presence or absence of CO_2.[2] A chemically treated indicator strip changes color revealing the presence or absence of exhaled CO_2. Deliver at least six breaths before taking the measurement since patients with gastric distention may produce higher levels of CO_2 in the esophagus and contribute to an inaccurate reading. Follow manufacturer's recommendations as these are designed for one-time use.

Reevaluation Adjuncts

A chest radiograph can determine the presence of a hemothorax, pneumothorax, or rib fractures and can help to confirm the position of the ETT.

Reevaluation and Post Resuscitation Care

Frequent reevaluation of airway patency and adequacy of ventilation is essential. Reassessment includes:

- Alertness or level of consciousness to determine the patient's ability to protect the airway

- Respiratory rate and pattern, work of breathing, and breath sounds

- Vital signs including pulse oximetry and capnography

- ABGs

- Response to interventions

- Monitor tolerance for and effectiveness of mechanical ventilation

- Reevaluation of ETT placement and the effectiveness of ventilation. Use the DOPE mnemonic to troubleshoot ventilator or capnography alarms:[27]

  ◦ **D**isplaced tube

  ◦ **O**bstructed or kinked tube

  ◦ **P**neumothorax

  ◦ **E**quipment failure, such as the patient becoming detached from the equipment or loss of capnography waveform

- Assess pain and sedation levels and provide pharmacologic and nonpharmacologic interventions to facilitate the effectiveness of breathing and ventilation

Definitive Care or Transport

Patients with airway or ventilation considerations may require the following transports:

- Alternative level of care (designated trauma center)

- Admission to an inpatient unit

- Transfer to the operating suite

Emerging Trends

As the science and evidence of trauma care continues to evolve, tools to improve patient outcomes continue to be trialed and refined. Until the evidence has been tested and replicated, controversies remain. Considerations related to the care of patients with airway and ventilation interventions include hyperoxia, visualizing the vocal cords and RSI medications.

Hyperoxia

Several studies have reported their findings regarding hyperoxia and patient outcomes. They include the following:

- A large, multicenter study of patients who experienced cardiac arrest and resuscitation reported clinical outcomes associated with hyperoxia within 24 hours of arriving to the intensive care unit (ICU). After controlling for variables of age, preadmission functional status, comorbidities, and vital signs, the hyperoxic patients had two times the in-hospital mortality than the patients who were normoxic.[12]

- Another study noted that in addition to reported hyperoxia, decreased hemodynamic stability may also contribute to poor outcomes resulting from the body's inability to deal with the free radical excess and resulting cellular injury.[28] This suggests that while high-flow oxygen is still indicated initially in all trauma patients, better outcomes depend on prompt titration of oxygen as indicated by SpO_2 and ABG values, maintaining the SpO_2 between 94% and 98% and PaO_2 between 100 and 200 mm Hg.[11,13]

- The 2010 American Heart Association (AHA) Guidelines, based on a review of scientific literature, emphasize the importance of 100% oxygen during resuscitation with the recommendation for early titration to maintain arterial oxyhemoglobin saturation equal to or above 94%[10]

- With demonstrated higher mortality at PaO_2 of 300 mm Hg and higher, the recommendation is that when SpO_2 is 100%, decrease supplemental oxygen to the minimum amount of oxygen necessary to maintain SpO_2 at or above 94%[10]

- In a study of 1,547 patients with traumatic brain injury (TBI), 43% had a PaO_2 higher than 200 mm Hg during the first 24 hours.[13] The authors made the following conclusions:[13]

  - Hyperoxia was related to worse short-term functional outcomes

  - Hyperoxia was connected to increased mortality rates

  - Both hypoxia and hyperoxia were detrimental to the short-term outcomes of patients with traumatic brain injuries

  - The reasons underlying these outcomes are not totally clear. However, oxygen-free radical toxicity brought on by the hyperoxia was suspected as a cause, and the authors suggested that limiting the duration of the use of high-flow oxygen may improve patient outcomes.

Laryngeal Manipulation to Visualize the Cords
Laryngeal manipulation of the thyroid cartilage can be used to help visualize the cords as an alternative to cricoid pressure. The preferred method is BURP: **b**ackward, **u**pward and **r**ightward **p**ressure.[2,5,29] Figure 6-9 illustrates this method.

RSI Pretreatment Medications
Several medications are used for pretreatment in RSI. Current evidence regarding their efficacy includes:

- Lidocaine is thought to blunt the cough reflex and bronchospasm that may be caused by intubation. Studies report that the cough reflex can be blocked using intravenous lidocaine 1.5 mg/kg.[30]

- Lidocaine is thought to mitigate the increase of intracranial pressure during intubation

  - In spite of conflicting evidence regarding this issue, lidocaine was found to be safe and it is recommended in patients for the potential benefit until there is evidence that demonstrates otherwise[2,30]

- Atropine is thought to reduce the chances of bradycardia that results from airway manipulation

Figure 6-9. The BURP Maneuver

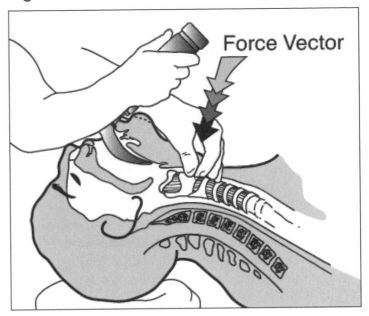

Reprinted from Noor, H. (n.d.). *Polytrauma and abdominal trauma: Essential management* [PowerPoint presentation]. Retrieved from http://www.hind.cc/6th%20MBBS/SURGERY/EndRotation/Dr.Hesham%20Noor/Polytrauma-and-abd-trauma.ppt

  - Some smaller studies have shown a reduction in heart rate even when patients took atropine. No strong evidence supports the routine use of atropine for pediatric intubation with succinylcholine.[2,30] It may be considered in children less than age 1 year.

- Opioids are thought to reduce increases in intracranial pressure, intraocular pressure, mean arterial pressure, myocardial oxygen consumption, and pulmonary artery pressure that result from intubation

- In one study of patients undergoing cardiac surgery, high-dose fentanyl caused thoracic and abdominal rigidity in 8% of patients. However, rigidity has not been reported in doses used in RSI.[2]

- If the patient is dependent on sympathetic response: exhibiting compensated or decompensated shock, or hemodynamic instability, pretreatment with fentanyl is avoided[31]

- Neuromuscular blocking agents have been commonly used to reduce the length and strength of muscle fasciculations and thought to potentially reduce postoperative muscle pain

  - Study results are varied with respect to any association between the use of neuromuscular blocking agents to prevent fasciculations or mitigate postoperative muscle pain[2]

Summary

Maintenance of an adequate airway is paramount for achieving optimal outcomes in the trauma patient. Assessment is the most important first step in the identification of any airway problem the trauma patient may experience; therefore, it is important for trauma nurses to learn this important skill. Recognition of the problem and anticipation of an impending problem are the primary focus. If an airway problem is not identified during the assessment, the results can be catastrophic for the patient. It is essential for trauma nurses to be able to quickly and accurately assess and recognize/identify certain life-threatening presentations and to intervene quickly. Familiarity with multiple types of airway adjuncts and their use is essential for nurses who care for trauma patients. A thorough understanding of the pathophysiology underlying adequate airway and ventilation will assist the trauma nurse to implement lifesaving interventions expediently.

Appendix 6-A. Seven P's of RSI

Phase	Description
Preparation	<ul><li>Gather and prepare supplies, medication, and equipment necessary for the RSI procedure</li><li>Ensure patency of vascular access and attach monitors and verify proper working order of the equipment</li><li>In anticipation of a potentially failed intubation during this step, prepare and have available any additional equipment that may be needed</li></ul>
Preoxygenation	<ul><li>Provide high-flow oxygen at the highest concentration available[7] to prepare the patient to tolerate the period of apnea without desaturation. Suggested strategies to prevent oxygen desaturation during intubation include:<ul><li>Place the patient in a heads-up position</li><li>If the patient is on a spine board, the reverse Trendelenburg position can be used. This also is helpful for bariatric patients.</li><li>Maintain airway patency with airway adjuncts</li><li>Use positive pressure ventilation for those patients unable to achieve SpO_2 at or above 94%</li></ul></li></ul>
Pretreatment	<ul><li>This is the phase during which medications can be administered to mitigate adverse effects associated with endotracheal intubation</li><li>The mnemonic LOAD (lidocaine, opioids, atropine, and defasciculating dose of neuromuscular blocking agents) has been used, but recent research has changed the practice of routine use of atropine and defasciculation dosing. These practices may be evaluated for use in certain cases, but are not recommended routinely. See "Trauma Care Considerations" for additional information.</li></ul>

Data from Blair,[7] Kahn et al.,[18] and Chan et al.[22]; and Skidmore-Roth, L. (2012). *Mosby's 2012 nursing drug reference* (25th ed.). St. Louis, MO: Mosby Elsevier.

Phase	Description
Paralysis with induction	The goal during RSI is to produce deep sedation and muscular relaxation quickly, but administer the sedative first to allow time for it to take effect. This will limit anxiety or panic that would result from paralysis if a neuromuscular blocking agent is given without sedation. If benzodiazepines are administered, have reversal agents available. • Etomidate • Ketamine • Midazolam • Propofol • Short-acting barbiturates (methohexital) Neuromuscular blocking agents used in RSI include: • Depolarizing agents (succinylcholine) ◦ Succinylcholine is a commonly used depolarizing agent. Use caution when administering this agent to certain trauma patients and monitor for the following: ‣ Hyperkalemia in patients in the acute phase of injury following burns, multiple trauma, extensive denervation of skeletal muscle, or upper motor neuron injury ‣ Malignant hyperthermia (can have an acute onset) ‣ Increased intraocular pressure in patients who have narrow angle glaucoma or a penetrating eye injury ‣ Bradycardia, which may progress to asystole: ‣ Incidence and severity of bradycardia higher in children ‣ Incidence more likely with a second dose ‣ Consider pretreatment with anticholinergic agents (atropine) to reduce the occurrence of bradyarrhythmias in children < 1 years old ◇ Have available for all trauma patients ‣ Muscle fasciculation may cause additional trauma in patients with fractures or muscle spasm ‣ Increased intragastric pressure results in regurgitation and possible aspiration of stomach contents • Nondepolarizing agents (rocuronium and vecuronium) ◦ Longer acting, so a definitive airway is crucial with their use ◦ Have fewer side effects than succinylcholine • Complications for all neuromuscular blocking agents ◦ Most serious complication is failure to successfully establish a definitive airway ◦ Patient requires bag-mask ventilations until the effects of the medications have worn off and the drive to breathe has returned ◦ Short-acting medications preferred

Data from Blair,[7] Kahn et al.,[18] and Chan et al.[22]; and Skidmore-Roth, L. (2012). *Mosby's 2012 nursing drug reference* (25th ed.). St. Louis, MO: Mosby Elsevier.

Phase	Description
Protection and Positioning	Protection • After the neuromuscular blocker is administered, the priorities are to protect the airway from aspiration and providing manual ventilation once spontaneous effort ceased • Monitor the patient's ventilatory status and oxygen saturation. If oxygen pretreatment was adequate and the SpO_2 remains within normal limits, assisted ventilations can be avoided to reduce the risk of regurgitation and aspiration. Once the neuromuscular blocking agent takes effect, intubation can be attempted. • If the SpO_2 falls below normal limits after the neuromuscular blockade takes effect, be prepared to assist ventilation with a bag-mask device. Administer breaths smoothly and gently to avoid gastric distention. • Orotracheal intubation in the trauma setting is a two-person procedure as one person is required to maintain manual cervical spinal stabilization
Placement with Proof	• Once intubation is completed, inflate the ETT cuff and secure the tube. See "Breathing Interventions Reassessment" for placement confirmation.
Post Intubation Management	• Secure the ETT with tape, ties, or a tube holder. A post-intubation chest radiograph may be useful to determine evidence of complications.

Data from Blair,[7] Kahn et al.,[18] and Chan et al.[22]; and Skidmore-Roth, L. (2012). *Mosby's 2012 nursing drug reference* (25th ed.). St. Louis, MO: Mosby Elsevier.

References

1. Copstead, L. E., & Banasik, J. (2013). *Pathophysiology* (5th ed.). St. Louis, MO: Saunders Elsevier.

2. Wall, R. M., & Murphy, M. F. (Eds.). (2012). *Manual of emergency airway management* (4th ed.). Philadelphia, PA: Lippincott Williams & Wilkins.

3. Goon, S. S., Stephens, R. C., & Smith, H. (2009). The emergency airway. *British Journal of Hospital Medicine, 70*(12), M186–M188.

4. Brain, J. D. (2006, August). Exchanging oxygen and carbon dioxide. In *The Merck manual home health handbook for patients and caregivers*. Whitehouse Station, NJ: Merck Sharp & Dohme. Retrieved from http://www.merckmanuals.com/home/lung_and_airway_disorders/biology_of_the_lungs_and_airways/exchanging_oxygen_and_carbon_dioxide.html

5. American College of Surgeons. (2012). Airway and ventilatory management. In *Advanced trauma life support student course manual* (9th ed., pp. 30–61). Chicago, IL: Author

6. Berg, M. D., Schexnayder, S. M., Chameides, L., Terry, M., Donoghue, A., Hickey, R. W., …Hazinski, M. F. (2010). Part 13: Pediatric basic life support: 2010 American Heart Association guidelines for cardiopulmonary resuscitation and emergency cardiovascular care. *Circulation, 122*(18), S962–S975.

7. Blair, A. E. (2012, December 4). Rapid sequence intubation in adults. *UpToDate.* Retrieved from http://www.uptodate.com/contents/rapid-sequence-intubation-in-adults

8. Lessig, M. L. (2006). The cardiovascular system. In J. G. Alspach (Ed.), *Core curriculum for critical care nursing* (6th ed., pp.185–380). St. Louis, MO: Saunders/Elsevier.

9. Wilkinson, J. M., & Treas, L.S. (2011). *Fundamentals of nursing* (2nd ed.). Philadelphia, PA: F. A. Davis Company

10. Perbedy, M. A., Callaway, C. W., Neumar, R. W., Geocadin, R. G., Zimmerman, J. L., Donnino, M., … Kronick, S. L. (2010). Part 9: Post-cardiac arrest care: 2010 Guidelines for Cardiopulmonary Resuscitation and Emergency Cardiovascular Care Science. *Circulation, 122*(18 Suppl 3), S768–S786.

11. O'Driscoll, B. R., Howard, L. S., & Davison, A. G. (2008). BTS guideline for emergency oxygen use in adult patients. *Thorax, 63*(Suppl VI), vi1–vi68.

12. Kilgannon, J. H., Jones, A. E., Shapiro, N. I., Angelos, M. G., Milcarek, B., Hunter, K., … Trzeciak, S. (2010). Association between arterial hyperoxia following resuscitation from cardiac arrest and in-hospital mortality. *Journal of the American Medical Association, 303*(21), 2165–2171.

13. Brenner, M., Stein, D., Hu, P., Kufera, J., Wooford, M., & Scalea, T. (2012). Association between early hyperoxia and worse outcomes after traumatic brain injury. *Archives of Surgery, 147*(111), 1042–1046.

14. Neumar, R. W., Otto, C. W., Link, M. S., Kudenchuk, P. J., Ornato, J. P., McNally, B., … Morrison, L. J. (2010). Part 8: Adult advanced cardiovascular life support: 2010 American Heart Association Guidelines for Cardiopulmonary Resuscitation and Emergency Cardiovascular Care. *Circulation, 122*(18 Suppl 3), S729–S767.

15. Keller, M. J. (2011). Excessive ventilation and oxygenation in resuscitation. *Caring in Motion.* Retrieved from http://www.seequip.com/BPWC/Documents/NREMTP%20Refresher/MAR%2012%20Excessive%20Ventilation%20&%20Oxygenation%20in%20resuscitation.pdf

16. Clark, D. Y. (2009). Oral airway insertion. In J. A. Proehl (Ed.), *Emergency nursing procedures* (4th ed., pp. 17–19). St. Louis, MO: Elsevier.

17. Lafferty, K., & Kulkarni, R. (2012, June 13). *Rapid sequence intubation.* Retrieved from http://emedicine.medscape.com/article/80222-overview

18. Kahn, R. M., Sharm, P. K., & Kaul, N. (2011). Airway management in trauma. *Indian Journal of Anaesthesia, 55*(5), 463-469.

19. Hung, O., & Murphy, M. F. (2011). *Management of the difficult and failed airway* (2nd ed.). New York, NY: McGraw-Hill.

20. Cohen, M. J. (2012). Towards hemostatic resuscitation: The changing understanding of acuter traumatic biology, massive bleeding, and damage-control resuscitation. *Surgical Clinics of North America, 92*(4), 877–891.

21. Dutton, R. (2008). Pathophysiology of trauma shock. *International Trauma Care, 18*(1), 12–15.

22. Chan, E. D., Chan, M. M., & Chan, M. M. (2013). Pulse oximetry: Understanding its basic principles facilitates appreciation of its limitations. *Respiratory Medicine, 107*(6), 789–799.

23. Valdez-Lowe, C., Ghareeb, S. A., & Artinian, N. T. (2009). Pulse oximetry in adults. *American Journal of Nursing, 109*(6), 52–59.

24. Schumann, L. L. (2013). Respiratory function and alterations in gas exchange. In L. E. Copstead & J. Banasik (Eds.), *Pathophysiology* (5th ed., pp. 449–474). St. Louis, MO: Elsevier.

25. Krauss, B., Silvestri, S., & Falk, J. L. (2012, October 15). Carbon dioxide monitoring (capnography). *UpToDate.* Retrieved from http://www.uptodate.com/contents/carbon-dioxide-monitoring-capnography

26. Moses, S. (2012, June 21). Oxygen saturation. In *Family practice notebook.* Retrieved from http://www.fpnotebook.com/Lung/Lab/OxygnStrtn.htm

27. Kleinman, M. E., Chameides, L., Schexnayder, S. M., Samson, R. A., Hazinski, M. F., Atkins, D. L., …Zaritsky, A. L. (2010). Part 14: Pediatric advanced life support: 2010 American Heart Association guidelines for cardiopulmonary resuscitation and emergency cardiovascular care. *Circulation, 122*, S876–S908.

28. Ackland, G. L., Dyson, A., & Singer, M. (2010). Arterial hyperoxia and in-hospital mortality after resuscitation from cardiac arrest. *Journal of the American Medical Association, 304*(13)m 1440.

29. Deakin, C. D., Morrison, L. J, Morley, P. T., Callaway, C. W., Kerber, R. E., Kronick, S. L., … Nolan, J. P. (2010). Part 8: Advanced life support: 2010 International Consensus on Cardiopulmonary Resuscitation and Emergency Cardiovascular Care Science with Treatment Recommendations. *Resuscitation, 81*(Suppl 1), e93–e174.

30. Staple, L. E., & O'Connell, K. J. (2013). Pediatric rapid sequence intubation: an in-depth review. *Pediatric Emergency Medicine Reports, 18*(1), 1–11.

31. Wade, T. (2012, April 12). *Fentanyl pretreatment in rapid sequence intubation.* Retrieved from http://www.tomwademd.net/2012/04/19/fentanyl-pretreatment-in-rapid-sequence-intubation/

Chapter 7 • Shock

Deborah A. Pentecost, MBA, BSN, RN
Sean G. Smith, BSN, RN, NREMT-P, FP-C, C-NPT, CCRN-CMC-CSC, CEN, CFRN, CPEN

Objectives:

Upon completion of this chapter, the learner will be able to:

1. Identify causes and characteristics of shock in the trauma patient.

2. Describe pathophysiologic changes as a basis for assessment of the trauma patient in shock.

3. Demonstrate nursing assessment priorities for the trauma patient in shock.

4. Plan appropriate interventions for the trauma patient in shock.

5. Evaluate the effectiveness of nursing interventions for the trauma patient in shock.

Introduction

Shock is defined as inadequate tissue perfusion, resulting from insufficient oxygen delivery, uptake, and utilization to meet the metabolic demands of cells and organs.[1] It is a dynamic process that begins when cells are hypoperfused, setting off a series of responses to preserve homeostasis and producing far-reaching effects on all systems and organs. The presence of shock, in its early stages, is likely to be subtle. If shock goes unrecognized and untreated, the hypoperfused cells shift from aerobic to anaerobic metabolism, which leads to life-threatening acidosis, tissue ischemia, and cellular death when coupled with the incomplete removal of metabolic waste products.

Shock is a complex state. A basic understanding of the concepts, types, and stages of shock as well as the body's response to inadequate tissue perfusion is essential for early recognition, early goal-directed interventions, and optimal care of the trauma patient in shock.

Classification and Etiology of Shock

Circulation in the human body is a closed system, consisting of the pump (the heart), the pipes (the vasculature), and the circulating fluid (the intravascular blood volume). The etiology of the different types of shock can be traced back to an issue with one of these three components.

Shock is classically delineated according to the cause, which falls into one of four categories: hypovolemic, obstructive, cardiogenic, and distributive (Table 7-1).

Hypovolemic Shock

Hypovolemic shock from hemorrhage is the leading cause of preventable deaths in trauma patients.[2,3] Hypovolemia is caused by a decrease in the amount of circulating blood volume.[4] In trauma, this typically results from hemorrhage but could result from a precipitous loss of volume, such as vomiting or diarrhea. Burn trauma can result in hypovolemic shock from damage to the cell membranes, leading to plasma and protein leakage. In hypovolemic shock, decreased circulating volume results in decreased preload. With less filling of the ventricles, heart muscle fibers stretch less at the end of the diastole. Starling's law states, in part, that with less stretching, there is less force of contraction, creating diminished cardiac output and less oxygenated blood being transported to the tissues, resulting in hypoperfusion.[1]

Goal-directed therapy for hypovolemic shock is aimed at replacing the type of volume the patient has lost in order to restore physiologic homeostasis (electrolytes with precipitous nonhemorrhagic losses or blood products with blood loss).[2] Not all hemorrhage involves obvious external bleeding. When solid organs and large bone structures are injured there can be a risk for concealed major blood loss, so it becomes imperative to consider the mechanism of injury, maintain a high index of suspicion for occult bleeding, and continually reassess for subtle signs of shock.

The physiologic responses related to the degrees of volume loss are listed in Table 7-2.

Obstructive Shock

Obstructive shock results from hypoperfusion of the tissue due to an obstruction in either the vasculature or heart. Goal-directed therapy is aimed at relieving the obstruction and improving perfusion. Tension pneumothorax and cardiac tamponade are two classic examples of obstructive shock that may result from trauma. Considerations for these include the following:[1]

- With tension pneumothorax, the increase in intrathoracic pressure leads to displacement of the

TNCC • Seventh Edition   73

vena cava, obstruction to atrial filling, decreased preload, and decreased cardiac output

- With cardiac tamponade, an accumulation of fluid within the inflexible pericardial sac impedes diastolic expansion and filling, which in turn, leads to a decrease in preload, stroke volume, cardiac output, and ultimately, end-organ perfusion

- Obstructive shock can also occur on the right side of the heart during systole caused by a venous air embolism in the pulmonary artery. If severe enough, this right ventricular outflow tract obstruction may precipitate shock causing increased intrathoracic pressure with resulting decreased cardiac output.

- Hyperventilation, which can occur in resuscitation, is a common iatrogenic cause of increased intrathoracic pressure resulting in compression of the heart and decreased cardiac output[5]

See Chapter 11, Thoracic and Neck Trauma, for additional information.

Cardiogenic Shock

Cardiogenic shock results from pump failure in the presence of adequate intravascular volume. There is a lack of cardiac output and end-organ perfusion secondary to a decrease in myocardial contractility and/or valvular insufficiency (aortic and/or mitral). Cardiogenic shock may be either chronic or acute in origin. Heart failure is one example of a chronic cause. Common acute etiologies include myocardial infarction (MI), dysrhythmias, or toxicologic pathologies. While trauma rarely causes cardiogenic shock, it is not unusual to observe MI or dysrhythmias and subsequent cardiogenic shock in the presence of trauma. For example, an individual may experience an MI while driving and, subsequently, is involved in a motor vehicle collision. When presented with a decreased cardiac output without volume loss in the context of trauma, assess the patient for signs of an MI or dysrhythmia, which are more common reasons for cardiogenic shock.

For the patient in cardiogenic shock, an excess of volume administration or an increase in afterload can result in pulmonary edema and increased myocardial ischemia. Successful emergent stabilization includes administering judicious fluid boluses to improve preload and inotropic support to improve contractility. If signs of fluid overload are present, afterload reduction may be indicated.[1,6] Blunt cardiac injury may present with similar assessment findings as MI. Injury or ischemia to myocardial tissue

Table 7-1. Classification of Shock Etiology and Underlying Defects

Classification	Etiology	Underlying Pathology
Hypovolemic	• Hemorrhage	• Whole blood loss
	• Burns	• Plasma loss
Cardiogenic	• Myocardial infarction	• Loss of cardiac contractility
	• Dysrhythmias	• Reduced cardiac output
	• Blunt cardiac trauma	• Loss of cardiac contractility and dysrhythmias
Obstructive	• Cardiac tamponade	• Compression of heart with obstruction to atrial filling
	• Tension pneumothorax	• Mediastinal shift with obstruction to atrial filling
	• Tension hemothorax	• Combination of compression of the heart and mediastinal shift
Distributive	• Neurogenic shock	• Loss of vasomotor tone due to decreases in sympathetic control
	• Anaphylactic shock	• Vasodilation of vessels due to immune reaction to allergens (release of histamine)
	• Septic shock	• Mediated by systemic inflammatory response syndrome (SIRS) with hypotension and perfusion abnormalities

Reprinted with permission from B. B. Jacobs.

or the conduction system could cause dysrhythmias and affect cardiac output. This is the most common cause of trauma-related cardiogenic shock, and goal-directed therapy includes inotropic support, antidysrhythmic medications, and correction or treatment of the underlying cause.[9]

Distributive Shock

Distributive shock occurs as a result of maldistribution of an adequate circulating blood volume with the loss of vascular tone or increased permeability. Diffuse vasodilation lowers the systemic pressure, creating a relative hypovolemia or reduction of the mean systemic volume and venous return to the heart or drop in preload, resulting in distributive shock. Causative factors include:[7]

- Anaphylactic shock typically resulting from a release of inflammatory mediators such as histamine, which contracts bronchial smooth muscle and increases vascular permeability and vasodilation

- Septic shock, which is caused by the systemic release of bacterial endotoxins, resulting in an increased vascular permeability and vasodilation

- Neurogenic shock that occurs with spinal cord injury (SCI) results in the loss of sympathetic nervous system control of vascular tone, which produces venous and arterial vasodilation[8]
  - Under normal homeostatic conditions, sympathetic and parasympathetic systems oppose each other allowing vasoconstriction and dilation to accommodate changing vascular volumes. With the loss of sympathetic nervous system input in SCI, unopposed vagal activity may result in decreased cardiac output through bradycardia.

In addition to providing controlled volume replacement, the treatment for distributive shock is to increase systemic vascular resistance. Medications, such as norepinephrine, dopamine, epinephrine, phenylephrine, and vasopressin, can be used to produce vasoconstriction. In some cases, atropine or transcutaneous pacing may be added to counteract parasympathetic bradycardia described. Treatment for septic shock includes the early administration of antibiotics and potential need for norepinephrine to vasoconstrict the peripheral vasculature, increase blood volume return to the heart, and improve cardiac output.[6]

Table 7-2. Estimated Blood Loss on a 70 kg Man Based on Initial Presentation

	Class I	Class II	Class III	Class IV
Blood loss (mL)	Up to 750	750–1,500	1,500–2,000	>2,000
Blood loss (% blood volume)	Up to 15%	15%–30%	30%–40%	>40%
Pulse rate (beats/min)	< 100	100–120	120–140	>140
Systolic blood pressure	Normal	Normal	Decreased	Decreased
Pulse pressure	Normal or increased	Decreased	Decreased	Decreased
Respiratory rate (breaths/min)	14–20	20–30	30–40	>35
Urine output (mL/h)	>30	20–30	5–15	Negligible
CNS/mental status	Slightly anxious	Mildly anxious	Anxious, confused	Confused, lethargic
Initial fluid replacement	Crystalloid	Crystalloid	Crystalloid and blood	Crystalloid and blood

Note: BPM indicates beats per minute; CNS, central nervous system.
From American College of Surgeons. (2012). *Advanced trauma life support student course manual* (9th ed.). Chicago, IL: Author.

Pathophysiology as a Basis for the Body's Response to Shock

Shock has many causes, classifications, and stages. Regardless of the cause, shock can be linked to one or more components of cardiac output. Cardiac output is the product of heart rate and stroke volume (Fig. 7-1). Stroke volume is affected by preload, which is a reflection of central venous pressure or the volume of blood returning to the heart at the end of diastole. Hypovolemia decreases preload, resulting in a loss in cardiac output. Afterload reflects the pressure the heart must overcome to pump blood into the circulation, or the systemic and pulmonary arterial pressures. Contractility is the ability of the ventricles to contract, forcefully ejecting blood. Different injuries can affect this contractility:[9]

- A tension pneumothorax can change intrathoracic pressure, causing an increase in afterload and compressing the heart and venae cavae, decreasing preload

- An injury to the myocardium or pericardial tamponade can limit the force of contraction and affect cardiac output

- Cardiac injury may cause bleeding in the pericardial space (cardiac tamponade) limiting the ability of the heart to contract and obstructing atrial filling

- A direct blunt force trauma to the heart can result in a dysrhythmia which can affect coordination of the cardiac cycle, decreasing cardiac output

In the early stages of shock, tissue perfusion and delivery of nutrients and oxygen are inadequate to meet the body's metabolic needs. To protect and maintain perfusion to essential organs, the body reacts by activating various compensatory mechanisms. For the short term, these compensatory mechanisms may improve tissue perfusion to some organs; however, it is accomplished primarily by shunting perfusion from other organs.[10] These responses can have a profound effect on microcirculation and vascular permeability if adequate perfusion is not restored. If the shock state is unrecognized, untreated, or prolonged or the protective mechanisms fail to restore perfusion, the patient progresses to irreversible shock. The cellular membrane loses its ability to maintain integrity, leading to cellular destruction and death, followed by a systemic inflammatory response, organ ischemia, end-organ damage, multiple organ dysfunction, and death.[4]

Early recognition and early goal-directed management of shock is essential to good outcomes and the prevention of organ failure and death.

Figure 7-1. The Relationship of Cardiac Output to Stroke Volume and Heart Rate

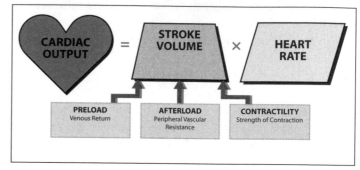

Cardiac output is the product of stroke volume and heart rate.

The human compensatory response includes a vascular component. As blood flow decreases and the arterial pressure falls below 80 mm Hg, oxygen delivery becomes impaired, resulting in decreased oxygen levels and increased carbon dioxide (CO_2) levels.[1] As a result of the lower blood pressure, a cascading response is set into motion to preserve tissue perfusion. The vascular response can be activated along two different pathways.

- Baroreceptor activation: Baroreceptors, found in the carotid sinus and along the aortic arch, are sensitive to the degree of stretch within the arterial wall. When the baroreceptors sense a decrease in stretch, they stimulate the sympathetic nervous system to release epinephrine and norepinephrine, causing stimulation of cardiac activity and constriction of blood vessels, which causes a rise in heart rate and diastolic blood pressure.[1]

- Chemoreceptor activation: Peripheral chemoreceptors consist of carotid and aortic bodies. Chemoreceptors detect changes in blood oxygen and CO_2 and pH.[1] When CO_2 rises or the oxygen level or pH falls, these receptors are activated and information is relayed to the central nervous system and to the cardiorespiratory centers in the medulla, which increases respiratory rate and depth and blood pressure.[1]

These changes in vital signs may seem subtle unless the trauma nurse is observant and alert to their presence. The increase of the diastolic blood pressure with a narrowing pulse pressure may be one of the first concrete measurements signaling that the patient's circulatory status is compromised and the body is trying to compensate. Recognizing this early shock response stage can be essential to preventing further tissue injury and progression of the shock state. Table 7-3 describes initial presentation by shock class.

Adrenal Gland Response

Activation of the sympathetic nervous system causes the adrenal glands to release the two catecholamines—epinephrine and norepinephrine:

- High levels of *epinephrine* cause smooth muscle relaxation in the airways and causes arteriole smooth muscle contraction (potentiating inotropic effect). Epinephrine also increases heart rate (positive chronotropic effect), peripheral vasoconstriction, and glycogenolysis (breakdown of glycogen stores in the liver into glucose for cellular use).

- *Norepinephrine* increases heart rate, vascular tone through alpha-adrenergic receptor activation, and blood flow to skeletal muscle and triggers the release of glucose from energy stores

In addition to the release of catecholamines, the adrenal glands stimulate the release of cortisol to raise blood glucose and promote renal retention of water and sodium.

Initially, sympathetic nervous system response and vasoconstriction is selective, shunting blood to the heart and brain and away from the skin and splanchnic circulation (gastric, small intestinal, colonic, pancreatic, hepatic, and splenic), increasing their risk for ischemia.[10] If shock is left untreated, compensatory mechanisms will begin to fail and blood flow will be reduced, resulting in lower blood pressure, reduction in organ perfusion and oxygen and CO_2 transport. Circulating lactic acid from anaerobic metabolism increases, resulting in acidosis and causing further injury to organs (Table 7-3).

Immune Response

The initial post-traumatic inflammatory response is both protective and essential for survival. Tissue hypoxia activates this response, and neutrophils are sent to the injury sites, activating signaling pathways that mobilize inflammatory cells. Tissue hypoxia also stimulates the secretion of multiple inflammatory mediators or biomarkers.[11]

An exaggerated immune inflammatory response can result from massive tissue injury and hemorrhage or a prolonged and untreated shock state. It can induce a generalized, acute inflammatory response that affects multiple organ systems and sets in motion a cycle of inflammation–tissue damage–inflammation that is driven by cytokines, chemokines, and products of damaged, dysfunctional, or stressed tissue.

The neutrophil's apoptosis may be inhibited, causing an accumulation of neutrophils that stimulate the release of inflammatory mediators. In other cells, apoptosis may be magnified, increasing cell death and worsening organ function. The neutrophils change and move from the capillaries into the interstitial space and trigger further release of free oxygen radicals and tissue destructive enzymes leading to additional tissue injury.[12] This process may start when hypoperfusion begins or during resuscitation. The organ systems most impacted are the lungs, liver, and kidneys, and unless organ and tissue hypoxia is corrected early, the inflammatory response becomes destructive, leading to organ failure and death.[12]

Table 7-3. Effects of the Sympathetic Nervous System Stimulation

Organ	Effect
Heart (muscle)	Increased force of contraction (positive inotropy)
Heart (rate)	Increased heart rate (positive chronotropy)
Peripheral vessels	Vasoconstriction
Pupils	Dilation
Sweat glands (cholinergic)	Increased secretion
Adrenal glands	Increased cortical and medullary secretion
Bronchi	Dilation
Kidneys	Renin secretion increased
Liver	Glycogenolysis (breakdown of stored glycogen)

Reprinted with permission from B. B. Jacobs

Pulmonary Response

During shock, the pulmonary system responds both to hypoperfusion and acidosis. The respiratory rate increases in an attempt to improve oxygen delivery to the tissue as well as to decrease the CO_2 level in order to maintain acid–base balance. Metabolic acidosis as a result of anaerobic metabolism results in this compensatory response of tachypnea and is one of the earliest responses to inadequately perfused tissue. If shock is left untreated, the pulmonary response may become ineffective, weaken, and fail, necessitating assisted ventilations.

Cerebral Response

As shock progresses, the primary goal of the body is to maintain perfusion to the vital organs—the midbrain, heart, and kidneys—shunting blood away from liver, bowel, skin, and muscle. Sympathetic stimulation has little effect on the cerebral and coronary vessels since they are capable of autoregulation.[13] Cerebral autoregulation maintains a constant cerebral vascular blood flow as long as the mean arterial pressure (MAP) is maintained in the range of 50 to 150 mm Hg.[2,11] When autoregulation in the brain fails, perfusion becomes dependent solely on pressure.[13] See Chapter 9, Brain, Cranial, and Maxillofacial Trauma, for additional information.

Renal Response

Hypoperfusion of the kidneys triggers a complex compensatory mechanism in the adrenal glands in an attempt to improve tissue perfusion that includes the following:[12]

- Renal ischemia causes the adrenal gland to increase production of renin
- Renin accelerates the production of angiotensin I
- Angiotensin I is then converted into angiotensin II in the lungs by angiotensin converting enzyme (ACE) produced by the vascular endothelium
- Angiotensin II effects include:
  - Potent vasoconstriction causing a rise in vascular resistance and arterial pressure
  - The release of aldosterone, which increases reabsorption of sodium and water in the distal tubules to increase intravascular volume
  - The stimulation of arginine vasopressin (AVP), also known as vasopressin, argipressin, or antidiuretic hormone (ADH), which further increases retention of water

Decreased urinary output may be noted, which can be an indication of poor renal perfusion and progression of the shock state. If shock is left untreated, it will progress to oliguria and renal failure.

Coagulopathy

Resuscitation-associated coagulopathy is associated with the trauma triad of death (Fig. 7-2). It includes:[14]

- Hypothermia
  - Impairs thrombin production and platelet function
- Acidosis
  - Impairs thrombin production
- Coagulopathy
  - Results in depletion of clotting factors through hemodilution and the impaired ability to produce clotting factors[15]

In the early 2000s, research demonstrated that in some cases, acute traumatic coagulopathy (ATC) began immediately at the time of injury and was not related to fluid resuscitation. This led to the development of damage control resuscitation or hemostatic resuscitation.[15] Studies show that severely injured patients with tissue hypoperfusion (base deficit < −6 mEq/L) developed ATC within 30 minutes of injury.[15] The tissue injury and hypoperfusion combine to prevent clot formation, which exacerbates the hemorrhagic shock state.[15]

Stages of Shock

There are three stages of shock: stage I (compensated), stage II (decompensated or progressive), and stage III (irreversible).[12] When low blood flow and poor tissue perfusion are detected, the body responds quickly. The patient may appear asymptomatic; however, compensatory mechanisms are working to maintain homeostasis. There is a narrow window of opportunity to rapidly intervene before the patient develops acidosis and decompensation, resulting in tissue death and organ dysfunction.

Shock is a complex, dynamic state. Blood pressure alone is not an indication of cardiac output and adequate perfusion. There are several endpoints of resuscitation that can be monitored proactively to recognize potential hemorrhage quickly and respond immediately. Appropriate and early management of traumatic bleeding is crucial as failure to initiate these interventions is the leading cause of death in trauma patients.[13]

Figure 7-2. Trauma Triad of Death

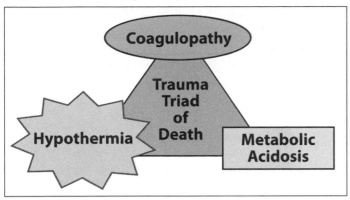

The combination of coagulopathy, hypothermia, and metabolic acidosis can be lethal for the trauma patient.

Stage I: Compensated Shock

In this stage, compensatory mechanisms are activated and the patient may begin to exhibit subtle changes in level of consciousness and vital signs, including:

- Anxiety, lethargy, confusion, and restlessness from oxygen being shunted to brainstem, maintaining survival function, and away from areas responsible for higher brain function

- Systolic blood pressure, usually within normal range

- A rising diastolic blood pressure, results in a narrowed pulse pressure, which is a reflection of peripheral vasoconstriction

- A bounding and/or slightly tachycardic pulse as a result of catecholamine release

- Increased respiratory rate, which could also be a result of pain or anxiety

- Decreased urinary output as the kidney works to retain fluid within the circulatory system

Stage II: Decompensated or Progressive Shock

Decompensated or progressive shock occurs when compensatory mechanisms begin to fail and are unable to support or improve perfusion.[7] Shock may still be reversible at this stage.[12] Signs and symptoms include:[7]

- level of consciousness deteriorates and the patient becomes obtunded or unconscious as the cells switch to anaerobic metabolism with increasing levels of lactic and pyruvic acids

- Normal or slightly decreased systolic blood pressure

- Narrowing pulse pressure that continues until peripheral vascular vasoconstriction fails to provide cardiovascular support

- Tachycardia greater than 100 beats/min

- Weak and thready pulses

- Rapid and shallow respirations as the lungs try to correct acidosis

- Cool, clammy, cyanotic skin as blood shunts to vital organs (may develop toward end of decompensated stage)

- Base excess not within normal range of –2 mEq/L to +2 mEq/L

- Serum lactate levels greater than 2 to 4 mmol/L[16]

Stage III: Irreversible Shock

Irreversible shock will lead to death without rapid intervention. Tissue and cells throughout the body become ischemic and necrotic, resulting in multiple organ dysfunction.[16] Signs and symptoms include:[7]

- Obtunded, stuporous, or comatose

- Marked hypotension and heart failure

- Bradycardia with possible dysrhythmias

- Decreased and shallow respiratory rate

- Pale, cool, and clammy skin

- Kidney, liver, and other organ failure due to continued hypoperfusion and ischemia

- Severe acidosis, elevated lactic acid levels, and worsening base excess on arterial blood gases (ABGs)

- Coagulopathies with petechiae, purpura, or bleeding

In spite of aggressive resuscitation at this level, it becomes increasingly difficult to restore tissue perfusion, correct the coagulopathies, and minimize organ damage. With whole blood loss, clotting factors are lost. Replacement with packed cells and saline without also transfusing with platelets and plasma further dilutes the patient's ability to clot.[4,17] The result is disseminated intravascular coagulopathy, multiple organ dysfunction syndrome, and death.

Usual Concurrent Injuries

Managing a patient with hemorrhagic hypovolemic shock requires goal-directed therapy aimed at controlling the blood loss and achieving hemostasis. Proactive consideration of possible internal hemorrhage can lead to earlier definitive management. While external bleeding necessitates rapid identification and control, it is important that it not serve as a distractor from the ongoing assessment. This is true of blunt trauma, either in isolation, or with a penetrating injury. Injuries to the liver, spleen, kidneys, large vessels, pelvis, and long bones may be the site of blood loss.

Early recognition and treatment can be achieved with the following:

- Consideration of concomitant injuries based on mechanism of injury (MOI) or bruising patterns (seatbelt injuries)
- Physical inspection for assessment findings of the bleeding in the abdomen, flank, or pelvis; hematuria; or rectal bleeding

In the presence of hemorrhagic shock, it is important to identify the source of the bleeding. Useful diagnostic tests include:[4]

- Chest and pelvic radiographs
- Focused assessment with sonography for trauma (FAST)
- Computed tomography (CT) scans for hemodynamically stable patients
- CT angiography to identify vascular sources of bleeding
- Diagnostic laparoscopy/exploratory laparotomy

Current Management Strategies

Damage Control Resuscitation

Damage control resuscitation (DCR) is a principle that focuses on prevention rather than intervention. Early recognition of the patient at risk for shock facilitates the use of goal-directed therapies.[17] It involves two strategies:[17]

- Hypotensive resuscitation
  - Studies suggest that the use of large volumes of crystalloid solution is associated with increased bleeding and decreased survival rates. This could be the result of hemodilution and decreased clotting factors.[3] Several studies have posited that delayed and restrictive administration of isotonic crystalloid solution in trauma patients (without head injury) may have better outcomes and lower mortality, by allowing the clotting cascade to work. This might limit the complications that lead to increased bleeding and re-bleeding, sometimes known as "popping the clot."[5] Plasma and blood products are the primary fluids to correct blood loss and inadequate coagulation.[4] The goal is not hypotension, but adequate resuscitation without producing hypertension.[4]
  - Additional research needs to be done to define hypotension, especially in older adults.[18] Some studies have indicated the threshold as a systolic blood pressure of 110 mm Hg, and the Centers for Disease Control and Prevention (CDC) recommends patients who are over 65 years old with a systolic blood pressure of 110 mm Hg are triaged to a trauma center.[19,20]

- Hemostatic resuscitation
  - The key to early goal-directed therapy is to optimize oxygenation and perfusion by preventing further losses through hemodilutional coagulopathy.[17] When hemorrhage occurs, clotting factors and platelets are lost along with red blood cells. Excessive use of isotonic crystalloids alone or replacing whole blood loss with only packed red blood cells can produce a hemodilutional coagulopathy in which the effective concentrations of both platelets and clotting factors are significantly reduced.[17] Hemorrhage control is optimized by giving component therapy, using both the transfusion of both packed red blood cells and fresh frozen plasma in a 1:1 ratio.[3] Platelets are added at a 1:1:1 ratio in the presence of actual or anticipated thrombocytopenia.[17]
  - Balanced fluid resuscitation is an approach to resuscitation that addresses all components that are lost with hemorrhage, including fluid, packed red blood cells and fresh frozen plasma while surgically controlling the source of bleeding.[21] It is crucial that hemorrhage control and balanced fluid resuscitation be initiated early.[4]

Fluid Resuscitation

The previous approach to fluid resuscitation in the patient with shock has been two large-bore intravenous (IV) catheters and rapid infusion of isotonic crystalloid solution. Following the initial fluid bolus, an assessment was repeated and if needed, blood transfusions were considered. This approach led to excessive volumes of crystalloid solution infusions, resulting in hemodilution, fewer circulating red blood cells to carry hemoglobin, worsening acidosis (due to anaerobic metabolism), dilution of coagulation factors, increased inflammatory response (due to large volumes of crystalloid), and potentially acute respiratory distress syndrome (ARDS), abdominal compartment syndrome and increased mortality.[3,4,23]

Current recommendations suggest a lesser volume of crystalloid solutions and use boluses to follow the principle of permissive hypotension.[17] Initial fluid management for the adult trauma patient should be a fluid resuscitation bolus of 1 to 2 L of warmed fluid, including fluid given by prehospital providers.[4] The patient's response to the initial fluid bolus should guide subsequent IV fluid administration.[4]

Massive Transfusion

The United States (U.S.) military first demonstrated that providing a balanced resuscitation (limited use of crystalloid solution) and following a massive transfusion protocol (MTP) with a defined blood-to-plasma ratio resulted in hemostasis and decreased mortality in hemorrhaging patients.[23] Similar findings have been achieved in civilian settings, and the U.S. Department of Defense is continuing research to determine the optimal ratio of blood-to-blood products.[3] Recognizing that a predefined MTP leads to early blood, plasma, and platelet transfusions with improved outcomes, the American College of Surgeons (ACS) delineated use of MTP as critical criteria for trauma centers in *Resources for Optimal Care of the Injured Patient*.[24] Success of the current MTP is dependent on early recognition and implementation, using a defined ratio of one part red blood cells to one part thawed plasma to one part platelets (1:1:1 ratio) and providing a detailed process for implementation. Limitations include the timing and immediacy of implementing the protocol and the availability of thawed plasma and platelets. More research is needed, but the 1:1:1 protocol seems to be directly related to improved survival rates.[3]

Calcium Chloride Replacement

Hypocalcemia is a concern with massive transfusion because citrate is added as a preservative to banked blood to prevent coagulation.[4] Citrate chelates, or binds with, calcium rendering it inactive. Because calcium is a vital part of the clotting cascade, hypocalcemia, as a result of massive transfusion, can actually worsen hypovolemic shock by permitting continued bleeding. Signs of hypocalcemia include cardiac dysrhythmias, muscle tremors, and seizures.[7,25] About 3 g of citrate is added to each unit of donated blood, and a healthy adult liver can metabolize citrate at a rate of 3 g every 5 minutes.[26] If the trauma patient requires more than one unit of blood every 5 minutes, anticipate citrate toxicity and hypocalcemia and prepare to replace losses with calcium gluconate or calcium choride.[26] If calcium chloride is used, monitor closely for infiltration as it can cause tissue necrosis.[25] Patients taking calcium-channel blockers (diltiazem) may be predisposed to cardiac dysrhythmias. Monitoring of calcium levels may be indicated earlier for these patients.[27]

Autotransfusion

Autotransfusion, or administration of the patient's own blood from the chest tube collection chamber, may be an option when transfusion is needed. Follow package recommendations, which usually suggest administration within 6 hours. Benefits include the following:[21]

- Transfused with the patient's own fresh whole blood, eliminating the risk of transfusion reaction
- Blood is at room temperature, with no waiting for blood products to warm
- Red blood cells in autotransfused blood may have better oxygen-carrying capacity, as older, banked blood may have red blood cells that have begun to degrade
- Lower cost
- Lower risk of communicable disease

Disadvantages of autotransfusion include:[22]

- The risk of contamination from a microorganism within the chest
- RBCs may become hemolyzed during hemorrhage
- Coagulation factors, including platelets and cryoprecipitate may be destroyed, increasing the D-dimer in the collected blood

Damage Control Surgery

Damage control surgery is a shift from rapid definitive surgery and complete repair to surgery that is intended to stop the bleeding, restore normothermia, and treat coagulopathy and acidosis; in other words, resuscitation from the trauma triad (Fig. 7-2).[15] Damage control surgery is recommended to last no longer than 90 minutes.[15] Definitive injury repair is accomplished later during planned or staged operations after the patient has been further resuscitated, stabilized, and warmed in the intensive care unit.

Tranexamic Acid

Tranexamic acid (TXA) is a synthetic version of the amino acid lysine. It is an antifibrinolytic that inhibits activation of plasminogen, a substance that is responsible for dissolving clots. TXA has been safely used to reduce intraoperative bleeding in elective medical and dental surgery and for the control of heavy menstrual bleeding.[28] The large, multicenter, multicountry study, Clinical Randomization of an Antifibrinolytic in Significant Hemorrhage (CRASH-2) evaluated 20,211 patients with or at risk of bleeding and found that TXA can be safely used to reduce the risk of death from bleeding in trauma patients.[17,29] Based on those findings, it is recommended that TXA be given early to be effective. It has considerable application in referral settings or during long transport times or in an austere environment.[29] At the time of writing, the U.S. Food and Drug Administration has not approved this medication for use in trauma, but with promising research results, look for approval and widespread use in the near future.[30]

Nursing Care of the Patient in Shock

Preparation and Triage

The American College of Surgeons Committee on Trauma (ACS-COT) considers a systolic blood pressure of 90 mm Hg or less in the prehospital setting as criteria for trauma team activation at the highest level.[24] One study found that a single systolic blood pressure reading of less than 105 mm Hg was associated with severe injuries that often required operative or endovascular treatment and admission to the intensive care unit (ICU). In light of this an isolated hypotensive blood pressure measurement in a prehospital setting is considered to be significant.[31]

Safe Practice, Safe Care

In the patient at risk for or experiencing traumatic shock, it is essential that assessment and intervention occur simultaneously and systematically. The primary survey is performed; life-threatening problems are treated and reassessed prior to moving to the next step and prior to moving to the secondary survey. Integrated ongoing assessments, history, physical examination, imaging and laboratory studies, and serial assessments are crucial to optimizing patient outcomes by anticipating potential blood loss from suspected or actual injuries, and having a proactive management plan that anticipates the patient's potential course.

Primary Survey and Resuscitation Adjuncts

Refer to Chapter 5, Initial Assessment, for the systematic approach to the nursing care of the trauma patient. The following assessment parameters are specific to patients with signs of shock.

A–Airway and Alertness

- Observe for restlessness and anxiety, which may be an early sign of shock

- Unresponsiveness in the trauma patient may be due to hypovolemia, not head trauma[4]

- A patient may experience uncompensated shock with a blood volume loss of 30% to 40% before becoming unresponsive[4]

- Use of alcohol and other substances make alterations in level of consciousness less useful in detecting early shock

B–Breathing and Ventilation

Inspect for:

- Increased work of breathing, which may indicate compensation for early hypovolemic shock and respiratory correction of metabolic acidosis

C–Circulation and Control of Hemorrhage

Inspect for:

- Active external bleeding

- Bruised, swollen, and deformed extremities

- A distended abdomen, which may indicate occult blood loss

Auscultate for:

- Diminished breath sounds (possible pneumothorax or hemothorax) or muffled heart tones (possible pericardial tamponade)

Palpate for:

- Central and peripheral pulses

  ○ Increased or bounding central pulses may indicate increased cardiac output and this can be the result of the release of catecholamines from the sympathetic nervous system in an effort to increase cardiac output

  ○ Peripheral pulses do not demonstrate a similar effect in the presence of hypovolemia due to vasoconstriction. Thus, strong central pulses combined with weak peripheral pulses may be indicative of shock.

  ○ Tenderness and rigidity in the abdomen and instability in the pelvis may be signs of occult hemorrhage

Interventions

- Administer supplemental oxygen via nonrebreather mask to achieve optimal oxygenation if not already completed as indicated in the assessment of the airway and breathing. Administer oxygen to maintain oxygen saturation (SpO_2) between 94% and 98%.[4]

- Control external hemorrhage with direct pressure

  ○ Tourniquets are a consideration if bleeding in the extremities is not controlled with direct pressure[4]

- A pelvic binder or sheeting is recommended for stabilization for suspected or confirmed unstable pelvic fracture. See Chapter 12, Abdominal and Pelvic Trauma, for more information.

- Insert two large-bore peripheral intravenous (IV) catheters

  ○ If IV access cannot be rapidly obtained, default to intraosseous (IO) access. This essential technique for early access during resuscitation is underused. IO and peripheral IV access allow for a more rapid infusion because the catheter length is shorter than a central line.[4]

○ If anticipating the need for use of a rapid volume infuser, check the manufacturer's recommendations for minimum catheter gauge needed for proper use

- Consider activation of the MTP (unmatched type O blood, thawed fresh frozen plasma, and platelets). See Appendix 7-A and 7-B for sample MTP protocols.

- Prevent hypothermia by warming resuscitation fluids to maintain the patient's temperature at 37°C (98.6°F)

  ○ Use a rapid infuser that warms the blood with blood tubing adequate to transfuse blood components maintaining the 1:1:1 replacement ratio

    ♦ Once hemostasis is achieved, it is estimated that one unit of packed red blood cells will increase hemoglobin by 1 g/dL and hematocrit by 3%[32]

    ♦ Use Rh-negative blood whenever possible. If O-negative blood is limited, O-positive blood can be administered to men and post-menopausal women. If O-positive blood is administered to premenopausal women, they may become sensitized to the Rh factor which may impact future pregnancies.[4]

D–Disability (Neurologic Status)
Assess for LOC. A decrease may be indicative of hypoxemia and uncontrolled internal bleeding.

E–Exposure and Environmental Control
Obtain the patient's temperature because hypothermia causes decreased tissue oxygenation, acidosis and increased coagulopathy, resulting in increased morbidity and mortality.

F–Full Set of Vital Signs
Blood Pressure Measurements
Systolic blood pressure does not directly reflect cardiac output, although trending vital signs may offer useful information regarding improved blood flow to the organs, and tissue oxygenation to guide continued care.[4] Additional measurements include:

- Frequent and serial blood pressure measurements to determine pulse pressure changes and monitor for signs of vascular compensatory mechanisms

- Blood pressure differences between the right and left arm, which may be a sign of thoracic aorta injury

A recent review of the literature reveals arterial readings as the gold standard for a dependable and precise blood pressure reading.[33] In adults experiencing trauma and shock, use of the standard non-invasive oscillometric blood pressure measurement has been described as appropriate.[33] However, measurement where the mean arterial pressure (MAP) is automatically calculated and trended is encouraged whenever it is available.[33]

G-Get Resuscitation Adjuncts
L–Laboratory Studies
The laboratory studies used to guide resuscitative efforts in shock include the following:

- Platelet count and clotting studies

- Serum lactate, anion gap, base deficit, and arterial blood gasses to assess acidosis

- Toxicology screen to help assess mental status and differentiate from head injury

- Calcium level when rapidly infusing large volumes of blood products

Additional blood specimens are needed including a type and crossmatch, hemoglobin and hematocrit, electrolytes, serum osmolarity, blood urea nitrogen, creatinine, amylase, and liver enzymes. These tests may be directly correlated to the shock pathophysiology and injuries; however, unlike serum lactate, platelets, and clotting factors, they are less useful in the initial treatment and more useful in ongoing reevaluation.

O–Oxygenation
Pulse Oximetry
The goal is to maintain a SpO_2 reading 94 to 98%.[34,35] As there are many variables that may skew pulse oximeter readings, including hemodilution and carbon monoxide exposure, it is essential that patient management decisions not be made on pulse oximetry values alone.

End-tidal Carbon Dioxide Monitoring
End-tidal carbon dioxide ($ETCO_2$) monitoring can be used to rapidly assess endotracheal tube placement, symptomatic pneumothoraxes, or other pulmonary pathologies. It may also be used to indirectly assess cardiac output as a function of pulmonary perfusion.[36] Continuous waveform capnography will provide a breath-to-breath analysis of both ventilation and perfusion and serve as a valuable adjunct during resuscitation and ongoing monitoring. Research shows that capnography indirectly measures cardiac output and can be used to monitor effectiveness of cardiopulmonary resuscitation and the return of spontaneous circulation.

Reevaluation
Determine if there is an early need for transport to a trauma center or to surgery.

Focused Assessment with Sonography for Trauma (FAST)

Following the primary survey, FAST examination may be used to rapidly and noninvasively assess for bleeding resulting from damage to the heart, liver, kidneys, and spleen.[17] FAST examination is also increasingly used to detect pneumothorax, especially tension pneumothorax.[17]

Portable Radiograph

If there is suspicion that the trauma patient has or is at risk for internal hemorrhage, chest and pelvic imaging can be performed in the resuscitation room to expedite early goal-directed management. This is true for patients who may have a sequestering hemorrhage in the highly vascular pelvis.

Secondary Survey and Reevaluation Adjuncts
H–History

Additional history to be collected when the patient is at risk for shock includes:

- What was the estimated blood loss at the scene?
- Was there any episode of blood pressure below 90 mm Hg during prehospital care?
- Does the patient have complaints of dizziness or other symptoms that might indicate the onset of shock?
- Does the patient have complaints of chest or abdominal pain?
- Is there a history of hypertension? Does the patient take any antihypertensive medication?
- Is there a history of anticoagulant therapy?
- Is there a history of anemia or other blood dyscrasia (hemophilia)?

Positive responses may provide clues regarding acute blood loss, and careful inspection with close monitoring can lead to early detection of shock. However, it is wise to assume that all trauma patients who present supine on a backboard are in compensated shock until it is proven otherwise.

Reevaluation Adjuncts
Diagnostic Studies
Diagnostic Peritoneal Lavage

Diagnostic peritoneal lavage (DPL) is not used frequently but continues to be an option when FAST examination or computed tomography (CT) is not available or the patient is too unstable to move for a CT scan. It is highly sensitive for bleeding within the abdominal cavity, and may also reveal free enteric contents.[37]

Computed Tomography

After stabilization and completion of the primary survey, CT is used to explore possible findings not seen on initial chest and abdominal radiography. Prepare the patient for intrafacility transport. See Chapter 23, Transition of Care for the Trauma Patient, for additional information. An important caveat is CT images are not required for transfer and should not delay transfer to a higher level of care if needed. Hemodynamically unstable trauma patients are high risk for deterioration during transport to radiology and imaging.[4]

Other Studies

Subsequent to achieving hemodynamic stability, echocardiography and a 12-lead electrocardiogram will provide additional cardiac assessment data.

Other selected reevaluation adjuncts specific to the trauma patient in shock include:

- Consider insertion of a urinary catheter to monitor urine output
  - Urine output is an important indicator of fluid volume status and organ perfusion and needs to be monitored hourly[17]
  - Adequate urinary output is a level of 0.5 mL/kg per hour (for the 70 kg adult patient)[4,17]
  - Output of less than 0.5 mL/kg per hour for two consecutive hours indicates oliguria[17]
- The use of vasoconstrictors and vasopressors is not indicated in hemorrhagic shock[4]

Reevaluation and Post Resuscitation Care

Reevaluation specific to shock includes the following:

- Oxygen saturation via pulse oximetry, $ETCO_2$ monitoring, and serial arterial blood gases (ABGs) provide ongoing assessment of oxygenation, ventilation, and perfusion
- Continued assessments are performed to monitor for rebleeding and previously unnoticed injuries and sources of hemorrhage as well as assessment to determine the effectiveness of resuscitative measures and adequate tissue perfusion. This may include frequent and repeated, focused assessment and additional imaging studies, such as CT or magnetic resonance imaging.
- Monitor urine output hourly to assess effective resuscitation and renal perfusion and function. Oliguria and an elevated blood urea nitrogen-to-creatinine ratio are signs of possible hypoperfusion.[4,17]
- Ongoing monitoring of hemoglobin, hematocrit, platelets, and clotting times may help to identify coagulopathy due to continued blood loss or hemodilutional effects of massive volume resuscitation

- Continued frequent monitoring and trending of goals and indicators of improved perfusion and optimal outcomes:
  - Signs of adequate perfusion to periphery
  - Adequate oxygen saturation
  - Normothermia
  - Normotension
  - Stable heart and respiratory rates
  - Controlled hemostasis
  - Normal serum pH
  - Decreasing serum lactate
  - Improved base excess

Definitive Care and Transport

Prepare the patient for surgical interventions to explore body cavities for occult blood loss, such as thoracotomy or laparotomy for the patient with continued hypotension despite ongoing resuscitation or uncontrollable hemorrhage from the torso.

Emerging Trends

As the science and evidence of trauma care continues to evolve, tools to improve patient outcomes continue to be trialed and refined. Evidence is tested and replicated, and new standards of care are transitioned into practice. This section on trauma care considerations explores some of the evidence and the potential significance to trauma patient care. In the care of patients in shock, evidence related to tourniquet use, prehospital shock scoring systems, and noninvasive monitoring will be discussed.

Tourniquet Use

Military experience and research has reinforced the use of tourniquets for limb injuries with uncontrolled hemorrhage. In 2008, a large study in a combat hospital reviewed the use of tourniquets to control hemorrhage on major limb injuries.[38] When tourniquets were appropriately and properly applied, the benefits outweighed the risks and reduced deaths. Direct pressure or pneumatic splinting devices are methods to control bleeding quickly. Kragh et al. studied the outcomes of patients who had tourniquets applied both in the prehospital setting and in military EDs.[39,40] A positive relationship was seen between lives saved and the early application of a tourniquet to stop major limb hemorrhage before clinical indications of shock were evident.[39] They also studied the impact of tourniquet application before and after the patient entered a shock state, and they concluded that prehospital tourniquet use was also strongly associated with saving lives. A few patients experienced transient nerve palsy at the level of the tourniquet, but no limbs were lost and no amputations resulted solely from tourniquet use.[39,40] The recommendation was that military and civilian emergency medical services providers be trained to appropriately apply tourniquets.[40]

Prehospital Shock Index

There are multiple issues confounding the early administration of blood products in patients with emergent hemorrhage. Aside from the obvious delays inherent in preparing blood products in patients in the early compensated phases of hemorrhagic shock, the need for transfusions may not be readily apparent, especially in the prehospital setting. Although not currently widely in use, ongoing research demonstrates the efficacy of deploying standardized prehospital scoring systems as clinical indicators, which allows for proactive preparation of unmatched type O blood and earlier progress to the therapeutic goals of hemostasis and oxygen delivery.[41,42]

Noninvasive Monitoring

Advances in technology have led to a growing number of noninvasive hemodynamic and cardiac output monitoring modalities and tools available for trauma resuscitation.

- Responsiveness to fluid resuscitation and cardiac output may be assessed comparing differences in pulse oximetry wave form amplitude (Pleth Variability Index)[43]
- Oxygen delivery at the tissue level can be assessed using near infrared spectroscopy[44]
- $ETCO_2$ monitoring, in the form of continuous wave form capnography, provides nearly instantaneous ongoing feedback related to ventilation. The recommended use for this technology is reflected in current American Heart Association guidelines.[45] However, in trauma patients, one study reported that the $ETCO_2$ was found to have a low correlation with the $PaCO_2$ and urged a search for improved strategies.[46]

Summary

Shock is a syndrome of impaired tissue perfusion and oxygenation. Mismatch between the supply and demand of oxygen and nutrients leads to ischemia at the cellular level, a transition to anaerobic metabolism and acidosis, and ultimately organ death. Shock may be classified into four broad categories: hypovolemic, obstructive, cardiogenic, and distributive. Hypovolemic shock and depletion of circulating volume secondary to hemorrhage is the most common and primary shock state observed in trauma and the leading cause of preventable death in trauma.[2,3,16] Regardless of the etiology, it is essential for the trauma nurse to rapidly recognize and intervene to optimize oxygen transport and tissue perfusion. Primary contributors to mortality in hemorrhagic shock include failure to recognize and failure to intervene early.[4] This leads to a shock state progressing and leading to the resuscitation complications of hypothermia, acidosis and coagulopathy. Early management of these concomitant variables is essential to ultimately optimizing patient outcomes in traumatic shock.

Appendix 7-A. Massive Transfusion Protocol–Hospital Example 1

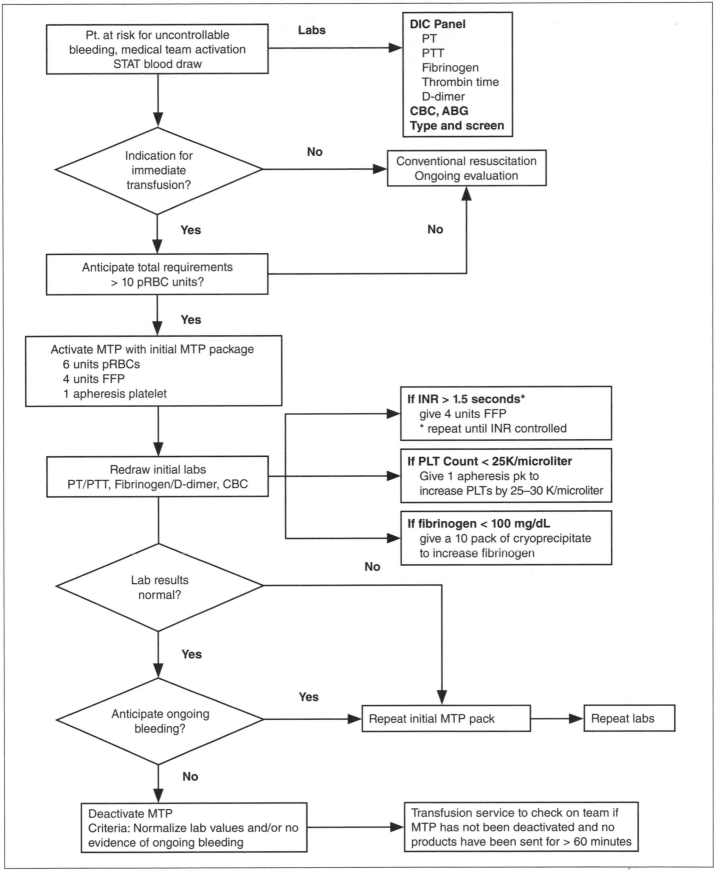

Reprinted from Young, P. P., Cotton, B. A., & Goodnough, L. T. (2011). Massive transfusion protocols for patients with substantial hemorrage. *Transfusion Medicine Reviews* 25(4), 293–303, *with permission from Elsevier.*

Appendix 7-A. Massive Transfusion Protocol–Hospital Example 2

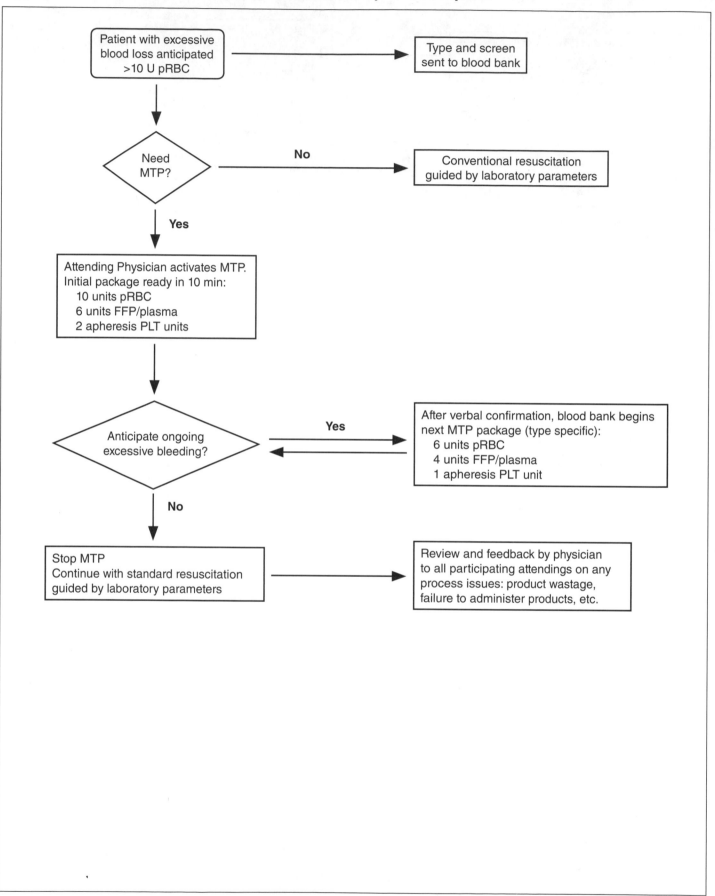

Reprinted from Young, P. P., Cotton, B. A., & Goodnough, L. T. (2011). Massive transfusion protocols for patients with substantial hemorrage. *Transfusion Medicine Reviews* 25(4), 293–303, *with permission from Elsevier.*

References

1. Klabunde, R.E. (2012). *Cardiovascular physiology concepts* (2nd ed.). Baltimore, MD: Lippincott, Williams, and Wilkins.

2. Santry, H. P., & Alam, H. B. (2010). Fluid resuscitation: Past, present, and future. *Shock, 33*(3), 229–241.

3. Young, P. P., Cotton, B. A., & Goodnough, L. T. (2011). Massive transfusion protocols for patients with substantial hemorrhage. *Transfusion Medicine Reviews, 25*(4), 293–303.

4. American College of Surgeons. (2012). Shock. In *Advanced trauma life support student course manual* (9th ed., pp. 62–81). Chicago, IL: Author.

5. Keller, M. J. (2011). *Excessive ventilation and oxygenation in resuscitation: Caring in motion 2011.* Retrieved from http://www.seeequip.com/BPWC/Documents/NREMTP%20Refresher/MAR%2012%20Excessive%20Ventilation%20&%20Oxygenation%20in%20resuscitation.pdf

6. Alarcon, L. H., Puyana, J. C., & Peitzman, A. B. (2013). Management of shock. In K. L. Mattox, E. E. Moore, & D. V. Feliciano (Eds.), *Trauma* (7th ed., pp. 189–215). New York, NY: McGraw Hill.

7. Calder, S. (2012). Shock. In Emergency Nurses Association, *Sheehy's manual of emergency care* (7th ed., pp. 213–221). St. Louis, MO: Mosby Elsevier.

8. Hall, J. A. (2011). *Textbook of medical physiology* (12th ed.). Philadelphia, PA: Sanders Elsevier.

9. Everson, F. (2012). Chest trauma. In Emergency Nurses Association, *Sheehy's manual of emergency care* (7th ed., pp. 407–417). St. Louis, MO: Mosby Elsevier.

10. deMoya, M. (2012, July). Shock and shock fluid resuscitation. In *The Merck manual for health care professionals.* Whitehouse Station, N.J.: Merck Sharp & Dohme. Retrieved from http://www.merckmanuals.com/professional/critical_care_medicine/shock_and_fluid_resuscitation/shock.html

11. Namas, R. A., Ghuma, A., Hermus, L., Zamora, R., Okonkwo, D. O., Billiar, T. R., & Vodovotz, Y. (2009). The acute inflammatory response in trauma/hemorrhage and traumatic brain injury: Current state and emerging prospects. *Libyan Journal of Medicine, 4*(3), 97–103.

12. Dutton, R. (2008). Pathophysiology of trauma shock. *International TraumaCare, 18*(1), 12–15.

13. Copstead, L. E., & Banasik, J. (2013). *Pathophysiology* (5th ed.) St. Louis, MO: Elsevier.

14. Mitra, B., Tullio, M. B., Cameron, P. A., & Fitzgerald, M. (2012). Trauma patients with the triad of death. *Emergency Medicine Journal, 29*(8), 622–625.

15. Cohen, M. J. (2012). Towards hemostatic resuscitation: The changing understanding of acute traumatic biology, massive bleeding and damage-control resuscitation. *Surgical Clinics of North America, 92*(4), 877–891.

16. Perel, P., Prieto-Merino, D., Shakur, H., Clayton, T., Lecky, F., Bouamra, O., ...Roberts, I. (2012). Predicting early death in patients with traumatic bleeding: Development and validation of prognostic model. *British Medical Journal, 345*, e5166. Retrieved from http://www.bmj.com/content/345/bmj.e5166

17. Cherkas, D. (2011). Traumatic hemorrhagic shock: Advances in fluid management. *Emergency Medicine Practice, 13*(11), 1–20.

18. Oyetunji, T. A., Chang, D. C., Crompton, J. G., Greene, W. R., Efron, D. T., Haut, E. R., ... Haider, A. H. (2011). Redefining hypotension in the elderly: Normotension is not reassuring. *Archives of Surgery, 146*(7), 865–869.

19. Eastridge, B. J., Salinas, J., McManus, J. G., Blackburn, L., Bugler, E. M., Cooke, W. H., ... Holcomb, J. B. (2007). Hypotension begins at 110 mm Hg: Redefining "hypotension" with data. *Journal of Trauma, 63*(2), 291–297.

20. Centers for Disease Control and Prevention. (2011). *2011 guidelines for field triage of injured patients.* Retrieved from http://www.cdc.gov/fieldtriage/pdf/DecisionScheme_Poster_a.pdf

21. Kahn, S., & Ander, D. (2013, March/April). Trauma Updates: Fluid resuscitation in traumatic hemorrhagic shock and blunt cerebrovascular injury. *Trauma Reports,* 1–11.

22. Salhanick, M., Corneille, M., Higgins, R., Olson, J., Michalek, J., Harrison, C., ... Dent, D. (2011). Autotransfusion of hemothorax blood in trauma patients: Is it the same as fresh whole blood? *The American Journal of Surgery, 202*(6), 817–822.

23. Davis, D. T., Johannigman, J. A., & Pritts, T. A. (2012). New strategies for massive transfusion in the bleeding trauma patient. *Journal of Trauma Nursing, 19*(2), 69–75.

24. American College of Surgeons. (2007). *Resources for optimal care of the injured patient.* Chicago, IL: Author.

25. Marett, B. E. (2012). Metabolic emergencies. In Emergency Nurses Association, *Sheehy's manual of emergency care* (7th ed., pp. 303–317). St. Louis, MO: Mosby Elsevier.

26. Murgo, M., & Leslie, G. (2012). Management of shock. In D. Elliott, L. Aitken, & W. Chaboyer (Eds.), *ACCCN's critical care nursing* (2nd ed., pp. 539-561). Chatswood, Australia: Mosby Elsevier.

27. Karch, A. M. (2013). *2013 Lippincott's nursing drug guide.* Philadelphia, PA: Wolters Kluwer Lippincott, Williams & Wilkins.

28. OTC tranexamic acid for heavy menstrual bleeding? (2011). *Drug & Therapeutic Bulletin, 49*(1), 6–8.

29. Shakur, H., Roberts, I., Bautista, R., Caballero, J., Coats, T., Dewan, Y., ... Yutthakasemsunt, S. (2010). Effects of tranexemic acid on death, vascular occlusive events, and blood transfusion in trauma patients with significant hemorrhage (CRASH-2): A randomised, placebo-controlled trial. *The Lancet, 376*(9734), 23–32.

30. U.S. Food and Drug Association. (2011). *Cyklokapron (tranexamic acid injection): Drug safety data.* Retrieved from http://www.accessdata.fda.gov/drugsatfda_docs/label/2011/019281s030lbl.pdf

31. Seamon, M. J., Feather, C., Smith, B. P., Kulp, H., Gaughan, J. P., & Goldberg, A. J. (2010). Just one drop: The significance of a single hypotension blood pressure reading during trauma resuscitations. *Journal of Trauma, 68*(6), 1289–1294.

32. Bittillier, A. (2010). Transfusion. In R. Aghababian (Ed.), *Essentials of emergency medicine* (p. 272–279). Sudbury, MA: Jones and Bartlett.

33. Barnason, S., Williams, J., Patrick, V. C., Storer, A., Brim, C., Leviner, C., ... Bradford, J. Y. (2012, December). *Clinical practice guideline: Non-invasive blood pressure measurement with automated devices.* Retrieved from http://www.ena.org/IENR/CPG/Documents/NIBPMCPG.pdf

34. O'Driscoll, B.R., Howard, L.S., & Davison, A.G. (2008). BTS guideline for emergency oxygen use in adult patients. *Thorax, 63*(Suppl 6), vi1–vi68.

35. Peberdy, M. A., Callaway, C. W., Neumar, R. W., Geocadin, R. G., Zimmerman, J. L., Donnino, M., Garbrielli, A., ... Kronick, S.L. (2010). Part 9: Post-cardiac arrest care: 2010 American Heart Association Guidelines for Cardiopulmonary Resuscitation and Emergency Cardiovascular Care. *Circulation, 122*(18 Suppl 3), S768–S786.

36. Gravenstein, J. S., Jaffe, M. B., Gravenstein, N., & Paulus, D. A. (Eds.). (2011). *Capnography* (2nd ed.). Cambridge, United Kingdom: Cambridge University Press.

37. Jagminas, L. (2012, June 18). *Diagnostic peritoneal lavage.* Retrieved from http://emedicine.medscape.com/article/82888-overview

38. Kragh, J. F., Walters, T. J., Baer, D. G., Fox, C. J., Wade, C. E., Salinas, J., & Holcomb, J. B. (2008). Practical use of emergency tourniquets to stop bleeding in major limb trauma. *The Journal of Trauma, 64*(2 Suppl), S38–S49.

39. Kragh, J., Walters, T., Baer, D., Fox, C., Wade, C., Salinas, J., & Holcomb, J. (2009). Survival with emergency tourniquet use to stop bleeding in major limb trauma. *Annals of Surgery, 249*(1), 1–7.

40. Kragh, J., O'Neill, M., Walters, T., Jones, J., Baer, D., Gershman, L., ... Holcomb, J. (2011). Minor morbidity with emergency tourniquet use to stop bleeding in severe limb trauma: Research, history, and reconciling advocates and abolitionists. *Military Medicine, 176*(7), 817–823.

41. Helwick, C. (2012, October 15). *Prehospital shock index predicts emergency blood transfusion.* Retrieved from http://www.medscape.com/viewarticle/772633

42. Vandromme, M. J., Griffin, R. L., Kerby, J. D., McGwin, G., Rue, L. W., & Weinberg, J. A. (2011). Identifying risk for massive transfusions in the relatively normotensive patients: Utility of the prehospital shock index. *Journal of Trauma, 70*(2), 388–390.

43. Cannesson, M., Besnard, C., Durand, P. G., Bohe, J., & Jacques, D. (2005). Relation between respiratory variations in pulse oximetry plethysmographic waveform amplitude and arterial pulse pressure in ventilated patients. *Critical Care, 9,* R562–R568.

44. Lipcsey, M., Woinarski, N. C., & Bellomo, R. (2012). Near infrared spectroscopy (NIRS) of the thenar eminence in anesthesia and intensive care. *Annals of Intensive Care, 2*(1), 11.

45. Neumar, R. W., Otto, C. W., Link, M. S., Kronick, S. L., Shuster, M., Callaway, C. W., … Morrison, L. J. (2010). Part 8: Adult advanced cardiovascular life support: 2010 American Heart Association Guidelines for Cardiopulmonary Resuscitation and Emergency Cardiovascular Care. *Circulation, 122,* S729–S767.

46. Warner, K. J., Cuschieri, J., Garland, B., Carlbom, D., Baker, D., Copass, M. K., … Bulger, E. M. (2009). The utility of early end-tidal capnography in monitoring ventilation status after severe injury. *Journal of Trauma, 66*(1), 26–31.

Chapter 8 • Pain

Marlene L. Bokholdt, MS, RN, CPEN
Audrey S. Cornell, PhD, RN, CNE

Objectives

Upon completion of this chapter, the learner will be able to:

1. **Describe the pathophysiologic and behavioral indicators of pain in the trauma patient.**

2. **Discuss the consequences of pain and inadequate pain management in the trauma patient.**

3. **Discuss nonpharmacologic nursing interventions for pain management in the trauma patient.**

4. **Compare opioid and non-opioid analgesics for pain management in the trauma patient.**

5. **Discuss pre-, intra-, and post-procedural responsibilities of the trauma nurse during procedural sedation.**

Preface

Knowledge of normal anatomy and physiology serves as a foundation for understanding anatomic derangements and pathophysiologic processes that may result from trauma. Before reading this chapter, it is strongly suggested that the learner review the following material. This material will not be covered in the lectures nor tested directly, but as foundational content, it may be the basis for some test questions and skill evaluation steps.

Anatomy

The Neurologic System

The components of the neurologic system involved with pain transmission are the neurons, neuron synapses, and neurotransmitters. The peripheral nervous system (PNS), spinal cord, central nervous system (CNS), and brain are also involved in transmission of pain.[1,3]

Neurons receive sensation in four ways:[1]

- Discriminative touch, which helps identify objects by feel

- Proprioception, which relates a sense of movement and position of the body within the environment

- Temperature, which senses heat and cold

- Nociception, which is the perception of pain and irritation (itch, sting, or tingle)

These sensory impulses travel along the neuron to the synapses and are carried through the release of neurotransmitters.[1]

Pain impulses travel to the dorsal horn of the spinal cord and up through the spinothalamic tracts, connecting with the thalamus and the reticular activating system (RAS) within the brain. The neospinothalamic tract consists of the A-delta fibers, and the paleospinothalamic tract consists of C fibers (Fig. 8-1). These tracts run through a section of the dorsal horn, which is divided into laminae I through VII. Laminae II and III, also known as the *substantia gelatinosa*, are dense with neurons and fibers, making them a primary area for pain transmission. Descending tracts modulate pain from the brain to the peripheral nervous system.[1–3]

Physiology

Nociception involves four inter-related processes: transduction, transmission, perception, and modulation.

Transduction

Pain begins with stimulation of the nociceptors, or first-order neurons, which activates the afferent pain pathway. Nociceptors are free sensory nerve endings that respond to chemical, mechanical, and thermal stimuli distributed within skin, muscle, joints, bones, arteries, and viscera. Transduction includes:

- Mechanical and thermal sensations stimulate nociceptors in response to direct tissue injury

- Chemical stimulation involves inflammatory responses and includes mediators such as potassium, lactate, histamine, and prostaglandins

  ◦ Prostaglandins have been identified as an important chemical mediator in regard to the use of nonsteroidal anti-inflammatory drugs (NSAIDs) as they work by blocking production of prostaglandins[3,4]

Transmission

Pain impulses are transmitted via nociceptors to fibers within the spinothalamic tracts.

- A-delta fibers carry pain impulses that are described as being sharp, stinging, or acute. They are fast,

Figure 8-1. Major Pathways for Pain Sensation

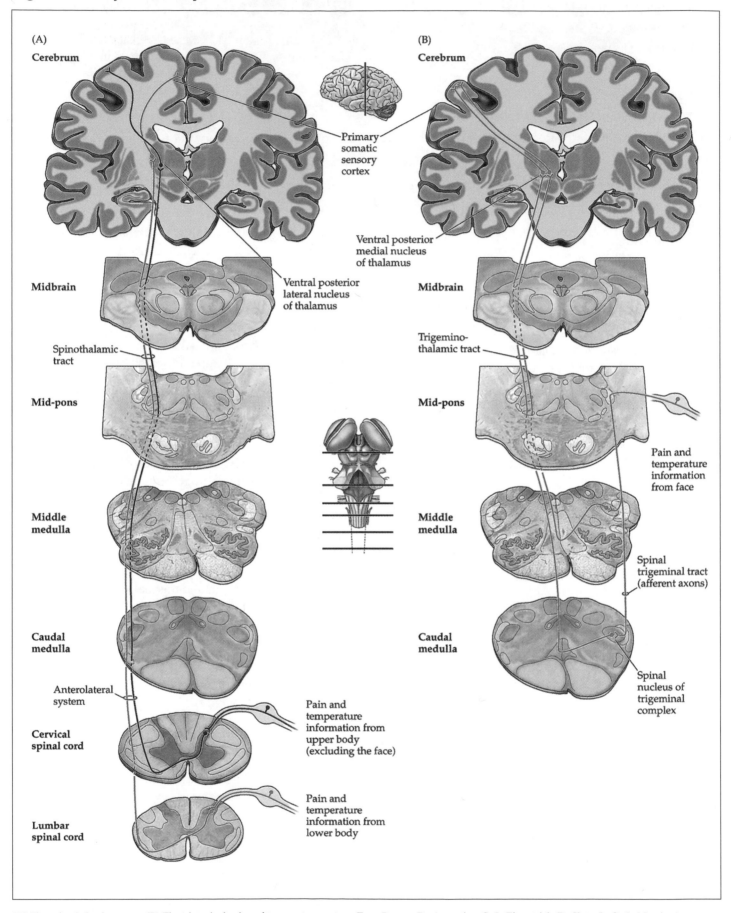

(A) The spinothalamic system. (B) The trigeminal pain and temperature system. *From* Purves, D., Augustine, G. J., Fitzpatrick, D., Katz, L. C., LaMantia, A., McNamara, J. O., & Williams, S. M. (Eds.). (2001). *Neuroscience* (2nd ed.). Sunderland, MA: Sinauer Associates.

well-localized pain impulses and ascend via the neospinothalamic tract to the lateral thalamus and somatosensory cortex.

- Pain from C fibers is described as dull, achy, or chronic. They are poorly localized pain fibers that travel via the paleospinothalamic tract to the midbrain and are responsible for reflexive responses. These fibers enter the spinal cord at the dorsal horn via the tract of Lissauer and cross to the anterior and contralateral portion of the gray matter within the cord.[3,4]

Perception

From the midbrain, the impulse is projected into higher order cortical areas of the brain for interpretation and perception. These complex mechanisms are poorly understood but provide the conscious awareness of pain. The cortical structure of the limbic system accounts for the emotional response, and the somatosensory areas of the cerebral cortex characterize the sensation (sharp, dull, aching, stinging). In terms of perception of pain, several concepts are important:

- *Pain threshold* is the level of stimulation at which perception occurs
- *Pain tolerance* is the level of pain an individual will withstand before seeking pain relief
- *Communication or expression of pain* can be verbal or nonverbal (see "Pain Assessment")

Modulation

Efferent neurons in descending pathways from the brainstem to the dorsal horn of the spinal cord contain neuromodulators that slow down or inhibit the pain impulse. This produces an analgesic effect or modulation of pain perception. An endorphin (endogenous morphine) is an inhibitory neuropeptide that attaches to opiate receptors on the plasma membrane of afferent neurons. This endogenous analgesia system can suppress strong pain signals at various stages of transmission, which may influence pain perception and sensation.[1-4]

Introduction

Pain is a complex physical and sensory process assessed as part of a complete evaluation of disease and injury. The International Association for the Study of Pain (IASP) defined pain as "an unpleasant sensory and emotional experience associated with actual or potential tissue damage."[5]

Because no specific tests measure pain, McCaffery and Beebe define pain as being subjective, stating "pain is whatever the person experiencing the pain says it is, existing whenever he or she says it does."[6] An understanding of the pain process assists in effective assessment and management of pain in the trauma patient.

Pain Theories

The *gate control theory* proposes that pain may be modulated by interneurons within the spinal cord, depending on which fibers are activated. Stimulation of the large A-beta cutaneous fibers was thought to close the gate on transmission of pain impulses from A-delta or C fibers. The A-beta fibers carry impulses from touch, which explains why massage, pressure, temperature, vibration, and rubbing a painful area can modulate the perception, lessening the pain. The gate control theory does not explain all pain types but has supported the use of many nonpharmacologic therapies for pain control such as ice, heat, and massage.[1-3,7,8]

The *neuromatrix theory* of pain proposes that each person's brain produces unique patterns of nerve impulses from a complex neural network with multidimensional inputs. These patterns may be triggered from peripheral sensory neurons or originate from the brain independently.[1] This theory explains patterns of pain with no discernible cause, such as phantom limb pain, and why people with similar injuries report differing levels and responses to pain.[8]

The *neuroplasticity theory* suggests that neurons can be permanently affected and reshaped by the experience of pain. This theory attempts to explain chronic pain, pain syndromes, and phantom pain.[7]

Types of Pain

There are two main types of pain: acute and chronic (Table 8-1).

Acute pain has a sudden onset, often has a clear source, is usually of short duration, and serves as a protective mechanism to alert the individual of a problem. Acute pain can activate the sympathetic nervous system (SNS) causing various physiologic changes. Classifications of acute pain are based on the source of origin and include the following:[1]

- Somatic pain originates from skin and musculoskeletal structures
- Visceral pain originates from organs and may lead to referred pain

- Referred pain occurs when afferent fibers from the affected organ (visceral pain pathway) converge at the same time on the same dorsal horn neurons as the somatic afferent fibers (skin or deep tissue sensation pathway). These visceral pain fibers come into contact with somatic nerve fibers and cause a pain sensation to travel to a point where the other nerves originated.[2,9,10]

Chronic pain is persistent pain usually lasting longer than 3 to 6 months, often long after expected healing, and may no longer have a clear cause. This pain may occur persistently or intermittently over an extended period of time. With intermittent chronic pain, the body may have physiologic responses similar to acute pain. With persistent chronic pain, the physiologic responses may adapt with little or no changes noted. Neuropathic pain is a form of chronic pain in which damage to the neurons or dysfunction of the neurons is the source of the pain, not stimulation of the receptors. Neuropathic pain may be further categorized into central and peripheral pain. Neuropathic pain may arise weeks or months after the injury, can be out of proportion to the severity of the damage to the tissues, and can present as a constant ache or intermittent bursts of shocking or stinging pain or both.[2,3,9]

Effects of Untreated or Undertreated Pain

Pain remains the most common reason patients come to the emergency department, and pain assessment and management continues to be a challenge in emergency care.[10,11] The term *oligoanalgesia* describes the concept of undertreatment of pain.[11] Multiple factors have been identified as contributing to inadequate pain management in the emergency department as outlined in Table 8-2.

Pathophysiologic Effects

There are common physiologic, behavioral, and psychological responses to pain. Knowing these responses can help the trauma nurse complete an assessment and to identify types of pain and cues of pain, particularly in the nonverbal patient. Table 8-3 describes some of these responses.

Table 8-1. Comparison of Acute and Chronic Pain

Characteristic	Acute Pain	Chronic Pain
Experience	An event	A state of existence
Source	External agent or internal disease	Unknown or treatment unsuccessful
Onset	Usually sudden	Sudden or develops insidiously
Duration	Transient (up to 6 mo)	Prolonged (months to years)
Pain identification	Painful and nonpainful areas generally well identified	• Painful and nonpainful areas less easily differentiated; change in sensation • Becomes more difficult to evaluate
Clinical signs	Typical response pattern with more visible signs	Response patterns vary with fewer overt signs (adaptation)
Significance	Informs person something is wrong	Person looks for significance
Pattern	Self-limiting or readily corrected	Continuous or intermittent; intensity may vary or remain constant
Course	Suffering usually decreases over time	Continuous or intermittent; intensity may vary or remain constant
Actions	Leads to actions to relieve pain	Leads to action to modify pain
Prognosis	Likelihood of complete relief	Complete relief usually not possible

Modified from Belden, J., DeFreiz, C., & Heuther, S. (2011). Pain, temperature, sleep, and sensory function. In S. Heuther & K. McCance (Eds.), *Understanding pathophysiology* (4th ed., pp. 324–329). St. Louis, MO: Mosby.
Reprinted and updated from Emergency Nurses Association. (2007). *Emergency nursing core curriculum* (6th ed.). St. Louis, MO: Saunders Elsevier.

Pain management can have long-term implications for healing, development of chronic pain, and perception of future incidents of pain for the trauma patient. Inadequate pain management can have a profound impact, both physiologic and psychological, such as the association of undertreated pain with post-traumatic stress disorder (Table 8-4). Some effects may be indiscernible from changes occurring from trauma. Rapid assessment and treatment of pain will enhance the assessment of the response to trauma.

Pain Assessment

The trauma patient experiencing pain needs prompt recognition and treatment. Pain management includes initial and ongoing assessment in order to evaluate pain status, achieve relief, and assess the response to interventions. In the patient experiencing trauma, limiting factors for assessment include diminished responsiveness and an inability to verbalize perception of pain. In these cases, the use of multiple assessment tools for accurate evaluation of pain is suggested.[12]

Self-report

The most reliable and valid tool for pain assessment is self-report,[1] which in acute pain assessment uses a scale, usually 0 to 10, to quantify the extent of the pain. Self-report and behavioral scales measure only the severity of pain. Multidimensional pain scales provide more depth including such aspects as quality, duration, aggravating and alleviating factors. These scales are more appropriate for chronic or cancer pain assessment but can also be useful in ongoing assessment of pain.[2,9] In the trauma setting, during the initial assessment, single-dimensional

Table 8-2. Inadequate Treatment of Pain in the Emergency Department

Causes of Oligoanalgesia	Effect
Failure to assess initial pain	Patients are not assessed for pain and thus not treated
Failure to implement guidelines and protocols	Protocols can decrease the time to analgesia by half
Failure to document pain	Improper documentation, no use of valid pain scales, no assessment before analgesia all contribute to inadequate pain management
Failure to meet patients' expectations	Patient expectation for pain relief is often very different from the achieved relief and many are discharged with unmet pain needs
Barriers to Treatment	**Effect**
Age bias	Children and older adult patients continue to be undertreated
Opiophobia	Many emergency care providers have a reluctance to prescribe opioids related to concerns regarding drug-seeking behavior, addiction or dependence, and masking of symptoms
ED environment	Interruptions and break in tasks often force providers to deviate from intended activity. This can mean pain management gets delayed.
ED culture and communication	Various cultures and languages can prevent accurate assessment of pain and delay of treatment

ED indicates emergency department.
Data from Motov & Khan[11] and Downey, L. A., & Zun, L. S. (2010). Pain management in the emergency department and its relationship to patient satisfaction. *Journal of Emergencies, Trauma, and Shock, 3*(4), 326–330; Hwang, W., Richardson, L. D., Harris, B., & Morrison, R.S. (2010). The quality of emergency department pain care for older adult patients. *Journal of the American Geriatric Society, 58*(11), 2122–2128; and Sinatra, R. (2010). Causes and consequences of inadequate management of acute pain. *Pain Medicine, 11*(12), 1859–1871.

scales are the most expedient. Examples of these self-report tools include:

- The Numeric Rating Scale (Appendix 8-A)
  - Patient rates his or her pain on a scale of 0 to 10
  - Zero represents no pain at all and 10 represents the worst possible pain
- The Visual Analog Scale (Appendix 8-B)

Table 8-3. Physiologic, Behavioral, and Psychological Responses to Pain

Response Type	Response
Sympathetic (acute pain)	• Increased systolic blood pressure • Increased heart rate and contractility • Increased respiratory rate • Cerebral vasodilation • Pupillary dilation • Increased alertness, rapid speech
Parasympathetic (chronic)	• Decreased systolic blood pressure, syncope • Decreased pulse rate • Variable respiratory patterns • Pupillary constriction • Slowed speech
Behavioral responses	• Withdrawal from stimuli • Moaning • Facial grimace • Crying • Agitation • Guarding
Psychological responses	• Anxiety • Depression • Anger • Fear • Exhaustion • Hopelessness • Irritability

Data from Sugarman[3] *and* Copstead & Banasik.[4]

- Colors and descriptors are plotted along a visual representation of the 0 to 10 scale
- The FACES Scale (Appendix 8-C)
  - Simple drawings of faces represent varying degrees of expression of pain
- For the nonverbal trauma patient who is alert, attempt alternate methods to elicit self-report such as gestures, eye blinks, hand grasps, or nodding of the head

Behavioral Assessment Tools

In the trauma setting, many patients may be unable to self-report and other tools are necessary.[13] Examples of behavioral assessment tools include:

- The FLACC Scale (Appendix 8-D)
  - Developed for the infant population
  - Validated for use in older children and adults who are nonverbal or have decreased level of consciousness[14,15]
  - Assesses
    - Facial expression
    - Leg position and movement
    - Activity
    - Crying
    - Consolability
  - Each parameter scored from 0 to 2 for a total of 0 to 10
- The Behavioral Pain Scale[16]
  - Can be used for intubated patients
  - Consists of three assessment components:
    - Facial expression
      - Relaxed – 1
      - Partially tightened – 2
      - Fully tightened – 3
      - Grimacing – 4
    - Upper limb movement
      - No movement – 1
      - Partially bent – 2
      - Fully bent with finger flexion – 3
      - Permanently retracted – 4
    - Compliance with ventilation
      - Tolerating movement – 1
      - Coughing with movement – 2
      - Fighting ventilator – 3
      - Unable to control ventilation – 4

- Each component scored from 1 to 4 for a maximum of 12[17,18]
- Critical-care Pain Observation Tool (CPOT) (Appendix 8-E)[19,20]
  - Intended for use in intubated or nonverbal patients unable to self-report
  - Consists of four assessment parameters:
    - Facial expression (0–2)
    - Body movements (0–2)
    - Muscle tension (0–1)
    - Compliance with ventilator (0–2)
  - Each parameter scored as above for a total of 0 to 7

Table 8-4. Physiologic Effects of Pain by System

System	Response
Cardiovascular	• Hypercoagulation • Increased cardiac workload • Increased oxygen demand
Respiratory	• Splinting • Hypoventilation • Hypercarbia • Respiratory acidosis • Increased risk of atelectasis and pneumonia
Musculoskeletal	• Impaired muscle function • Immobility • Fatigue • Muscle spasm
Gastrointestinal	• Decreased motility
Genitourinary	• Decreased urinary output • Urinary retention • Fluid overload
Endocrine	• Increased release of hormones and mediators
Metabolic	• Glucogenesis • Hyperglycemia • Glucose intolerance • Insulin resistance • Muscle protein catabolism • Increased lipolysis
Immune	• Depressed response

Data from Polomano,[1] Sugarman,[2] and Copstead & Banasik.[4]

Pain Management

Pain management is a multifactorial, interdisciplinary, and ongoing process. Some considerations and recommendations for pain management in the trauma patient include:[21]

- Pain management should begin as soon as possible. Administration of medications and nonpharmacologic interventions should not be delayed for a diagnosis of the pain etiology, other testing, or procedures.

- Optimum management involves the combined use of nonpharmacologic interventions, opioid, non-opioid, and adjuvant medications. Patients with an addictive disease have special needs to be considered in order to ensure adequate and safe delivery of analgesia. Unusual behaviors may indicate under-treatment of pain and not the presence of addiction.

- Analgesic protocols developed with physician–nurse collaboration are recommended with consistent evaluation of patient response to pain relief interventions

Nonpharmacologic Interventions

Most often, nonpharmacologic interventions are thought to be used to manage minor pain. However, they also play an important role in the management of severe pain. Simple techniques such as elevation of an injured extremity, application of ice, or positioning with a pillow can contribute to relief. Nonpharmacologic interventions can be categorized as physical and cognitive-behavioral. Table 8-5 outlines additional examples of nonpharmacologic interventions.

In the pediatric population, distraction techniques to keep a patient's mind off of the pain can be particularly effective. These are described in Table 8-6.

Discharge education includes teaching the patient how to use the available options, support and reinforcement of their correct use, and evaluation and documentation of the effectiveness of the intervention.[9,22,23]

Pharmacologic Interventions

The World Health Organization (WHO) developed guidelines for effective pain management (Fig. 8-2). Originally intended for use in managing cancer pain, some concepts apply to the trauma setting. In this three-step approach, pain management is based on severity, with additional pharmacologic resources at each step.[22,23]

- Step 1: Non-opioids for mild pain rating (1–3)
  - Acetaminophen
  - Ibuprofen
  - Ketorolac
  - Naproxen
- Step 2: Weak opioids for mild to moderate pain rating (4–6)
  - Codeine
  - Nalbuphine
- Step 3: Strong opioids for moderate to severe pain rating (7–10)
  - Morphine
  - Fentanyl
  - Hydromorphone

Adjuvant medications are medications that were not originally developed for pain management but have been found to be effective when used in combination with analgesics. These medications include antiemetics, anxiolytics, antidepressants, anticonvulsants, corticosteroids, laxatives, and stimulants.[24] Use of these medications needs to be evaluated at each step of the pain relief ladder.

Some multisystem trauma patients will present with acute and/or severe pain, and it is important that they are adequately and promptly treated for that pain. In addition to self-report, assess the physiologic and behavioral responses to pain before and after medication administration to determine the effectiveness. Nonpharmacologic pain interventions can always be combined with pharmacologic interventions to augment pain relief.

In patients with a lesser degree of injury, an analgesic trial may be attempted. If pathologic conditions or injuries exist or procedures are initiated that may cause pain, modify both nonpharmacologic and pharmacologic

Table 8-5. Nonpharmacologic Pain Management

Physical	Cognitive-Behavioral
• Cold/heat therapy	• Emotional support
• Positioning	• Family presence
• Massage	• Imagery
• Immobilization	• Distraction
• Elevation	• Music
• Covering open wounds	• Relaxation
	• Biofeedback
	• Breathing control
	• Play

Table 8-6. Pediatric Distraction Techniques

Technique	Description
Music therapy	Play soothing music, children's songs
Toys	Kaleidoscopes, soap bubbles, glitter wands, puppets
Caregiver aid	Telling stories, singing songs, or counting out loud
Deep breathing	Have child focus on the inhalation and exhalation phases of each breath
Relaxation	Massage or gentle rocking while speaking softly to the child
Blowing away the pain	Have child pretend to blow out candles or use bubbles or pinwheels
Imagery	Talk child through a pleasant scenario; describe details such as a cool breeze or beautiful colors
Positive self-talk	Coach the child to say positive statements such as "I can do it" or "I'm doing great"

Data from Emergency Nurses Association.[14]

Figure 8-2. World Health Organization Pain Relief Ladder.

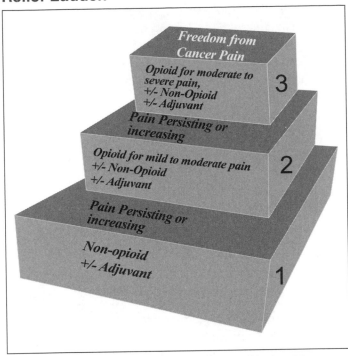

From World Health Organization. (n.d.). *WHO's pain ladder for adults.* Retrieved from http://www.who.int/cancer/palliative/painladder/en/

interventions according to the intensity of the suspected pain. Considerations include the following:

- Begin with nonpharmacologic and non-opioid interventions

- Monitor the physiologic and behavioral response for changes

- If there is no change, attempt to rule out other causes and consider adding a low-dose opioid if the patient's condition allows

- Continue to reassess and evaluate responses to each intervention for changes indicating improvement in pain management and behavior indicating pain relief

- In severe pain, this interval approach is not appropriate, and immediate use of intravenous opioid medications may be indicated

Procedural Sedation

Procedural sedation is the process of administering sedative or dissociative medications so the patient can withstand procedures that are too painful, uncomfortable, or anxiety-producing to tolerate without medication. Because sedatives do not have an analgesic effect, if the procedure is expected to be painful, include analgesia as part of procedural sedation. Anxiolytics may also be used in place of or in addition to analgesia for mild anxiety or to assure patient cooperation.[9,11]

Procedural sedation and anesthesia involves four levels of consciousness with defined characteristics (Table 8-7):[23,25]

- Minimal sedation (anxiolysis) is a medication-induced state in which cognitive function and coordination may be impaired, but cardiovascular and ventilatory functions are unaffected

- Moderate sedation (formerly called conscious sedation) is a medication-induced depression of consciousness in which patients can respond purposefully to verbal commands and independently maintain a patent airway. Cardiovascular and respiratory function are maintained, but emergency equipment is readily available.

- Deep sedation is a medication-induced depression of consciousness but differs from moderate sedation because patients cannot be easily awakened but can respond purposefully after repeated or painful stimulation. Cardiovascular function is maintained, but spontaneous ventilation and maintenance of airway patency may require assistance.

- General anesthesia is a medication-induced loss of consciousness; patients cannot be aroused, even with painful stimulation. Cardiovascular function may be impaired; spontaneous ventilation is often inadequate and the patient is unable to maintain airway patency. Airway and ventilatory support is required.

There are considerations to make prior to, during, and after the procedure in regards to sedation. Follow organizational policies regarding procedural sedation.

Prior to the Procedure

- Assist with education and counseling for the patient and family regarding the procedure, medications to be given, expected length of time, what he or she may experience, risks, benefits, and alternatives[11,25]

- Perform a focused history and physical assessment in collaboration with the provider in order to identify allergies, the potential for a difficult airway, or previous experience with anesthesia or sedation[11,25]

  ○ The American Society of Anesthesiologists recommends limiting last oral intake of clear liquids to 2 hours and of solid food or milk to 6 hours before the procedure[26]

- Assure all necessary medications, supplies, and equipment are readily available and in working order, including, but not limited to the following:[11,23,25]

  ○ Oxygen and oxygen delivery devices

  ○ Suction and suction devices

- Monitoring, including cardiopulmonary, pulse oximetry, and capnography
- Resuscitation equipment, including bag-mask device, airways, and intubation equipment
- Resuscitation medications
- Sedatives, analgesics, anxiolytics, and reversal agents

• Assure adequate and competent personnel are present, including the following:

- A provider who is trained and experienced in procedural sedation at the anticipated level (may require credentialing in some jurisdictions) and is able to rescue the patient from one level deeper than intended
    - Because it exists on a continuum, the exact level of sedation needed cannot always be predicted, so preparation should include anticipation of the patient experiencing deeper sedation than expected
    - This provider is trained and credentialed to intervene with rescue techniques, including advanced airway management
- A registered nurse who administers medications for procedural sedation
    - This nurse has demonstrated competency in all aspects of procedural sedation, patient monitoring, and resuscitation
    - This nurse is responsible for monitoring the patient's condition and level of sedation and is not involved in procedural tasks, such as immobilization or application of splinting material or dressings. Procedural care is performed by another nurse.

• Discuss family presence with the patient, if possible, and determine if the family would like to remain during the procedure. If so, provide support and information for the family.

• Plan with the sedation team for anticipated issues, review the intended procedure and assure each member is aware of assigned tasks

• Participate in a time out to assure accuracy of all plans immediately before administration of medications

- The time out process was implemented in order to decrease the number of wrong patient, wrong surgery, and wrong site incidences
- With necessary personnel in attendance, the team leader calls time out just prior to the procedure to verify the name of the patient, the procedure to be performed, and the location of the procedure

Table 8-7. Definitions of General Anesthesia and Levels of Sedation*

	Minimal Sedation Anxiolysis	Moderate Sedation/ Analgesia (Conscious Sedation)	Deep Sedation/ Analgesia	General Anesthesia
Responsiveness	Normal response to verbal stimulation	Purposeful[†] response to verbal or tactile stimulation	Purposeful[†] response following repeated painful stimulation	Unarousable even with painful stimulus
Airway	Unaffected	No intervention required	Intervention may be required	Intervention often required
Spontaneous ventilation	Unaffected	Adequate	May be inadequate	Frequently inadequate
Cardiovascular function	Unaffected	Usually maintained	Usually maintained	May be impaired

*Monitored Anesthesia Care does not describe the continuum of depth of sedation; rather it describes "a specific anesthesia service in which an anesthesiologist has been requested to participate in the care of a patient undergoing a diagnostic or therapeutic procedure."
† Reflex withdrawal from a painful stimulus is NOT considered a purposeful response.
From American Society of Anesthesiologists. (2009). *Continuum of depth of sedation: Definition of general anesthesia and levels of sedation/analgesia.* Retrieved from http://www.asahq.org/For-Members/Standards-Guidelines-and-Statements.aspx

During the Procedure

- If the patient is expected to respond during the procedure, continue communication, distraction, and assessment of pain and anxiety. Prepare to administer additional sedation or analgesia as needed.
- Continue to support and inform family members, either in the procedure room or waiting elsewhere

After the Procedure

- Continue to monitor vital signs and assess the patient until he or she regains the preprocedural level of consciousness
- Plan for and manage ongoing and postprocedural pain and anxiety
- Assess for the severity of pain and discuss pain relief goals with the patient
- Perform teaching regarding expectations from receiving sedative medications
- Plan for care following discharge or admission

- Provide teaching for the patient and family regarding medications to be taken at home
- Continue nonpharmacologic pain management

Summary

Pain assessment and management, including procedural sedation, are vital components of the trauma nursing process and when undertaken with the goal of optimal pain relief, negative physiologic, emotional, and psychological effects can be minimized. Traumatic injuries can be painful immediately and may develop into chronic pain syndromes. Effective management in the acute phase can promote healing, bolster immunity, limit fear and anxiety, and affect future experiences with pain.[11]

Familiarity with pain management and procedural sedation practice recommendations and position statements can provide the trauma nurse with additional information regarding this aspect of patient care. Box 8-1 lists online resources for pain management and procedural sedation recommendations and guidelines.

Box 8-1. Online Resources for Pain Management and Procedural Sedation

	Organization	Website
Pain Management	American Society of Pain Management Emergency Nurses Association: American College of Emergency Physicians	www.aspmn.org www.ena.org www.acep.org
Procedural Sedation	American Society of Anesthesiologists	www.asahq.org

Appendix 8-A. Numeric Rating Scale

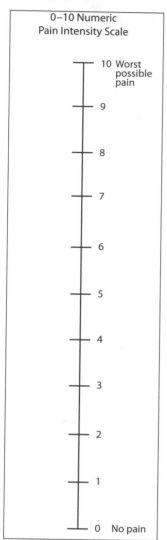

0–10 Numeric
Pain Intensity Scale

- 10 Worst possible pain
- 9
- 8
- 7
- 6
- 5
- 4
- 3
- 2
- 1
- 0 No pain

From Gelinas, C., Fillion, L., & Puntillo, K. A. (2009). Item selection and content validity of the Critical-Care Pain Observation Tool for non-verbal adults. *Journal of Advanced Nursing, 65*(1), 203–216.

Appendix 8-B. Visual Analog Pain Scale

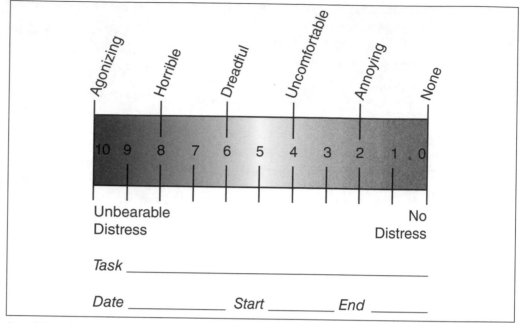

Agonizing · Horrible · Dreadful · Uncomfortable · Annoying · None

10 9 8 7 6 5 4 3 2 1 0

Unbearable Distress

No Distress

Task _____

Date _____ Start _____ End _____

From Adams, C. (n.d.). *How to use a visual analog pain scale.* Retrieved from http://ergonomics.about.com/od/ergonomicbasics/ss/painscale.htm

Appendix 8-C. The FACES Pain Rating Scale

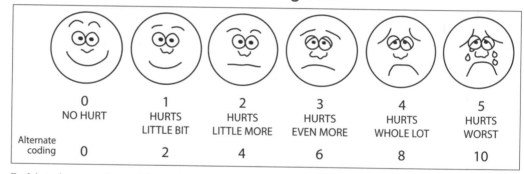

0 NO HURT	1 HURTS LITTLE BIT	2 HURTS LITTLE MORE	3 HURTS EVEN MORE	4 HURTS WHOLE LOT	5 HURTS WORST
Alternate coding 0	2	4	6	8	10

Explain to the person that each face is for a person who feels happy because he has no pain (hurt) or sad because he has some or a lot of pain. **Face 0** is very happy because he doesn't hurt at all. **Face 1** hurts just a little bit. **Face 2** hurts a little more. **Face 3** hurts even more. **Face 4** hurts a whole lot. **Face 5** hurts as much as you can imagine, although you don't have to be crying to feel this bad. Ask the person to choose the face that best describes how he is feeling. From Hockenberry, M. J., & Wilson, D. (2009). *Wong's essentials of pediatric nursing* (8th ed.). St. Louis, MO: Mosby. Used with permission. Copyright Mosby.

Appendix 8-D. The FLACC Scale

		DATE/TIME					
Face	0 - No particular expression or smile 1 - Occasional grimace or frown, withdrawn, disinterested 2 - Frequent to constant quivering chin, clenched jaw						
Legs	0 - Normal position or relaxed 1 - Uneasy, restless, tense 2 - Kicking, or legs drawn up						
Activity	0 - Lying quietly, normal position, moves easily 1 - Squirming, shifting back and forth, tense 2 - Arched, rigid, or jerking						
Cry	0 - No cry (awake or asleep) 1 - Moans or whimpers, occasional complaint 2 - Crying steadily, screams or sobs, frequent complaints						
Consolability	0 - Content, relaxed 1 - Reassured by occasional touching, hugging, or being talked to, distractable 2 - Difficult to console or comfort						
	TOTAL SCORE						

From Merkel, S. I., Voepel-Lewis, T., Shayevitz, J. R., & Malviya, S. (1997). The FLACC: A behavioral scale for scoring postoperative pain in young children. *Pediatric Nursing, 23*(3), 293–297.

Appendix 8-E. The Critical-care Pain Observation Tool

Component and Indicator	Description	Scale
Behavioral component		**Choose one score**
Facial expression	• No muscle tension observable in patient's face	Relaxed, neutral 0
	• Frowning	Tense 1
	• Brow lowering • Levator contraction/Orbit tightening • Eyes tightly closed/Eyes opened • Mouth opened • Flushing/Other	Grimacing 2
Body movements	• Does not move at all	Absence of movements 0
	• Slow, cautious movements	Protection 1
	• Touching pain site/Rubbing pain site • Trying to reach pain site, tubes/Touching tubes • Seeking attention by tapping on the bed with legs or arms • Pulling tubes • Attempting to sit up • Fidgeting • Not following commands/Striking at staff • Trying to climb out of bed • Other	Restlessness 2
Muscle tension	• No muscle tension observable	Relaxed 0
	• Tense or rigid at rest when being stimulated (turned)	Tense, rigid 1
Compliance with the ventilator	• Alarms not activated, easily ventilated	Tolerating ventilator, movements 0
	• Coughing/Alarms stop spontaneously	Coughing but tolerating 1
	• Asynchrony: blocking ventilation, alarms frequently activated	Fighting ventilator 2
Sub-total		___/7

From Gelinas, C., Fillion, L., & Puntillo, K. A. (2009). Item selection and content validity of the Critical-Care Pain Observation Tool for non-verbal adults. *Journal of Advanced Nursing, 65*(1), 203–216.

References

1. Polomano, R.C. (2010). Neurophysiology of pain. In B. St. Marie (Ed.), *Core curriculum for pain management nursing* (2nd ed., pp. 63–90). Dubuque, IA: Kendall Hunt Publishing Co.

2. Sugerman, R. A. (2010). Structure and function of the neurologic system. In K. L. McCance, & S. E. Huether (Ed.), *Pathophysiology: The biologic basis for disease in adults and children.* (6th ed., pp. 442-480). Philadelphia, PA: Mosby.

3. Copstead, L. E., & Banasik, J. (2013). *Pathophysiology* (5th ed.). St. Louis, MO: Elsevier.

4. Wilkinson, J., & Treas, L. (2010). *Fundamentals of nursing* (2nd ed.). Philadelphia, PA: F. A. Davis.

5. International Association for the Study of Pain. (2012, May 22). *IASP taxonomy.* Retrieved from http://www.iasp-pain.org/Content/NavigationMenu/GeneralResourceLinks/PainDefinitions/default.htm

6. McCaffery, M., & Beebe, A. (1989). *Pain: Clinical manual for nursing practice.* St. Louis, MO: Mosby.

7. Cope, D. K. (2010). Intellectual milestones in our understanding and treatment of pain. In S. M. Fishman, J. C. Ballantyne, & J. P. Rathmell (Eds.), *Bonica's management of pain* (4th ed.) [Kindle edition]. Philadelphia, PA: Wolters Kluwer/Lippincott, Williams and Wilkins.

8. Helms, J. E., & Barone, C. P. (2008). Physiology and treatment of pain. *Critical Care Nurse, 28*(6), 38-49.

9. Jarzyna, D., Wagner, K. D., & Arzouman, J. (2010). Acute pain in the high acuity patient. In K. D. Wagner, K. L. Johnson, & M. G. Hardin-Pierce (Eds.), *High-acuity nursing* (5th ed., pp. 59–90). Upper Saddle River, NJ: Pearson.

10. Czarnecki, M. L., Turner, H. N., Collins, P. M., Doellman, D., Wrona, S., & Reynolds, J. (2011). Procedural pain management: A position statement with clinical practice recommendations. *Pain Management Nursing, 2,* 95–111.

11. Motov, S. M., & Khan, A. (2009). Problems and barriers of pain management in the emergency department: Are we ever going to get better? *Journal of Pain Research, 2,* 5–11.

12. Herr, K., Coyne, P.J., McCaffery, M., Manworren, R., & Merkel, S. (2011). Pain assessment in the patient unable to self-report: Position statement with clinical practice recommendations. *Pain Management Nursing, 12*(4), 230–250.

13. Bergman, C. L. (2012). Emergency nurses' perceived barriers to demonstrating caring when managing adult patients' pain. *Journal of Emergency Nursing, 38*(3), 218–225.

14. Emergency Nurses Association. (2012). *Emergency nursing pediatric course provider manual* (4th ed.) Des Plaines, IL: Author.

15. Voepel-Lewis, T., Zanotti, J., Dammeyer, J. A., & Merkel, S. (2010). Reliability and validity of the face, legs, activity, cry, consolability behavioral tool in assessing acute pain in critically ill patients. *American Journal of Critical Care, 19*(1), 55–61.

16. Ahlers, S. J., van der Veen, A. M., van Dijk, M., Tibboel, D., Knibbe, C. A. (2010). The use of the Behavioral Pain Scale to assess pain in conscious sedated patients. *Anesthesia and Analgesia, 110*(1), 127–133.

17. Cade, C. H. (2008). Clinical tools for the assessment of pain in sedated critical ill adults. *Nursing in Critical Care 13*(6), 288–297.

18. Pudas-Tahka, S. M., Axelin, A., Aantaa, R., Lund, V., & Salantera, S.(2009). Pain assessment tools for unconscious or sedated intensive care patients: A systematic review. *Journal of Advanced Nursing, 65*(5), 946–956.

19. Keane, K.M. (2012). Validity and reliability of the critical care pain observation tool: A replication study. *Pain Management Nursing.* Retrieved from http://www.painmanagementnursing.org/article/S1524-9042(12)00018-5/abstract

20. Gelinas, C., Fillion, L., & Puntillo, K. A. (2009). Item selection and content validity of the Critical-Care Pain Observation Tool for non-verbal adults. *Journal of Advanced Nursing, 65*(1), 203–216.

21. Air & Surface Transport Nurses Association, American Academy of Emergency Medicine, American Association of Critical Care Nurses, American College of Emergency Physicians, American Nurses Association, American Radiological Nurses Association, American Society for Pain Management Nursing, Emergency Nurses Association, and National Association of Children's Hospital and Related Institutions. (2008, March 20). *Procedural sedation consensus statement.* Retrieved from http://www.ena.org/SiteCollectionDocuments/Position%20Statements/Procedural_Sedation_Consensus_Statement.pdf

22. American Society for Pain Management Nursing, Emergency Nurses Association, American College of Emergency Physicians, and American Pain Society. (2009, July). *Optimizing the treatment of pain in patients with acute presentations* [position statement]. Retrieved from http://www.ena.org/SiteCollectionDocuments/Position%20Statements/Pain_Mgmt_pol.pdf

23. McGuire, L. L. (2010). Pain: The fifth vital sign. In D. D. Ignatavicius, & M. L. Workman (Eds.), *Medical-surgical nursing: Patient-centered collaborative care.* St. Louis, MO: Saunders.

24. Portenoy, R. K., Ahmed, E., & Keilson, Y. Y. (2013, April 9). Cancer pain management: Adjuvant analgesics (coanalgesics). *UpToDate.* Retrieved from http://www.uptodate.com/contents/cancer-pain-management-adjuvant-analgesics-coanalgesics

25. American Society of Anesthesiologists. (2011). *Statement on granting privileges for administration of moderate sedation to practitioners who are not anesthesia professionals.* Retrieved from http://www.asahq.org/For-Members/Standards-Guidelines-and-Statements.aspx

26. American Society of Anesthesiologists. (2011). Practice guidelines for preoperative fasting and the use of pharmacologic agents to reduce the risk of pulmonary aspiration: Application to healthy patients undergoing elective procedures: An updated report by the American Society of Anesthesiologists Committee on Standards and Practice Parameters. *Anesthesiology, 114*(3), 495–511.

Chapter 9 • Brain, Cranial, and Maxillofacial Trauma

Jill C. McLaughlin, MSN, RN, CEN, CPEN

Objectives

Upon completion of this chapter, the learner will be able to:

1. Describe the mechanisms of injury associated with brain, cranial, and maxillofacial trauma.

2. Describe pathophysiologic changes as a basis for assessment of the trauma patient with brain, cranial, and maxillofacial injuries.

3. Demonstrate the nursing assessment of the trauma patient with brain, cranial, and maxillofacial injuries.

4. Plan appropriate interventions for the trauma patient with brain, cranial, and maxillofacial injuries.

5. Evaluate the effectiveness of nursing interventions for the trauma patient with brain, cranial, and maxillofacial injuries.

Preface

Knowledge of normal anatomy and physiology serves as a foundation for understanding anatomic derangements and pathophysiologic processes that may result from trauma. Before reading this chapter, it is strongly suggested that the learner review the following material. This material will not be covered in the lectures nor tested directly, but as foundational content, it may be the basis for some test questions and skill evaluation steps.

Anatomy and Physiology of the Brain, Cranium, and Face

Scalp

The scalp consists of five layers of tissue. These layers can be remembered using the mnemonic **SCALP**: **s**kin, **c**onnective tissue, **a**poneurosis (galea aponeurotica), **l**oose areolar tissue, and **p**ericranium.[1] The scalp provides a protective covering and absorbs some energy transferred during an injury event. Since the scalp is highly vascular, lacerations or tears can result in profuse bleeding.

Skull

The skull, formed by the cranial bones (frontal, ethmoid, sphenoid, occipital, parietal, and temporal) and the facial bones, provides protection to the contents within the cranial vault. The cranial bones are relatively thick (up to 6 mm) with the exception of the temporal bone. Because of the thickness of the cranium, the skull may not fracture when struck by excessive force. However, the lack of flexibility prevents absorption of energy, and the force is transmitted to the parenchyma and vascular structures of the brain, causing injury without skull fracture. The base of the skull forms three depressions: the anterior, middle, and posterior fossae. Significant force is required to fracture the base of the skull.[2] The internal surface of the skull is rough and irregular. When excess energy is applied to the head and face, the brain moves across these rough inner surfaces, resulting in contusions, lacerations, and shearing injuries.[1,3]

Meninges

The meninges consist of three layers of protective coverings—the **p**ia mater, **a**rachnoid membrane, and **d**ura mater—that **PAD** the brain and spinal cord. The pia mater, the innermost layer, firmly attaches to the brain and spinal cord. The arachnoid membrane is thin and transparent. The dura mater, the outermost layer, is a tough, fibrous membrane that adheres to the internal surface of the skull.

The choroid plexus in the lateral and third ventricles of the brain produces cerebrospinal fluid (CSF) that circulates around the brain beneath the arachnoid membrane (subarachnoid space) and through the central canal of the spinal cord.[4] The CSF cushions and protects the brain and spinal cord. Arteries, including the middle meningeal arteries, are located above the dura mater. Small bridging veins lie beneath the dura mater. Potential spaces may expand following injury that occurs above the dura (epidural) or below the dura (subdural). Subdural bleeding may be less evident in patients who have brain atrophy or widening of the subdural space associated with normal aging or diseases such as alcoholism.[4]

Tentorium

The tentorium cerebelli is formed as part of the dura mater and extends from the occipital bone to the center of the cranium. The tentorium divides the cranial vault into two compartments—supratentorial and infratentorial. The supratentorial compartment contains the cerebral hemispheres in the anterior and middle fossae. The infratentorial compartment contains the lower parts of the brainstem (pons and medulla) and the cerebellum in the posterior fossa. The upper part of the brainstem (midbrain) and the oculomotor nerve (cranial nerve [CN] III) pass through a gap in the tentorium. Injury or edema near the tentorium gap may cause compression and shifting of the brainstem structures and the oculomotor nerve against the tentorium.

Brain

The two cerebral hemispheres are divided into the frontal, parietal, temporal, and occipital lobes. The lobes are responsible for judgment, reasoning, social restraint, and voluntary motor functions (frontal); sensory functions and spatial orientation (parietal); speech, auditory, and memory functions (temporal); and vision (occipital).[5]

The diencephalon connects the two cerebral hemispheres with the midbrain and includes the thalamus, hypothalamus, subthalamus, and epithalamus. These subcortical structures play major roles in hormonal regulation and metabolic functions, including temperature regulation; release of hormones from the pituitary gland and adrenal cortex; emotional behaviors such as fear, rage, and pleasure; and activation of the sympathetic and parasympathetic nervous systems.[2,4,6]

The three divisions of the brainstem are the midbrain, pons, and medulla. The reticular activating system (RAS) is composed of clusters of specialized neural tissue that originate in the midbrain and pons. The RAS is primarily responsible for wakefulness or consciousness while the medulla and the pons are responsible for vital functions such as cardiovascular function and respiration. Injury to the brainstem is associated with changes in consciousness and impairment in vital functions, specifically blood pressure, heart rate, and respiration.[4]

The cerebellum is located in the posterior fossa and lies behind the brainstem and beneath the cerebral hemispheres. The cerebellum has extensive neural connections with the spinal cord, midbrain, and cerebral hemispheres.[2,6] Primary functions of the cerebellum include voluntary and involuntary muscle coordination, movement, balance, and posture.

Cranial Nerves

There are 12 pairs of cranial nerves (CNs). The olfactory nerve (CN I) consists of a group of nerves located within a fiber tract that connect the nasal mucosa to the olfactory bulb. The optic nerve (CN II) originates in the retina and is considered a fiber tract once it leaves the optic chiasm. Millions of optic fibers then branch out to the occipital and temporal lobes. The brainstem is the point of origin for CNs III through X and XII, and they all exit via the skull foramina, leaving the cranial vault through the base of the lower brain. This shared exit pathway increases the risk for compression injury to the nerve tissue with subsequent swelling and tissue damage.[7] The accessory nerves (CN XI) have both a cranial and spinal component.

Face

The face is divided into functional thirds. The upper third of the face includes the lower portion of the frontal bone, supraorbital ridge, nasal glabellar region, and frontal sinuses. The middle third (midface) includes the orbits, maxillary sinuses, nasal bone, zygomatic bones, temporal bones, and basal bone of the maxilla. The lower third includes the basal bone of the mandible and the teeth-bearing bones of the maxilla and mandible. The muscles covering the facial bones contribute to facial movements and expressions. Muscles covering the mandible assist with mastication and jaw movement.

Blood Supply

The brain contains a large vascular supply. Arterial blood travels to the brain via two pairs of arteries: the right and left internal carotid and the right and left vertebral arteries. Venous blood drains via the jugular veins. Blood supply to the face originates from the internal and external carotid arteries. The external carotid arteries also supply blood to the neck.[8] Injury resulting in uncontrolled hemorrhage from any of these blood vessels may be life threatening.[4,6]

Blood-brain Barrier

The blood-brain barrier is a network of blood vessels and cells surrounding the brain that act as a filter for the central nervous system and controls the exchange of oxygen, carbon dioxide, and metabolites between the blood and brain.[9]

Cerebral Blood Flow

The brain uses approximately 20% of the body's total oxygen supply and is heavily dependent upon glucose metabolism for energy.[4] The brain does not have the ability to store essential nutrients; therefore, it requires a continuous supply of both oxygen and glucose through the cerebral blood flow (CBF). The brain can self-regulate to maintain CBF through a process that is complex, multifaceted, and not well understood.[8,10] The autoregulatory mechanisms originate in the cerebral arterioles, which cause arteriole vasodilation or constriction. These mechanisms respond to changes in carbon dioxide levels and arterial pressure and fluctuations in cellular needs of the tissue.

Carbon dioxide (CO_2) is a primary regulator of blood flow to the brain and a strong vasodilator. At higher than normal levels, $PaCO_2$ causes cerebral vasodilation, thus increasing cerebral blood volume and perfusion.[6,9,10] Conversely, if the level of $PaCO_2$ decreases, cerebral vasoconstriction results, reducing blood volume and perfusion, subsequently decreasing intracranial pressure (ICP). Initially the brain responds to the hypoxemia by increasing oxygen extraction from blood. When hypoxia becomes acute (PaO_2 less than 50 mm Hg), cerebral vasodilation occurs and blood flow increases.[8]

Intracranial Pressure

Brain tissue occupies approximately 80% of the cranial vault, arterial and venous blood approximately 10%, and CSF approximately 10%. These volumes are relatively fixed, and together they create a normal ICP of 0 to 15 mm Hg. Small changes in individual volumes can occur without affecting ICP or changing the constant total volume. Sustained ICP greater than 20 mm Hg is considered abnormal.[6,11] According to the Monro-Kellie doctrine, as the volume of one component expands, the volume of one or both of the other components must decrease to maintain a constant ICP.[6] The intracranial compensation is limited because the cranial vault is inflexible. Even small increases in total volume may cause significant increases in ICP, resulting in a decrease in CBF and a decrease in CPP.

Cerebral Perfusion Pressure

Adequate perfusion of oxygen and supply of nutrients (glucose) to the brain tissue is dependent on the CPP and CBF. CPP is defined as the pressure gradient across the brain tissue, or the difference between the pressures of the cerebral artery and venous vessels. It is a primary determinant of CBF[4,6,12] and is reflected as the following: CPP = MAP – ICP

Cerebral autoregulation maintains a constant cerebral vascular blood flow as long as the mean arterial pressure (MAP) is maintained in the range of 50 to 150 mm Hg.[2,10] When autoregulation in the brain fails, perfusion becomes dependent solely on pressure. Normal cerebral perfusion pressure (CPP) is 60 to 100 mm Hg, and acceptable CPP is between 50 and 70 mm Hg.[11,13] When the CPP is between 50 and 160 mm Hg, autoregulation maintains a steady state.[2,8,11]

When autoregulation fails, perfusion of the brain depends on the MAP. If maintenance of MAP is disrupted (such as in hemorrhage and hypovolemia), the body's compensatory mechanisms may not be able to sustain a sufficient CPP. With a brain injury that results in an increased ICP, a normal MAP may not be sufficient to maintain CPP. A CPP of less than 60 mm Hg has been associated with poor outcomes because arterial pressure is unable to overcome the increased pressure gradient to deliver oxygen and nutrients.[13] One report suggests that in patients with ischemia, it is advisable to maintain the CPP above 70 mm Hg.[13]

Loss of autoregulation can result in cerebral and brainstem ischemia, which initiates a central nervous system ischemic response, known as Cushing response. Cushing response is characterized by a triad of assessment findings: widening pulse pressure, reflex bradycardia, and diminished respiratory effort. The response is partially an attempt to increase the MAP against an elevated ICP, ultimately trying to cause a rise in CPP.[6]

Introduction

Epidemiology

Traumatic brain injury (TBI) is a significant public health problem. According to recent United States (U.S.) data, 1.7 million individuals sustain a TBI annually.[1,12] Of the 1.3 million people seen and treated in emergency departments for TBI, 75% were classified as minor trauma, 15% were moderately injured, and 10% were severely injured.[1,12] TBI contributes to 30.5% of the injury-related deaths in the U.S.[12] Around 10% of TBIs are caused by violence, including gunshots and interpersonal violence.[15] The three most common causes of facial fracture injury are assaults, falls, and motor vehicle collisions (MVCs).[14]

Mechanism of Injury

Injuries are classified as blunt or penetrating.

- Blunt injuries result from falls, MVCs, sports-related injuries, and recreation- and recreational vehicle–related injuries. Falls are the most frequent cause of TBI.[16]

- Penetrating injuries may occur from firearms or exploding objects or projectiles. See Chapter 4, Biomechanics, Kinematics, and Mechanisms of Injury, for more information.

Primary injury to brain tissue may result from several factors, including:

- Compressive or direct impact force with injury to the tissue under the point of impact on the skull

- Acceleration/deceleration forces creating a pressure wave resulting in energy transfer to several sites within the brain

- Severe rotation or spinning that causes shearing or tensile force resulting in tearing of cellular structures and bleeding

- A blast from an explosive device creating a pressure wave and contused tissue

- Penetrating injury from a sharp object or firearm causing severe, irreparable damage to brain cells, blood vessels, and protective tissues around the brain

- Lacerations as the brain moves across the irregular, rough base of the skull

- Fractures of the skull and facial bones

Risk Factors

Certain risk factors contribute to the risk of sustaining a brain injury. These include:

- Age: Children ages 0 to 4 years old, young adults 15 to 24 years old, and adults over 75 years old are at high risk[15]

- Risk-taking behaviors such as reckless or impaired driving, extreme sports, or violence[17]

- Improper use of or refusal to use automobile safety restraint systems,[18] approved protective helmets,[17] or protective equipment in sports[19,20]

- Anticoagulant therapy

- Use of substances that may cause dizziness, imbalance, or delayed response times, such as the following:

  ○ Alcohol

  ○ Medications (opioids)

  ○ Illicit substances

Usual Concurrent Injuries

Individuals with brain or craniofacial injuries are at risk for concurrent injury to the cervical spinal cord and vertebral column.[1] Facial injuries may be associated with severe bleeding due to vascular disruption. Bony injuries may entrap nerves causing injury to the underlying structures and present as ocular trauma.

Types of Injury

Brain injury is classified as primary or secondary injury. Primary injuries result from a direct transfer of energy and include:

- Skull and craniofacial fractures

- Intracranial lesions (contusions or mild traumatic brain injury)

- Lacerations, tearing, and shearing injuries and bleeding into the brain (epidural or subdural hematomas)

Secondary injury is caused by complex pathophysiologic changes that include the following:[4,21]

- Hypotension

- Hypoxemia

- Hypercarbia

- Cerebral edema

- Increased ICP

- Decreased CPP

- Cerebral ischemia

The goal of caring for the patient who has experienced head trauma is to prevent or limit secondary injury and the catastrophic cascade of events that result from those conditions, including death.

Pathophysiology as a Basis for Assessment Findings

Pathophysiologic concepts that affect the patient with brain, cranial, or maxillofacial injuries include issues related to the following:

- Hypotension and CBF

- Hypoxia and hypercarbia

- ICP

Hypotension and Cerebral Blood Flow

If injury causes the CPP to fall outside the range between 50 and 160 mm Hg, the brain loses its ability to autoregulate, and CBF becomes directly dependent on MAP for perfusion.[4] If the trauma patient is bleeding and becomes hypotensive, the MAP is unable to produce a perfusing CPP and the brain tissue becomes hypoxic. The hypoperfused brain becomes ischemic and suffers irreversible damage while the patient experiences dizziness and confusion, becoming unresponsive and comatose.[8] A single episode of hypotension (systolic blood pressure < 90 mm Hg) can be harmful to patient outcomes.[6,21] In the context of severe head injuries, hypotension has been linked to more than double the mortality as compared to normotensive patients.[21]

If autoregulation fails and the MAP is elevated, edema can result, which can be disastrous when occurring with a brain injury. Therefore, it is important to maintain blood pressure and MAP within normal limits.

Hypercarbia and Hypoxia

CO_2 causes vasodilation, which can have a powerful, but reversible effect on CBF. Hypercapnia causes significant dilation of cerebral arterial vasculature and increased blood flow; hypocapnia causes constriction and decreased blood flow.[8] This is notable as it relates to bag-mask–assisted ventilation and hyperventilation of the intubated patient. Hyperventilation reduces the $PaCO_2$, causing cerebral vasoconstriction and hypoperfusion and may result in cerebral ischemia.[1] Hypercarbia ($PaCO_2 > 45$ mm Hg) promotes vasodilation and increases ICP, so it is also to be avoided.[1,22]

A brief period of hyperventilation may be indicated if the patient demonstrates signs of impending herniation (unilateral or bilateral pupillary dilation, asymmetric pupillary reactivity, or abnormal posturing). This is only a temporizing measure until definitive interventions are implemented.[1,13] Hypocapnia can cause harm and is limited to emergency management of life-threatening intracranial hypertension awaiting definitive measures.

Signs and symptoms of hypoxia may initially be obscured by the brain's ability to compensate by extracting more oxygen from the blood.[7] Early changes in mental status may be vague. It is crucial to be aware of the potential for deterioration. A single episode of hypoxemia (apnea or $PaO_2 < 60$ mm Hg) can be detrimental to patient outcome.[6,21] By the time that a patient demonstrates symptoms of hypoxia, the damage may be irreversible.

Intracranial Pressure

As ICP rises, CPP decreases, resulting in cerebral ischemia, hypoxemia, and lethal secondary insult.[4,21] Small elevations in blood pressure and MAP are attempts by the body to protect against brain ischemia in a patient with elevated ICP. Intricate physiologic alterations result in a decreased PaO_2 and increased $PaCO_2$, both of which act to dilate cerebral blood vessels, increasing CBF. Those combined with an expanding hematoma, inflammation, or edema of the brain parenchyma result in increases in ICP and herniation.[4] ICP sustained at greater than 20 mm Hg and unresponsive to treatment are associated with poor outcomes.[1] Increased ICP produces signs and symptoms that are predictable and sequential.
Early assessment findings of increased ICP include:[4]
- Headache

- Nausea and vomiting

- Amnesia
- Behavior changes (impaired judgment, restlessness, or drowsiness)
- Altered level of consciousness (hypo- and hyperarousability)

Late assessment findings of increased ICP include:
- Dilated, nonreactive pupils
- Unresponsiveness to verbal or painful stimuli
- Abnormal motor posturing (flexion, extension, or flaccidity)
- Cushing response[1,4,22]
  - Widening pulse pressure
  - Reflex bradycardia
  - Decreased respiratory effort

Nursing Care of the Patient with a Brain, Cranial, and Maxillofacial Injury

Refer to Chapter 5, Initial Assessment, for the systematic approach to the nursing care of the trauma patient. The following assessment parameters are specific to patients with brain, cranial, or maxillofacial injuries.

Preparation and Triage

The Centers for Disease Control and Prevention's Field Triage Criteria suggest including the presence of anticoagulation medication as a triage parameter.[23] As part of the prehospital report, ask if the patient takes anticoagulation medications. These medications have the ability to cause uncontrolled hemorrhage in the older trauma patient, so it becomes essential to identify the possible need for treating this condition in the primary survey as part of controlling hemorrhage. Data indicate that patients who take anticoagulation medications, such as warfarin and aspirin, and experience a head trauma have higher potential for injury and death than patients not taking those medications.[24]

Primary Survey and Resuscitation Adjuncts
A–Airway and Alertness
- Rigid cervical collars may contribute to an increase in ICP as the collars can interfere with venous outflow and cause increased pain and discomfort to the patient.[25] The fit of the rigid collar may need to be adjusted.

- Assess the patient using AVPU mnemonic: A patient response other than alert may be associated with a brain injury

- Be prepared to assist with early endotracheal intubation for patients who are unable to protect their airway, especially those with facial injuries and bleeding

B–Breathing and Ventilation

- If the patient is alert, administer oxygen at 15 L/min via nonrebreather mask with a tight-fitting seal and reservoir bag
- Titrate for normoxia and maintain SpO_2 between 94% and 98% (see Chapter 6, Airway and Ventilation, for additional information)[1,26–30]
- As needed, support ventilation using a bag-mask device and attached oxygen reservoir at 15 L/min with a breath every 5 to 6 seconds (10–12 ventilations/min) unless otherwise prescribed by the physician[27]
  ○ Deliver each breath over 1 to 2 seconds with just enough tidal volume to achieve chest rise[31]

C–Circulation and Control of Hemorrhage

- If applying direct pressure to bleeding sites, avoid pressure in the area over a depressed skull fracture
- If possible, avoid hypotension
  ○ The goal of fluid support is to maintain hemodynamic stability while avoiding fluid overload
  ○ Vasopressors may be indicated to maintain CPP
- The role of hypertonic saline solution (3%–5%) in maintaining normovolemia and normotension without infusing large volumes of fluid is controversial[19,26,32]

D–Disability (Neurologic Status)

- Assess pupillary size and response to light
  ○ A unilaterally fixed and dilated pupil may indicate oculomotor nerve compression from increased ICP and herniation syndrome
  ○ Bilaterally fixed and pinpoint pupils may indicate an injury at the pons or the effects of opioids
  ○ A moderately dilated pupil with sluggish response may be an early sign of herniation syndrome
- Assess the Glasgow Coma Scale (GCS) score[33] or FOUR (Full Outline of UnResponsiveness) Score[34] (Table 9-1)
  ○ Intubation is recommended if the GCS score is less than 8 or the level of consciousness decreases acutely[1,4,21,35]

Glasgow Coma Scale

The GCS score ranges from 3 to 15 and provides a measure of the patient's level of consciousness as well as a predictor of morbidity and mortality after brain injury.[4] The patient's total score derives from the patient's response to three aspects that are independently measured:

- BEST eye opening
- BEST verbal response
- BEST motor response[36]

The motor component of the GCS score is the most sensitive subscore for identifying patients with severe brain injury.[1,6,37] The initial GCS score provides a baseline score, and repeated assessments determine whether the patient's neurologic status is improving or deteriorating.

One or more limbs may be immobilized due to the effects of sedation, pharmacologic paralysis, fractures, brain or spinal cord injury, or other circumstances. Avoid misinterpreting a grasp reflex or postural adjustment as a response to a command. Remember the BEST response is to be measured. This is particularly important when one limb's response is better than the others, or the patients move their eyelids purposefully yet have paralysis from the neck down. However, the GCS becomes limited as a reliable tool when the patient is intubated.[35] See Chapter 5, Initial Assessment, for more information.

FOUR Score

The FOUR score ranges from 0 to 16 and provides greater neurologic detail than the GCS score (Fig. 9-1).[34] The patient's total score results from a summative score of four components of response that include:

- Eye response
- Motor response
- Brainstem reflexes
- Respiration

All components of the FOUR score can be rated in patients with or without an endotracheal tube. Therefore, the score may have advantages with use in the critical care setting. Early research of the score's predictive reliability and validity is promising.[38]

In patients who are mechanically ventilated, assessment is done preferably when $PaCO_2$ is within normal limits. No adjustments are made to the ventilator while the patient is being graded. Assess the pressure waveform on spontaneous respiration or when the patient triggers the ventilator's R1 rate (the rate above the ventilator rate). When the patient breathes at ventilator rate R0 (the patient does not have a rate above the ventilator rate), a standard apnea test may be needed.[37]

Table 9-1. Comparison of the Glasgow Coma Scale and the FOUR Score

Glasgow Coma Scale		FOUR Score	
Eye opening		**Eye response**	
4 =	Spontaneous	4 =	Eyelids open or opened, tracking, or blinking to command
3 =	To speech	3 =	Eyelids open but not tracking
2 =	To pain	2 =	Eyelids closed but open to loud voice
1 =	None	1 =	Eyelids closed but open to pain
Best verbal response		0 =	Eyelids remain closed with pain
5 =	Oriented	**Motor response**	
4 =	Confused conversation	4 =	Thumbs up, fist or peace sign
3 =	Inappropriate words	3 =	Localizing to pain
2 =	Incomprehensible sounds	2 =	Flexion response to pain
1 =	None	1 =	Extension response to pain
Best motor response		0 =	No response to pain or generalized myoclonus status
6 =	Obeys commands	**Brainstem reflexes**	
5 =	Localizes to pain	4 =	Pupil and corneal reflexes present
4 =	Withdrawal (normal flexion)	3 =	One pupil wide and fixed
3 =	Abnormal flexion (decorticate)	2 =	Pupil or corneal reflexes absent
2 =	Extension (decerebrate)	1 =	Pupil and corneal reflexes absent
1 =	None	0 =	Absent pupil, corneal and cough reflex
		Respiration	
		4 =	Not intubated, regular breathing pattern
		3 =	Not intubated, Cheyne-Stokes breathing pattern
		2 =	Not intubated, irregular breathing
		1 =	Breathes above ventilator rate
		0 =	Breathes at ventilator rate or apnea

Data from Jagoda et al.[33] and Wijdicks et al.[3]

Figure 9-1. FOUR Score

Eye Response (E)

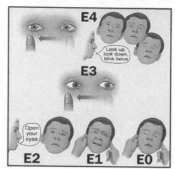

E4 Eyelids open or opened, tracking or blinking to command
E3 Eyelids open but not tracking
E2 Eyelids closed, opens to loud voice, not tracking
E1 Eyelids closed, opens to pain, not tracking
E0 Eyelids remain closed with pain

Motor Response (M)

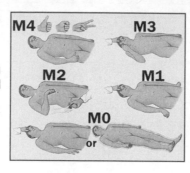

M4 Thumbs up, fist, or peace sign to command
M3 Localizing to pain
M2 Flexion response to pain
M1 Extensor posturing
M0 No response to pain or generalized myoclonus status epilepticus

Brainstem Reflexes (B)

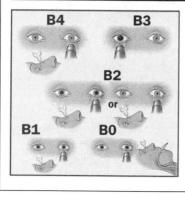

B4 Pupil and corneal reflexes present
B3 One pupil wide and fixed
B2 Pupil or corneal reflexes absent
B1 Pupil and corneal reflexes absent
B0 Absent pupil, corneal, and cough flex

Respiratory Response (R)

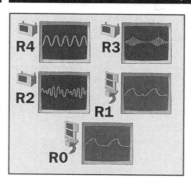

R4 Not intubated, regular breathing pattern
R3 Not intubated, Cheyne-Stokes breathing pattern
R2 Not intubated, irregular breathing pattern
R1 Breathes above ventilator rate
R0 Breathes at ventilator rate or apnea

E–Exposure and Environmental Control

Hypothermia in combination with shock can have a deleterious effect on oxygenation of brain tissue (see Chapter 7, Shock, for more information). However, there is some evidence that therapeutic hypothermia in patients with severe brain injury may result in a reduction in both morbidity and mortality.[35] See "Emerging Trends" for more information.

G–Get Resuscitation Adjuncts

- Obtain an arterial blood gas (ABG)
- Monitor end-tidal carbon dioxide ($ETCO_2$) as recommended
- Avoid inserting a gastric tube through the nose and insert it through the oral cavity if facial or basilar skull fractures are suspected[1]

Reevaluation

Determine if the patient is a candidate for immediate surgery or meets criteria for transport to a trauma center. Any head-injured patient with evidence of neurologic deficits meets the criteria for transport if the services and expertise are not available.[23]

The patient's blood pressure is a determinant for subsequent approach to care:[1]

- In the adult patient, intracranial hemorrhage will rarely produce a volume of blood loss large enough to produce hypotension. If hypotension is present, the priority is to determine another cause of bleeding.

- If the patient is normotensive with a neurologic deficit (unequal pupils or asymmetric motor examination), the priority is to obtain a computed tomography (CT) scan

- In borderline cases, it is preferable to obtain a head CT prior to any surgery (laparotomy or thoracotomy)

Secondary Survey and Reevaluation Adjuncts
H–History

History-taking questions specific to patients with suspected brain, cranial, or maxillofacial injuries include the following:

- If conscious, what are the patient's complaints?
  - Headache, nausea and vomiting, and amnesia (may be early signs of increased ICP)

- If the patient's level of consciousness is altered, does the history suggest head trauma?
  - Impact to the head or face
  - Post-injury lucid interval
- Was there any vomiting or other signs and symptoms of a brain or cranial injury?
- Was there any loss of consciousness (LOC)? How long?
- Does the patient have amnesia from the injury event?

H–Head-to-toe Assessment
Inspect for:
- Inspect the craniofacial area for ecchymoses or contusions
  - Basilar skull fractures can produce bleeding that may not be evident until several hours after the injury. These collections of blood under the tissue may become apparent in one of three areas:[39]
    - Periorbital ecchymoses, also known as raccoon eyes, indicates an anterior fossa fracture
    - Mastoid process ecchymoses, also known as battle sign, indicates a middle fossa fracture
    - Hemotympanum, blood behind the tympanic membrane, may indicate a middle fossa fracture
- Inspect the craniofacial area for symmetry, flattening of the face, or malocclusion[40]
  - Asymmetrical facial appearance can indicate soft tissue injury or facial fracture
  - Flattening of the face or a dish-like appearance is consistent with Le Fort fractures
  - Malocclusion may be a sign of mandibular fracture
- Inspect the nose and ears for drainage
  - Test otorrhea/rhinorrhea for cerebral spinal fluid (CSF)[41–46]
    - β_2-Transferrin is a test that requires fluid to be sent to the laboratory and is considered the gold standard for identifying CSF otorrhea or rhinorrhea
    - Two tests can be performed rapidly to give a general suspicion of CSF leak, but have high rates of false positives and are considered unreliable
      - Halo sign: Place fluid on clean gauze and a classic ring forms if it is CSF. Tears, water and saline may also produce a halo if mixed with blood.
      - Glucose: Test for the presence of glucose, which is high in CSF, but also can be in nasal drainage

- Assess extraocular eye movements (EOMs) to test the function of CNs III, IV, and VI
  - The ability to perform EOMs indicates the brainstem is intact
  - In the presence of facial fractures, the inability to perform EOMs may indicate a trapped nerve
- Observe for abnormal motor posturing (abnormal flexion, abnormal extension) or flaccidity

Palpate for:
- Palpate the cranial area gently for the following:
  - Point tenderness
  - Depressions or deformities
  - Hematomas
- Assess all four extremities for the following:
  - Bilateral motor function, muscle strength, and abnormal motor posturing
  - Sensory function

Selected Brain, Cranial, and Maxillofacial Injuries

Coup/Contrecoup Injury
When the head strikes a solid object, a sudden deceleration force may result in bony deformity and injury to cranial contents.[47] Within the cranial vault, a pressure wave is generated at the point of impact, which may tear tissue and cause injury at the site of impact (coup injury). As the pressure wave travels across the cranial contents and dissipates, injury may occur on the side opposite the impact (contrecoup injury).[3] It is possible to suffer this type of head injury without a direct blow to the head.

Assessment findings include:[3]
- Altered level of consciousness
- Behavioral, motor, or speech deficits
- Abnormal motor posturing
- Signs of increased ICP

Focal Brain Injuries
Focal brain injuries occur in a localized area with grossly observable and identifiable brain lesions. These lesions may expand causing damage to other areas of the brain or result in secondary brain injury from increased ICP.[1,6,22] Focal brain injuries include cerebral contusion, intracerebral hematoma, epidural hematoma, subdural hematoma, and herniation syndromes.

Cerebral Contusion

A cerebral contusion is damaged brain tissue usually caused by blunt trauma. Most cerebral contusions are located in the frontal and temporal lobes, but they may also occur in tissue beneath a depressed skull fracture. Contusions begin as the capillaries within the brain tissue are damaged, resulting in hemorrhage, infarction, necrosis, and edema. Significant contusions with swelling may cause a midline shift within the cranial vault. The maximum effects of contusion and edema formation usually peak 18 to 36 hours after injury.[1,6,22] Delayed hemorrhage or formation of intracranial hematomas may occur.

Intracerebral Hematoma

Intracerebral hematomas occur deep within the brain tissue, may be single or multiple, and may be associated with cerebral contusions.[4,6,22] Similar to cerebral contusions, most intracerebral hematomas are located in the frontal and temporal lobes. They may create a significant mass effect, increase ICP, and result in neurologic deterioration. Assessment findings include:[4,6,22]

- Progressive and often rapid decline in level of consciousness
- Headache
- Signs of increasing ICP
- Pupil abnormalities
- Contralateral hemiparesis, hemiplegia, or abnormal motor posturing

Epidural Hematoma

An epidural hematoma results from a collection of blood that forms between the dura mater and the skull. The hematoma is frequently (90%) associated with fractures of the temporal or parietal skull that lacerate the middle meningeal artery.[4,22] Since the source of bleeding is arterial, blood can accumulate rapidly, and the expanding hematoma may cause compression of underlying brain tissue, rapid rise in ICP, decreased CBF, and secondary brain injury. Significant epidural hematomas require immediate surgical intervention. The most common causes of epidural hematoma are MVCs and falls, but they can also be the result of sports-related injuries.[48]

Assessment findings include:[4]

- Transient LOC followed by a lucid period lasting minutes to hours
- Headache and dizziness
- Nausea and vomiting
- Contralateral hemiparesis, hemiplegia, or abnormal motor posturing (flexion or extension)
  - Extension is associated with brainstem herniation and poor outcomes[4]
- Ipsilateral unilateral fixed and dilated pupil
- Rapid deterioration in neurologic status

Subdural Hematoma

A subdural hematoma results from a collection of blood formed immediately beneath the dura mater usually following acceleration, deceleration, or combination forces. Subdural hematomas are usually caused by tearing of the bridging veins and associated direct injury to the underlying brain tissue. Subdural hematomas may be acute or chronic.

Acute Subdural Hematoma

Patients with acute subdural hematomas generally manifest signs and symptoms within 72 hours of the injury event.[39] The hematoma can cause reduction in cerebral blood flow.[39] This is commonly the type of bleed sustained by athletes who suffer a catastrophic head injury.[48] Assessment findings in patients with acute subdural hematomas include:[4,49]

- Severe headache
- Changes in level of consciousness
- Ipsilateral dilated or nonreactive pupil
- Contralateral hemiparesis

Chronic Subdural Hematoma

Chronic subdural hematomas are frequently associated with minor injury in older adults, patients taking anticoagulation medications, and patients with chronic alcohol use. This increased incidence is due to brain atrophy, fragility of the bridging veins, and coagulation alterations.[4,49] The onset of signs and symptoms and effect on neurologic function vary depending on the size and rapidity of the hematoma formation.[39] The assessment findings in patients with chronic subdural hematomas develop over time and may not be evident until up to 2 weeks after the injury event. They include:[39]

- Altered or steady decline in level of consciousness
- Headache
- Loss of memory or altered reasoning
- Motor deficit: Contralateral hemiparesis, hemiplegia, or abnormal motor posturing or ataxia
- Aphasia
- Ipsilateral unilateral fixed and dilated pupil
- Incontinence
- Seizures[4,6]

Herniation Syndrome

Herniation is a shifting of brain tissue with displacement into another compartment as the result of bleeding or edema. This shift compresses, tears, or shears the vasculature, decreasing perfusion.[4] Supratentorial herniation is most common in trauma. Assessment findings include:[4,22]

- Asymmetric pupillary reactivity
- Unilateral or bilateral pupillary dilation
- Abnormal motor posturing
- Other evidence of neurologic deterioration (loss of normal reflexes, paralysis, or change in level of consciousness)

The two major types of supratentorial herniation are named by the site of herniation:

- Uncal transtentorial herniation—the uncus of the temporal lobe is displaced unilaterally over the tentorium into the posterior fossa causing a shift of the mid-brain to the opposite side[6]
- Central or transtentorial herniation—the cerebral hemispheres are pushed downward through the tentorial notch directly compressing the brainstem[6]

Diffuse Injuries

Diffuse TBIs occur over a widespread area. They may not always be identifiable on radiograph or CT imaging because the damage involves contusions or shearing and stretching of the microvasculature, not a localized hematoma.[6] These injuries commonly follow a direct blow to the head and very often are sports-related. They may also occur after a blow to the body.[50] Patients who sustain these injuries may have varying degrees of symptoms that last from minutes to hours. Assessment findings include:

- Transient LOC
- Headache and dizziness
- Nausea and vomiting
- Confusion and disorientation
- Memory loss and concentration difficulty
- Irritability and fatigue

These diffuse TBIs are currently classified based on GCS scores along with loss of consciousness, amnesia, and other symptoms.[1]

Mild Traumatic Brain Injury (mTBI)[1,39]

Mild TBI was formerly known as concussion. Assessment findings include:

- GCS score of 13 to 15
- Brief (< 30 min) LOC
- Post-traumatic amnesia of less than 24 hours
- No change on neuroimaging studies[51]

Moderate Traumatic Brain Injury[1,39]

Assessment findings include:

- GCS score of 9 to 12
- Wide variety of symptoms, including alterations in consciousness, confusion, amnesia, and focal neurologic deficits[52]
- May deteriorate to severe head injury over time, so monitor patients closely

Severe Traumatic Brain Injury[1,39]

Assessment findings include:

- GCS score of 8 or less
- Significant alteration in consciousness
- Abnormal pupillary response
- Abnormal motor posturing[52]

Second Impact Syndrome

Second impact syndrome refers to a condition that occurs when the patient suffers a second mild TBI before recovery from the first. It is rare but usually fatal, especially in the pediatric population.[38] The second impact causes loss of autoregulation leading to cerebral edema. Recent reports note that legislation has been enacted to protect athletes from second impact syndrome.[32]

Postconcussive Syndrome

Patients who sustain a mild TBI may develop postconcussive syndrome. Typically, postconcussive syndrome manifests several days or months after the head trauma. Signs and symptoms usually resolve but may persist for long periods of time. These patients may require ongoing evaluation, treatment, and extended rehabilitation before they are able to return to their previous level of athletic participation or other activities.[52] As it cannot be determined who will develop postconcussive syndrome, education related to this condition is included in patient discharge instructions with information regarding when to return for care. Assessment findings include:[53]

- Nausea
- Dizziness and persistent headache
- Memory and judgment impairment, as well as attention deficits

- Insomnia and sleep disturbance
- Loss of libido
- Anxiety, irritability, depression, and emotional lability
- Noise and light oversensitivity
- Attention or concentration problems[54]

Diffuse Axonal Injury

Diffuse axonal injury (DAI) is widespread microscopic damage, primarily to the axons, from diffuse shearing, tearing, or compressive stresses from rotational or acceleration/deceleration mechanisms of injury (MOI).[6,22] The damage may also result following hypoxic or ischemic insults from the initial trauma.[1] The injury presents as diffuse, microscopic, hemorrhagic lesions, and cerebral edema, which may be detected on magnetic resonance imaging (MRI). Deeper brain structures, the brainstem, and RAS are most at risk for injury, which commonly results in prolonged coma. The brain injury is graded as mild, moderate, or severe.[1,5,22,52] Severe DAI has significant morbidity and mortality. Assessment findings include:[22]

- Unconsciousness
  - In mild DAI, unconsciousness may last 6 to 24 hours
  - In severe DAI, unconsciousness may persist for weeks or months or continue as a persistent vegetative state
- Increased ICP
- Abnormal motor posturing
- Hypertension (systolic blood pressure between 140 and 160 mm Hg)
- Hyperthermia with temperature between 104°F and 105°F (40°C and 40.5°C)
- Excessive sweating
- Mild to severe memory loss; cognitive, behavioral, and intellectual deficits

Penetrating Injuries

Penetrating injuries to the brain can be devastating, and it is essential to discover the site and extent of the injury. CT and angiography are preferred along with vascular imaging as necessary.[1] The presence of a large contusion, hemorrhage, or hematoma, especially when both hemispheres are involved, is associated with increased mortality.[1] Keep the following in mind when dealing with penetrating injuries to the brain:

- Leave any protruding penetrating objects in place and stabilize them
- Prepare for surgery to evacuate the hematoma

Craniofacial Fractures
Skull Fractures
The significance of a skull fracture is the considerable force it takes to cause the injury. They can occur in the skull vault or the base. Types of skull fractures include the following:

- Linear skull fracture
  - A non-displaced fracture of the cranium
  - Assessment findings may include:[39]
    - Headache
    - Surrounding soft tissue injury
    - Possible decreased level of consciousness
- Depressed skull fracture
  - Extends below the surface of the skull and may cause dura mater laceration and brain tissue injury
  - Assessment findings may include:[39]
    - Headache
    - Surrounding soft tissue injury
    - Palpable depression of skull over fracture site
    - Possible open fracture
    - Possible decreased level of consciousness
- Basilar skull fracture
  - Fracture of any of the five bones in the base of the skull
  - Can result in punctures or lacerations to brain tissue or cranial nerves and CSF leakage
  - May result in laceration of the dura mater and open passage of CSF, placing the patient at risk for infections such as meningitis, encephalitis, or brain abscess
  - Occurs concurrently with facial fractures
  - Cerebral arteriography or CT angiography: Used to identify and manage the bleeding
  - Assessment findings may include:[39]
    - Headache
    - Altered level of consciousness
    - CSF rhinorrhea or otorrhea
    - Periorbital ecchymoses (raccoon eyes)
    - Mastoid ecchymoses (battle sign)
    - Bleeding behind the tympanic membrane (hemotympanum)
    - Facial nerve palsy (CN VII injury)

Maxillary Fractures

The LeFort classification system provides precise definitions of maxillary fractures (Fig. 9-2).[55]

- LeFort I is a transverse maxillary bone fracture that occurs above the level of the teeth and results in a separation of the teeth from the maxilla. Assessment findings include:[55]

  - Independent movement of the maxilla from the rest of the face

  - Slight swelling of the maxillary area

  - Lip laceration or fractured teeth

  - Malocclusion

- A LeFort II fracture is a pyramidal maxillary bone fracture involving the mid-face area.[55] The apex of the fracture transverses the bridge of the nose. The two lateral fractures of the pyramid extend through the lacrimal bone of the face and ethmoid bone of the skull into the median portion of both orbits. The base of the fracture extends above the level of the upper teeth into the maxilla. Assessment findings include:[55]

  - Massive facial edema

  - Nasal swelling with obvious fracture of the nasal bones

  - Malocclusion

  - CSF rhinorrhea

- A LeFort III fracture is a complete craniofacial separation involving the maxilla, zygoma, orbits, and bones of the cranial base.[55] Assessment findings include:[55]

  - Massive facial edema

  - Mobility and depression of zygomatic bones

  - Ecchymoses

  - Diplopia

  - Open bite or malocclusion

Mandibular Fractures

Mandibular fractures occur to the horseshoe-shaped lower jawbone that attaches to the cranium at the temporomandibular joints. The common fracture sites are at the canine and third molar tooth and the angle of the mandible and the condyles. They can be open or closed, have multiple breaks on the same bone, or be impacted (one fragment pushed into another).[56] Assessment findings include:[56]

- Malocclusion

- Inability to open the mouth (trismus)

- Pain, especially on movement

- Facial asymmetry and a palpable step-off deformity

Figure 9-2. LeFort Fractures

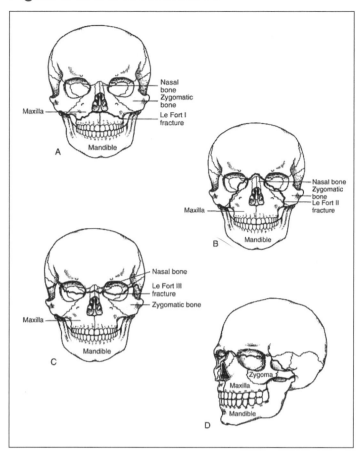

From Emergency Nurses Association. (2013). *Sheehy's manual of emergency care* (7th ed.) St. Louis, MO: Mosby Elsevier, *reprinted with permission.*

- Edema or hematoma formation at the fracture site

- Blood behind, or ruptured tympanic membrane

- Anesthesia of the lower lip

Interventions for the Patient with Brain, Cranial, or Maxillofacial Trauma

- Position the patient as guided by institutional protocols, keeping in mind the status of the cervical spine

  - Elevation of the patient's head of bed by 30 degrees is recommended to decrease ICP.[6,21] The spine board may be tilted in reverse Trendelenberg at 30 degrees.

  - Position the head midline to facilitate venous drainage. Rotation of the head can compress the neck veins and result in venous engorgement and decreased venous drainage.[6]

- Prepare for insertion of an ICP monitoring device and then monitor the ICP according to institutional protocols. A brain tissue oxygenation monitoring device can be inserted at the same time as ICP monitor placement (Fig. 9-3). Indications for ICP monitoring include:[21]

- Severe TBI (GCS score 3–8) with an abnormal CT scan on admission
- Severe TBI (GCS score 3–8) with normal CT scan and two or more of the following:
  - Age older than 40 years
  - Unilateral or bilateral abnormal posturing
  - Systolic blood pressure less than 90 mm Hg
- Administer mannitol, as prescribed
  - Rule out other injuries before administering. Administration via bolus may be more effective than continuous infusion.[1,21,34,57]
  - Indications for mannitol include acute neurologic deterioration such as dilated pupils, loss of consciousness, or hemiparesis while the patient is being monitored. Weigh the risks.[1]
  - Not for use with active intracranial bleeding
    - It is not for use in hypotensive patients since it will not lower ICP in hypovolemia and is a potent osmotic diuretic[1]
- Administer anticonvulsant medication, as prescribed
  - Posttraumatic epilepsy occurs in about 15% of patients with severe head injuries.[1] Seizure activity increases ICP and cerebral metabolic rate.[4,6,21]
  - Indications for seizure prophylaxis include:
    - Depressed skull fracture
    - Seizure at the time of injury
    - Seizure on arrival to the emergency department
    - History of seizures
    - Penetrating brain injury
    - Severe head injury
    - Acute subdural hematoma
    - Acute epidural hematoma
- Fever is a result of a change in the thermoregulatory set point, while an elevated temperature from brain injury is from a disruption in thermoregulation. For this reason, antipyretics are not effective at treating hyperthermia related to acute brain injury.[7] A cooling blanket or ice packs may be used. If fever is present as a result of an inflammatory process, antipyretics may be useful.
- Hyperthermia increases ICP and cerebral metabolic rate. Avoid causing shivering with the cooling process; shivering increases the cerebral metabolic rate and may precipitate a rise in ICP.
- Do not pack the ears or nose if a CSF leak is suspected

- Administer tetanus prophylaxis, as needed
- Assist with wound repair as indicated
- Administer other medications, as prescribed
  - Analgesics or sedatives may be indicated for pain or agitation
  - If the change in mental status is suspected to be the result of an overdose, naloxone may be given for opioid use, and flumazenil for benzodiazepine use. Use caution for either of these medications as abrupt withdrawal from long-term opioid use or reversal of benzodiazepine use as an anticonvulsant both may precipitate seizures, causing further deterioration.[58]
  - Administer antibiotics, as prescribed

Reevaluation Adjuncts

Radiographic Studies
- CT scans[4,6]
  - Patient movement may produce artifact and result in an inaccurate CT reading. Patient movement may be a result of seizures, inability to cooperate based on mental status changes, or inappropriate flexion or extension.
  - Sedation may be administered as prescribed
    - Closely monitor patients who have received sedation or neuromuscular blocking medications during a CT procedure
- Magnetic resonance imaging (MRI)
  - MRI is not typically used in the acute resuscitation phase. It may be indicated to provide better delineation of a patient's injury and prognosis.
- Angiography
  - Angiography may be indicated if vascular injury is known or suspected
- Skull series
  - Radiographs of the skull are generally not needed, especially if CT scan is available

Laboratory Studies
- Coagulation studies
  - Analysis of coagulation status may be helpful in directing the management for those patients taking anticoagulants or for timing of insertion of ICP monitoring devices
- Blood alcohol and urine toxicology screens

Figure 9-3. Treatment Algorithm: Clinical Practice Guidelines for the Nursing Management of Adults with Severe TBI

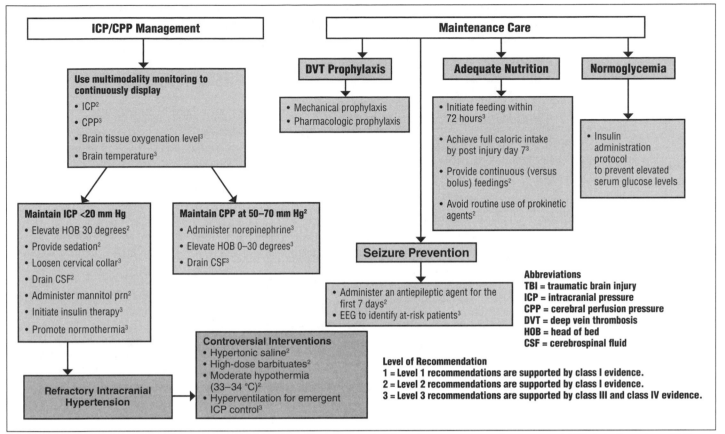

From American Association of Neuroscience Nurses. (2008). *Nursing management of adults with severe traumatic brain injury: AANN clinical practice guideline series*. Chicago, IL: Author.

○ These studies may be helpful to determine the presence or absence of alcohol or other substances that may contribute to an altered mental status

Reevaluation and Post Resuscitation Care

Reevaluation of the patient with brain, cranial, or maxillofacial trauma includes:

- Serial scoring of the GCS or FOUR score for patients with a GCS score less than 15 (crucial for early detection of patient deterioration[1])

- Frequent reassessment of pupils

- ABG trending

- Trends in vital signs, especially blood pressure, respiratory rate and pattern, temperature, SpO_2, and end-tidal carbon dioxide

- Reevaluation for the development of the following:

  ○ Headache, nausea, vomiting, and seizure activity

  ○ Changes in motor or sensory function

  ○ Response to interventions such as fluid administration and diuretic therapy

Continuous ICP Monitoring

Continuous ICP monitoring is important for assessing brain injury and the response of the patient to treatment. The addition of a brain tissue oxygenation monitoring device can provide early detection of secondary brain injury such as cerebral hypoxia and possible ischemia. This oxygenation device reflects oxygen delivery to the cerebral tissues as well as monitors the temperature of the brain tissue. Any change in brain tissue can alter cerebral metabolism and affect CBF and ICP. The monitoring system can detect poor oxygenation to the brain tissue before changes can be detected in the ICP. With this early detection, early management can result in a better patient outcome.[59]

Definitive Care or Transport

Consider the need to transport the patient to a trauma center and/or prepare the patient for operative intervention, hospital admission, or transfer, as indicated.

Emerging Trends

As the science and evidence of trauma care continues to evolve, tools to improve patient outcomes continue to be trialed and refined. Evidence is tested and replicated, and new standards of care are transitioned into practice. This section on trauma care considerations explores some of the evidence and the potential significance to trauma patient care. Regarding the care of patients with brain, cranial, and maxillofacial injuries, the use of the GCS and therapeutic hypothermia are discussed.

Validity and Reliability of the Glasgow Coma Scale

The GCS has long been considered the gold standard by which other scoring systems are compared.[60] Recently the GCS has come under question with regard to inter-rater reliability and lack of prognostic utility. An additional limitation of the GCS is the inability to accurately assess intubated patients and difficulty in assessing aphasic patients due to the requirement of a verbal component.[61]

The FOUR score was developed in 2005 and assesses four variables as noted earlier. Since all components of the FOUR score can be rated even when patients are intubated, this scoring system may have advantages for use in trauma patients (Table 9-1). The authors noted advantages of the FOUR score as compared to the GCS were it can account for intubated patients with substitute scores, identify a locked-in state, and detect the presence of a vegetative state.[34] The FOUR score has been validated as a useful assessment tool in both adults and pediatrics and across multiple hospital settings.[62–64] A limitation is that it was initially only validated at the Mayo Clinic.[60]

Therapeutic Hypothermia for Traumatic Brain Injury

With the development of technology to measure the temperature within the brain parenchyma, it was noted that patients with severe TBI commonly have a brief drop in temperature during ischemia. With reperfusion, this temperature returned to normal. Research focused on determining if this phenomenon was protective or reactive. Several studies produced conflicting results with more evidence that mild to moderate cooling (32° to 34°C) reduces morbidity in the adult patient when therapy is maintained for at least 72 hours after injury or until ICP has stabilized for 24 hours.[65–67] One study in children demonstrated worse outcomes with hypothermia.[68]

Summary

Approximately 1.7 million individuals sustain a TBI each year. Early intervention and appropriate resuscitation is crucial to prevent or minimize the effects of secondary brain injury. Secondary brain injury may result from a hypoxic event, cerebral edema, hypotension, or increased ICP. Facilitating oxygenation and ventilation are priorities in treating patients with TBI. Frequently reassessing the patient's neurologic status will minimize the effects of any neurologic deterioration.

References

1. American College of Surgeons. (2012). *Advanced trauma life support student course manual* (9th ed.). Chicago, IL: Author.

2. Sugerman, R. A. (2010). Structure and function of the neurologic system. In K. L. McCance & S. E. Huether (Eds.), *Pathophysiology: The biologic basis for disease in adults and children* (6th ed., pp. 442–480). St. Louis, MO: Mosby.

3. Hunt, J. P., Marr, A. B., & Stuke, L.E. (2013). Kinematics. In K. L. Mattox, E. E. Moore, & D. V. Feliciano (Eds.), *Trauma* (7th ed., pp. 2–17). New York, NY: McGraw-Hill.

4. Copstead, L. E., & Banasik, J. L. (Eds.). (2013). *Pathophysiology* (5th ed., pp. 898–921). St. Louis, MO: Elsevier Saunders.

5. Ball, J., Bindler, R., & Cowen, K. (2012). *Principles of pediatric nursing: Caring for children* (5th ed.). Upper Saddle River, NJ: Pearson Education.

6. McQuillan, K. A., & Thurman, P. A. (2009). Traumatic brain injuries. In K. A. McQuillan, M. B. Flynn Makic, & E. Whalen (Eds.), *Trauma nursing: From resuscitation through rehabilitation* (4th ed., pp. 448–518). Philadelphia, PA: W. B. Saunders.

7. Stim, E. (2010, September 23). *The cranial nerves – Smell/vision/eye/face/visceral/taste.* Retrieved from http://physiciansnotebook.blogspot.com/2010/09/912-cranial-nerves-smellvisioneyefacevi.html

8. Cipolla, M. J. (2009). Control of cerebral blood flow. In *The cerebral circulation.* San Rafael, CA: Morgan & Claypool Life Sciences. Retrieved from http://www.ncbi.nlm.nih.gov/books/NBK53082/

9. Hall, J. E. (2011). Cerebral blood flow, cerebrospinal fluid, and brain metabolism. In *Guyton and Hall textbook of medical physiology* (12th ed., pp. 743–752). St. Louis, MO: W. B. Saunders.

10. Peterson, E. C., Wang, Z., & Britz, G. (2011). Regulation of cerebral blood flow. *International Journal of Vascular Medicine, 2011,* 823525

11. Slazinski, T. (2011) Intracranial and fiberoptic catheter insertion, intracranial pressure monitoring care, troubleshooting, and removal. In D.J.L.M. Wiegand (Ed.) *AACN procedure manual for critical care* (6th ed., pp. 802–809). St. Louis, MO: Elsevier Saunders.

12. Centers for Disease Control and Prevention. (2012, March 23). *How many people have TBI?* Retrieved from http://www.cdc.gov/traumaticbraininjury/statistics.html

13. Haddad, S. H., & Arabi, Y. M. (2012). Critical care management of severe traumatic brain injury in adults. *Scandinavian Journal of Trauma, Resuscitation and Emergency Medicine, 20,* 12.

14. Allareddy, V., & Nallia, R. P. (2011). Epidemiology of facial fracture injuries. *Journal of Oral and Maxillofacial Surgery, 69*(10), 2613–2628.

15. Mayo Clinic. (2012, October 12). *Traumatic brain injury: Causes.* Retrieved from http://www.mayoclinic.com/health/traumatic-brain-injury/DS00552/DSECTION=causes

16. Faul, M., Xu, L., Wald, M.M., & Coronado, V.G. (2010). *Traumatic brain injury in the United States: Emergency department visits, hospitalizations, and deaths 2002–2006.* Atlanta, GA: Centers for Disease Control and Prevention.

17. Leather, N.C. (2009). Risk-taking behavior in adolescence: A literature review. *Journal of Child Healthcare, 13*(3), 295–304.

18. National Highway Traffic Safety Administration. (2010). *Traffic safety facts 2010: A compilation of motor vehicle crash data from the Fatality Analysis Reporting System and the General Estimates System*. Washington, DC: U.S. Department of Transportation.

19. Centers for Disease Control and Prevention. (2012, July 27). *Concussion and mild TBI*. Retrieved from http://www.cdc.gov/concussion/

20. Centers for Disease Control and Prevention. (2012, September 24). *Heads up: Concussion*. Retrieved from http://www.cdc.gov/concussion/headsup/index.html

21. Brain Trauma Foundation. (2007). Guidelines for the management of severe traumatic brain injury 3rd edition: Cerebral perfusion thresholds. *Journal of Neurotrauma, 24*(Suppl 1), S59–S64.

22. Boss, B. J. (2010). Alterations in cognitive systems, cerebral hemodynamics and motor function. In K. L. McCance & S. E. Huether (Eds.), *Pathophysiology: The biologic basis for disease in adults and children* (6th ed., pp. 525-582). St. Louis, MO: Mosby.

23. Sasser, S. M., Hunt, R. C., Faul, M., Sugarman, D., Pearson, W. S., Dulski, T., ... Lerner, E. B. (2012). Guidelines for field triage of injured patients: Recommendations of the National Expert Panel on Field Triage, 2011. *MMWR Recommendations and Reports, 61*(RR-1), 1–20.

24. Peck, K. A., Sise, C. B., Shackford, S. R., Sise, M. J., Calvo, R. Y., Sack, D. I., ... Schehter, M. S. (2011). Delayed intracranial hemorrhage after blunt trauma: Are patients on preinjury anticoagulants and prescription antiplatelet agents at risk? *Journal of Trauma, 71*(6), 1600–1604.

25. Stone, M. B., Tubridy, C. M., & Curran, R. (2010). The effect of rigid cervical collars on internal jugular vein dimensions. *Academic Emergency Medicine, 17*(1), 100–102.

26. Kilgannon, J. H., Jones, A. E., Shapiro, N. I., Angelos, M. G., Milcarek, B., Hunter, K., ... Trzeciak, S. (2010). Association between arterial hyperoxia following resuscitation from cardiac arrest and in-hospital mortality. *Journal of the American Medical Association, 303*(21), 2165–2171.

27. Wall, R. M., & Murphy, M. F. (Eds.). (2012). *Manual of emergency airway management* (4th ed.). Philadelphia, PA: Lippincott Williams & Wilkins.

28. Perbedy, M. A., Callaway, C. W., Neumar, R. W., Geocadin, R. G., Zimmerman, J. L., Donnino, M., ... Kronick, S. L. (2010). Part 9: Post-cardiac arrest care: 2010 American Heart Association Guidelines for Cardiopulmonary Resuscitation and Emergency Cardiovascular Care. *Circulation, 122*(18 Suppl 3), S768–S786.

29. O'Driscoll, B. R., Howard, L. S., & Davison, A. G. (2008). BTS guideline for emergency oxygen use in adult patients. *Thorax, 63*(Suppl VI), vi1–vi68.

30. Brenner, M., Stein, D., Hu, P., Kufera, J., Wooford, M., & Scalea, T. (2012). Association between early hyperoxia and worse outcomes after traumatic brain injury. *Archives of Surgery, 147*(111), 1042–1046.

31. Neumar, R.W., Otto, C.W., Link, M.S., Kronick, S.L., Shuster, M., Callaway, C.W.,...Morrison, L.J. (2010). Part 8: Adult advanced cardiovascular life support: 2010 American Heart Association guidelines for cardiopulmonary resuscitation and emergency cardiovascular care. *Circulation, 122*, S729–S767.

32. Su, J. K., & Ramirez, J. F. (2012). Management of the athlete with concussion. *The Permanente Journal, 16*(2), 54–56.

33. Jagoda, A. S., Bazarian, J. J., Bruns, J. J., Cantrill, S. V., Gean, A. D., Howard, P. K., ... Whitson, R. R. (2008). Clinical policy: Neuroimaging and decision making in adult mild traumatic brain injury in the acute setting. *Annals of Emergency Medicine, 52*(6),714–748.

34. Wijdicks, E., Bamlet, W., Maramottom, B., Manno, E., & McClelland, R. (2005). Validation of a new coma scale: The FOUR score. *Annals of Neurology, 58*, 585–593.

35. Brain Trauma Foundation. (2007). Guidelines for the management of severe traumatic brain injury 3rd edition: Blood pressure and oxygenation. *Journal of Neurotrauma, 24*(Suppl 1), S7–S13.

36. Teasdale, G., & Jennent, B. (1974). Assessment of coma and impaired consciousness. A practical scale. *Lancet, 2,* 81–84.

37. Ross, S. E. , Leipold, C., Terregino, C., & O'Malley, K. F. (1998). Efficacy of the motor component of the Glasgow Coma Scale in trauma triage. *Journal of Trauma, 45,* 42–44.

38. Kramer, A. A., Wijdicks, E. F., Snavely, V. L., Dunivan, J. R., Naranjo, L. L., Bible, S., ... Dickess, S. M. (2012). A multicenter prospective study of interobserver agreement using the Full Outline of Unresponsiveness score coma scale in the intensive care unit. *Critical Care Medicine, 40*(9), 2671–2676.

39. Welch, K. C. (2011, June). *CSF leaks*. Retrieved from http://care.american-rhinologic.org/csf_leaks

40. Meagher, R. J., & Young, W. F. (2013, March 1). *Subdural hematoma*. Retrieved from http://emedicine.medscape.com/article/1137207-overview

41. Prosser, J. D., Vender, J. R., & Solares, C. A. (2011). Traumatic cerebrospinal fluid leaks. *Otolaryngology Clinics of North America, 44,* 857–873.

42. Welch, K. C., Caballlero, N., & Stankiewicz, J. (2013, April 29). *CSF rhinorrhea*. Retrieved from http://emedicine.medscape.com/article/861126-overview

43. Sunder, R. & Tyler, K. (2013). Basal skull fracture and the halo sign. *Canadian Medical Association Journal, 185*(5), 416.

44. Gibson, A. and Boswell, K. (2011). Facial trauma: Challenges, controversies, and therapeutic options. *Trauma Reports: Evidence-based Medicine for the ED, 12*(2), 1–11.

45. McCudden, C. R., Senior, B. A., Hainsworth, S., Oliveira, W., Silverman, L. M., Bruns, D. E., & Hammett-Stabler, C. A. (2013). Evaluation of high resolution gel β2-transferrin for detection of cerebrospinal fluid leak. *Clinical Chemistry and Laboratory Medicine, 51*(2), 311–315.

46. Sherif, C., DiLeva, A., Gibson, D., Pakrah-Bodingbauer, B., Widhalm, G., Krusche-Mandl, I., ... Matula, C. (2011). A management algorithm for cerebrospinal fluid leak associated with anterior skull base fractures: Detailed clinical and radiological follow-up. *Neurosurgical Review, 35,* 227–238.

47. Berg, R. A., Hemphill, R., Aufderheide, T. P., Cave, D. M., Hazinski, M. F., Lerner, E. B., ... Swor, R. A. (2010). Part 5: Adult basic life support: 2010 American Heart Association guidelines for cardiopulmonary resuscitation and emergency cardiovascular care. *Circulation, 122*(18 Suppl 3), S685–S705.

48. Zuckerman, S. L., Kuhn, A., Dewan, M. C., Morone, P. J., Forbes, J. A., Solomon, G. S., & Sills, A. K. (2012). Structural brain injury in sports-related concussion. *Neurosurgical Focus, 33*(6), 1–12.

49. McLaughlin, J. C. (2013). Head trauma. In Emergency Nurses Association, *Sheehy's manual of emergency care* (7th ed., pp. 379–406). St. Louis, MO: Mosby Elsevier.

50. Levine, Z. (2010). Mild traumatic brain injury. Part 2: Concussion management. *Canadian Family Physician, 56*(7), 658–662.

51. Anderson-Barnes, V.C., Weeks, S., & Tsao, J.W. (2010). Mild traumatic brain injury update. *Continuum: Lifelong Learning Neurology, 16*(6), 17–26.

52. Post, A. F., Boro, T., & Ecklund, J. M. (2013). Injury to the brain. In K. L. Mattox, E. E. Moore, & D. V. Feliciano (Eds.), *Trauma* (7th ed., pp. 356–376). New York, NY: McGraw-Hill.

53. Prigatano, G. P., & Gale, S. D. (2011). The current status of postconcussion syndrome. *Current Opinion in Psychiatry, 24*(3), 243–250.

54. Brain Trauma Foundation. (2007). Guidelines for the management of severe traumatic brain injury 3rd edition: Hyperosmolar therapy. *Journal of Neurotrauma, 24*(Suppl 1), S14–S20.

55. Moe, K. S., Byrne, P., Kim, D. W., & Tawfilis, A. R. (2012, February 2). *Maxillary and Le Fort fractures*. Retrieved from http://emedicine.medscape.com/article/1283568-overview#a0104

56. Laub, D. R. (2012, June 4). *Mandibular fractures*. Retrieved from http://emedicine.medscape.com/article/1283150-overview

57. Wakai, A., Roberts, I., & Schierhout, G. (2007). Mannitol for acute traumatic brain injury: *Cochrane Database of Systematic Reviews*, (1), CD001049.

58. Karch, A. M. (2012). *2013 Lippincott's nursing drug guide*. Philadelphia, PA: WoltersKluwer Lippincott, Williams & Wilkins.

59. Hession, D. (2008). Management of traumatic brain injury: Nursing practice guidelines for cerebral perfusion and brain tissue oxygenation (PbtO2) systems. *Pediatric Nursing, 34*(6), 470–472.

60. Kornbluth, J., & Bhardwaj, A. (2011) Evaluation of coma: A critical appraisal of popular scoring systems. *Neurocritical Care, 14*(1), 134–143.

61. Green, S. M. (2011). Cheerio, laddie! Bidding farewell to the Glasgow Coma Scale. *Annals of Emergency Medicine, 58*(5), 427–430.

62. Sadaka, F., Patel, D., & Lakshmanan, R., (2012) The FOUR score predicts outcome in patients after traumatic brain injury. *Neurocritical Care, 16,* 95–101.

63. Cohen, J. (2009). Interrater reliability and predictive validity of the FOUR score coma scale in a pediatric population. *Journal of Neuroscience Nursing, 41*(5), 261–267.

64. Iyer, V., Mandrekar, J., Danielson, R., Zubkov, A., Elmer, J., & Wijdicks, E. (2009). Validity of the FOUR score coma scale in the medical intensive care unit. *Mayo Clinic Proceedings, 84*(8), 694 –701.

65. Fox, J. L., Vu, E. N., Doyle-Waters, M., Brubacher, J. R., Abu-Laban, R., & Hu, Z. (2009). Prophylactic hypothermia for traumatic brain injury: A quantitative systematic review. *Canadian Journal of Medicine, 12*(4), 355–364.

66. Wilson, J. R. F., & Green, A. (2009). Acute traumatic brain injury: A review of recent advances in imaging and management. *European Journal of Trauma and Emergency Surgery, 2,* 176–185.

67. Sacho, R. H., & Childs, C. (2008). The significance of altered temperature after traumatic brain injury: An analysis of investigations in experimental and human studies: Part 2. *British Journal of Neurosurgery, 22*(4), 497–507.

68. Hutchison, J. S., Ward, R. E., Lacroix, J., Hebert, P. C., Barrow, M. A., Bohn, D. J.,…Skippen, P. W. (2008). Hypothermia therapy after traumatic brain injury in children. *New England Journal of Medicine, 358*(23), 2447–2456.

Chapter 10 • Ocular Trauma

Darcy Egging, MS, RN, C-ANP, CEN

Objectives

Upon completion of this chapter, the learner will be able to:

1. Describe mechanisms of injury associated with ocular trauma.

2. Summarize pathophysiologic changes as a basis for assessment of the trauma patient with ocular injuries.

3. Demonstrate the nursing assessment of the trauma patient with ocular injuries.

4. Plan appropriate interventions for the trauma patient with ocular injuries.

5. Evaluate the effectiveness of nursing interventions for the trauma patient with ocular injuries.

Preface

Knowledge of normal anatomy and physiology serves as a foundation for understanding anatomic derangements and pathophysiologic processes that may result from trauma. Before reading this chapter, it is strongly suggested that the learner review the following material. This material will not be covered in the lectures nor tested directly, but as foundational content, it may be the basis for some test questions and skill evaluation steps.

Anatomy and Physiology of the Eye

The eye consists of various structures, both external and internal. It is protected by the orbital bones and the eyelids. The globe of the eye consists of multiple layers. The white outer layer, the *sclera,* can be easily seen without specialized equipment. The *cornea*, a transparent, multilayered convex structure, covers the iris and pupil. The globe consists of the anterior and posterior chamber and the vitreous chamber (Fig. 10-1).

The *conjunctiva,* which is a mucous membrane, covers the sclera and inner surface of the eyelid. Tears are secreted from the lacrimal glands in the upper eyelids and lubricate and protect the eye. These tears drain through the punctum located at the inner canthus of the eye.[1-3]

The *vitreous humor* is located behind the lens and fills most of the eye. The anterior chamber is located between the cornea and iris and is filled with aqueous humor. *Aqueous humor* is a watery substance that supports the cornea and lens. The cornea is an avascular layer of tissue that covers the iris and pupil. The iris is the colored portion of the eye and is positioned between the cornea and the lens. The lens is located behind the iris, and its primary function is to focus light on the retina. The cornea and lens gather light and bend it to make a clear image, whereas the iris adjusts the size of the pupil to accommodate the intensity of the light.

Figure 10-1. Anatomy of the Eye

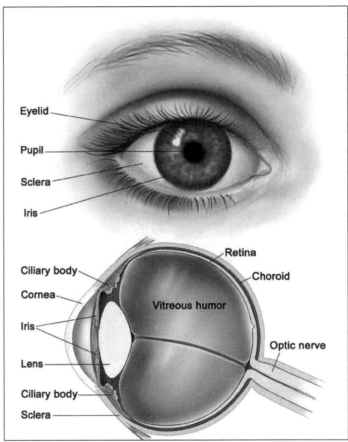

Copyright Therese Winslow. Reprinted with permission.

The retina is located at the back of the globe and contains rods and cones, which help the eye to see images. The macula and fovea are located within the retina. The macula is the dark spot on the fundus of the eye that provides for clear and distinct vision, whereas the fovea is where vision is the sharpest. The optic disc exits the back of the eye to form the optic nerve; it appears as a pale round area with a large number of blood vessels (Fig. 10-2).[1-4]

Figure 10-2. Fundus of the Eye

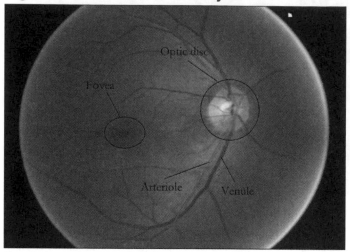

From Retinography. (2005, March 31). Retrieved from http://en.wikipedia.org/wiki/File:Retinography.jpg. This file is licensed under the Creative Commons Attribution-Share Alike 3.0 Unported license.

The movement of the eye is controlled by four rectus muscles and two oblique muscles. The eye is innervated by cranial nerves (CNs) II, III, IV, V, and VI. Eye movement is controlled by CNs III, IV, and VI (Table 10-1).[5–7] CN VII innervates the eyelids to close, and CN III innervates them to open. Ptosis (eyelid drooping) occurs due to oculomotor nerve (CN III) palsy. The blood supply to the eye comes from the ophthalmic artery, which branches off to form the central retinal artery. The majority of venous drainage occurs through the superior and inferior ophthalmic veins.[3]

Introduction

Epidemiology of Eye Trauma

Ocular trauma is not usually associated with increased mortality; however, disability and overall quality of life are key drivers for understanding the impact of this type of trauma. Ocular trauma may or may not be an isolated injury. An estimated 2% to 6% of all trauma patients who are hospitalized have some type of ocular injury.[8] Around

2 to 3 million eye injuries occur annually. The United States (U.S.) Eye Injury Registry reports that most eye injuries occur in the home (40%–50%).[9,10] Eye injuries also occur at sporting events, in industrial settings, and on streets and highways.[9,10] The mean age for ocular trauma is less than 30 years, and males are at higher risk. Blunt trauma is the most prevalent mechanism of injury (MOI) followed by injury from sharp objects and motor vehicle collisions (MVCs).[11] Trauma sustained in the workplace is usually caused by a sharp object. Airbag deployment, air gun (BB gun) injury, and fireworks injuries contribute to the types of injuries seen with ocular trauma.[9] It is estimated that three-quarters of all individuals who sustained ocular trauma did not wear protective eyewear.[9,10,12]

Mechanisms of Injury

Ocular trauma can be classified as *blunt, penetrating,* or *burn.* Another method of classifying ocular trauma is to designate it as *mechanical or nonmechanical.*

- Mechanical injuries may be either perforating or nonperforating. These injuries may be caused by blunt force, sharp objects, and foreign bodies.

- Nonmechanical injury is usually associated with an ocular burn and includes thermal, chemical, and radiation injury[13]

The literature is divided regarding the terminology to use when describing ocular trauma. The Birmingham Eye Trauma Terminology (BETT)[14] system, used to describe mechanical trauma, has been endorsed by the American Academy of Ophthalmology, International Society of Ocular Trauma, and U.S. Eye Injury Registry. This system begins with the simple question: Is the globe intact? If the globe remains intact, the injury is a closed globe injury and is classified as a contusion or *lamellar laceration,* which is a partial thickness wound of the eye. If the globe is not intact, it is an open globe injury and referred to as one of the following:[14]

Table 10-1. Primary Movement and Innervations of Extraocular Muscles

Extraocular Muscle	Primary Eye Movement	Innervation
Medial rectus	Toward nose (adduction)	Oculomotor (CN III)
Lateral rectus	Away from nose (abduction)	Abducent (CN VI)
Superior rectus	Upward (elevation)	Oculomotor (CN III)
Inferior rectus	Downward (depression)	Oculomotor (CN III)
Superior oblique	Medial rotation	Trochlear (CN IV)
Inferior oblique	Lateral rotation	Oculomotor (CN III)

Note: CN indicates cranial nerve.
Data from Robinett & Kahn[3] and Bord & Linden.[19]

- Penetrating laceration
- Perforating laceration
- Full-thickness laceration
- Rupture

The *British Medical Journal Best Practice*[15] classifies contusions as injuries around the eye caused by blunt trauma with no open wounds and lamellar lacerations as wounds to the cornea or sclera that have not penetrated the full thickness of the globe wall.

Open globe injuries are classified as either lacerations or ruptures. These injuries penetrate through the eye wall and are described as a through-and-through injury to the cornea, sclera, or both. Open globe lacerations can be further categorized as penetrating, intraocular foreign body, or perforating. Penetrating is defined as having an entrance wound, an intraocular foreign body as when foreign objects are present, and perforating as having an entrance and exit wound.[14,16]

As noted, variations exist in ocular injury classification. Therefore, the use of a standardized ocular injury classification system is essential when communicating with other healthcare professionals. Refer to your organization's preferred system of classification if applicable.

Usual Concurrent Injuries

Ocular injuries often present as isolated events; however, associated head, face, or neck trauma may also be present. Assessment and intervention for airway, breathing, circulation, and disability take precedence over ocular assessment and interventions. The patient who presents at triage with ocular trauma may be high priority depending upon the MOI and risk for vision loss.

Nursing Assessment of the Patient with Ocular Trauma

The priority is to complete the primary survey. When life-threatening injuries have been addressed, the ocular examination can be performed. All eye injuries, even the most minor, require a visual acuity examination.

Primary Survey

See Chapter 5, Initial Assessment, for the systematic approach to nursing care of the trauma patient. The following assessment parameters are specific to patients with ocular injuries.

Secondary Survey
H-History
Questions to ask regarding events surrounding the ocular trauma include:
- When and where did the incident occur?
- Was the patient wearing protective eyewear or any type of corrective eyewear?
- What was the MOI: blunt, penetrating, or foreign body injury?
  - If blunt, what was the cause (baseball hitting the eye)?
  - If penetrating, what was the material that caused the injury (metallic or organic)?
    - If still in the eye, metallic foreign objects can cause permanent staining
    - Organic material carries a high incidence of infection
- Did the trauma cause a change in vision? What are those changes: blurring, double vision, or loss of vision?
- Is the patient having pain? Ask for both a description and location of that pain.
- Was there a chemical exposure? What type of chemical (acid or alkali)? Was any type of treatment or decontamination performed prior to arrival?[17]
- Does the patient wear glasses, contact lenses, or both? Is there a history of ocular surgery?
- Does the patient have other medical conditions that may affect vision, such as diabetes, glaucoma, or macular degeneration?
- What medications are taken? Note any eye medications including eye drops.
- Is the patient's tetanus status up to date?[18,19]

Ocular Assessment
The ocular assessment is performed in a systematic manner beginning with the external structures.

Inspect for:
- Assess for symmetry of the head, face, orbits, and eyelids
- Observe for lacerations, abrasions, contusions, swelling, and the presence of foreign material
- Evert the upper eyelid and inspect for any potential foreign body[18–20]
- Do not force the eye open if penetrating trauma is suspected[18–20]

Palpate for:

- Tenderness or step-offs, which may indicate a fracture

Visual Acuity

Visual acuity is a fundamental part of the ocular examination. Key elements to assess while performing the examination include the following:

- Ask about the patient's vision

  - What can the patient see? Ask the patient to describe his or her vision (blurry, decreased, or normal).

- Use a Snellen chart to assess visual acuity (Table 10-2).

  - Position the chart 20 feet away from the patient

  - If he or she is unable to stand, use a handheld Snellen chart held 14 inches from the patient's face

  - If the patient cannot read the chart, ask the patient what he or she can see: fingers, objects, light, or shadows?

  - Alternatives to the Snellen chart for those who do not read English are the directional E chart and object chart (Figs. 10-3 & 10-4)

Extraocular Movements

A quick assessment of extraocular movements (EOM) can be conducted by asking the patient to follow an object (finger, light, etc.) with his or her eyes without moving the head. Assess the ability to perform, looking at smoothness of movement, symmetry, and speed (Fig. 10-5). Each position is significant for CN evaluation. If nystagmus is present, determine if it is the patient's baseline or if it began since the traumatic incident. Conditions that may affect the patient's ability to perform the EOM evaluation include:

- CN disruption

- Extraocular muscle entrapment

- Increased intraocular pressure (IOP)[3,19]

Pupil Examination

Assess pupils for shape, size, reactivity, and symmetry. Up to 25% of the general population have unequal pupils (anisocoria); this is a benign physiologic condition.[19,21] Causes of anisocoria are trauma, uncal herniation, oculomotor nerve (CN III) palsy, medications, and some nebulizers (ipratropium).[3,21] Pupils are normally round; an oval pupil may indicate a tumor, retinal detachment, or previous injury. A teardrop-shaped pupil suggests a globe rupture, with the tip of the teardrop pointing to the rupture site. Pupils are tested using a penlight in a darkened room; test both direct and consensual reactivity. Normal pupillary response is a brisk constriction with both pupils constricting to the same size.[3,19,22]

Table 10-2. Examples of Visual Acuity Examination

Vision Level	Examination
20/20	Standing at 20 ft, patient can read what the normal eye can read at 20 ft
20/20 2	Standing at 20 ft, the patient can read what the normal eye can read at 20 ft; however, patient missed 2 letters
20/200	• At 20 ft, patient can read what the normal eye can read at 200 ft • Considered legally blind if reading is obtained while wearing glasses or contact lenses
10/200	• If the patient is unable to read letters on the Snellen chart, have patient stand at half distance to the chart • Record findings from distance at which the patient is standing over the smallest line he or she can read
CF/3 ft	Patient can count fingers at a maximum distance of 3 ft
HM/4	Patient can see hand motion at a maximum distance of 4 ft
LP/position	Patient can perceive light and determine the direction from which it is coming
LP/no position	Patient can perceive light but is unable to determine the direction from which it is coming
NLP	Patient unable to perceive light

Data from Robinett & Kahn[3] and Bord & Linden.[19]

Figure 10-3. E Chart

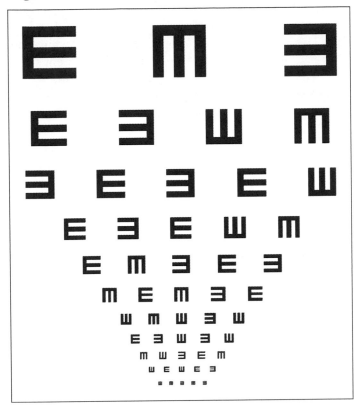

From Digital Eye Chart. (n.d.). *Tumbling E's chart.* Retrieved from http://www.digitaleyechart.com/ex_4.html

Figure 10-4. Children's Visual Acuity Chart

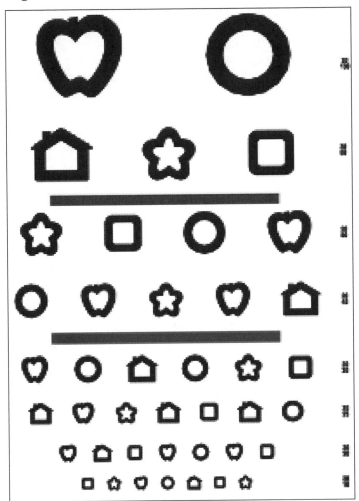

Image courtesy of Precision Vision.

Figure 10-5. Innervation and Movement of Extraocular Muscles

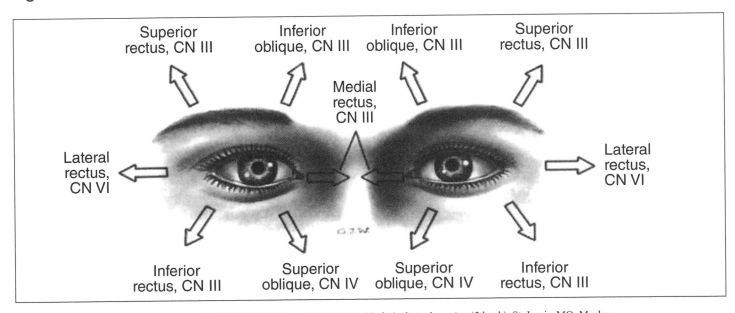

From Thompson, J. M., McFarland, G. K., Hirsch, J. E., & Tucker, S. M. (2002). *Mosby's clinical nursing* (5th ed.). St. Louis, MO: Mosby.

Anterior Segment Examination

The anterior segment consists of the sclera, conjunctiva, cornea, anterior chamber, iris, lens, and ciliary body. Inspect the sclera and conjunctiva for redness, swelling, discharge, foreign bodies, and lacerations. Assess the anterior chamber by shining a light tangentially; the chamber is normally clear and well defined. The lens is normally clear; if it appears cloudy, suspect the presence of a cataract.[3,19,22] A handheld blue light or a slit lamp can be used to assess the cornea after it is stained with fluorescein dye.

Fluorescein Examination

Fluorescein is a staining agent used to determine if there are defects to the cornea of the eye (foreign bodies, abrasions, lacerations, and infections). Have the patient remove contact lenses prior to staining. Staining is performed by touching the tip of a moistened fluorescein strip in the fornix of the lower lid and instructing the patient to blink several times before aiming the blue light over the cornea. Defects to the cornea will appear bright green under the blue light.[22,23]

Slit Lamp Examination

The slit lamp examination is a major component of the eye assessment. It is contraindicated in patients who cannot sit upright or if a globe rupture is suspected.[20] The slit lamp is a microscope that magnifies the structures of the eye (Fig. 10-6). Various light beams are used to visualize the structures of the eye and to identify any injuries. Although the nurse may not perform the examination, it is essential to understand how to set up for the procedure and ensure that the equipment is functioning properly.[23,24]

Ophthalmoscope Examination

The ophthalmoscope is used to look at the fundus, optic nerve, disc, and the major blood vessels (Fig. 10-2). If possible, dim the lights to allow the patient's pupil to dilate, or the physician may dilate the pupil with either an ophthalmic sympathomimetic or a cycloplegic agent. Sympathomimetic agents stimulate the dilator muscle of the iris, whereas the cycloplegic agents block the parasympathetic stimulus that constricts the iris. Cycloplegic agents stop the ciliary muscle from contracting.[3,24,25] If the patient is having a difficult time keeping his or her eyes open, topical anesthetics may be used. It is important to note that these medications are not sent home with the patient since use without medical supervision puts the patient at risk for inhibited corneal healing.

Figure 10-6. Slit Lamp

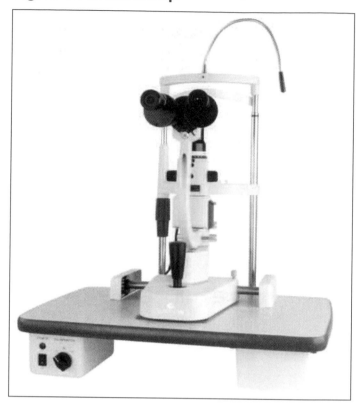

Image courtesy of US Ophthalmic.

Intraocular Pressure Measurement

IOP is fairly stable; however, if the production of aqueous humor exceeds the outflow in cases such as glaucoma and hyphema, IOP is increased. The opposite, or decreased IOP, results from a decrease in the production of fluid or by a disruption in the globe. IOP measurement is routinely performed in patients who have loss of vision, suspected glaucoma, or blunt trauma. Normal pressure readings are between 10 and 20 mm Hg.[19,20,22,23] IOP measurement is contraindicated for patients suspected of globe rupture or with penetrating trauma.

IOP is measured using a tonometer. Types of tonometry include:

- *Electronic indentation tonometry* (Tono-pen) (Fig. 10-7): This is an electronic device that uses a disposable latex cover. The Tono-pen is touched to the cornea three to four times and the findings are averaged. This device can be difficult to use. Prior to the procedure, anesthetic drops are administered as prescribed.

- *Applanation tonometry* (Goldmann applanation): This procedure is used by most ophthalmologists and optometrists and is usually found on the slit lamp[19,20,22,23,26,27]

Figure 10-7. Electronic Indentation Tonometry (Tono-pen)

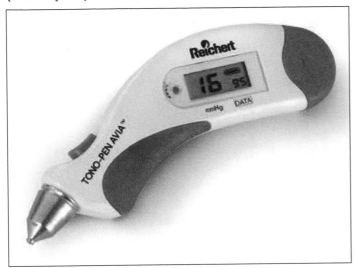

Image courtesy of Reichert Technologies.

- *Impression tonometry* (Direct Schiotz tonometer): This device places a small plunger onto the cornea for measurement. It is not commonly used due to difficulty with sterilization and questionable accuracy.

Selected Eye Emergencies

Lid Injury

With any eyelid injury, inspect the eye for concurrent injuries such as hyphema, globe rupture, and corneal abrasion. The literature reports that lacerations requiring a specialist can be closed up to 48 hours after the initial injury without adverse effects.[18,20,28-30] Obtain an ophthalmology consultation for lacerations to the following:

- Lacrimal area
- Lid margins
- Inner surface of the eyelids and those involving the tarsal plate
- Muscular structures

Complications from an improperly closed lid laceration include:[18,20,28-30]

- Ptosis
- Notched lid margins
- Trichiasis (misdirected eyelashes)
- Lagophthalmos (incomplete eye closure)
- Corneal exposure

Corneal Injury

Corneal Abrasion

A corneal abrasion is damage to the corneal epithelium, which is highly innervated and results in a great deal of pain. Corneal abrasions are frequently seen in the emergency department and can be caused by objects such as contact lenses, fingernails, and environmental debris. If the injury is work related, the patient may be at high risk for globe penetration due to a high-speed foreign body. Abrasions are relatively easy to see once the eye is stained with fluorescein.[18-20,31]

Assessment findings include:

- Photophobia and tearing
- Pain
- Injected conjunctiva or redness of the eye
- Lid swelling
- Complaint of a foreign body sensation in the eye

Treatment includes:[19]

- Topical ophthalmic antibiotics
  - If caused by contact lenses, treat for *Pseudomonas*
- Cycloplegic ophthalmic agent to decrease spasms and pain
- Topical ophthalmic nonsteroidal anti-inflammatory drugs (NSAIDs), such as ketorolac or diclofenac, to reduce swelling
- Oral analgesics
- No patching; evidence shows abrasions heal faster if unpatched[32]
- Follow-up with an ophthalmologist in 24 hours

Corneal Laceration

Corneal lacerations involve one or more layers of the cornea. A slit lamp is used to visualize the cornea, as small lacerations can be easily missed. Treat small corneal lacerations similarly to a corneal abrasion. Larger lacerations need referral and possible surgery.[19,20,22] Undiagnosed corneal lacerations can result in traumatic cataracts and decreased vision.

Assessment findings include:

- Pain out of proportion to findings (small lacerations may spontaneously close and will be difficult to find)
- Decreased vision
- Symptoms similar to corneal abrasion

Treatment includes:
- Obtaining an ophthalmologic consult
- Administering ophthalmic medications similar to those for corneal abrasion

Corneal Foreign Bodies

Corneal foreign bodies routinely consist of metal, plastic, or wood. They are usually superficial and can be easily removed. Assess for the potential of a high-speed foreign body and penetration of the globe. The assessment findings for foreign bodies are similar to corneal abrasion, and removal may result in a corneal abrasion.[18–20,22]

Assessment findings include:
- Photophobia and tearing
- Pain
- Injected conjunctiva
- Lid swelling

Treatment includes:
- Administering topical anesthetic
- Removing a foreign body
- Use of discharge medications including:
  - Topical ophthalmic antibiotics
  - Cycloplegics
  - Oral analgesia

Intraocular Foreign Body

An intraocular foreign body is considered a true eye emergency, and early intervention is essential. It is important to determine the composition of the foreign body (metallic, wood, or vegetative) to assist in determining what type of diagnostic testing and treatment are needed.

Assessment findings include:
- Compromised visual acuity
- Pain
- Misshapen pupils (possible)

Interventions:[33]
- Elevating the head of the bed
- Obtaining an ophthalmologic consult
- Immobilizing the foreign body if it is large with potential to become unstable
- Limit concomitant eye movement by patching the unaffected eye
- Performing globe closure as soon as possible[20]

- Administering systemic and topical ophthalmic antibiotics
- Administering systemic analgesics

Postoperative infection, vision loss, and retinal detachment are common complications associated with intraocular foreign bodies.[33]

Blunt Trauma to Orbit

Periorbital Contusion (Black Eye)

Use eyelid retractors to open the eye if necessary (this ensures there is no pressure on the globe). Assess the anterior chamber. A flat appearance may be indicative of a globe rupture. A head and neck computed tomography (CT) scan may be indicated to rule out concomitant injuries based on the mechanism of injury and symptoms. An orbital CT may be indicated to accurately evaluate orbital injuries.[33]

Assessment findings include:
- Eyelid swelling and bruising initially with ecchymosis developing later
- Decreased vision secondary to swelling
- Pain
- Possible hyphema
- Decreased EOM secondary to *blowout fracture* (a fracture of the orbital floor that can cause muscle and or nerve entrapment)[19]

Interventions:[18–20,22]
- Elevating the head of the bed
- Applying cold compresses
- Providing pain management
- Informing the patient that it may take two to three weeks to resolve the injury

Orbital Fracture

Orbital fractures are usually a result of a direct blow to the eye. The orbital floor and ethmoid bones are the weakest parts of the orbit and at high risk for fracture.[18–20,22] A complication of this type of fracture is entrapment of the inferior rectus or inferior oblique muscle.[18,19] Orbital fractures are not considered an ophthalmologic emergency unless there is impaired vision or globe rupture.

Assessment findings include:
- Periorbital ecchymosis
- Diplopia
- Enophthalmos
- Infraorbital numbness
- Decreased EOM

Treatment includes:

- Oral antibiotics
- Cool compresses
- Ophthalmologic consultation with possible surgical repair if the patient continues to have diplopia or enophthalmos 1 to 2 weeks after swelling has decreased
- Discharge instruction including advising the patient to avoid blowing the nose, sneezing, and/or performing a Valsalva maneuver (bearing down)

Hyphema

Hyphema is a collection of blood in the anterior chamber of the eye classified as traumatic or spontaneous. Hyphemas are graded 1 to 4 based on the amount of blood present in the chamber. Table 10-3 describes the hyphema grading system.[18–20,22]

Assessment findings include:

- Pain and photophobia
- Noticeable collection of blood in the anterior chamber
- Blurry vision (due to blood in the anterior chamber)
- Increased IOP, nausea, and severe pain with grade 4 hyphema

Treatment includes:[19]

- Elevating the head of the bed to 30 degrees
- Protecting the eye with a metal shield
- Providing pain management
- Topical ophthalmic cycloplegics and ophthalmic steroids, ophthalmic beta-blockers if IOP is elevated
- Recommended admission if the hyphema is greater than 30% (most patients discharged with close follow-up recommended)
  - Instruct the patient to avoid aspirin and nonsteroidal anti inflammatory drugs (NSAIDs) as they increase the risk for re-bleeding
  - The risk for re-bleed is greatest three to five days after injury

Retrobulbar Hematoma

Retrobulbar hematoma is a rare occurrence secondary to blunt trauma. It is a hemorrhage into the retrobulbar space (behind the globe) that occurs in a small percentage of patients with non-displaced orbital fractures. Bleeding causes increased pressure behind the globe, which causes an elevation in IOP that compresses the optic nerve and blood vessels. Early recognition is imperative to save vision.[18–20,22] This is a true ophthalmologic emergency.

Table 10-3. Grading Traumatic Hyphema

Grade	Type of Trauma
Grade 1	Blood occupying less than one third of the anterior chamber
Grade 2	Blood occupying ⅓ to ½ of the anterior chamber
Grade 3	Blood occupying ½ but less than total filling of the anterior chamber
Grade 4	Blood occupying the entire anterior chamber

Data from Firat, P. G., Doganay, S., Cumurcu, T., Demirel, S., & Kutukde, D. (2012). Anterior segment complications in ocular contusion. *Journal of Trauma and Treatment, 1*, 101. doi:10.4172/jtm.1000101

Assessment findings include:

- Severe pain
- Decreased vision
- Reduced eye movement
- IOP greater than 40 mm Hg

Treatment includes:

- Emergency decompression via lateral canthotomy indicated with IOP greater than 40 mm Hg

Globe Rupture

When a full thickness injury occurs to the cornea or sclera, or both, it is termed a *globe rupture* and considered a genuine emergency. Once the diagnosis is confirmed, it is important to protect the area from further injury.[28] The most common area of rupture is at the limbus, where the sclera is the thinnest.[18–20,22,29]

Assessment findings include:

- Anterior chamber appearing flat or shallow
- Irregular or teardrop-shaped pupils or the presence of what looks like a secondary pupil due to a tear in the ciliary body (referred to as traumatic iridodialysis)
- Periorbital ecchymosis
- Decreased visual acuity and EOM
- Severe subconjunctival hemorrhage
- Nausea
- Pain that may be difficult to assess depending on patient condition and MOI

Treatment includes:
- Avoidance of any type of pressure on the globe—do not perform tonometry
- Application of a rigid shield to protect the affected eye[28,34]
- Administration of antiemetics to decrease the risk for vomiting, which increases IOP
- Avoiding the use of ophthalmic drops or medications[34]
- Consultation by ophthalmology

Ocular Burns

Ocular burns can be the result of chemical, thermal, or radiant sources, and chemical burns are considered a true emergency. Saving the eyesight requires immediate irrigation of the eye. It takes precedence over completion of a history, pH of the eye, and thorough assessment.[35] Alkaline products cause liquefaction necrosis and produce burns that are deeper than acid burns. Acidic burns are less severe, causing immediate damage through coagulation necrosis, which ultimately forms a barrier to deeper penetration. See Table 10-4 for common chemical agents.[17,19,22]

Table 10-4. Common Chemical Products

Alkalis
• Lye
• Oven cleaner
• Ammonia
• Dishwasher detergent
• Calcium carbonate
• Sodium or potassium hydroxide
• Ammonium hydroxide
• Sodium tripolyphosphate

Acids
• Toilet cleaner
• Pool cleaners
• Vinegar
• Rust removal agents
• Sulfuric acid
• Sodium hypochlorite
• Acetic acid
• Hydrofluoric acid

Data from Spector & Fernandez.[17]

Assessment findings include:
- Chemosis (swelling of the sclera)
- Conjunctival irritation
- Corneal clouding (opacification of the cornea indicating a severe burn)
- Pain

Treatment and reevaluation includes:
- Irrigating the area until pH returns to normal range—depending on exposure severity, alkaline burns may require at least 2 L of irrigation
- Determining a baseline pH of the eye—normal is 7.0 to 7.3 or neutral[353]
- Administering topical ophthalmic antibiotics and cycloplegics
- Administering tetracaine drops for pain
- Visual acuity reassessment

Ultraviolet Keratitis

Ultraviolet keratitis, a radiation burn also known as welder's burn or snow blindness, occurs when ultraviolet lights absorbed by the cornea cause damage to corneal epithelial cells. This damage produces keratitis, conjunctivitis, or both. Effects are usually cumulative, and it may take up to two days before the patient experiences symptoms.[17,19,22]

Assessment findings include:
- Severe pain and photophobia
- Conjunctival irritation and tearing
- Decreased visual acuity

Treatment includes:
- Topical ophthalmic antibiotics
- Cycloplegics
- Oral analgesics

General Nursing Interventions

General nursing interventions for ocular trauma include the following:
- If foreign body penetrates the globe, stabilize and immobilize
- Elevate the head of the bed to decrease IOP
- Assist with procedures and administer medications as directed
- Update the patient's tetanus status

Selected Ocular Interventions

Foreign Body Immobilization

If a foreign body penetrates the globe, stabilize and immobilize the object until it can be removed during surgery. Take care to avoid applying any pressure to the globe. Place a protective shield over the eye or stabilize with fluff dressings or shields made specifically for this purpose. Consider patching the unaffected eye to prevent consensual movement.[23,24]

Foreign Body Removal

Foreign body removal is a common problem in the ED. This can be a simple or complex procedure. Assess the eye for perforation and determine if the foreign body is easily visible. MOI is helpful in determining the probability of an intraocular penetrating foreign body. If the patient says he or she felt something in the eye after rubbing it or that something fell or blew into the eye, he or she is at low risk for a globe penetrating injury. The patient who presents with a MOI of grinding metal or other materials, blast injury, or any other mechanism that is considered high velocity is at a greater risk for having a penetrating injury.[23,24]

The results of the physical examination may help to determine whether the foreign body is superficial or has penetrated the cornea. Symptoms that usually indicate an intraocular foreign body are irregular pupil, shallow anterior chamber, and a positive Seidel test. Pain is not always present with a globe penetration. The slit lamp can be used for magnification when removing a superficial foreign body. Consult an ophthalmologist immediately, and keep the patient calm with the eye protected from any type of pressure if a penetrating intraocular foreign body is suspected. Do not attempt tonometry.[23,24]

To remove a simple foreign body, the physician everts the upper eyelid (Fig. 10-8). If the foreign body is under the eyelid, a moistened cotton-tipped applicator can be used for removal. If the foreign body is imbedded in the cornea, a 25–gauge needle can be used for removal (Fig. 10-9). If the foreign body is metallic and a rust ring is present, an eye spud or Burr drill may be indicated.[23,24]

Contact Lens Removal

Contact lens removal is a simple procedure to perform. Determine whether the lens is hard or soft. Ask the patient to point to where they feel the lens. The patient may think he or she feels the lens when what actually is felt is a corneal abrasion that occurred secondary to trying to remove the lens. If the lens is not readily visible, stain the eye with fluorescein dye to help identify the location. Note that if fluorescein is used, it can permanently stain a soft contact.

Hard contacts can be removed by expulsion (Fig.10-10) or by using a suction cup applicator specifically made for the removal of this type of lens. Soft contacts can be removed by using gloved fingers to squeeze the lens (Fig.10-11). After removing the lens, the patient needs to be assessed for a corneal abrasion and instructed not to wear the contacts until symptoms have resolved or until follow-up examination has confirmed healing.[19,23,24]

Eye Irrigation

Irrigation is used for the removal of chemicals, foreign bodies, and other debris from the eye. It is contraindicated in patients who may have a ruptured globe. Prior to the procedure, check the pH of the eye, and then instill ophthalmic anesthetic drops unless contraindicated. Use either warmed normal saline or Ringer's lactate solution. Solution is warmed only to body temperature 37°C (98.6°F) to limit the risk of thermal injury.[36] A Morgan lens or intravenous tubing may be used to direct flow. Keep in mind that the shorter the tubing, the greater the flow and pressure. When using intravenous tubing, direct the stream across the eye from the inner to the outer canthus of the eye. Irrigation is continued until the pH reaches neutral (7.0–7.3).[37–39]

Reevaluation Adjuncts

Radiographic and Other Diagnostic Procedures

- It is helpful to establish what type of injury and/or foreign body is involved in order to determine the appropriate diagnostic procedure

- Plain films are used to assess for foreign bodies and fractures of the facial structures, excluding orbits

- The gold standard for the evaluation of mid-face and orbit trauma is a CT scan

- A CT scan may be indicated if metallic material is suspected

Figure 10-8. Upper Eyelid Everted Showing Foreign Body

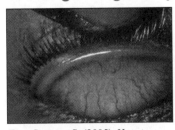

From Stevens, S. (2005). How to evert the upper eyelid and remove a sub-tarsal foreign body. *Community Eye Health Journal, 18*(55), 110.

Figure 10-9. Corneal Foreign Body

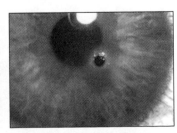

From Stevens, S. (2005). How to remove a corneal foreign body. *Community Eye Health Journal, 18*(55), 110.

Figure 10-10. Removal of Hard Contact Lens

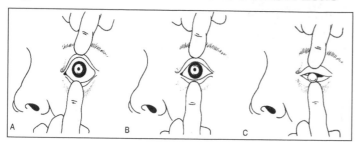

From Egging[19], *with permission.*

Figure 10-11. Removal of Soft Contact Lens

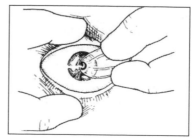

From Egging[19], *with permission.*

- If wood or a vegetative foreign body is suspected, magnetic resonance imaging (MRI) is the most appropriate imaging method to use; however, MRI is minimally useful in the acute setting. Plain films and CT scans are not helpful if vegetative foreign bodies are suspected.[18,20]

Reevaluation

Reevaluation for ocular trauma includes injuries and effectiveness of interventions including:

- Visual acuity

- Pain

Definitive Care or Transport

Definitive care for ocular trauma includes the following:

- Consult or follow-up with ophthalmology

- Discharge teaching

  ○ Educate the patient on the correct method of instilling ocular medication

  ○ Inform the patient of any symptoms that might indicate the need to seek additional care

Summary

Assessment of patients presenting to the emergency department with an ocular complaint include a visual acuity exam, visual inspection, palpation, pupil and EOM assessment, and fundoscopic examination. Further assessment may include fluorescein staining, upper lid eversion, and possible measurement of IOP as indicated. Screen for tetanus and update if necessary. Since ocular injuries may be life-altering, it is important for the emergency nurse to obtain a history, remembering that ocular burns, globe rupture, and retrobulbar hematoma are true emergencies and require immediate assessment and intervention to save the patient's vision. Patient education is essential to minimize further damage and preserve sight.

References

1. Root, T. (2009). Basic eye anatomy. In *OphthoBook: The free ophthalmology textbook*. Retrieved from http://www.ophthobook.com/chapters/anatomy

2. *Rapid review anatomy reference guide: A guide for self testing and memorization* (3rd ed.). (2010). Skokie, IL: Anatomical Chart Company.

3. Robinett, D. A., & Kahn, J. H. (2008). The physical examination of the eye. *Emergency Medicine Clinics of North America, 26*(1), 1–16.

4. Shuster, C. J. (n.d.). *Physiology of vision*. Retrieved from http://faculty.madisoncollege.edu/cshuster/ap1/eye_physiology_handout.pdf

5. Duong, D. K., Leo, M. M., & Mitchell, E. L. (2008). Neuro-ophthalmology. *Emergency Medicine Clinics of North America, 26*(1), 137–180.

6. Gilroy, A. M., MacPherson, B. R., & Ross, L. M. (2008). Orbit & eye. In *Atlas of anatomy* (pp. 506–519). New York, NY: Thieme Medical Publishers.

7. Reeves, A. G., & Swenson, R. S. (2008). Extraocular movement. In *Disorders of the nervous system: A primer*. Hanover, NH: Dartmouth Medical School. Retrieved from http://www.dartmouth.edu/~dons/part_1/chapter_4.html

8. Scruggs, D., Scruggs, R., Stukenborg, G., Netland, P.A., & Calland, J. F. (2012). Ocular injuries in trauma patients: An analysis of 28,340 trauma admissions in the 2003–2007 National Trauma Data Bank National Sample Program. *Journal of Trauma and Acute Care Surgery, 73*(5), 1308–1312.

9. American Academy of Ophthalmology. (2008, July). *Eye injuries: Recent data and trends in the United States*. Retrieved from http://www.aao.org/newsroom/guide/upload/eye-injuries-bkgrnderlongversfinal-l.pdf

10. Weaver, J., & Good, G. (2009). Environmental vision. In *Optometric care within the public health community*. Cadyville, NY: Old Post Publishing. Retrieved from http://webpages.charter.net/oldpostpublishing/oldpostpublishing/Section%202,%20Principles%20of%20Public%20Health/Sect%202,%20Environmental%20Vision%20by%20Weaver%20and%20Good.pdf

11. Owens, P. L., & Mutter, R. (2011, May). *Emergency department visits related to eye injuries, 2008*. (AHRQ statistical brief #112). Retrieved from http://www.hcup-us.ahrq.gov/reports/statbriefs/sb112.pdf

12. American Academy of Ophthalmology. (2009, May). *Eye health statistics at a glance*. Retrieved from http://www.aao.org/newsroom/press_kit/upload/Eye-Health-Statistics-June-2009.pdf

13. Hodge, C., & Lawless, M. (2008). Ocular emergencies. *Australian Family Physician, 37*(7) 506–509.

14. Kuhn, F., Morris, R., Mester, V., & Witherspoon, C. D. (2008). Terminology of mechanical injuries: The Birmingham Eye Trauma Terminology (BETT). In F. Kuhn (Ed.), *Ocular traumatology* (pp. 3–11). New York, NY: Springer.

15. Eye trauma. (2012, June 12). *BMJ Best Practice*. Retrieved from http://bestpractice.bmj.com/best-practice/monograph/961.html

16. Lima-Gomez, V., Blanco-Hernandez, D.,& Rojas-Dosal, J. (2010). Ocular trauma score at the initial evaluation of ocular trauma. *Cirugia y Cirujanos, 78*(3), 209–213.

17. Spector, J., & Fernandez, W. G. (2008). Chemical, thermal, and biological ocular exposures. *Emergency Medicine Clinics of North America, 26*(1), 125–136.

18. Bord, S. P., & Linden, J. (2008).Trauma to the globe and orbit. *Emergency Medicine Clinics of North America, 26*(1), 97–123.

19. Egging, D. (2008). Ocular emergencies. In P. K. Howard & R. A. Steinmann (Eds.), *Sheehy's emergency nursing: Principles and practice* (6th ed., pp. 602–615). St. Louis, MO: Mosby Elsevier.

20. Alteveer, J., & Lahmann, B. (2010). An evidence-based approach to traumatic ocular emergencies. *Emergency Medicine Practice, 12*(5), 1–24.

21. Eggenberger, E. R. (2012, April 3). *Anisocoria*. Retrieved from http://emedicine.medscape.com/article/1158571-overview

22. Walker, R. A., & Adhikari, S. (2011). Eye emergencies. In J. E. Tintinalli, J. Stapczynski, O. J. Ma, D. Cline, R. Cydulka, & G. Meckler (Eds.), *Tintinalli's emergency medicine* (7th ed., pp. 1517–1549). New York, NY: McGraw Hill Medical.

23. Babineau, M. R., & Sanchez, L.D. (2008). Ophthalmologic procedures in the emergency department. *Emergency Medicine Clinics of North America, 26*(1), 17–34.

24. Knopp, K. J., Dennis, W. R., & Hedges, J. R. (2010). Ophthalmologic, otolaryngologic and dental procedures. In J. R. Roberts & J. R. Hedges (Eds.), *Clinical procedures in emergency medicine* (5th ed., pp. 1141–1177). Philadelphia, PA: Saunders.

25. Root, T. (2009). History and physical. In *OphthoBook: The free ophthalmology textbook*. Retrieved from http://www.ophthobook.com/chapters/historyphysical

26. Doherty, M. D., Carrim, Z. I., & O'Neill, D. P. (2012). Diaton tonometry: An assessment of validity and preference against Goldmann tonometry. *Clinical and Experimental Ophthalmology, 40*(4), e171–e175.

27. O'Keefe, K. P. (2011, October 16). Essential ophthalmologic procedures and examination. *American College of Emergency Physicians 2011 Scientific Assembly*. Retrieved from http://webapps.acep.org/sa/Syllabi/SU-101.pdf

28. American College of Surgeons. (2012). Ocular trauma. In *Advanced Trauma Life Support Student Course Manual*. (9th ed., pp. 311–315). Chicago, IL: Author

29. Magauran, B. (2008). Conditions requiring emergency ophthalmologic consultation. *Emergency Medicine Clinics of North America, 26*(1), 233–238.

30. Trott, A. T. (2012). Special anatomic sites. In *Wounds and lacerations emergency: Care and closure* (4th ed., pp. 137-160). Philadelphia, PA: Mosby Elsevier.

31. Dargin, J. M., & Lowenstein, R. A. (2008). The painful eye. *Emergency Medicine Clinics of North America, 26*(1), 199–216.

32. Turner, A., & Rabiu, M. (2006). Patching for corneal abrasion. *Cochrane Database of Systematic Reviews*, (2), CD004764.

33. Carvounis, P. E., & Chu, Y. I. (2013). Eye. In K. L. Mattox, E. E. Moore, & D. V. Feliciano (Eds.), *Trauma* (7th ed., pp. 377–394). New York, NY: McGraw-Hill.

34. Acerra, J., & Golden, D. J. (2012, July 30). *Globe rupture and treatment*. Retrieved from http://emedicine.medscape.com/article/798223-treatment#a1126

35. D'Alessandro, D. (2010, March 22). Why do you check the pH of the eye after chemical exposure? Retrieved from http://www.pediatriceducation.org/2010/03/22/why-do-you-check-the-ph-of-the-eye-after-chemical-exposure/

36. Knoop, K. J., Dennis, W. R., & Hedges, J. R. (2010). Ophthalmologic procedures. In J. R. Roberts & J. R. Hedges (Eds.), *Clinical procedures in emergency medicine* (5th ed., pp. 1141–1177). Philadelphia, PA: Saunders Elsevier.

37. Kiechle, F. L. (Ed.). (2009, May). Q&A: What is the reference range for pH of the eye? *CAP Today*. Retrieved from http://www.cap.org/apps/cap.portal?_nfpb=true&cntvwrPtlt_actionOverride=%2Fportlets%2FcontentViewer%2Fshow&_windowLabel=cntvwrPtlt&cntvwrPtlt%7bactionForm.contentReference%7d=cap_today%2F0509%2F0509_qa.html&_state=maximized&_pageLabel=cntvwr

38. Pokhrel, P. K., & Loftus, S. A. (2007). Ocular emergencies. *American Family Physician, 76*(6), 829–836.

39. Shea, S. S. (2007). Ocular and maxillofacial trauma. In K. S. Hoyt & J. Selfridge-Thomas (Eds.), *Emergency nursing core curriculum* (6th ed., pp. 848–878). St. Louis, MO: Saunders Elsevier.

Chapter 11 • Thoracic and Neck Trauma

Michael W. Day, MSN, RN, CCRN

Objectives

Upon completion of this chapter, the learner will be able to:

1. Describe the mechanisms of injury associated with thoracic and neck trauma.

2. Describe pathophysiologic changes as a basis for assessment of the trauma patient with thoracic and neck injuries.

3. Demonstrate the nursing assessment of the trauma patient with thoracic and neck injuries.

4. Plan appropriate interventions for the trauma patient with thoracic and neck injuries.

5. Evaluate the effectiveness of nursing interventions for the trauma patient with thoracic and neck injuries.

Preface

Knowledge of normal anatomy and physiology serves as a foundation for understanding anatomic derangements and pathophysiologic processes that may result from trauma. Before reading this chapter, it is strongly suggested that the learner review the following material. This material will not be covered in the lectures nor tested directly, but as foundational content, it may be the basis for some test questions and skill evaluation steps.

Anatomy and Physiology of the Thoracic Cavity and Neck

Respiratory System

Three processes transfer oxygen from the atmosphere to the lungs and bloodstream. They include ventilation, diffusion, and perfusion as discussed in Chapter 6, Airway and Ventilation.

The upper airway consists of the nose, oropharynx, larynx, and trachea. The lower airway consists of the bronchi, bronchioles, and alveoli with its associated capillaries.

The thoracic cavity extends from the top of the sternum to the diaphragm and is enclosed by the sternum, ribs, and costal cartilage. The main thoracic structures are the lungs and the mediastinum. The mediastinum is the space between the sternum, thoracic vertebrae, and diaphragm. The heart, pericardium, thoracic aorta, superior and inferior vena cava, phrenic and vagus nerves, and other vascular structures are found within the mediastinum. The correlation of thoracic surface landmarks and the underlying structures are important in the physical assessment of the chest (Fig. 11-1).[1]

Figure 11-1. Chest and Anatomic Landmarks

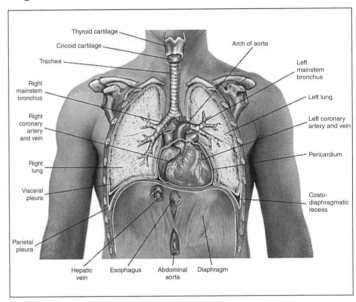

From Seidel, H. M., Ball, J. W., Dains, J. E., & Benedict, G. W. (2006). *Mosby's guide to physical examination* (6th ed.). St. Louis, MO: Mosby.

See Chapter 6, Airway and Ventilation, for a detailed description of the physiology of ventilation.

Heart and Thoracic Great Vessels

The heart is enclosed within the mediastinum, with the right ventricle behind the sternum and the left ventricle anterior to the thoracic vertebrae. The heart is surrounded by the pericardium. The two layers of the pericardium consist of a tough, outer layer and a thinner, serous layer closely adhering to the heart. The space between the two layers contains approximately 25 mL of lubricating pericardial fluid that allows the heart to expand and contract without causing friction against surrounding structures.[1]

Cardiac output is a product of heart rate (HR) and stroke volume (SV) (cardiac output = HR × SV). See Chapter 7, Shock for more information. SV, in turn, is affected by the following:

- Preload: The passive stretching force of the ventricles during diastole, also known as end-diastolic pressure

  ○ Preload is directly related to the amount of blood volume that is returned to the heart

  ○ If there is less volume, the ventricles will not have much stretch, decreasing preload

- Afterload: The resistance of the system (either systemic or pulmonary) that the ventricles must overcome in order to eject blood

  ○ Intrathoracic pressure affects right ventricular pressure as it contracts against the pulmonary system

  ○ The patient's blood pressure and elasticity of the peripheral vasculature affect left ventricular pressure

- Myocardial contractility: The amount of force exerted by contracting ventricles

  ○ Factors affecting myocardial contractility include preload and sympathetic nervous system stimulation

Injury to the myocardium can affect any one of these functions, resulting in decreased cardiac output and the ability to perfuse oxygenated blood to the tissues.

The thoracic aorta carries oxygenated blood from the heart to the body and is located in the mediastinum. The three segments of the thoracic aorta are the ascending aorta, the aortic arch, and the descending aorta (Fig. 11-3). The ascending aorta is the portion located most proximal to the heart. The aortic arch extends from the ascending to the descending thoracic aorta and is the source for both the carotid and subclavian arteries. The descending aorta continues distally from the aortic arch and constricts slightly at the aortic isthmus, where it is held in place by the ligamentum arteriosum, the left mainstem bronchus, and the paired intercostal arteries. The aortic isthmus is the transition from the more mobile aortic arch to the relatively fixed descending aorta and is less able to tolerate rapid acceleration and/or deceleration forces. It is most often the site of aortic injury.[2]

Neck

The neck contains several important anatomic structures relative to its size (Fig. 11-2). It is commonly divided into three zones, based on bony and superficial landmarks (Fig. 11-4):

- Zone I extends from the sternal notch and clavicle up to the cricothyroid cartilage

Figure 11-2. Anatomy of the Neck

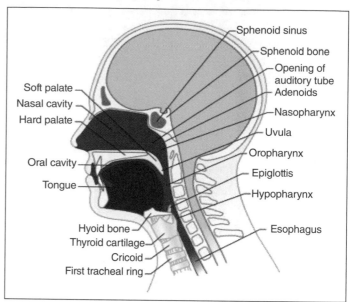

From Miller, R. D., Eriksson, L. I., Fleisher, L., Wiener-Kronish, J. P., & Young, W. L. (2010). *Miller's anesthesia* (7th ed.). Philadelphia, PA: Churchill Livingstone.

Figure 11-3. Anatomy of the Descending and Abdominal Aorta

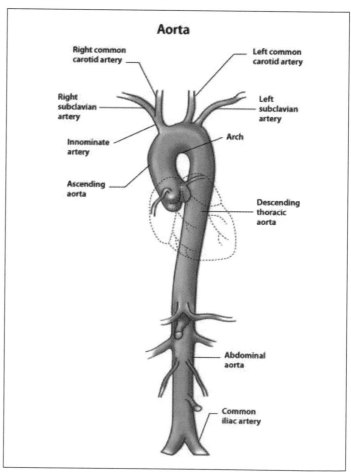

From Lee Memorial Health System. (n.d.). *About your heart: Your aorta.* Retrieved from http://www.leememorial.org/cardiaccare/about/aorta.asp

Figure 11-4. Zones of Neck Injury

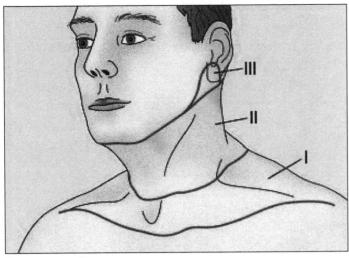

From Gross et al.[20]

- Zone II extends from the cricothyroid cartilage upward to the angle of the mandible
- Zone III extends from the angle of the mandible to the base of the skull

The neck's anatomic structures are contained within two fascial layers. The superficial fascia contains the platysma muscle, which protects the underlying structures. If the platysma is damaged, injury to the structures beneath is suspected. The deep cervical fascia supports the muscles, vessels, and organs of the neck. The compartments formed by the fascia may limit external bleeding but may also allow a hematoma to form, which may compromise the airway.

The vascular supply for the brain and the brain stem arises from the vertebral and internal carotid arteries (Fig. 11-5).

Nerve roots from C5 through T1 merge, forming the brachial plexus, which in turn, subdivides and merges to form the multiple nerves that are responsible for the arm and hand function, such as the axillary, musculocutaneous, median, radial, and ulnar nerves (Fig. 11-6).

Introduction

Epidemiology

Thoracic and neck trauma can cause significant life-threatening injuries necessitating emergent intervention. Motor vehicle collisions (MVCs), involving automobiles, motorcycles, and pedestrians account for over half of blunt injuries to the neck and chest.[3] Penetrating injuries to the neck in adults are most commonly caused by personal assaults with firearms and stabbings.[4] However, in children, most penetrating neck trauma is unintentional, such as falling on sharp objects or MVCs.[4] Interpersonal violence is increasingly a more common cause of thoracic trauma.[4]

Figure 11-5. The Vascular Supply to the Brain

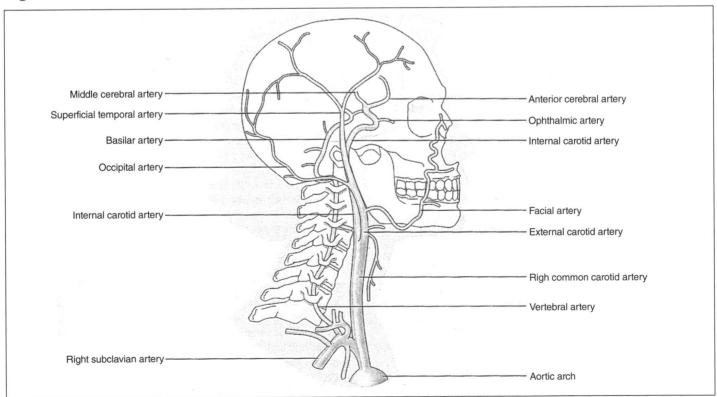

From Copstead, L. E., & Bansik, J. L. (Eds.). (2010). *Pathophysiology* (4th ed.). Philadelphia, PA: Saunders Elsevier.

Figure 11-6. Nerves Responsible for Arm and Hand Functions

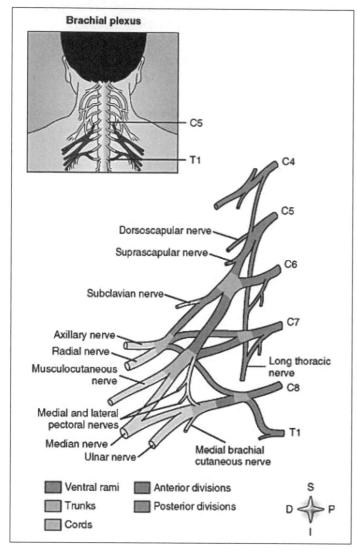

Brachial plexus

C5
T1

Dorsoscapular nerve
Suprascapular nerve
Subclavian nerve
Axillary nerve
Radial nerve
Musculocutaneous nerve
Medial and lateral pectoral nerves
Median nerve
Ulnar nerve

C4
C5
C6
C7
Long thoracic nerve
C8
T1
Medial brachial cutaneous nerve

Ventral rami   Anterior divisions
Trunks   Posterior divisions
Cords

S
D — P
I

From Thibodeau, G. A., & Patton, K. T. (2003). *Anatomy and physiology* (5th ed.). St. Louis, MO: Elsevier Health Sciences.

Biomechanics and Mechanisms of Injury

While MVCs are the most common cause of thoracic trauma, other mechanisms of injury (MOI) include falls, crush injuries, assaults, gunshot and stabbing wounds, and pedestrian-versus-vehicle collisions.[3] Additional considerations include the following:

- Energy forces associated with acceleration and deceleration can result in devastating injury to the major vessels as the body makes impact, yet the internal organs stay in motion. Due to the descending aorta's fixation at the ligamentum arteriosum, it is susceptible to being torn.[2]

- Mechanical energy forces applied to the thorax can cause rib fractures, pulmonary contusion, pneumothorax, hemothorax, and blunt cardiac injury. The sternum and first and second ribs are relatively more resistant to energy forces when they are injured.

As more force is required to damage these structures, there is increased risk of injury to the underlying structures.

- Direct blunt injury to the myocardium may result in ventricular perforation or rupture, and can often be fatal

- Penetrating injury to the heart commonly injures the right ventricle due to its anterior position in the thoracic cavity

Usual Concurrent Injuries

Thoracic injuries are often associated with life-threatening conditions, such as airway disruption, impaired breathing, or impaired circulation. Thoracic trauma is most often associated with head, spine, extremity, and abdominal injuries. Thoracic skeletal injuries are often linked with specific injuries (Table 11-1). Penetrating thoracic trauma can occur with penetrating abdominal trauma due to the movement of the diaphragm in and out of the thoracic cavity. If a penetrating thoracic wound is found below the fourth intercostal space, penetration into the abdominal cavity is suspected until proven otherwise.[5]

Neck injuries may be isolated but may also be associated with head, cervical spine, or upper thoracic injuries. Identifying the specific zone of neck injury is helpful in identifying the potential structures injured, the need for diagnostic studies and the surgical management approach. Injuries to the neck may occlude the airway, interrupt blood flow to the brain, or cause cervical spinal cord injury. Because of the possibility of concurrent cervical spinal injuries, patients with neck injuries are immobilized and assessed for cervical spinal injury.

Pathophysiology as a Basis for Assessment Findings

Ineffective Ventilation

Trauma to the thoracic cavity and structures within can result in ineffective ventilation. Any loss of integrity to the lungs or diaphragm may compromise normal respiration. A punctured lung, pulmonary bleeding, rib and sternal fractures can interfere with the mechanics of breathing, from both increased intrathoracic pressure and pain.

Rib and sternal fractures can also result in damage to underlying organs. Lung contusions cause interstitial and alveolar edema. Lacerations to the lung allow for the accumulation of blood in the interstitial and alveolar spaces. Oxygen and carbon dioxide (CO_2) diffusion across the alveolar membrane is impaired by interstitial and alveolar edema or blood. Damaged alveoli and capillary injuries produce abnormalities in the ventilation to perfusion ratio.[6]

Table 11-1. Thoracic Skeletal Fractures and Associated Injuries

Fractures	Associated Injuries
Sternal fractures	• Blunt cardiac injury
First and second rib fractures	• Great vessel injuries • Brachial plexus injuries • Head and spinal cord injuries
Multiple rib fractures and flail chest	• Pulmonary contusion • Pneumothorax • Hemothorax
Lower rib fractures (7–12)	• Liver (right-sided fractures) • Spleen (left-sided fractures)

Data from Wall et al.[31] and Melendez, S. L., & Doty, C. I. (2012, September 24). *Rib fracture.* Retrieved from http://emedicine.medscape.com/article/825981-overview

Penetrating injury to the chest wall and lacerated lung tissue can cause the loss of normal negative intrapleural pressure. Thus, the collection of air or blood in the pleural space causes lung collapse. The degree of collapse depends on the extent of the air or blood that collects in the pleural space and the severity of the underlying lung injury.

The airway can be easily compromised or occluded due to neck trauma. Edema or hematomas from disrupted blood vessels following a neck injury may narrow or completely obstruct the upper airway. Tears or lacerations of the tracheobronchial tree disrupt the integrity of the upper and lower airway. Patients with these injuries initially present with dramatic symptoms, such as signs of airway obstruction, hemoptysis, cyanosis, and subcutaneous emphysema from massive air leaks into the tissue of the face, chest, and neck.

Ineffective Circulation

Air or blood that continues to accumulate in the thoracic cavity causes an increase in intrapleural pressure on that side of the chest. If this pressure is allowed to expand without intervention, it can produce a mediastinal shift which compresses the heart and great vessels, resulting in a decrease in venous return (preload) and subsequent decrease in cardiac output. The increased pressure can also compress the opposite lung, further decreasing ventilation. The patient usually exhibits signs of increased work of breathing, tachypnea, shortness of breath, tachycardia, hypotension, and a unilateral decrease in breath sounds on the injured side.[7] Neck vein distension from the increased intrathoracic pressure and tracheal deviation caused by the mediastinal shift are late signs and may not be clearly evident.[6]

Injury to the heart or great vessels can be fatal from an immediate uncontrolled hemorrhage. Direct injury to the heart may cause damage to the tissue, reduce myocardial contractility, and ultimately lead to a reduction in cardiac output. The rapid accumulation of even small amounts of blood in the pericardial sac (pericardial tamponade) may result in compression of the heart, making it difficult for the heart to fill during diastole, resulting in decreased cardiac output. Assessment findings include hypotension, tachycardia, muffled heart sounds, and neck vein distension.[8]

Injury to the arteries in the neck causes decreased blood flow to the brain, subsequently producing cerebral hypoxia and neurologic deficits. Penetrating injuries to certain neck vessels (carotid or vertebral arteries or vertebral, brachiocephalic, and jugular veins) may cause rapid exsanguination.

Nursing Care of the Patient with Thoracic or Neck Trauma

Refer to Chapter 5, Initial Assessment, for the systematic approach to the nursing care of the trauma patient. The following assessment parameters are specific to patients with thoracic or neck injuries.

Primary Survey and Resuscitation Adjuncts
A–Airway and Alertness
Assessment
Inspect for:
- Injuries to the neck that may indicate edema or blood in the airway
- Signs of injury that may obstruct or impede the patient's ability to maintain a patent airway
  - Swelling
  - Hematoma
  - Subcutaneous emphysema
  - Impaled objects
  - Lacerations
  - Bleeding
  - Tracheal deviation

Auscultate for:

- Hoarseness or stridor may be signs of tracheal injury and airway narrowing

Interventions

- Apply direct pressure to bleeding sites
- Stabilize any impaled objects
- Prepare to assist with a definitive airway as indicated

Cervical Spinal Stabilization

There is a risk for cervical spinal injury concurrently with neck trauma. Whenever trauma to the neck occurs, take care to immobilize the cervical spine until injury can be ruled out.

B–Breathing and Ventilation

Assessment

Inspect for:

- Chest wall injuries that may severely impair the adequacy of breathing, such as open chest wounds or flail segments
  - May require the removal of debris or blood from the skin to avoid overlooking any wounds
- Breathing effectiveness and rate of respiration
- Symmetrical or paradoxical chest wall movement
- Evidence of blunt or penetrating trauma to the thorax or upper abdomen

Auscultate for:

- Equality of bilateral breath sounds
- Unilateral or generalized diminished breath sounds

Percuss for:

- Dullness or hyperresonance of the chest

Palpate for:

- Tenderness
- Swelling or hematoma
- Subcutaneous emphysema
- Bony crepitus (possible fractured ribs or sternum)
- The suprasternal notch of the trachea to assess for tracheal deviation

Interventions

- Begin administering oxygen at 15 L/min via a closely fitted nonrebreather mask attached to an oxygen reservoir
- As soon as the patient is stabilized, maintain SpO_2 between 94% and 98%[9–12]

- Prepare to monitor and titrate oxygen delivery to maintain normoxia. See Chapter 6, Airway and Ventilation, for information regarding hyperoxia.
- Implement selected interventions based on assessment findings

C–Circulation and Control of Hemorrhage

If there is a high degree of suspicion for cardiac injury. Auscultate for:

- Muffled heart sounds or murmurs

Palpate for:

- Central pulses
  - Compare quality between left and right and lower and upper extremities
- External jugular veins for distention as a potential sign of cardiac tamponade
- Extremities for motor and sensory function
  - Lower extremity paresis or paralysis may indicate an aortic injury[2]

Reevaluation

If assessment findings lead to the suspicion of uncontrolled internal bleeding, a chest radiograph or focused assessment with sonography for trauma (FAST) examination may be indicated. Determine if the patient needs immediate definitive operative intervention or transport.

Chest Radiograph

A supine chest radiograph will likely identify any significant pneumothorax. If a hemothorax is suspected, the position of the patient during the test directly influences the reading. If the patient is supine, blood will likely spread throughout the affected side, creating general opacification. If the patient is upright, the air-fluid boundary will appear horizontally.[13] If a potential spinal cord injury has been ruled out, an upright chest radiograph can be used to evaluate a hemothorax. Chest radiographs may suggest an aortic injury but cannot confirm or rule out the diagnosis.[2]

Focused Assessment with Sonography for Trauma

A FAST examination may be indicated to detect the presence of pericardial blood and heart wall motion. See Chapter 12, Abdominal and Pelvic Trauma, for more information on performing the FAST examination.

Emergency Thoracotomy

An emergency thoracotomy may be necessary when a patient with penetrating chest trauma arrives with unstable vital signs or impending arrest.[1] Indications for performing this invasive procedure in the resuscitation room include a pericardial tamponade necessitating evacuation, immediate control of massive intrathoracic bleeding, penetrating trauma with a witnessed cardiac arrest permitting open cardiac massage, or with massive hemorrhage in the peritoneal cavity necessitating cross-clamping of the aorta.[5] In order to determine the need or success of resuscitative thoracotomy in the emergency department, the American College of Surgeons (ACS) notes that a "qualified" surgeon must be present at the time of the patient's arrival.[5] Emergency thoracotomy is rarely successful in patients with blunt chest trauma.[1]

Secondary Survey and Reevaluation Adjuncts

H–History
Questions specific to patients with thoracic or neck injuries include:

- Is the patient complaining of the following?

  ○ Dyspnea

  ○ Dysphagia

  ○ Dysphonia

- Was there a cardiac event prior to the injury?

- If cardiopulmonary resuscitation (CPR) is being performed, when was it started?

  ○ This information is important in determining the indications for performing an emergency thoracotomy or when to consider withdrawal of support.

Selected Neck and Thoracic Injuries

Tracheobronchial Injury
Tracheobronchial trauma is most likely to be caused by penetrating mechanisms.[14,15] The majority of penetrating injuries occur in the proximal trachea. Direct blows to the neck or clothesline-type injuries are common mechanisms for blunt tracheobronchial trauma. Diagnosis is based on assessment findings and confirmed with bronchoscopy or computed tomography (CT) for large disruptions. Bronchoscopy can be used to help advance an endotracheal tube past the injury to assure adequate ventilation.[16]

Assessment Findings[16]
- Dyspnea, tachypnea

- Hoarseness

- Subcutaneous emphysema in the neck, face or upper thorax

- Pneumothorax, possibly tension pneumothorax

- Hemoptysis

- Decreased or absent breath sounds

- Signs and symptoms of airway obstruction

Interventions
Attempts at endotracheal intubation may cause further injury or contribute to airway occlusion. Anesthesiology, if available, may reduce the risk of intubation injury. Other approaches that may minimize trauma to the airway include flexible endoscopy or a smaller endotracheal tube (ETT).

Blunt Esophageal Injury
Injury to the esophagus is rare as a result of blunt trauma.[17]

Assessment Findings
- Air in the mediastinum with possible widening

- Concurrent left pneumothorax or hemothorax

- Esophageal matter in a chest tube

- Subcutaneous emphysema

Interventions
- Prepare for surgery

Neck Trauma
Neck trauma may result in injuries to airway structures (trachea or larynx), blood vessels (subclavian, jugular, carotid, and vertebral), esophagus, endocrine glands (thyroid and parathyroid), thoracic duct, and brachial plexus. Mechanisms of injury may be either blunt or penetrating. Examples of blunt trauma include direct blows or clothesline-type injury to the neck region. Penetrating trauma may be caused by either sharp instruments or missile injuries (gunshot wounds). Neck trauma may damage significant airway or vascular structures or the spinal column.

Assessment Findings
- Dyspnea, tachypnea

- Hemoptysis (coughing up blood)

- Subcutaneous emphysema (by palpation or auscultation)

- Decreased or absent breath sounds

- Penetrating wounds or impaled objects

- Bruits

- Active external bleeding

- Neurologic deficits, (aphasia or loss of extremity movement or sensation)

- Dysphonia

- Dysphagia

Interventions

- Stabilize any impaled objects
- Control external bleeding with direct pressure
- Continuously monitor for continued bleeding or expanding hematomas
- Prepare for surgery

Rib and Sternal Fractures

Rib fractures are found in 4% to 10% of all hospitalized trauma patients and are one of the most frequent diagnoses in trauma admissions.[18] If the patient has fractures of the right lower ribs, suspect the possibility of underlying injury to the liver, while fractures of the left lower ribs may indicate injuries to the spleen. With any displaced rib fracture, lung contusion or laceration is possible. Sternal fractures are usually caused by a blow to the anterior chest. Due to the force required to fracture the sternum, most of these fractures are not isolated and may be associated with multiple rib or thoracic spine fractures.[19] A severely displaced sternal fracture may indicate serious cardiac injury.

Assessment Findings

- Dyspnea
- Localized pain on movement, palpation, or inspiration
- Patient assumes a position of comfort, which splints the chest wall to reduce pain
- Paradoxical chest wall movement
- Chest wall contusions
- Bony crepitus or deformity

Interventions

- Assess for signs of injury to underlying organs
- Administer supplemental oxygen as needed
- Administer analgesia to promote adequate chest expansion and depth of respiration

Flail Chest

While there is no consensus on the definition, flail chest is often classified as two or more fractures of three or more adjacent ribs and/or sternal fractures, creating a free-floating fractured segment (Fig. 11-7).[16,20,21] This flail segment may move paradoxically, drawing in with chest expansion and pushing out with exhalation. This paradoxical chest movement can be limited by surrounding musculature, making it generally more easily detected with palpation than with inspection.[22] Ineffective ventilation in flail chest is caused by several factors:

- Pain that causes the patient to splint, with rapid, shallow breathing

Figure 11-7. Flail Chest

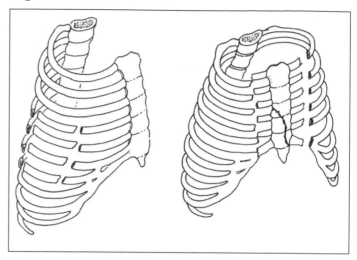

Reprinted from Marx, J. A. (2009). *Rosen's emergency medicine* (7th ed.). St. Louis, MO: Mosby Elsevier.

- Inefficiency of the muscles of respiration as the flail segment pulls in the opposite direction, decreasing tidal volume and secretion removal
- Associated injury from jagged rib fragments, including parenchymal laceration, pulmonary contusion, pneumothorax, or hemothorax

Assessment Findings

- Dyspnea
- Chest wall pain
- Chest wall contusions
- Paradoxical movement of the chest
  - If the patient is splinting as a response to pain, this may be difficult to visualize
  - Once the patient has received pain medication, it may be more visible

Interventions

- Prepare for intubation and ventilator support

Simple Pneumothorax

A simple pneumothorax can be caused by blunt trauma. Air escapes from the injured lung into the pleural space, and negative intrapleural pressure is lost, resulting in a partial or complete collapse of the lung.[16]

Assessment Findings

- Dyspnea, tachypnea
- Tachycardia
- Decreased or absent breath sounds on the injured side
- Chest pain

Interventions

A simple pneumothorax is treated based on the size, presence of symptoms and stability. For those patients who are asymptomatic and stable, observation, with or without oxygen is often adequate. Supplemental oxygen promotes reabsorption of pleural air. For patients with larger pneumothoraces or who are unstable or likely to deteriorate, a chest tube is placed to evacuate the pleural air and maintain the lung expansion.[23]

Open Pneumothorax

An open pneumothorax can be the result of a penetrating wound through the chest wall causing air to be trapped in the intrapleural space. During inspiration air enters the pleural space through the wound, as well as through the trachea.

Assessment Findings

In addition to the assessment findings of a simple pneumothorax, the following may also be present:

- Subcutaneous emphysema (air escaping from the lung into the subcutaneous tissue)

- Chest wound that creates a sucking sound on inspiration

Interventions

- Completely cover open chest wounds with a nonporous dressing (plastic wrap, petroleum jelly gauze) and tape securely on three sides. This measure is temporary with variable effectiveness and definitive repair is completed as quickly as possible in the form of a chest tube and wound closure or surgical repair.[5]

- Monitor for the potential risk of tension pneumothorax

- If signs and symptoms of a tension pneumothorax develop after the application of the dressing, remove the dressing and reevaluate the patient

Tension Pneumothorax

A tension pneumothorax occurs when air enters the intrapleural space but cannot escape on expiration. The increasing intrathoracic pressure causes the lung on the injured side to collapse. If the pressure is not relieved, the mediastinum can shift toward the uninjured side, compressing the heart, great vessels, and ultimately the opposite lung. An alert, responsive patient may be able to compensate for a short time by increasing their respiratory rate, tidal volume, and chest expansion. A sedated and intubated patient may not be able to mount this response. As the intrathoracic pressure rises, venous return is hampered, cardiac output decreases, and hypotension occurs.[19]

Assessment Findings

- Anxiety or severe restlessness

- Severe respiratory distress

- Significantly diminished or absent breath sounds on the injured side

- Hypotension

- Distended neck, head, and upper extremity veins (may not be evident if the patient has experienced significant blood loss)

- Tracheal deviation or a shift toward the uninjured side

- Cyanosis (late sign)

Interventions

- Immediate decompression is indicated for patients who exhibit the assessment findings of a tension pneumothorax. If the patient is relatively stable, an immediate and rapid chest radiograph may confirm the diagnosis.[16]

- Immediately prepare for needle thoracentesis

  ○ A 14-gauge needle is inserted into the second intercostal space in the midclavicular line on the affected side over the top of the rib to avoid the neurovascular bundle that runs under the rib (Fig. 11-8). See "Emerging Trends" for additional information.

- Prepare for chest tube placement, which is the definitive treatment

Figure 11-8. Insertion Sites for Needle Thoracentesis and Chest Tubes

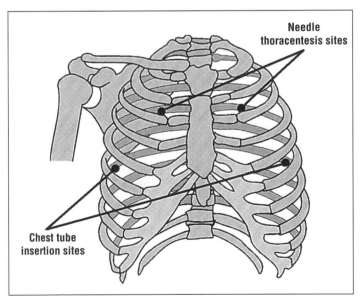

Possible insertion sites for needle thoracentesis and chest tubes.

Hemothorax

A hemothorax is caused by blood accumulating in the intrapleural space. It results from injury to multiple structures including the lung, costal blood vessels, great vessels and other structures. Hemothorax may also result from laceration to the liver or spleen combined with an injury to the diaphragm. A massive hemothorax is defined as the rapid accumulation of more than 1,500 mL of blood in the intrapleural space.[24]

Assessment Findings

- Anxiety or restlessness
- Dyspnea, tachypnea
- Chest pain
- Signs of shock such as tachycardia, cyanosis, diaphoresis, and hypotension
- Decreased breath sounds on the injured side

Interventions

- Prepare for a needle thoracentesis and chest tube insertion
- Ensure two, large-caliber IV catheters are patent and blood is available before thoracentesis to treat large volume blood loss if needed. If immediate open thoracotomy is performed, chest tube insertion is deferred.
- The chest tube is inserted at the fifth intercostal space at the anterior or midaxillary line (Fig. 11-8).[5,25] After the chest tube is inserted, it is connected to a chest drainage system.

Pulmonary Contusion

Pulmonary contusions most commonly occur as a result of a rapid deceleration or direct blunt impact, such as MVCs and falls.[26] A contusion develops when capillary blood leaks into the lung parenchyma, with edema, and inflammation. The contusion may be localized or diffuse. The degree of respiratory insufficiency is related to the size of the contusion, the severity of the injury to the alveolar-capillary membrane, and the development of subsequent atelectasis. The subtle assessment findings associated with pulmonary contusions usually develop over time rather than immediately after injury.[16]

Assessment Findings

- Dyspnea
- Ineffective cough
- Increased work of breathing
- Hypoxia
- Chest pain
- Chest wall contusions or abrasions

Interventions

- Maintain SpO_2 between 94% and 98% for adequate oxygenation and to avoid hyperoxia.[27] See Chapter 6, Airway and Ventilation, for additional information.
- Minimize or use intravenous fluids (IV) judiciously
- Prepare for possible intubation and ventilation support

Blunt Cardiac Injury

Blunt cardiac injury includes myocardial contusion and, less commonly, injury to the ventricular septum, coronary arteries or cardiac valves.[2] This type of injury usually occurs from a direct impact or compression of the thoracic cavity. The majority of blunt cardiac injuries are caused by MVCs, with motorcycle collisions, falls, and blast injuries being other common mechanisms.[28] Maintain a high index of suspicion for blunt cardiac injury in a patient with an abnormally poor cardiovascular response to their injuries.

Assessment Findings

- Electrocardiogram (ECG) abnormalities, including premature ventricular contractions, atrial fibrillation, S-T segment changes, ischemia, or atrioventricular block[18]
- Chest wall contusion
- Chest pain

Interventions

- Monitor the heart rate, and rhythm, and treat dysrhythmias
- Monitor the patient continuously because the signs and symptoms may not be immediately evident

Cardiac Tamponade

Cardiac tamponade is a collection of blood in the pericardial sac. Typically, the MOI for cardiac tamponade is penetrating trauma, but it can also occur with blunt trauma. Blood that collects between the heart and nondistensible pericardial sac, as little as 50 mL, compresses the heart and decreases the ability of the ventricles to fill, subsequently causing decreased SV and cardiac output.[16] The decrease in cardiac output is related to both the amount of blood in the pericardial sac and its rate of accumulation.

Assessment Findings[29]

- Beck triad
  - Hypotension
  - Distended neck veins
  - Muffled heart sounds
    - May be difficult to assess and may be absent[2]
- Chest pain
- Tachycardia or pulseless electrical activity

- Dyspnea

- Cyanosis

- Pulsus paradoxus greater than 10 mm Hg[17]

Interventions

- Prepare for pericardial decompression:

  ◦ A 3- to 4-cm incision is made just to the left of the xiphoid process[2]

  ◦ Needle pericardiocentesis may also be used to relieve the symptoms of cardiac tamponade, but it is only a temporary solution. Any patient experiencing a pericardial tamponade and needing a pericardiocentesis, requires surgical evaluation of the heart.[5]

Aortic Disruption

Injuries to the thoracic aorta are usually caused by blunt trauma but may also be caused by penetrating trauma. The aortic isthmus is the most frequently injured site of the aorta.[18] Deaths from aortic injury most commonly occur at the scene, with mortality rates of 75% to 90%.[2] Of those patients who survive to hospitalization, 75% are hemodynamically stable but up to 50% die prior to repair.[2]

Assessment Findings

- Fractures of the sternum, first or second rib, or scapula

- Cardiac murmurs

- Back or chest pain

- Unequal extremity pulse strength or blood pressure (significantly greater in the upper extremities)

- Hypotension

- Tachycardia

- Skin changes

  ◦ Diaphoresis

  ◦ Pallor

  ◦ Cyanosis

- Paraplegia (due to disruption of spinal perfusion from aortic injury)

- Radiographic findings include:

  ◦ Widened mediastinum

  ◦ Right-sided tracheal deviation

  ◦ Left hemothorax

Interventions

- Prepare for surgery or angiography

- Consider a massive transfusion protocol (see Chapter 7, Shock, for more information)

Ruptured Diaphragm

A ruptured diaphragm is a potentially life-threatening injury. It can be the result of blunt or penetrating trauma, but most commonly occurs from high-speed MVCs.[30] The left hemidiaphragm is more likely to be affected because the right hemidiaphragm is protected by the solid mass of the liver. When the diaphragm is ruptured, the abdominal contents can herniate into the thoracic cavity, compressing the lung and obstructing the patient's ability to take a breath. If left untreated, it may lead to respiratory compromise.[14]

Penetrating trauma below the fourth intercostal space indicates a potential for ruptured diaphragm and concurrent abdominal injury. Without increased awareness and a thorough assessment, this injury may go unrecognized.[14] Penetrating trauma to the lateral chest walls and flanks are also associated with diaphragmatic injuries due to the close proximity, steep slope, and large surface area of the diaphragm.

Assessment Findings

- Dyspnea or orthopnea

- Dysphagia

- Abdominal pain

- Sharp epigastric or chest pain radiating to the left shoulder (Kehr sign)

- Bowel sounds auscultated in the lung fields on the injured side

- Decreased breath sounds on the injured side

Interventions

- Prepare for surgery

Reevaluation

Imaging Studies

- A thoracic CT scan can reveal injuries to the thoracic skeletal structure, pulmonary parenchymal, and the aorta

  ◦ CT angiography scans have replaced aortography for evaluating aortic injures, with sensitivity and negative predictive values approaching 100%[2]

  ◦ Some facilities have the capability to perform a cardiac gated CT. This specialty test is for a more detailed review looking for an aortic injury.[31]

- Bronchoscopy, laryngoscopy, or esophagoscopy may be indicated in certain neck injuries

- Angiography may be used to evaluate suspected vascular injuries in the chest

Other Studies

- ECG to identify possible injury to the myocardium

- An elevated central venous pressure (CVP) may be noted in patients with tension pneumothorax or cardiac tamponade. Patients with hypovolemia may have low CVP.

- Echocardiography provides an accurate assessment of the cardiac function (wall motion, valvular function, estimated cardiac output) and for the presence of pericardial fluid. Transesophageal echocardiography is the most accurate form of this technology.

Chest Drainage Systems

Consider the following when managing a chest drainage system:

- Be familiar with the facility's equipment and policies and procedures due to variations across products

- Cover the insertion site securely with tape. Tape all tubing connections between the patient and the chest drainage system to prevent inadvertent disconnection

- Obtain a chest radiograph to verify correct tube placement

- Maintain the chest drainage system below the level of the chest to facilitate the flow of drainage and prevent reflux back into the pleural space. For those systems with a water seal, keep the collection chamber upright to prevent loss of the water seal.

- Coil the tubing gently on the bed without any dependent loops or kinks, maintaining the collection chamber below the level of the heart[32]

- Assess and document the following using the FOCA mnemonic: **f**luctuation in the water seal chamber, **o**utput, **c**olor of drainage, and the presence of an **a**ir leak

- Troubleshooting for problems should follow the DOPE mnemonic (**d**islodgement, **o**bstruction, **p**neumothorax, **e**quipment failure)

- Notify the physician of the following and anticipate the need for surgery:[3]

  - If the initial chest drainage is greater than 500 mL

  - If there is a continuing blood loss of more than 200 mL per hour for 2 to 4 hours

- During patient transport, clamping of the chest tube is contraindicated since it may cause the development of a tension pneumothorax

Autotransfusion

There are risks inherent in receiving a blood transfusion, including infection and anaphylactic reaction. An alternate method for replacing red blood cells with oxygen-carrying capacity is autotransfusion, or the collection of the one's own blood for reinfusion. There are specific indications and contraindications for autotransfusion and this modality of treatment remains a controversial intervention.[5,33] See Chapter 7, Shock, for more information.

Reevaluation and Post Resuscitation Care

Reevaluation of the patient with thoracic or neck trauma includes monitoring the following:

- Airway patency, respiratory effort, and ventilation adequacy

- Signs of developing tension pneumothorax following the application of an occlusive dressing

- Neck hematomas for signs of expansion

- Vital signs

- Chest tube drainage systems for the amount of drainage and any change in drainage characteristics

- ABGs

Definitive Care or Transport

Prepare for surgery, admission, or transport to a trauma center.

Emerging Trends

As the science and evidence of trauma care continues to evolve, tools to improve patient outcomes continue to be trialed and refined. Evidence is tested and replicated, and new standards of care are transitioned into practice. This section on trauma care considerations explores some of the evidence and the potential significance to trauma patient care. In the care of patients with thoracic and neck trauma, needle decompression placement is discussed.

Needle Decompression Placement

The usual approach to needle decompression is to insert the needle at the second intercostal space, midclavicular line. However, the failure rate using that approach has been reported as high as 58%.[34,35] The failure rate in female patients is also higher due to the thickness of their chest wall.[36] Researchers report that using the placement of fifth intercostal space, anterior axillary line increased the likelihood of success, since the chest wall is commonly thinner in that area.[34–36] Additionally, the length of the catheter contributed to successful decompression. Researchers found that with variations in chest wall thickness based on age, gender, and body mass index, the success rate for needle decompression with the standard 4.5-cm catheter was significantly less than with the 5-cm or 8-cm catheter.[5,34–38]

Summary

Thoracic and neck trauma both have the potential to cause immediate life-threating alterations in airway, breathing and circulation. Understanding the anatomy, mechanism of injury, and pathophysiology related to these injuries can prepare the trauma nurse to accurately and rapidly assess for and proactively and effectively intervene with life-threatening injuries to affect optimal patient outcomes.

References

1. Frawley, P. M. (2009). Thoracic trauma. In K. A. McQuillan, M. B. F. Makic, & E. Whalen (Eds.), *Trauma nursing: From resuscitation through rehabilitation* (4th ed., pp. 614–677), Philadelphia, PA: Elsevier Mosby.

2. Cook, C. C., & Gleason, T. G. (2009). Great vessel and cardiac trauma. *Surgical Clinics of North America, 89,* 797–820.

3. Everson, F. P. (2013). Chest trauma. In Emergency Nurses Association, *Sheehy's manual of emergency care* (7th ed., pp. 407–418). St. Louis, MO: Mosby Elsevier.

4. Mayglothling, J., & Legome, E. (2013, January 4). Initial evaluation and management of penetrating thoracic trauma in adults. *UpToDate.* Retrieved from http://www.uptodate.com/contents/initial-evaluation-and-management-of-penetrating-thoracic-trauma-in-adults

5. American College of Surgeons. (2012). *Advanced trauma life support student course manual* (9th ed.). Chicago, IL: Author.

6. Schumann, L. L. (2013). Respiratory function and alterations in gas exchange. In L. E. Copstead & J. Banasik (Eds.), *Pathophysiology* (5th ed., pp. 449–474). St. Louis, MO: Elsevier Saunders.

7. American Academy of Orthopaedic Surgeons. (2010). *Advanced assessment and treatment of trauma.* Burlington, MA: Jones and Bartlett.

8. Bethel, J. (2008). Tension pneumothorax. *Emergency Nurse, 16*(4), 26–29.

9. Wall, R. M., & Murphy, M. F. (Eds.). (2012). *Manual of emergency airway management* (4th ed.). Philadelphia, PA: Lippincott Williams & Wilkins.

10. Perbedy, M. A., Callaway, C. W., Neumar, R. W., Geocadin, R. G., Zimmerman, J. L., Donnino, M., … Kronick, S. L. (2010). Part 9: Post-cardiac arrest care: 2010 America Heart Association Guidelines for Cardiopulmonary Resuscitation and Emergency Cardiovascular Care. *Circulation, 122*(18 Suppl 3), S768–S786.

11. Kilgannon, J. H., Jones, A. E., Shapiro, N. I., Angelos, M. G., Milcarek, B., Hunter, K., … Trzeciak, S. (2010). Association between arterial hyperoxia following resuscitation from cardiac arrest and in-hospital mortality. *Journal of the American Medical Association, 303*(21), 2165–2171.

12. Brenner, M., Stein, D., Hu, P., Kufera, J., Wooford, M., & Scalea, T. (2012). Association between early hyperoxia and worse outcomes after traumatic brain injury. *Archives of Surgery, 147*(111), 1042–1046.

13. Snaith, B., & Hardy, M. (2012, March). The chest radiograph: trauma and intervention. *Synergy: Imaging, Therapy, and Practice,* 13–18.

14. Morgan, B. S., Watcyn-Jones, T., & Garner, J. P. (2010). Traumatic diaphragmatic injury. *Journal of the Royal Army Medical Corps, 156,* 139–144.

15. Glazer, E. S., & Meyerson, S. L. (2008). Delayed presentation and treatment of tracheobronchial injuries due to blunt trauma. *Journal of Surgical Education, 65*(3), 302–308.

16. Bernardin, B., & Troquet, J. M. (2012). Initial management and resuscitation of severe chest trauma. *Emergency Medicine Clinics of North America, 30*(3), 377–400.

17. Roodenburg, B., & Roodenburg, O. (2011). Chest trauma. *Anaesthesia & Intensive Care Medicine, 12*(9), 390–392.

18. Hossain, M., Ramavath, A., Kulangara, J., & Andrew, J. G. (2010). Current management of isolated sternal fractures in the UK: Time for evidence based practice? A cross-sectional survey and review of literature. *Injury, 41,* 495–498.

19. Molnar, T. F. (2010). Surgical management of chest wall trauma. *Thoracic Surgical Clinics, 20,* 475–485.

20. Gross, K. R., Collier, B. R., Riordan, W. P., & Morris, J. A. (2012). Wilderness trauma and surgical emergencies. In P. S. Auerbach (Ed.), *Wilderness medicine* (6th ed., pp. 411–433). Philadelphia, PA: Elsevier Mosby.

21. Bjerke, H. S. (2012, January 20). *Flail chest.* Retrieved from http://emedicine.medscape.com/article/433779-overview

22. Wilson, B. (2011). Where we have been, where we are now, and where we are going: Preliminary results with operative fixation of flail chest. *Journal of Trauma Nursing, 18*(1), 18–23.

23. Daley, B.J., Bhimji, S., Bascom, R., Benninghoff, M. G., & Alam, S. (2013, June 18). *Pneumothorax*. Retrieved from http://emedicine.medscape.com/article/424547-overview

24. Mowery, N. T., Gunter, O. L., Collier, B. R., Diaz, J. J., Haut, E., Hildreth, A., .. Streib, E. (2011). Practice management guidelines for management of hemothorax and pneumothorax. *The Journal of Trauma, 70,* 510–518.

25. Shlamovitz, G. Z. (2012, May 8). *Tube thoracostomy*. Retrieved from http://emedicine.medscape.com/article/80678-overview

26. Cohn, S. M., & Dubose, J. J. (2010). Pulmonary contusion: An update of recent advances in clinical management. *World Journal of Surgery, 34,* 1959–1970.

27. Moses, S. (2012, June 21). *Oxygen saturation*. Retrieved from http://www.fpnotebook.com/lung/Lab/OxygnStrtn.htm

28. Berg, R., Talving, P., & Inaba, K. (2011). Cardiac rupture following blunt trauma. *Trauma, 13*(1), 35–45.

29. Khandaker, M. H., Espinosa, R. E., Nichimura, R. A., Sinak, L. J., Hayes, S. N., Mellduni, R. M., & Oh, J. K. (2010). Pericardial disease: Diagnosis and management. *Mayo Clinic Proceedings, 85*(6), 572–593.

30. Galketiya, K. P, Kerr, J. N., & Davis, I. P. (2012). Blunt diaphragmatic rupture–a rare injury in blunt thoracoabdominal trauma. *Journal of Gastrointestinal Surgery, 16*(9), 1805–1806.

31. Wall, M. J., Tsai, P.I., Gilani, R., & Mattox, K.L. (2010). Challenges in the diagnosis and management of unusual presentation of blunt injury to the ascending aorta and aortic sinuses. *Journal of Surgical Research, 163*(2), 176–178.

32. Singer, M., & Webb, A. R. (2009). *Oxford handbook of critical care* (3rd ed.). Oxford, United Kingdom: Oxford University Press.

33. Kaplan, L. J., & Maerz, L. L. (2012, June 6). *Transfusion and autotransfusion*. Retrieved from http://emedicine.medscape.com/article/434176-overview

34. Inaba, K., Branco, B., Eckstein, M., Shatz, D., Martin, M., Green, D., … Demetriades, D. (2011). Optimal positioning for emergent needle thoracostomy: A cadaver-based study. *Journal of Trauma, 71*(5), 1099–1103.

35. Inaba, K., Ives, C., McClure, K., Branco, B., Eckstein, M., Shatz, D., … Demetriades, D. (2012). Radiologic evaluation of alternative sites for needle decompression of tension pneumothorax. *Archives of Surgery, 147*(9), 813–818.

36. Zengerink, I., Brink, P., Laupland, K., Raber, E., Zygun, D., & Kortbeek, J. (2008). Needle thoracostomy in the treatment of a tension pneumothorax in trauma patients: What size needle? *Journal of Trauma, 64*(1), 111–114.

37. Sanchez, L.D., Straszewski, S., Saghir, A., Khan, A., Horn, E., Fischer, C., … Camacho, M.A. (2011). Anterior versus lateral needle decompression of tension pneumothorax: Comparison by computed tomography chest wall measurement. *Academic Emergency Medicine, 18,* 1022–1026.

38. Stevens, R. L., Rochester, A. A., Busko, J., Blackwell, T., Schwartz, D., Argenta, A., & Sing, R. F. (2009). Needle thoracostomy for tension pneumothorax: Failure predicted by chest computed tomography. *Prehospital Emergency Care, 13,* 14–17.

Chapter 12 • Abdominal and Pelvic Trauma

Arvie M. Webster, MSN, RN, CEN
Cynthia M. Bratcher, BSN, RN, CEN

Objectives

Upon completion of this chapter, the learner will be able to:

1. Describe the mechanisms of injury associated with abdominal and pelvic trauma.

2. Describe pathophysiologic changes as a basis for the assessment of the trauma patient with abdominal and pelvic injuries.

3. Demonstrate the nursing assessment of the trauma patient with abdominal and pelvic injuries.

4. Plan appropriate interventions for the trauma patient with abdominal and pelvic injuries.

5. Evaluate the effectiveness of nursing interventions for the trauma patient with abdominal and pelvic injuries.

Preface

Knowledge of normal anatomy and physiology serves as a foundation for understanding anatomic derangements and pathophysiologic processes that may result from trauma. Before reading this chapter, it is strongly suggested that the learner review the following material. This material will not be covered in the lectures, nor tested directly, but as foundational content, it may be the basis for some test questions and skill evaluation steps.

Anatomy and Physiology of the Abdomen and Pelvis

Peritoneal Cavity

The peritoneal cavity is located between the parietal peritoneum and visceral peritoneum and contains serous fluid. This fluid lubricates the visceral peritoneum and reduces friction between organs and the peritoneum. It consists of water, proteins, electrolytes, and solutes that are derived from interstitial fluid in adjacent tissues and plasma from local blood vessels.

The peritoneal cavity is closed in males, with the reproductive organs located outside of this space. In females, the cavity contains the fallopian tubes and uterus, communicating to the extraperitoneal space via the vagina.

Abdominal Solid Organs

Liver

The liver is the largest solid organ in the body, weighing approximately 1,200 to 1,600 g.[1] It is located in the right upper quadrant at the level of the sixth to tenth ribs, along the right costal margin under the diaphragm.[1] It is divided into a right and left lobe by the falciform ligament, which also attaches it to the anterior abdominal wall.[1,2] The round ligament is the remnant of the umbilical cord and follows the path of the falciform ligament, attaching the inferior surface of the liver to the umbilicus.[1] The Glisson capsule encases the liver and contains blood vessels, lymphatics, and nerves.[1] In swollen and diseased livers, the capsule enlarges and leaks fluid into the peritoneal space, which is known as *ascites*.[1]

The liver is extremely vascular, receiving blood from both venous and arterial sources. A healthy liver filters about 1.7 L of blood per minute and at any given moment can hold about 13% of the body's blood supply.[3] The hepatic artery branches from the abdominal aorta and provides 400 to 500 mL per minute of oxygenated blood, 25% of total cardiac output.[1] The hepatic portal vein receives venous blood from the small bowel, spleen, pancreas, and stomach. This nutrient-rich, deoxygenated blood accounts for 70%, or 1,000 to 1,200 mL per minute, of blood entering the liver. The liver then filters out toxins, takes the nutrients, and returns the blood to the heart via the hepatic veins.[1]

Hepatocyte cells located within the liver are capable of regeneration, allowing the liver to repair its own damaged tissue. Other cells in the liver store and metabolize lipids, transport nutrients, produce bilirubin and glucose, act as bactericides, convert amino acids to carbohydrates by converting ammonia to urea, and secrete electrolytes, lipids, lecithin, cholesterol, and bile.[1] Metabolized fats within the liver include vitamin K, which is necessary for blood clotting. Other clotting factors produced in the liver are thrombin and fibrinogen.[1]

Spleen

The spleen is the largest of the secondary lymph organs, weighing approximately 150 g.[1] The encapsulated organ is located in the left upper quadrant at the level of the ninth and eleventh ribs and curves around a portion of the stomach.[1] It has several functions including filtering and cleansing the blood, supplying lymphocytes to stimulate an immune response to blood-borne microorganisms, and serving as a blood reservoir.[1] The spleen stores 200 to 300 mL of blood, leading to hemodynamic instability quickly if the organ is damaged.[1] The splenic artery branches from the descending aorta and supplies blood to the spleen.[1] Incoming blood circulates through the spleen's numerous compartments and back to the circulatory system through the splenic vein, which drains into the portal vein.[1]

Presence of the spleen is not necessary for life, but its absence causes several adverse effects on the body.[1] An asplenic patient is at risk for leukocytosis, decreased levels of circulating iron, diminished immunologic response to bacteria, and increased defective blood cell production.[1] In an effort to decrease these adverse effects, surgeons have evolved their practice to salvage the spleen when possible after trauma.[4]

Gallbladder

The gallbladder is a sac-like organ located on the inferior surface of the liver.[1] Its primary function is to store and concentrate bile between meals.[1] It is part of the biliary system and works closely with the liver. Alterations in liver function may create alterations in gallbladder function. Blood in the gallbladder can block the cystic ducts causing acute cholecystitis.[2]

Pancreas

The pancreas is approximately 20 cm long with its head touching the curve of the duodenum and its tail touching the spleen.[1] The middle portion, called the body, is located behind the stomach and in front of the spinal column.[1,5] The pancreas is one of the only organs to have dual endocrine and exocrine function. The endocrine function secretes insulin, glucagon, somatostatin, and pancreatic polypeptide, while the exocrine function secretes alkaline fluids used in digestion.[1] The alkaline secretion neutralizes acidic chyme (partially digested food) from the stomach as it passes into the duodenum.[1] This allows for absorption of fat by the bowel.[1] Secretions from the pancreas drain into a network of ducts leading to the pancreatic duct, emptying into the common bile duct, and finally into the duodenum.[1]

Blood is supplied to the pancreas through branches of the celiac and superior mesenteric arteries (SMAs).[1] Venous blood drains from the pancreatic head via the portal vein, and the body and tail drain via the splenic vein.[1] Hormonal pancreatic secretions, such as insulin, pass through the portal vein to the liver.[1]

Abdominal Hollow Organs
Stomach

The stomach is a hollow, muscular organ and is divided into three portions: the upper, called the fundus; the middle, called the body; and the lower, called the antrum. The stomach's primary responsibility is to aid digestion.[1] It is responsible for storing food, secreting digestive enzymes, and propelling chyme into the duodenum.[1] The stomach is situated in different areas of the abdomen depending on the person's body habitus and body position. When in a supine position, it is located in the intrathoracic abdomen, and it extends into the lower abdomen when standing.[6]

The sympathetic and parasympathetic nervous systems innervate the stomach.[1] The fibers originating from inside the stomach are intrinsic and are stimulated by local stimuli.[1] The fibers originating outside of the stomach are extrinsic and reside in the brain nerve center, which is controlled by the vagus nerve.[1]

Blood is supplied to the stomach through a branch from the celiac artery.[1] It drains from the right side of the stomach through the splenic vein and from the left side through the gastric vein.[1] The acidity of the stomach creates a low-growth bacterial environment; however, medications such as proton pump inhibitors lower gastric acidity and can lead to increased bacterial growth.[6] Patches of bacterial growth and undigested food can increase the risk of perforation and peritoneal contamination.[6]

Small Bowel

Spanning 5 to 6 m in length, the small bowel is divided into three sections: the duodenum, jejunum, and ileum.[1,6] The duodenum begins at the pylorus of the stomach and ends at the ligament of Treitz, which also suspends the jejunum.[1] The end of the jejunum and beginning of the ileum is not marked by a landmark but is identified by an increase in lumen diameter.[6] The ileocecal valve is located at the end of the ileum and controls the flow of digested food into the large bowel.[1]

The duodenum is attached to the posterior abdominal wall in the retroperitoneum.[1] The jejunum and ileum are suspended from the abdominal wall by a membrane called the mesentery.[1] Blood is supplied to the duodenum via the gastroduodenal artery, while the ileum and jejunum are supplied by the SMA, which originates behind the pancreas.[1,6] Parasympathetic nerve fibers regulate secretion, motility, pain sensation, and intestinal reflexes, while sympathetic nerve fibers inhibit motility and cause vasoconstriction.[1]

The primary function of the small bowel is digestion and absorption, which occurs through segmentation and peristalsis. Chyme from the stomach enters the duodenum where pancreatic enzymes, intestinal brush border enzymes, and bile salts combine to aid in digestion.[1] Peristaltic motions at the end of the ileum signal the ileocecal valve to open, permitting chyme to enter the large bowel.[1]

Large Bowel

The large bowel extends approximately 1.5 m and is composed of the cecum, appendix, colon, rectum, and anus.[1] After passing through the ileocecal valve, chyme enters the cecum. From there, it travels through the ascending colon, the transverse colon, the descending colon, and the sigmoid colon through O'Beirne sphincter to the rectum.[1] Waste exits through the internal and then the external anal sphincter.[1] Anaerobic bacteria are located in the colon and assist in the breakdown of food.[7] Finally, the large bowel absorbs the last of the nutrients and reabsorbs any needed water before the waste is expelled from the body.[7]

Pelvis and Pelvic Organs

The pelvis is a ring formed by the sacrum and two innominate bones (Fig. 12-1). Each bone is formed by the fusion of the ilium, ischium, and pubis. They are connected posteriorly to the sacrum at the sacroiliac points and are joined anteriorly at the symphysis pubis. The stability of the pelvis is maintained by ligaments. The pelvis is a weight-bearing structure and provides protection to the lower abdominal and pelvic viscera.

Bladder, Ureters and Urethra

The bladder is a hollow, sac-shaped organ composed of smooth muscle fibers situated in the cradle of the pelvis located anterior to the rectum in both sexes and anterior to the uterus in women.[1] When full, the bladder expands into the abdomen, and when empty, it lies in the pelvic cavity. The urethra serves as a conduit for urine from the bladder, exiting through the meatus. Ureter injuries are rare in blunt trauma. In penetrating trauma, signs of ureter trauma are nonspecific.

Reproductive Organs

In males, reproductive organs are primarily external and include the testes, vas deferens, seminal vesicles, ejaculatory ducts, and the penis as well as the prostate and bulbourethral glands. The scrotum is a pouch of skin that

Figure 12-1. The Pelvis

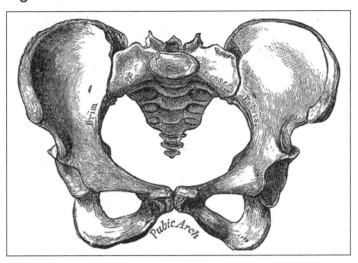

Adapted from Gray, H. (1918). *Gray's anatomy of the human body* (20th ed.). Philadelphia, PA: Lea & Febiger.

contains the testes and parts of the spermatic cords.[8] The prostate gland surrounds the neck of the bladder and part of the urethra. The urethra is longer and more exposed in males, making it more prone to injury than in females. The perineum is that portion between the scrotum and anus.

In females, reproductive organs are internal (uterus, vagina, fallopian tubes, and ovaries) and external (labia, mons, and perineum).[9] The female internal reproductive organs are located in the pelvic cavity and are supported by the pelvic floor. The vagina is thin-walled and can be easily lacerated. Blood supply to the female reproductive organs comes from uterine and ovarian arteries that extend from the internal iliac arteries and aorta. The perineum, the area between the vagina and anus, helps to support the pelvic contents.

Abdominal and Pelvic Vasculature

Abdominal vascular injuries primarily stem from the viscera, the mesentery, and the major abdominal vessels. The four major areas for bleeding are the midline retroperitoneum, the upper lateral retroperitoneum, the pelvic retroperitoneum, and the portal retrohepatic area (Table 12-1).[7] Vascular injuries are common in penetrating abdominal trauma, can cause active hemorrhage, and result in retroperitoneal, mesenteric, or portal hematomas.

Blood loss within the pelvis can be the result of lacerations from fragments of fractured bone or tearing and lacerations to vascular structures. Uncontrolled blood loss may occur from major vessels such as the external iliac arteries. Significant arterial injuries occur in approximately 20% of pelvic fractures.[10] More commonly, bleeding occurs in the hypogastric vascular distribution, which is a rich network of smaller arterial branches in

Table 12-1. Major Sites of Hemorrhage in Abdominal Trauma

Zone 1: Midline Retroperitoneum
• Proximal superior mesenteric artery • Proximal renal artery • Superior mesenteric vein • Infrarenal abdominal aorta • Infrahepatic inferior vena cava
Zone 2: Upper Lateral
• Renal artery • Renal vein
Zone 3: Pelvic
• Iliac artery • Iliac vein
Zone 4: Portal
• Portal vein • Hepatic artery • Retrohepatic vena cava

Data from Dente & Feliciano.[7]

communication with multiple collateral vessels supplying various pelvic structures.

Retroperitoneal Organs

Kidneys

Each kidney is approximately 11 cm long, 5 to 6 cm wide, and surrounded by a capsule.[1] The kidneys are located in the retroperitoneal area along the posterior abdominal wall outside of the peritoneal cavity and on either side of the vertebral column.[1] The poles extend from the twelfth thoracic to the third lumbar vertebrae.[1] The kidneys are responsible for balancing solute and water transport, excretion of metabolic waste, conservation of nutrients, and regulation of acids and bases.[1] The kidneys also act as an endocrine organ because they secrete renin, erythropoietin, and 1,25-dihydroxyvitamin D3—the hormones responsible for blood pressure regulation, production of erythrocytes, and calcium metabolism.[1] Urine is the product of the kidneys after filtration, reabsorption, and secretion of fluid from the glomeruli and tubules.[1]

The kidneys receive 1,000 to 1,200 mL of blood a minute, which is approximately 20% of cardiac output.[1] Twenty percent of plasma filtered from blood at the glomerulus is measured in units of time known as the glomerular filtration rate (GFR). GFR is directly related to renal blood flow, which is autoregulated by intrinsic mechanisms and determines perfusion to other organs in the body.[1] When mean arterial pressure (MAP) drops, blood flow to the kidneys is decreased, which results in decreased renal blood flow and organ perfusion.

Introduction

Hemorrhage continues to be a leading cause of preventable death in the trauma patient.[11] Since the abdomen and pelvis contain a large number of vascular structures, control of internal hemorrhage is a major priority during the assessment of circulation and perfusion. Significant blood loss can be sequestered in the abdominal and pelvic cavities before any obvious signs and symptoms present in the patient. The priority for the trauma nurse is to be proactive and maintain a high index of suspicion for any potential life-threatening injuries in this area.

Epidemiology

The mortality rate resulting from abdominal trauma is 10% to 30%, and hemorrhagic shock is considered a therapeutic emergency.[12] Blunt and penetrating trauma are the most common causes of abdominal trauma; however, the exact frequency of blunt abdominal trauma is unknown.[13] Trauma to hollow viscus organs is more frequently seen along with a severe related injury in a solid organ, particularly the pancreas.[13] According to the National Center for Injury Prevention and Control, penetrating abdominal trauma is present in 35% of patients admitted to urban trauma centers and as many as 12% of those admitted to suburban or rural trauma centers.[14]

Pelvic trauma often results in a fracture. Older adults with pelvic fractures have a 20% mortality rate, and these are often the result of a fall.[15] Pelvic and hip fractures are common injuries after falling, and 37% of these low-impact injuries are severe.[16] Patients with pelvic or hip fractures may have poor outcomes; 25% will never return to their pre-fall health status, and a similar number die within a year of injury.[17]

Mechanisms of Injury

The mechanism of injury (MOI) for abdominal and pelvic trauma is classified as blunt or penetrating. The extent of injuries sustained is associated with the type and strength of force applied and the tissue density and tensile strength of the structure receiving the energy (solid organs vs.

hollow organ vs. vascular structure). Table 12-2 describes common mechanisms of injury in abdominal trauma.

Blunt Trauma

Blunt abdominal and pelvic trauma usually results from motor vehicle collisions (MVCs), falls, and assaults.[18] The most frequently injured organs are the spleen (40% –55%), liver (35%–45%), and small bowel (5%–10%).[19] These MOI cause specific injury patterns to the various organs. These include the following:

- Lacerations to the solid organs[18,20]

  - Encapsulated organs—such as the liver, spleen, and kidneys—are more likely to lacerate due to their semi-elastic capsule[20]

  - The pancreas is prone to lacerations in blunt trauma from a compression injury due to the location in the body[19]

- Rupture of air-filled hollow organs—such as the stomach, small bowel, large bowel, uterus, and bladder—can be the result of a sudden increase in intra-abdominal pressure[18,20]

- Tearing or shearing from sudden deceleration or acceleration force causing extreme stress on fixed sites in the abdomen can result in injury. Those relatively unyielding fixed sites succumb to the force and result in a tearing or avulsion injury.

  - Organs most susceptible to this type of injury include the small bowel, large bowel, ureters, urethra, and esophagus[20]

  - Examples include lacerations of the liver and spleen where the supporting ligaments are fixed to their abdominal structures[19]

  - Also prone to injury are multiple vascular sites such as vessels of the kidneys and liver[18]

- Fractures of the pelvis occur as a result of a fall or MVC

  - Closed lateral compression forces resulting from a MVC can cause internal rotation of the pelvis.[19] Incidence is approximately 60% to 70%.[19]

  - Open book fracture occurs as a result of anterior-posterior compression forces resulting from a direct crush, vehicle-versus-pedestrian collision, or fall from a height of more than 12 feet in adults. Incidence is about 15% to 20%.[19] This type of fracture can cause opening of the pelvic ring, tearing of the vascular venous complex or the internal iliac artery, and uncontrolled hemorrhage.[19]

Penetrating Trauma

Penetrating trauma is usually the result of gunshot wounds (GSWs) or stab wounds but can also occur due to impaled foreign bodies from blasts or explosions that can penetrate the body when under enough force.[19] See Chapter 4, Biomechanics, Kinematics, and Mechanisms of Injury, for more information. Penetrating injuries can be further classified as low-velocity or high-velocity.

- Stab wounds and low-velocity GSWs cause tissue damage by lacerating and cutting and create a tract of damage from the missile. About 60% of these wounds penetrate into the peritoneal cavity.[21]

- High-velocity GSWs result in increased kinetic energy transfer and thus more injury to the abdominal viscera, including missile tract damage, blast tissue damage, and cavitation[21]

- Injuries sustained as a result of GSWs are more likely to require surgical intervention than stab wounds since 85% of anterior GSWs penetrate the peritoneum[21]

  - Any GSW below the nipple line is considered an abdominal injury and requires exploratory laparotomy[22]

  - Stab wounds below the nipple line are assessed on the basis of the patient's hemodynamic stability and/or the presence of fascial penetration to determine if surgical intervention is warranted[19]

  - Wounds are documented according to size and distinguishing characteristics without reference to whether they are entrance or exit wounds[23]

Usual Concurrent Injuries

The abdominal and pelvic cavities are filled with an intricate network of organs, vessels, and other structures. Blunt or penetrating force to one area of the abdomen or pelvis often results in injury to more than one organ, vessel, or structure.[24] Concurrent injuries may include:

- Thoracic injuries due to the adjacent anatomic structures[19]

  - Any injury sustained from the nipple line to the inguinal crease raises concern for both abdominal and thoracic injuries, especially in penetrating trauma

  - Injuries to the aorta may include injuries to both thoracic and abdominal structures

- Diaphragm injuries in penetrating trauma to the abdomen

- Liver and spleen injuries from fractured ribs

- Lower extremity fractures: Common in high-energy blunt force trauma

Table 12-2. Abdominal and Pelvic Mechanism of Injury History with Implications for Injury

Type of Mechanism	History Questions	Implication for Injury
MVC	What was the type of crash? • Lateral impact (T-bone) • Rear end • Frontal	Provide further clues regarding suspected concurrent injuries

	• Was the patient restrained?
	• What type of restraint?
	  ◦ Lap belt
	  ◦ Lap belt and shoulder harness
	  ◦ Airbag deployment
	• Was it properly positioned?
		Improper placement may cause compression and rupture of hollow organs and vasculature, as well as laceration of solid organs

	Was the patient ejected?	• Ejection from a compartment may cause penetrating injury in addition to blunt injury. Rapid deceleration can cause vessels to stretch and shear, causing tears, dissection, rupture, or aneurysm formation. • Acceleration injuries can result in a hyperextension of the neck, producing "whiplash" type injuries
	What was the speed of the vehicle?	Speed will influence the severity of injuries
	• What was the extent of vehicular damage? • How long was extrication?	Extent of damage and length of extrication give an indication of the amount of energy transferred into the passenger compartment and ultimately the patient's body
	What was the patient's location within the vehicle?	Location together with extent and type of crash give clues for body position and areas possibly injured

Note: MVC indicates motor vehicle collision; GSW, gunshot wound.

Table 12-2. Abdominal and Pelvic Mechanism of Injury History with Implications for Injury (Continued)

Type of Mechanism	History Questions	Implication for Injury
Falls	How far did the patient fall?	Falls from heights over 3 times the height of a child or 12 to 20 feet for an adult are associated with increased injury severity and may require transfer to a trauma center
	On what type of surface did the patient land?	Type of surface gives indication of severity of energy impact
	What body part was the point of impact?	The body part impacted will be the focal point of assessment. If the patient landed on his or her feet, energy will be transferred from the feet through the entire body to the head.
Assault/Struck by an Object	Where on the body was the patient struck?	Location of the point of impact will be the focus of the assessment
	Has the patient undergone bariatric or other abdominal/pelvic surgery?	Previous surgery to the abdomen may have weakened the musculature and the protection they provide
Penetrating Trauma	What type of weapon or object was used?	Stab wounds traverse adjacent structures
	• In GSWs, what was the distance from the assailant? What was the caliber and velocity of the weapon? Was special ammunition used, such as exploding, armor-piercing, or buckshot? • What was the estimated blood loss at the scene?	GSWs may cause additional injuries based on their trajectory, cavitation effect, and bullet fragmentation[18]

Note: MVC indicates motor vehicle collision; GSW, gunshot wound.

- Pelvic fractures: Frequently associated with injuries to the pelvic organs and accompanied by hemorrhage in the highly vascular structures of the abdomen and pelvis

Pathophysiology as a Basis for Assessment Findings

Hemorrhage

Injuries to the abdominal and pelvic organs and vasculature can cause significant bleeding and uncontrolled hemorrhage. It is important to quickly identify the source of bleeding and control the hemorrhage in order to save the patient's life. Abdominal distention may be an indication of bleeding into the peritoneal cavity. Since several liters of blood are required to affect abdominal girth, distention may be a late sign of uncontrolled internal hemorrhage.[25]

Pressure from bleeding in the encapsulated, highly vascular spleen and liver may cause rupture, which leads to uncontrolled hemorrhage and change in the contour of the abdomen. The lower portion of the aorta may be torn, resulting in absence of pulses in the lower extremities. The very vascular venous plexus in the pelvis may be torn as a result of acceleration/deceleration energy forces, resulting in uncontrolled internal hemorrhage and initiation of the body's compensatory mechanisms. See Chapter 7, Shock, for more information.

Pain

Pain can influence the trauma nurse's ability to determine an accurate assessment of the abdomen. Pain, rigidity, and guarding or spasms of the abdominal musculature are classic signs of intra-abdominal pathology.[18]

Sudden movement of the irritated peritoneal membranes against the abdominal wall produces rebound tenderness and patient guarding. Causes of peritoneal membrane irritation include:

- The presence of blood
- Chemical peritonitis as a result of leakage of gastric contents
- Possible enzyme spillage from the pancreas into the bowel and/or peritoneal cavity
- Bacterial contamination from bowel contents

Chemical, bacterial, or enzyme leakage into the peritoneum can result in damage to surrounding tissues, leading to inflammation, necrosis, and tissue death.

Referred Pain

Pain travels along nerve pathways (see Chapter 8, Pain, for more information) and may result in pain that is referred to a different body part. Classic examples include:

- Pain radiating to the left shoulder (Kehr sign)
- Pain referred to the testicle that may be indicative of duodenal injury
- Pain that may be referred from one quadrant of the abdomen to another during palpation, making it important to begin palpation away from the initial site of pain and assessing the painful area last

Nursing Care of the Patient with Abdominal and/or Pelvic Trauma

Primary Survey

Complete the primary survey and address any life-threatening injuries before proceeding to the physical assessment of the abdomen and pelvis during the head-to-toe assessment of the secondary survey. However, the assessment of circulation during the primary survey includes early evaluation of suspected uncontrolled internal hemorrhage in the abdomen and pelvis.[19] In those cases, an emergent abdominal or pelvic assessment may be performed to include a radiograph of the pelvis and/or a focused assessment with sonography for trauma (FAST) examination.[19]

See Chapter 5, Initial Assessment for the systematic approach to the nursing care of the trauma patient. The following assessment parameters are specific to abdominal or pelvic injuries.

Resuscitation Adjuncts

A drop in serial hemoglobin and hematocrit (H&H) may indicate ongoing bleeding. Monitor coagulation studies throughout massive blood transfusions to guide indications for blood component administration. If the patient is receiving massive transfusions, it is important to monitor electrolytes, particularly potassium and calcium since they can be affected by the administration of banked blood. Causes of these electrolyte disturbances are:

- Potassium is released from cellular destruction that occurs naturally as banked blood ages. As potassium is predominately an intracellular ion, serum potassium levels rise.
- Calcium citrate is used in banked blood to prevent clotting. This citrate binds with free calcium reducing serum levels.

Secondary Survey
H–Head-to-toe Assessment
Inspect for:

- Asymmetry, abnormal contour, and abdominal distention of the abdominal wall

- Pooling on the side on which the patient is lying due to gravity (if the patient is in a supine position, the blood will start to pool in the retroperitoneal space)

- Location of contusions, abrasions, open wounds, or lacerations to provide a clue to underlying injuries

    - In GSWs, observe for signs of a retained projectile

    - Lap belt ecchymosis (seatbelt sign) is associated in 20% of mesenteric, bowel, and lumbar spine injuries[25]

    - Periumbilical ecchymosis (Cullen's sign) and flank ecchymosis (Grey Turner's sign) are late indicators of retroperitoneal bleeding[25]

- Presence of spasm or involuntary guarding

- Presence of blood at the urinary meatus and/or perineal ecchymosis

Auscultate for:

- Bowel sounds for presence, hypoactivity, and absence

    - Bowel sounds may be decreased and/or absent when fluid or blood irritates the peritoneum[18]

    - Diminished bowel sounds raise an index of suspicion for intra-abdominal bleeding[18]

Percuss for:

- Dullness over solid organs, such as the liver, and hyperresonance over hollow organs, such as the stomach

- Abnormal findings

    - Dullness in the hollow organs, which may indicate fluid or a solid mass

    - Hyperresonance, which indicates air over solid organs

    - Tenderness upon percussion, which is a peritoneal sign and requires further evaluation[25]

Palpate for:

- Bilateral femoral pulses for presence and symmetry

- Pelvic stability

    - In obvious pelvic fractures, testing for stability is deferred[19]

    - Gentle pressure over the iliac wings downward and medially reveals laxity or instability[19]

    - Apply pressure only once, since any movement can result in further hemorrhage[19]

- Rectal examination

    - This may reveal a high-riding prostate. Classic presentation for urethral injuries in males is blood in the urinary meatus, a high-riding prostate, or a scrotal hematoma. Absence of these signs does not rule out a urethral injury.[10]

General Interventions for All Patients with Abdominal and Pelvic Trauma

- Begin hemodynamic monitoring for patients with suspected abdominal or pelvic trauma

- Anticipate blood transfusions and balanced volume resuscitation. See Chapter 7, Shock, for more information.

- Avoid insertion of a urinary catheter if there is any sign of urethral injury, including blood at the urethral meatus or any difficulty in passing the catheter.[26] See Chapter 5, Initial Assessment, for additional information.

Selected Abdominal Injuries

Selected abdominal injuries are described below and outlined in Table 12-3.

Hepatic Injuries

The size, location, and vascular composition of the liver make it the most frequently injured organ in the abdomen as a result of blunt and penetrating mechanisms combined.[2] In blunt trauma, the organ may lacerate from increased abdominal pressure. Bleeding may be contained by the capsule encasing the liver, resulting in a hematoma, or the capsule may be disrupted, resulting in a laceration. The hematoma or laceration is graded to demonstrate the extent of the injury (Table 12-4). Grade I indicates minor trauma, while grade VI is the most severe.[2]

Assessment Findings

- Ecchymosis around the umbilicus (Cullen sign) or in the right upper quadrant

- Tenderness, guarding, or rigidity in the right upper quadrant[21]

- Fractures at ribs nine through 12 on the right side of the body raising suspicion for underlying injury

- Elevated liver function tests (LFTs)

Table 12-3. Selected Abdominal Injuries Assessment, Diagnostics, and Definitive Care

	Liver	Spleen	Pancreas	Small Bowel	Large Bowel & Rectum	Stomach & Esophagus
Assessment						
Inspect abdomen	• Nipple line to mid-abdomen, right side • Lacerations • Abrasions • Contusions • Open wounds	• LUQ • Lacerations • Abrasions • Contusions • Open wounds	• Epigastric area radiating to the back, extending to the LUQ • Pain initially minimal, becoming increasingly worse	• Left side of the abdomen • Lacerations • Abrasions • Contusions • Open wounds	• Pelvic and abdominal areas • Lacerations • Abrasions • Contusions • Open wounds	• Neck, chest, and epigastric area • Lacerations • Abrasions • Contusions • Open wounds
Bowel sounds	Hypoactive or absent	Hypoactive or absent	Hypoactive or absent	Hypoactive or absent	Hypoactive or absent	Hypoactive or absent
Palpation	• RUQ tenderness • Muscle rigidity • Spasm • Involuntary guarding	• LUQ tenderness • Left shoulder pain • Muscle rigidity • Spasm • Involuntary guarding	• Abdominal tenderness with deep palpation	• Peritoneal irritation including rebound tenderness and guarding	• Abdominal tenderness or rebound tenderness	• Esophageal: neck, chest, shoulders, or abdomen • Gastric: Pain in epigastric area
Percussion	Dullness	Dullness	Dullness	Dullness	Dullness	Dullness

Note: CT indicates computed tomography; DPL/DPA, diagnostic peritoneal lavage/diagnostic peritoneal aspirate; FAST, focused assessment with sonography for trauma; H&H, hemoglobin and hematocrit; LFT, liver function test; LUQ, left upper quadrant; RUQ, right upper quadrant.

Table 12-3. Selected Abdominal Injuries Assessment, Diagnostics, and Definitive Care (Continued)

	Liver	Spleen	Pancreas	Small Bowel	Large Bowel & Rectum	Stomach & Esophagus
Reevaluation Adjuncts (Diagnostics)						
Radiographs and other diagnostic tests	• Fractures, ribs 9–12	• Repeat CT imaging to assess for ongoing bleeding	• CT 80% sensitive; Missed diagnosis may occur	• CT • DPL/DPA • FAST (least sensitive)	• CT with oral, IV, and rectal contrast • DPL/DPA • Sigmoidoscopy	• Abdominal radiographs • CT • DPA/DPL • FAST (least sensitive)
Laboratory studies	• LFTs • Coagulation profiles	• Serial H&H	• Amylase elevated, but not definitive to diagnose	—	—	—
Definitive care	• Nonoperative management • Operative management	• Nonoperative management • Operative management	• Nonoperative management • Operative management	• Nonoperative management • Operative management	• Operative management	• Operative management

Note: CT indicates computed tomography; DPL/DPA, diagnostic peritoneal lavage/diagnostic peritoneal aspirate; FAST, focused assessment with sonography for trauma; H&H, hemoglobin and hematocrit; LFT, liver function test; LUQ, left upper quadrant; RUQ, right upper quadrant.

Definitive Care

- Nonoperative management is the standard of care in hemodynamically stable patients who sustain blunt liver injuries[2]

  - Patients sustaining high-grade liver injuries with large hemoperitoneum, or that show extravasation of contrast on computed tomography (CT), do not require immediate surgical treatment.[2] These patients may be observed but are at higher risk for failure of nonoperative management and are frequently monitored with serial abdominal exams.[2]

  - Patients who have a finding of contrast extravasation may be managed with embolization by interventional radiology[2]

- For patients with penetrating liver injuries and patients with blunt abdominal trauma with signs of hemodynamic instability, surgery is indicated. Appropriate fluid resuscitation and interventions to promote hemostasis are essential in preparation for surgery.[2] Risks during surgery include disruption of the natural tamponade process due to the evacuation of large amounts of blood with resulting hypovolemia.[2]

Splenic Injuries

The spleen has minimal elasticity and flexibility. That, in combination with its high vascularity, makes it the most frequently injured organ from blunt trauma.[19,27] Similar to the liver, the spleen is an encapsulated organ that can lacerate under sudden, increased abdominal pressure. Splenic injuries are suspected in patients who sustain an energy transfer or blow to the left side of the body.[22] Splenic injuries are categorized using Grade I for lowest severity through Grade V for highest severity (Table 12-5).

Assessment Findings

- Abrasions, contusions, ecchymoses, lacerations, or open wounds in the left upper quadrant

- Abdominal distention, asymmetry, abnormal contour, and a tight abdomen

- Tenderness, guarding, or rigidity in left upper quadrant[21]

- Abdominal tenderness in the left upper quadrant or pain in the left shoulder when lying supine or in the Trendelenburg position

- CT scan findings that may indicate splenic injury such as:[28]

  - Hemoperitoneum: Localized fluid collections around the spleen can be highly suggestive of hemoperitoneum. Briskly bleeding splenic lacerations may establish blood density fluid throughout the abdomen.

  - Hypodensity: Hypodense regions represent areas of parenchymal disruption, intraparenchymal hematoma, or subcapsular hematoma

  - Contrast blush or extravasation: Contrast blush describes hyperdense areas within the splenic parenchyma that represent traumatic disruption or

Table 12-4. Liver Injury Scale

Grade	Injury Description
I	• Hematomas: Subcapsular and nonexpanding; affects < 10% of surface area • Lacerations: < 1 cm parenchymal depth and nonbleeding
II	• Hematomas: 10%–50% of subcapsular surface < 1 cm intraparenchymal hematoma • Lacerations: Capsular tear with active bleeding; 1–3 cm in length
III	• Hematomas: > 50% surface area or actively bleeding; ruptured subcapsular or parenchymal hematoma; intraparenchymal hematoma > 10 cm or expanding • Lacerations: > 3 cm deep into parenchyma
IV	• Ruptured parenchymal hematomas with active bleeding or parenchymal disruption involving 25%–75% of a hepatic lobe
V	• Parenchymal disruption involving > 75% of hepatic lobe • Vascular injury involving retrohepatic cava or juxtahepatic venous injury
VI	• Hepatic avulsion with avulsion from vascular structures

Data from Bacidore, V. (2009). Abdominal and urinary trauma. In P. K. Howard & R. Steinmann (Eds.), *Sheehy's emergency nursing: Principles and practice* (6th ed., pp. 301–312). St. Louis, MO: Mosby/Elsevier.

pseudoaneurysm of the splenic vasculature. Active extravasation of contrast implies ongoing bleeding and the need for urgent intervention.

Definitive Care

Management of splenic injury has trended toward nonoperative or conservative treatment. Nonoperative management includes:

- Continuous monitoring with serial abdominal examinations and H & H laboratory studies
- Frequent monitoring and immediate notification of the surgeon if there are signs of shock or changes in the abdominal examination

While this varies from institution to institution, patients with the following parameters are usually candidates for observation:[29]

- Stable hemodynamic signs
- Stable hemoglobin levels during the next 12 to 48 hours
- Minimal transfusion requirements (≤ 2 units)
- Splenic laceration grade I or II without evidence of a blush on CT scan
- Age less than 55 years
- Alert and able to give feedback during abdominal examination

Operative management considerations include the following:

- For instances in which patients have significant injury to other systems, surgical intervention may be considered even in the presence of the previously noted findings

- A total splenectomy may be indicated in patients who resist stabilization efforts or have a severe splenic injury[28]
- In patients who are stable, every effort is made to preserve part or all of the splenic tissue, and operative procedures can range from direct pressure and packing to embolization to splenorrhaphy or partial removal of the spleen[28]

Postoperative Considerations

One unique postoperative risk following splenectomy is pneumococcal sepsis.[22] The asplenic compromised immune system has difficulty destroying encapsulated bacteria such as *Streptococcus pneumonia*, *Neisseria meningitides*, and *Haemophilus influenza*. Therefore, vaccination against these bacteria is required. Following splenectomy, patients are encouraged to receive annual influenza vaccines and meningococcal and pneumococcal vaccines every five years (the initial dose can be given before discharge from the hospital).

Pancreatic Injuries

Due to its location in the abdominal cavity, fewer than 10% of patients who sustain a pancreatic injury will have a single-system injury.[5] Pancreatic injuries in blunt trauma are a result of the pancreas being crushed between the anterior abdominal wall and the spinal column, which also raises the index of suspicion for concurrent spinal fractures.[5] Patients with penetrating pancreatic injury often sustain concurrent duodenal injuries.[5]

Table 12-5. Spleen Injury Scale

Grade	Injury Description
I	• Hematomas: Subcapsular involving < 10% surface area and nonexpanding • Laceration: Capsular tears < 1 cm into parenchymal depth and nonbleeding
II	• Hematomas: Subcapsular involving 10%–50% of the surface area or < 5 cm diameter • Lacerations: Capsular tear 1–3 cm into parenchymal depth with active bleeding
III	• Hematomas: Greater than 50% surface area and expanding, or a ruptured subcapsular or parenchymal hematoma with active bleeding • Lacerations: > 3 cm into parenchyma with active bleeding or involving the trabecular vessels
IV	• Lacerations involving hilar vessels producing major devascularization (> 25% spleen)
V	• Completely shattered spleen; hilar vascular injury with total devascularization

Data from Bacidore, V. (2009). Abdominal and urinary trauma. In P. K. Howard & R. Steinmann (Eds.), *Sheehy's emergency nursing: Principles and practice* (6th ed., pp. 301–312). St. Louis, MO: Mosby/Elsevier.

Assessment Findings

- Serial serum amylase levels increasing over time may indicate a potential pancreatic injury, but this does not constitute a definitive diagnosis[22]
- Serial abdominal examinations are performed in conjunction with the serial serum amylase levels to appropriately confirm pancreatic injury
  - Slight abdominal pain and tenderness becoming more significant within 48 hours of injury[3,5,21]
  - Pain located in the epigastric area radiating to the back[22]
  - Abdominal tenderness present on deep palpation
  - Increasing or worsening abdominal wall muscle rigidity, spasm, or involuntary guarding

Definitive Care

- Nonoperative management is a growing trend in pancreatic injuries. Management consists of complete bowel rest, nutritional support, and serial CT scanning with observation.[6]
- Pseudocyst formations may be managed with percutaneous drainage[5]
- Pancreatic ductal injuries may occur as a result of trauma, and ductal injuries at or distal to the neck are treated with a distal pancreatectomy[5]
- Complications from pancreatic injury include secondary hemorrhage, pancreatic fistula, and abdominal abscess.[5] Signs and symptoms of infection will often occur seven to ten days after injury and usually include fever, elevated white blood cell count, and nausea and vomiting.[5]

Small Bowel Injuries

The force applied to the abdomen from the lap belt compresses the small bowel between the abdominal wall and spine and can cause a rupture of the bowel[6] or hematoma, resulting in edema of the bowel wall with decreased lumen size, which puts the patient at risk for obstruction.[28] Sudden deceleration forces can cause tearing of the small bowel at its fixed points; the most common is at the ligament of Treitz.[6,23] Transverse fractures of the spine in the lumbar region, known as Chance fractures, also increase suspicion for a small bowel injury due to the force required to result in fracture.[6] Lumen content of the small bowel has a neutral pH and is relatively sterile.[6] Due to low bacteria growth and minimal spillage of contents from a penetrating injury, clinical findings for small intestinal perforation may be delayed.[6]

Assessment Findings

- Seatbelt sign or bruising to the abdomen from a seatbelt
- Rebound tenderness and guarding[6]
- Muscle spasm or rigidity in the epigastric area or left upper quadrant
- Presence of bile or food fibers on diagnostic peritoneal lavage/diagnostic peritoneal aspirate (DPL/DPA) in the hemodynamically unstable patient mandating laparotomy[17,19]
- CT scan provides information about the presence of free fluid or air in the abdominal cavity
- Tachycardia, hypotension, elevated white cell count, increased serum amylase, or metabolic acidosis that may indicate risk for a missed hollow viscus injury[6]

Definitive Care

- Nonoperative management includes serial abdominal examinations[6]
- Operative management occurs in patients who exhibit signs of peritonitis or hemodynamic instability
  - Diagnostic laparoscopy can be helpful to inspect abdominal spaces for spillage and to examine the loops of bowel[23]
  - Large-volume fluid resuscitation can cause swelling of the bowel resulting in an inability to replace the loops of bowel in the peritoneal cavity and close the abdominal wall at the conclusion of the surgical procedure

Large Bowel Injuries

Injuries to the large bowel occur from penetrating wounds[30] or as a result of blunt trauma. Blunt trauma energy to the large bowel may cause it to rupture from a sudden increase in intraluminal pressure, be torn from fixation points on other structures, or avulse from the abdominal wall.[30]

Retroperitoneal colon injuries, caused by penetrating trauma to the back, may take up to 24 hours or more to manifest as abdominal tenderness or signs of infection begin to develop.[29]

Assessment Findings

- Peritoneal irritation
- Hypovolemic shock
- Evisceration of bowel

Definitive Care

If significant injury is found, the patient may undergo a primary bowel repair or a diverting colostomy, depending on the severity of the injury.[30] A diverting colostomy may be closed within weeks with uncomplicated healing of the bowel.[22]

Rectal Injuries

Rectal injuries are often sustained as a result of penetrating injury, such as GSWs or stab wounds to the pelvic or gluteal area.[30] Rectal injuries are uncommon in blunt trauma.[30] Immediate signs of peritonitis are common in anterior and lateral rectal wall injuries but delayed in posterior wall injuries of the rectum.[30]

Assessment Findings

- Bleeding from and around the rectum
- Scrotal hematoma
- Foreign objects

Definitive Care

Sigmoidoscopy is used in diagnosing rectal injuries but may not detect an injury in an unprepared bowel.[30] It is a useful modality to assist in the removal of foreign objects from the rectum.[30] Rectal injuries are often managed with a colostomy and distal rectal washout.[22]

Gastric and Esophageal Injuries

Injuries to the stomach occur in 20% of patients with a penetrating mechanism to the abdomen.[6,22] In blunt trauma, only 1% of patients sustain gastric perforation. Since a significant force is required to rupture the stomach, the trauma nurse may identify other concurrent injuries.[6] Esophageal injury is most common in the cervical and thoracic regions.[6]

Assessment Findings

- Tenderness, guarding, or rigidity[6,21]
  - Present primarily in the epigastric area for gastric injuries
  - For esophageal injuries, pain that may radiate to the neck, chest, shoulders, or throughout the abdomen
- Bloody drainage from a nasogastric or orogastric tube that may indicate a gastric injury[6]

Definitive Care

Gastric injuries require operative management.[6]

Selected Pelvic Cavity and Pelvis Injuries

Reproductive Organs

While injuries to the reproductive organs are not life-threatening in the nonpregnant patient, they can produce significant loss and crisis for the patient and significant others. Genital trauma is seen with injuries to the perineum, pelvis, bladder, penis, vagina, or rectum. Surgical repair generally provides good results; external genitalia injuries may be treated with compression dressings and wound irrigation to preserve tissue viability.

Male Genitalia[31]

Testes are generally spared from injury due to their mobility and tough capsular covering; however, a direct blow to the testes can produce contusion or rupture. Injuries to the scrotum may result in avulsion injuries resulting in tissue loss. Trauma to the penis may result from blunt injuries, strangulation, penetrating injuries, or amputation. A penile fracture is the result of such trauma with rupture of the tunica albuginea, subsequent hemorrhage, and hematoma formation. Urethral injuries occur concurrently in 10% to 30% of penile fractures.[31] Foreign objects or human hair constricting the penis may result in strangulation injuries. Penetrating injuries involve the urethra in 22% of cases.[31] Amputation of the penis can produce profound psychological impact along with physical injuries and requires a team of urologists, plastic surgeons, and psychiatrists to address the resulting injuries.[31]

Female Genitalia[31]

Female reproductive organ injuries result from straddle injuries, pelvic fractures, MVCs, sexual violence, and powered personal watercraft events or penetrating injuries. Straddle injuries or sexual violence may result in hematoma formation. Pelvic fractures can cause vaginal and perineal lacerations. Vaginal tears may result from personal watercraft events when pressurized water enters the swimsuit. These injuries may extend to the intra-abdominal, perianal, or perineal areas. Penetrating trauma may injure the uterus, ovaries, or fallopian tubes.

Bladder and Urethral Injuries

Blunt force intense enough to cause the bladder to rupture may cause other injuries such as pelvic fracture.[18] Ruptured full bladders may result in leakage of urine into surrounding pelvic tissue, the vulva, or scrotum. Extraperitoneal rupture involves lacerations below the pelvic peritoneum while in intraperitoneal rupture, the pelvic peritoneum is violated.

The male urethra is divided into two segments: posterior and anterior.[23] Posterior segment injuries are associated with pelvic fracture, while anterior are associated with straddle trauma.[23] Urethral injury in females is usually the result of the urethra tearing away from the neck of the bladder.[23] In females, consider a pelvic fracture or vaginal laceration as potential concurrent injuries.[26]

Assessment Findings

- Urge to urinate with an inability to void[23]
- Blood at the urethral meatus[26]
- Rebound tenderness in the suprapubic area
- Displacement of the prostate gland, known as a high-riding prostate[31]

Definitive Care

Definitive care is determined based on the extent of injury sustained. If pelvic fracture is present, obtain urology and orthopedic surgery consults. Extraperitoneal bladder injuries are treated with urethral or suprapubic catheter drainage, while intraperitoneal bladder injury requires surgical intervention to close the multilayer injury.[23]

Gluteal Injuries

Penetrating injuries to this area are associated with up to a 50% incidence of significant intra-abdominal injuries, including certain rectal injuries.[19]

Pelvic Fractures

There are three main patterns of injury leading to pelvic fractures (Table 12-6). Pelvic fractures are classified as either stable or unstable:

- Stable fractures do not involve the pelvic ring or have minimal displacement of the pelvic ring
- Unstable fractures are two or more fractures of the pelvic ring that have outward rotational displacement[32]

Unstable pelvic fractures increase the volume of the pelvic cavity and can be life threatening in the presence of large-volume blood loss and/or injury to the genitourinary system. Bleeding may originate from lacerated veins or arteries, or from the fracture itself. Disruption of the iliolumbar vein causes bleeding in 60% of patients with unstable pelvic fractures, and posterior fractures are more likely than anterior fractures to cause bleeding.[33] Bleeding may be significant enough to cause hypovolemic shock, and the patient may require a massive blood transfusion. Pelvic fractures may be open or closed, and open pelvic fractures have a significantly higher mortality rate.[34]

Assessment Findings

- Shortening of the leg
- External rotation of the leg[19]
- Blood at the urinary meatus or hematuria
- Pelvic instability and/or pain
- Unexplained hypotension or evidence of hypovolemic shock

Definitive Care

Significant resources are required for the management of the patient with severe and/or open pelvic fracture with hemorrhage. Consider early transfer to a trauma center.

- Internal rotation of the lower limbs will help gain pelvic stabilization.[19] This is used with some external pelvic stabilization device, as described below.
- A folded sheet around the pelvis that is clamped or tied at the front of the patient or a commercially prepared binder or sling may improve alignment of the pelvis, control hemorrhage, and aid in patient comfort[19,33,35]

Table 12-6. Patterns of Pelvic Fractures

Pattern	Fractures		
Pattern	• Lateral compression • Closed • 60%–70% frequency	• Anterior-posterior compression • Open book • 15%–20% frequency	• Vertical shear • 5%–15% frequency
Mechanism	• Motor vehicle collision	• Auto vs. pedestrian collision • Motorcycle collision • Crush injury • Fall from height	• Fall from height

Data from American College of Surgeons.[19]

- Some literature recommends that pelvic binders or sheets be applied at the level of the greater trochanter and symphysis pubis (Fig. 12-2)[19,33,36]

Renal Injuries

Renal injuries are classified into five grades, with Grade I being minor and Grade V being severe (Table 12-7).[31] Renal injuries occur in 10% of patients who sustain abdominal trauma.[20] Maintain a high index of suspicion for renal injuries in the presence of blunt injuries to the flank, deceleration force, and fall from heights.[31] Penetrating trauma to the flank, pelvis, and lower chest also raises suspicion for renal trauma.[31]

Assessment Findings

- Turner sign, which is ecchymosis over the flank at the level of the 11th and 12th ribs

- Hematuria: Common, but absence does not rule out renal injury[31]

- Flank tenderness, costovertebral angle tenderness, or palpable flank mass

- Structural damage or leakage of contrast on intravenous pyelogram (IVP)[23]

  - If the patient is hemodynamically unstable and unable to go to the CT suite, a single-infusion IVP can be performed in the resuscitation area, followed by a complete study once the patient is stable[23]

Figure 12-2. Use of a Pelvic Binder

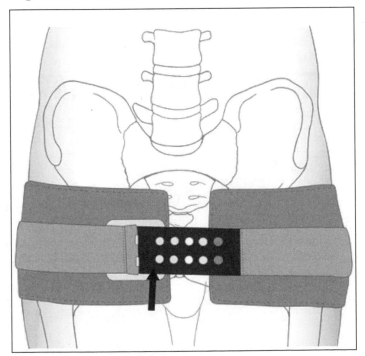

From Hak, D., Smith, W., & Suzuki, T. (2009). Management of hemorrhage in life-threatening pelvic fracture. *The Journal of The American Academy of Orthopaedic Surgeons, 17*(7), 447–457

- Positive urine dipstick for microscopic blood or leukocyte esterase[31]

- Abnormal or elevated blood urea nitrogen and creatinine

Definitive Care

Treatment varies depending on injury severity. Approximately 90% of renal injuries are minor and do not require surgical intervention.[23] Anticipate a nephrology consultation in more severe renal injuries. Surgical repair is required within 12 hours to salvage an ischemic kidney.[23]

Reevaluation Adjuncts for Abdominal and Pelvic Trauma

Laboratory Studies

Laboratory studies specific for diagnosis in abdominal and pelvic trauma include the following:

- LFTs to assess the extent of damage to the liver

- Coagulation studies to assess liver function and development of disseminated intravascular coagulopathy (DIC)

- Serum amylase for suspected pancreatic injury

- Urinalysis to assess for presence of blood or leukocyte esterase

- Urine pregnancy test to assess status in females of reproductive age

- Gastric contents studies to assess for blood

- Stool analysis to assess for blood

Imaging Studies

Chest, abdomen, and pelvis radiographic images are inexpensive, simple, and commonly performed at the bedside. However, interpreting diagnostic procedures can be difficult, and repeat studies or more than one modality may be needed. The use of radiographs can be limited, due in part to patient positioning, body habitus, or technician technique:

- An upright chest radiograph can be used to determine the presence of pneumoperitoneum[19]

- An abdomen or pelvic radiograph may be obtained to identify a retained foreign body or separation of bowel loops by fluid or air, or to determine the source of blood loss[19]

- An abdominal radiograph may demonstrate free air[23] indicative of perforated viscera

Imaging studies for bladder and urethral injuries include the following:

- CT cystograms are used to diagnose an intraperitoneal or extraperitoneal bladder rupture. Contrast media is instilled via the urinary catheter followed by CT scanning[26,30]

- Urethrograms are generally performed prior to insertion of a urinary catheter when a urethral injury is suspected.[18] Contrast media is instilled into the urethra at the meatus. Detection of contrast media within the bladder indicates adequate instillation. Leakage from the urethral tract demonstrates urethral disruption.[19]

FAST Examination

FAST is a portable ultrasound that demonstrates excellent sensitivity in identifying intra-abdominal blood or fluid (Fig. 12-3).[37] An ultrasound wand is placed over the bladder, liver, and splenic area to assess for fluid.

- When there is 1 L of fluid (blood) in the peritoneum, the FAST examination can be 90% to 100% sensitive[7]

- However, volumes less than 400 mL are rarely identified by the examiner[2]

- A negative FAST examination does not rule out injury, and serial FAST examinations or CT imaging may be required

- A positive FAST examination indicates fluid present in the abdomen, and surgical intervention may be indicated

- A FAST examination is not as sensitive as CT imaging or DPL for gastric or small bowel injuries[6]

- A FAST examination is limited when determining injury to structures located in the retroperitoneal space[37]

The advantages of the FAST examination are that it does not use radiation and is not invasive, so the patient is not exposed to radiation or risk for infection.[36] The limitations of the FAST examination include its inability to assess for retroperitoneal bleeding and hollow viscus injury.[19] Successful use of FAST requires provider education and practical experience for consistency, accuracy, and competency.

Computed Tomography

Abdominal CT examination is the most widely used diagnostic tool in the hemodynamically stable trauma patient with blunt injury.[19]

- Abdominal CT can detect hemoperitoneum as well as help determine the extent of organ injury, spinal and pelvic fractures, and vascular injury[19]

- CT will not directly reveal injury to hollow viscus organs but will show free air, bowel wall thickening, extravasation of contrast, intraperitoneal fluid in the absence of solid organ injury, and mesenteric fat stranding[19]

- CT is used less frequently for penetrating trauma due to a lower sensitivity for diagnosing hollow organ injuries and retroperitoneal hemorrhage[19]

  - Penetrating trauma accompanied by any degree of hematuria generally calls for CT scanning[3,31]

Table 12-7. Renal Injury Scale

Grade	Injury Description
I	• Contusion: Microscopic or gross hematuria may be present, but urologic studies normal • Hematoma: Subcapsular, nonexpanding without parenchymal laceration
II	• Hematoma: Nonexpanding perirenal hematoma confined to the renal retroperitoneum • Laceration: > 1 cm depth of renal cortex without urinary extravasation
III	• Laceration: > 1 cm in parenchymal depth of renal cortex without collecting system rupture or urinary extravasation
IV	• Lacerations extending through the cortex, medulla, and collecting system • Vascular injuries involving the main renal artery or vein with contained hemorrhage
V	• Completely shattered kidney • Vascular injury includes avulsion of renal hilum, which devascularizes the kidney

Data from Bacidore, V. (2009). Abdominal and urinary trauma. In P. K. Howard & R. Steinmann (Eds.), *Sheehy's emergency nursing: Principles and practice* (6th ed., pp. 301–312). St. Louis, MO: Mosby/Elsevier.

Figure 12-3. Focused Assessment with Sonography for Trauma

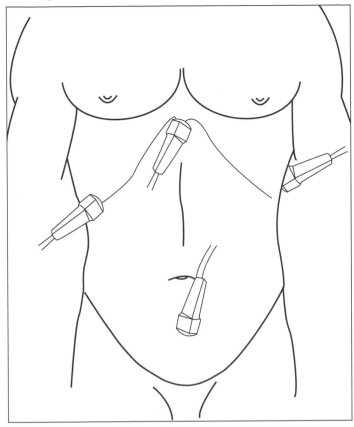

Four sites viewed during FAST examinations.

- Abdominal CT scans have an 80% sensitivity in diagnosing pancreatic injuries, which is considered low[5]
  - Due to the well-protected location of the pancreas, a delayed or missed diagnosis may occur.[5] Patients who have an initial negative CT but continue to have persistent abdominal pain, fever, or elevated amylase may require a repeat CT.[5] Air and fluid accumulation over time may change findings on repeat CT to aid in the diagnosis of a pancreatic injury.[5]
- CT is useful to determine splenic injury[28]
- Contrast may be required to identify abdominal injuries
  - Intravenous (IV) contrast is required to accurately identify solid organ injury on CT imaging[37]
  - Oral contrast is useful in assessing hollow viscus injury; however, it requires administration 30 minutes prior to CT to coat the small bowel[37]
  - A CT scan using oral, IV, and rectal contrast, called a triple contrast CT, is used to diagnose colon injuries[2,30]
- CT imaging is not used in hemodynamically unstable patients because surgical exploration or angiography are indicated for timely identification of the source of bleeding and embolization[19]

Angiography

Angiography is the use of injected low osmolar contrast media to assess for tears or leaks in the vasculature. Angiography has been a useful treatment modality in nonoperative management of blunt and penetrating solid organ and vascular injuries.[19]

- Selected patients for angiography are based on physical findings and CT imaging[19]
- Prime candidates for angiography are hemodynamically stable patients without peritoneal signs but with evidence of solid organ injury on CT imaging[19]
- The risks associated with angiography involve adverse reactions to the contrast and contrast-induced nephropathy[33]

Embolization to stop bleeding within solid organs or vessels is an interventional radiology procedure that can provide hemostasis without surgical intervention.[10] Occlusion balloons are inserted into arteries temporarily to prevent further hemorrhage and preserve end-organ perfusion.[10] A microcoil, such as Gelfoam slurry, is inserted through a microcatheter at the site of bleeding to embolize the vessel.[10] If unable to stop the bleeding, a larger coil or an occlusion device may be necessary.[10]

Embolization is also used to control bleeding arteries and reduce the need for surgical intervention.[23] It is often used for patients with pelvic fractures as the best option for definitive management of pelvic hemorrhage.[19,33]

Diagnostic Peritoneal Aspirate/Diagnostic Peritoneal Lavage

DPL/DPA is recommended for hemodynamically unstable patients, those considered too unstable to transport to CT, or those unable to participate in serial abdominal examinations.[38] The sensitivity of these procedures is extremely high, nearly 100%, but it is invasive and may cause unnecessary surgical intervention since surgery is not always indicated for intra-abdominal bleeding.[37] The procedure requires operator expertise, and when CT and/or ultrasound are available, this adjunct is not often used.[19] Another limitation of DPL/DPA is that it detects bleeding but does not identify the injured organ or structure.[37] Current practice reflects decreased use of DPL/DPAs with increased use of FAST and CT. DPL/DPA may be useful in unstable patients who have an equivocal FAST examination.[37]

- The presence of feces indicates potential need for surgical intervention
- The presence of bile or food fibers during DPL/DPA is an indication for immediate surgical exploration[19]

The Procedure

During the DPA, a small incision is made midline below the umbilicus, a catheter is inserted, aspiration is performed, and if 10 mL or more of gross blood is aspirated, it is considered positive and the procedure ends. If no gross blood is obtained upon aspiration, a DPL is performed with an infusion of one L of fluid which is then drained back into the empty container by lowering it below the level of the patient.[30] A positive DPL is defined as the presence of red blood cells in the returned irrigant solution of at least 100,000 mm.[32]

Selected Nursing Considerations for the Trauma Patient Undergoing Radiologic Evaluation

It is a priority to remove metal objects such as zippers or piercings to optimize the radiographic image and prevent injury to the patient. The nurse will need to monitor the patient's condition during movement and manipulation for the examination.

Specific nursing considerations include:

- CT scan
  - Administer oral contrast if indicated, and monitor for aspiration following contrast administration
    - Consider the patient's level of consciousness and aspiration risk when administering oral contrast
    - Requirements for oral and IV contrast in CT imaging vary among facilities, so be familiar with organizational policy
  - Prepare the patient for transfer from the resuscitation room to the CT scan, and monitor the patient while in the CT suite
  - Prophylactic administration of N-acetylcysteine in patients with a serum creatinine above 1.2 mg/dL undergoing contrast-enhanced CT scan, along with hydration, can reduce the risk of contrast-induced nephropathy[38]
- FAST examination
  - Since the pelvic view identification and sensitivity is increased when the bladder is distended, FAST is performed prior to placement of the urinary catheter, if not contraindicated[19]
  - Availability of a water-based transducer gel is necessary
- DPL/DPA
  - Prior to the procedure, the trauma nurse inserts a urinary catheter to decompress the bladder, and a gastric tube to decompress the stomach
  - Specimens may be sent to the lab for analysis of content and cell count

- Ongoing monitoring of the patient for complications such as perforation is necessary[22]
- Angiography
  - Prepare the patient for transport to interventional radiology and monitor the patient while in the radiology suite and for adverse reactions to contrast
  - Monitor the access site for signs of post-procedural bleeding

Reevaluation and Post Resuscitation Care

Assessment and identification of abdominal and pelvic injuries may be challenging since patients may not always present with immediate pain or obvious injury. Continuous evaluation and ongoing assessment is required. Ecchymosis may take several hours before presentation, and peritoneal signs such as abdominal pain on palpation may be delayed for up to 24 hours after initial injury. Ongoing, frequent, systematic assessments are essential to detect potential missed injuries. These include the following:

- Primary survey serial assessments (ABCDE)
- Monitoring of vital signs for uncontrolled hemorrhage and shock
- Pain assessment
- Frequent reevaluation of identified injuries and serial abdominal examinations to assess for additional injuries
- Trending of appropriate laboratory studies as needed for nonoperative management

Summary

Abdominal and pelvic trauma can be the result of blunt or penetrating trauma. Solid organs—including the spleen, liver, and pancreas—are more frequently injured by blunt trauma; hollow organs—such as the small and large bowel—are more frequently damaged by penetrating mechanisms. Subtle assessment findings that are similar in a variety of abdominal and pelvic injuries necessitate frequent, serial examinations to detect changes.

The bony structures of the pelvis are more frequently injured by blunt trauma. The pelvis can be the source of significant hemorrhage resulting in increased mortality. Patients who are hemodynamically unstable should be closely evaluated for pelvic hemorrhage and other sources of bleeding. Bleeding from concurrent injuries also contributes to the risk of increased mortality. Immediate definitive treatment is imperative to impact the mortality associated with massive pelvic hemorrhage. Early intervention by nurses includes early administration of blood products to replace blood loss and control of further bleeding. It is important that trauma nurses remain vigilant in the monitoring of these patients to identify and correct any life-threatening compromises to circulation and perfusion.

References

1. McCance, K., Huether, S., Brashers, V., & Rote, N. (2010). *Pathophysiology: The biologic basis for disease in adults and children* (6th ed.). Maryland Heights, MO: Mosby Elsevier.

2. Fabian, T., & Bee, T. (2013). Liver and biliary tract. In K. L. Mattox, E. E. Moore, & D. V. Feliciano (Eds.), *Trauma* (7th ed., pp. 539–580). Chicago, IL: McGraw-Hill.

3. Li, W. W. (2008). The liver: An amazing organ. *The Inside Tract,* (166), 8–9. Retrieved from http://www.badgut.org/downloads/inside-tract-issue-166.pdf

4. Wisner, D. (2013). Injury to the spleen. In K. L. Mattox, E. E. Moore, & D. V. Feliciano (Eds.), *Trauma* (7th ed., pp. 561–580). Chicago, IL: McGraw-Hill.

5. Biffl, W. L. (2013). Duodenum and pancreas. In K. L. Mattox, E. E. Moore, & D. V. Feliciano (Eds.), *Trauma* (7th ed., pp. 603–619). Chicago, IL: McGraw-Hill.

6. Diebel, L. (2013). Stomach and small bowel. In K. L. Mattox, E. E. Moore, & D. V. Feliciano (Eds.), *Trauma* (7th ed., pp. 581–602). Chicago, IL: McGraw-Hill.

7. Dente, C. J. & Feliciano, D. V. (2013). Abdominal vascular injury. In K. L. Mattox, E. E. Moore, & D. V. Feliciano (Eds.), *Trauma* (7th ed., pp. 632–654). Chicago, IL: McGraw-Hill.

8. Gray, H. (2000). The male genital organs. In *Gray's anatomy of the human body.* Bartleby.com. Retrieved from http://education.yahoo.com/reference/gray/subjects/subject/258

9. Jadack, R. A. (2013). Female genital and reproductive function. In L. E. Copstead & J. L. Banasik (Eds.), *Pathophysiology* (5th ed., pp. 654–669). St. Louis, MO: Elsevier Saunders.

10. Velmahos, G. C. (2013). Pelvis. In K. L. Mattox, E. E. Moore, & D. V. Feliciano (Eds.), *Trauma* (7th ed., pp. 655–668). Chicago, IL: McGraw-Hill.

11. Pfeifer, R., Tarkin, I.S., Rocos, B., & Pape, H. C. (2009). Patterns of mortality and causes of death in polytrauma—Has anything changed? *Injury, 40*(9), 907–911.

12. Guillon, F. (2011). Epidemiology of abdominal trauma. In P. Taourel (Ed.), *CT of the acute abdomen.* Berlin, Germany: Springer-Verlag.

13. Udeani, J., Salomone, J. A., Keim, S. M., Legonme, E. L., & Salomone, J. P. (2012, September 20.). *Blunt abdominal trauma.* Retrieved from http://emedicine.medscape.com/article/1980980-overview

14. Offner, P., Stanton-Maxey, K. J., & Bjerke, S. (2012, January 23). *Penetrating abdominal trauma.* Retrieved from http://emedicine.medscape.com/article/2036859-overview

15. Dechert, T., Duane, T., Frykberg, B., Aboutanos, M., Malhotra, A., & Ivatury, R. (2009). Elderly patients with pelvic fracture: Interventions and outcomes. *The American Surgeon, 75*(4), 291–295.

16. American College of Surgeons. (2012). Geriatric trauma. In *Advanced trauma life support student course manual* (9th ed.). Chicago, IL: Author.

17. Adams, P. E., Martinez, M. E., Vickerie, J. L., & Kirzinger, W. K. (2011). Summary health statistics for the U.S. populations: National Health Interview Survey, 2010. *Vital and Health Statistics, 10*(251), 1–117.

18. Howard, P. K. & Steinmann, R. A. (Eds.). (2010). *Sheehy's emergency nursing: Principles and practice* (6th ed.) St. Louis, MO: Mosby.

19. American College of Surgeons. (2012). Abdominal and pelvic trauma. In *Advanced trauma life support student course manual* (9th ed., pp. 122–147). Chicago, IL: Author.

20. Criddle, L. (2011). *TCAR: Trauma care after resuscitation.* Scappoose, OR: The Laurelwood Group.

21. Hunt, J. P., Marr, A. B., & Stuke, L. E. (2013). Kinematics. In K. L. Mattox, E. E. Moore, & D. V. Feliciano (Eds.), *Trauma* (7th ed., pp. 2–17). Chicago, IL: McGraw-Hill.

22. Wallis, A., Kelly, M., & Jones, L. (2010). Angiography and embolisation for solid abdominal organ injury in adults—A current prospective. *World Journal of Emergency Surgery, 5*(18), 1–13.

23. Jones, K. M. (2008). Abdominal injuries. In K. A. McQuillan, M. B. Flynn Mackic, & E. Whalen (Eds.), *Trauma nursing: From resuscitation through rehabilitation* (4th ed., pp. 678–705). St. Louis, MO: Saunders.

24. Ferri, F. (2010). *Ferri's best test: A practical guide to clinical laboratory medicine and diagnostic imaging* (2nd ed.). Philadelphia, PA: Mosby Elsevier.

25. Evans, T., & Murphy, C. (2010). Genitourinary trauma: Etiology, imaging, and emergency management. *Trauma Reports, 11*(2), 1–16.

26. Van der Vlies, C., Van Delden, O., Punt, B., Ponsen, K., Reekers, J., & Goslings, J. C. (2010). Literature review of the role of ultrasound, computed tomography, and transcatheter arterial embolization for the treatment of traumatic splenic injuries. *Cardiovascular Interventional Radiology, 33,* 1079–1087.

27. Maung, A. A., & Kaplan, L. J. (2012, August 16). Management of splenic injury in the adult trauma patient. *UpToDate.* Retrieved from http://www. uptodate.com/contents/management-of-splenic-injury-in-the-adult-trauma-patient

28. Bjerke, H. S., & Bjerke, J. S. (2012, January 20). *Splenic rupture treatment & management.* Retrieved from http://emedicine.medscape.com/article/432823-treatment

29. Hoyt, K. S., & Selfridge-Thomas, J. (2007). *Emergency nursing core curriculum* (6th ed.). St. Louis, MO: Saunders Elsevier.

30. Demetriades, D. & Inaba, K. (2013). Colon and rectal trauma. In K. L. Mattox, E. E. Moore, & D. V. Feliciano (Eds.), *Trauma* (7th ed., pp. 620–631). Chicago, IL: McGraw-Hill.

31. Coburn, M. (2013). Genitourinary trauma. In K. L. Mattox, E. E. Moore, & D. V. Feliciano (Eds.), *Trauma* (7th ed., pp. 669–708). Chicago, IL: McGraw-Hill.

32. Anwar, R., Tuson, K., & Khan, S. A. (2008). Fractures of the pelvis. In *Classification and diagnosis in orthopedic trauma* (pp. 127–130). New York, NY: Cambridge University Press.

33. Cullinane, D. C., Schiller, H. J., Zielinski, M. D., Bilaniuk, J. W., Collier, B. R., Como, J., ... & Wynne, J. L. (2011). Eastern Association for the Surgery of Trauma practice management guidelines for hemorrhage in pelvic fracture—Update and systematic review. *Journal of Trauma, 71*(6), 1850–1868.

34. American College of Surgeons. (2012). Musculoskeletal trauma. In *Advanced trauma life support student course manual* (9th ed., pp. 206–223). Chicago, IL: Author.

35. Schmitt, B. D. (2011, September 15). *Leg injury.* Retrieved from http://www.ohsu.edu/xd/health/services/doernbecher/patients-families/health-information/md4kids/symptom-index/leg-injury.cfm?WT_rank=23

36. Prasarn, M. L., Small, J., Conrad, B., Horodyski, N., Horodyski, M., & Rechtine, G. R. (2012). Does application position of the T-POD affect stability of pelvic fractures? *Journal of Orthopaedic Trauma.* [Epub ahead of print.]

37. Hirschberg, A. (2013). Trauma laparotomy: Principles and techniques. In K. L. Mattox, E. E. Moore, & D. V. Feliciano (Eds.), *Trauma* (7th ed., pp. 512–528). Chicago, IL: McGraw-Hill.

38. Wu, M. Y., Hsiang, H. F., Wong, C. S., Yao, M. S., Li, Y. W., Hsiang, C. Y., ... Tam, K. W. (2013). The effectiveness of N-acetylcysteine in preventing contrast-induced nephropathy in patients undergoing contrast-enhanced computed tomography: A meta-analysis of randomized controlled trials. *International Urology and Nephrology.* [Epub ahead of print].

Chapter 13 • Spinal Cord and Vertebral Column Trauma

Melanie Crowley, MSN, RN, CEN

Objectives

Upon completion of this chapter, the learner will be able to:

1. Describe mechanisms of injury associated with spinal cord and/or vertebral column trauma.

2. Describe pathophysiologic changes as a basis for assessment of the trauma patient with spinal cord and/or vertebral column injuries.

3. Demonstrate the nursing assessment of the trauma patient with spinal cord and/or vertebral column injuries.

4. Plan appropriate interventions for the trauma patient with spinal cord and/or vertebral column injuries.

5. Evaluate the effectiveness of nursing interventions for the trauma patient with spinal cord and/or vertebral column injuries.

Preface

Knowledge of normal anatomy and physiology serves as a foundation for understanding anatomic derangements and pathophysiologic processes that may result from trauma. Before reading this chapter, it is strongly suggested that the learner review the following material. This material will not be covered in the lectures nor tested directly, but as foundational content, it may be the basis for some test questions and skill evaluation steps.

Anatomy and Physiology of the Spinal Cord and Vertebral Column

Spinal Cord

The spinal cord is the communication structure between the body and the brain. It arises from the brain stem, extending through the foramen magnum and descending downward to the second lumbar vertebra. The adult spinal cord is 40 to 50 cm long and one to 1.5 cm in diameter. It is responsible for the two-way communication between the brain and the peripheral nervous system. Two consecutive rows of nerve roots emerge from each side— the dorsal root and the ventral root. These nerve roots join distally to form 31 pairs of spinal nerves. The end of the spinal cord, the conus medullaris, is cone shaped. Spinal nerves continue from the conus medullaris forming a nerve bundle known as the cauda equina.[1]

The spinal cord is divided into the cervical, thoracic, lumbar, and sacral regions. When viewed in a cross section, the spinal cord has a butterfly- or H-shaped core (Fig. 13-1). It contains a central mass of gray matter that is divided into three paired horns: the ventral (anterior),

Figure 13-1. Cross Section of the Spinal Cord

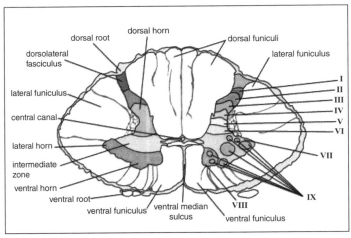

Schematic drawing showing the cytoarchitectural lamination of the lower cervical section of the human spinal cord.
Copyright 2007 Encyclopedia Britannica, Inc.

the intermediolateral, and the dorsal (posterior). The horns of the spinal cord are responsible for voluntary motor activity. The ventral horn provides the motor components of the spinal nerves. The intermediolateral horn contains the preganglionic sympathetic fibers of the thoracic, lumbar, and sacral spine. The dorsal horn contains peripheral sensory neurons.[2,3] Surrounding the gray matter is the white matter, which consists of myelinated nerve fibers and forms three columns: the anterior, the lateral, and the posterior.[2,3] Each column contains ascending sensory tracts that carry impulses up the spinal cord to the brain and descending motor tracts that carry motor impulses down the spinal cord.

Motor Function

Impulses are conducted between the brain and the spinal cord through the upper motor neurons.[1] The upper motor neurons form two major systems: the corticospinal tract (Fig. 13-2), which is responsible for fine motor skills, and the extracorticospinal tract, which is responsible for gross motor movement (Table 13-1).[1,3] Upper motor neurons cross at the medulla of the brain stem to the opposite side and descend in the corticospinal tract. This is the basis for loss of movement on the contralateral side from a head injury. Some fibers descend through the white matter on the same side and cross at specific spinal cord segments, resulting in ipsilateral loss of movement.[1,4] Impulses that originate in the upper motor neurons are conducted to the lower motor neurons in the spinal cord and innervate the skeletal muscle groups. The cervical nerve fibers from the corticospinal tract, located in the central portion of the ventral horn, innervate the upper extremities. The sacral fibers from the corticospinal tract, located in the peripheral portion of the ventral horn, innervate the lower extremities.[1,2,3]

Sensory Function

Sensory pathways include those impulse routes that can be combined into spinal reflex arcs (sensory) or those transmitted to higher centers in the brain to be interpreted (cortical).

The Reflex Arc

The reflex arc is a stimulus-response mechanism that does not require ascending or descending spinal cord pathways to the cerebral cortex to function. Examples of reflex arcs include deep tendon reflexes (patellar reflex) and the withdrawal reflex to avoid physical injury (reflexive withdrawal from a hot surface before pain is registered or catching oneself from falling). The reflex arc is the only part of the neural path with withdrawal responses. The stimulus continues to travel up the spinothalamic tract to

Figure 13-2. Corticospinal Tracts

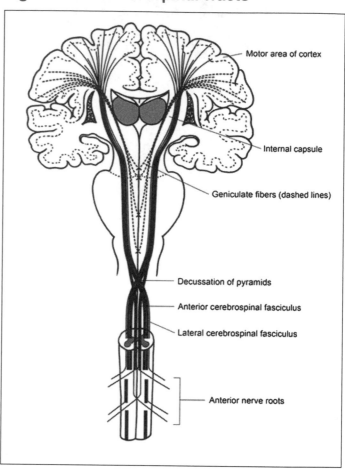

Labels: Motor area of cortex; Internal capsule; Geniculate fibers (dashed lines); Decussation of pyramids; Anterior cerebrospinal fasciculus; Lateral cerebrospinal fasciculus; Anterior nerve roots

Reprinted from Bican, O., Minager, A., & Pruitt, A. (2013). The spinal cord: A review of functional neuroanatomy. *Neurologic Clinics, 31*(1), 1–18, *with permission from Elsevier.*

the cortex, registering pain or imbalance.[5] The essential structures of the reflex arc include the following:[3]

- Receptor (sense organ, cutaneous end organ, or neuromuscular spindle)
- Afferent (sensory) neuron

Table 13-1. Motor and Sensory Spinal Nerve Tracts

Nerve Tracts	Origin	Function	Location in Spinal Cord
Descending tracts Corticospinal (pyramidal)	Cerebral cortex	Voluntary motor	Anterolateral
Ascending tracts Spinothalamic	Sensory receptors located throughout the body	• Pain • Temperature • Crude touch	Anterolateral
Posterior (dorsal) tracts	Sensory receptors located throughout body	• Proprioception • Fine touch • Two-point discrimination	Posterior (dorsal)

Data from Banasik.[5]

- Association (interneuron) neuron
- Efferent (motor) neuron
- Effector neuron (muscle, tendon, or gland that produces response)

An anatomically and physiologically intact reflex arc will function even if there is disruption of spinal cord function above the level of the reflex.[3,6]

Cortical Sensation

Cortical sensation includes simple sensation and deep sensation. Pain, touch, and temperature are known as simple sensations since they have discrete sensory organs, such as the skin. Information from general somatic receptors in the skin is conducted over small diameter fibers of the spinal nerves into the dorsal horn of the spinal cord gray matter. Pain and temperature fibers enter the spinal cord and travel within one to two spinal segments, and then cross before ascending in the spinothalamic tract.[7] Light touch sensation fibers cross immediately upon entering the spinal cord and then ascend in the spinothalamic tract.[7]

Deep sensation includes proprioception, vibration sensation, and deep muscle pain.[4] These afferent (ascending) impulses transmit sensory information by entering the spinal cord via the dorsal roots and ascend in a tract of the spinal cord, depending on the type of sensation. Proprioception and vibration fibers ascend via the posterior column and cross in the medulla. These sensations are referred to as cortical because they require an intact cerebral hemisphere to interpret the impulses.[7]

Spinal Nerves

There are 31 pairs of spinal nerves, including eight cervical, twelve thoracic, five lumbar, five sacral, and one coccygeal. Each pair of spinal nerves exits the spinal cord bilaterally, and each has a dorsal and ventral root. The dorsal root transmits sensory impulses, whereas the ventral root transmits motor impulses. The dorsal root of each nerve innervates particular dermatomes in the body (Fig. 13-3).

The cervical nerves innervate the head, diaphragm, neck, shoulders, and upper arms.[3] The thoracic nerves innervate the thorax, abdomen, and portions of the buttocks and upper arm. The intercostal muscles are innervated by spinal nerves T1 through T12. The lumbar nerves innervate the groin region and lower extremities. The sacral nerves S3 to S5 supply the perianal muscles, which control voluntary contraction of the external bladder sphincter and the external anal sphincter (Table 13-2).[3,6]

Figure 13-3. Dermatomes

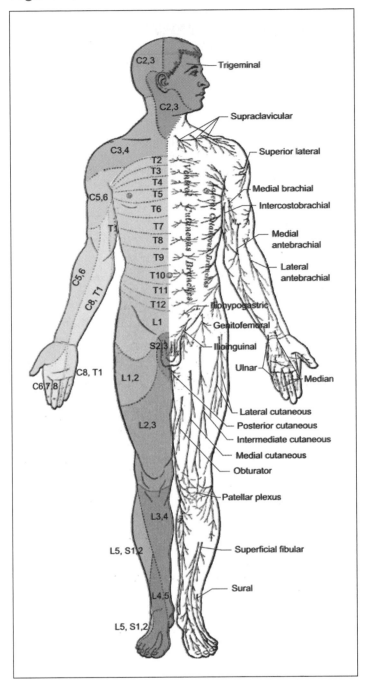

From Haggstrom, M. (2010, October 17). *Dermatomes and cutaneous nerves-anterio.* Retrieved from http://commons.wikimedia.org/wiki/File: Dermatomes_and_cutaneous_nerves_-_anterior.png#

Nerve Plexuses

A plexus is an integral part of the nervous system where nerves converge in small groups. These nerve clusters connect the peripheral and central nervous systems, allowing signals to travel from the brain and spinal cord to the rest of the body. Without these connections, the brain would not be able to communicate with the rest of the body.[5] There are four major nerve plexuses:

Table 13-2. Spinal Nerve Segments and Areas of Innervation

Spinal Nerve Segment	Area Innervated
C5	Area over the deltoid
C6	Thumb
C7	Middle finger
C8	Little finger
T4	Nipple
T8	Xiphisternum
T10	Umbilicus
T12	Symphysis pubis
L4	Medial aspect of the calf
L5	Web space between the first and second toes
S1	Lateral border of the foot
S3	Ischial tuberosity area
S4 and S5	Perianal region

Data from McGee.[7]

- The *cervical* plexus is formed by the first four cervical nerves, which innervate the muscles of the neck and shoulders. In addition, the phrenic nerve arises from C3, C4, and C5, which innervates the diaphragm.[5]

- Spinal nerves C5 to C8, along with T1, form the *brachial* plexus, which supplies motor control and sensation to the arm, wrist, and hand.[3,4] The brachial plexus branches include the ulnar and radial nerves.

- Spinal nerves L1 to L4 form the *lumbar* plexus, which gives rise to the femoral nerve and innervates the anterior portion of the lower body

- Spinal nerves L5 to S4 form the *sacral* plexus, which is the origin of the sciatic nerve. The sacral plexus innervates the posterior portion of the lower body.[3,6]

Autonomic Nervous System
The autonomic nervous system (ANS) fibers innervate smooth muscle, cardiac muscle, and glands, controlling involuntary vital functions such as blood pressure, heart rate, body temperature, appetite, fluid balance, gastrointestinal motility, and sexual function.[1]

The ANS has two subdivisions. The parasympathetic nervous system originates from nerves in the craniosacral regions of the central nervous system, and the sympathetic nervous system originates from the thoracolumbar region of the spinal cord. The parasympathetic division regulates bodily function under normal body conditions. Sympathetic system activity increases during physiologic and psychological stress. Specific responses from autonomic stimulation are dependent on the type and number of receptors located within a tissue, organ, or system. The generalized responses resulting from stimulation of both of these systems are listed in Table 13-3.[3,6]

Vertebral Column
The vertebral column is held together by ligaments and contains 33 vertebrae, including seven cervical, twelve thoracic, five lumbar, five sacral, and four coccygeal vertebrae (Fig. 13-4).[5]

Figure 13-4. The Spine

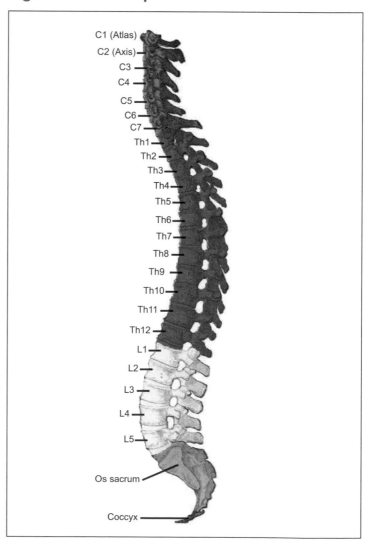

From Gille, U. (2006, October 16). *Gray 11-Vertebral column-coloured.* Retrieved from http://commons.wikimedia.org/wiki/File:Gray_111_-_Vertebral_column-coloured.png

The typical vertebra is composed of a weight-bearing body and a vertebral arch. The arch is made of two pedicles (right and left), two laminae, four articular processes (facets), two transverse processes, and one spinous process (Fig. 13-5). The spinous process can be felt when palpating the back. Together, the arch and the body form an enclosure called the *vertebral foramen* that encircles and protects the spinal cord.[3]

Cervical Vertebrae

The cervical vertebrae are the smallest and most mobile. The first cervical vertebra, the *atlas*, supports the weight of the head and articulates with the occipital condyles of the skull. The atlas is different from the other vertebrae because it has no spinous process or vertebral body. In addition, the foramen opening for the spinal cord is larger than in the rest of the vertebrae. The *axis*, C2, has a perpendicular projection called the odontoid process, or *dens*. The atlas articulates with the axis on the odontoid process.

Thoracic Vertebrae

The thoracic vertebrae, T1 through T12, attach to the ribs, which limits flexion and extension but permits more rotation than the lumbar region and less than the cervical region. The vertebrae in this region are strong, and additional support is provided by the ribs.

Lumbar, Sacral, and Coccygeal Vertebrae

The five lumbar vertebrae (L1–L5) are the largest and strongest in the vertebral column.[3] This area of the spine has some freedom of movement and rotation but not as much as the cervical region. The five sacral vertebrae (S1–S5) fuse together to form the sacrum—a solid bone that fits like a wedge between the bones of the hip. The final four coccygeal vertebrae are fused together to form the coccyx.[3,4,6]

Table 13-3. Effects of Sympathetic and Parasympathetic Stimulation[3,5]

Target Tissue, Organ, or System	Result of Sympathetic Stimulation	Result of Parasympathetic Stimulation
Skin	• ↑ Secretions from sweat glands • Piloerection	N/A
Cardiac	• ↑ Heart rate, conduction, and contractility • Coronary artery dilation	• ↓ Heart rate, conduction, and contractility • Coronary artery constriction
Vascular	• Peripheral vasoconstriction	N/A
Respiratory	• ↑ Respiratory rate • Bronchial dilation • Pulmonary vascular constriction	• Bronchial constriction
Hepatic	• ↑ Glycogen breakdown and synthesis of new glucose	• Promotes glycogen synthesis
Stomach and Intestines	• ↓ Motility and tone • Sphincter contraction • ↓ Gastric secretions and mesenteric blood flow	• ↑ Motility and tone • Sphincter relaxation • ↑ Gastric secretions
Renal	• ↑ Renin secretion • Vascular constriction causes ↓ urinary output	N/A
Adrenal medulla	• Catecholamines, norepinephrine, and epinephrine released from adrenal glands	N/A

Figure 13-5. The Vertebrae

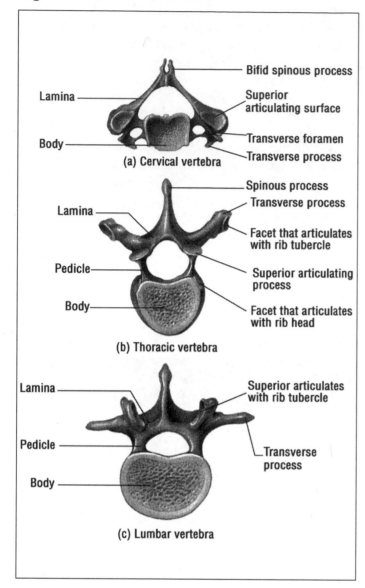

(a) Cervical vertebra
- Lamina
- Body
- Bifid spinous process
- Superior articulating surface
- Transverse foramen
- Transverse process

(b) Thoracic vertebra
- Lamina
- Pedicle
- Body
- Spinous process
- Transverse process
- Facet that articulates with rib tubercle
- Superior articulating process
- Facet that articulates with rib head

(c) Lumbar vertebra
- Lamina
- Pedicle
- Body
- Superior articulates with rib tubercle
- Transverse process

From Barker, E. (2007). *Neuroscience nursing* (3rd ed.). St. Louis, MO: Mosby Elsevier.

Ligaments and Intervertebral Discs

The vertebral bodies are connected by a series of ligaments that provide support and stability for the vertebral column. The anterior and posterior longitudinal ligaments are major ligaments that run the length of the vertebral column and hold the discs and vertebral bodies in position. The ligaments help to prevent the vertebral column from experiencing excessive flexion and extension. The spinous and transverse processes act as points of attachment for muscles and other ligaments. Fibrocartilaginous discs are located between the vertebral bodies and act as shock absorbers during weight bearing and as articulating surfaces for the subsequent vertebral bodies. The more flexible cervical and lumbar regions contain thicker intervertebral discs.[4,6]

Vascular Supply

Blood is supplied to the spinal cord from branches of the vertebral arteries and the aorta. Primarily, the cord is perfused from the anterior and posterior spinal arteries, which branch off from the vertebral artery at the cranial base.[1,4] Injuries to the cord or surrounding area can lacerate these arteries, resulting in hematoma formation that may compress the cord. Injury to the vessels can be devastating because collateral circulation does not develop in this area.[3]

Introduction

All trauma patients with multiple injuries are at risk for spinal cord injury (SCI), regardless of the presence or absence of neurologic deficit on arrival. Given the significant impact a SCI places on the health and ability of the individual, it is essential that trauma nurses who care for these patients maintain adequate spinal immobilization or manual stabilization when caring for these patients in order to avoid any excessive manipulation of the spine until injury can be ruled out.

Epidemiology

In 2009, the average age of a survivor of a SCI was 40.2 years, indicating an increase over recent years.[7] Explanations for this include improved survival rates for older populations. Most injuries are seen in young adult males.[8]

Mechanisms of Injury and Biomechanics

Spinal injuries occur as a result of penetrating or blunt trauma. The causes include:[8]

- Motor vehicle collisions (MVCs), 39.2%
- Falls, 28.3%
- Sports, work-related incidents, and other incidents, 17.9%
- Violence, 14.6%

Most injuries to the spinal cord or vertebral column are the result of blunt injuries from acceleration or deceleration forces. Rapid acceleration or deceleration energy forces may push the spinal column or supporting structures beyond the usual range of motion.[12] Four distinct types of forces can be applied to the vertebral column: hyperextension, hyperflexion, rotation, or axial loading forces. Table 13-4 summarizes those forces and their associated injuries.

Penetrating injuries result from gunshot wounds (GSW) that cause disruption in the integrity of the vertebral column. Stab wounds do not usually cause instability of the vertebral column; however, the wounding object may damage the spinal cord and/or nerve roots.

Types of Injuries

The cervical spine is the most common site for injury.[3] Fifty-five percent of spinal injuries occur to the cervical vertebrae; 15% of injuries occur to the thoracic vertebral area; and the thoracolumbar junctions and lumbosacral are each involved 15% of the time.[9] Extreme forces are required to produce fractures and dislocations in the thoracic region of the vertebral column; therefore, fractures of the thoracic vertebrae can be frequently accompanied by a SCI.[6]

Usual Concurrent Injuries

Concurrent injuries include closed head injuries, long-bone fractures, thoracic injuries, and abdominal injuries.[12] Approximately 5% of patients with brain injury have an associated spinal injury, and 25% of patients with spinal injury have some mild brain injury.[9] When a patient incurs a cervical spinal fracture, there is risk for a second noncontiguous vertebral column fracture 10% of the time.[9] Thoracic injuries may be associated with thoracic vertebral injuries.[3] Pelvic fractures are frequently associated with injuries to the lumbar spine. A fall from a height, resulting in calcaneus fracture, is an additional pattern of injury associated

Table 13-4. Mechanisms of Injury to the Vertebral Column

Mechanism of Injury	Etiology of Injury (Cause)	Result of Injury (Effect)	Example	Common Location of Injury
Hyperextension	Backward thrust of the head beyond the anatomic capacity of the cervical vertebral column	• Damage to anterior ligaments ranging from stretching to ligament tears • Bony dislocations	Rear-end MVC resulting in whiplash	Cervical spine
Hyperflexion	Forceful forward flexion of the cervical spine with the head striking an immovable object	• Wedge fractures • Facet dislocations • Subluxation (due to ligament rupture) • Teardrop, odontoid, or transverse process fractures	Head-on MVC with head striking windshield, creating a starburst effect	Cervical spine
Rotational	A combination of forceful forward flexion with lateral displacement of the cervical spine	• Rupture of the posterior ligament and/or anterior fracture • Dislocation of the vertebral body	MVC to front or rear lateral area of vehicle resulting in conversion of forward motion to a spinning-type motion	Cervical spine
Axial loading	Direct force transmitted along the length of the vertebral column	• Deformity of the vertebral column • Secondary edema of the spinal cord, resulting in neurologic deficits	Diver striking head on bottom of pool	T12–L2

Note: MVC indicates motor vehicle collision.
Data from Boss, B. J. (2010). Disorders of the central and peripheral nervous system and the neuromuscular junction. In K. L. McCance & S. E. Huether (Eds.), *Pathophysiology: The biologic basis for disease in adults & children* (6th ed., pp. 583–646). St. Louis, MO: Mosby; and Jackson, A. B., Dijker, S. M., Deviv, O. M., & Poczatek, R. B. (2004). A demographic profile of new traumatic spinal cord injuries: Change and stability over 30 years. *Archives of Physical Medicine and Rehabilitation, 85,* 1740–1748.

with compression fractures of the lumbar vertebrae.[10] Patients with SCIs often have decreased or altered sensation and/or proprioception, making it difficult to identify other potentially serious injuries.

Seatbelts applied incorrectly may be associated with concurrent injuries. Serious injury to the anterior neck may be associated with the use of diagonal torso belts alone. Lumbar vertebral fractures or dislocations may result from the use of a lap belt only.[10]

Pathophysiology as a Basis for Assessment Findings

A SCI usually begins with sudden, traumatic application of force to the spinal column or supporting structures. Displaced bone fragments, damaged disc material, or torn ligaments result in bleeding into the vertebral column or spinal cord tissue. Primary and secondary mechanisms of injury are involved in the pathophysiology of acute SCI. Both may result in neurologic dysfunction.

Primary Injury

Primary injury typically refers to the initial mechanical damage to the spinal cord and includes:

- Laceration or puncture of the cord from displaced or jagged bone fragments

- Crushed or contused disc material

- Stretching or crushing of the spinal cord

- Torn or strained ligaments

- Bleeding into the vertebral column or spinal cord tissue

- Direct injury to the cord including:

  ° Cord concussion: A transient dysfunction of the spinal cord lasting 24 to 48 hours. This injury may be observed in patients with preexisting degenerative disease and resultant narrowing of the vertebral foramen.[1,2]

  ° Cord contusion: Bruising of the neural tissue causing edema, ischemia, and possible infarction of tissue from cord compression. The degree of neurologic deficit is dependent on the size, location, and local physiologic changes related to the bleeding.[1,2]

  ° Cord transection: Complete disruption of the neural elements. With cord transections, all cord-mediated functions below the level of the injury are permanently lost.[2]

  ° Incomplete cord transection: An interruption in the vascular perfusion to the spinal cord may result in cord ischemia or necrosis. Ischemia results in temporary deficits. Prolonged ischemia results in necrosis of the spinal cord with permanent neurologic deficits.[2]

Secondary Injury

The progressive cell damage that results from biochemical and cellular reactions due to inflammatory response, hemorrhage, hypoperfusion, and hypoxemia in SCI is considered secondary injury.[11] Understanding the pathophysiology related to secondary injury is essential to implementing patient interventions to reduce the amount of cell loss, minimize the secondary injury cascade, and optimize the patient's functional outcome.

Table 13-5. Neurogenic and Spinal Shock

	Neurogenic Shock	Spinal Shock
Precipitating injury	• Spinal cord injury at T6 or above	• Spinal cord injury at any level
Pathophysiology	• Temporary loss of vasomotor tone and sympathetic innervation	• Transient loss of reflex (flaccidity) below the level of injury
Duration	• Temporary, often < 72 hrs	• Variable
Signs/Symptoms	• Hypotension • Bradycardia • Loss of ability to sweat below level of injury	• Flaccidity • Loss of reflexes • Bowel and bladder dysfunction

Data from American College of Surgeons[7] and Bawa & Fayssoux.[10]

Vascular System Response (Neurogenic Shock)

Neurogenic shock occurs with damage to the spinal cord, commonly at T6 or higher, which results in disruption of the sympathetic regulation of vagal tone leading to loss of vascular resistance and generalized vasodilation (Table 13-5). Peripheral vasodilation, reduced systemic vascular resistance, decreased venous return, decreased cardiac output, and lowered blood pressure occur due to loss of vascular tone.[1,2,4,12] Although the patient experiences hypotension, it is not the result of a change in blood volume.[6] The blood volume is redistributed or pooled in the vasodilated peripheral vasculature, which is neurogenic shock. See Chapter 7, Shock, for more information.

Assessment findings include:
- Bradycardia
  - Sympathetic innervation to the heart is lost[3]
  - The body is unable to respond to hypovolemia with a tachycardic response, resulting from an unopposed parasympathetic vagal response
- Hypotension
  - As the reduction in blood flow becomes more widespread, with venous pooling in the periphery, self-regulation is compromised, and blood pressure falls[3]
- Warm, normal skin color
  - This is due to peripheral vasodilation
- Core temperature instability
  - This is due to peripheral vasodilation

Because the effectiveness of vasoconstriction is compromised, along with hypotension and resulting decreased venous blood, circulation to the spinal cord decreases. This results in loss of function, which can last from several hours to several days.[3]

Nervous System Response (Spinal Shock)

Spinal shock occurs when normal activity in the spinal cord at and below the level of the injury ceases because of a disruption or inhibition of impulses in the spinal cord.[1] See Table 13-5. When the spinal cord is injured, a cascade of events takes place:
- Blood supply to the cord can be disrupted
- Axons are severed or damaged
- Conduction of electrical activity of neurons and axons is also compromised
- All of the above result in loss of function, which can last from several hours to several days

Spinal shock results in a complete loss of reflex function below the level of the injury.[1,9,10] A transient hypotensive period and poor venous circulation may be seen.[1] Disruption in the thermal control centers results in sweating and a lack of ability to regulate body temperature.[1]

Onset is usually immediate or soon after the injury. The timing of resolution of spinal shock is debatable. One model shows spinal shock occurring in four phases and resolution delayed up to 12 months after injury.[12] The intensity and duration of spinal shock varies with the severity and level of the lesion. These changes are most prominent at the level of the injury and in the two cord segments above and below it.[1]

Additional assessment findings include:
- Transient loss of muscle tone (flaccidity) and complete or incomplete paralysis with loss of reflexes and sensation at or below the level of the injury
- Bowel and bladder dysfunction
- The return of sacral reflexes, bladder tone, and the presence of hyperreflexia indicates the resolution of spinal shock[1]
- The presence of rectal tone and intact perineal sensation indicates sacral sparing

Immune (Inflammatory) Response

Once the spinal cord is damaged, the immune or inflammatory system is activated. How immune cells function once they enter the damaged spinal cord is poorly understood. Additional factors to the immune response include:
- Within minutes of the injury, endothelial cells that line the blood vessels in the spinal cord become edematous[1,5]
- The combination of leaking, swelling, and sluggish blood flow prevents the normal delivery of oxygen and nutrients to neurons[1,5]
- Edema in the white matter impairs cord circulation and leads to the development of ischemic areas
- The resulting cellular ischemia may cause a temporary loss of function

Spinal cord neurons do not regenerate; therefore, severe injury with cellular death may result in the following assessment findings:
- Temporary or permanent loss of function
- Flaccidity
- Loss of reflexes

Other Related Pathophysiologic Changes

Respiratory System
- Respiratory arrest: Injury to the cord at C3 to C5 can cause loss of phrenic nerve function, resulting in a paralyzed diaphragm and inability to breathe
- Hypoventilation: Injury to the spinal cord between T1 and T11 may result in the loss of intercostal muscles and decreased respiratory effort. Loss of innervation from T7 to T12 may result in loss of the use of abdominal muscles for support of breathing.

Pain
- The ability to perceive pain may be disrupted and result in an inadequate physical assessment. See Chapter 8, Pain, for more information.

Selected Vertebral Column and Spinal Cord Injuries

Spinal Cord Injuries
Spinal cord injuries (SCIs) are classified according to the following:[9]
- Level of injury
- Severity of neurologic deficit
- Spinal cord syndromes

Level of Injury
The vertebral level is the level of vertebrae where the injury occurred. However, the neurologic injury level is determined by clinical assessment and is the lowest level that has positive sensory and motor function.[8] The vertebral level may not be the same as the neurologic level since the spinal cord tracts are not exactly synonymous with the level of vertebrae. Level of injury usually refers to the neurologic level.

The sensory level is the point of demarcation where there is no or decreased sensation below and normal sensation above.

Severity of Neurologic Deficit
SCI can be characterized as an incomplete or complete lesion.

Incomplete Spinal Cord Lesion
Selected incomplete lesions are referred to as specific incomplete spinal cord syndromes (Fig. 13-6). Comparison of motor and sensory function of bilateral upper and lower extremities is important to discern the exact cord syndrome. These cord syndromes include:
- Central cord syndrome: Characterized by loss of motor function in the upper extremities that is greater than that of the lower extremities. There is often sacral sparing. Bladder function may be affected.
- Anterior cord syndrome: Loss of pain and temperature sensation with weakness, paresthesia, and urinary retention
- Brown-Sequard syndrome: Contralateral loss of pain and temperature sensation and ipsilateral paralysis with reduced touch sensation (occurrence is rare)

A patient with an incomplete SCI has some sensory and/or motor function below the level of the injury. Sacral sparing represents some structural integrity of the lowest sacral segments of the spinal cord at S4 and S5.[13] Sacral sparing is identified by the following:[13]

Figure 13-6. Incomplete Spinal Cord Syndromes

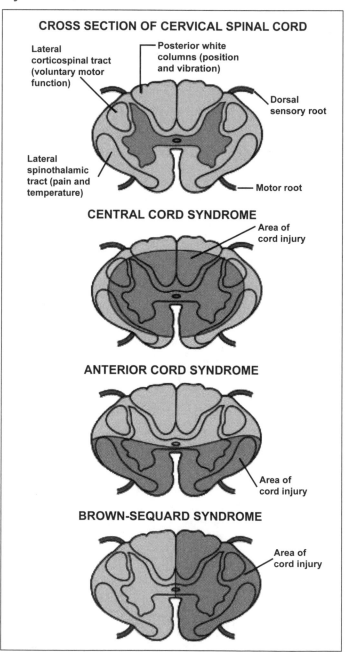

From Marx, J. A. (2009). *Rosen's emergency medicine* (7th ed.). St. Louis, MO: Mosby Elsevier.

- Intact perianal sensation
- Voluntary anal sphincter tone
- Voluntary great toe flexor function

It is important to recognize that a patient with an incomplete lesion may not exhibit sacral sparing in the presence of spinal shock. As spinal shock resolves, sacral sparing may become evident.

Complete Spinal Cord Lesions

Patients with a complete SCI lose all motor and sensory function at and below the level of the lesion. Assess for the following:[1,10]

- Absent motor function below the level of the injury
- Flaccid paralysis and bilateral external rotation of the legs at the hips
- Absent sensory function below the level of the injury, such as loss of pain, touch, temperature, pressure, vibration, and proprioception
- Loss of all reflexes below the level of the injury
- Loss of ANS function
  - Hypotension resulting in venous pooling in the extremities
  - Bradycardia
  - Poikilothermia primarily related to the absence of sympathetic tone and inability of the patient to shiver or sweat to regulate body temperature
  - Loss of voluntary bowel and bladder function
- Paralytic ileus with abdominal distention
- Priapism
- Respiratory depression

Vertebral Column Injuries

Vertebral column injuries are described as fractures, subluxations/dislocations, and penetrating injuries. They are further classified as stable or unstable.[9]

Atlas and Axis Fractures

The atlas vertebra, C1, and the axis vertebra, C2, provide a wide range of motion. Table 13-6 describes four fractures and dislocations of this region. Almost one third of SCIs result from excessive energy transfer to C1 and C2 and can result in death.[9,14] Most fatal cervical spinal injuries occur at the craniocervical junction with associated subluxation or dislocation causing loss of central innervation to the phrenic nerve resulting in apnea.[9,12] The risk of neurologic injury secondary to spinal cord injury increases with age-related degenerative changes such as rheumatoid arthritis, ankylosing spondylitis, and spinal stenosis, the specific mechanism of injury, and location of the injury.[15]

Vertebral Fracture Stability

Vertebral fractures are frequently classified as stable or unstable. Spinal stability is defined as the following:[16]

- No potential for progressive impingement or injury to the spinal cord
- No potential for displacement of injured bony area during the healing process
- No displacement or angulation from normal physiologic loading after healing has occurred

The integrity of ligamentous and bony structures will dictate the stability of the vertebral column. The loss of ligamentous integrity can result in an unstable spinal injury and subsequent damage to the spinal cord or nerve roots.[12] During resuscitation, treat these patients as though they have an unstable injury and maintain spinal immobilization until SCI can be ruled out (Table 13-6).

Subluxation or Dislocation

Injuries to the anterior and posterior ligaments may produce unilateral or bilateral facet dislocation, resulting in dislocation of the vertebrae. If the vertebrae are not completely dislocated, the injury is termed a subluxation. Dislocations and subluxations may occur simultaneously with a fracture.

Vertebral Body Fractures

Vertebral fractures most often occur in the vertebral body itself or in combination with another part of the vertebrae. The mobility of the cervical and lumbar regions results in an increased frequency of these injuries.[1,10] Fractures of the transverse or spinous processes of the vertebrae are considered minor vertebral fractures. These injuries do not typically result in associated neurologic compromise and are considered mechanically stable. However, significant forces are required to cause these fractures, therefore, abdominal injuries may be associated with these injuries.[3]

Vertebral fractures of the thoracic and lumbar spine are typically caused by high-energy trauma, and spinal cord damage with neurologic deficits can result. However, osteoporosis can place the older adult at risk with low-energy trauma. The unique anatomic and functional features of each vertebral region result in specific injuries. Greater force is required to fracture the thoracic vertebrae due to the support provided by the sternum, and the ribs.[11] However, the relative immobility of the thoracic spine as compared to the flexibility of the lumbar spine can result in a fracture at the thoracolumbar junction (T11–L1) most often a result of acute hyperflexion and rotation.[9] These fractures result in an unstable fracture and they are vulnerable to rotational

Table 13-6. C1 and C2 Fractures and Dislocations

Fracture/Dislocation	Mechanism of Injury	Description	Clinical Considerations
(C1) Atlanto-occipital dislocation	• Hyperflexion with distracting injury	• Dislocation of atlas from the occipital bone	• Commonly fatal • Common cause of death in abusive head trauma
(C1) Atlas fracture, Burst fracture, or Jefferson fracture	• Axial loading forces transmitted from occiput to spine	• Disrupts anterior and posterior rings of C1 • Lateral displacement of lateral masses • Spinal cord involvement rare	• Treat as unstable until definitive evaluation
(C1) Rotary Subluxation	• May occur spontaneously or with minor trauma	• Persistent rotation of the head (torticollis)	• Most often seen in children • Immobilize in the rotated position
(C2) Odontoid fracture Hangman's fracture	• Hyperextension	• Occurs in about 20% of axis fractures • C2 posterior elements are affected	• Consider transverse ligament injury • Maintain external immobilization until definitive evaluation

Adapted from American College of Surgeons (2012). Advanced trauma life support student course manual (9th ed.) Chicago, IL: Author; and Davenport, M. (2013, March 19). Cervical spine fracture in emergency medicine. Retrieved from http://emedicine.medscape.com/article/824380-overview.

movement so great care is required when logrolling these patients.[9] See Table 13-7 for more information.

Nursing Care of the Patient with Spinal Cord or Vertebral Column Injuries

Preparation and Triage
Safe Practice, Safe Care
When considering the nursing care of the trauma patient from the perspective of SCI, a vital aspect to safe care is the suspicion that a vague history may indicate a mechanism for spinal injury. An unwitnessed near drowning may be a diving injury. The unconscious patient may have fallen. The infant arriving with seizures and unresponsive may have suffered abusive head trauma, which can include a SCI. If the mechanism is unclear, treat these patients as though they have a SCI until cleared.

Triage
There are many reasons the patient with a suspected or confirmed SCI may warrant a high acuity rating for triage, including alterations in vital signs from neurogenic shock, diminished respiratory effort from loss of innervation of the muscles of ventilation, and alterations in level of consciousness from concurrent head injury.

Primary Survey and Resuscitation Adjuncts
Refer to Chapter 5, Initial Assessment for the systematic approach to the nursing care of the trauma patient. The following assessment parameters are specific to patients with spinal cord and vertebral column injuries.

A–Airway and Alertness
Cervical spinal immobilization is always a part of the airway and alertness assessment, but nowhere else is it more important than with the patient with a strong mechanism of injury or indication for spinal injury. Patients with distracting injuries (significant blood loss, open fractures) and those with questionable intoxication or altered mental status are presumed to have sustained a vertebral injury until proven otherwise.[12]

Assessment
Assess immobilization devices for correct placement and proper fit. Once immobilization is verified, additional assessment of spinal cord integrity may be deferred until the primary survey is complete.

Intervention
Apply manual stabilization as necessary throughout the primary and secondary surveys, such as when removing the collar to examine the neck.

Table 13-7. Thoracic Vertebral Fractures

Fracture	Mechanism of Injury	Description
Anterior compression (Wedge)	• Axial loading • Flexion	• Anterior portion rarely > 25% shorter than the posterior body • Most are stable
Burst (Comminuted)	• Vertical axial compression	• Comminuted fracture of vertebral body • May result in spinal cord injury • Unstable
Chance fracture (Seatbelt fracture)	• Hyperflexion	• Horizontal fracture lines with injury to bone and ligaments • Suspect injuries to organs in the peritoneal cavity • Certain types are unstable
Fracture–dislocation	• Extreme flexion	• Disruption of the pedicles, facets and lamina of the thoracic or lumbar vertebrae • Subluxation can result in complete neurologic deficit • Unstable • Relatively uncommon

Adapted from American College of Surgeons (2012). *Advanced trauma life support student course manual* (9th ed.) Chicago, IL: Author; and Reither, G. T. (2011, January 7). *Vertebral fracture.* Retrieved from http://emedicine.medscape.com/article/248236-overview#a0104.

B–Breathing and Ventilation
Assessment
Shallow respirations or evidence of increased work of breathing may indicate a cervical or thoracic SCI. Cervical SCIs can impair the patient's ability to breathe due to loss of phrenic nerve function and use of the diaphragm and thoracic SCIs can result in loss of function of the muscles of respiration (intercostals).

Intervention
Be prepared to support inadequate respiratory effort with bag-mask ventilation.

C–Circulation and Control of Hemorrhage
Assessment
- Differentiate signs of hypovolemic shock from signs of neurogenic shock

  - Neurogenic shock presents with assessment findings of impaired cardiac output accompanied by bradycardia and a normal or strong pulse

  - Hypovolemic shock is characterized by tachycardia with a weak peripheral pulse[9]

Intervention
- Use care when administering intravenous fluids (IV) to the patient in neurogenic shock in order to avoid pulmonary edema

- If there is no improvement in hypotension with fluid resuscitation, consider inotropic support[10]

D–Disability (Neurologic Status)
Assessment
- Be aware that Glasgow Coma Scale (GCS) motor response score may not be reliable in the patient with a spinal cord injury

- Ineffective breathing from poor muscular function may result in anxiety

E–Exposure and Environmental Control
Assessment
Anticipate temperature instability with neurogenic shock and peripheral vasodilation

G–Get Resuscitation Adjuncts
P–Pain Assessment and Management
Lack of pain may be a significant finding if SCI is suspected based on mechanism of injury or identified injuries.

Reevaluation
For known SCIs, early evaluation for interfacility transfer is recommended. If transfer is indicated, delegate or begin preparation before continuing to the secondary assessment. The American College of Surgeons (ACS) supports transferring the patient with a known or suspected SCI to a specialized center or trauma center. Spinal immobilization during transport must be ensured.

Secondary Survey
H–History
Questions specific to patients with spinal or vertebral injuries include the following:
- Was there a mechanism of injury that is strongly associated with SCI?

- What symptoms were noted in the field: pain in the head or neck, numbness, tingling, loss of motor activity of the extremities, loss of bladder or bowel control? Have the symptoms changed since arrival?

- What medications are currently used? Will any affect the assessment parameters in the patient with SCI (changes in heart rate and blood pressure)?

- Is there any past medical history that is significant? Does the patient have diabetic neuropathy that may affect the central nervous system examination? Is there a history of spinal injury, stenosis, arthritis, or osteoporosis that may increase the suspicion of injury despite a minor mechanism of injury?

Documentation that reflects an accurate and thorough initial assessment and history will facilitate trending of signs and symptoms. The absence of these symptoms with subsequent development later may indicate expansion of a hematoma or edema formation.

H–Head-to-toe Assessment
Neck and Cervical Spine
Palpate for:
- Use a second person to maintain manual stabilization of the cervical spine while removing the collar for palpation.[9] Reapply the collar after assessment and determine proper placement.

- Gently palpate the neck for pain, tenderness, crepitus, subcutaneous emphysema, or step-off deformities between vertebrae

Pelvis/Perineum
Inspect for:
- Assess for the presence of priapism. This may be a sign of loss of sympathetic nervous system control and stimulation of the parasympathetic nervous system.

Extremities

Inspect for:
- Ask the patient to wiggle the toes and fingers and to lift the arms and legs to assess extremity movement and control
  - The inability to perform gross extremity movement indicates a lesion above the level of injury. Table 13-8 lists normal extremity movement with associated levels of innervation.

Palpate for:
- Palpate all extremities for the presence of crepitus, step-off deformity, or early development of edema
- Palpate skin temperature
  - Skin is warm and dry in neurogenic shock, as opposed to cool and moist in hypovolemic shock
  - If there is concomitant hemorrhage, skin may become cool
- Assess all four extremities for muscle strength
  - Muscle strength is usually graded from 5 (normal) down to 0 (total paralysis)[9]
  - Assess muscle strength bilaterally, upper and lower for comparison[10]
- Assess sensory function; loss of sensation can affect the patient's ability to identify areas of pain or fractures
  - Assess the patient's response to pain
    - Use a pinprick to determine levels of sensory function. Begin distally and proceed proximally to aid in localizing the level of injury.[10]
  - Assess the patient's response to pressure
    - Use the head of a pin to determine response to pressure
  - Assess proprioception.
    - This can be tested by moving the great toe up, down, or in a neutral position and asking the patient to describe the position[10]

I–Inspect Posterior Surfaces

Inspect for:
- Logroll the patient to assess the vertebral column for deformity, tenderness, or open wounds, or impaled objects, maintaining spinal precautions

Table 13-8. Assessment of Innervation Levels

Movement	Innervation
Extend and flex arms	C5 to C7
Extend and flex legs	L2 to L4
Flexion of foot; extension of toes	L4 to L5
Tighten anus	S3 to S5

Palpate for:
- Palpate the entire vertebral column gently for pain, tenderness, crepitus, or step-off deformities between vertebrae
- Assess for rectal tone
  - An alternative to a digital rectal exam (DRE) is to ask the alert patient to squeeze the buttocks together
  - In the unconscious patient, palpate the anal sphincter
- Assess for sacral sparing
  - The presence of perianal sensation and anal sphincter tone when seen in conjunction with focal deficits represents an incomplete SCI[12]
- Assess for reflexes
  - In the presence of spinal shock, the patient may present with areflexia
  - A Babinski or plantar reflex is a pathologic response in anyone ages one year of age or older due to dysfunction of upper motor neurons of the corticospinal tract. See Chapter 17, Special Populations: The Pediatric Trauma Patient, for more information.
  - Deep tendon reflexes are tested with a reflex hammer by tapping sharply on the tendon and observing for a jerk or contraction of the muscle

Reevaluation Adjuncts
Diagnostic Procedures
Radiographic Studies

Anticipate a computed tomography (CT) scan of the cervical, thoracic, and lumbar spine as indicated. If cross table imaging of the cervical spine is used, verify visualization of all cervical vertebrae through T1.

Unless contraindicated, magnetic resonance imaging may be used to evaluate ligamentous and cord injuries.[4]

Medications

Administer steroids, as prescribed, for non-penetrating injuries.[17] See "Emerging Trends" for more information.

Reevaluation and Post Resuscitation Care

Reevaluation includes trending of neuromuscular status, maintaining homeostasis and further reevaluation to determine the type and degree of injury. These include:

- Maintain cervical spinal immobilization

- Monitor breathing effectiveness. Patients with disruption of the innervation to the intercostal muscles develop respiratory fatigue and must be monitored closely.

- Monitor changes in sensory and motor function

- Monitor temperature to avoid hypothermia

Definitive Care or Transport

If the decision has not already been made, reassess and prepare for interfacility transfer as needed. Careful attention is given to cervical spine immobilization during transport.

Emerging Trends

As the science and evidence of trauma care continues to evolve, tools to improve patient outcomes continue to be trialed and refined. Evidence is tested and replicated, and new standards of care are transitioned into practice. This section on trauma care considerations explores some of the evidence and the potential significance to trauma patient care. In the care of patients with spinal cord and vertebral column injuries, evidence related to cervical spinal clearance, steroid use in SCIs, stem cell research, and hypothermia for SCIs are discussed.

Cervical Spine Clearance

The prevalence of cervical spinal injuries is less than 3% following blunt trauma.[18,19] A timely and accurate diagnosis is imperative.[18] There remains some ambiguity around the optimal approach to diagnosing cervical spinal injuries.[18–21] A more conservative approach to diagnose cervical spinal injuries is to obtain imaging studies on all trauma patients.[18] Other guidelines recommend using a screening tool to identify those patients with a significant likelihood of clinically important cervical spinal injuries.[18,20] The appropriate screening tool is sensitive, with a low rate of false positives.[18]

Two clinical decision tools are available to assess the patient's need for cervical spine imaging following trauma: the Canadian C-Spine Rule and the National Emergency X-Radiography Utilization Study (NEXUS) (Appendix 13-A). The aim of both tools is to reduce the unnecessary imaging.[18,20,22] A study published in the *Canadian Medical Association Journal* compared the two screening tools and found the Canadian C-spine

Rule to have better diagnostic accuracy than the NEXUS criteria.[18] The American College of Surgeons Committee on Trauma (ACS-COT) offers guidelines for cervical spinal injury screening (Table 13-9).

Methylprednisolone Use in Spinal Cord Injuries

There is some controversy regarding steroid use in patients with SCIs. Historically, high-dose steroid administration has been reported to minimize the effects of certain biochemical responses; other sources call into question the risk-benefit ratio of routine use of steroids.[17]

Three clinical trials conducted by the National Acute Spinal Cord Injury Study (NASCIS) over the past 25 years have investigated steroid use in patients with SCI.

A recent study by Hurlbert et al.[23] found evidence that showed significant adverse effects associated with the administration of high-dose steroids, including death, and does not recommend methylprednisolone use in treating acute SCI.

Stem Cell Research

Stem cells are unspecialized cells capable of regenerating or proliferating through cell division and can be induced to become tissue- or organ-specific cells.[24] In comparison, nerve cells do not usually repair, duplicate, or replicate; however, stem cells are very proliferative.[25] Demyelization has been documented as a secondary degenerative component of SCIs; however, there are few studies in humans that reflect the exact consequences on rehabilitation of patients with SCI.[26,27] Chronic demyelination has been observed in the human spinal cord following SCI, suggesting that demyelination contributes to functional disabilities.[26,28] The use of neural stem cells to promote remyelination of nerve cells appears to be promising based on their ability to promote axonal regeneration by development of a foundation for growing axons in the area of ischemia and/or injury.[24,27,29] Stem cell research in the patient with SCI is ongoing. Currently, there are multiple types of cells used in stem cell research; not all types of cells will have the same effects.[26] Identification of the approach that will have maximal benefit in SCI is ongoing.[27,29]

Hypothermia

Therapeutic hypothermia remains an experimental clinical approach; however, research and randomized trials are continuing to evaluate therapeutic interventions. Its use in the treatment of SCIs has demonstrated beneficial effects in reducing localized edema and ischemic changes. However, additional research is needed to provide conclusive evidence for the efficacy of its use. Several

Table 13-9. ACS Guidelines for Screening Patients with Suspected Spine Injury

Cervical Spine Injury

If the patient exhibits paraplegia or quadriplegia, think spinal instability

In patients who are awake, alert, not under the influence, and have no neurologic abnormalities:
- If there is no presence of neck pain, midline tenderness, or distracting injury, an acute cervical spine fracture or instability is unlikely
  - After removing the collar and performing a manual palpation of the neck, if there is no pain, and the patient is able to move their neck without pain, imaging is not necessary
- If neck pain and midline tenderness are present, imaging is necessary. Multi-detector axial CT is recommended where available. The alternative is lateral, AP, and open mouth odontoid radiographs of the cervical spine and axial CT of any suspicious areas or the lower cervical spine if not well-visualized on radiographs. Views must include the spine down to T1.
  - If images are normal the cervical collar can be removed. If suspicion for injury remains, replace the collar and consult a spine specialist.

In patients who have an altered level of consciousness or are nonverbal (children who cannot describe their symptoms):
- Multi-detector axial CT is recommended where available
- The alternative is the same as above, with CT optional in children
- If the cervical spine is normal, the cervical collar can be removed after evaluation by a physician

When in doubt, leave the collar on.

Consult a physician skilled in evaluating and managing patients with spine injuries when spine injury is suspected or determined.

Evaluate patients with neurologic deficits (paraplegia or quadriplegia) rapidly and remove them from the spine board as soon as possible.

In patients who require surgery prior to the completion of a complete spine evaluation:
- Transport the patient carefully and assume an unstable spine injury is present
- Leave the cervical collar on and logroll the patient to and from the operating table
- Remove the patient from the spine board as early as is safely possible
- Inform the anesthesiologist and surgical team of the status of the spine evaluation

Vertebral Column Spine Injury

Paraplegia or sensory loss at the level of the chest or abdomen may indicate spinal instability.

In patients who are awake, alert, not under the influence, and have no neurologic abnormalities and midline thoracic or lumbar back pain or tenderness:
- Palpate and inspect the entire spine. If no tenderness is present on palpation or ecchymosis noted over the spinous processes, unstable fracture is unlikely and imaging may not be necessary.

In patients with spine pain or tenderness on palpation or if they have neurologic deficits, an altered level of consciousness, or suspected intoxication:
- AP and lateral radiographs are recommended
- Thin-cut axial CT is recommended if suspicious areas are seen on radiographs
- Ensure films are good quality and read by an experienced physician prior to spine clearance

Consult a physician skilled in evaluating and managing patients with spine injuries when spine injury is suspected or determined.

Adapted from American College of Surgeons.[9]

clinical studies using animal models have shown the use of therapeutic hypothermia to be promising in patients with severe cervical SCI.[18,30-33] Moderate hypothermia (33°C) introduced systemically by intravascular cooling strategies has been shown to be safe and provides some improvement of long-term recovery of function.[18,30-33]

Summary

Blunt and penetrating injuries to the bony vertebral column may result in fractures, subluxations, or dislocations of the vertebral column. Knowledge of the pattern of injury—including the type of forces applied to the vertebral column and the resulting flexion, extension, or rotation—is important during the assessment of the trauma patient.

Although there are currently many studies examining the ischemic damage to the spinal cord and regeneration of the myelinated nerve fibers, there is no substitution for the initiation and maintenance of cervical spine immobilization and good skin care in the emergency department.

Appendix 13-A. Clearing the Cervical Spine

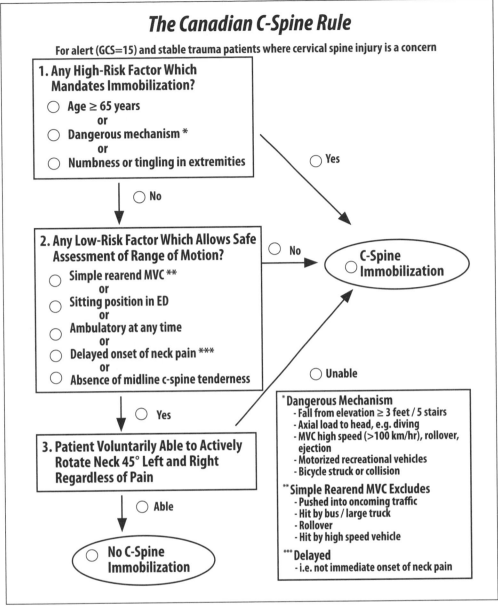

The Canadian C-Spine Rule

For alert (GCS=15) and stable trauma patients where cervical spine injury is a concern

1. Any High-Risk Factor Which Mandates Immobilization?
- ○ Age ≥ 65 years
  - or
- ○ Dangerous mechanism *
  - or
- ○ Numbness or tingling in extremities

○ Yes →

↓ ○ No

2. Any Low-Risk Factor Which Allows Safe Assessment of Range of Motion?
- ○ Simple rearend MVC **
  - or
- ○ Sitting position in ED
  - or
- ○ Ambulatory at any time
  - or
- ○ Delayed onset of neck pain ***
  - or
- ○ Absence of midline c-spine tenderness

○ No →

○ **C-Spine Immobilization**

↓ ○ Yes

○ Unable →

3. Patient Voluntarily Able to Actively Rotate Neck 45° Left and Right Regardless of Pain

↓ ○ Able

○ **No C-Spine Immobilization**

*Dangerous Mechanism
- Fall from elevation ≥ 3 feet / 5 stairs
- Axial load to head, e.g. diving
- MVC high speed (>100 km/hr), rollover, ejection
- Motorized recreational vehicles
- Bicycle struck or collision

**Simple Rearend MVC Excludes
- Pushed into oncoming traffic
- Hit by bus / large truck
- Rollover
- Hit by high speed vehicle

***Delayed
- i.e. not immediate onset of neck pain

Clement et al.[34]

The NEXUS Criteria for Cervical Spine Clearance
• No posterior midline cervical spine tenderness is present
• No evidence of intoxication is present
• The patient has a normal level of alertness
• No focal neurologic deficit is present
• The patient does not have a painful distracting injury

Davenport, M. (2013, March 19). *Cervical spine fracture workup.* Retrieved from http://emedicine.medscape.com/article/824380-workup

The Canadian C-Spine Rule and the National Emergency X-radiography Utilization Study created criteria for clearing patients at low risk for unstable fractures or ligamentous injury to reduce unnecessary imaging in this population. Each institution may have its own policies guiding cervical spine clearance, but the two examples above are provided for reference. Please refer to your institution's policies.

References

1. Sugarman, R. A. (2010). Structure and function of the neurologic system. In K. L. McCance & S. E. Huether (Eds.), *Pathophysiology: The biologic basis for disease in adults and children* (6th ed., pp. 442–480). St. Louis, MO: Mosby Elsevier.

2. Russo, T. A. (2008). Spinal cord injuries. In K. A. McQuillan, M. B. Flynn Mackic, & E. Whalen (Eds.), *Trauma nursing: From resuscitation through rehabilitation* (4th ed., pp. 565–613). St. Louis, MO: Saunders.

3. Seeley, R. R., VanPutte, C., Regan, J., & Russo, A. (2011). *Anatomy & physiology* (9th ed.). Boston, MA: McGraw-Hill.

4. Waxman, S. G. (2010). *Correlative neuroanatomy.* New York, NY: McGraw-Hill.

5. Banasik, J. L. (2013). Structure and function of the nervous system. In L. E. Copstead & J. L. Banasik (Eds.), *Pathophysiology* (5th ed., pp. 857–897). St. Louis, MO: Elsevier Saunders.

6. Tortora, G. J., & Derrickson, B. H. (2012). *Principles of anatomy & physiology* (13th ed.). New York, NY: Wiley Publishing.

7. McGee, S. (2012). Examination of the sensory system. In *Evidence-based physical diagnosis* (3rd ed., pp. 567–580). Philadelphia, PA: Elsevier.

8. National Spinal Cord Injury Statistical Center. (2012, February). *Spinal cord injury facts and figures at a glance.* Retrieved from https://www.nscisc.uab.edu/PublicDocuments/fact_figures_docs/Facts%202012%20Feb%20Final.pdf

9. American College of Surgeons. (2012). Spine and spinal cord trauma. In *Advanced trauma life support student manual* (9th ed., pp. 174–193). Chicago, IL: Author.

10. Howard, P. K. & Steinmann, R. A. (Eds.). (2010). *Sheehy's emergency nursing principles and practice* (6th ed.). St. Louis, MO: Mosby.

11. Dietrich W. D., Cappuccino, A., & Cappuccino, H. (2011). Systemic hypothermia for the treatment of acute cervical spinal cord injury in sports. *Current Sports Medicine Reports, 10*(1), 50–54. doi:10.1249/JSR.0b013e318205e0b3.

12. Bawa, M., & Fayssoux, R. (2013). Vertebrae and spinal cord. In K.L. Mattox, E. E. Moore, & D. V. Feliciano (Eds.), *Trauma* (7th ed., pp. 430–460). New York, NY: McGraw-Hill.

13. Freeman Somers, M. (2010). *Spinal cord injury: Functional rehabilitation* (3rd ed.). Upper Saddle River, NJ: Pearson.

14. Zhang, S., Wadhwa, R., Haydel, J., Toms, J., Johnson, K., & Guthikonda, B. (2013). Spine and spinal cord trauma: Diagnosis and management. *Neurologic Clinics, 31*(1), 183–206.

15. Aresco, C., & Stein, D. M. (2010). Cervical spine injuries in the geriatric patient. *Clinical Geriatrics, 18*(2), 30–35.

16. Gupta, M. C., Benson, D. R., & Keenan, T. L. (2009). Initial evaluation and emergency treatment of the spine-injured patient. In B. D. Browner, B. Jupiter, A. M. Levine, P. G. Trafton, & C. Krettek (Eds.), *Skeletal trauma: Basic science, management, and reconstruction* (4th ed., pp. 729–752). Philadelphia, PA: Saunders Elsevier.

17. Bracken, M. B. (2012). Steroids for acute spinal cord injury. *Cochrane Database of Systemic Reviews,* (1), CD001046. doi:10.1002/14651858.CD001046.pub2.

18. Michaleff, Z. A., Maher, C. G., Verhagen, A. P., Rebbeck, T., & Lin, C. C. (2012). Accuracy of the Canadian C-spine Rule and NEXUS to screen for clinically important cervical spine injury in patients following blunt trauma: A systematic review. *Canadian Medical Association Journal, 184*(16), E867–E876. doi:10.1503/cmaj.120675.

19. Halpern, C. H., Milby, A. H., Guo, W., Schuster, J. M., Gracias, V. H., & Stein, S. C. (2010). Clearance of the cervical spine in clinically unevaluable trauma patients. *Spine, 35,* 1721–1728.

20. Como, J. J., Diaz, J. J., Dunham, C. M., Chiu, W. C., Duane, T. M., Capella, J. M., ...Winston, E. S. (2009). Practice management guidelines for identification of cervical spine injuries following trauma: Update from the Eastern Association for the Surgery of Trauma Practice Management Guidelines Committee. *Journal of Trauma, 67,* 651–659.

21. Rose, M. K., Rosal, L. M., Gonzalez, R. P., Rostas, J. W., Baker, J. A., Simmons, J. D., ... Brevard, S. B. (2012). Clinical clearance of the cervical spine in patients with distracting injuries: It is time to dispel the myth. *Journal of Trauma and Acute Care Surgery, 73,* 498–502.

22. Hoffman, J. R., Mower, W. R., Wolfson, A. B., Todd, K. H., & Zucker, M. I. (2000). Validation of a set of clinical criteria to rule out injury to the cervical spine in patients with blunt trauma. *New England Journal of Medicine, 343,* 94–99.

23. Hurlbert, R. J., Hadley, M. N., Walter, B. C., Aarabi, B., Dhall, S. S., Gelb, D. E., ... Theodore, N. (2013). Pharmacological therapy for acute spinal cord injury. *Neurosurgery, 72,* 93–105.

24. The National Institutes of Health Resource for Stem Cell Research. (2009, April 28). *Stem cell basics.* Retrieved from http://stemcells.nih.gov/info/basics/

25. Becker, D., & McDonald, J. W. 3rd. (2012). Approaches to repairing the damaged spinal cord: Overview. *Handbook of Clinical Neurology, 109,* 445–461. doi:10.1016B978-0-444-52137-8.00028-0

26. Kim, B. G., Hwang, D. H., Lee, S. I., Kim, E. J., & Kim, S.U. (2007). Stem cell-based cell therapy for spinal cord injury. *Cell Transplantation, 16,* 355–364.

27. Li, J., & Lepski, G. (2013). Cell transplantation for spinal cord injury: A systematic review. *BioMed Research International, 2013,* 786475. Retrieved from http://dx.doi.org/10.1155/2013/786475

28. Watson, R. A., & Yeung, T. M. (2011). What is the potential for oligodendrocyte progenitor cells to successfully treat human spinal cord injury? *BMC Neurology, 11,* 113.

29. Thomas, K.E. & Moon, L.D.F. (2011). Will stem cell therapies be safe and effective for treating spinal cord injuries? *British Medical Bulletin 2011; 98:* 127-142.

30. Dietrich, W.D. 3rd. (2009). Therapeutic hypothermia for spinal cord injury. *Critical Care Medicine, 37*(7 Suppl), S238–S242. doi: 10.1097/CCM.0b013e3181aa5d85

31. Maybhate, A., Hu, C., Bazley, F. A., Yu, Q., Thakor, N. V., Kerr, C. L., & All, A. H. (2012). Potential long-term benefits of acute hypothermia after spinal cord injury: Assessments with somatosensory-evoked potentials. *Critical Care Medicine, 40*(2), 573–579. doi: 10.1097/CCM.0b013e318232d97e.

32. Ahmad, F., Wang, M. Y., & Levi, A. D. (2013). Hypothermia for acute spinal cord injury-A review. *World Neurosurgery,* [Epub ahead of print]. doi: 10.1016/j.wneu.2013.01.008

33. Dietrich, W. D., Levi, A. D., Wang, M., & Green, B. A. (2011). Hypothermic treatment for acute spinal cord injury. *Neurotherapeutics, 8*(2), 229–239.

34. Clement, C. M., Stiell, I. G., Davies, B., O'Connor, A., Brehaut, J. C., Sheehan, P., ... Beland, C. (2011). Perceived facilitators and barriers to clinical clearance of the cervical spine by emergency department nurses: A major step towards changing practice in the emergency department. *International Emergency Nursing, 19,* 44–52.

Chapter 14 • Musculoskeletal Trauma

Cynthia M. Bratcher, BSN, RN, CEN

Objectives

Upon completion of this chapter, the learner will be able to:

1. Describe the mechanisms of injury associated with musculoskeletal trauma.

2. Describe pathophysiologic changes as a basis for assessment of the trauma patient with musculoskeletal injuries.

3. Demonstrate the nursing assessment of the trauma patient with musculoskeletal injuries.

4. Plan appropriate interventions for the trauma patient with musculoskeletal injuries.

5. Evaluate the effectiveness of nursing interventions for the trauma patient with musculoskeletal injuries.

Preface

Knowledge of normal anatomy and physiology serves as a foundation for understanding anatomic derangements and pathophysiologic processes that may result from trauma. Before reading this chapter, it is strongly suggested that the learner review the following material. This material will not be covered in the lectures nor tested directly, but as foundational content, it may be the basis for some test questions and skill evaluation steps.

Anatomy and Physiology of the Musculoskeletal System

The musculoskeletal system provides support, protection, and functional movement to the human body. The system includes bones, joints integrated with tendons, ligaments, cartilage, vessels, and nerves, and muscle. Bones store minerals and lipids and produce blood cells in the red marrow.[1]

Bones and Supporting Structures

Bones are composed of several different types of tissue: cartilage, dense connective tissue, epithelium, adipose tissue, and nervous tissue:[2]

- *Cartilage* is a matrix of cells capable of trapping water, which allows the cartilage to rebound after being compressed, providing strength. Following bones, cartilage is the firmest structure in the body.

- *Dense connective tissue* includes protein fibers that form thick bundles of collagen fibers for structures such as tendons and ligaments. Tendons connect muscles to bones, and ligaments connect bones to bones.

- *Epithelial tissue* covers and protects deeper tissue surfaces

- *Adipose tissue* contains lipids and functions to insulate, store energy, and protect against injury

- *Nervous tissue* is characterized by its ability to conduct electrical signals

The two primary types of bone tissues are compact and spongy (cancellous). *Compact bone* is the strongest form of bone tissue. It is dense and more rigid than cancellous bone and forms the shaft of long bones and the exterior covering of other bones. *Cancellous bone* is located in the interior of the bones, and macroscopic spaces between lattice-like columns help make bone lighter. Cancellous tissue is located along stress lines and aids in the bone's resistance to stress without breaking. Cancellous tissue in hips, vertebrae, ribs, sternum, and the ends of long bones is the storage center for red bone marrow and the location of the bone's blood cell production in adults.[3]

Classification of Bones

The adult human body contains 206 bones; however, infants and children have more bones because some fuse together as the body develops. Most bones can be classified into five categories: long, short, flat, irregular, and sesamoid.[4]

- *Long bones* have greater length than width and have a slight curve for strength. Compact bone tissue comprises the shaft of long bones. Long bones include the femur, tibia, fibula, humerus, radius, and ulna.

- *Short bones* are more cube-shaped and consist of cancellous bone except at the surface, which has a thin layer of compact bone. Carpal and tarsal bones are classified as short bones.

- *Flat bones* are usually thin and have a surface of compact bone surrounding a layer of cancellous bone.

The cranial bones, the sternum, and the ribs are flat bones.

- *Irregular bones* are complex-shaped bones; the vertebrae, hip bones, and some facial bones are irregular bones.

- *Sesamoid bones* are small bones that develop in tendons for protection from excessive wear. The largest sesamoid bone is the patella.[5]

Structure of Bone

The structural components of long bones are as follows (Fig. 14-1):

- Epiphysis—the distal and proximal ends of the bone

- Epiphyseal plate—a layer of cartilage that allows for bone growth and ossifies when growth stops after puberty and adolescence[6]

- Diaphysis—the main portion of the bone

- Articular cartilage—a thin layer of cartilage that covers the epiphysis where a bone forms a joint with another bone

- Periosteum—the connective tissue that covers the bone except at articular surfaces

- Medullary cavity—the space within the diaphysis that contains yellow bone marrow in adults[1]

Joints, Tendons, and Ligaments

Joints are classified into three types: synovial, cartilaginous, and fibrous.

- *Synovial joints* have a fluid-filled synovial cavity, and the bones are held together with connective tissue and ligaments. Synovial joints allow free movement and are located at the knee, elbow, and hip.

- *Cartilaginous joints* have no synovial cavity, and cartilage holds the bones together. Cartilaginous joints allow little or no movement and are found at the sternum and vertebra.

- *Fibrous joints* have no synovial cavity, and fibrous connective tissue holds the bones together. They allow little or no movement and are found in the skull, tibia, and fibula.

Other structures support the musculoskeletal system, including tendons, ligaments, and skeletal muscle.

- *Tendons* are cords of dense tissue that attach muscles to bones and control movement of the extremity by extension or flexion of the muscle groups. The tendon pulls the distal bone in the direction of the muscle group movement.

Figure 14-1. Structural Components of Long Bones

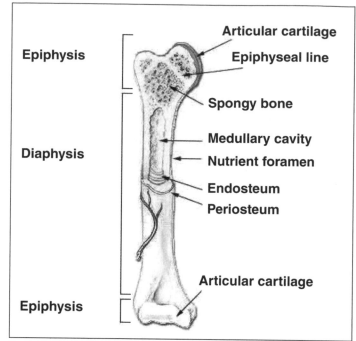

From http://www.daviddarling.info/encyclopedia/B/bone.html

- Ligaments are fibrous capsules that are arranged in parallel bundles of dense connective tissue and are highly resistant to strains. In joints, bones are held together primarily through the strength of ligaments.

- *Skeletal muscle* has striations of dark and light bands containing connective tissues, which surround muscle fibers, blood vessels, and nerves. Skeletal muscle attaches to bone by fibrous connective tissue or tendons.

Blood and Nerve Supply

Bone is highly vascular. Periosteal arteries supply blood to the periosteum and outer part of compact bones, and metaphyseal arteries supply the bone marrow of long bones. Veins are located in the diaphysis, the epiphysis, and the periosteum. The metaphyseal and epiphyseal arteries supply red bone marrow and bone tissue.[3]

Bone is also highly innervated. The periosteum contains many sensory nerves that carry pain sensations. These nerves are sensitive to tearing or tension that can result in severe pain with fracture.

Introduction

Epidemiology

According to the Centers for Disease Control and Prevention (CDC), one third of patients presenting for emergency treatment have an injury due to fractures, sprains, or strains.

Mechanisms of Injury (MOI)

Musculoskeletal trauma can cause single-site or multisystem injuries and is considered high priority when hemodynamic or neurovascular compromise is present. Injury mechanisms include falls, motor vehicle collisions (MVCs), assaults, sports activities, and home- and work-related activities. Falls are the leading cause of musculoskeletal injury in all age groups except teens and young adults. Falls are the leading cause of injury-related death after age 72 years.[7,8] See Chapter 18, Special Populations: The Older Adult Trauma Patient, for more information.

Fall Risk

With falls, comorbidities increase the likelihood of poor healing and complications, and have a high mortality rate, so it is important to evaluate what precipitated the fall. Consider if the fall was the result of the following:

- A mechanical event (trip or slip)
- A comorbid event (cardiovascular, myocardial infarction, syncope)
- Medication use
- Alcohol use

Drinking two to four alcoholic beverages daily can decrease bone mass and bone mineral density and increase fall risk with potential for fractures of the forearm, spine, iliac crest, and greater trochanter.[9]

Types of Injuries

The extremities are the most common site of traumatic injuries.[10] Injuries may involve bone, soft tissue, muscles, nerves, tendons, blood vessels, and joint spaces. Musculoskeletal injuries include fractures, dislocations, amputations, sprains, strains, penetrating injuries, ligament tears, tendon lacerations, and neurovascular compromise. Common injuries include:

- Falling onto outstretched hands (FOOSH)
- Calcaneus fractures in jumps or falls with a feet-first landing: Axial loading forces that diffuse upward, compressing vertebral bodies and resulting in thoracolumbar vertebral fractures
- Fractures of the patella as a result of high-impact trauma (passenger compartment intrusion or when the occupant is thrown forward into the dashboard of the vehicle)
- Fractures of the leg are often accompanied by knee injuries
- Femur fractures, hip fractures and dislocations, and popliteal artery damage associated with knee trauma[11]
- Bilateral tibia and fibula fractures as a result of pedestrian-versus-vehicle injuries: If the pedestrian is struck by a larger vehicle (sport utility vehicle, van, or truck), suspect pelvic injuries[12]

Concurrent Injuries

Musculoskeletal injuries can be predictors of concurrent injuries, and knowledge of concurrent injury patterns help the trauma nurse identify and properly assess for primary and concurrent injuries. In the presence of an open fracture, there is a 70% incidence of associated non-skeletal injury.[13] Table 14-1 describes injuries associated with musculoskeletal trauma.[13]

Table 14-1. Injuries Associated with Musculoskeletal Injuries

Injury	Missed or Associated Injury
Clavicular or scapular fracture / Fracture and/or dislocation of the shoulder	• Major thoracic injury, especially pulmonary contusion and rib fractures
Fracture/dislocation of the elbow	• Brachial artery injury • Median, ulnar, and radial nerve injury
Femur fracture	• Femoral neck fracture • Posterior hip dislocation
Knee dislocation or displaced tibial plateau fracture	• Popliteal artery and nerve injuries
Calcaneal fracture	• Spine injury or fracture • Fracture-dislocation of hindfoot • Tibial plateau fracture
Open fracture	• Associated nonskeletal injury

Pathophysiology as a Basis for Assessment Findings

Blood Loss

Musculoskeletal trauma can result in large-volume hemorrhage, which is the leading cause of preventable death in trauma.[10,13] Fractures of the femoral shaft resulting from high-energy forces are often associated with other injuries and open wounds. Patients with femur fractures can lose up to two or three units of blood as a result of the injury, which can be life threatening.[14]

Musculoskeletal injuries disrupt capillaries and cellular membranes. Hemorrhage in the area surrounding the injury may be visible or occult. As arterial blood flow becomes obstructed, tissue oxygenation decreases, resulting in tissue ischemia and cellular death. During this progression, pain increases, and pulses may become more difficult to palpate. The extremity becomes pale, cyanotic, and cool, and capillary refill time increases.[15,16]

Nerve Injury

Bone or joint displacement can compress surrounding nerves, causing pathophysiologic changes distal to the injury. Compressed or lacerated nerves interrupt conduction pathways, blocking or delaying nerve impulses. Nerve injury can result in alterations in pain sensation and partial or complete loss of motor and sensory function distal to the injured nerve. Increased pain, even when pulses remain present, is a sign of worsening cellular hypoxia, and is often the first sign of increased compartment pressures.[10]

Selected Musculoskeletal Injuries

See Chapter 15, Surface and Burn Trauma, for information on soft tissue injuries.

Figure 14-2. Types of Fractures

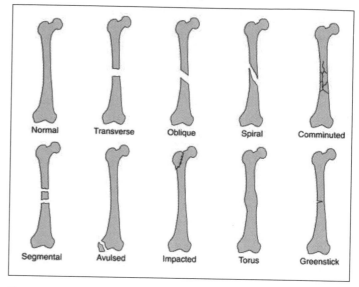

From Roberts, J. (2007). Fractures. In The Merck Manual for Healthcare Professionals. Retrieved from http://www.merckmanuals.com/professional/injuries_poisoning/fractures_dislocations_and_sprains/fractures.html?qt=fractures&alt=sh

Fractures

A fracture is a complete or incomplete interruption in the continuity of the bone cortex. Table 14-2 outlines the classification of fractures. Figure 14-2 illustrates each type of fracture.

Femur Fractures

Major trauma is often the cause of femoral shaft fractures, which can occur in the proximal, distal, or midshaft femur. Femur fractures can result in significant blood loss, which has the potential to cause shock, especially when combined with comorbid factors.[13]

Assessment findings of femur fractures include:[17]

- Pain and the inability to bear weight
- Shortening of the affected leg

Table 14-2. Classification of Fractures

Fracture	Description
Open	Fracture site is accompanied by compromised skin integrity near or over the fracture.
Closed	Skin is intact over or near fracture site.
Complete	Bony cortex is completely interrupted.
Incomplete	Bony cortex is not completely interrupted.
Comminuted	Bone is splintered into fragments.
Greenstick	Bone bends or is buckled.
Impacted	Bone is wedged into distal and proximal fracture sites.
Displaced	Bone fracture sites are not aligned.

- Internal or external rotation
- Edema
- Deformity of the thigh
- Evidence of hypovolemic shock may or may not be present

Open Fractures

All open fractures are considered contaminated due to exposure to the environment and are at risk for infection. These sites of injury have poor wound healing with a risk of osteomyelitis and sepsis. Table 14-3 describes the classification of open fractures. Open wounds near a joint may indicate joint space involvement, and some open fractures with neurologic injury, prolonged ischemia, and muscle damage may require amputation.[15]
Assessment findings of open fractures include:[18]
- Open wound over or near a fracture
- Open wound with protrusion of bone
- Pain
- Neurovascular compromise
- Controlled or severe bleeding

Amputations

Amputations may be partial or complete and usually involve the digits, the lower leg, the hand, or the forearm.[19] The priority is to focus on the overall assessment and resuscitation of the patient to establish and maintain hemodynamic stability, including control of hemorrhage.

Assessment findings of an amputation include:[19]
- Obvious tissue loss
- Pain
- Controlled or severe bleeding
  - Partial amputations may have more severe bleeding than complete amputations because with a complete amputation, the severed arteries retract[19]
- Evidence of hypovolemic shock may or may not be present

Crush Injury

A crush injury of a large muscle can be the result of prolonged compression, entrapment, or a crushing blow. Direct muscle injuries may lead to muscle ischemia and ultimately cell death with release of myoglobin and other cellular components (potassium). This injury can result in several complications, including compartment syndrome, hyperkalemia, and rhabdomyolysis.

Crush injuries can also cause hemorrhage from the damaged tissue, destruction of muscle and bone tissue, fluid loss resulting in hypovolemic shock and infection.

Table 14-3. The Gustilo Classification of Open Fractures

Type	Description
I Low energy injury	Wound < 1 cm
	Fracture: Simple transverse or oblique with skin pierced by bone spike
	Minimal soft tissue damage
	Clean wound
II Moderate energy injury	Wound > 1 cm
	Moderate contamination
	Fracture: Moderate comminution/ crush injury
	Moderate soft tissue damage
III High energy injury	High energy injury
	High degree of contamination
	Fracture: Severe comminution and instability
	Extensive soft tissue damage involving muscle, skin, and neurovascular structures, or amputation
IIIA	Soft tissue coverage of fracture is adequate
IIIB	Extensive injury to or loss of soft tissue, periosteal stripping, and exposure of bone
	Massive contamination
IIIC	Any open fracture associated with arterial injury that must be repaired regardless of degree of soft tissue injury

Data from Kim & Leopold[18] and Walsh, C. R. (2008). Musculoskeletal injuries. In K.A. McQuillan, M. B. Flynn Mackic, & E. Whalen (Eds.), *Trauma nursing: From resuscitation through rehabilitation* (4th ed., pp. 735–779). St. Louis, MO: Saunders.

Compartment Syndrome

Compartment syndrome is a serious complication of musculoskeletal injury and involves increased pressure inside a fascial compartment (Fig. 14-3). This increased pressure can inhibit blood flow, leading to muscle and nerve damage or destruction. Elevated compartment pressures are commonly caused by hematoma formation secondary to fractures from increased pressure or decreased space.[16] Increased pressure may occur from internal or external sources. Internal sources of pressure include hemorrhage or edema from fractures or crush injuries; external sources of pressure include casts,

Figure 14-3. Compartments of the Lower Leg

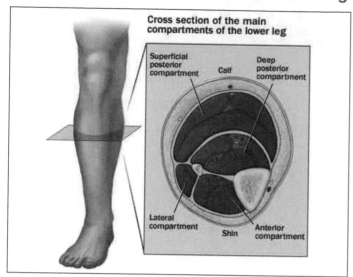

Cross section of the main compartments of the lower leg

Superficial posterior compartment
Calf
Deep posterior compartment
Lateral compartment
Shin
Anterior compartment

From The Mayo Clinic (n.d.). *Chronic exertional compartment syndrome.* Retrieved from http://www.mayoclinic.com/health/medical/IM00124

dressings, traction splints, or air splints. The increased pressure compromises blood flow to nerves, blood vessels, and muscles, resulting in cellular ischemia.

The muscles of the lower leg or forearm are the most frequent sites of compartment syndrome, but it can occur in any fascial compartment.[15,16] The degree of damage is dependent upon the amount of pressure and the length of time perfusion is compromised within the compartment. Muscle necrosis can occur within 4 to 6 hours, resulting in permanent loss of function or amputation.[15,16] The length of time to cellular death is shortened with higher pressures. Measured compartment pressure elevation confirms compartment syndrome. Basing the diagnosis on the loss of palpable pulse may result in tissue damage, as this is often a late sign.[16] Frequent reassessment and identification of neurovascular compromise can improve patient outcomes.

Assessment Findings

Initial findings in compartment syndrome are a feeling of tightness, pain when the muscle is stretched, and rigidity on palpation. The six P's associated with compartment syndrome can be useful, but other than pain and pressure, the others are late signs and damage may already be irreversible.[20] The six P's include:

- **Pain:** A hallmark sign of compartment syndrome is pain out of proportion to the extent of the injury. Pain on passive range of motion of the affected compartment can indicate development of or existing compartment syndrome.

- **Pressure:** The compartment or limb will feel tight or tense upon palpation. The skin may appear taut and shiny as the skin stretches.

- **Pallor:** Poor skin color and cool temperature indicate poor perfusion. Delayed capillary refill may also indicate decreased perfusion.

- **Pulses:** Pulses can remain normal in the presence of compartment syndrome. Weak or absent pulses are late signs of compartment syndrome.[15]

- **Paresthesia:** Numbness, tingling, or loss of sensation may occur as nerves and blood vessels are compressed. With loss of sensation, there may be a relief of pain. This is indicative of a worsening perfusion, not an improvement.

- **Paralysis:** Motor dysfunction signifies injury to the nervous system[16]

Hyperkalemia

Potassium exists predominately in the intracellular space, so cellular destruction releases large amounts of potassium resulting in hyperkalemia, placing the patient at risk for cardiac dysrhythmias.[21] Potassium levels peak at about 12 hours after injury.[22] This may be seen in the initial resuscitation period following a prolonged extraction or delayed transport. See Chapter 24, Post Resuscitation Care in the Emergency Department, for more information.

Rhabdomyolysis

Significant muscle damage and cellular destruction releases myoglobin, a muscle protein, into the bloodstream. Since myoglobin is excreted in the kidneys, the risk of acute renal failure is high in patients with crush injury.[23] The classic triad of assessment findings includes:[24]

- Muscle pain, numbness, or changes in sensation
- Muscle weakness or paralysis
- Dark red, or brown urine

Other assessment findings include:[24]

- Extensive soft tissue edema and bruising
- General weakness or malaise
- Evidence of hypovolemic shock, which may or may not be present
- Elevated creatinine kinase levels

Treatment of rhabdomyolysis is focused on early intervention with aggressive fluid resuscitation to flush out myoglobin to prevent renal failure. It is recommended to maintain the patient's urinary output at 100 mL per hour until the myoglobinuria is resolved.[13]

Joint Dislocations

Dislocations occur when the articulating surfaces of the joint become separated. These can cause nerve injury because of the anatomic proximity of nerves to the affected joint.

Assessment findings of joint dislocations include:
- Inability to move the affected joint
- Joint deformity
- Pain
- Edema
- Abnormal range of motion
- Neurovascular compromise: Diminished or absent pulses; diminished sensory function

Specific joint dislocations can have unique manifestations. These include:
- Dislocated hip joints[25]
  - Often associated with significant trauma
  - Complications of a hip dislocation include:
    - Avascular necrosis of the femoral head
    - Sciatic nerve compression
    - Permanent disability
  - Reduction of the dislocated hip is a priority as soon as the patient is stabilized
- Ankle dislocations may require immediate realignment to restore circulation[26]
- Dislocations of the knee may result in the following:[27]
  - Peroneal nerve injury
  - Constriction of the popliteal artery and vein if reduction of the dislocation is delayed
  - Popliteal artery damage that may not become apparent for several hours; frequent vascular checks recommended

Nursing Care of the Patient with Musculoskeletal Trauma

Primary Survey
See Chapter 5, Initial Assessment, for the systematic approach to care of the trauma patient. The following assessment parameters are specific to musculoskeletal injuries.

Secondary Survey
H–History
The MOI can reveal clues to specific trauma patterns, especially those that occur to certain components of the skeletal structure. It is useful to know where the energy force was applied and the location of pain. Attempt to reconstruct the event to determine the extent of injury, as well as any potential injuries that may not be apparent. See Chapter 4, Biomechanics, Kinematics, and Mechanisms of Injury, for more information.

Components of the history may include:
- MVCs
  - Extent of damage to the vehicle
  - Point of impact on the vehicle
  - Patient location within the vehicle and location at scene
  - Ejection from vehicle
  - Airbag deployment
  - Use of a seat belt
- Pedestrian hit by vehicle
  - Speed of the vehicle upon impact
  - Height or size of the vehicle
  - Vehicle point of impact
  - Patient point of impact
  - Dragged by vehicle
- Falls
  - Height of the fall
  - Landing surface: Concrete, gravel, sand, grass, etc.
  - Point of impact: Feet, head, back, etc.
- Crush injuries
  - Weight of crushing object
  - Length of time compressed: Longer periods of compression increase risk of rhabdomyolysis
  - Body part or parts affected
- Blast injuries
  - Distance between the patient and the point of blast
  - Flying debris

H–Head-to-toe Assessment
Head
- Sudden vision changes may indicate a possible fat embolism in the cerebral vasculature[28]

Chest
- Assess for a fat embolism within the pulmonary vasculature, which is a potential complication of long-bone fractures. It may be evidenced by acute respiratory difficulty in a patient with multiple injuries.[28]

Extremities

Inspect and palpate for:

- Active, uncontrolled bleeding

- Integrity of the injured area, noting any breaks in the skin and soft tissue abnormalities that may indicate fractures or dislocations

- Deformity or angulation of the extremity

- Color, position, and any obvious differences in the injured extremity as compared to the uninjured extremity, such as shortening, rotation, displacement, or loss of function

The six P's can be helpful to guide the trauma nurse's neurovascular assessment of the extremity:[29]

- Pain

  - Field splints should be removed, at least partially, for assessment

  - Palpate the entire length of each extremity for pain or tenderness

  - Assess the quality of pain at identified points

  - Assess the active and passive range of motion of all extremities. Note pain with movement.

- Pallor

  - Assess the color and temperature of the injured extremity

  - Pallor, delayed capillary refill, and a cool extremity may indicate vascular compromise in a normothermic environment

- Pressure

  - The skin may appear shiny as tissue becomes stretched

  - Palpate the extremity for firmness of compartments and for muscle spasms

- Pulses

  - Palpate pulses proximal and distal to the injury

  - Bilateral pulse comparison is necessary to determine quality of the pulse

  - The presence of a pulse does not rule out compartment syndrome

- Paresthesia

  - Assess for abnormal sensations such as burning, tingling, and numbness. Ischemic pain is often described as burning.

- Paralysis

  - Assess range of motion to determine motor function. Neurologic function is related to mobility.

  - Extremities with obvious injury may require deferment of the range of motion assessment due to the risk of increased damage to muscles and nerves

Interventions

Interventions for musculoskeletal injuries include:

- Control of hemorrhage by direct pressure, compression dressings, or tourniquets for severe, life-threatening injuries

- Immobilizing the affected extremity to prevent further bleeding, injury, and pain

Splinting

Splinting is usually performed during or after the secondary survey, depending on the risk to the patient. Remove clothing and jewelry prior to splinting and immobilization. Abnormalities that indicate the possible need for splinting include:

- Pain

- Deformity

- Bony crepitus

- Edema

- Circulatory compromise

Splinting can also be used to stabilize an impaled object.

Types of splints include:

- Rigid splints, such as cardboard, plastic, or metal splints: Pad to prevent pressure injury to bony prominences

- Soft splints or air splints

- Traction splints: Applied for femur or proximal tibial fractures

- Custom splints with fiberglass casting materials

Guidelines for splint application include the following:[30]

- If the patient has an obvious deformity or bony protrusion, do not attempt repositioning of the limb

- Assess pulse, temperature, color, and pulse quality before and after each attempt to immobilize the limb or move the patient

  - Note any losses of a previously palpable pulse; changes in temperature, color, or pulse quality; or increases in pain

  - If present, repositioning of the extremity may be indicated. Remove the splints and notify the physician.

- Elevate the extremity

  - If compartment syndrome is suspected, elevate the limb to the level of the heart.[31] Avoid elevating the limb higher than the heart, as this can reduce circulation and tissue perfusion.[32]

- If compartment syndrome is not a risk, elevate above the level of the heart to reduce pain and swelling

- Assess and treat pain to include administration of pain medications as prescribed

- Prepare for procedural sedation following institutional policy when indicated

- Immobilize the joint

  - When applying a splint or other immobilizing device, include joints above and below the deformity

  - Avoid movement of the fractured extremity, which can increase bleeding and the risk of fat embolism or can result in an inadvertent open fracture

- Apply ice to reduce swelling and pain for 20 minutes. Do not place ice directly on the skin. Ice can be reapplied hourly as necessary.[33]

  - If compartment syndrome is suspected, ice is strongly contraindicated, as it can exacerbate already compromised perfusion

Interventions for Selected Injuries
Open Fracture

- Cover open wounds with saline-soaked dressings[34]

- Administer antibiotics as ordered

- Administer tetanus prophylaxis according to current CDC guidelines

Amputation

- Apply direct pressure over bleeding or compress the artery above the bleeding site

- Elevate the extremity

- Tourniquets can be used when pressure and elevation fail to control bleeding

  - Pneumatic tourniquets (similar to large blood pressure cuffs) may be required for stabilization of complex injuries[13]

  - Tourniquets are placed as close to the amputation site as possible to limit ischemia and nerve compression of extremity

  - Release the tourniquet as soon as the hemorrhage is controlled[10]

  - Recent studies have shown that tourniquets are valuable as a lifesaving measure for amputations with uncontrolled bleeding[35]

- Remove dirt or debris from the amputated part and the residual limb

  - *Residual limb* refers to the part of the body that remains after an amputation—for instance, the part of the thigh that remains following an above-the-knee amputation is the residual limb[36]

- Keep the amputated part cool by wrapping it in slightly saline-moistened sterile gauze, and then place it in a sealed plastic bag

  - The bag containing the amputated part is then placed in a second bag containing ice water

  - Do not allow the amputated part to freeze or be submerged in liquid

  - Label the bag with appropriate patient identifiers[35]

- Administer antibiotics as ordered

- Administer tetanus prophylaxis according to current CDC guidelines

Crush Injury and Compartment Syndrome

- Administer an intravenous isotonic crystalloid solution to increase urinary output to 100 mL per hour to enhance the excretion of myoglobin[13]

- Remove casts, splints, or dressings

- Elevate the limb only to the level of the heart to promote circulation[31]

- Initiate noninvasive hemodynamic monitoring to observe for cardiac dysrhythmias

- Prepare for measuring fascial compartment pressure. This is typically performed by a physician inserting a large-caliber needle or catheter into the fascia of the involved muscle and attaching it to a manometer or intracompartmental pressure monitor. A noninvasive method of measuring compartmental pressure is by using near-infrared spectroscopy to measure decreased tissue blood flow.[37] Normal pressure is 0 to 8 mm Hg. Elevated readings of 30 to 40 mm Hg are suggestive of ischemia to muscles and nerves.

- Anticipate a fasciotomy, if indicated, to decompress the compartment to prevent muscle and/or neurovascular damage and loss of the limb. Surgical debridement or amputation may also be necessary.

Reevaluation Adjuncts to the Secondary Survey

Additional diagnostic studies for patients with musculoskeletal trauma include the following:

- Anterior posterior and lateral radiographs of the injured extremity are necessary. Some fractures can only be seen from one angle, which may require an additional oblique view. The images need to include the joints above and below the injury.

- Computed tomography (CT) can be used for more definitive evaluation of musculoskeletal trauma and for assessment of damage to surrounding organs

- Angiography can be performed to identify tears or compressions in the vasculature of the injured extremity

- Noninvasive near-infrared spectroscopy to measure decreased tissue blood flow can be useful to diagnose compartment syndrome

Reevaluation

Refer to Chapter 5, Initial Assessment, for a description of reevaluation of the trauma patient.

Additional evaluations related to musculoskeletal injuries include:

- The six P's
- Urinary output and presence of myoglobin

Definitive Care or Transport

Prepare the patient for definitive stabilization, operative intervention, hospital admission, or transfer. Definitive stabilization includes:

- Closed or open reduction
- Traction
- External fixators
- Casting

Summary

Extremity injuries are usually addressed during the secondary survey. However, some injuries may be life threatening and require immediate intervention for uncontrolled hemorrhage during the primary survey. Consideration is also given to injuries that may result in functional disability and loss of limb. The secondary survey is carefully conducted in order to identify all injuries. Early intervention for suspected fractures to include neurovascular assessment before and after any splint application can help to prevent further injury. Pain is important to consider in musculoskeletal injuries, and splinting and pain medication can be effective means of pain management.

A systematic approach to the assessment and reassessment of the trauma patient assists in the identification of musculoskeletal injuries and life-threatening sequelae to improve the overall outcome for the patient.

References

1. Yale Medical Group. (n.d.). *Anatomy of the bone.* Retrieved from http://www.yalemedicalgroup.org/stw/Page.asp?PageID=STW022760

2. Seeley, R., VanPutte, C., Regan, J., & Russo, A. (Eds.). (2011). Skeletal system: Bones and bone tissue. In *Seeley's anatomy & physiology* (9th ed., pp. 109–147). New York, NY: McGraw-Hill.

3. Tortora, G. J., & Derrickson, B. (2012). The skeletal system: Bone tissue. *Principles of anatomy and physiology* (13th ed., pp. 182–207). Hoboken, NJ: Wiley.

4. Tortora, G. J., & Derrickson, B. (2012). The skeletal system: The axial skeleton. *Principles of anatomy and physiology* (13th ed., pp. 208–254). Hoboken, NJ: Wiley.

5. *Mosby's medical dictionary* (9th ed.). (2009). St. Louis, MO: Mosby Elsevier.

6. Gunn, A. (2009). *Essential forensic biology* (2nd ed.). West Sussex, United Kingdom: John Wiley and Sons.

7. Centers for Disease Control and Prevention. (2012, July). *FASTSTATS–Accidental or unintentional injuries.* Retrieved from http://www.cdc.gov/nchs/fastats/acc-inj.htm

8. American College of Surgeons. (2012). Geriatric trauma. In *Advanced trauma life support student course manual* (9th ed., pp. 272–285). Chicago, IL: Author.

9. Maurel, D. B., Boisseau, N., Benhamou, C. L., & Jaffre, C. (2012). Alcohol and bone: Review of dose effects and mechanisms. *Osteoporosis International, 23*(1), 1–16.

10. Rush, R. M., Arrington, E. D., & Hsu, J. R. (2012). Management of complex extremity injuries: Tourniquets, compartment syndrome detection, fasciotomy, and amputation care. *Surgical Clinics of North America, 92*(4), 987–1007.

11. Anwar, R., Tuson, K., & Khan, S. A. (2008). Knee and leg. In *Classification and diagnosis in orthopedic trauma* (pp. 160–174). New York, NY: Cambridge University Press.

12. Desapriya, E., Subzwari, S., Sasges, D., Basic, A., Alidina, A., Turcotte, K., & Pike, I. (2010). Do light truck vehicles (LTV) impose greater risk of pedestrian injury than passenger cars? A meta-analysis and systematic review. *Traffic Injury Prevention, 11*(1), 48–56.

13. American College of Surgeons. (2012). Musculoskeletal trauma. In *Advanced trauma life support student course manual* (9th ed., pp. 206–223). Chicago, IL: Author.

14. Mirza, A., & Ellis, T. (2004). Initial management of pelvic and femoral fractures in the multiply injured patient. *Critical Care Clinics, 20,* 159–170.

15. Porth, C. (2011). Disorders of the skeletal system: Trauma, infections, neoplasms, and childhood disorders. In *Essentials of pathophysiology: Concepts of altered health states* (3rd ed., p. 1096–1129). Philadelphia, PA: Wolters Kluwer/Lippincott Williams & Wilkins.

16. Percival, T., White, J., & Ricci, M. (2011). Compartment syndrome in the setting of vascular injury. *Perspectives in Vascular Surgery and Endovascular Therapy, 23*(2), 119–124.

17. Aukerman, D. F., Deitch, J. R., Ertl, J. P., & Ertl, W. (2011, December 5). *Femur injuries and fractures.* Retrieved from http://emedicine.medscape.com/article/90779-overview

18. Kim, P. H., & Leopold, S. S. (2012). Gustilo-Anderson classification. *Clinical Orthopaedics and Related Research, 470,* 3274–3279.

19. Langdorf, M. I., Kahn, J. A., & King, L. (2011, August 11). *Replantation.* Retrieved from http://emedicine.medscape.com/article/827648-overview

20. Rasul, A. T. (2013, May 9). *Acute compartment syndrome clinical presentation.* Retrieved from http://emedicine.medscape.com/article/307668-clinical#a0256

21. Copstead, L.E., & Banasik, J. (2013). *Pathophysiology* (5th ed.). St. Louis, MO: Saunders Elsevier.

22. Criddle, L. M. (2003). Rhabdomyolysis: Pathophysiology, recognition, and management. *Critical Care Nurse, 23,* 14–32.

23. Harbrecht, B., Rosengart, M., Zenati, M., Forsythe, R., & Peitzman, A. (2007). Defining the contribution of renal dysfunction to outcome after traumatic injury. *The American Surgeon, 73*(8), 836–840.

24. Cervellin, G., Comelli, I. & Lippi, G. (2010). Rhabdomyolysis: Historical background, clinical, diagnostic and therapeutic features. *Clinical Chemistry and Laboratory Medicine, 28*(6), 749–756.

25. Anwar, R., Tuson, K., & Khan, S. A. (2008). Hip and thigh. In *Classification and diagnosis in orthopedic trauma* (pp. 134–136). New York, NY: Cambridge University Press.

26. Keany, J. E., & McKeever, D. (2012, October 29). *Ankle dislocation in emergency medicine.* Retrieved from http://emedicine.medscape.com/article/823087-overview#a0199

27. Kelleher, H. B., & Mandavia, D. (2013, May 16). *Knee dislocation.* Retrieved from http://emedicine.medscape.com/article/823589-overview

28. American College of Surgeons. (2012). Appendix A: Ocular trauma. In *Advanced trauma life support student course manual* (9th ed., pp. 311–315). Chicago, IL: Author.

29. Johnston-Walker, E., & Hardcastle, J. (2011). Neurovascular assessment in the critically ill patient. *Nursing in Critical Care, 16*(4), 170–177.

30. Hoyt, K. S. (2009). Plaster and fiberglass splinting. In J. A. Proehl (Ed.) *Emergency nursing procedures* (4th ed., pp. 622–633). St Louis, MO: Saunders Elsevier.

31. Cerepani, M. J. (2010). Orthopedic and neurovascular trauma. In P. K. Howard & R. A. Steinmann (Eds.), *Sheehy's emergency nursing: Principles and practice* (6th ed., pp. 313–339). St. Louis, MO: Mosby Elsevier.

32. Farrow, C., Bodenham, A., & Troxler, M. (2011). Acute limb compartment syndromes. *Continuing Education in Anaesthesia, Critical Care & Pain, 11*(1), 24–28.

33. Schmitt, B. D. (2011, September 15). *Leg injury.* Retrieved from http://www.ohsu.edu/xd/health/services/doernbecher/patients-families/health-information/md4kids/symptom-index/leg-injury.cfm?WT_rank=23

34. Mauffrey, C., Bailey, J. R., Bowles, R. J., Price, C., Hasson, D., Hak, D. J., & Stahel, P. F. (2012). Acute management of open fractures: Proposal of a new multidisciplinary algorithm. *Orthopedics, 35*(10), 877–881.

35. Mamczak, C.N., Born, C.T., Obremskey, W.T., & Dromsky, D.M. (2012). Evolution of acute orthopaedic care. *Journal of the American Academy of Orthopaedic Surgeons, 20*(Suppl 1), S70–S73.

36. Sears, B. (2012, July 31). *Residual limb.* Retrieved from http://physicaltherapy.about.com/od/amputationrehabilitation/g/Residual-Limb.htm

37. Starks, I., Frost, A., Wall, P., & Lim, J. (2011). Is a fracture of the transverse process of L5 a predictor of pelvic fracture instability? *Journal of Bone & Joint Surgery, 93*(7), 967–969.

Chapter 15 • Surface and Burn Trauma

Cathy Provins-Churbock, PhD, RN, ANCP-BC, CCNS, CCRN

Objectives

Upon completion of this chapter, the learner will be able to:

1. Describe the mechanisms of injury associated with surface and burn trauma.

2. Describe pathophysiologic changes as a basis for assessment of the trauma patient with surface and burn injuries.

3. Demonstrate the nursing assessment of the trauma patient with surface and burn injuries.

4. Plan appropriate interventions for the trauma patient with surface and burn injuries.

5. Evaluate the effectiveness of nursing interventions for the trauma patient with surface and burn injuries.

Preface

Knowledge of normal anatomy and physiology serves as a foundation for understanding anatomic derangements and pathophysiologic processes that may result from trauma. Before reading this chapter, it is strongly suggested that the learner review the following material. This material will not be covered in the lectures nor tested directly, but as foundational content, it may be the basis for some test questions and skill evaluation steps.

Anatomy and Physiology of the Integumentary System

The integumentary system, or skin, is the largest organ in the body and is composed of the epidermis, dermis, and hypodermis (Fig. 15-1). The integumentary system serves many vital functions including:

- Protection from environmental hazards, including infection

- Thermoregulation

- Sensory perception

Epidermis

The epidermis is the outermost layer of skin and the body's first line of defense to environmental threat. It is composed of epithelial cells, is avascular, and receives nourishment from the dermis. The epidermis is thin in most areas but is thicker on the soles of feet, hands, or other areas routinely exposed to pressure and friction.[1] The epidermis of the skin is composed of two or more cellular layers and is constantly shedding cells from the outer layer and developing new cells from the basal cell layer. The epidermal layer of the skin regenerates at a rate of complete replacement every month or faster following an injury. With an intact basal cell layer, regeneration is possible.[1]

Dermis

The dermis is located directly beneath the epidermis and is often referred to as "true skin." It has a strong extracellular matrix and is thicker than the epidermis. The three components of the dermis are *collagen,* a protein that gives skin its mechanical strength, *elastin,* a substance that gives the skin stretch and flexibility, and *ground substance,* which helps to cushion and lubricate the skin.[2,3]

The dermis has two layers. The reticular dermis, the deeper layer, contains nerve endings, hair follicles, sweat and sebaceous glands, and blood vessels. The papillary dermis, the superficial layer, aids in healing and provides nourishment to the epidermis.[3,4] This layer of skin is highly vascular and plays a role in fluid, electrolyte, and body temperature regulation.[3,5] Unlike the epidermis, the dermis does not continuously regenerate new cells. Repair of damaged dermal cells is dependent on the inflammatory and wound healing processes, especially fibroblast infiltration of the area.

Hypodermis

The subcutaneous tissue, sometimes referred to as the hypodermis or superficial fascia, lies beneath the dermis. This layer is rich in fat and connective tissue and attaches the dermis to the underlying structures. It functions as a heat insulator, nutrition supplier, and mechanical shock absorber.[2] Excess fatty tissue, which is not vascular in nature, can delay or complicate wound healing.

Figure 15-1. Layers of the Skin and Depth of Burn Wound

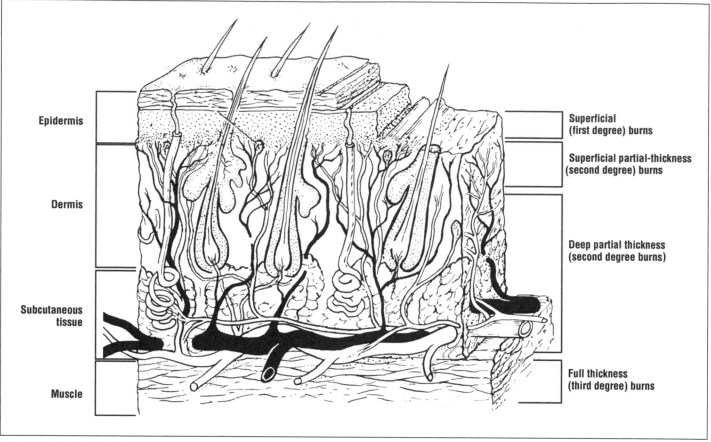

The layers of the skin and which are affected depending on the depth of a burn injury.

Wound Healing
Wound healing is a four-phase process:[6]
- Hemostasis
  - Platelet activation and aggregation is triggered
  - Clotting factors are released, beginning the clotting cascade
  - Vasoconstriction occurs
  - A clot is formed
- Inflammatory phase
  - Vasodilation and capillary permeability increase perfusion to the wound
  - White blood cells infiltrate the area, removing cellular debris and foreign material, and fighting infection
- Proliferative phase
  - There is a proliferation and lateral migration of epithelial cells combined with collagen to resurface the wound bed
  - Granulation tissue forms; the time needed depends on depth and severity of wound
  - Tensile strength improves
- Maturation phase
  - This can take days to years, depending on when the wound fibroblasts leave the site
  - Tensile strength continues to increase
  - Collagen models scar tissue, reducing size and visibility

Capillary and Fluid Dynamics
As noted, the dermis plays a role in fluid and electrolyte balance. Four pressures within the interstitium and the vasculature play a role in the fluid and electrolyte status of the body including the skin and its structures.[1] These are described in Table 15-1.

In patients with large burns to the skin, these pressures are disrupted. Due to this disruption, capillary leak of fluid from the intravascular and interstitium occurs and can result in hypovolemia, shock, and death.

Table 15-1. Pressures Involved in Capillary and Fluid Dynamics

Pressure	Function
Hydrostatic pressure	• Pushes fluid out of the capillary into the interstitium
Plasma colloid osmotic pressure	• Pulls fluid into the capillary
Interstitial fluid pressure	• Pulls fluid out of the capillary when the pressure is negative • Pushes fluid into the capillary when pressure is positive
Interstitial fluid colloid osmotic pressure	• Pulls fluid into the capillary

Data from Copstead & Banasik.[1]

Surface Trauma

Introduction

Surface trauma is defined as a disruption in the normal integumentary system. It may be the patient's primary traumatic injury but more often occurs concurrently in a patient with multisystem trauma. Surface trauma includes:

- Abrasions
- Avulsions
- Contusions and hematomas
- Lacerations
- Puncture wounds
- Frostbite

Surface trauma can involve the skin and the supporting and underlying structures such as muscles, tendons, ligaments, blood vessels, and nerves. It is essential that these seemingly minor injuries not be minimized, as they can result in hemorrhage, loss of limb, and death secondary to infection.

Mechanisms of Injury

The mechanisms of injury (MOIs) for surface injuries are:

- Falls
- Motor vehicle collisions (MVCs)
- Impact with objects
- Overexertion and strenuous movements
- Cutting or piercing objects
- Natural and environmental factors
- Foreign bodies
- Exposure to chemicals or caustic substances

MOI is essential to predicting injury patterns in the trauma patient and assessment findings can provide clues to potential underlying tissue and organ damage. See Chapter 4, Biomechanics, Kinematics, and Mechanisms of Injury, for more information.

Pathophysiology as a Basis for Assessment Findings

The wound healing process is complex and requires meticulous and ongoing assessment and monitoring to prevent infection, which remains a leading cause of death.[7]

Patients at highest risk for infectious complications include:[6]

- Infants
- Older adults
- Smokers or others with impaired oxygenation and perfusion
- Patients who are immunocompromised
- Patients with diabetes
- Patients with existing vascular disease

Trauma patients with these comorbidities or risk circumstances often benefit from referral to wound clinics that specialize in optimizing the wound healing process with specialized therapies such as leech therapy, hyperbaric oxygen treatments, negative pressure wound therapy, and specialty dressings (silver-impregnated products).

Nursing Care of the Patient with Surface Trauma

When caring for trauma patients, keep in mind that surface injuries may be a distraction, especially if extensive and obvious, from subtle, but potentially more life-threatening injuries such as an ineffective airway.

Primary Survey

The primary survey and all life-threatening injuries are addressed and the patient is stabilized before addressing surface trauma. Refer to Chapter 5, Initial Assessment, for the systematic approach to the nursing care of the trauma patient. The following assessment parameters are specific to patients with surface trauma injuries.

Secondary Survey

H–History

Questions to ask during history taking include, but are not limited to, the following:

- Was the cause of the injury from a clean or dirty source?
- Was the cause of the wound an animal bite and if so, is the animal known? Is there a risk of rabies exposure?
- Is there a risk of a retained foreign body?
- Is there possible tendon involvement and does the patient have full or partial range of motion?
- Is there possible nerve involvement and does the patient have sensation at the site?
- Was the injury intentional or unintentional?
- Does the patient have a history of medical conditions that may impact wound healing (diabetes)?
- What medication is the patient taking (anticoagulants, antihypertensives, steroids)?
- Is the patient's tetanus status up to date?

H–Head-to-toe Assessment

Inspect for:

- The location and type of the wound and any associated injuries
- The effectiveness of hemostasis
- The depth, length, and size of the wound
- The color of the tissue and surrounding tissue
- The extent of denuded tissue and underlying structures involved
- Tissue swelling and/or deformity and presence of foreign bodies
- Evidence of any apparent wound contamination or presence of exudate

Palpate for:

Assessment findings suspicious for compartment syndrome including:[8]

- Pain
  - Hallmark of compartment syndrome when out of proportion for the injury
  - Often occurs before changes in pulse, color, and temperature of distal limb
- Weak or absent distal pulses
- Delayed capillary refill
- Firmness on palpation of muscle and soft tissue in surrounding area
- Distal skin cool to touch
- Distal skin pale or cyanotic
- Decrease in patient sensation

The six P's mnemonic helps the trauma nurse to remember components of the neurovascular assessment: pain, pallor, pulses, paresthesia, paralysis, and pressure. See Chapter 14, Musculoskeletal Trauma, for more information.

Interventions

The immediate goal in treating surface trauma is to obtain and maintain hemostasis. This is accomplished by applying direct pressure to the site.[9] For cases that are not resolved by direct pressure, cauterization and suture ligation of isolated vessels may be necessary. In patients who experience limb injuries where bleeding cannot be controlled with direct pressure, tourniquets have been used successfully.[8] See Chapter 7, Shock, and Chapter 14, Musculoskeletal Trauma, for more information.

Selected Surface Trauma Injuries

Abrasion

An abrasion is a partial- or full-thickness wound that denudes the skin.[10] Commonly occurring with falls and bicycle or motorcycle collisions, abrasions can be mild or severe and vary in surface area and depth depending on the mechanism and force involved. Road burn or abrasions, resulting from a low-side crash or laying down a motorcycle, is one example of an abrasion involving a large surface area. If the area becomes embedded with gravel and dirt, it can cause a tattoo effect on the skin and require vigorous wound cleansing and debridement to remove the foreign bodies, avoid skin discoloration, and reduce the risk for infection.

Avulsion

Avulsions are full-thickness wounds caused by a tearing or ripping of skin and soft tissue.[11] The wound edges are not well approximated.[10] They often involve fingers, scalps, and noses and can occur as a result of working with machinery or from motor vehicle collisions. A degloving injury is an avulsion where the skin and tissue is removed, exposing underlying structures, including bone, tendons, and ligaments.[11,12] Degloving injuries commonly affect the extremities and scalp.

Avulsions can occur in bone fractures when soft tissue is torn away from the bone. The extent of these injuries can impact other systems. For example, one of the prognostic indicators for limb salvage after tibia–fibula fracture is consideration of the magnitude of avulsed tissue from the bone shaft.[13] When soft tissue is avulsed, the bone may not receive adequate nutrients through the circulation. Exposed bone and mangle injuries are at highest risk for infection. Treatment for avulsions depends on the body part and the amount of tissue avulsed. Simple wound care may be adequate as in a simple skin avulsion, but more extensive avulsions, such as degloving injuries, may require surgical intervention for grafting or amputation.[10]

Contusion and Hematoma

A contusion is a closed wound in which a ruptured blood vessel or capillary bed hemorrhages into the surrounding tissue.[7] A hematoma occurs when blood leaks under the skin surface and often forms a palpable mass (blood clot) under the skin.[7]

Treatment requires analysis of the force required to produce the contusion and the potential for trauma to underlying structures such as compression injury to arteries and nerves, causing ischemia.

Laceration

Lacerations are open wounds that result from shearing forces through the dermis and epidermis with potential involvement of the underlying structures such as muscles, tendons, and ligaments.[10] Common causes of laceration include injuries from tools or machinery. Exploration of deeper lacerations is required to assess the integrity of underlying structures and to evaluate for foreign bodies. Lacerations differ from cuts or incisions, which have clean, well-approximated edges such as from a knife or broken glass.

Puncture Wound

Puncture wounds are caused by penetration of objects into tissues. Injuries result from various mechanisms including:

- Superficial wounds, such as stepping on a tack
- Deeper injuries such as stab wounds[10]
- Injuries from foreign bodies or implements
- Animal and human bites

Although puncture wounds may appear minor, there is a potential risk for infection and underlying tissue or organ damage, especially with injuries caused by high pressure, such as a nail gun injury. These types of wounds are referred to as missile injuries.[10] See Chapter 4, Biomechanics, Kinematics, and Mechanisms of Injury, for more information.

When a patient experiences a missile or impalement injury, the foreign body is often more deeply embedded and involves underlying tissue. Large foreign bodies are removed after underlying structures have been assessed. Hemorrhage can result after embedded objects are removed because the item may be providing a means of hemostasis. For example, a piece of glass embedded in the hand may be placing pressure on a branch of a capillary, which is serving to control bleeding. Premature removal of the glass results in bleeding. Large impaled objects are often removed in the operating room by trauma surgeons who can repair damage to deep tissue and vessels.

Puncture wounds carry a high infection rate.[5] Risk factors for infection include:

- Large or deep wounds
- Contaminated wounds (bite wounds)
- Wounds with osseous involvement
- High-pressure injuries
- Wounds more than 6 hours old
- Human and animal bites are of particular concern due to the risk for infection. Rabies, although rare, does occur and is a consideration when managing animal bite wounds. If the animal is known to the patient or family but not current with immunizations or if the animal is unknown or wild, rabies prophylaxis and antibiotic therapy may be indicated.[10]

Frostbite[14]

Frostbite occurs when exposure to cold causes tissue to freeze and ice crystals to form. Vasoconstriction causes reduced perfusion and injury to the endothelial layer of blood vessels, and a thrombus can form. Frostbite is classified according to depth and type of tissue involved. Levels of frostbite include:

- Partial thickness: Skin becomes hyperemic and edematous. Some tingling may be felt.
- Deep partial thickness: Clear blisters begin to form. If blood is present in the blister, it may suggest full thickness damage to the skin.
- Full thickness: Total skin necrosis reaches into the subcutaneous tissue and involves muscle and bone. Skin turns black, and dry hard eschar forms.

Interventions

- Initial treatment consists of quickly rewarming over a period of 15 to 30 minutes in water that is at a temperature of 40°C to 42°C (104°F to 107.6°F) [13]
  - Start treatment only after it can be confirmed that the affected area will not be at risk for frostbite again after it is rewarmed as incomplete thawing and refreezing can cause further injury[14,15]
  - Administer pain medication as the rewarming process can be painful[14,15]
  - Avoid any friction or rubbing to preserve tissue integrity
  - If possible, immerse the area in warm water 40°C to 42°C (104°F to 107.6°F).[5,14,15] Use a method where the temperature of the water can be maintained within the appropriate range, such as a whirlpool with circulating water.
- Extract fluid in clear blisters to reduce further damage. Blisters that are hemorrhagic are maintained intact.[15]
- Guard against further injury to the area. For example, affected extremities can be splinted.
- Prevent or limit the risk of thrombus formation
  - Administer aspirin or non-steroidal medications
  - In early trials the use of tissue plasminogen activator (tPA) has been effective in maintaining perfusion and decreasing the need for amputation[15]

Reevaluation Adjuncts

Radiographic Studies
Obtain plain films prior to wound closure to evaluate wounds for foreign bodies and assess for underlying fractures or joint penetration from any foreign body.[7]

Laboratory Studies
- A complete blood count (CBC) may be obtained to assess blood loss
- A white blood cell count (WBC) can be used to screen for evidence of possible infection

- Wound culture and sensitivity may be useful especially in wounds more than 8 hours old to guide appropriate antibiotic therapy[10]

Wound Care
The goals of wound care include the following:
- Promote wound healing
- Prevent complications (infection, limited range of motion)
- Maintain function
- Minimize scar formation

Three basic classifications of closure are used for wound healing: primary, secondary, and tertiary (Fig. 15-2):[16]
- Primary wound closure is used for wounds with well-approximated borders and minimal tissue destruction. Simple closure techniques, such as suturing, are used
- Secondary wound closure is used for infected wounds in which the edges are not well approximated. Gauze packing or wound drains may need to be used. This method of repair requires formation of granulation tissue from the base of the wound upwards.

Figure 15-2. Wound Healing

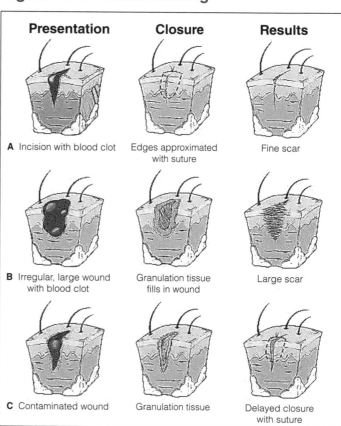

Types of wound healing. A, Primary intention. B, Secondary intention. C, Tertiary intention. Reprinted from Howard, P. K., & Steinmann, R. (Eds.). (2009). *Sheehy's emergency nursing: Principles and practice* (6th ed.). St. Louis, MO: Mosby Elsevier.

- Tertiary wound closure is used for deep wounds that have become infected or wounds that were initially allowed to granulate with secondary intention. After this granulation, secondary sutures may be used to bring wound edges together to promote healing.[16]

Nursing considerations include:
Superficial wounds may be cleaned with normal saline.[2]
- Dirty or deep wounds require some disinfection. Follow organizational policy regarding use of cleansing solutions.
- Anesthesia may be required when removing gravel or other foreign materials from the wound[2]
  ◦ Avoid using lidocaine with epinephrine on fingers, toes, or any other area where vasoconstriction could cause impaired distal blood circulation
  ◦ Digital blocks using bupivacaine (Marcaine) or lidocaine may be used for finger or toe injures
- Hair removal from around the wound is done with scissors or clippers. Shaving is not recommended due to risk of potential for infection.[17,18]
- Wound irrigation can reduce the bacterial contamination of the wound and prevent infection. Use a copious amount of sterile normal saline. Low-pressure irrigation, such as with a bulb syringe, will help to remove large contaminants, but high-pressure irrigation works best for smaller contaminants and bacteria. Take care to not destroy viable tissue.[19]

Reevaluation and Post Resuscitation Care

Reevaluation and ongoing assessment of new wounds include:
- The ability of the patient to maintain hemostasis of the wound
- The effectiveness of the wound closure modality

Definitive Care or Transport

Provide the patient and family with education including:
- Signs and symptoms of infection including fever, opening of the wound site, draining from the wound, excessive pain or swelling at the site, or numbness or tingling at sites distal to the wounds
- Bathing information with bandage or dressing supplies
- When to report signs and symptoms to their primary care providers
- Instructions regarding suture removal and follow-up
- Infection prevention

Burn Trauma

Introduction

Burn injuries can have a lifelong impact on patients due to loss of function, scarring, and psychological trauma. Caring for this patient population can be challenging for the trauma nurse because in addition to life-threatening situations necessitating immediate attention, hypothermia, hypercarbia, and hypoxia may develop. Pain management for these patients can also be difficult. Lengthy recovery, chronic pain, and scarring are also common in this patient population.

Epidemiology

According to the World Health Organization (WHO), non-fatal burn injuries are a leading cause of morbidity worldwide.[20] In the United States, 69% of all burn injuries occurred in the home.[21] Cooking is the primary cause of residential fires, whereas smoking caused the most fire-related deaths.[21] Alcohol intoxication is implicated as a contributing factor in as many as 40% of fire-related deaths.[22]

Mechanism of Injury and Biomechanics

Burns are injuries to tissues caused by heat, friction, electricity, radiation, or chemicals.[23] In order of prevalence, the most common mechanisms of burn injury for persons ages 5 years and older are:[24]
- Fire/flames
- Scald injuries
- Contact with hot objects

Scalds are the most common mechanism of injury (80%) in young children. Burns from flames are more common for children between ages 6 and 16 years.[25]

Burns are intentional or unintentional. Pattern burns (such as from a cigarette or identifiable object) or immersion burns—such as circumferential and sharply demarcated burns to both feet—should raise suspicion of possible maltreatment. See Chapter 20, Special Populations: The Interpersonal Violence Trauma Patient, for more information.

Burns are classified as:
- Thermal
- Chemical
- Electrical
- Radiation

Thermal Burns

Thermal burns result from contact with hot objects but can also occur as the result from steam, smoke, or thermal flash burns.

Scald burns are thermal burns that result from a wet substance, such as steam or water, and injury severity depends on the temperature of the substance and the length of exposure. For instance, the safety standard for the maximum temperature of U.S. residential water heaters is 120°F (48.8°C).[24] At this temperature, it will take an average of 5 minutes to cause a full thickness burn on the skin of an adult.[24] By comparison, hot beverages (coffee, tea, etc.) average 160°F to 180°F (71°C to 82°C) and can cause full thickness burns on contact.[24]

Chemical Burns

Chemical burns account for 4% of admissions to burn units in developed countries and up to 14% in underdeveloped countries.[27] Chemical burns are classified as acids or alkalis. Acids are organic or inorganic substances that cause coagulation necrosis. Examples include hydrofluoric acid, carbonic acid, and white phosphorus. Alkalis cause extensive tissue damage by dissolving protein and collagen and result in deep tissue destruction and necrosis. Examples of alkaline agents include anhydrous ammonia, cement, hydrocarbons, and tar.

Electrical Burns

The cause of electrical burns includes direct exposure to electrical current or a lightning strike. Electrical current can be either direct (DC) or alternating (AC). DC is commonly found in batteries, solar panels, and fuel cells. AC is commonly found in homes and businesses and used in medical devices and electronics. Electrical burns are the second leading cause of occupational-related death. Persons who work in the construction or electrical fields experience two thirds of all electrical injuries.[28]

Radiation Burns

Common causes of radiation burns include the sun, such as a sunburn, or radiation beams used to treat cancer patients.

Usual Concurrent Injuries

Patients with selected MOIs can be at risk for an inhalation injury, including loss of airway, respiratory failure, and death. Patients that present with thermal burns from fires that occurred in a small or enclosed space are at especially high risk. Other concurrent injuries may be determined by reviewing the MOI and pertinent details from the scene. For example, if the patient jumped from a building during a fire, assess for fractures and organ hemorrhage. If the burn was sustained in a motor vehicle collision, assess for additional injuries related to the collision. Consider a blunt traumatic injury if the MOI was a blast event. See Chapter 4, Biomechanics, Kinematics, and Mechanisms of Injury, for additional information.

Pathophysiology as a Basis for the Assessment Findings of Burn Trauma

The external injury resulting from burn trauma is the destruction of the skin. However, the internal injuries are of equal, if not more concern in these patients and are described below.

Airway Patency

Burns to tissue can cause massive edema and airway edema is life threatening. A hoarse voice, carbonaceous sputum, burns around the mouth or nares, or stridor may indicate burns to the airway.

Hypoxia, Asphyxia, and Carbon Monoxide Poisoning

Hypoxia can result from an inhalation injury or from carbon monoxide poisoning.[29]

Asphyxia occurs from breathing decreased amounts of oxygen in the inspired air, as a result of being in a closed space where oxygen is being consumed by the fire.

Carbon monoxide (CO) is a colorless, odorless, and tasteless gas released into the air during a fire. CO, which has a higher affinity to the hemoglobin molecule than oxygen, will replace the oxygen, resulting in carboxyhemoglobin and reducing the oxygen content of the blood. The patient may complain of headache and nausea or confusion. CO poisoning can also result in coma or death.[30] In assessing the patient with CO poisoning, oxygenation and oxygen saturation are best measured with arterial blood gases (ABGs).[31] The pulse oximeter will not differentiate hemoglobin bound to oxygen from hemoglobin bound to CO, making it unreliable.[31] Treat the patient with CO poisoning with oxygen until carboxyhemoglobin levels drop to below 10%. For severe cases, hyperbaric oxygen may be indicated.[31]

Pulmonary Injury

Pulmonary injury doubles the mortality of patients with burns.[30] The process of pulmonary injury includes:[30]

- Inhalation of the products of combustion such as particles of carbon and noxious fumes

- Damage to the mucosal cells of the bronchioles

- Increased permeability of cell membranes allowing leakage causing impaired gas exchange

- Sloughing of dead cells obstructing the airways

- Decreased production and/or loss of surfactant, resulting in alveolar collapse
- Acute lung injury or acute respiratory distress syndrome (ARDS)
- Secondary complications such as pneumonia

Clinical evidence of a pulmonary injury may not be immediately evident during the resuscitation phase,[30] so it is crucial that the trauma team identify those patients at risk and proactively manage and protect the airway.

Capillary Leak Syndrome[32]

Edema formation is one of the more challenging management issues of treating burn injuries. The inflammatory response occurs both locally and systemically and results in a shift of fluid from the intravascular fluid into the interstitial space,[33] sometimes referred to as "third-spacing." In burned tissue, mediators such as histamine, serotonin, prostaglandins, blood products, complement components, and kinins act to increase the vascular permeability of the capillary membrane.[33] This increased permeability, referred to as *capillary leak,* allows nearly all elements of blood, except for red blood cells, to pass through the damaged membranes. In areas of undamaged tissue, there can be increased permeability due to the release of the histamines and kinin. Burns greater than 20% total body surface area (TBSA) are most commonly vulnerable to this capillary leak.[33]

During capillary leak, almost half of the fluid infused during resuscitation can seep from the veins into the tissue.[33] This can last for 6 to 12 hours after the burn injury when the capillary membranes begin to repair and leakage begins to decrease.[33] However, the edema can last much longer. The rate of fluid lost from intravascular spaces depends on patient age, burn size and depth, intravascular pressures, and time elapsed since the burn.[8]

The inflammatory response results in the release of numerous substrates that leads to further edema and potential cardiac collapse. These include the following:[8]
- Release of histamine and prostaglandin leads to vasodilation and increased capillary permeability
- Thromboxane A2, a vasoconstrictive substance, causes platelet aggregation and expansion of the zone of coagulation
- Bradykinin causes increased permeability of the venules, and oxygen-free radicals damage the endothelial cells, which are the basement membrane of new tissue

Mechanical Obstruction

Circumferential burns to the chest may reduce the ability of the patient to breathe deeply.

Loss of Skin Integrity

Loss and destruction of the skin layer results in the loss of vital functions including thermoregulation and protection against infection. Assessment of the burn surface reveals three surrounding zones of injury (Fig. 15-3):[34]
- Zone of coagulation
  - This is the most severely damaged center of the burn and is often necrotic in nature
  - Debridement of this necrotic tissue is essential for wound healing as it is not capable of regeneration
  - Skin grafting is a consideration for burns involving the zone of coagulation
- Zone of stasis
  - This zone surrounds the zone of coagulation
  - Tissue in this area has been moderately damaged, resulting in decreased tissue perfusion and edema
  - If wound treatment is timely and appropriate, this tissue may improve to a zone of hyperemia; if not, it may deteriorate to a zone of coagulation
- Zone of hyperemia
  - This is the outermost area
  - Due to the inflammatory process, there is increased blood flow to this area resulting in the best chance for tissue viability

Hypothermia

Patients can become hypothermic because the normal integumentary function of temperature regulation is disrupted. Hypothermia can help lead to clotting and bleeding disorders such as disseminated intravascular coagulation (DIC).

Figure 15-3. Zones of Injury

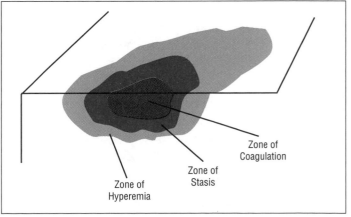

Zones of injury in burns.

Nursing Care of the Patient with Burn Trauma

Severe burns can distract from the more subtle and more life-threatening co-existing injuries such as an ineffective airway. It is imperative that the trauma team maintain focus on treating life threats before treating the burn.

Refer to Chapter 5, Initial Assessment, for the systematic approach to the nursing care of the trauma patient. The following assessment parameters are specific to patients with burn injuries.

Primary Survey and Resuscitation Adjuncts

A–Airway and Alertness

- Assess that patient is alert and can maintain a patent airway

- If patient is unable to protect the airway, ensure a patent airway

- If fire is the mechanism for a thermal burn, inspect for evidence of soot, carbonaceous sputum, or singed nasal hairs, which might indicate an inhalation injury. If present, consider prophylactic intubation.

B–Breathing and Ventilation

- Begin administering oxygen at 15 L/min via a closely fitted mask attached to an oxygen reservoir[35–40]

- After the primary survey is complete, maintain SpO_2 between 94% and 98%[35–40]

- Ensure effective ventilation

- For CO poisoning not responsive to bag-mask ventilations at the highest oxygen concentrations, consider hyperbaric oxygen

C–Circulation and Control of Hemorrhage

- Avoid vascular access over burned tissue

- Follow a fluid resuscitation guideline for calculating the amount of fluid needed (see "Emerging Trends" for additional information)

- Use only partial-thickness or full thickness burns to determine the percent of TBSA for the formula

Adult Fluid Replacement Guidelines[41]

- In adults with flame, scald and chemical burns that are over 20% Total Body Surface Area (TBSA) begin fluid resuscitation with Ringer's lactate solution at 2 mL/kg/percentage of TBSA[41]

- Excessive fluid resuscitation can result in complications such as cerebral edema, pulmonary edema, abdominal compartment syndrome, and ARDS[42]

- Half of the fluid is given in the first 8 hours from time of burn injury, and the remainder is given in the remaining 16 hours

- In an adult, maintain urinary output at 0.5 mL/kg or approximately 30 to 50 mL per hour (always consider the patient's urinary output, comorbidities, and physiologic response prior to initiating fluid resuscitation)

- Table 15-2 provides a sample calculation using this formula

Some patients may require higher fluid requirements than recommended calculations. They include:

- Infants and children

- Older adults

- Patients with inhalation injury

- Patients with high-voltage injuries

- Intoxicated patients

Pediatric Fluid Replacement Guidelines[41]

- For children younger than 14 years or weighing less than 40 kg, give 3 mL/kg per percentage of TBSA, half during the first 8 hours and the remaining half over the next 16 hours

Table 15-2. Adult Fluid Replacement Recommendations

Adult Fluid Recommendation
Formula: Weight in kg × 2 mL × % TBSA = the total amount of fluid to be infused in 24 hrs from the time of injury • Give half of the calculated total during the first 8 hrs • Give the remaining half over the next 16 hrs
Example: A 100-kg patient has sustained a 50% TBSA burn
Calculation • 100 kg × 2 = 200 mL • 200 mL × 50% TBSA burn = 10,000 mL to be infused over the first 24 hours from the time of the burn • 5,000 mL (10,000/2 = 5,000) given in the first 8 hrs • 5,000 mL will be infused over the remaining 16 hrs

Note: TBSA indicates total body surface area.

- For children weighing less than 40 kg, maintain the urinary output at 1 mL/kg per hour

- A glucose infusion or maintenance fluids with glucose may be needed to prevent or treat hypoglycemia

- Ringer's lactate solution is recommended for children weighing more than 10 kg. In patients who weigh less than 10 kg, use dextrose 5% in Ringer's lactate solution.[41]

E–Exposure and Environmental Control
Maintenance of body temperature is crucial in patients with burns since they have lost their protective skin barrier.

Exposure [41, 43]
- Remove all clothing and jewelry, especially rings and bracelets that may cause constriction as the extremity swells

- For superficial burns less than 10% TBSA cool burned tissue

  ◦ Cool with wet cloths with room temperature sterile water for 5 minutes

- Do not apply ice to the skin as it may cause additional tissue damage

- Do not immerse in water

Environmental Control
- Use blankets to keep the patient warm

- Use caution with cooling interventions as it may contribute to hypothermia

- Burns cause an increase in metabolism, which can affect medication dosing needs

G-Get Resuscitation Adjuncts
L–Laboratory Studies
Laboratory studies for patients with burns include the following:
- ABGs and oxygenation content of the blood

- Carboxyhemoglobin levels[44]

  ◦ Normal non-smoker: 0% to 3%

  ◦ Normal smoker: 0% to 15%

  ◦ Toxic: 25% to 35%

  ◦ Lethal: over 60%

M–Monitoring
- Monitor hemodynamic parameters including central venous pressure or right atrial pressure, to determine fluid status

- Continuous cardiac monitoring for dysrhythmias for patients with electrical burns is also recommended

- Insert a urinary catheter to monitor effectiveness of fluid resuscitation

Table 15-3. American Burn Association Burn Injury Referral Criteria

ABA Burn Injury Referral Criteria
• Partial thickness burns greater than 10% TBSA
• Burns that involve the face, hands, feet, genitalia, perineum, or major joints
• Third degree burns in any age group
• Electrical burns, including lightning injury
• Chemical burns
• Inhalation injury
• Burn injury in patients with preexisting medical disorders that could complicate management, prolong recovery, or affect mortality
• Any patient with burns and concomitant trauma (such as fractures) in which the burn injury poses the greatest risk of morbidity or mortality ◦ In such cases, if the trauma poses the greater immediate risk, the patient may be initially stabilized in a trauma center before being transferred to a burn unit. Physician judgment will be necessary in such situations and should be in concert with the regional medical control plan and triage protocols.
• Burned children in hospitals without qualified personnel or equipment for the care of children
• Burn injury in patients who will require special social, emotional, or rehabilitative intervention

Excerpted from Guidelines for the Operation of Burn Centers (pp. 79-86), Resources for Optimal Care of the Injured Patient 2006, Committee on Trauma, American College of Surgeons
Reprinted from American Burn Association. (n.d.). *Burn center referral criteria.* Retrieved from http://www.ameriburn.org/BurnCenterReferralCriteria.pdf

Table 15-4. Differentiating Depth of Wounds

Depth	Appearance	Sensation	Healing Time
Superficial	• Dry, red • Blanches with pressure	• Painful	• 3–6 days
Superficial partial-thickness	• Blisters • Moist and weeping • Red • Blanches with pressure	• Painful to temperature and air	• 7–21 days
Deep partial-thickness	• Blisters • Wet or waxy dry • Patchy to cheesy white to red in color • Does not blanch with pressure	• Perceptive of pressure only	• Greater than 21 days • Usually requires grafting
Full-thickness	• Waxy white to leathery gray to charred and black • No blanching with pressure	• Perceptive of deep pressure only	• Requires surgical grafts
Fourth degree (full thickness)	• Extends into fascia and or muscle	• Perceptive of deep pressure only	• Requires surgical grafts

Data from Black, J. M, & Hawks, J. H. (2009). *Medical-surgical nursing: Clinical management for positive outcomes* (8th ed.). St. Louis, MO: Elsevier and Wolf, S. E. (2009). Burns. In *The Merck manual for health care professionals*. Retrieved from http://www.merckmanuals.com/professional/injuries_poisoning/burns/burns.html

Table 15-5. Modified Lund and Browder Chart

Burned Area	Age (years)					
	1	1–4	5–9	10–14	15	Adult
	Total Body Surface (%)					
Head	19	17	13	11	9	7
Neck	2	2	2	2	2	3
Anterior trunk	13	13	13	13	13	13
Posterior trunk	13	13	13	13	13	13
Right buttock	2.5	2.5	2.5	2.5	2.5	2.5
Left buttock	2.5	2.5	2.5	2.5	2.5	2.5
Genitalia	1	1	1	1	1	1
Right upper arm	4	4	4	4	4	4
Left upper arm	4	4	4	4	4	4
Right lower arm	3	3	3	3	3	3
Left lower arm	3	3	3	3	3	3
Right hand	2.5	2.5	2.5	2.5	2.5	2.5
Left hand	2.5	2.5	2.5	2.5	2.5	2.5
Right thigh	5.5	6.5	8	8.5	9	9.5
Left thigh	5.5	6.5	8	8.5	9	9.5
Right leg	5	5	5.5	6	6.5	7
Left leg	5	5	5.5	6	6.5	7
Right foot	3.5	3.5	3.5	3.5	3.5	3.5
Left foot	3.5	3.5	3.5	3.5	3.5	3.5

The Modified Lund and Browder Chart is one method used to determine the total body surface area burned in adult and pediatric patients.

N–Nasogastric or Orogastric Tube Insertion

In patients who have burns over 20% TBSA, consider a gastric tube because of the high probability of gastric distension, nausea and vomiting.[41]

O–Oxygenation and Ventilation

Pulse oximetry cannot differentiate oxygen-bound hemoglobin from carboxyhemoglobin and readings will not be accurate in the presence of carbon monoxide. Laboratory analysis of arterial blood gases and carboxyhemoglobin levels is needed to trend changes.

P–Pain Assessment and Management

- Burns can be very painful, thus pain management is a priority. See Chapter 8, Pain, for more information
- Burns cause an increase in metabolism, which can affect medication dosing needs

Reevaluation

Consider transfer to a burn center (Table 15-3) or facility with hyperbaric therapy

Secondary Survey

The sections below discuss the secondary survey and management of the patient with thermal burns. See "Selected Burn Injuries" for a discussion of electrical and chemical burns.

H–History

- Example questions specific to patients with thermal burn injuries are as follows:
  - If MOI was a fire, where was the fire located (indoors or outdoors)?
  - Did the fire occur in a structure? If so, what type (car, house, commercial structure)?
  - How long was the patient in the burning structure?
  - Was there exposure to chemicals?
  - Were there others injured in the fire?
  - Was there a fall or did the patient jump and have associated injuries?
  - Was there a blast?

H–Head-to-toe Assessment

Determine depth, extent, and location of the burn wound.

Depth of the Burn

- The depth of the burn is reflective of the layers of skin and tissue affected (Table 15-4). In assessing depth remember that the dermis is the vascular layer, so superficial burns, which affect the epidermis, will not bleed.[34]

- Initial assessment is completed to begin fluid resuscitation. Definitive assessment of depth may change over the course of the first 24 to 48 hours of the wound.[33]

Extent of the Burn

- Determine the extent of partial- and full-thickness burn injury using one of the following:
  - Modified Lund and Browder Chart is based on age and burned area (Table 15-5)
  - The Rule of Nines (Fig. 15-4) divides the body into areas of 9% or multiples of 9%, except for the perineum, which is 1%
  - Rule of Palms is used to measure small or scattered burns. A 1% burn is considered to be the size of the patient's hand (including fingers).[41]
- The percentage of TBSA is essential to calculating fluid resuscitation

Figure 15-4. Rule of Nines

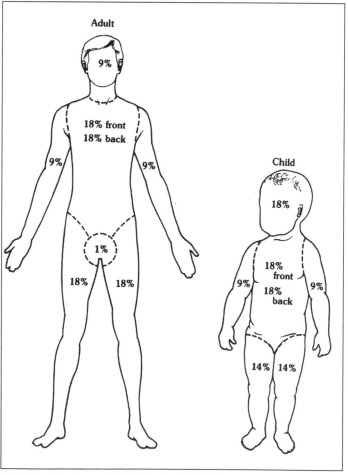

The Rule of Nine in an adult (left) and a child (right).

Location of Burn

Burns identified as high risk include:[33]

- Circumferential
  - Assess for increasing pressure to structures under circumferential burns
  - Prepare for escharotomies to chest wall or extremities
  - Eschar creates restrictive movement and can result in failure to ventilate and/or loss of limb or life
- Perineal
  - High risk for contamination or infection
- Hands or feet
  - High risk for strictures and necessitate intense rehabilitation

Interventions[33]

- Assess and manage pain
- Cover wounds with clean, dry dressings or sheets to minimize exposure to air currents, which can be painful
- Elevate extremity to the level of the heart (not above) to promote circulation and assist in reduction of edema
- If maltreatment is suspected, further investigation and notification of social or child protective services is warranted
- Administer tetanus prophylaxis as indicated
- Consider psychological support for the patient and family

Reevaluation Adjuncts
Laboratory Studies

Ongoing laboratory studies for patients with burns include:

- ABGs with carboxyhemoglobin to follow trends
- Blood glucose in infants and young children as hypoglycemia may occur due to reduced glycogen stores
- CBC, especially WBC, as an indicator of infection
- Electrolytes including potassium and magnesium
- Blood urea nitrogen and creatinine as indicators of renal function
- Creatinine kinase as an indicator of rhabdomyolitis

Selected Burn Injuries

Electrical Burns
H–History

If the patient has experienced an electrical burn, it is important to determine the following:

- The type of current and voltage
  - AC is more dangerous than DC since it causes tetany, which can result in the person tightening his or her grip on the source of current thus increasing the exposure[45]
  - The higher the voltage involved, the greater the degree of internal thermal injury
- The surface area at point of contact to help identify areas and extent of burn injury
- Identify points of contact to anticipate organs damaged along the path of the current
- Duration of contact with source to help determine the possible extent of internal injury
- Any loss of consciousness and any concurrent injuries pertinent to the MOI

H–Head-to-toe Assessment

It is difficult to assess the damage from electrical burns for much of it may be internal. The electrical current enters the body at point of skin contact and travels throughout the body with the potential to damage all types of tissue including bones, muscles, blood vessels, and nerves—the least resistant to electrical current—before exiting the body. Assessment findings include:

- Wounds or burns to the body (Fig. 15-5)
  - Document the assessment of the wounds and do not label the wounds "exit" or "entrance"

Figure 15-5. Electrical Burn

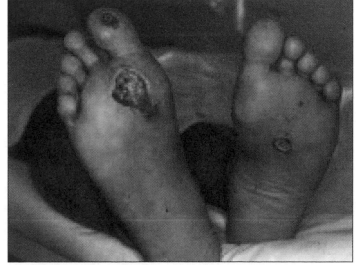

From Cushing & Wright.[43]

- Cardiac dysrhythmias
  - Analyze T-wave for changes associated with hyperkalemia
- Rhabdomyolysis with myoglobinuria (see Chapter 24, Post Resuscitation Care in the Emergency Department, for more information)
  - Urine with myoglobin will appear dark red or brown
  - Myoglobin levels
  - Acute kidney injury
  - Renal failure
- Fractures
- Seizures

Diagnostic Studies
- If myoglobin is detected in the urine, obtain a blood sample to screen for myoglobin
- Creatine kinase levels may be helpful in determining muscle damage
- Consider ABGs with bicarbonate levels for patients with rhabdomyolysis who require alkalization of the urine

Interventions
- Consider cervical spine immobilization based on MOI
- Treatment for myoglobinuria includes:
  - Administer an infusion of sodium bicarbonate to alkalize the urine, which promotes the excretion of the myoglobin[45]
  - Consider administration of Mannitol, an osmotic diuretic to help flush the kidneys of myoglobin[45]
- Monitor cardiac rate and rhythm in patients with high voltage exposure
- Monitor for signs and symptoms of compartment syndrome and prepare for fasciotomy as indicated
- Monitor compartment pressures and splint extremities with severe burns
- Consider tetanus immunization

Chemical Burns
Preparation
The first consideration with chemical burns is the safety of the trauma team. Use of personal protective equipment (PPE) will limit the serious risk of a cross exposure of the chemical agent especially during decontamination.

Patient Decontamination
- Decontamination of dry chemical exposure can generally be accomplished by removal of the patient's clothing. Use caution not to scatter any of the stimulus or causative agent with removal of clothing and jewelry.
- Lightly brush any remaining dry chemical away
- Then dilute by flushing with liberal amounts of water[41]

H-History
- Dry powder and chemical fumes can also cause inhalation injuries.

When a patient presents with a chemical burn, it is important to determine the following:
- The type of chemical (acid or alkali)
  - The container with content information can be useful in identifying chemicals
- The concentration and volume of chemical
- The route and duration of exposure
- The direct effects of the chemical such as obvious burning
- Risk for potential systemic effects

Interventions
- Support oxygenation and ventilation and consider the presence of inhalation injury
- Neutralize the chemical by irrigating the skin until the pH is normal
  - Normal human skin pH is about 5.3
  - Tap water may be used, with low pressure to avoid tissue injury[46]
  - For extensive acid or alkali burns it may require several hours of irrigation to achieve neutral pH[46]
  - Avoid hypothermia by using tepid water
- Debride any blisters caused by a chemical exposure[47]
- With tar or asphalt, stop the burning process by using water until the tar or asphalt is cool to the touch, and then use petroleum to assist in removal of the agent[41]
- Phenols are an acidic form of alcohol and poorly soluble in water. They are found in a majority of household disinfectants and chemical solvents. For patients with phenol burns, provide copious irrigation with water followed by 50% polyethylene glycol (PEG). PEG increases the solubility of phenols in water. Phenol burns can cause a thick eschar to the affected area, if not removed quickly.[41]
- For hydrofluoric acid (used for glass etching) burns, irrigate for at least 30 minutes[41]

- Because hydrofluoric acid can cause depletion of calcium, assess levels

- For information on burns to the eyes, see Chapter 10, Ocular Trauma, for more information

Reevaluation of the Patient with Burn Injury

Provide frequent and ongoing reevaluation of the following:
- The effectiveness of airway and ventilation with ongoing ability of the patient to protect the airway and perform adequate ventilation

- The effectiveness of fluid resuscitation as evidenced by hemodynamic stability and urine output[41]

  - Monitor urine output every hour

- All associated injuries and the effectiveness of the interventions

- The patient's temperature to maintain euthermia

- Skin, pulmonary, and systemic signs and symptoms of infections

- Patient's pain level and medication effectiveness

Post Resuscitation Care

Wound Care

- Initial wound care varies with the type of wound and includes debridement, topical wound care products, and dressings. This may be done in the ED, operating room, or ICU.

- Burn debridement and dressing procedures are very painful, and IV pain medication should be administered before and during the process. Monitor patients closely after the procedures for respiratory depression.

- Wound care depends on the location, depth, and extent of the burn

  - Superficial burns may require topical antibiotics but rarely dressings[34]

  - Skin grafting may be required for deeper wounds[34]

- Wound healing for larger burns may require weeks or months of inpatient hospital care

- Reevaluate the effectiveness of interventions

Definitive Care and Transport

Consider transfer to a burn center. If transferring the patient to a burn center, coordinate with the receiving burn team to determine recommended wound care prior to transfer.

The American Burn Association (ABA) recommends:
- Avoid delays in transport to a burn center

- Do not debride burns or bullae

- Do not apply creams, ointments, or topical antibiotics which may cause difficulty in assessing the extent of the burn

Emerging Trends

As the science and evidence of trauma care continues to evolve, tools to improve patient outcomes continue to be trialed and refined. Evidence is tested and replicated, and new standards of care are transitioned into practice. This section on trauma care considerations explores some of the evidence and the potential significance to trauma patient care. In the care of patients with surface and burn injuries, fluid resuscitation formulas will be discussed.

Fluid Resuscitation Formulas

Multiple formulas are outlined in the literature with regard to fluid resuscitation.[42,48] These formulas describe the use of crystalloid, colloid, hypertonic fluid, fresh frozen plasma and volume expanders. While no one formula has emerged as the standard of practice, most agree that the effectiveness of resuscitation is measured based on urinary output.[30,41,42]

Commonly used formulas include the following:
- The American Burn Association recommends beginning fluid resuscitation with Ringer's lactate solution at 2 mL/kg/percentage of TBSA[41]

- The Parkland Formula determines the fluid to administer with the following: 4 mL/kg of Ringer's lactate solution multiplied by the percentage TBSA

  - Administer the first half of the fluid over the first 8 hours, from time of burn injury, not arrival to ED, and the remaining half in the next 16 hours[34,41]

- The Modified Brooke Formula recommends beginning burn shock resuscitation at 2 mL of fluid multiplied by body weight (in kg) multiplied by percentage of TBSA[34,41]

- The American College of Surgeons (ACS) recommends 2 to 4 mL/kg per percentage TBSA in the first 24 hours[30]

Summary

The integumentary system is the largest organ in the body. The skin serves many vital functions, such as heat regulation, fluid and electrolyte regulation, and sensory relay. It is also the body's first line of defense against environmental hazards. Surface and burn trauma results in alteration of these normal functions.

Trauma resuscitation of the patients with skin trauma requires the same resuscitation strategies used for other trauma patients. Once the trauma victim with surface or burn trauma is stabilized wound care becomes the primary concern. Infection is a leading cause of morbidity and mortality in these patients. The treatment goal for these patients is to promote wound healing, maintain function, prevent complications, minimize disfiguring scars and optimize the patient's return to activities of daily living.

References

1. Copstead, L.E., & Banasik, J. (2013). *Pathophysiology* (5th ed.). St. Louis, MO: Elsevier.

2. Goldberg, M. T., & Smith, L. R. (2012). Anatomy and physiology of the skin. In *Wound management and healing* (2nd ed., pp. 1–7). Brockton, MA: Western Schools.

3. Wysocki, A. B. (2012). Anatomy of skin and soft tissue. In R. A. Bryant & D. P. Nix (Eds.), *Acute and chronic wounds: Current management concepts* (4th ed.). St. Louis, MO: Mosby Elsevier.

4. Habif, T. P. (2010). *Clinical dermatology: A color guide to diagnosis and therapy* (5th ed.). St. Louis, MO: Mosby Elsevier.

5. Burns, T., Breathnach, S., Cox, N., & Griffiths, C. (2010). *Rook's textbook of dermatology* (8th ed.). Oxford, United Kingdom: Wiley-Blackwell.

6. Doughty, D. B., & Sparks-DeFriese, B. (2012). Wound-healing physiology. In R. A. Bryant & D. P. Nix (Eds.), *Acute and chronic wounds: Current management concepts* (4th ed.). St. Louis, MO: Mosby Elsevier.

7. Williams, F. N., Herndon, D. N., Hawkins, H. K., Lee, J. O., Cox, F. A., Kulp, G. A., Jeschke, M. G. (2009). The leading causes of death after burn injury in a single pediatric burn center. *Critical Care, 13,* R183.

8. Mattox, K. L., Moore, E. E., & Feliciano, D. V. (2013). *Trauma* (7th ed.). New York, NY: McGraw-Hill.

9. Solheim, J. (2013). Assessment and stabilization of the trauma patient. In Emergency Nurses Association, *Sheehy's manual of emergency care* (7th ed., pp. 365–378). St. Louis, MO: Mosby Elsevier.

10. Hoyt, K. S, & Selfridge-Thomas, J. (Eds.). (2007). *Emergency nursing core curriculum* (6th ed.). St. Louis, MO: Saunders Elsevier.

11. Makic, M. B. F., & McQuillan, K. A. (2009). Wound healing and soft tissue injuries. In K. A. McQuillan, M. B. F. Makic, & E. Whalen (Eds.), *Trauma nursing: From resuscitation through rehabilitation* (4th ed.). St. Louis, MO: Saunders Elsevier.

12. Herr, R. D. (2013). Wound management. In Emergency Nurses Association, *Sheehy's manual of emergency care* (7th ed., pp. 147–160). St. Louis, MO: Mosby Elsevier.

13. Scalea, T., Dubose, J., Moore, E. E., West, M., Moore, F. A., McIntyre, R., … Feliciano, D. (2011). Western Trauma Association critical decisions in trauma: Management of the mangled extremity. *Journal of Trauma and Acute Care Surgery, 72*(1), 86–93.

14. Wheeless, C. R. (2012, May 22). Frost bite. In *Wheeless' textbook of orthopaedics.* Retrieved from http://www.wheelessonline.com/ortho/frost_bite

15. Mecham, C. C., Cheng, D., Thompson, T., & Yakobi, R. (2013, January 24). *Frostbite treatment and management.* Retrieved from http://emedicine.medscape.com/article/926249-treatment

16. Denke, N. J. (2010). Wound management. In P. K. Howard & R. A. Steinmann, *Sheehy's emergency nursing: Principles and practice.* St. Louis, MO: Mosby Elsevier.

17. Reichman, D. E., & Greenburg, J. A. (2009). Reducing surgical site infections: A review. *Reviews in Obstetrics & Gynecology, 2*(4), 212–221.

18. Centers for Disease Control and Prevention. (2011, May 2). *Guideline for prevention of surgical site infection, 1999.* Retrieved from http://www.cdc.gov/hicpac/SSI/004_SSI.html

19. Gabriel, A. (2011, May 19.) Wound irrigation. Retrieved from http://emedicine.medscape.com/article/1895071-overview

20. World Health Organization. (2012, May). *Burns: Fact sheet no. 365.* Retrieved from http://www.who.int/mediacentre/factsheets/fs365/en/

21. Ahrens, M. (2012, August). *Home structure fires.* Retrieved from http://www.nfpa.org/itemDetail.asp?categoryID=2685&itemID=58320&URL=Research/Statistical%20reports/Occupancies/&cookie_test=1

22. U.S. Fire Association. (2009, March 20). *Focus on fire safety: Alcohol and fire.* Retrieved from http://www.usfa.fema.gov/citizens/focus/alcohol.shtm

23. Burns. (2008). *Gale encyclopedia of medicine.* Retrieved from http://medical-dictionary.thefreedictionary.com/Burns

24. American Burn Association. (2012). *National Burn Repository: Report of data from 2002–2011.* Chicago, IL: Author. Retrieved from http://www.ameriburn.org/2012NBRAnnualReport.pdf

25. Lloyd, E., Rodgers, B. C., Michener, M., & Williams, M. S. (2012). Outpatient burns: Prevention and care. American Family Physician, 85(1), 25–32.

26. American Burn Association. (n.d.). *Scald injury prevention: Educator's guide.* Retrieved from http://www.ameriburn.org/Preven/ScaldInjuryEducator%27sGuide.pdf

27. Pruitt, V. M. (2006). Work-related burns. *Clinics in Occupational and Environmental Medicine, 5*(2), 423–433, ix–x.

28. U.S. Bureau of Labor Statistics. (2012, September 20). *Census of fatal occupational injuries summary, 2011.* Retrieved from http://www.bls.gov/news.release/cfoi.nr0.htm

29. Centers for Disease Control and Prevention. (2012, October 12). *Carbon monoxide poisoning.* Retrieved from http://www.cdc.gov/co/faqs.htm

30. American College of Surgeons. (2012). Thermal injuries. In *Advanced trauma life support student course manual* (9th ed., pp. 230–245). Chicago, IL: Author.

31. Shochat, G. M., & Lucchesi, M. (2012, June 11). *Carbon monoxide toxicity treatment and management.* Retrieved from http://emedicine.medscape.com/article/819987-overview

32. Stein, D. M., & Scalea, T. M. (2012). Capillary leak syndrome in trauma: What is it and what are the consequences? *Advances in Surgery, 46*(1), 237–253.

33. Oliver, R. I. (2012, February 1). *Burn resuscitation and early management.* Retrieved from http://emedicine.medscape.com/article/1277360-overview

34. Makic, M. B. F., & Mann, E. (2009). Burn injuries. In K. A. McQuillan, M. B. F. Makic, & E. Whalen (Eds.), *Trauma nursing: From resuscitation through rehabilitation* (4th ed.). St. Louis, MO: Saunders Elsevier.

35. Wall, R. M., & Murphy, M. F. (Eds.). (2012). *Manual of emergency airway management* (4th ed.). Philadelphia, PA: Lippincott Williams & Wilkins.

36. American College of Surgeons. (2012). Airway and ventilator management. In *Advanced trauma life support student course manual* (9th ed., pp. 30–61). Chicago, IL: Author.

37. Perbedy, M. A., Callaway, C. W., Neumar, R. W., Geocadin, R. G., Zimmerman, J. L., Donnino, M., Kronick, S. L. (2010). Part 9: Post-cardiac arrest care: 2010 American Heart Association Guidelines for Cardiopulmonary Resuscitation and Emergency Cardiovascular Care. *Circulation, 122*(18 Suppl 3), S768–S786.

38. O'Driscoll, B. R., Howard, L. S., & Davison, A. G. (2008). BTS guideline for emergency oxygen use in adult patients. *Thorax, 63*(Suppl), vi1–vi68.

39. Kilgannon, J. H., Jones, A. E., Shapiro, N. I., Angelos, M. G., Milcarek, B., Hunter, K., Trzeciak, S. (2010). Association between arterial hyperoxia following resuscitation from cardiac arrest and in-hospital mortality. *Journal of the American Medical Association, 303*(21), 2165–2171.

40. Brenner, M., Stein, D., Hu, P., Kufera, J., Wooford, M., & Scalea, T. (2012). Association between early hyperoxia and worse outcomes after traumatic brain injury. *Archives of Surgery, 147*(111), 1042–1046.

41. American Burn Association. (2011). *Advanced burn life support provider manual.* Chicago, IL: Author.

42. Warden, G. D. (2012). Fluid resuscitation and early management. In D. N. Herndon (Ed.), *Total burn care* (4th ed., pp. 115–124). St. Louis, MO: Elsevier.

43. Jenkins, J. A., & Schraga, E. D. (2011, September 26). Management of thermal burns. Retrieved from http://emedicine.medscape.com/article/769193-overview

44. Thaniyavarn, T., & Eiger, G. (2012, October 25). *Carboxyhemoglobin.* Retrieved from http://emedicine.medscape.com/article/2085044-overview

45. Cushing, T. A., & Wright, R. (2013, April 2). *Electrical injuries in emergency medicine.* Retrieved from http://emedicine.medscape.com/article/770179-overview

46. Cox, R. D. (2010, June 28). *Chemical burns in emergency medicine treatment and management.* Retrieved from http://www.emedicine.medscape.com/article/769336-treatment#a1126

47. Palao, R., Monge, I., Ruiz, M., & Barret, J. P. (2010). Chemical burns: Pathophysiology and treatment. *Burns, 36*(3), 295–304.

48. Granger, J. P, Estrada, C. M., & Abramo, T. J. (2009, January). An evidence-based approach to pediatric burns. *EB Medicine.* Retrieved from http://www.ebmedicine.net/topics.php?paction=showTopic&topic_id=186858

Chapter 16 • Special Populations: The Pregnant Trauma Patient

Rebecca A. Steinmann, APN, CCNS, CCRN, CEN, CPEN, FAEN

Objectives

Upon completion of this chapter, the learner will be able to:

1. Describe mechanisms of injury associated with the pregnant trauma patient and fetus.

2. Describe physiologic and developmental changes as a basis for assessment of the pregnant trauma patient and fetus.

3. Demonstrate the nursing assessment of the pregnant trauma patient and fetus.

4. Plan appropriate interventions for the pregnant trauma patient and fetus.

5. Evaluate the effectiveness of nursing interventions for the pregnant trauma patient and fetus.

Introduction

Trauma is not only the leading cause of death among women of child-bearing age, it is the leading nonobstetric cause of maternal death and disability during pregnancy.[1] It is estimated that 7% of all pregnancies are complicated by trauma, with death occurring in 6% to 7% of the population of injured mothers.[1] Most injuries occur in the final trimester of pregnancy and are relatively minor in nature.[2] The hormonal and physiologic differences during the gestational period appear to provide a survival advantage to the injured mother over her nonpregnant injured peers.[3] Pregnancy alters the pattern of injury, and the gravid patient is more prone to abdominal trauma as gestation progresses.

Head injury and hemorrhagic shock remain the leading causes of maternal death.[4] The most common cause of fetal death is maternal death. Major trauma is associated with a 40% to 50% risk of fetal loss[4]; this rate increases to 80% fetal mortality in the presence of maternal shock.[1] Evidence suggests that premature delivery, low birth weight, and fetal demise are post-traumatic issues, even when the mother experiences no or minor injuries.[5] Placental abruption and preterm delivery are the most common causes of fetal mortality and morbidity secondary to minor trauma.

Resuscitation priorities for the injured pregnant patient are identical to those of the nonpregnant patient. Assessment of the pregnant trauma patient is complicated by maternal anatomic and physiologic adaptations designed to nourish the second patient, the fetus. During the resuscitative phase of treatment, pregnancy should not limit or restrict any diagnostic or pharmacologic treatment. Optimal resuscitation of the mother affords the best fetal outcome. It is important to access obstetric expertise early in the resuscitation process as the trauma team simultaneously manages two patients—the mother and the fetus.

Mechanisms of Injury and Biomechanics

Blunt trauma is responsible for the vast majority of maternal injuries. The most common mechanisms of injury (MOI) include motor vehicle collisions (MVCs), falls, and physical maltreatment or interpersonal violence. MVCs are responsible for the highest proportion of life-threatening injuries.[5] Falls, which become increasingly common as pregnancy progresses, account for the majority of minor injuries.[5] The incidence of intentional injury from interpersonal violence rises during pregnancy, commonly manifested as direct assaults to the gravid abdomen.[5] Penetrating trauma is most commonly due to gunshot wounds.[5] Stab wounds are less common and carry a better prognosis for both the mother and fetus.

The potential for direct injury to the fetus increases with each trimester. With blunt maternal abdominal trauma or pelvic fractures, assess for fetal injuries, including skull fractures and intracranial hemorrhage. Clavicle and long-bone injuries may also occur in utero. Firearm injury to the maternal abdomen and uterus are frequently associated with fetal injury and death.

Anatomic and Physiologic Changes During Pregnancy as a Basis for Assessment Findings

Anatomic and physiologic changes in pregnancy can confound the typical assessment findings associated with trauma. Understanding these changes is critical to the accurate assessment and evaluation of the pregnant trauma patient.

Cardiovascular Changes

- Pregnancy results in a hypervolemic, hyperdynamic state. Total blood volume increases, improving maternal tolerance to hemorrhage. The pregnant patient can lose up to 30% to 40% of her circulating volume before a significant drop in blood pressure occurs.[4]

- Resting heart rate increases 10 to 20 beats per minute to help meet the increased metabolic demands of mother and fetus and results in increased cardiac output

- Increased hormonal levels (estrogen, prostaglandins) cause vasodilation, resulting in a decrease in systemic vascular resistance and pulmonary vascular resistance. Peripheral resistance decreases, causing a small decrease in systolic blood pressure and a more marked decrease in diastolic blood pressure.[2] The pregnant patient in shock may appear warm and dry due to this vasodilation.

- Supine hypotension syndrome (aortocaval compression) may occur after 20 weeks' gestation as the aorta and inferior vena cava are compressed by the uterus and its contents when the patient is supine. Venous return decreases, and cardiac output falls. The patient may report acute nausea and dizziness, appearing pale and diaphoretic.

- Uterine blood flow increases from approximately 50 mL/min in the nonpregnant state to 500 mL/min at term.[6,7] Engorged pelvic vessels increase the risk of retroperitoneal hemorrhage with maternal pelvic fractures.[8]

- Catecholamine-mediated vasoconstriction of uterine vessels in response to hemorrhage shunts blood to the mother and away from the fetus. Fetal hypoperfusion, evidenced by fetal tachycardia or bradycardia and changes in fetal movement, can occur before signs of maternal shock.

Respiratory Changes

- Capillary engorgement of upper respiratory passages increases the risk of nasopharyngeal bleeding and upper airway obstruction

- Minute ventilation—the amount of air inhaled and exhaled in 1 minute—increases as respiratory rate and tidal volume—the amount of air moved in and out with each breath—increase

- Oxygen consumption increases, placing the mother and fetus at increased risk for hypoxia

- As the gravid uterus presses on the diaphragm, functional capacity decreases, and the pregnant patient breathes at a faster rate, decreasing the partial pressure of carbon dioxide (PCO_2) levels, resulting in a state of respiratory alkalosis[8]

- As the diaphragm is pushed upwards by the expanding uterus, the lungs shorten and functional reserve decreases. Chest tube placement is one to two intercostal spaces higher.[9]

Hematologic Changes

- By the 30th week of pregnancy, the amount of circulating plasma increases 30-50% above its original volume, resulting in a dilutional or physiologic anemia and a proportional decrease in hematocrit.[8]

- An increase in fibrinogen levels and clotting factors results in a hypercoagulable state that increases the risk for thromboembolism and disseminated intravascular coagulation (DIC)[8]

Gastrointestinal Changes

- Abdominal organs are displaced laterally and cephalad by the enlarging uterus

- Abdominal wall muscles are stretched and lax and may mask typical findings of guarding and rigidity. Abdominal palpation is less reliable.

- Bowel sounds are less audible

- Prolonged emptying time of the gastrointestinal tract increases the risk of aspiration

- Increase in gastric secretions makes the gravid patient more prone to gastric reflux, passive regurgitation, and aspiration

Renal Changes

- Urinary stasis increases the risk for urinary tract infection

- Urinary frequency increases due to the increase of renal blood flow and resulting increased glomerular filtration rate. The mother feels additional pressure as the uterus compresses the bladder.

Musculoskeletal Changes
- Softening and relaxation of sacral ligaments and pubic symphysis make the pelvis more flexible
- The widening pelvis and heavy abdomen results in an unsteady gait, predisposing the gravid patient to falls[9]

Selected Injuries and Emergencies

Preterm Labor
Preterm labor is the most common obstetric complication in the pregnant trauma patient, occurring in up to 25% of patients.[4] Contractions are usually noted in alert patients but may go undetected in unconscious or intubated patients.

Assessment findings for preterm labor include:
- Uterine contractions of more than six per hour
- Abdominal or low back pain, pressure, or cramping
- Vaginal bloody show or bleeding
- Cervical dilation and/or effacement

Abruptio Placentae
Abruptio placentae, or placental abruption, is the premature separation of a portion of the placenta from the uterine wall, disrupting maternal-fetal circulation. Acceleration/deceleration forces can shear the relatively inelastic placenta from the elastic uterus resulting in abruption. Effects on the fetus depend on the amount of functional placenta that remains attached to the uterine wall. Any blunt abdominal trauma places the pregnant patient at risk. Maternal mortality is low; however, fetal mortality rates are as high as 30% to 68%.[2]

Assessment findings for abruptio placentae include:[4,10]
- Vaginal bleeding (occurs in 80% of cases;[10] usually dark red)
- Abdominal or back pain (sudden onset, sharp, constant)
- Fetal distress (alteration in fetal heart rate and rhythm)
- Uterine irritability and rigidity with tetanic contractions (board-like uterus)
- Preterm labor
- Maternal shock presentation disproportionate to the amount of visible vaginal bleeding
- Rising fundal height
- DIC developing as late as 48 hours after initial trauma

Uterine Rupture
Actual tearing or laceration of the uterus is rare but may occur in patients with extreme compression injury or with a history of prior cesarean sections.[4] Uterine rupture is associated with high maternal and fetal mortality.

Assessment findings for uterine rupture include:[11]
- Sudden onset of sharp abdominal or suprapubic pain
- Asymmetry of the uterus: It is possible to palpate two masses or fetal extremities outside the uterus
- Diaphragmatic irritation
- Maternal shock
- Slowing or absent fetal heart tones
- Vaginal bleeding (may or may not be present)

Maternal Cardiopulmonary Arrest/Fetal Delivery
If any moribund patient is at gestation of 24 weeks or more, the accepted standard age of fetal viability, it is important to consider a perimortem cesarean section.[1] Delivery of the fetus may improve the effectiveness of resuscitative efforts when the uterus is no longer gravid and potentially causing aortocaval compression.[12] Estimation of gestational age and assessment of fetal heart activity can be rapidly obtained while cardiopulmonary resuscitation is being performed. To optimize fetal outcome, it is recommended that cesarean section be initiated within 4 minutes of maternal arrest and the fetus be delivered within 5 minutes of any unsuccessful maternal resuscitative attempts (the "five-minute rule" adopted by the American Heart Association).[13] It is essential that a team capable of neonatal resuscitation be present. Begin Basic Life Support and Advanced Life Support protocols and continue throughout the cesarean section:[13]
- Perform chest compressions higher on the sternum, slightly above the center of the sternum
- Displace the uterus laterally during chest compressions to minimize aortocaval compression

Nursing Care of the Pregnant Trauma Patient

Primary Survey
See Chapter 5, Initial Assessment for the systematic approach to care of the trauma patient. The following assessment parameters are specific to pregnant trauma patients.

A–Airway and Alertness
Consider the supine position as it may affect the airway and fetal circulation. A 15-degree tilt of the spine board to either side can release pressure on the inferior vena cava.[14]

Secondary Survey
H–History
- What was the MOI?
  - For events related to MVCs:
    - Was the patient wearing a safety restraint device?
    - How was the restraint positioned?
  - For falls:
    - What was the height of the fall?
    - What was the surface on which the patient landed?
    - Which body part impacted the surface?
- When was the last normal menstrual period? Consider the possibility of pregnancy in any female of childbearing age.
- When is the expected date of confinement (EDC)? To estimate the EDC, count back 3 months from the first day of the last known menstrual period and add 7 days.
- What problems or complications have occurred during this or other pregnancies?
- Is there a possibility of more than one fetus?
- Is there vaginal bleeding?
- Are uterine contractions or abdominal pain present?
- Is there fetal activity?
  - If available, begin monitoring as soon as possible to trend fetal heart rate
- Is there a suspicion that injuries have been caused by interpersonal violence?

H–Head-to-toe Assessment
Inspect for:
- The shape and contour of the abdomen: A change in shape may indicate concealed hemorrhage or uterine rupture
- Signs of fetal movement
- Vaginal bleeding or the presence of amniotic fluid around the perineum
  - The patient may describe having had a sudden gush of fluid. This may be an indication of a spontaneous bladder void or premature rupture of amniotic membranes.
- Crowning or any abnormal fetal presentation at the vaginal opening

- Prolapse of the cord is rare. If present, relieve cord compression immediately. If positioning the mother to relieve pressure on the cord is contraindicated, manual displacement of the presenting part of the cord may be needed.

Auscultate for:
- Fetal heart tones and rate
  - The pregnant patient, with an increase in circulating blood volume can better compensate for blood loss. Fetal distress may be the first indication of maternal shock.
  - Fetal heart rate is an indicator of the well-being of both the mother and fetus. The normal range for fetal heart rate is between 120 and 160 beats per minute. Fetal heart tones may be heard using a Doppler ultrasound by 10 to 14 weeks' gestation.[16]
  - Continuous fetal monitoring (cardiotocography) is recommended for all pregnant patients of more than 20 weeks' gestation[1]

Palpate for:
- The height of the fundus
  - Fundal height is an indicator of gestational age. The fundus is measured in centimeters from the symphysis pubis to the top of the fundus and approximates the number of weeks of gestation. The fundal height reaches the symphysis at 12 weeks, the umbilicus at 20 weeks, and the costal margin at 36 weeks (Fig. 16-1).[16] Generally a fundus that is palpable between the umbilicus and the xiphoid is consistent with a viable fetus.[16]
- Tenderness or contractions of the uterus or abdomen

Interventions
Maternal stabilization is the priority, thus initial interventions are focused on resuscitation of the mother. Interventions specific to the pregnant trauma patient include:
- Obtain obstetric consultation in all cases of injury in pregnant patients[1]
- Position the patient on either side tilted at least 15 degrees to prevent supine hypotension from aortocaval compression if she is greater than 20 weeks' gestation. Either side will relieve the compression.
  - Displace the uterus from the vena cava as it may increase cardiac output up to 30%.[4,14] The patient can be tilted at least 15 degrees using a spine board or hip wedge, or it can be equally effective to manually displace the uterus to either side.[14]

Figure 16-1. Uterine Size and Location Reflecting Gestational Age

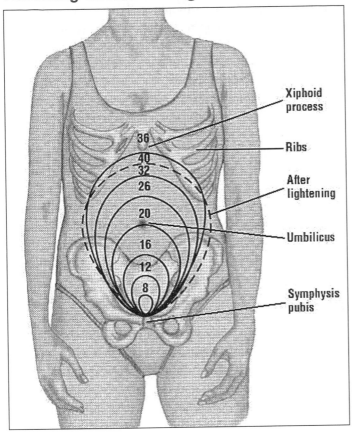

Xiphoid process

Ribs

After lightening

Umbilicus

Symphysis pubis

36
40
32
26
20
16
12
8

Reprinted with permission from Gorrie, T. M., McKinney, E. S., & Murray, S. S. (1998). Uterine growth pattern during pregnancy. In *Foundations of maternal-newborn nursing* (2nd ed., pp. 411). Philadelphia, PA: W. B. Saunders.

- Monitor uterine contractions in all pregnancies greater than 20 weeks' gestation

  ○ Tocolytic agents such as magnesium sulfate or terbutaline may be effective in halting preterm labor of the hemodynamically stable patient[4]

- Initiate continuous fetal monitoring (cardiotocography) early in the resuscitation of the mother for pregnancies at 20 weeks' gestation or more[1]

  ○ Cardiotocography monitors both the fetal heart rate and uterine contractions

  ○ It is essential that a healthcare provider experienced in the interpretation of fetal monitoring be present to assist in the care of the patient

  ○ An abnormal fetal heart rate or heart rate response to contraction may be the result of maternal hypovolemia or hypoxia, possible placental separation, or uterine rupture

- Consider emergency cesarean section if the presence of the fetus compromises maternal stability or if fetal distress is not alleviated by other methods

Reevaluation Adjuncts

Diagnostic Procedures

Patients and members of the healthcare team are often concerned about possible adverse effects from radiation on the fetus. Fetal radiation dose without shielding is 30% of that to the mother.[1] Exposure to less than 5 rad has not been associated with an increase in fetal anomalies or pregnancy loss[1] (Table 16-1). It is important to shield the fetus for all radiographic films or computed tomography (CT) studies, except for those of the pelvis or lumbar spine. Consider a consultation with the radiologist to assist in calculating the estimated radiation dose to the fetus when multiple diagnostic radiographs are performed.[1] Imaging procedures not associated with ionizing radiation are recommended instead of radiographs whenever possible.

Ultrasound

Ultrasound involves the use of sound waves and is not a source of ionizing radiation. Uterine views are being incorporated with the focused assessment with sonography for trauma (FAST) at some trauma facilities to screen for pregnancy in patients who cannot communicate or do not know if they are pregnant. A more comprehensive ultrasound may be performed during the secondary survey to determine the following:

- Gestational age
- Fetal weight
- Fetal heart rate and variability
- Placental location

Sonography has demonstrated poor sensitivity for diagnosing placental abruption, missing 50% to 80% of these injuries.[15]

Laboratory Studies

Laboratory studies to consider in the pregnant trauma patient include the following:

- Prothrombin time and partial thromboplastin time and serial coagulation studies
- Beta human chorionic gonadotropin (βHCG)

  ○ It is recommended that all female patients of childbearing age with significant trauma have a pregnancy test and be shielded for radiologic imaging whenever possible.[1] βHCG in blood confirms pregnancy as early as 1 to 2 weeks after conception and in urine 2 to 4 weeks after conception.

- Kleihauer-Betke (KB) test

  ○ The KB serum test detects fetal red cells in the maternal circulation, indicating hemorrhage of fetal blood through the placenta. A KB analysis is recommended for all pregnant patients of more than 12 weeks' gestation.[1]

Table 16-1. Estimated Fetal Exposure for Various Radiographic Studies

Examination Type	Estimated Fetal Dose per Examination (rad)
Plain radiograph	
• Cervical spine	0.002
• Chest (two views)	0.00007
• Pelvis	0.04
• Thoracic spine	0.009
• Lumbosacral spine	0.359
Computed tomography scans	
• Head	< 0.05
• Chest	< 0.1
• Abdominopelvic	2.6

Adapted from Barraco et al.[1]

- Not only is the KB test important in determining the need to administer Rh immune globulin when the mother is Rh negative and the fetus is Rh positive to prevent maternal alloimmunization, but studies have demonstrated that the KB test is an important predictor of abuptio placentae and preterm labor[1]

Diagnostic Peritoneal Lavage

Diagnostic peritoneal lavage (DPL) can be safe in pregnant trauma patients.[6] To minimize risks of visceral injury, the open technique of DPL is preferred.[4] Insert a gastric tube and urinary catheter prior to the procedure.

Additional Selected Reevaluation Adjuncts

- Pelvic examination

  - The cervix is assessed to determine if the cervical os is closed and the membranes are intact. If not, there is a risk for preterm delivery and the patient may need to be admitted.

  - Test any obvious fluid in the vaginal vault for presence of amniotic fluid. The pH of amniotic fluid is 7.5; the pH of urine is 4.6 to 6.[16]

- Provide psychosocial support and realistic reassurance related to the well-being of the fetus; allay maternal and family concerns related to fetal safety during diagnostic procedures

- Screen the patient for intimate partner violence

Reevaluation and Post-resuscitation Care

In addition to those assessments described in Chapter 5, Initial Assessment, reevaluation includes:

- Monitor amount of uterine and/or vaginal blood loss

- Measure and record fundal height every 30 minutes

- Monitor fetal heart rate and activity and assess uterine activity

  - Use cardiotocographic monitoring for a minimum of 6 hours in all women of greater than 20 weeks' gestation who experience trauma.[1] This is commonly initiated in the emergency department and continued in the labor and delivery or inpatient area.

Definitive Care or Transport

Prepare patient for hospital admission, operative intervention, or transfer, as indicated.

Summary

The consequences of trauma during pregnancy include:
- Maternal or fetal injury
- Preterm labor and delivery
- Maternal or fetal hemorrhage
- Uterine rupture
- Maternal or fetal death

The pregnant trauma patient presents the team with unique challenges and responsibilities assessing and managing two patients—the mother and fetus. The resuscitation priorities for the injured pregnant patient are identical to those of any injured patient. Fetal well-being is dependent on adequate blood flow to the uterus and placenta; therefore, the best chance for fetal survival is optimum resuscitation of the mother.

References

1. Barraco, R. D., Chiu, W. C., Clancy, T. V., Como, J. J., Ebert, J. J., Hess, L. Weiss, P. M. (2010). Practice management guidelines for the diagnosis and management of injury in the pregnant patient: The EAST practice management guidelines work group. *Journal of Trauma, 69*(1), 211–214.

2. Chang, A. K. (2011, July 22). *Pregnancy trauma*. Retrieved from http://emedicine.medscape.com/article/796979-overview

3. John, P. R., Shiozawa, A., Haut, E. R., Efron, D. T., Haider, A., Cornwell, E. E., & Chang, D. (2011). An assessment of the impact of pregnancy on trauma mortality. *Surgery, 149*(1), 94–98.

4. Hill, C. C. (2009). Trauma in the obstetrical patient. *Women's Health, 5*(3), 269–285.

5. Fischer, P. E., Zarzaur, B. L., Fabian, T. C., Magnotti, L. J., & Croce, C. A. (2011). Minor trauma is an unrecognized contributor to poor fetal outcomes: A population-based study of 78,522 pregnancies. *Journal of Trauma, 71*(1), 90–93.

6. Greiss, F. C. (2008). Uterine and placental blood flow. In *Global library of women's medicine*. Retrieved from http://www.glowm.com/section_view/heading/Uterine%20and%20Placental%20Blood%20Flow/item/197

7. Knudson, M. M., & Yeh, D. D. (2013). Trauma in pregnancy. In K. L. Mattox, E. E. Moore, & D. V. Feliciano (Eds.), *Trauma* (7th ed., pp. 709–724). New York, NY: McGraw-Hill.

8. Ruffolo, D. C. (2009). Trauma care and managing the injured pregnant patient. *Journal of Obstetrics, Gynecology, and Neonatal Nursing, 38*(6), 704–714.

9. Repasky, T. M. (2010). Obstetric trauma. In P. K. Howard & R. A. Steinmann (Eds.), *Sheehy's emergency nursing: Principles and practice* (6th ed., pp. 382–392). St. Louis, MO: Mosby.

10. Clark, A., Bloch, R., & Gibbs, M. (2011). Trauma in pregnancy. *Trauma Reports, 12*(3), 1–11.

11. Gaufberg, S. V. (2011, May 19). *Emergent management of abruptio placentae*. Retrieved from http://emedicine.medscape.com/article/795514-overview

12. Kilpatrick, S. J. (2012, March 6). Trauma in pregnancy. *UpToDate*. Retrieved from http://www.uptodate.com/contents/trauma-in-pregnancy

13. Vanden Hoek, T. L., Morrison, L. J., Shuster, M., Donnino, M., Sinz, E., Lavonas, E. J., … Gabrielli, A. (2010). Part 12: Cardiac arrest in special situations: 2012 American Heart Association Guidelines for Cardiopulmonary Resuscitation and Emergency Cardiovascular Care. *Circulation, 122*(18 Suppl 3), S829–S861.

14. Smith, L. G. (2009). The pregnant trauma patient. In K. A. McQuillan, M. B. Flynn Makic, & E. Whalen (Eds.), *Trauma nursing: From resuscitation through rehabilitation* (4th ed., pp. 780–809). St Louis, MO: Saunders.

15. Bernstein, M. P. (2008). Imaging of traumatic injuries in pregnancy. *American Roentgen Radiologic Society, 2*, 203–210.

16. American College of Surgeons (2012). *Advanced trauma life support student course manual* (9th ed.) Chicago, IL: Author.

Chapter 17 • Special Populations: The Pediatric Trauma Patient

Robin Goodman, MSN, RN, CPEN

Objectives

Upon completion of this chapter, the learner will be able to:

1. Describe mechanisms of injury associated with the pediatric trauma patient.

2. Describe anatomic, physiologic, and developmental characteristics as a basis for assessment of the pediatric trauma patient.

3. Demonstrate the nursing assessment of the pediatric trauma patient.

4. Plan appropriate interventions for the pediatric trauma patient.

5. Evaluate the effectiveness of nursing interventions for the pediatric trauma patient.

Introduction

Epidemiology

Despite a shift toward pediatric-specific injury prevention and a reduction of overall pediatric deaths due to injury, trauma continues to be the leading cause of death in children ages 1 to 19 years.[1,2] Medical spending in children ages 5 to 14 years is principally due to injury, and for every trauma-related death, more than 1,000 children are treated or receive medical consultation for non-fatal injury.[3,4] Current data estimate that 9.2 million children require medical care annually for treatment of unintentional injuries. In 2009, approximately 9,000 children died from and 225,000 were hospitalized for unintentional injuries.[5] Additional considerations are the lifelong need for medical and mental health services for survivors, productivity losses, and the costs associated with caregivers' lost earnings.[5] Research has also shown that throughout the United States (U.S.), a majority of emergency departments lack pediatric-specific training and equipment to meet the needs of this special population and a majority of injured children are managed at adult-focused facilities.[6–8] These statistics clearly highlight the need for pediatric trauma awareness, education, and preparedness.

Mechanisms of Injury and Biomechanics

Pediatric traumatic events often result in multisystem organ injury. Greater force is distributed throughout the body of pediatric patients as a result of trauma due to the patient's reduced body mass.[4,5,9–11] This force is transmitted through pliable, incompletely calcified bones, limited connective tissues, weaker abdominal walls, organs that are in closer proximity to other organs and structures, and the pediatric patient's smaller physical stature, resulting in multisystem injury. Knowledge of injury patterns in children allows clinicians to better anticipate, identify, and rapidly intervene in an effort to improve outcomes in the pediatric trauma patient.[7] Table 17-1 outlines these patterns. Additional considerations include the following:

- Blunt trauma from motor vehicle collisions, (MVCs) suffocation, drowning, and fires and/or burns are the leading causes of injury-related death among children ages 14 and under[2,3]

- Traumatic brain injury (TBI) accounts for more pediatric fatalities than injuries to other organ systems[2,3,9,12]

- Nonfatal injuries in children ages 14 years and under are most often attributable to unintentional falls[2]

- Penetrating trauma, most frequently from firearms, most often affects adolescents and carries a high mortality rate[2]

- Sports- and recreational-related injuries in children demonstrate a significant correlation with traumatic brain injury and musculoskeletal injuries. These injuries continue to play a significant role in nonfatal, unintentional injuries in pediatric patients.[13]

- Injury from child maltreatment reaches across all age groups and both genders, so it is important for the trauma nurse to maintain a high awareness for potential abuse in all pediatric trauma patients. (See Chapter 20, Special Populations: The Interpersonal Violence Trauma Patient, for additional information).

Childhood Growth and Development

Understanding normal childhood growth and development is essential when caring for pediatric trauma patients. Considerations regarding the pediatric patient's overall body size, larger body surface area, and physiologic and immunologic immaturity make up the foundation of care provided to the injured child.[7] Principles such as cephalocaudal and proximodistal define a child's development.[5,11,14]

- In children, development begins at the head and moves down towards the lower portions of the body in a cephalocaudal progression. This can be seen in the relatively larger size of the head in infants and young children in comparison to their overall body size and in the development of sensory and motor functions that begin in the upper portions of the body before the lower.

- Proximodistal development patterns begin from the core of the child's body and move outward as the child grows. An example of this development pattern is a child's control of gross motor movements prior to fine motor control. Understanding these principles helps the trauma nurse to successfully approach, properly assess, and safely care for the pediatric patient.[13,14]

Knowing expected growth and developmental milestones will help the trauma nurse to identify any deviation from established norms. Appendix 17-A describes childhood development.

Another reason it is vital that the trauma nurse is familiar with these developmental milestones is to identify any incongruity in stated mechanisms of injury (the 3-week-old who presents following a fall from a changing table because he or she rolled off when a 3-week-old has not reached the milestone of rolling over).

Children with special healthcare needs often develop at different rates and may have baseline assessment data that differs from accepted norms. Compare assessment findings to baseline with the caregiver.

Anatomic, Physiologic, and Developmental Differences in Pediatric Trauma Patients

Anatomic and physiologic characteristics unique to the pediatric patient present significant clinical implications. Maintaining an awareness and understanding of these differences can help the trauma nurse to optimize care and improve patient outcomes. These unique characteristics are reviewed within each section of the initial assessment.

Table 17-1. Common Mechanisms of Injury and Associated Patterns of Injury in Pediatric Patients

Mechanism of Injury	Common Patterns of Injury
Pedestrian struck by a vehicle	• Low speed: Lower extremity fractures • High speed: Multiple trauma, head and neck injuries, lower extremity fractures
Automobile occupant	• Unrestrained: Scalp and facial lacerations, head and neck injuries, and multiple trauma • Properly restrained: Chest and abdomen injuries, lumbar spinal fractures
Fall from a height	• Low: Upper extremity fractures • Medium: Head and neck injuries, upper and lower extremity fractures • High: Upper and lower extremity fractures, head and neck injuries, multiple trauma
Fall from a bicycle	• Without helmet: Surface abrasions, scalp and facial lacerations, head and neck lacerations • With or without a helmet: Upper extremity fractures • Striking handlebar: Internal abdominal injuries

Adapted from American College of Surgeons. (2012).[12]

Selected Developmental Differences[14]

- Children and adolescents are easily distracted, have a limited grasp of cause and effect, and lack experience with situations that can cause traumatic injury

- Young children have difficulty judging the speed and distance of oncoming vehicles

- Young children may have trouble localizing sound and recognizing sounds of danger

- The visual field is primarily at eye level, which is lower in children

- Toddlers and school-aged children are egocentric and believe that if they see the car, the driver sees them

Nursing Care of the Pediatric Trauma Patient

See Chapter 5, Initial Assessment for the systematic approach to care of the trauma patient. The following assessment parameters are specific to pediatric trauma patients.

Preparation and Triage

Safe Practice, Safe Care

Because of its complex nature, trauma care creates significant potential for medical errors; the unique anatomic, physiologic, and developmental characteristics of the pediatric patient can further compound this potential.[15] Performing a systematic, multisystem assessment in the pediatric patient, despite mechanism of injury (MOI) allows for easier recognition of multi-organ trauma and rapid intervention in life-threatening injuries.

Patient Equipment

Preparation to care for the injured pediatric patient includes the availability of necessary pediatric-specific equipment (Appendix 17-B) and reference material including normal vital sign ranges by age (Table 17-2), scales configured to read *only* in kilograms help facilitate a thorough assessment. Length-based resuscitation tapes, and guides to appropriately sized equipment and medication dosing promote accurate treatment. The Emergency Nurses Association (ENA), with the support of other professional healthcare associations, has emphasized the importance of weighing children in kilograms.[16]

Nursing Preparation

- Pediatric-specific education (ENPC) and training for trauma nurses can provide them with an understanding of the unique patient population and the preferred management principles

- Competency evaluations for all clinical staff to include pediatric skills and skills related to the care of the child with special healthcare needs will increase the trauma team's ability to provide excellent care to the pediatric trauma patient

- Regular reviews of pediatric trauma cases can assist the trauma team to identify learning, equipment, and policy needs

Facility Preparation

- Review the care environment, protocols, and guidelines to ensure a proper pediatric focus and safety

Table 17-2. Normal Vital Sign Ranges by Age

Respiratory Rate (breaths/min)	
Age	**Rate**
Infant	30–60
Toddler	24–40
Preschooler	22–34
School-age child	18–30
Adolescent	12–16

Heart Rate (beats/min)		
Age	**Awake Rate**	**Sleeping Rate**
Newborn to 3 months	85–205	80–160
3 months to 2 years	100–190	75–160
2 to 10 years	60–140	60–90
>10 years	60–100	50–90

Data from American Heart Association.[22]

- Ensure policies and agreements are in place for appropriate transfers to definitive care (burn center, pediatric trauma center)

Triage

- Pediatric assessment triangle (PAT)
  - The PAT is an across-the-room assessment that is completed within 3 to 5 seconds, evaluating:
    - General appearance
      - Muscle tone: Is there normal tone or is the patient limp and floppy?
      - Interactiveness: Does the patient recognize and interact with the caregiver?
      - Consolability: Does the patient respond to soothing attempts by caregiver?
      - Look or gaze: Does the patient maintain visual contact with the caregiver and turn toward the nurse upon entering the room?
      - Speech or cry: Is there a continuous or high-pitched cry or no crying at all?
    - Work of breathing
      - Inadequate or excessive
      - Nasal flaring
      - Retractions
      - Accessory muscle use
      - Abnormal upper airway sounds
      - General respiratory rate too fast or too slow
      - Position of comfort (tripod, sitting up)
    - Circulation to the skin
      - Color
      - Mottling or central or peripheral cyanosis
      - Diaphoresis

Primary Survey and Resuscitative Adjuncts

While the priorities for the initial assessment of the pediatric trauma patient are the same as they are in the adult patient, anatomic and physiologic differences as well as normal patterns of pediatric growth and development impact the pediatric patient's response to injury. Survival rates in pediatric trauma patients can be directly correlated with rapid airway management, initiation of ventilatory support, and early recognition and response to intracranial and intra-abdominal hemorrhage.[13] Encourage the caregiver to remain with the child during the initial assessment to help calm the child and gain cooperation during the initial assessment phase.

A—Airway and Alertness

Anatomic and Physiologic Characteristics

- Infants are obligate nose breathers until 4 to 6 months of age, and may more easily develop respiratory distress as a result of nasal congestion[17]
- A smaller airway diameter may cause minimal amounts of blood, edema, mucous, and/or foreign objects to partially or completely impede the airway[17]
- The tongue size is larger in relation to the oral cavity and may require the use of a tongue depressor, positioning, and/or oral adjuncts to maintain airway patency[17]
- A shortened trachea and neck means there is a narrow margin for movement of the endotracheal tube (ETT) before dislodgement, which may lead to increased incidence of right main stem bronchus intubation or inadvertent extubation[17]
- The cricoid cartilage is C-shaped allowing for potential increased risk for compression and subsequent airway obstruction with hyperextension or hyperflexion of the neck[11,14]
- A large occiput results in passive flexion of the cervical spine while in a supine position which may occlude the airway[17]
- A large, heavy head, lax neck ligaments, and more flexible joints all contribute to greater energy impact to the neck with angular momentum forces. These characteristics can increase the risk for both head and cervical spinal injuries.[18]
- Lax neck ligaments and incompletely calcified vertebrae place the pediatric patient at higher risk for injury to the spinal cord without a fracture, or spinal cord injury without radiographic abnormalities (SCIWORA)[14]
- Vertebral bodies are wedged anteriorly and may tend to slide forward or sublux with flexion due to acceleration/deceleration forces

Assessment

Use AVPU to assess the pediatric patient. See Chapter 5, Initial Assessment, for more information.
  - An alert older infant or toddler will recognize his or her caregiver, be cautious of strangers, and may not respond to commands, which is a normal response
- Loose and/or missing teeth may be normal findings in school-aged children and not the result of oral trauma
  - Assess for bleeding sockets
  - Loose teeth can be more easily dislodged and pose a risk for aspiration
- Assess for cyanosis in the oral mucous membranes

- It is a significant finding and indicative of central cyanosis due to either severe respiratory or circulatory issues

Interventions

- Frequent suctioning or placement of a nasal airway may be required to keep the pharynx clear of secretions and improve ventilation

- When inserting an oral airway in the unconscious patient by the anatomic insertion method, use a tongue blade and a direct insertion technique with the oral airway curving downward to avoid damage to the soft palate and to limit the potential for subsequent bleeding[19]

- Previous recommendations suggested the use of uncuffed tubes in children under the age of 8 years due to the risk of ischemic damage to the tracheal mucosa from potential compression between a cuff and the cricoid ring. However, endotracheal tube (ETT) cuffs are now designed to be high-volume and low-pressure and produce a seal at a lower pressure, and use of cuffed tubes in young children is increasing in EDs and pediatric intensive care units (PICU). Be sure to follow guidelines regarding air leak and cuff pressure monitoring.[20,21]

- Secure the ETT at the lip at a depth equal to three times the diameter of the tube until definitive placement can be verified by chest radiograph[22]

- Gastric tubes decrease gastric distension and facilitate diaphragmatic function and chest expansion, and improve ventilation[22]

Cervical Spinal Immobilization
Assessment

- Inspect the position of the infant and/or child's occiput in relationship to the body on the spine board to assure alignment. Pad the upper back to horizontally align the external auditory meatus to the shoulders.

- Assess for appropriate sizing and application of rigid cervical collars to maintain cervical spine stabilization

Interventions

- Remove the infant from the safety seat while maintaining cervical spinal stabilization

  ○ One team member stabilizes the infant's head and neck from behind the infant seat, while another lays the infant seat down with the back resting on the stretcher, removing it from the foot of the stretcher

B–Breathing and Ventilation
Anatomic and Physiologic Characteristics

- Respiratory rates are faster, as a result of their increased basal metabolic rate (Table 17-2) and contribute to overall insensible fluid losses resulting in a greater risk for hypovolemia, further exacerbated in the presence of hemorrhage

- An increased metabolic rate inefficiently uses oxygen; limited reserves are quickly depleted in times of physiologic stress such as trauma

- Children with respiratory distress may increase their respiratory rate and exhibit signs of increased work of breathing to maximize ventilation. This requires a large amount of energy, and the patient will fatigue once physiologic reserves are exhausted leading to rapid decompensation.

- Due to a horizontally oriented rib cage and weak chest wall and intercostal muscles, young children have smaller tidal volumes with decreased ability to increase their volume during periods of distress[23]

- Alveoli are fewer and smaller creating a reduced area for gas exchange in younger children. Existing alveoli have less elastic recoil and lack supportive tissue.[23]

- Younger children have a flat-shaped diaphragm and since it is the primary muscle for ventilation, gastric distension can greatly limit ventilation[23]

- Thin chest walls contribute to the transmission of breath sounds from one side of the chest to the other potentially masking the presence of pneumothorax, hemothorax, and/or tension pneumothorax[14,18,24]

- Younger pediatric patients normally use the abdominal muscles for breathing. Those experiencing abdominal pain may exhibit alterations in respiratory patterns, such as shallow respirations and expiratory grunting.[25]

Assessment

- Inspect for increased work of breathing

  ○ Nasal flaring

  ○ Retractions:

    • Site: substernal, intercostal, suprasternal, or supraclavicular

    • Severity: mild, moderate, or severe

  ○ Head bobbing

  ○ Expiratory grunting

  ○ Accessory muscle use: sternocleidomastoid or trapezius

- Infants normally are diaphragmatic breathers and the diaphragm is considered a primary muscle of breathing, not accessory
- Auscultate for:
  ◦ An appropriately sized stethoscope can assist with the accuracy of auscultating the lung fields and lessen the transmission of lung sounds across the chest

Interventions

- Blow-by oxygen does not meet oxygen requirements nor provide beneficial ventilatory support in the injured child. A tight-fitting, nonrebreather mask with an attached reservoir is recommended for trauma patients.[6]
- If gastric distention develops from either assisted ventilations or air swallowing, a gastric tube can relieve the distention, optimizing lung expansion

C–Circulation and Control of Hemorrhage

Systemic hypovolemia can produce secondary brain injury and is the single worst risk factor for devastating brain injury.[9,13]

Anatomic and Physiologic Characteristics

- Heart rates vary by age (Table 17-2)
- Children are largely comprised of water and can easily become dehydrated
- The myocardium is less compliant in pediatric patients. In order to maintain cardiac output, heart rate increases to meet systemic demands. A strong compensatory response, as evidenced by tachycardia, may maintain cardiac output in times of increased systemic need for an extended amount of time. When compensatory mechanisms are exhausted, decompensation is sudden and rapid.

Tachycardia and delayed capillary refill of more than 2 seconds are signs of poor tissue perfusion in the pediatric trauma patient.[22] The initial compensatory mechanism to increase cardiac output is to increase the heart rate in response to hemorrhagic shock. Tachycardia is followed by systemic vasoconstriction to increase systemic vascular resistance, resulting in delayed capillary refill, weak distal pulses, and cool, mottled extremities.

- Systemic vasoconstriction results from stimulation of the sympathetic nervous system, which can maintain adequate systolic blood pressure despite significant blood loss
- Because children have a larger blood volume to weight ratio, a small volume loss can more quickly result in circulatory compromise than in adult patients[14]
  ◦ Hypovolemic shock as a result of hemorrhage is the most common form of shock in the pediatric trauma patient.[17] Hypotension (Table 17-3) is a late finding, reflecting blood loss of approximately 30% and indicates severe compromise to organ perfusion.[22]

Assessment

- Palpate central and peripheral pulses. For purposes of determining the need for cardiopulmonary resuscitation, the brachial pulse is palpated in those under the age of one year.
- Assess for capillary refill (normal 2 seconds or less). Blanch the forehead, sole of the foot, or palm of the hand and observe time to refill. A nail bed can be used on the older child or adolescent.[24]
- Perform frequent serial assessments and comparison of central and peripheral pulses to determine stability, improvement, or worsening of circulation and perfusion
- Jugular vein distension (JVD) can be difficult to assess in young children and infants due to their short necks

Interventions

- Rapid vascular access with peripheral intravenous (IV) access or intraosseous (IO) access is the priority of care for a patient in shock. It is not necessary to attempt IV access before the use of the IO route. If peripheral perfusion is compromised, IO access may be the best and first choice.[24]
- Immediate, rapid infusion of 20 mL/kg of warmed isotonic crystalloid solution over 5 to 10 minutes with a three-way stopcock and a 20 mL syringe (for a patient weighing 5 kg, fill the 20 mL syringe 5 times to deliver a 20 mL/kg bolus) in the tubing system is

Table 17-3. Hypotension by Systolic Blood Pressure and Age

Age	Systolic blood pressure (mm Hg)
Term neonates (0–28 days)	< 60
Infants (1–12 months)	< 70
Children 1–10 years (5th percentile blood pressure)	< 70 + (age in years x 2)
Children > 10 years	< 90

From American Heart Association.[22]

an effective way to deliver specific fluid quantities in the injured pediatric patient[14]

- After each bolus of isotonic crystalloid solution assess bilateral breath sounds for crackles or other signs of fluid excess. Infants and children with congenital heart defects are susceptible to fluid overload.[14]

- Assess for continued signs of shock. There is not adequate evidence at this time to recommend an acceptable total resuscitation volume in the pediatric patient. As with any trauma patient, consideration is given for balanced resuscitation to include blood and blood component therapy.

D–Disability (Neurologic Status)
Anatomic and Physiologic Characteristics
- A positive Babinski reflex is a normal finding in the young infant

  - When the sole of the foot is stimulated in a line from the heel to the small toe, the large toe moves upward and the other toes fan out

- The normal body position in an infant is slightly flexed, with the arms and legs pulled in to the core

- The head of the infant and young child is proportionately larger in comparison to overall body size in young children. By age 2 years, the head has achieved 80% of the adult size.[14]

- Smaller subarachnoid space and a decreased volume of cerebrospinal fluid (CSF) results in less cushioning for the brain in the event of an injury

- Infants have unfused cranial sutures and open fontanels that allow for expansion. This means a larger volume of blood can be lost into the cranial vault before assessment findings of increased intracranial pressure develop.

- Restlessness, crying, fussiness, agitation, and irritability may be signs of decreased cerebral perfusion

- Normal intracranial pressures are as follows:[14]

  - Infants: 2 to 6 mm Hg

  - Young children: 3 to 7 mm Hg

  - Older children: 0 to 15 mm Hg

Assessment
- Consider any alterations in level of consciousness to be the result of cerebral hypoxia until proven otherwise

- Restlessness, anxiety, fussiness, crying, irritability, and combativeness can be early signs of hypoxia in the pediatric patient. Be concerned about the older infant and toddler who should express fear or anxiety

Figure 17-1. Positive Babinski Reflex

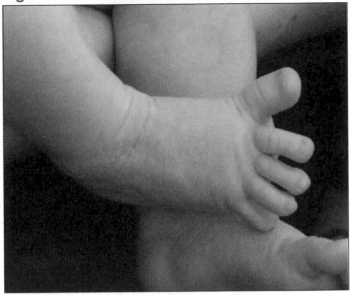

A positive Babinski reflex is normal in infants. The large toe points upward and the other toes fan out.
From Babinksi-newborn.jpg. (2008, October 1). Retrieved from https://commons.wikimedia.org/wiki/File:Babinski-newborn.jpg. *File licensed under the Creative Commons Attribution-Share Alike 3.0 unported license.*

toward a stranger and does not. This may be an altered level of consciousness.[18]

- Calculate the Pediatric Glasgow Coma Scale score (Table 17-4)

Interventions
- Consider a bedside glucose to determine if any change in level of consciousness may be related to hypoglycemia

- Prepare for endotracheal intubation for noted changes in mental status that may indicate decreased cerebral blood flow, hypoxia, or fatigue

- Hyperventilation ($PaCO_2$ < 35 mm Hg) causes cerebral vasoconstriction and decreases cerebral blood flow and is contraindicated in patients with traumatic brain injury (TBI). In patients that continue to demonstrate signs and symptoms of increased intracranial pressure (ICP) despite interventions moderate prophylactic hyperventilation (maintain $PaCO_2$ 30–35 mm Hg) can be initiated but usually only as a temporary rescue measure for signs of impending brain herniation.[4,12,14,22] See Chapter 9, Brain, Cranial, and Maxillofacial Trauma, for more information.

E–Exposure and Environmental Control
Anatomic and Physiologic Characteristics
- Children have a large body surface area–to–body mass ratio that increases insensible losses through surface evaporation

Table 17-4. Pediatric Glasgow Coma Scale

Response	Child (1 – 5 years)	Infant (< 1 year)	Score
Eye opening	Spontaneous	Spontaneous	4
	To speech	To speech	3
	To pain only	To pain only	2
	No response	No response	1
Best verbal response	Oriented, appropriate	Coos and babbles	5
	Confused	Irritable cries	4
	Inappropriate words	Cries to pain	3
	Incomprehensible sounds	Moans to pain	2
	No response	No response	1
Best motor response*	Obeys commands	Moves spontaneously and purposefully	6
	Localizes painful stimulus	Withdraws to touch	5
	Withdraws in response to pain	Withdraws in response to pain	4
	Flexion in response to pain	Abnormal flexion posture to pain	3
	Extension in response to pain	Abnormal extension posture to pain	2
	No response	No response	1

*If patient is intubated, unconscious, or preverbal, the most important part of this scale is motor response. Motor response should be carefully evaluated.
From American Heart Association.[22]

- Young children, specifically infants with a higher percentage of brown adipose tissue, an inability to shiver, and an immature thalamus have limited ability to regulate temperature[26]

- Lesser amounts of body fat allow for rapid dissipation of body heat when exposed to surrounding environment

- Hypothermia results in increased oxygen consumption and subsequent hypoxia or acidosis if left uncorrected[27]

- Hypothermia complicates coagulopathies in the injured pediatric patient and has been correlated to increase risk of morbidity and mortality in severely injured pediatric patients[4]

- Children have thinner skin and higher rates of insensible water losses. Because of this they are more susceptible to dehydration, increased severity of burn injuries, and more rapid absorption of dermal toxins.[28]

Assessment
- During clothing removal, take note of any signs or patterns of injuries that might raise an index of suspicion for maltreatment

Interventions
- Consider continuous temperature monitoring (urinary catheter thermometer, rectal temperature probe) due to the pediatric patient's sensitivity to heat loss

- A radiant warmer with servo control can provide heat in response to the infant's body temperature while allowing full access for necessary interventions

- Clothing removal may be upsetting to the pediatric patient. Provide age-appropriate explanations and maintain privacy (Appendix 17-A).

F–Full Set of Vital Signs/Family Presence
- Use appropriately sized equipment to obtain accurate vital signs

- Respiratory and heart rates can vary with activity, anxiety, and crying. Attempt to measure vital signs when the pediatric patient is calm and count both for a full minute.
  - Assess while the caregiver holds the child
  - Count respirations before close interaction or hands-on assessment
  - Use toys or bright objects to distract the infant during the assessment

- With the use of automated blood pressure devices assure correct sizing of equipment and measure when the patient is calm

  ◦ Adjust monitor settings to reflect pediatric or infant parameters

  ◦ Results may be inaccurate with movement or extreme values

  ◦ Validate with manual blood pressure

- Promote family-centered care and recognize that the pediatric patient's family may not just include the caregiver

- Advocate for and encourage family presence at the bedside throughout the emergency department stay, especially during invasive procedures and resuscitation. Research supports the development and implementation of structured family-presence programs in the emergency setting.[29] These programs have been shown to have positive effects on patients and caregivers and do not negatively impact clinical care with regards to efficiency and outcomes.[29,30]

Resuscitation Adjuncts
G–Get Resuscitation Adjuncts
L–Laboratory Analysis

- Use pediatric-specific tubes that can accommodate smaller volumes of blood

- Bedside serum glucose testing and repeat evaluation as needed

- The metabolic demands of children are higher than in adults, and glycogen stores in the liver can be limited. Physiologic stress may rapidly deplete glycogen stores resulting in hypoglycemia and causing decreased cardiac contractility, alteration in the level of consciousness, seizures, and acidosis.

M–Monitoring

- Use appropriately sized pediatric equipment

- Use non-invasive monitors with caution, knowing that movement and crying, poor perfusion, and extreme values can affect the readings

- Change monitor alarm settings to reflect normal pediatric parameters for age-based respiratory rate, heart rate, SpO_2, and blood pressure

N–Nasogastric or Orogastric Tube Consideration

- Crying and bag-mask ventilation can cause children to swallow air and gastric distention. Consider decompression with a nasogastric or orogastric tube if not already completed with endotracheal intubation.

- Select appropriate sizes with the use of length-based resuscitation tape

O–Oxygenation

- Apply the pulse oximeter probe to a warm extremity for the most accurate results

  ◦ A warm pack around the hand or foot may help

  ◦ Other possible locations in the pediatric patient include the side of the hand, the earlobe, or the forehead

P–Pain Assessment and Management

- Pain has been consistently shown to be poorly assessed and managed in pediatric trauma patients[31,32]

- Children may have difficulty localizing the source(s) of pain and may not be able to effectively communicate that they are experiencing pain

- Environmental and emotional factors can potentiate the pain experience in pediatric patients

Assessment and Interventions

- Use age and developmentally appropriate pain scales to assess for pain in all injured pediatric patients. See Chapter 8, Pain, for more information.

- Provide distraction techniques and comfort items. See Chapter 8, Pain, for further information.

- Advocate for appropriate levels of pain management in all injured pediatric patients

- Assess for signs and symptoms of traumatic stress

Reevaluation

- Assess for the need of pediatric surgical services, intensive care, or specialists (burn center) at this time and prepare for transport if indicated

- Determination of the Pediatric Trauma Score (Table 17-5) may aid in the determination if the need for transfer to a pediatric trauma center exists[13]

Secondary Survey and Reevaluation Adjuncts
H–History

- Obtain additional pertinent history information (Table 17-6)

  ◦ Include the caregiver's perception of the child

  ◦ For the child with special healthcare needs, vital signs, work of breathing, color, and mental status may vary from norms. The caregiver should be able to give a description of baseline status for assessment comparison.

- Additionally, the caregiver may have important insight into the injury

Table 17-5. The Pediatric Trauma Score

Assessment Component	Pediatric Trauma Score		
	+2	+1	-1
Weight	Weight > 20 kg	10–20 kg	< 10 kg
Airway	Normal	Oral or nasal airway, oxygen	Intubated, cricothyroidotomy, or tracheostomy
Systolic blood pressure	> 90 mm Hg, good peripheral pulses and perfusion	50–90 mm Hg, carotid/femoral pulses palpable	< 50 mm Hg, weak or no pulses
Level of consciousness	Awake	Obtunded or any loss of consciousness	Coma, unresponsive
Fracture	None seen or suspected	Single, closed	Open or multiple
Cutaneous	None visible	Contusion, abrasion, laceration < 7 cm not through fascia	Tissue loss, any gunshot wound or stab wound through fascia

From Tepas, J. J. 3rd, Mollitt, D. L., Talbert, J. L., & Bryant, M. (1987). The pediatric trauma score as a predictor of injury severity in the injured child. *Journal of Pediatric Surgery*, 22(1), 14–18.

H–Head-to-toe Assessment

Older infants, toddlers, and preschool-aged children may respond better to a least invasive to most invasive approach to assessment rather than a head-to-toe progression.

- Head
  - Palpate the infant for full or bulging fontanels
- Chest
  - The pediatric patient's ribs are more cartilaginous, so fractures are not common. When present, rib fractures indicate significant force transmitted across the chest with the high possibility of damage to underlying structures.
  - A mobile mediastinum allows a greater degree of shift to the right or left in the presence of pneumothorax, hemothorax, and/or tension pneumothorax
- Abdomen
  - Anatomic and physiologic characteristics
    - The abdominal muscles are thin and less developed, so abdominal organs are not well protected
    - The liver is more anterior and less protected by the ribs
    - The kidneys are more mobile and less protected by fat
    - The sigmoid colon and ascending colon are more mobile within the peritoneum and at greater risk for deceleration injuries
    - The duodenum has an increased vascular supply; injury can lead to increased blood loss[14]
  - Assessment
    - Inspect the abdomen for distention. Determine if distension may be gastric dilatation from swallowing air while crying or with bag-mask assisted ventilations.
    - Crying interferes with the assessment for guarding, tenderness, and rigidity. Provide distraction, involve the caregiver, or take the time for the patient to become calm before assessing.
- Pelvis and genitalia
  - The shallow depth of the pelvis increases risk for bladder rupture, particularly when full[33]
  - Assessing for rectal tone in the pediatric patient can be upsetting and can contribute to a reduction in the patient's cooperation, potentially limiting ongoing systemic assessments
    - Assess by observing for an anal wink with rectal temperature unless contraindicated
    - Perform this last and include the caregiver to comfort and hold the patient at the end of the assessment

Table 17-6. CIAMPEDS Mnemonic

Definition	Description
C–Chief complaint	• Reason for the pediatric patient's ED visit and duration of complaint (fever for past 2 days)
I–Immunizations	• Evaluation of the pediatric patient's current immunization status • Evaluation of completion of all scheduled immunizations for the patient's age • Documentation if immunizations not received due to religious or cultural beliefs
I–Isolation	• Evaluation of the pediatric patient's exposure to communicable diseases (meningitis, chickenpox, shingles, whooping cough, and tuberculosis) • Respiratory isolation placement upon ED arrival of pediatric patients with active disease or who are potentially infectious • Evaluation of other exposures (lice, scabies)
A–Allergies	• Evaluation of the pediatric patient's previous allergic or hypersensitivity reactions • Documentation of reactions to medications, foods, products (latex), and environmental allergens, including type

M–Medications	• Evaluation of the pediatric patient's current medication regimen, including prescription medications, over-the-counter medications, and herbal and dietary supplements, including:
	  ○ Dose administered
	  ○ Time of last dose
	  ○ Duration of use

P–Past medical history	• Review of the pediatric patient's health status, including prior illnesses, injuries, hospitalizations, surgical procedures, and chronic physical and psychiatric illnesses
	• Evaluation of alcohol, tobacco, drug, or other substance use as appropriate
	• Medical history of the neonate should include prenatal and birth history:
	  ○ Maternal complications during pregnancy or delivery
	  ○ Infant's gestational age and birth weight
	  ○ Number of days infant remained in the hospital after birth
	• Medical history of the post-menarche female should include date and description of her last menstrual period
	• Medical history for sexually active patients should include the following:
	  ○ Type of birth control used
	  ○ Barrier protection
	  ○ Prior treatment for sexually transmitted infections
	  ○ Gravida (pregnancies) and para (births, miscarriages, abortions, and living children)

P–Caregiver's impression of the pediatric patient's condition	• Evaluation of the caregiver's concerns and observations of the patient's condition • Significant when evaluating the child with special healthcare needs • Consideration of cultural differences that may affect the caregiver's impressions

Table 17-6. CIAMPEDS Mnemonic (Continued)

Definition	Description

E–Events surrounding the illness or injury	• Evaluation of the onset of the illness or circumstances and mechanism of injury
	• Time and date injury occurred
	  ◦ M: Mechanism of injury, including the use of protective devices (seatbelts and helmets)
	  ◦ I: Injuries suspected
	  ◦ S: Signs in the prehospital environment
	  ◦ T: Treatment by prehospital providers
	• Description of circumstance leading to injury
	• Witnessed or unwitnessed
	• Illness
	  ◦ Length of illness, including date and day of onset and sequence of symptoms
	  ◦ Treatment provided before ED visit

D–Diet	• Assessment of the pediatric patient's recent oral intake and changes in eating patterns related to the illness or injury • Time of last meal and last fluid intake • Changes in eating patterns or fluid intake • Usual diet: Breast milk, type of formula, solid foods, diet for age and developmental level, and cultural differences • Special diet or dietary restrictions
S–Symptoms associated with the illness or injury	• Identification of symptoms and progression of symptoms since the onset of the illness or injury event

Note: ED indicates emergency department.
From Emergency Nurses Assocation.[14]

• Extremities
   ◦ Pediatric patients have pliable, incompletely calcified bones that may mask significant underlying trauma
   ◦ Greenstick and buckle/torus fractures of the bones occur frequently in children due to the pliability and cartilaginous nature of young bones
   ◦ Because of the ossification process in children, comparison views for extremity radiographs will assist in identifying injury[14]

Reevaluation Adjuncts
Radiographic Studies
Cervical Spinal Trauma
The National Emergency X-Radiography Utilization Study (NEXUS) criteria for cervical spine clearance have demonstrated mixed results in sensitivity in the pediatric population.[18,34–36] Because young pediatric patients rarely meet the criteria, those under 8 years of age may require alternate diagnostic approaches, such as computed tomography (CT). The use of plain cervical radiographs may be useful in limiting exposure to ionizing radiation in children. However, CT may still be required if the films are not definitive.[35,37–41]

Maintain full spinal immobilization if symptoms exist, even in the face of negative radiographs or CT imaging. SCIWORA can be diagnosed with magnetic resonance imaging.

Head Trauma

CT scans have become the standard to evaluate for traumatic injuries in the pediatric patient. Recent research shows that ionizing radiation exposure via CT scanners during assessment of blunt trauma correlate with an increased life-long risk of leukemia and solid tumor cancers.[39,40,42] Children ages 0 to 5 years are most susceptible to ionizing radiation exposure; therefore, consider the benefit and cumulative radiation dose of each imaging study in this group. Because the diagnostic value of these images can be crucial when needed, the Pediatric Emergency Care Applied Research Network (PECARN) released guidelines for use of CT in children with head injuries to minimize risk and eliminate unnecessary scans.[36]

Abdominal Trauma

For abdominal trauma in the pediatric patient, diagnostic options continue to evolve. The current recommendations include:

- To assess for free air in penetrating abdominal trauma, use CT and upright abdominal radiograph

- For moderate or severe blunt abdominal trauma:[18]

  ○ Obtain a CT in the stable patient

  ○ Use focused assessment with sonography in trauma (FAST) or surgical exploration in the unstable patient

Focused Assessment with Sonography in Trauma

The use of FAST in pediatric patients has limited sensitivity for identifying peritoneal bleeding but can be useful for the hypotensive patient that is too unstable for CT. The practice is rapidly evolving as studies begin to support its use in pediatric trauma management and trauma physicians and surgeons develop expertise with the technology.[43]

Diagnostic Peritoneal Lavage

Diagnostic peritoneal lavage (DPL) is no longer considered the preferred diagnostic method to rule out intra-abdominal bleeding in children. Accuracy and expertise with FAST has lessened the popularity of the more invasive DPL.[43]

Selected Injury Findings
Head Injury

- Suspect severe brain injury in a pediatric trauma patient with bulging fontanels.[4] Head ultrasound or CT may be indicated for the infant with bulging fontanel.[4]

- Persistent vomiting post-trauma can be an indication of increased ICP

Traumatic Brain Injury

- The assessment goal is to determine if the pediatric patient with TBI requires medical or surgical intervention or if observation and discharge teaching may be indicated

- The PECARN criteria (Fig. 17-2) can identify those patients that require observation only, limiting ionizing radiation exposure[40]

Cervical Spinal Injury

- If any signs or symptoms of SCI are present, despite negative radiographic evidence, assume that an unstable spinal injury exists and maintain cervical spinal immobilization

- Appropriate, early removal of cervical collars promotes comfort, decreases anxiety and fear, decreases risk for skin breakdown, and may lower the risk of aspiration in pediatric patients[39–41]

Abdominal Trauma

- Because pediatric patients are more susceptible to abdominal injury, bruising or abrasions to the abdomen may indicate the need for CT or serial assessments[12]

- The liver, spleen, and kidneys have less protection from the ribs and overlying muscle and fat and carry the highest risk of injury of the abdominal organs[14]

- Management is based upon the hemodynamic stability of the patient, stability of the injured organ, and the need for continued blood replacement therapy. Liver and spleen injuries are managed nonoperatively in the hemodynamically stable pediatric trauma patient.[44] Preservation of the spleen is of utmost importance in this population due to its immunologic functions.[4,44] Even if surgery is required, the focus is on repair and hemostasis, not removal.

Musculoskeletal Trauma

- Injuries involving the growth plates may result in growth abnormalities and lifelong implications (length discrepancies in arms or legs, scoliosis, kyphosis, gait disturbances). For the pediatric patient with a growth plate injury, expect referral to an orthopedic specialist for follow-up.

Maltreatment

(See Chapter 20, Special Populations: The Interpersonal Violence Trauma Patient, for more information)
Suspect maltreatment with certain musculoskeletal injury patterns such as:

- Injuries of differing stages of healing and injuries not supported by the reported MOI

- Rib, scapular, or sternal fractures that require a great deal of force

Figure 17-2. PECARN Algorithm

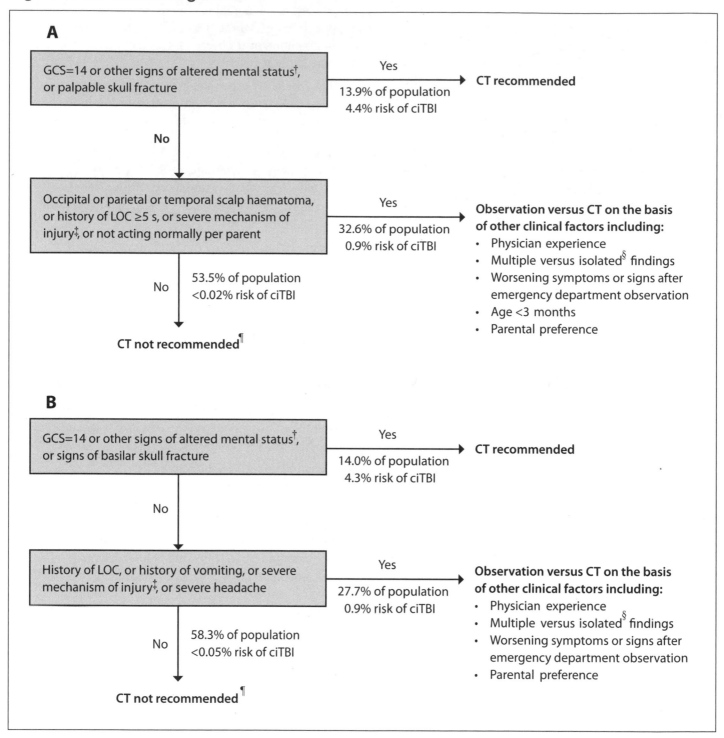

Figure 17-2: Suggested CT algorithm for children younger than 2 years (A) and for those aged 2 years and older (B) with GCS scores of 14-15 after head trauma. *From:* PECARN.org ciTBI indicates clinically important traumatic brain injury; GCS, Glasgow Coma Scale; loss of consciousness. *Data are from the combined derivation and validation populations. †Other signs of altered mental status: agitation, somnolence, repetitive questioning, or slow response to verbal communication. ‡Severe mechanism of injury: motor vehicle crash with patient ejection, death of another passenger, or rollover; pedestrian or bicyclist without helmet struck by a motorized vehicle; falls of more than 0.9 m (3 feet) (or more than 1.5 m [5 feet] for panel B); or head struck by a high-impact object. §Patients with certain isolated findings (with no other findings suggestive of traumatic brain injury), such as isolated LOC, isolated headache, isolated vomiting, and certain types of isolated scalp hematomas in infants older than 3 months, have a risk of ciTBI substantially lower than 1%. ¶Risk of ciTBI exceedingly low, generally lower than risk of CT-induced malignancies. Therefore, CT scans are not indicated for most patients in this group.

- If the MOI does not indicate this level of force, suspect maltreatment

- Transverse, oblique, and spiral fractures

- Bilateral or symmetrical fractures, bruising, or abrasions

Burn Trauma (See Chapter 15, Surface and Burn Trauma, for more information)

Assessment

- Pediatric patients with facial or neck burns or a history of enclosed space inhalation may require rapid airway management as a result of the edema and inflammation in the airway

- Commonly used methods for calculating burn size in children include the following:

  - The modified Lund and Browder chart[45,46]

    - Considered most accurate

    - First choice of most burn centers

  - The Pediatric Rule of Nines[12,45–47]

    - Most widely used

    - Accounts for the proportionally larger head of the young child

    - May be slightly adjusted by burn centers based on patient age

    - For purposes of determining a higher level of care, can be used for patients up to age 15 years at which point the adult Rule of Nines is more accurate

  - The palmar method[12,45,46]

    - The patient's palm from the crease of the wrist to the tips of the fingers roughly equivalent to 1%

    - Best for small or scattered burns

Interventions

- Stop the burning process.

  - For superficial burns less than 10% total burn surface area (TBSA) cool water may be used for 3 to 5 minutes[47]

  - **Never** use ice or iced water[47]

- Provide fluid resuscitation as indicated

  - The Parkland formula is used to calculate fluid resuscitation in pediatric burn patients and is used when an area of greater than 15% to 20% TBSA exists[14,18]

  - The Parkland formula for children is 3 mL Ringer's lactate solution multiplied by weight in kilograms multiplied by percent of TBSA including only deep partial thickness or full thickness burns (3 mL x weight in kg x %TBSA = 24-hour fluid requirement)[47]

  - Administer the first half of the fluid over the first 8 hours and the remaining half in the next 16 hours

  - Adequacy of fluid resuscitation is measured by a minimum urine output of 1 to 2 mL/kg/hour[18]

  - Young children require maintenance IV fluids in addition to burn resuscitation fluids to meet increased metabolic demands and prevent hypoglycemia and acidosis[4,12]

- Keep patients covered to prevent heat loss

  - Hypothermia increases metabolic demands and contributes to coagulopathy development

  - Wet dressings are removed promptly and all efforts to keep the patient warm are instituted

- Pain management includes the following:

  - Cover all burns to prevent pain from air current across exposed nerves

  - Opioid treatment should be considered early. Reassess the patient for pain and relief often as medication absorption can be unpredictable with fluid shifts.[14]

Refer patients to burn center per established guidelines for follow-up (see Chapter 15, Surface and Burn Trauma, for more information)

Psychosocial Aspects

- Untreated pain has been shown to increase the risk for post-traumatic stress disorder and heighten future pain responses in children[31]

- In the presence of multiple injury and stress, larger doses of analgesia may be required to manage pain during procedural modalities. Ongoing reevaluation is essential.[32]

- Understanding emotional development is important when caring for the pediatric patient in the immediate post-trauma phase. An age and developmentally appropriate approach facilitates a complete assessment of the pediatric patient's response to traumatic stress.

- Research indicates that families of pediatric trauma patients experience significant stress. Initiate social support services as early as possible to assist families in their time of crisis.[31]

Disaster Management (See Chapter 22, Disaster Management, for more information)

- Disaster preparedness incorporates addressing pediatric needs including equipment and resources for staff that emphasizes weight-based medication principles, anatomic and physiologic differences in children, normal vital sign ranges, nutritional support, family reunification processes, and mental health resources[7]

- Ideally, these resources are easily available for the trauma team, in any mass casualty incident that includes pediatric patients

- Young children and those with limited physical mobility or developmental delays may not be able to remove themselves from unfolding disaster events

- Children's proximity to the ground and increased respiratory rate may make them more vulnerable to some chemical and biologic agents

- Thinner skin in pediatric patients leads to increased systemic absorption of biologic and chemical agents

- JumpSTART is a widely used pediatric mass casualty triage tool and is discussed more thoroughly in Chapter 22, Disaster Management[48]

- Children may need additional assistance during the decontamination process

- Use warmed water during decontamination to prevent hypothermia

- Suggestions to promote identification and reunification include:

  - Documentation of clothing, backpacks, bags, jewelry, and other identifying objects carried or worn by the patient before removal before decontamination

  - Permanent marker on the child's skin can also be used to record important identifying characteristics

Reevaluation and Post Resuscitation Care

- Ongoing assessment and evaluation of interventions include frequent, serial reevaluation of the primary survey, monitoring for changes in vital signs, and continued reevaluation and management of pain and identified injuries. These, along with monitoring urine output, will help to guide therapy.

- Continue to monitor and treat serum glucose levels for hypoglycemia, specifically in infants and young children who deplete glycogen stores rapidly

Patient Safety

Safety of the injured pediatric patient in an adult care setting can be resource consuming but is essential to prevent further injury. Infants and younger children may need constant supervision in the absence of a caregiver and require cribs or isolettes to help prevent the risk for fall from a stretcher. Other risks for falls include older children who may attempt to remove themselves from cervical spine immobilization devices or may attempt to ambulate unassisted while under the effects of opioids and/or with compromised balance from an injury.

Social services may be necessary to promote family reunification if the patient arrives without a primary caregiver. A child life therapist and child life techniques can be helpful to promote normalcy and calm during difficult procedures.

Definitive Care or Transport

- Consider the need for transfer to a pediatric trauma center or burn center early in the care and management of the pediatric patient for best outcomes (see Chapter 15, Surface and Burn Trauma, for more information)

- Assessment of the pediatric patient's status, injuries, and needs for definitive care are considered when deciding the necessary configuration of the transport team. Pediatric patients have better outcomes and fewer unplanned events when transported by a specialized pediatric team.[49]

- Provide follow-up and clear discharge instructions, including gradual and incremental return to play information for all patients diagnosed with traumatic brain injury to include concussions. Returning to play while symptoms remain, places the patient at risk for secondary brain injury which is more likely to be fatal in the pediatric patient.[50]

- Have contact information readily available for referral to the closest pediatric trauma center for transfer or consult

Injury Prevention

Injury prevention programs and discussions have played a key role in the overall reduction of childhood injuries.[11] In the U.S., injury prevention is considered a public health priority. To support the integral role of injury prevention in trauma management, the American College of Surgeons (ACS) requires that Level I and Level II trauma centers establish injury prevention programs as part of overall trauma programs.[12] Successful programs include community involvement to analyze local pediatric-specific trauma statistics, development of initiatives relevant to the local population, and advocacy for child safety legislation within their communities. The American Academy of Pediatrics (AAP) has resources available regarding a wide variety of injury prevention programs.[32,51] Injury prevention campaigns such as "Head's Up," "Back to Sleep," and programs related to seatbelts, safety seat, helmets, water safety, and smoke detector legislation have worked to increase awareness and decrease unintentional injuries in pediatric patients.[6]

Summary

Pediatric trauma care requires familiarity with the unique responses of the injured pediatric patient. The systematic approach of the primary survey is the same for adults and children, but the clinical manifestations for complications and interventions may vary based on age, size, and development. Knowledge of normal growth and development assists the trauma nurse in approaching the pediatric patient and providing appropriate care. Family-centered care in the adult population is important; in pediatrics, it is vital. Identification of the primary caregivers and integration of their perspectives and input into care can promote optimal pediatric trauma care. Box 17-1 provides Internet resources related to the care of pediatric patients.

Box 17-1. Internet Resources

Internet Resource	Web Address
Emergency Nurses Association	www.ena.org
Society of Trauma Nurses	www.traumanurses.org
American Academy of Pediatrics	www.aap.org
American College of Emergency Physicians	www.acep.org
American College of Surgeons	www.facs.org/trauma
Pediatric Trauma Society	www.pediatrictraumasociety.org
EMSC National Resource Center	www.childrensnational.org/emsc
Centers for Disease Control and Prevention	www.cdc.gov/injury
Injury Free Coalition	www.injuryfree.org
Safe Kids	www.safekids.org
Sage Diagram (free TBSA calculator)	www.sagediagram.com
Image Gently Campaign	www.pedrad.org/associations/5364/ig

Appendix 17-A. Childhood Development

Physical and Motor Development	Intellectual or Psychosocial Development	Language Development	Pain	Death
Infant Development (Ages 1 Month–1 Year)				
Growth: period of most rapid growth; infant weight gain, around 28.3g/day; weight doubles by the age of 6 mos and triples by the age of 1 year	Trust vs. mistrust (Erikson): when physical needs are consistently met, infants learn to trust self and environment; common fears (after the age of 6 mos) include separation and strangers	Sensorimotor period: infants learn by the use of their senses and activities	Infants do experience pain; the degree of pain perceived is unknown	Infants do not understand the meaning of death; the developing sense of separation serves as a basis for a beginning understanding of the meaning of death
Toddler Development (Ages 1–2 Years)				
Growth: rate significantly slows down, accompanied by a tremendous decrease in appetite; general appearance is potbellied, exaggerated lumbar curve, wide-based gait, increased mobility, and hallmark of physical development in the toddler	Autonomy vs. shame and doubt (Erikson): increasing independence and self-care activities; expanding the world with which the toddler interacts; need to experience joy of exploring and exerting some control over body functions and activity while maintaining support of "anchor" (primary caregiver); common fears include separation, loss of control, altered rituals, and pain	Sensorimotor period: cognition and language not yet sophisticated enough for children to learn through thought processes and communication	No formal concept of pain related to immature thought process and poorly developed body image; react as intensely to painless procedures as to those that hurt, especially when restrained; intrusive procedures, such as taking a temperature, are distressing; react to pain with physical resistance, aggression, negativism, and regression; rare for toddlers to fake pain; verbal responses concerning pain are unreliable	Understanding of death still limited; belief that loss of significant others is temporary; reinforced by developing sense of object permanence (objects continue to exist even if they cannot be seen); repeated experiences of separations and reunions; magical thinking; and TV shows (cartoon characters)

Reprinted from *Emergency Nurses Association*.[14]

Appendix 17-A. Childhood Development (Continued)

Physical and Motor Development		Intellectual or Psychosocial Development	Language Development	Pain		Death
			Preschool Development (Ages 3–5 Years)			
Growth: weight gain of 2 kg/year; height gain of 6–8 cm per year; usually are half adult height by the age of 2 years; general appearance of "baby fat" and protuberant abdomen disappear		Initiative vs. guilt (Erikson): greater autonomy and independence; still intense need for caregivers when under stress; initiate activities, rather than just imitating others; age of discovery, curiosity, and development of social behavior; sense of self as individual; common fears include mutilation, loss of control, death, dark, and ghosts	Preoperational (Piaget): time of trial-and-error learning; egocentric (experiences from own perspective); understand explanations only in terms of real events or what their senses tell them; no logical or abstract thought; coincidence confused with causation; magical thinking continues; difficulty distinguishing between reality and fantasy; may see illness or injury as punishment for "bad" thoughts or behavior; imaginary friends; fascination with superheroes and monsters	Pain perceived as punishment for bad thoughts or behavior; difficulty understanding that painful procedures help them get well; cannot differentiate between "good" pain (resulting from treatment) and bad pain (resulting from injury or illness); react to painful procedures with aggression and verbal reprimands ("I hate you" and "You're mean")		Incomplete understanding of death fosters anxiety because of fear of death; death is seen as an altered state of consciousness in which a person cannot perform normal activities, such as eating or walking; perceive immobility, sleep, and other alterations in consciousness as deathlike states; associate words and phrases ("put to sleep") with death; death is seen as reversible (reinforced by TV and cartoons); unable to perceive inevitability of death as the result of limited time concept; view death as punishment

Reprinted from *Emergency Nurses Association.*[14]

Appendix 17-A. Childhood Development (Continued)

Physical and Motor Development	Intellectual or Psychosocial Development	Language Development	Pain	Death
School-Aged Children (Ages 6–10 Years)				
Growth: relatively latent period	Industry vs. inferiority (Erikson): age of accomplishment, increasing competence, and mastery of new skills; successes contribute to positive self-esteem and a sense of control; need parental support in time of stress (may be unwilling or unable to ask); common fears include separation from friends, loss of control, and physical disability	Concrete operations (Piaget): beginning of logical thought; deductive reasoning develops; improved concept of time; awareness of possible long-term consequences of illness; more sophisticated understanding of causality; still interpret phrases and idioms at face value	Reaction to pain affected by past experiences, parental response, and the meaning attached to it; better able to localize and describe pain accurately; pain can be exaggerated because of heightened fears of bodily injury, pain, and death	Concept of death more logically based; understand death as the irreversible cessation of life; view death as a tragedy that happens to others, not themselves; when death is an actual threat, may feel responsible for death and experience guilt
Adolescent Development (Ages 11–18 Years)				
Growth: for females, growth spurt begins at the age of 9.5 years; for males, growth spurt begins at the age of 10.5 years; at puberty, secondary sex characteristics begin to develop between the ages of eight and 13 years for females and between the ages of 10 and 14 years for males	Identity vs. role confusion (Erikson): transition from childhood to adulthood; quest for independence often leads to family dissension; major concerns: establishing identity and developing mature sexual orientation; risk-taking behaviors include feeling that nothing bad can happen to them; common fears include changes in appearance or functioning, dependency, and loss of control	Concrete to formal operations (Piaget): memory fully developed; concept of time well understood; adolescents can project to the future and imagine potential consequences of actions and illnesses; some adolescents do not achieve formal operations	Can locate and quantify pain accurately and thoroughly; often hyperresponsive to pain; reacts to fear of changes in appearance or function; in general, highly controlled in responding to pain and painful procedures	Understanding of death similar to that of adults; intellectually believe that death can happen to them but avoid realistic thoughts of death; many adolescents defy the possibility of death through reckless behavior, substance abuse, or daring sports activities

Reprinted from *Emergency Nurses Association*.[14]

Guidelines for Care of Children in the Emergency Department

This checklist is based on the American Academy of Pediatrics (AAP), American College of Emergency Physicians (ACEP), and Emergency Nurses Association (ENA) 2009 joint policy statement "Guidelines for Care of Children in the Emergency Department," which can be found online at http://aappolicy.aappublications.org/cgi/reprint/pediatrics;124/4/1233.pdf. Use the checklist to determine if your emergency department (ED) is prepared to care for children.

Administration and Coordination of the ED for the Care of Children

○ *Physician Coordinator for Pediatric Emergency Care.* The pediatric physician coordinator is a specialist in emergency medicine or pediatric emergency medicine; or if these specialties are not available then pediatrics or family medicine, appointed by the ED medical director, who through training, clinical experience, or focused continuing medical education demonstrates competence in the care of children in emergency settings, including resuscitation.

○ *Nursing Coordinator for Pediatric Emergency Care.* The pediatric nurse coordinator is a registered nurse (RN), appointed by the ED nursing director, who possesses special interest, knowledge, and skill in the emergency care of children.

Physicians, Nurses and Other Healthcare Providers Who Staff the ED

○ Physicians who staff the ED have the necessary skill, knowledge, and training in the emergency evaluation and treatment of children of all ages who may be brought to the ED, consistent with the services provided by the hospital.

○ Nurses and other ED healthcare providers have the necessary skill, knowledge, and training in providing emergency care to children of all ages who may be brought to the ED, consistent with the services offered by the hospital.

○ Baseline and periodic competency evaluations completed for all ED clinical staff, including physicians, are age specific and include evaluation of skills related to neonates, infants, children, adolescents, and children with special healthcare needs. (Competencies are determined by each institution's medical and nursing staff privileges policy.)

Guidelines for QI/PI in the ED

○ The QI/PI plan shall include pediatric specific indicators.
○ The pediatric patient care-review process is integrated into the ED QI/PI plan. Components of the process interface with out-of-hospital, ED, trauma, inpatient pediatric, pediatric critical care, and hospital-wide QI or PI activities.

Guidelines for Improving Pediatric Patient Safety

The delivery of pediatric care should reflect an awareness of unique pediatric patient safety concerns and are included in the following policies or practices:

○ Children are weighed in kilograms.
○ Weights are recorded in a prominent place on the medical record.
○ For children who are not weighed, a standard method for estimating weight in kilograms is used (e.g., a length-based system).
○ Infants and children have a full set of vital signs recorded (temperature, heart rate, respiratory rate) in medical record.
○ Blood pressure and pulse oximetry monitoring are available for children of all ages on the basis of illness and injury severity.
○ A process for identifying age-specific abnormal vital signs and notifying the physician of these is present.
○ Processes in place for safe medication storage, prescribing, and delivery that includes precalculated dosing guidelines for children of all ages.
○ Infection-control practices, including hand hygiene and use of personal protective equipment, are implemented and monitored.
○ Pediatric emergency services are culturally and linguistically appropriate.
○ ED environment is safe for children and supports patient- and family-centered care.
○ Patient identification policies meet Joint Commission standards.
○ Policies for the timely reporting and evaluation of patient safety events, medical errors, and unanticipated outcomes are implemented and monitored.

Guidelines for ED Policies, Procedures, and Protocols

Policies, procedures, and protocols for the emergency care of children should be developed and implemented in the areas listed below. These policies may be integrated into overall ED policies as long as pediatric specific issues are addressed.

○ Illness and injury triage.
○ Pediatric patient assessment and reassessment.

Produced by the AAP, ACEP, ENA, the EMSC National Resource Center, and Children's National Medical Center

1

Guidelines for ED Policies, Procedures, and Protocols, Cont.

- Documentation of pediatric vital signs and actions to be taken for abnormal vital signs.
- Immunization assessment and management of the under-immunized patient.
- Sedation and analgesia, including medical imaging.
- Consent, including when parent or legal guardian is not immediately available.
- Social and mental health issues.
- Physical or chemical restraint of patients.
- Child maltreatment and domestic violence reporting criteria, requirements, and processes.
- Death of the child in the ED.
- Do not resuscitate (DNR) orders.
- Family-centered care:
  - Family involvement in patient decision-making and medication safety processes;
  - Family presence during all aspects of emergency care;
  - Patient, family, and caregiver education;
  - Discharge planning and instruction; and
  - Bereavement counseling.
- Communication with the patient's medical home or primary care provider.
- Medical imaging, specfically policies that address pediatric age- or weight-based appropriate dosing for studies that impart radiation consistent with ALARA (as low as reasonably achievable) principles.

Polices, Procedures, and Protocols for All-Hazard Disaster Preparedness

Policies, procedures, and protocols should also be developed and implemented for all-hazard disaster-preparedness. The plan should address the following preparedness issues:

- Availability of medications, vaccines, equipment, and trained providers for children.
- Pediatric surge capacity for injured and non-injured children.
- Decontamination, isolation, and quarantine of families and children.
- Minimization of parent-child separation (includes pediatric patient tracking and timely reunification of separated children with their family).
- Access to specific medical and mental health therapies, and social services for children.
- Disaster drills which include a pediatric mass casualty incident at least every two years.
- Care of children with special healthcare needs.
- Evacuation of pediatric units and pediatric subspecialty units.

Policies, Procedures, and Protocols for Patient Transfers

- Written pediatric inter-facility transfer procedures should be established.

Guidelines for ED Support Services

Radiology capability must meet the needs of the children in the community served. Specifically:

- A process for referring children to appropriate facilities for radiological procedures that exceed the capability of the hospital is established.
- A process for timely review, interpretation, and reporting of medical imaging by a qualified radiologist is established.

Laboratory capability must meet the needs of the children in the community served, including techniques for small sample sizes. Specifically:

- A process for referring children or their specimens to appropriate facilities for laboratory studies that exceed the capability of the hospital is established.

Guidelines for Equipment, Supplies, and Medications for the Care of Pediatric Patients in the ED

- Pediatric equipment, supplies, and medications are appropriate for children of all ages and sizes (see list below), and are easily accessible, clearly labeled, and logically organized.
- ED staff is educated on the location of all items.
- Daily method in place to verify the proper location and function of equipment and supplies.
- Medication chart, length-based tape, medical software, or other systems is readily available to ensure proper sizing of resuscitation equipment and proper dosing of medications.

Medications

- atropine
- adenosine
- amiodarone
- antiemetic agents
- calcium chloride
- dextrose (D10W, D50W)
- epinephrine (1:1000; 1:10,000 solutions)
- lidocaine
- magnesium sulfate
- naloxone hydrochloride
- procainamide
- sodium bicarbonate (4.2%, 8.4%)
- topical, oral, and parenteral analgesics
- antimicrobial agents (parenteral and oral)
- anticonvulsant medications
- antidotes (common antidotes should be accessible to the ED)
- antipyretic drugs
- bronchodilators
- corticosteroids
- inotropic agents
- neuromuscular blockers
- sedatives
- vaccines
- vasopressor agents

Produced by the AAP, ACEP, ENA, the EMSC National Resource Center, and Children's National Medical Center

2

Appendix 17-B. Guidelines for Care of Children in the Emergency Department (Continued)

Equipment/Supplies: General Equipment

- ○ patient warming device
- ○ intravenous blood/fluid warmer
- ○ restraint device
- ○ weight scale in kilograms (not pounds)
- ○ tool or chart that incorporates weight (in kilograms) and length to determine equipment size and correct drug dosing
- ○ age appropriate pain scale-assessment tools

Equipment/Supplies: Monitoring Equipment

blood pressure cuffs
- ○ neonatal
- ○ infant
- ○ child
- ○ adult-arm
- ○ adult-thigh

- ○ doppler ultrasonography devices

- ○ electrocardiography monitor/defibrillator with pediatric and adult capabilities including pads/paddles
- ○ hypothermia thermometer
- ○ pulse oximeter with pediatric and adult probes
- ○ continuous end-tidal CO2 monitoring device

Equipment/Supplies: Vascular Access

arm boards
- ○ infant
- ○ child
- ○ adult

catheter-over-the-needle device
- ○ 14 gauge
- ○ 16 gauge
- ○ 18 gauge
- ○ 20 gauge
- ○ 22 gauge
- ○ 24 gauge

intraosseous needles or device
- ○ pediatric
- ○ adult

- ○ IV administration sets with calibrated chambers and extension tubing and/or infusion devices with ability to regulate rate and volume of infusate

umbilical vein catheters
- ○ 3.5F
- ○ 5.0F

central venous catheters (any two sizes)
- ○ 4.0F
- ○ 5.0F
- ○ 6.0F
- ○ 7.0F

intravenous solutions
- ○ normal saline
- ○ dextrose 5% in normal saline
- ○ dextrose 10% in water

Equipment/Supplies: Fracture-Management Devices

extremity splints
- ○ femur splints, pediatric sizes
- ○ femur splints, adult sizes

- ○ spine-stabilization devices appropriate for children of all ages

Equipment/Supplies: Respiratory

endotracheal tubes
- ○ uncuffed 2.5 mm
- ○ uncuffed 3.0 mm
- ○ cuffed or uncuffed 3.5 mm
- ○ cuffed or uncuffed 4.0 mm
- ○ cuffed or uncuffed 4.5 mm
- ○ cuffed or uncuffed 5.0 mm
- ○ cuffed or uncuffed 5.5 mm
- ○ cuffed 6.0 mm
- ○ cuffed 6.5 mm
- ○ cuffed 7.0 mm
- ○ cuffed 7.5 mm
- ○ cuffed 8.0 mm

feeding tubes
- ○ 5F
- ○ 8F

laryngoscope blades
- ○ straight: 0
- ○ straight: 1
- ○ straight: 2
- ○ straight: 3
- ○ curved: 2
- ○ curved: 3

- ○ laryngoscope handle

magill forceps
- ○ pediatric
- ○ adult

nasopharyngeal airways
- ○ infant
- ○ child
- ○ adult

oropharyngeal airways
- ○ size 0
- ○ size 1
- ○ size 2
- ○ size 3
- ○ size 4
- ○ size 5

stylets for endotracheal tubes
- ○ pediatric
- ○ adult

suction catheters
- ○ infant
- ○ child
- ○ adult

tracheostomy tubes
- ○ 2.5 mm
- ○ 3.0 mm
- ○ 3.5 mm
- ○ 4.0 mm
- ○ 4.5 mm
- ○ 5.0 mm
- ○ 5.5 mm

- ○ yankauer suction tip

bag-mask device, self inflating
- ○ infant: 450 mL
- ○ adult: 1000 mL

masks to fit bag-mask device adaptor
- ○ neonatal
- ○ infant
- ○ child
- ○ adult

Equipment/Supplies: Respiratory, Continued		Equipment/Supplies: Specialized Pediatric Trays or Kits

Equipment/Supplies: Respiratory, Continued

clear oxygen masks
- ○ standard infant
- ○ standard child
- ○ standard adult
- ○ partial nonrebreather infant
- ○ nonrebreather child
- ○ nonrebreather adult

nasal cannulas
- ○ infant
- ○ child
- ○ adult

nasogastric tubes
- ○ infant: 8F
- ○ child: 10F
- ○ adult: 14-18F

laryngeal mask airway
- ○ size: 1
- ○ size: 1.5
- ○ size: 2
- ○ size: 2.5
- ○ size: 3
- ○ size: 4
- ○ size: 5

Equipment/Supplies: Specialized Pediatric Trays or Kits

- ○ lumbar puncture tray (including infant/pediatric 22 gauge and adult 18-21 gauge needles)

- ○ supplies/kit for patients with difficult airway (supraglottic airways of all sizes, laryngeal mask airway, needle cricothyrotomy supplies, surgical cricothyrotomy kit)

- ○ tube thoracostomy tray

chest tubes:
- ○ infant: 10-12F
- ○ child: 16-24F
- ○ adult: 28-40F

- ○ newborn delivery kit, including equipment for resuscitation of an infant (umbilical clamp, scissors, bulb syringe, and towel)

- ○ urinary catheterization kits and urinary (indwelling) catheters (6F–22F)

4

References

1. American Academy of Pediatrics. (2008). Management of pediatric trauma. *Pediatrics, 121,* 849–854.

2. Centers for Disease Control and Prevention. (2012). Vital signs: Unintentional injury deaths among persons aged 0–19 years—United States, 2000–2009. *Morbidity and Mortality Weekly Reports, 61,* 270–276. Retrieved from http://www.cdc.gov/mmwr/pdf/wk/mm61e0416.pdf

3. American College of Surgeons. (2012). *National Trauma Data Bank 2012: Pediatric report.* Retrieved from http://www.facs.org/trauma/ntdb/pdf/ntdb-pediatric-annual-report-2012.pdf

4. Guner, Y. S., Ford, H. R., & Upperman, J. S. (2010). Pediatric trauma. In H. C. Pape, A. B. Peitzman, C. W. Shwab, & P. V. Giannoudis (Eds.), *Pediatric trauma and polytrauma in the pediatric patient* (pp. 331–356). New York, NY: Springer.

5. Reuter-Rice, K., & Bolick, B. N. (Eds.). (2012). *Pediatric acute care a guide for interprofessional practice.* Burlington, MA: Jones & Bartlett Learning.

6. Beaudin, M., Daugherty, M., Geis, G., Moody, S., Brown, R. L., Garcia, F., & Falcone, R. A. Jr. (2012). Assessment of factors associated with the delayed transfer of pediatric trauma patients: An emergency physician survey. *Pediatric Emergency Care, 28,* 758–763.

7. Gausche-Hill, M. (2009). Pediatric disaster preparedness: Are we really prepared? *Journal of Trauma, 67*(2 Suppl), S73–S76.

8. Centers for Disease Control and Prevention, National Center for Health Statistics. (2006, February 28). *More work needed to ensure U.S. hospitals equipped and staffed to handle pediatric emergency patients* [press release]. Retrieved from http://www.cdc.gov/nchs/pressroom/06facts/pediatricemergency.htm

9. Wesson, D. E. (Ed.). (2006). *Pediatric trauma pathophysiology, diagnosis, and treatment.* New York, NY: Taylor & Francis Group.

10. Cordle, R. J. & Cantor, R. M. (2010). Pediatric trauma. In J. A. Marx, R. S. Hockberger, & R. M. Walls (Eds.), *Rosen's emergency medicine concepts and clinical practice* (7th ed., pp. 262–280). Philadelphia, PA: Mosby Elsevier.

11. London, M. L., Ladewig, P.W., Ball, J.W., & Bindler, R.C. (Eds.). (2010). *Maternal and child nursing care* (3rd ed.). Upper Saddle River, NJ: Pearson/Prentice Hall.

12. American College of Surgeons (2012). *Advanced trauma life support student course manual* (9th ed.). Chicago, IL: Author.

13. Centers for Disease Control and Prevention. (2011). Nonfatal traumatic brain injuries related to sports and recreation activities among persons aged ≤ 19 years—United States, 2001–2009. *Morbidity and Mortality Weekly Reports, 60,* 1337–1342. Retrieved from http://www.cdc.gov/mmwr/preview/mmwrhtml/mm6039a1.htm

14. Emergency Nurses Association. (2012). *Emergency nursing pediatric course provider manual* (4th ed.). Des Plaines, IL: Author.

15. Williams, B. G., Hlaing, T., & Aaland, M. O. (2009). Ten-year retrospective study of delayed diagnosis of injury in pediatric trauma patients at a level II trauma center. *Pediatric Emergency Care, 25,* 489–493.

16. Emergency Nurses Association. (2012, March). *Weighing pediatric patients in kilograms* [position statement]. Retrieved from http://www.ena.org/SiteCollectionDocuments/Position%20Statements/WeighingPedsPtsinKG.pdf

17. Roskind, C. G., Dayan, P. S., & Klein, B. L. (2011). Acute care of the victim of multiple trauma. In R. M. Kliegman, B. F. Stanton, J. W. St. Geme, N. F. Schor, & R. E. Behrman (Eds.), *Nelson textbook of pediatrics* (19th ed., pp. 333–341). Philadelphia, PA: Elsevier Saunders.

18. Fleisher, G. R., & Ludwig, S. (Eds।). (2010). *Textbook of pediatric emergency medicine* (6th ed.). Philadelphia, PA: Wolters Kluwer/Lippincott, Williams, & Wilkins

19. Veyckemans, F. (2011). Anesthesia equipment. In B. Bissonette, B. J. Anderson, A. Bosenberg, T. Engelhardt, L. J. Mason, & J. D. Tobias (Eds.), *Pediatric anesthesia* (pp. 594–668). Shelton, CT: People's Medical Publishing.

20. Kleinmann, M. E., de Caen, A. R., Chameides, L., Atkins, D. L., Berg, R. A., Berg, M. D., Zideman, D. (2010). Part 10: Pediatric basic and advanced life support: 2010 international consensus on cardiopulmonary resuscitation and emergency cardiovascular care science with treatment recommendations. *Circulation, 122,* S466–S515.

21. Santillanes, G., & Gausche-Hill, M. (2008). Pediatric airway management. *Emergency Clinics of North America, 26,* 961–975.

22. American Heart Association. (2011). *Pediatric advanced life support: Provider manual.* Dallas, TX: Author.

23. Sarnaik, A. P., & Heidemann, S. M. (2011). Respiratory pathophysiology and regulation In R. M. Kliegman, B. F. Stanton, J. W. St. Geme, N. F. Schor, & R. E. Behrman (Eds.), *Nelson textbook of pediatrics* (19th ed., pp. 1419–1421). Philadelphia, PA: Elsevier Saunders.

24. Hockenberry, M. J. (2011). Communication and physical assessment of the child. In M. J. Hockenberry & D. Wilson (Eds.), *Wong's nursing care of infants and children* (9th ed., pp. 117–178). St. Louis, MO: Elsevier Mosby.

25. Luckett, T. R. & Hays, S. R. (2013). Analgesia, sedation, and neuromuscular blockade. In M. F. Hazinski (Ed.), *Nursing care of the critically ill child* (3rd ed., pp.77–99). St. Louis, MO: Elsevier Mosby.

26. Wheeler, B. J. (2011). Health promotion of the newborn and family. In M. J. Hockenberry & D. Wilson (Eds.), *Wong's nursing care of infants and children* (9th ed., pp. 227–278). St Louis, MO: Elsevier Mosby.

27. Ewald, M. B., & Baum, C. R. (2010). Environmental emergencies. In G. R. Fleisher & S. Ludwig (Eds.), *Textbook of pediatric emergency medicine* (6th ed., pp. 783–804). Philadelphia, PA: Wolters Kluwer/Lippincott, Williams, & Wilkins.

28. Greenbaum, L. A. (2011). Maintenance and replacement therapy. In R. M. Kliegman, B. F. Stanton, J. W. St. Geme, N. F. Schor, & R. E. Behrman (Eds.), *Nelson textbook of pediatrics* (19th ed., pp. 242–245). Philadelphia, PA: Elsevier Saunders.

29. O'Connell, K. J., Farah, M. M., Spandorfer, P., & Zorc, J. J. (2007). Family presence during pediatric trauma team activation: An assessment of a structured program. *Pediatrics, 120,* e565–e574.

30. Egging, D., Crowley, M., Arruda, T., Proehl, J., Walker-Cillo, G., Papa, A., Walsh, J. (2009, December). *Emergency nursing resource: Family presence during invasive procedures and resuscitation in the emergency department.* Retrieved from http://www.ena.org/IENR/CPG/Documents/FamilyPresenceCPG.pdf

31. Gold, J. I., Kant, A. J., & Kim, S. H. (2008). The impact of unintentional pediatric trauma: A review of pain, acute stress, and posttraumatic stress. *Journal of Pediatric Nursing, 23,* 81–91.

32. Twycross, A. (2010). Managing pain in children: Where to from here? *Journal of Clinical Nursing, 19,* 2090–2099.

33. Shore, B. J., Plamer, C. S., Bevin, C., Johnson, M. B., & Torode, I. P. (2012). Pediatric pelvic fracture: A modification of a preexisting classification. *Journal of Pediatric Orthopedics, 32,* 162–168.

34. Viccellio, P., Simon, H., Pressman, B. D., Shah, M. N., Mower, W. R., & Hoffman, J. R. (2001). A prospective multicenter study of cervical spine injury in children. *Pediatrics, 108,* e20. Retrieved from http://pediatrics.aappublications.org/content/108/2/e20.full.pdf

35. Garton, H. J., & Hammer, M.R. (2008). Detection of pediatric cervical spine injury. *Neurosurgery, 62*(3), 700–708.

36. Ehrlich, P. F., Wee, C., Drongowski, R, & Rana, A.R. (2009). Canadian C-spine Rule and the National Emergency X-Radiography Utilization Low-Risk Criteria for C-spine radiography in young trauma patients. *Journal of Pediatric Surgery, 44*(5), 987–991.

37. Rana, A. R., Drongowski, R., Breckner, G., & Ehrlich, P. F. (2009). Traumatic cervical spine injuries: Characteristics of missed injuries. *Journal of Pediatric Surgery, 44*(1), 151–155.

38. Silva, C. T., Doria, A.S., Traubici, J., Moineddin, R., Davila, J., & Shroff, M. (2010). Do additional views improve the diagnostic performance of cervical spine radiography in pediatric trauma? *American Journal of Roentgenology, 194*(2), 500–508.

39. Mueller, D. L., Hatab, M., Al-Senan, R., Cohn, S. M., Corneille, M. G., Dent, D. L., Stewart, R. M. (2011). Pediatric radiation exposure during the initial evaluation for blunt trauma. *The Journal of Trauma, 70,* 721–731.

40. Nigrovic, L. E., Rogers, A. J., Adelgais, M., Olsen, C. S., Leonard, J. R., Jaffe, D. M., & Leonard, J. C. (2012). Utility of plain radiographs in detecting traumatic injuries of the cervical spine in children. *Pediatric Emergency Care, 28,* 426–432.

41. Kuppermann, N., Holmes, J. F., Dayan, P. S., Hoyle, J. D., Atabaki, S. M., Holubkov, R., Wootton-Gorges, S. L. (2009). Identification of children at very low risk of clinically-important brain injuries after head trauma: a prospective cohort study. *The Lancet, 374,* 1160–1170.

42. Brunetti, M. A., Mahesh, M., Nabaweesi, R., Locke P., Ziegfeld, S., & Brown, R. (2011). Diagnostic radiation exposure in pediatric trauma patients. *Journal of Trauma, 70,* E24–E28.

43. Tuggle, D. W., & Kreykes, N. S. (2013). The pediatric patient. In K. L. Mattox, E. E. Moore, D. V. Feliciano (Eds.) *Trauma* (7th ed., pp. 859–873). New York, NY: McGraw-Hill.

44. Marwan, A., Harmon C. M., Georgeson, K. E., Smith, G. F., & Muensterer, O. J. (2010). Use of laparoscopy in the management of pediatric abdominal trauma. *Journal of Trauma, 69,* 761–764.

45. Ribbens, K. A. & DeVries (2013). Burns. In Emergency Nurses Association, *Sheehy's manual of emergency care* (7th ed., pp. 453–462). St. Louis, MO: Elsevier

46. Antoon, A. Y. & Donovan, M. K. (2011). Burn injuries. In R. M. Kliegman, B. F. Stanton, J. W. St. Geme III, N. F. Schor, & R. E. Behrman (Eds.), *Nelson textbook of pediatrics* (19th ed.) [Kindle edition]. Philadelphia, PA: Elsevier

47. American Burn Association. (2011). *Advanced burn life support provider manual.* Chicago, IL: Author.

48. Romig, L. E. (2012). *The JumpSTART pediatric MCI triage tool.* Retrieved from http://www.jumpstarttriage.com/

49. Orr, R. A., Felmet, K. A., Han, Y., McCloskey, K. A., Dragotta, M. A., Bills, D. M., Watson, R.S. (2009). Pediatric specialized transport teams are associated with improved outcomes. *Pediatrics, 124,* 40–48.

50. Centers for Disease Control and Prevention. (2012, September 24). *Heads Up: Concussion.* Retrieved from http://www.cdc.gov/concussion/headsup/index.html

51. American Academy of Pediatrics. (n.d.). *Injury, violence, and poison prevention.* Retrieved from http://www2.aap.org/sections/ipp/

Chapter 18 • Special Populations: The Older Adult Trauma Patient

Catherine Jagos, MSN-Ed, RN

Objectives

Upon completion of this chapter, the learner will be able to:

1. Describe mechanisms of injury associated with the older adult trauma patient.

2. Describe age-related anatomic and physiologic changes as a basis for assessment of the older adult trauma patient.

3. Demonstrate the nursing assessment of the older adult trauma patient.

4. Plan appropriate interventions for the older adult trauma patient.

5. Evaluate the effectiveness of nursing interventions for the older adult trauma patient.

Introduction

Epidemiology

The percentage of the population over the age of 65 increases annually, and by 2040, 20% of the United States (U.S.) population will fall into this category.[1] Trauma in older adults is also increasing, and it is estimated that by the year 2050, almost 39% of trauma patients will be 65 years and older.[2] Data for 2010 show that trauma was among the top 10 causes of death in this population.[3] Older adults have increased morbidity and mortality and experience more severe injuries, most likely due to increased comorbidities. Because of this, the injuries result in complications and major disability, requiring longer stays and consumption of more resources.[4] For trauma patients over 80 years of age, a minor trauma can result in a major disability.[1]

Due in part to an emphasis on preventative medicine and improved healthcare, older adults not only live longer, they live independently and remain more active. Despite advancing age, a number of older adults still participate in sports and continue to drive their own automobiles.[1]

The approach and priorities remain the same when caring for the older adult trauma patient; however, special consideration is given to factors that might complicate care in this population. Since an injury in an older adult, regardless of its severity, may result in a poor outcome,[5] it becomes important to consider and address the following factors:

- Normal pathophysiologic changes as a result of aging
- Comorbidities
- Medications
- Lower physiologic reserve

In addition to these factors, it is also important to understand common mechanisms of injury of trauma in this population.

Mechanisms of Injury in the Older Adult

Falls and injuries due to motor vehicle collisions (MVCs) and traffic, including pedestrian-related collisions, are the most common causes of trauma and injury death in adults 65 years and older.[3]

Falls

In the older adult population, falls are the leading cause of injury-related death and the leading cause of hospital admissions for trauma.[6] Falls in this patient population are primarily low-energy trauma (LET) events[7] and occur from a standing height or lower, often as a result of conditions such as wet surfaces, poor lighting, inadequate footwear, and cluttered pathways. An older adult is often undertriaged after experiencing a LET fall from a standing height.[7] Most falls occur at home (60%) with an additional 30% occurring in the community and 10% in nursing homes or other institutions,[8] often while the older adult patient is engaged in everyday activities such as walking on stairs, going to the bathroom, or working in the kitchen.

Falls can also occur as a result of the following:

- Syncope due to dysrhythmias, venous pooling, orthostatic hypotension, hypoxia, anemia, or hypoglycemia
- Alcohol and medications (antihypertensives, antidepressants, diuretics, and hypoglycemia agents)
- Changes in postural stability, balance, motor strength, and coordination
- Slower reaction times
- Poor visual acuity and visual attention

Mortality from falls among older men and women has increased sharply over the past decade. Falls account for 25% of all hospital admissions and 40% of all nursing home admissions; 40% of those admitted do not return to independent living and 25% die within a year.[8] Regarding falls, women tend to be injured more easily, but men have higher rates of mortality.[9]

Mortality and disability can be affected by the under triage of older patients. Falls, or LET, and high-energy trauma, such as MVCs, are categorized and often triaged differently, but the mortality and morbidity rates are similar for both types. Patients with LET should be triaged at a higher level of urgency until they are assessed and all the predisposing factors (medications, medical history) are considered.[7]

The most common injuries resulting from falls in the older adult include:[6]

- Lacerations

- Traumatic brain injuries (TBIs)

- Fractures, especially to the hip[10]

After a fall, many older adults cannot get up without assistance, which can result in further complications. When a person falls and lies motionless for many hours, the weight of the body results in compression of muscle tissue, placing the patient at risk for rhabdomyolysis (see Chapter 14, Musculoskeletal Trauma, for more information). Rhabdomyolysis can lead to many serious complications including:[11,12]

- Acute renal failure

- Hyperkalemia and other electrolyte imbalances

- Fluid shifting, hypovolemic shock

- Fat embolism and acute respiratory distress syndrome (ARDS)

- Coagulopathies (disseminated intravascular coagulopathy [DIC] and fibrinolysis)

- Sepsis and multiple organ dysfunction syndrome (MODS)

Motor Vehicle Collisions

Driving patterns change as people age, and older adults tend to drive fewer miles and prefer local roads to expressways and highways.[13] Independence is very important, and many older adults continue driving even after the age of 80.[14] The Centers for Disease Control (CDC) and Prevention list MVCs as the second most common mechanism of trauma in the older adult.[3] Although the older adult may have more driving experience, normal age-related physiologic changes can impact the ability to drive. These include changes in vision, hearing, perception, muscle flexibility, and reflexes.[13]

MVCs involving older adult drivers are less likely to be related to alcohol use and speed. Instead the physiologic changes noted above affect the older adult's ability to drive safely in the following situations:[13]

- At intersections (due to limited peripheral vision)

- Merging into traffic when another vehicle is traveling faster (due to reduced reaction time)

- When another car is in the older driver's blind spot (due to limited peripheral vision and kyphosis)

- When it is dark (due to loss of visual acuity)

According to Labib et al.,[14] the most commonly injured body regions in the older adults involved in MVCs were the head, chest, and cervical spine. Table 18-1 describes physiologic changes in older adults that may increase their risk of injury. Additional considerations include:

- In MVCs, there is an increase in sternal fractures from seatbelts in patients over 65 years of age[15]

- Rib fractures are common and increase the morbidity of the older trauma patient, leading to acute respiratory problems such as respiratory failure, pneumonia, and pleural effusion.[15,16] As the number of ribs fractured increases, so does mortality.

- Lower cervical injuries are common, and minor head injury can result in a significant intracranial injury

- Older patients presenting with hip fractures from a major trauma are more likely to hemorrhage[15]

The older adult can experience the same injury patterns as their younger counterpart but require a lengthier recovery time, which may result in increased deaths.[7]

Pedestrian-related Collisions

The third most common cause of trauma in the older adult population is as a pedestrian struck by a vehicle.[3] Older adults are at high risk for pedestrian-related collisions and have higher rates of morbidity and mortality.[17,18] See Chapter 4, Biomechanics, Kinematics, and Mechanisms of Injury, for more information.

Age-related physiologic changes also can contribute to these pedestrian-related collisions, including:[19,20]

- Kyphosis that can decrease cervical range of motion, limiting the older adult's ability to see oncoming traffic or crossing signals

- Inability to walk quickly
- Reduced reaction time
- Decreased hearing
- Loss of visual acuity and peripheral vision

Age-related Anatomic and Physiologic Changes

Two categories of factors impact the older patient's response to illness and injury. Non-modifiable changes occur as a result of the natural aging process (Table 18-1), while others are due to modifiable factors, such as lifestyle.

Non-modifiable factors that occur through aging can impact how the older adult responds to stress, illness, temperature, medications, trauma, and blood loss. Each patient is unique in his or her response to aging, illness, and injury.

Modifiable factors that influence the older adult's ability to respond to illness and injury include:
- Lifestyle
  - Use of alcohol or tobacco
  - Use of illicit drugs
  - Misuse of prescription medication
- Diet
  - Healthy diet
  - Failure to eat due to illness or depression, loss of appetite, or financial restrictions
- Exercise
  - Ambulatory (use of non-slip surfaces and assistive devices)
  - Non-ambulatory (active with seated exercise or sedentary)

Nursing Care of the Older Adult Trauma Patient

Refer to Chapter 5, Initial Assessment for the systematic approach to the nursing care of the trauma patient. The following assessment parameters are specific to the older adult trauma patient.

Preparation and Triage

Prehospital and ED triage of the older adult can be challenging. According to Calloway and Wolfe,[21] MOI and vital signs can be misleading triage tools in older adult trauma patients because they are susceptible to significant injuries from relatively minor mechanisms (LET).[7]

Primary Survey and Resuscitation Adjuncts

A–Airway and Alertness

In opening and clearing the airway of the older adult patient, also assess for the following:[21]
- Decreased gag reflex and diminished cough reflex
- Presence of dentures or partials
- Possible neurologic sequelae due to strokes, such as a loss or decrease in the function of the glossopharyngeal or hypoglossal nerves resulting in diminished control in swallowing and tongue movement

Interventions
- Since loss of muscle mass, osteoporosis, osteoarthritis, and kyphosis can contribute to discomfort and skin breakdown in the older patient, consider padding bony areas and facilitate removal from the spine board as quickly as possible
- Keep in mind that the mucosa is thinner in older adults and the older patient may be on anticoagulant therapy, so use caution when inserting an oral or nasal airway and when suctioning. Either of these can result in swelling, bleeding, or hemorrhage.[4,21]

B–Breathing and Ventilation
- Assess and monitor the work of breathing as there may be lack of physiologic reserve
- Consider early ventilatory support
- Consider leaving dentures in place if they are well-fitting and the patient requires bag-mask ventilation as they may aid in a tighter-fitting mask[22]
- Use care during intubation since arthritis and osteoporosis have the following effects:
  - Limited visualization of the vocal cords from decreased mobility with the jaw thrust
  - Increase the possibility of cervical spine injury during instrumentation[21]

C–Circulation and Control of Hemorrhage

The maintenance of homeostasis in an older adult trauma patient can be difficult. With limited cardiac reserve, older adults may deteriorate quickly without exhibiting the usual expected changes in vital signs, urinary output, and physiologic responses.[22]

Table 18-1. Anatomic and Physiologic Changes in the Older Adult

System	Changes with Aging
Airway	• Atrophy of oral mucosa may lead to loose or poorly fitting dentures (full or partial) that may obstruct the airway • Relaxed musculature of the oropharynx may result in aspiration • Decreased gag and cough reflexes predispose the older adult to aspiration, infection, and bronchospasm • Temporomandibular and cervical arthritis make intubation more difficult
Cervical spine	Older adults are predisposed to cervical injury and/or discomfort from the rigid spine board due to: • Osteoporosis • Changes in bone density • Osteopenia • Development of spinal stenosis • Increasing rigidity C4 to C6 levels; lever action causes fractures above and below • Rigidity from neurologic disorders (Parkinson disease) • Kyphosis limits cervical range of motion, inhibiting the ability to see oncoming traffic or crossing signals
Breathing	• Older adults experience a loss of strength in the muscles of respiration and diminished endurance • Rib calcification decreases inspiratory and expiratory force, chest expansion, increases respiratory rate, and reduces tidal volume • Respiratory fatigue occurs more easily, resulting in hypoxia • Older adults have a decreased ability to compensate for hypoxia • Higher rate of complications, even following minor thoracic injuries including pulmonary edema, atelectasis, and pneumonia • Small airways lose recoil, resulting in potential airway collapse, air trapping, and uneven distribution of ventilation • Pain, injury, and extended supine positioning can reduce arterial oxygen saturation and cardiac output

Circulation	• There is a limited ability to increase heart rate and cardiac output in response to physiologic stress
	  ○ A heart rate of > 90 beats/min may indicate significant physiologic stress
	  ○ Orthostatic hypotension results from loss of sensitivity of baroreceptors
	• Hypoperfusion is poorly tolerated due to declining cardiac reserve
	• Left ventricular thickening decreases filling capacity and delays filling time
	• Muscle mass reduction results in decreased contractility
	• Reduction in total body water increases risk for dehydration
	• Anemia is caused by nutritional deficiencies, chronic inflammatory disease, and chronic renal disease

Table 18-1. Anatomic and Physiologic Changes in the Older Adult (Continued)

System	Changes with Aging

Neurologic	• Brain tissue atrophy results in the following:
	  ○ Stretching parasagittal bridging veins, predisposing them to tearing with injury
	  ○ Additional space in the cranial vault, resulting in substantial bleeding before the onset of symptoms
	  ○ Higher incidence of chronic subdural hematomas
	  ○ Other factors, including:
	    ♦ Anticoagulant therapy (warfarin, dabigatran)
	    ♦ Antiplatelet therapy (aspirin)
	    ♦ Alcohol abuse, adding to brain atrophy and causing liver damage that can increase bleeding tendencies
	• Nerve cells transmit more slowly reducing reflexes and sensation, leading to problems with movement, safety, and pain perception and control

Skin and Tissue	• Diminished autonomic response and thinner skin limit thermoregulation (impaired heat conservation, production, and dissipation)
	• Increased risk of skin breakdown results from:
	  ○ Skin aging from lifestyle, diet, heredity, sun exposure, and other habits (smoking)
	  ○ Breakdown of elastin
	  ○ Obesity
	  ○ Loss of subcutaneous fat, thinning of the skin
	  ○ Decreased ability to sweat
	  ○ Immobility

Renal	• A decreased number of nephrons limits the ability to concentrate urine • Diminished sense of thirst leads to dehydration
Musculoskeletal	Fat and fibrous tissue replaces lean body mass, so only 15% of the total body mass is muscle by age 75, producing the following effects: • Diminished force of contractile muscle • Increased weakness and fatigue • Poor exercise tolerance • Slower, limited movement • Slower and shorter gait, unsteadiness
Endocrine	• Thyroid function drops, slowing metabolism • Parathyroid levels rise, increasing risk of osteoporosis • Metabolic syndrome increases, blunting the effects of insulin • Aldosterone production drops, predisposing orthostatic hypotension and dehydration

Data from O'Connor & Hackenschimdt[18], Smith & Cotter[19], and Lynch[22]; Evans, R. W. (2009). *Headache*. Retrieved from http://www.rwevansmd.com/EvansPublictations/AACP%20headache%202009.pdf; Scheetz, L. J. (2011). Life-threatening injuries in older adults. *AACN Advanced Critical Care, 22*(2), 128–139; Aresco, C., & Stein, D. (2010). Cervical spine injuries in the geriatric patient. *Clinical Geriatrics, 30–35.* Retrieved from http://www.clinicalgeriatrics.com/articles/Cervical-Spine-Injuries-Geriatric-Patient; and Dugdale, D. C. (2012, September 2). *Aging changes in hormone production*. Retrieved from http://www.nlm.nih.gov/medlineplus/ency/article/004000.htm

The normal older adult's heart and baroreceptors have a limited response to the body's normal release of catecholamines (adrenaline and norepinephrine), which are needed to increase heart rate and cardiac output.[22] The addition of medications such as beta-blockers and cardiac glycosides can further limit this response. Regardless of the history of the older adult patient, a heart rate of greater than 90 beats per minute may indicate significant physiologic stress and increases the risk of mortality.[23]

Interventions

- Consider smaller fluid boluses with reassessment for signs of fluid overload (increased work of breathing or crackles on auscultation of lung sounds) after every bolus

- Consider early administration of packed red blood cells to increase oxygen carrying capacity[4,20,21]

- If indicated, initiate hemorrhage control measures such as pressure dressings and vitamin K for control of internal and external bleeding if the patient takes any anticoagulant medications

- Trend endpoints of resuscitation as well as lactate and/or base deficit levels

Cardiac dysfunction may be the cause or result of trauma in the older adult. Any complaint of chest pain warrants further investigation for either a pathophysiologic or traumatic cause. When assessing the older adult patient ask questions including:

- Did the pain begin before the injury, possibly precipitating the injury?

- Did the pain begin directly after the trauma possibly indicating tissue damage?

- Was there shortness of breath or any other symptoms prior to the chest pain?

D–Disability (Neurologic Status)

Head trauma can result in both acute and chronic subdural hematoma. Cerebral atrophy causes tension on the parasagittal bridging veins making them more susceptible to rupture and increasing the risk for subdural hematoma even with minor trauma to the head. There is also an increased incidence of intracerebral hematomas, which may be caused by anticoagulant use.

Severe head injury with hypotension is associated with high mortality.[24,25] Cerebral atrophy causes increased space within the skull and allows bleeding to accumulate before the patient exhibits signs and symptoms of increased intracranial pressure (ICP). Consider the following:

- Maintain a high index of suspicion for bleeding to the brain

- Consider the need for computed tomography (CT) of the brain early in the resuscitation

- Continuously monitor the patient for signs of increased ICP

Altered mental status in the older adult patient may have several possible causes aside from the traumatic injury. Changes in neurologic status require a full investigation to rule out the following:

- Hypoglycemia

- Hypoxia

- Hyperthermia or hypothermia

- Anxiety, disorientation, agitation, and confusion

- Dementia or mental health issue

If a head injury is suspected, the trauma management is the same, and early CT is recommended. Close monitoring and frequent reorientation are needed for the confused patient.

E–Exposure and Environmental Control

Older adults are at a greater risk for hypothermia and resulting complications. According to Ghazzawi,[23] 3.6% of older adults admitted to the hospital are hypothermic. As the adult ages, normal body temperature becomes more difficult to regulate (Table 18-1).[23] Situations contributing to the risk of compromised thermoregulation include:

- Loss of subcutaneous fat and thinning of the skin

- Decreased ability to sweat

- Neurologic changes

- Chronic cardiac or thyroid conditions

- Poor nutrition

- Psychotropic medications

The risk is increased when the older adult is exposed to temperature extremes at the site of the trauma or in the ED. The patient may present with either hypothermia or hyperthermia. When obtaining a history from the patient, family, or emergency medical services, the location of the trauma is important. For instance, was there prolonged extraction from the vehicle with or exposure to high or low temperatures?

Hyperthermia should also be considered, especially following a fall where exposure and environmental temperature is a factor. Signs and symptoms include:

- Headache
- Vertigo
- Syncope
- Dehydration
- Rapid respirations
- Confusion
- Agitation
- Delirium
- Hallucinations
- Convulsions

Interventions

Because maintenance of normothermia is so important in the older adult trauma patient, regulate the ambient temperature in the trauma room as needed, apply warm blankets, and administer warmed intravenous fluid. When using mechanical warming devices, such as forced air blankets or fluid warmers, monitor the temperature closely to avoid thermal burns to fragile skin.

Resuscitation Adjuncts
F–Full Set of Vital Signs

In addition to comorbidities and medication history, baseline changes in respiration and pulse may be present in the older adult's vital signs.

G–Get Resuscitation Adjuncts
L–Laboratory Studies

It is important to perform prothrombin time (PT), partial thromboplastin time (PTT), and coagulation studies, as use of anticoagulants, such as aspirin, is common among older adults. Use of alcohol and changes in the liver can also affect clotting. An increased international normalized ratio (INR) has been associated with increased mortality in the older adult trauma patient.[26]

M–Monitoring

An electrocardiogram (ECG) may be indicated particularly if there is a history of cardiac disease or if the patient has since developed signs and symptoms of myocardial ischemia surrounding the traumatic event.

P–Pain Assessment and Management

The older adult trauma patient who is anxious, confused, or has dementia may not be able to accurately report pain, so it is important for trauma nurses to assess behavioral cues, subtle signs of discomfort, and common pain responses to injuries. Older adults are frequently undermedicated due to the failure to appropriately assess for pain and the fear of overmedicating.[27] See Chapter 8, Pain, for more information.

When using opioids for pain relief, such as morphine or hydromorphone (Dilaudid), consider the following:

- Obtain an accurate body weight prior to starting opioid administration and calculate doses accordingly
- Use of smaller doses is indicated. Remember "start low, go slow."
- Monitor closely for decreased respirations
- Monitor level of consciousness and any reports of dizziness

Since some age-related compromise to the respiratory system exists, the failure to aggressively manage pain from rib contusions and fractures results in increased respiratory complications and disability.[20]

Reevaluation

- Consider early transfer to a trauma center
- If signs of internal hemorrhage are present, consider a chest and/or pelvis radiograph

Secondary Survey and Reevaluation Adjuncts
H–History

For the older adult patient, a pertinent medical history is crucial. In addition to the findings in the primary survey, it is important that the trauma nurse ask about a patient's comorbidities and all current and recently discontinued medications. Include questions about multiple prescribers, compliance, or obstacles to taking prescribed medications.

Comorbidities

As a result of advances in medicine, more adults are living longer with chronic diseases and comorbidities, necessitating the use of multiple medications. These comorbidities, as well as medication effects, impact the number and severity of complications and the mortality and morbidity of an older patient.

Older adult patients average six or more preexisting conditions,[9] so it is important for the trauma nurse to consider that impact on patient assessment and interventions. Comorbidities may result in a cascade of effects, where one system impacts another, resulting in increased morbidity and mortality.[9] Other factors contribute to the morbidity and mortality of older adult trauma patients. Cirrhosis, coagulopathy, ischemic heart disease, chronic obstructive pulmonary disease, diabetes, renal disease, and malignancy all increase mortality risk in older adults.[16]

Comorbid factors to be assessed in the older trauma patient when there is a fall include:[9]
- Acute problems
  - Cardiac disease, such as myocardial infarction or arrhythmia
  - Stroke
  - Postural hypotension
  - Hypovolemia
- Chronic problems
  - Neurologic disease, such as dementia or parkinsonism
  - Neuropathy
  - Balance problems that can occur post stroke or brain injury
  - Medication such as analgesics, antihistamines, anticoagulants, sleeping aids, or antidepressants

In addition to the aging process, comorbidities can decrease the physiologic reserve in the older adult trauma patient.[8] In other words, the body loses its ability in times of stress to function above its basic level. This is the result of the sympathetic response being circumvented by cardiac disease, pacemakers, or medications. The inability to increase heart rate in order to compensate for decreased volume can conceal the fact that a patient is hemorrhaging, so it is essential for the trauma nurse to consider the complete presentation and history to obtain a true representation of the patient's condition.

Loss of physiologic reserve is a primary factor resulting in the following:[21]
- Increased complications
- Decreased independence
- Increased morbidity or mortality following a traumatic event

Medications
Medication effects can also be contributing and complicating factors in trauma in the older adult. Therefore, it is important to obtain a current list of medications, herbal supplements, and over-the-counter medications during history taking:[15]

- Antihypertensives
  - Beta-blockers are used to treat hypertension and cardiac arrhythmias. They can prevent the increase in heart rate that is an expected response in patients with hypovolemia, shock states, pain, or stress.
- Anticoagulants (aspirin, clopidogrel [Plavix], warfarin [Coumadin], enoxaparin [Lovenox], dabigatran [Pradaxa] and heparin)
  - These medications are the most frequently prescribed in the older adult[28] and increase the possibility of intracranial, internal, or retroperitoneal bleeding
- Diabetes medications
  - If a patient is taking any diabetes medications, a change in the level of consciousness or mentation may be due to abnormal blood sugar levels
- Analgesics
  - Pain medication that depresses the central nervous system (CNS), such as opioids, can be the cause of a traumatic injury by impairing balance and judgment
  - Check the patient for any extra pain patches that he or she may have forgotten to remove
  - Ask if the patient has received any pain medications in the past
    - If so, what was prescribed, how much, and how did the patient respond or react?
    - Did the medication cause excessive sedation?
    - What, if any, adverse effects did the patient experience?
  - Observe for behaviors of misuse of a medication
- Nitroglycerin
  - Use can increase the chance of injury secondary to a drop in blood pressure

H–Head-to-toe Assessment
Urinary Catheter Consideration
Insertion of a urinary catheter to assess output related to circulation and renal function may increase the risk of a catheter-acquired urinary tract infection (CAUTI), which is more common and can result in more severe complications in the older adult population. Consider alternate methods of output measurement before inserting a urinary catheter.[29]

I–Inspect Posterior Surfaces
To help prevent pressure sores and decrease the discomfort associated with being immobilized on a spine board, expedite clearing the cervical spine so the patient may be removed as quickly as possible. It has been

reported that in the older adult even 30 to 45 minutes of lying on a spine board can cause skin breakdown.[30] Physiologic changes due to osteoporosis, osteoarthritis, and kyphosis increase the discomfort of the rigid spine board in older adults and the loss of subcutaneous fat and thinning of the skin provides less padding. The skin's blood vessels are more fragile resulting in easier bruising, bleeding under the skin, and skin tears in the older adult. Once off the board, frequent turning may help to prevent the formation of pressure sores.

Reevaluation and Post Resuscitation Care

The older adult has a limited physiologic reserve, so frequent reevaluations are important to determine any changes in vital signs, pain, injuries, the effectiveness of the interventions that were implemented as well as reassessment of the primary survey.

Definitive Care or Transport

Length of Stay and Adverse Events

Increased length of stay in the emergency department has been associated with poorer outcomes and increased mortality across all trauma patient populations,[31] but in the older adult trauma patient, ED boarding is more likely to result in an adverse event.[32] As noted above, the older adult tends to take more medications and have more comorbidities; and these factors increase the chance of an adverse event while waiting for an inpatient bed.[32] One study notes that boarding older, sicker patients in the ED is not recommended due to these outcomes.[32]

Elder Maltreatment

According to the American Psychological Association (APA), around 2.1 million older adults in the U.S. are victims of physical abuse, emotional abuse, neglect, or other forms of maltreatment.[33] For this reason, when an older adult who was injured at home or in a nursing facility presents to the ED, the patient should be assessed for signs of elder maltreatment.

As older adults acquire more physical limitations, they become more vulnerable to maltreatment. Limitations in mobility, vision, and hearing can make them a target. Mental or physical ailments may add to stress for caregivers.[33]

Visits related to healthcare may be the only human contact the older adult has other than with the abuser.[33] Fear of retribution, losing their home, or isolation often keeps older adults from self-reporting instances of elder maltreatment. For every case of elder maltreatment that is reported to authorities, an estimated five cases have not been reported.[33] Recent research suggests that older adults who have been abused tend to die earlier than those who are not, even in the absence of chronic conditions or life-threatening disease.[34]

Suspected maltreatment is reported according to individual facility protocol. Healthcare workers are mandated reporters in the U.S. When assessing all older adult patients, use the following strategies to help determine if the patient is a victim of maltreatment:

- Completely undress the patient and inspect for any signs of physical abuse or neglect
- Observe and listen to interactions between the patient and the caregiver
- Ask questions directly to the patient and listen to answers. Avoid allowing the caregiver to answer for the older adult.
- Ask if the patient feels safe at home
- Compare the injuries to the history and reported mechanism for concurrence or discrepancy

Signs of potential elder maltreatment include:[33,34]

- Frequent arguments or tension between the caregiver and the older adult
- Reported changes in personality or behavior in the older adult when abuser is present
- Caregiver's refusal to allow the older adult to be seen alone
- Caregiver's dismissive attitude or statements about injuries
- History of visiting different EDs for repeated injuries
- Threatening, belittling, or controlling behavior by the caregiver
- Behavior from the older adult that mimics dementia, such as rocking, sucking, or mumbling to oneself

See Chapter 20, Special Populations: The Interpersonal Violence Trauma Patient, for more information regarding signs and symptoms of maltreatment.

Summary

Normal age-related changes can complicate the assessment of the older adult trauma patient. Any presence of comorbidity and individual response to illness and injury make each patient unique. Failure to recognize the impact of those age-related changes, acknowledge the medications history and understand the older adult's response to physical and emotional stress can result in poorer outcomes. For an older adult with multiple injuries, early consideration of transfer to a trauma center may reduce mortality and morbidity.

References

1. Blumenthal, J., Plummer, E. & Gambert, S, (2010). Trauma in the elderly: Causes and prevention. *Clinical Geriatrics, 21–24.* Retrieved from http://www.clinicalgeriatrics.com/articles/Trauma-Elderly-Causes-and-Prevention

2. Pandya, S., Yelon, J., Sullivan, T., & Risucci, D. (2011). Geriatric motor vehicle collision survival: The role of institutional trauma volume. *Journal of Trauma, 70*(6), 1326–1330

3. Centers for Disease Control and Prevention. (2010). *10 leading causes of injury deaths by age group highlighting unintentional injury deaths, United States – 2010.* Retrieved from http://www.cdc.gov/injury/wisqars/pdf/10LCID_Unintentional_Deaths_2010-a.pdf

4. Cutugno, C. (2011). The 'graying' of trauma care: Addressing traumatic injury in older adults. *American Journal of Nursing, 111*(11), 40–48.

5. Bourg, P., Richey, M., Salottolo, K., & Mains, C. (2012). Development of a geriatric resuscitation protocol, utilization compliance, and outcomes. *Journal of Trauma Nursing, 19*(1), 51–56.

6. Centers for Disease Control and Prevention. (2012, September 20). *Falls among older adults: An overview.* Retrieved from http://www.cdc.gov/HomeandRecreationalSafety/Falls/adultfalls.html

7. Fair, L. R., Donatelli, N. S., & Somes, J. (2012). Accurate triage and specialized assessment needs of the geriatric trauma patient who experiences low-energy trauma. *Journal of Emergency Nursing, 38*(4), 378–380.

8. Jayasinghe, N. (2011, March 29). *Addressing falls prevention among older adults, part I: Understanding why falls happen.* Retrieved from http://www.hss.edu/professional-conditions_addressing-falls-prevention-older-adults-understanding.asp

9. Kaplan, J. L., &. Porter R.S. (Eds.). (2011). *The Merck manual of diagnosis and therapy* (19th ed.). Whitehouse Station, NJ: Merck, Sharp, & Dohme.

10. Centers for Disease Control and Prevention. (2010, September 10). *Hip fractures among older adults.* Retrieved from http://www.cdc.gov/HomeandRecreationalSafety/Falls/adulthipfx.html

11. Jagodzinski, N. A., Weerasinghe, C., & Porter, K. (2010). Crush injuries and crush syndrome – a review. Part 1: The systemic injury. *Trauma, 12,* 69–88.

12. Jagodzinski, N.A., Weerasinghe, C., & Porter, K. (2010). Crush injuries and crush syndrome – a review. Part 2: The local injury. *Trauma, 12,* 133–148.

13. National Institute on Aging. (n.d.). *Older drivers: How aging affects driving.* Retrieved from http://nihseniorhealth.gov/olderdrivers/howagingaffectsdriving/01.html

14. Labib, N., Nouh, T., Winocour, S., Deckelbaum, D., Banici, L., Fata, P., … Khwaja, K. (2011). Severely injured geriatric population: Morbidity, mortality, and risk factors. *Journal of Trauma, 71*(6), 1908–1914

15. Aschkenasy, M. T., & Rothenhaus, T. C. (2006) Trauma and falls in the elderly. *Emergency Medicine Clinics of North America, 24,* 413–432.

16. Chang, T. T., & Schecter, W. P. (2007). Injury in the elderly and end-of-life decisions. *Surgical Clinics of North America, 87*(1), 229–245.

17. U.S. Department of Transportation. (2009). *Traffic safety facts 2009.* Retrieved from http://www-nrd.nhtsa.dot.gov/Pubs/811402EE.pdf

18. O'Connor, P., & Hackenschmidt, A. (2008). Geriatric pedestrian versus auto trauma: An age-old problem. *Journal of Emergency Nursing, 34*(2), 177–179.

19. Smith, C.M., & Cotter, V.T. (2012). Age-related changes in health. In M. Boltz, E. Capezuti, T. Fulmer, & D. Zwicker (Eds.), *Evidence-based geriatric nursing protocols for best practice* (4th ed., pp. 23–47). New York, NY: Springer Publishing

20. Bartley, M. K., &. Shiflett, L. (2010). Handle older trauma patients with care. *Nursing 2010, 40*(8), 24–29.

21. Callaway, D., & Wolfe, R. (2007). Geriatric trauma. *Emergency Medicine Clinics of North America, 25,* 837–860.

22. Lynch, A. (2009). Trauma in older people. In E. Cole (Ed.), *Trauma care: Initial assessment and management in the emergency department* (pp. 217–230). West Sussex, U.K.: Blackwell Publishing.

23. Ghazzawi, H. (2007, April 18). *Hypothermia causing multi system complications in elderly patient with femur neck fracture.* Retrieved from http://www.orthogate.org/cases/trauma/hypothermia-causing-multi-system-complications-in-elderly-patient-with-femur-neck-fracture.html

24. Brain Trauma Foundation. (2007). Guidelines for the management of severe traumatic brain injury 3rd edition: Cerebral perfusion thresholds. *Journal of Neurotrauma, 24*(Suppl 1), S59–S64.

25. McQuillan, K. A., & Thurman, P. A. (2009). Traumatic brain injuries. In K. A. McQuillan, M. B. Flynn Makie, & E. Whalen (Eds.), *Trauma nursing: From resuscitation through rehabilitation* (4th ed., pp. 448–518). Philadelphia, PA: W. B. Saunders.

26. Williams T. M., Sadjadi, J., Harken, A. H., & Victorino, G. P. (2008). The necessity to assess anticoagulation status in elderly injured patients. *Journal of Trauma, 65*(4), 772–777.

27. Jermyn, R.T., Janora, D. M., & Surve, S. A. (2010). Assessment and classification of pain in the elderly patient. *Clinical Geriatrics, 16–19.* Retrieved from http://www.clinicalgeriatrics.com/articles/Assessment-and-Classification-Pain-Elderly-Patient

28. Robert-Ebadi, H., Le Gal, G., & Righini, M. (2009). Use of anticoagulants in elderly patients: Practical recommendations. *Clinical Interventions in Aging, 4,* 165–177.

29. Voss, A.M.B. (2009). Incidence and duration of urinary catheters in hospitalized older adults: Before and after implementing a geriatric protocol. *Journal of Gerontological Nursing, 35*(6), 35–41.

30. Somes, J., & Donatelli, N. S. (2010). Geriatric emergency nursing: Case study. *Journal of Emergency Nursing, 36*(3), 260–262.

31. Mowery, N. T., Dougherty, S. D., Hildreth, A. M, Holmes, J. H., Chang, M. C., Martin, R. S., … Miller, P. R. (2011). Emergency department length of stay is an independent predictor of hospital mortality in trauma activation patients. *Journal of Trauma, 70*(6), 1317–1325.

32. Liu, S. W., Thomas, S. H., Gordon, J. A., Hamedani, A. G., & Weissman, J. S. (2009). A pilot study examining undesirable events among emergency department-boarded patients awaiting inpatient beds. *Annals of Emergency Medicine, 54*(3), 381–385.

33. American Psychological Association. (n.d.). *Elder abuse and neglect: In search of solutions.* Retrieved from http://www.apa.org/pi/aging/eldabuse.html

34. Sellas, M.I. & Krouse, L. (2011, June 8). *Elder abuse treatment & management.* Retrieved from http://emedicine.medscape.com/article/805727-treatment#a1126

Chapter 19 • Special Populations: The Bariatric Trauma Patient

Jessie M. Moore, MSN, APRN

Objectives

Upon completion of this chapter, the learner will be able to:

1. Describe mechanisms of injury associated with the bariatric trauma patient.

2. Describe pathophysiologic changes as a basis for assessment of the bariatric trauma patient.

3. Demonstrate the nursing assessment of the bariatric trauma patient.

4. Plan appropriate interventions for the bariatric trauma patient.

5. Evaluate the effectiveness of nursing interventions for the bariatric trauma patient.

Introduction

The word *bariatric* comes from the Greek word baro for weight[1] and describes patients who are overweight; however, more specific definitions are necessary to identify and classify the bariatric patient and discuss trauma care for this patient population.

The World Health Organization (WHO) uses body mass index (BMI) to define the degree to which a person is considered overweight.[2] BMI is calculated by dividing a person's weight in kilograms by height in meters squared. The WHO makes the following obesity classifications:[2]

- Underweight: BMI less than 18.5 kg/m²
- Normal weight: BMI between 18.5 kg/m² and 24.9 kg/m²
- Overweight: BMI between 25 kg/m² and 29.9 kg/m²
- Obese: BMI of 30 kg/m² or greater

When a patient reaches a BMI of 40 kg/m² or greater, they are categorized as morbidly obese, as the patient's health is often significantly impacted by diseases such as hypertension, hyperlipidemia, obstructive sleep apnea, diabetes, and others.[3] Many of these disorders may also be present at lower BMI levels although a higher BMI increases the risk of these diseases and others. In children and teens, age- and gender-specific tables are used and take into account developmental changes to determine BMI and degree of obesity.[4]

For the purposes of this chapter, the *bariatric patient* is typically a patient with a BMI of 30 kg/m² or greater, unless otherwise specified.

Epidemiology

The rates of obesity are increasing in the United States (U.S.) and around the world. From 2009 to 2010, 35.7% of adults and 16.9% of children in the U.S. were identified as obese.[5] Worldwide, obesity has increased in developed countries, with rates of obesity in Mexico now comparable to the U.S., and lower, yet significant rates of obesity are seen in Korea, Japan, and China. Figure 19-1 shows the increase in levels of obesity in countries in North America, Europe, and Asia.[6] Australia shows similar growth in obesity rates, and in 2012, 25% of Australian adults were considered obese.[7]

Increasing numbers of bariatric trauma patients present to the emergency department (ED) for care. Both physicians and nurses report challenges in the assessment and care of this group including vital sign measurement, venipuncture, intravenous (IV) cannulation, patient positioning and mobilization, and other general procedures.[8] Difficulty finding appropriately sized equipment is common.[1] Education regarding this population can assist the trauma nurse to be better prepared to care for these patients.

Mechanisms of Injury and Biomechanics

Studies related to patterns and severity of injury in bariatric patients show mixed data over the past two decades. Early studies described BMI as an independent risk factor for mortality and other adverse outcomes following blunt trauma.[9] More recent studies found that once injured, bariatric patients have an increased incidence of complications. With sprains, strains, and dislocations, bariatric patients have higher rates of hospitalization than patients of more normal weights.[10] There is evidence that bariatric patients died after the initial 72–hour post-injury period with researchers attributing this delayed mortality not to obesity but to comorbid diseases, such as diabetes, and BMI is no longer considered an independent risk factor for death.[11]

There are several factors associated with the higher mortality in the bariatric patient, including higher incidence of specific injuries, the inability to use or improper fit of safety equipment and practices, and comorbidities in patients with increased BMI.[12] Studies found increased mortality for bariatric patients involved in frontal vehicular collisions.[13] Specific injuries more common in the bariatric patient include head, thoracic, abdominal, lower extremity fractures, particularly distal femur, torso and proximal arm injuries.[14–16] While bariatric patients may initially sustain fewer injuries, the injuries tend to be more severe. These patients have longer hospital and intensive care unit (ICU) lengths of stay, with worse survival rates than for patients who are of a normal weight.[14,17,18]

One of the largest studies to date found an increased mortality rate among both moderately and morbidly obese drivers in severe motor vehicle collisions (MVCs).[19] This may result from a decrease in seatbelt usage in morbidly obese drivers and passengers.[20] Inappropriate or inadequate restraint points for body habitus and different energy distribution have been offered as theories for these injury patterns.[21] Little research regarding MVC mechanics includes data related to increased BMI.[9,13] Automotive safety systems and crash test simulations are based on standard height and weight projections of a BMI of 25.[9,15] Patients who wore seatbelts experienced fewer injuries in patients of all weights.[22]

Comorbid conditions and factors associated with bariatric patients, such as sleep apnea, decreased endurance and reserve, diabetes, and gastroesophageal reflux disease (GERD) affect the risk for and response to injury. Patients with sleep apnea have a sevenfold risk for vehicular collisions, due to drowsiness while driving.[23] The bariatric patient with limited endurance and reserve is at greater risk for falls and delayed recovery from decreased mobility.[10,15,24] Diabetes affects sensation of injury, healing, and metabolism. Patients with GERD have a higher risk of aspiration and pneumonia, which can delay recovery from injury.[25]

Figure 19-1. World Obesity Rates

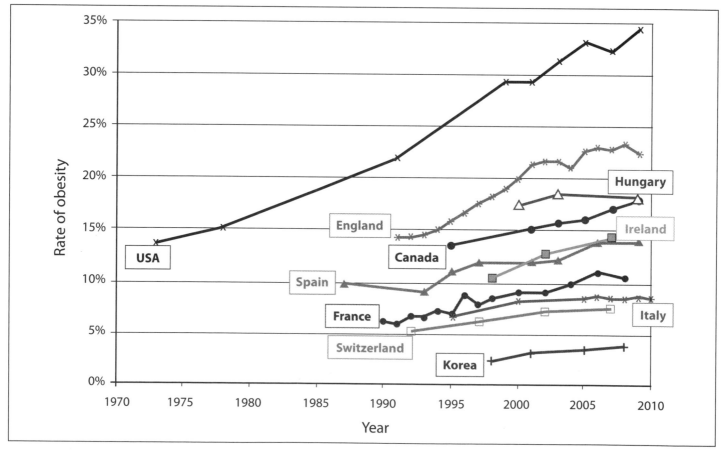

From Organisation for Economic and Co-operative Development.[6]

Obese children have also been found to have an increased risk of upper and lower extremity injuries, and obese children aged 2 to 5 years have an increased risk for severe head and thoracic injuries.[20]

Pathophysiologic Differences in the Bariatric Trauma Patient

Bariatric patients with BMI greater than 40 kg/m[2] can have both functional and physiologic differences from normal weight patients, which may contribute to poorer outcomes following traumatic injury.[24] Distribution of fat is also an important factor, as central or abdominal adipose tissue has been associated with dyslipidemia, diabetes, and cardiovascular disease.[26] This type of adipose tissue is now known to have active endocrine function, which contributes hormonally to the development of these disorders.[26]

Airway changes in patients with a BMI of greater than 30 kg/mm[2] can include increased cervical fat and a larger neck circumference, increased fat distribution in the soft tissues of the oropharynx, increased tongue size, and relaxation of airway muscles narrowing the opening and risking airway collapse with compromise.[4] The airway of a patient of normal weight is often maintained best in a supine position; for the bariatric patient, the opposite may be true. In the supine position, a narrowed airway may become obstructed. Figure 19-2 shows the difference between the airway of a bariatric patient and a normal weight counterpart.[27] Obstructive sleep apnea (OSA) is frequently a result of these changes, as the relaxation of pharyngeal musculature and weight of the tongue during sleep cause intermittent airway occlusion in the narrowed opening.[4,27]

Reduction in functional residual capacity, vital capacity, and total lung capacity can be as high as 25% to 30% in the bariatric patient.[28] Closure of the smaller airways leads to collapsed alveoli and a chronic state of atelectasis in the bases of the lungs.[28] Bariatric patients may compensate with increased respiratory rates, often up to 40% higher than patients of normal weight.[28,29] Work of breathing can also be up to 40% higher in the overweight patient and 250% higher in the morbidly obese patient.[28] Respiratory efforts are made more difficult by intra-abdominal size and pressure, which displaces the diaphragm. The weight of the chest wall adds to the work of breathing. These changes lead to obesity hypoventilation syndrome (OHS), also known as OSA, causing increased systemic and pulmonary artery pressures, increased left and right ventricular pressures, and increased cardiac output, which can cause right-sided heart failure and pulmonary hypertension.[28]

Hypertension, dyslipidemia, and coronary artery disease are frequent comorbidities.[28]

Bariatric patients who are morbidly obese have a higher baseline intra-abdominal pressure,[30] especially those who are apple-shaped (central adiposity). This is associated with a multitude of comorbid conditions including:[30]

- Respiratory compromise and OHS

- Hypertension and cardiovascular disease

- Gastroesophageal reflux disease (GERD)

- Urinary stress incontinence

Fig. 19-2. Airways of a Normal Body Weight Patient and an Obese Patient

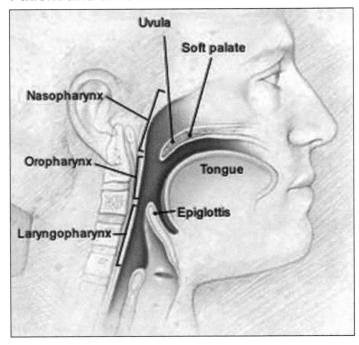

A. The airway of a normal body weight patient. *From* Welliver & Bednarzyk.[27]

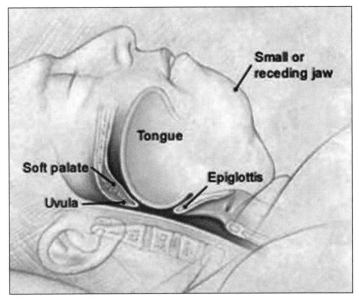

B. The airway of an obese patient. *From* Welliver & Bednarzyk.[27]

- Idiopathic intracranial hypertension (formerly pseudotumor cerebri)
- Deep vein thrombosis (DVT)
  - Delayed venous return resulting from increased intra-abdominal pressure creates a high risk for deep venous thrombosis (DVT) and pulmonary embolus in the bariatric patient
  - Compromise from injury and/or decreased mobility due to lower extremity injury further increases the risk.
  - Increased levels of leptin, a hormone secreted by fat cells, in the bariatric patient has been shown to increase platelet aggregation[26]

Pharmacokinetic factors associated with obesity will affect medication metabolism and pharmacodynamics. Bariatric patients have both increased lean body mass and fat mass. Blood flow to adipose tissue is approximately 5% of circulatory volume, with 73% directed to the viscera and 22% to lean tissue.[31] Muscle tissue holds more water than fat tissue does, and medications that are hydrophilic are distributed more to lean tissue and less to adipose tissue. In general, hydrophilic medications should be dosed on ideal body weight (IBW) and not on actual weight.[31] Lipophilic medications are better absorbed by adipose tissue and are more frequently dosed on actual body weight (ABW).[31] They will have a longer half-life for elimination, prolonging the effects. This is often referred to as a *resedation effect* when related to anesthesia or analgesic medications, as the slower elimination continues the effect of the medication longer than might be expected. Renal function is also a factor in medication clearance, especially in patients with comorbidities of diabetes or hypertension.[31]

Obesity causes alterations in joint cartilage and bone metabolism. The ankle joints are subject to 4.5 times body weight during walking and 10 times body weight during running,[32] leading to early development of osteoarthritic disorders.[33] Lower extremity fractures tend to be more complex in the bariatric patient due to these degenerative changes.[32] Table 19-1 outlines both physiologic changes seen in obesity and signs and symptoms related to these changes.

Nursing Care of the Bariatric Trauma Patient

Preparation

It is important to be prepared before the trauma patient's arrival with a variety of appropriate sizes of equipment such as stretchers, blood pressure cuffs, and cervical spine collars. Education regarding the special considerations of caring for bariatric patients can also serve as a foundation for the trauma team to provide competent, safe, and sensitive trauma care.

Primary Survey and Resuscitative Adjuncts

Bariatric patients with lower BMI levels may be able to adequately compensate with little noticeable difference in their assessment parameters. As the BMI level increases, expect physiologic and functional changes to become increasingly severe. The initial assessment is focused on establishing a baseline to determine which findings can be attributed to a known, suspected pre-injury cause and which may be related to potential traumatic injury.

A–Airway and Alertness
Assessment

Bariatric patients are at high risk for gastric reflux or aspiration, especially in patients with altered levels of consciousness.

Interventions
- Cervical spinal immobilization
  - Blanket rolls, and tape can be used to assist immobilization.[4,24] Commercially available immobilization devices may not fit the bariatric patient with a shorter, thicker neck.
  - Anticipate the need for additional personnel when logrolling or repositioning the patient
- Airway
  - Use a two-handed bilateral jaw-thrust with airway adjuncts for optimal airway control[34]
  - Anticipate the need for early intubation if airway compromise is a risk
  - The reverse Trendelenburg position will benefit both airway maintenance and work of breathing[28]
- Place the patient in a position with the head elevated during intubation with the external auditory canal parallel with sternal notch to allow for better visualization of pharyngeal landmarks.[34,35] This position is known as the *ramped* position (Fig. 19-3). Blankets can be used to elevate the head and torso into this position.
- Awake intubation using fiberoptic technology may be preferable as it preserves pharyngeal and laryngeal muscle tone.[28,33,35] Fiberoptic visualization also provides a superior view of the glottis in many patients.[35]
- Selection of the provider with the most experience in difficult airway management is recommended[33,36]

Rapid Sequence Intubation

Rapid sequence intubation (RSI) dosage for bariatric patients remains controversial.

Table 19-1. Pathophysiologic Changes Related to Obesity and Morbid Obesity

System	Alterations	Related Disorder (Comorbid Disease)	Signs and Symptoms Affecting Trauma Patients
Pulmonary/Airway	• Respiratory insufficiency due to chest wall weight, decreased chest wall compliance, and increased airway resistance[28,51]	• Increased work of breathing	• Dyspnea with very mild exertion, positional dyspnea
	• IAP leads to elevated diaphragm, chronic atelectasis	• Obesity hypoventilation syndrome, also known as obstructive sleep apnea	• Higher baseline respiratory rate
	• Narrowed airway, larger tongue, relaxed pharyngeal muscle • Nocturnal gastric reflux	• Asthma	• Oxygen saturation likely lower in supine position • Hypoxia, hypercapnea • Daytime drowsiness common in undiagnosed sleep apnea; may contribute to MVCs

Note: BMI indicates body mass index; BUN, blood urea nitrogen; ECG, electrocardiogram; IAH, intra-abdominal hypertension; IAP, intra-abdominal pressure; MVCs, motor vehicle collisions

Table 19-1. Pathophysiologic Changes Related to Obesity and Morbid Obesity (Continued)

System	Alterations	Related Disorder (Comorbid Disease)	Signs and Symptoms Affecting Trauma Patients
Cardiovascular	Ventricular remodeling:[26] • Left ventricle hypertrophy and decreased compliance • Increased cardiac output • Diastolic dysfunction	• Hypertension	Muffled heart sounds
	Accelerated rate of coronary atherosclerosis	• Right- and left-sided heart failure	Compensatory tachycardia
	Increased IAP thought to contribute to development of hypertension as well as lower extremity circulatory disorder	• Pulmonary hypertension	ECG changes: • PR, QRS, and QT intervals prolonged • ST depression, or flattening of T waves • Low QRS voltage
	Venous insufficiency	• Varicose veins	
	Elevated blood viscosity due to increased leptin	• Venous stasis • Pulmonary embolism	Arrhythmias • Higher incidence of atrial fibrillation • Premature ventricular contractions common • Edema in the lower extremities • Skin ulceration, lymphedema • Dyspnea, leg, or chest pain
Endocrine	Elevated insulin levels and resistance to endogenous insulin, cholesterol production	• Metabolic syndrome • Type 2 diabetes • Dyslipidemia • Polycystic ovarian syndrome	Elevated blood glucose levels

Note: BMI indicates body mass index; BUN, blood urea nitrogen; ECG, electrocardiogram; IAH, intra-abdominal hypertension; IAP, intra-abdominal pressure; MVCs, motor vehicle collisions

Table 19-1. Pathophysiologic Changes Related to Obesity and Morbid Obesity (Continued)

System	Alterations	Related Disorder (Comorbid Disease)	Signs and Symptoms Affecting Trauma Patients
Musculoskeletal	Weight-bearing joint deterioration due to excess weight	• Osteoarthritis	Degenerative symptoms including: • Joint pain, particularly lower hips, knees, and ankles • Limited range of motion of extremities • Limited flexibility
	Compression of spinal vertebrae due to weight load	• Low back pain	Back pain, neurologic symptoms
	• Increase in uric acid • Gait and balance changes related to weight distribution with increased BMI	• Gout	• Pain, swelling, redness of affected area • Decreased mobility
Gastrointestinal	Increased IAP, inability of lower esophageal sphincter to withstand this pressure	• Gastroesophageal reflux	Reports reflux from awake patient or potential aspiration symptoms in altered consciousness
	Increased liver size due to fatty deposits	• Nonalcoholic fatty liver disease	Elevated liver function studies, often asymptomatic
	Abdominal muscle wall weakness, increased IAP	• Hernias	Pain, bulging on palpation of abdomen
Genitourinary	Insulin resistance and IAP causation	• Renal dysfunction	Elevated BUN and creatinine levels
	Increased urinary bladder pressure related to IAP	• Urinary stress incontinence	Urinary urgency, leakage
Neurologic	Increased intracranial pressure due to IAH	• Idiopathic intracranial hypertension (pseudotumor cerebri)	Headaches, visual disturbances

Note: BMI indicates body mass index; BUN, blood urea nitrogen; ECG, electrocardiogram; IAH, intra-abdominal hypertension; IAP, intra-abdominal pressure; MVCs, motor vehicle collisions

Table 19-1. Pathophysiologic Changes Related to Obesity and Morbid Obesity (Continued)

System	Alterations	Related Disorder (Comorbid Disease)	Signs and Symptoms Affecting Trauma Patients
Skin	Venous stasis lower extremities	• Cellulitis	Early breakdown of skin in moist area, and areas of pressure points, including occiput
	Excess skin accumulation	• Intertrigo under skin folds	
Psychological		• Depression • Low self-esteem • Social isolation	

Note: BMI indicates body mass index; BUN, blood urea nitrogen; ECG, electrocardiogram; IAH, intra-abdominal hypertension; IAP, intra-abdominal pressure; MVCs, motor vehicle collisions.

- Evidence at this time supports using lean body weight (LBW) for induction agents, IBW for rocuronium and other nondepolarizing agents, and total body weight (TBW) for succinylcholine.[34,35] Table 19-2 can be used to rapidly estimate medication dosages in emergent situations.

- Monitor the patient closely for desaturation. Increased oxygen consumption leads to rapid desaturation in the obese patient; a patient with a higher BMI may desaturate in as little time as one minute, compared to six minutes in a patient of normal weight[34]

- Placing the patient in reverse Trendelenburg to 25 degrees prolongs the safe apnea time, as does preoxygenation with a bag-mask device[34]

If intubation is unsuccessful, a supraglottic device such as the laryngeal mask airway (LMA) or multilumen airway is acceptable for use in the bariatric patient.[34,35] Other useful devices include an endotracheal tube introducer (ETTI).

Tracheal access may be necessary in patients when intubation fails. Surgical cricothyrotomy is the technique of choice.[34] Use of an endotracheal tube (ETT) is recommended, as the standard cricothyrotomy tube may be too short.[34] Tracheostomy is less desirable in this patient population due to increased complications and procedure difficulty.[28]

B–Breathing and Ventilation
Assessment
- Inspect for:
  - Increased work of breathing, especially when in a supine position: Weakened respiratory muscles may quickly lead to fatigue and respiratory failure
  - Monitor level of consciousness; lethargy, mental status changes, and restlessness that may indicate hypoxia
- Auscultate for:
  - Breath sounds
    - Can be muffled through additional soft tissue[33]
    - Displace skin folds over the lung area to auscultate lung sounds

Interventions
- As soon as the cervical spine is cleared, place the patient in an upright position to improve access and chest excursion
  - Placing the patient in a lateral left position or elevating the head of the bed in reverse Trendelenburg position at 45 degrees may help the patient with adequate ventilation[26,28]

Figure 19-3. Ramped Position for Better Visualization with Intubation

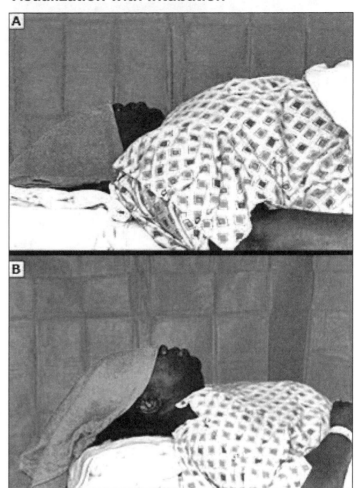

A, Patient in normal position.
B, Patient in ramped position.
From Arbelaez et al.[35]

- Anticipate potential use of bilevel positive airway pressure (BiPAP)
  - This can be a useful intervention prior to intubation to provide adequate ventilation, especially in patients with a history of sleep apnea[33]
  - BiPAP can be useful in patients with flail chest injury or acute pulmonary embolism[37]
  - Prior to application, assure that the patient has an intact swallow function, gag reflex, and cough mechanism[37]
- Use two-person bag-mask ventilation with oropharyngeal or nasopharyngeal airways in place, unless contraindicated, if manual ventilation is required[34,37]

Table 19-2. Ideal Body Weight and Approximate Lean Body Weight in Obesity (Adult)

	Height (in)	Height (cm)	IBW* (kg)	Approximate LBW in class III obesity† (kg)
Female (Adult)	60	152	46	52
	65	165	57	60
	70	178	68	70
	75	191	80	80
Male (Adult)	60	152	50	63
	65	165	62	73
	70	178	76	85
	75	191	89	97
	80	203	103	112

Note: BMI indicates body mass index; IBW, ideal body weight; LBW, lean body weight; TBW, total body weight.
*IBW male = 50 + (2.3 × height in inches over 5 feet); IBW female = 45.5 + (2.3 × height in inches over 5 feet).
†Approximate LBW in class III obesity (BMI 40–45 kg/m²) for dosing emergency medications; LBW estimate (kg) = (9270 × TBW)/(A + B × BMI) where A and B are 6,680 and 216 respectively for males and 8,780 and 244 respectively for females.
From Arbelaez et al.[35]

C–Circulation and Control Hemorrhage
Assessment
- Palpate for:
  - Subcutaneous emphysema over chest wall is significant, as auscultation of breath sounds and percussion may not be as useful in detecting chest injuries due to the effects of subcutaneous tissue in muffling accurate sound transmission from the lungs[4]

Interventions
- Monitor the volume of fluid resuscitation closely to avoid overload since some bariatric patients with cardiac comorbidities may not tolerate aggressive fluid administration[4]
- Use guided ultrasound for catheter placement if there is difficulty obtaining intravenous (IV) access[8]
- Consider use of intraosseous (IO) access devices. External jugular cannulation attempts may be impaired due to increased adipose tissue in the neck area; however, if landmarks can be visualized, the sites can be used after the cervical spine has been cleared.
- Burn management may require higher levels of fluid replacement, and patients will be at high risk of infection[38]

Resuscitative Adjuncts
F–Full Set of Vital Signs
- An accurate blood pressure in the bariatric patient can be a challenge
  - Use an appropriately sized cuff

- A cuff that is too small can produce a false high pressure reading.[26,39] See Table 19-3 for a chart of correct cuff sizes.[39]
  - The forearm can be used for blood pressure measurement; however, results may be higher than pressures taken in the upper arm[40]
  - Obtaining the correct cuff size for the forearm is essential, and the circumference of the forearm should be measured midway between the elbow and wrist
  - Center the cuff between the elbow and wrist with arm supported at the level of heart[39]
- Palpation of anatomic landmarks for electrocardiogram (ECG) leads in bariatric patients may be difficult,[41] and leads should be placed under breast area tissue when possible. Greater chest circumference will cause lead placement that is wider than on a standard-sized person; however, the landmarks of the midclavicular and midaxillary lines are the same for all patients.

G–Get Resuscitation Adjuncts
- L–Laboratory Studies
  - Laboratory studies for bariatric patients include the following:
    - Additional laboratory studies related to comorbid conditions as indicated
    - Arterial blood gases (ABGs) to evaluate ventilation status

Table 19-3. Correct Cuff Size Based on Arm Circumference

Arm Circumference* (cm)	Cuff size (cm)
22–26	Small adult, 12 × 22
27–34	Adult, 16 × 30
35–44	Large adult, 16 × 36
45–52	Adult–thigh, 16 × 42

*Arm circumference is measured midway between acromion and olecranon.
From Rauen et al.[39]

- Liver function studies and renal studies to compare to baseline values and rule out significant pathology

- N–Nasogastric or Orogastric Tube Consideration

  - If a patient's history includes recent bariatric surgery, blind placement of a nasogastric or orogastric tube is contraindicated as it may disrupt the suture lines of the new stomach or perforate the smaller stomach. Tubes may be safely placed using fluoroscopy if indicated.[42]

- O–Oxygenation and Ventilation

  - Continuously monitor oxygenation status and capnography

    - Higher concentrations of supplemental oxygen may be necessary to achieve adequate oxygenation

    - Conversely, obese patients have higher rates of chronic obstructive pulmonary disorder (COPD), so the risk of hyperoxia includes loss of ventilatory drive as well as hyperoxia. Monitor and maintain SpO_2 between 94 and 98%[11]

- P–Pain Assessment and Management

  - Pain medication dosing is based on IBW or normal weight parameters and not on actual weight.[26] Lipophilic medications are taken up by adipose tissue and released slowly back into the blood stream. Medications which are lipophilic—including benzodiazepines, propofol, and fentanyl—should be titrated according to effects and patient response monitored closely.[26]

Emergency Resuscitation

While obesity can make resuscitation efforts more challenging, no modifications to basic or advanced life support procedures are recommended by the American Heart Association's Advanced Cardiac Life Support Guidelines.[43] Defibrillation is best accomplished using a biphasic defibrillator, which delivers energy from one contact point or pad to the other and then reverses direction back to the source. There is no current evidence that supports the need for higher energy levels, larger pads, or any change in the algorithm with defibrillation.[44]

Secondary Survey
H–History
The trauma nurse should consider several questions when obtaining the history of a bariatric patient.

- What is the patient's current weight and height?

  - Weight may be used for adequate medication dosing. Studies have shown that physician and nurse abilities to estimate a patient's weight within 10% of actual weight occurs only 33% to 50% of the time, and patient estimates are most accurate.[8,45]

  - Use of a bed or stretcher with weight measurement capability is ideal for the bariatric patient who may lack mobility. Check equipment for upper weight limits before use.

- What medical problems does the patient have?

  - Known medical history and potential undiagnosed conditions are both important factors

  - Be alert for signs of comorbidities that have yet to be identified

    - Ask about increased thirst, urination, dry mouth, headaches, or fatigue that may indicate metabolic syndrome or elevated glucose levels

    - Symptoms such as snoring, daytime drowsiness and fatigue, frequent night awakening, observed apnea, or a choking sensation during sleep can indicate undetected sleep apnea[41]

- Does the patient have a history of bariatric surgery?

  - A patient who has undergone surgery may be in one of several stages of weight loss, have achieved limited success, or have rebounded with weight gain some time after the original surgery

  - Determine the type of procedure, any complications, and when it was performed

  - Patients who have not been compliant with dietary and vitamin recommendations may have deficiencies in their protein or vitamin levels. Patients who have undergone gastric bypass, for example, are more likely to have iron and B12 deficiency and may have a baseline anemia that affects laboratory studies.

- What medications is the patient taking?
  - Bariatric patients may be currently treated for several comorbid conditions. It is important to determine the patient's use of the following:
    - Antidiabetic medications, including last dose
    - Diuretics
    - Antihypertensives
    - Antilipidemics
    - Anticoagulants and salicylates
    - Antianginals, including calcium-channel blockers, beta-adrenergic blockers, and nitrates
    - Antacids and histamine antagonists
    - Antidepressants
    - Bronchodilators and corticosteroids
    - Appetite suppressants: May cause tachycardia, increased blood pressure, paresthesia, dyspepsia, and abdominal pain, which can be confused with trauma-related injury symptoms[38]
    - Chronic pain medications, including nonsteroidal anti-inflammatory medications
  - Because of altered absorption following bariatric surgery, many patients may be taking vitamin supplements
  - Ask about over-the-counter (OTC) medications, alternative and herbal remedies, and the use of energy supplements or drinks

H–Head-to-toe Assessment
Peripheral pulses may need to be assessed using Doppler ultrasound.[26]

Reevaluation Adjuncts
Thromboembolism Prevention
The bariatric patient is at higher risk for embolus formation and for serious complications from thromboembolism. Standard prevention measures include antiembolism stockings and compression devices, prophylactic anticoagulant therapy, and early mobilization.

Patients who are discharged with reduced mobility after fractures may need anticoagulation as well as discharge instruction related to signs and symptoms of thromboembolism. Fracture stabilization choices may be altered due to the need for custom-fit splints, which allow for anticipated swelling that is likely to occur.[32] Bariatric patients with a BMI greater than 40 kg/m² will need specialty beds to help prevent complications of immobility.

Computed Tomography
Be aware of weight limits and size restrictions of the CT scanning equipment. Prepare alternative options in advance.

Staff and Patient Safety

Staff safety during procedures is a consideration when caring for bariatric patients. The weight of an extremity in a bariatric patient with a BMI greater than 40 kg/m² may exceed the safe lifting load for a single caregiver, and lifting devices should be used to help prevent staff and patient injury in all aspects of care. Consideration should be given to preplanning and training in the use of techniques and devices to assist in transfer, positioning, and nursing care procedures.

Lateral transfer devices should be used to help prevent skin shearing and staff injury. Such devices include slider boards and friction-reduction devices, as well as air-assisted lateral transfer aids. Friction-reduction sheets and air transfer cushions need to be placed on the stretcher prior to patient use. With the lateral air transfer device, air flows through the inflated mattress to provide a thin cushion of air to move the patient laterally, reducing the work of transfer.[46]

Key components of providing a safe environment for the bariatric patient include:
- Knowing the weight capacity of conventional equipment (stretchers, wheelchairs, toilets)
- Familiarity with safe use of bariatric equipment available in the department
- Demonstrating confidence in the ability to safely care for the bariatric patient to the patient and to other caregivers

Patient Dignity

Bariatric patients often experience discrimination and bias in the healthcare setting.[47] Physicians, nurses, and other staff members may have negative beliefs and opinions about causes of obesity and characteristics of the obese patient, which can translate into care that lacks sensitivity or even displays open prejudice. The challenges of providing care to a bariatric patient can also lead to frustration for the trauma nurse. This behavior may be perceived by the patient as a negative reaction directed at them.

Important considerations in providing sensitive care for the bariatric patient include:

- Protect patient privacy—provide adequately sized gowns and draping, and obtain patient weight in a discreet manner

- Demonstrate tact regarding weight issues—references to "large size," "big boy," "obesity," or "excess fat" are often offensive to bariatric patients. Terms such as "weight problem" or "excess weight" are often less emotionally charged.

- Be sensitive to the bariatric patient's past encounters with healthcare providers. Many bariatric patients have suffered embarrassment from use of improperly sized equipment, insensitive comments, and even openly discriminatory behavior. Be aware of nonverbal communication.

A heightened sensitivity to these issues is needed in the care of the bariatric patient to overcome self-protective barriers and develop a trusting relationship that will facilitate care.[33,48]

Reevaluation and Post Resuscitation Care

Continued assessment of the airway and oxygenation are the highest priority in the bariatric trauma patient, to include monitoring for the following:

- Signs of impending airway or respiratory compromise

- Signs of gastric reflux, which can lead to pulmonary aspiration particularly in a supine patient

- Signs and symptoms of pulmonary embolism, since both obesity and trauma are independent risk factors for this complication[12]

Due to the numerous challenges in evaluation and treatment of the bariatric patient, prolonged immobilization can occur.[49] Ongoing reevaluation includes monitoring for the following:

- Pressure-induced rhabdomyolysis from muscle breakdown (see Chapter 14, Musculoskeletal Trauma)

- Acute compartment syndrome in compromised extremities (see Chapter 14, Musculoskeletal Trauma)

- Skin breakdown, particularly on the occiput area of the head and between skin folds in bariatric patients, along with areas of bony prominence[50]

- If using BiPAP, monitor for the following:[37]

  ○ Skin breakdown across the bridge of the nose due to mask pressure

  ○ Gastric insufflation and potential regurgitation and aspiration

Disposition or Transport

Bariatric centers of excellence are located throughout the United States. Consider if the patient needs to be cared for at a trauma center and/or bariatric center of excellence.

Summary

Trauma nurses encounter increasing numbers of trauma patients who are overweight or obese. This bariatric patient population is a vulnerable group due to the presence of functional and physiologic changes, and at high risk of airway and breathing complications. Standard assessments and interventions may need to be modified, and equipment needs to be available for use in a variety of sizes. Trauma care goals are aimed at diagnosis and management of injury, despite challenges presented by body habitus and limited diagnostic capabilities, while preserving the dignity of the patient.

References

1. Berger, E. (2007). Emergency departments shoulder challenges of providing care, preserving dignity for the "super obese." *Annals of Emergency Medicine, 50*(4), 443–445.

2. World Health Organization. (2012, May). *Obesity and overweight. Fact sheet Number 311.* Retrieved from http://www.who.int/mediacentre/factsheets/fs311/en/index.html

3. Copstead, L. E., & Banasik, J. (Eds.). (2013). *Pathophysiology* (5th ed.). St. Louis, MO: Elsevier Saunders.

4. Ogden, C. L., Carroll, M. D., Kit, B. K., & Flegal, K. M. (2012). Prevalence of obesity in the United States, 2009–2010. *National Center for Health Statistics Data Brief,* (82), 1–8.

5. Organization for Economic and Co-operative Development. (2012). *Obesity update 2012.* Retrieved from http://www.oecd.org/health/healthpoliciesanddata/49716427.pdf

6. Australian Institute of Health and Welfare. (n.d.). *Australia's health 2012.* Retrieved from http://www.aihw.gov.au/australias-health/

7. Kam, J. & Taylor, D. M. (2010). Obesity significantly increases the difficulty of patient management in the emergency department. *Emergency Medicine Australasia, 22*(4), 316–322.

8. Kent, R. W., Forman, J. L., & Bostrom, O. (2010). Is there really a "cushion effect"? A biomechanical investigation of crash injury mechanisms in the obese. *Obesity, 18*(4), 749–753.

9. Matter, K. C., Sinclair, S. A., Hostetler, S. G., & Xiang, H. (2007). A comparison of the characteristics of injuries between obese and non-obese inpatients. *Obesity, 15*(10), 2384–2390.

10. Mica, L., Keel, M., & Trentz, O. (2012). The impact of body mass index on the physiology of patients with polytrauma. *Journal of Critical Care, 27*(6), 722–726.

11. Diaz, J. J., Norris, P. R., Collier, B. R., Berkes, M. B., Ozdas, A., May, A., K., Morris, J. A. (2009). Morbid obesity is not a risk factor for mortality in critically ill trauma patients. *Journal of Trauma, 66*(1), 226–231.

12. Mica, L., Keel, M., & Trentz, O. (2012). The impact of body mass index on the physiology of patients with polytrauma. *Journal of Critical Care, 27*(6) 722–726.

13. Ryb, G. E., & Dischinger, P. C. (2008). Injury severity and outcome of overweight and obese patients after vehicular trauma: A Crash Injury Research and Engineering Network (CIREN) study. *Journal of Trauma, 64*(2), 406–411.

14. Maheshwari, R., Mack, C. D., Kaufman, R. P., Francis, D. O., Bulger, E., M., Nork, S. E., & Henley, M. B. (2009). Severity of injury and outcomes among obese trauma patients with fractures of the femur and tibia: A crash injury research and engineering network (CIREN) study. *Journal of Orthopaedic Trauma, 23*(9), 634–639.

15. Evans, D. C., Stawicki, S. P., Davido, H. T., & Eiferman, D. (2011). Obesity in trauma patients: Correlations of body mass index with outcomes, injury patterns, and complications. *The American Surgeon, 77*(8), 1003–1008.

16. Tagliaferri, F., Compagnone, C., Yoganandan, N., & Gennarelli, T. A. (2007). Traumatic brain injury after frontal crashes: Relationship with body mass index. *Journal of Trauma, 66*(3), 727–729.

17. Dossett, L. A., Heffernan, D., Lightfoot, M., Collier, B., Diaz, J. J., Sawyer, R. G., & May, A. K. (2008). Obesity and pulmonary complications in critically injured adults. *Chest, 134*(5), 974–980.

18. Bonatti, H., & Calland, J. F. (2008). Trauma. *Emergency Medicine Clinics of North America, 26*, 625–648.

19. Jehle, D., Gemme, S., & Jehle, C. (2012). Influence of obesity on mortality of drivers in severe motor vehicle crashes. *American Journal of Emergency Medicine, 30*, 191–195.

20. Toevs, C. C. (2010). Trauma in obese patients. *Critical Care Clinics, 26*, 689–693.

21. Brown, C. V., Rhee, P., Neville, A. L., Sangthong, B., Salim, A., & Demetriades, D. (2006). Obesity and traumatic brain injury. *Journal of Trauma, 61*(3), 572–576.

22. Zarzaur, B. L. & Marshall, S. W. (2008). Motor vehicle crashes obesity and seat belt use: A deadly combination? *Journal of Trauma, 64*(2), 412–419.

23. Meroz, Y., & Gozal, Y. (2007). Management of the obese trauma patient. *Anesthesiology Clinics, 25*, 91–98.

24. Greenleaf, R. M. & Altman, D. T. (2011). Evaluation and treatment of spinal injuries in the obese patient. *Orthopedic Clinics of North America, 42*, 85–93.

25. Gaude, G. S. (2009). Pulmonary manifestation of gastroesophageal reflux disease. *Annals of Thoracic Medicine, 4*(3), 115–123.

26. Peavy, W. C. (2009). Cardiovascular effects of obesity: Implications for critical care. *Critical Care Nursing Clinics of North America, 21*(3), 293–300.

27. Welliver, M., & Bednarzyk, M. (2009). Sedation considerations for the nonintubated obese patient in critical care. *Critical Care Nursing Clinics of North America, 21*(3), 341–352.

28. Siela, D. (2009). Pulmonary aspects of obesity in critical care. *Critical Care Nursing Clinics of North America, 21*(3), 301–310.

29. Littleton, S.W. (2012). Impact of obesity on respiratory function. *Respirology, 17*(1), 43–49.

30. Malbrain, M. L., & De Iaet, I. E. (2009). Intra-abdominal hypertension: Evolving concepts. *Clinics in Chest Medicine, 30*(1), 45–70.

31. Astle, S. M. (2009). Pain management in critically ill obese patients. *Critical Care Nursing Clinics of North America, 21*(3),323–339.

32. Chaudry, S. & Egol, K. A. (2011). Ankle injuries and fractures in the obese patient. *Orthopedic Clinics of North America, 42*, 45–53.

33. Wolf, L. (2008). The obese patient in the ED. *American Journal of Nursing, 108*(12), 77–81.

34. Dargin, J., & Medzon, R. (2010). Emergency department management of the airway in obese adults. *Annals of Emergency Medicine, 56*(2), 95–104.

35. Arbelaez, C., Bartels, S., & Brown, C. A. (2012, July 19). Emergency airway management in the morbidly obese patient. *UptoDate.* Retrieved from http://www.uptodate.com/contents/emergency-airway-management-in-the-morbidly-obese-patient

36. Sifri, Z. C., Kim, H., Lavery, R., Mohr, A., & Livingston, D. H. (2008). The impact of obesity on the outcome of emergency intubation in trauma patients. *Journal of Trauma, 65*(2), 396–400.

37. Hostetler, M. A. (2008). Use of noninvasive positive-pressure ventilation in the emergency department. *Emergency Medical Clinics of North America, 26*, 929–939.

38. Geiling, J. (2010). Critical care of the morbidly obese in disaster. *Critical Care Clinics, 26*, 703–714.

39. Rauen, C. A., Chulay, M., Bridges, E., Vollman, K. M., & Arbour, R. (2008). Seven evidence-based practice habits: Putting some sacred cows out to pasture. *Critical Care Nurse, 28(2), 98-124.*

40. McFarlane, J. (2012). Blood pressure measurement in obese patients. *Critical Care Nurse 32*(6), 70–73.

41. Sinha, A. C. (2009). Some anesthetic aspects of morbid obesity. *Current Opinion in Anesthesiology, 22*, 442–446.

42. MacDonald, K. G. (2008) Early complications of bariatric surgery. In K. B. Jones, K. D. Higa, & J. C. Pareja (Eds.), *Obesity surgery: Principles and practice* (pp. 307–311). New York, NY: McGraw Hill.

43. Vanden Hoak, T. L., Morrison, L. M., Shuster, M., Donnino, M., Sinz, E. K., Lavonas, E. J., Gabrielli, A. (2010). Part 12: Cardiac arrest in special situations: 2010 American Heart Association Guidelines for Cardiopulmonary Resuscitation and Emergency Cardiovascular Care. *Circulation, 122*, S829–S861.

44. McFarlane, J. (2012). Defibrillation of obese patients. *Critical Care Nurse, 32*(2), 73–74.

45. Lin, B. W., Yoshida, D., Quinn, J., & Strehlow, M. (2009). A better way to estimate adult patients' weights. *American Journal of Emergency Medicine, 27*, 1060–1064.

46. Hunt, D. G. (2007). Evaluating equipment and techniques for safe perioperative positioning of the morbidly obese patient. *Bariatric Nursing and Surgical Patient Care, 2(1), 57–63.*

47. Poon, M. Y., & Tarrant, M. (2009). Obesity: Attitudes of undergraduate student nurses and registered nurses. *Journal of Clinical Nursing, 18*, 2355–2365.

48. Bejciy-Spring, S. M. (2008). RESPECT: A model for the sensitive treatment of the bariatric patient. *Bariatric Nursing and Surgical Patient Care*, 3(1), 47–56.

49. Baskerville, J. R., & Moore, R. K. (2012). Morbidly obese patients receive delayed ED care: Body mass index greater than 40 kg/m² have longer disposition times. *American Journal of Emergency Medicine, 30*, 737–740.

50. Rush, A. (2009). Bariatric care: Pressure ulcer prevention. *Wound Essentials, 4*, 68–74.

51. McCallister, J. W., Adkins, E. J., & O'Brien, J. M. (2009). Obesity and acute lung injury. *Clinical Chest Medicine, 30*, 495–508.

Chapter 20 • Special Populations: The Interpersonal Violence Trauma Patient

Cynthia Blank-Reid, MSN, RN, CEN
Marlene L. Bokholdt, MS, RN, CPEN

Objectives

Upon completion of this chapter, the learner will be able to:

1. Identify the risk factors and assessment characteristics of patients experiencing interpersonal violence.

2. Discuss nursing responsibilities in the care of the patient experiencing interpersonal violence.

3. Apply appropriate medical and forensic interventions for the patient who has experienced interpersonal violence.

4. Summarize the role of the nurse in support of prevention programs for interpersonal violence.

Introduction

A Unique Challenge

Violence in society is a complex, multi-faceted problem with many contributing issues. In some ways violence may be compared to a chronic disease that is related to lifestyle and environment. People who experience interpersonal violence do not always report the actual mechanism of injury (MOI), but they are often treated in the emergency department (ED) where trauma nurses and teams have the unique opportunity to assess for and identify these injuries, report according to jurisdictional and organizational policies, protect and care for these patients in a safe environment, and advocate for their well-being.

Some of the challenges related to treating patients who experience interpersonal violence are the factors associated with it, including drug and alcohol use[1,2] and mental illness.[3,4] Since the ED environment can be chaotic, tense, and unpredictable, the patient, family, visitors, and staff may all be at risk for violence.

Epidemiology

The World Health Organization (WHO) has identified two distinct categories of interpersonal violence:

- *Family and intimate partner violence* typically occurs within a family unit or between partners, including child maltreatment, intimate partner violence, and elder maltreatment

- *Community violence* occurs between people who may be strangers or acquainted but are not related. This includes youth violence, random violence, rape or sexual violence, and institutional violence in schools, workplaces, prisons, and care facilities.[2]

Overall, violence in the United States (U.S.) has dropped in the past 15 years. Serious violent crimes against youth dropped 77% between 1994 and 2010.[5] Intimate partner violence dropped 64% in the same time period.[6] However, there are segments of the population where violence has risen. Violence against those with disabilities is four to ten times higher than those without disabilities.[7] Assaults on adults with cognitive disabilities doubled from 2009 to 2011.[8]

Risk Factors

Interpersonal violence is seen across all cultures and environments. However, there are some characteristics that place certain people at higher risk for being subjected to violence. These risk factors include:[6–10]

- Age

- Pregnancy

- Those requiring dependent care

- Disability

Age

The very young and the very old have been identified as at high risk for interpersonal violence and maltreatment, as well as young women ages 18 to 34 years and some adolescents. Additional age-related considerations include the following:

- Children are at risk due to their level of dependency on the caregiver, small size, and the inability to defend themselves or communicate.[10] Children who have an irritable temperament or are developmentally disabled also have a higher risk for maltreatment.[10] See Chapter 17, Special Populations: The Pediatric Trauma Patient, for more information.

- Older adults are vulnerable to maltreatment for many of the same reasons as pediatric patients. The older adult population may also be unable to voice complaints of abuse due to embarrassment, guilt, cultural and language barriers, or distrust of law enforcement. Additionally, they may fear losing their present living arrangement or acts of retribution by the perpetrator.[10] See Chapter 18, Special Populations: The Older Adult Trauma Patient, for additional information.

- Young women have been identified as a population at high risk for interpersonal violence. Reports of data regarding this population vary slightly over recent years. Before 2007, the highest rates were among women ages 18 to 24 years.[6] Since that time, the highest rates of interpersonal violence have been identified in women ages 25 to 34 years.[6]

- The adolescent dating population has been identified at risk for intimate partner violence. In one metropolitan center in 2010, a study revealed 10% of the reports for intimate partner violence were under the age of 18.[11]

Pregnancy
In a review of literature, Symes[2] found several studies revealing higher rates of intimate partner violence among pregnant women. As many as 16% of pregnant women in the U.S. experience intimate partner violence.[2]

Those Requiring Dependent Care
Persons who receive dependent care are commonly those individuals who live in either residential or correctional facilities. This population—who by choice, need, or also for legal reasons reside in a supervised, custodial, or care facility—are in a vulnerable position for interpersonal violence. In all of these situations, others possess some type of authority (physical, financial, and emotional) over the individual. Being aware of this information raises awareness of the trauma nurse to the importance of assessing for injuries consistent with maltreatment in this patient population.

Disability
People with disabilities exhibit certain physical and/or behavioral traits due to the nature of their disability. This makes recognizing the signs and symptoms of abuse and neglect difficult in this population.[12] Occasionally, the abuse of persons with developmental disabilities may be interpreted as a result of well-intentioned but unsuccessful attempts by the caregiver to ensure the person's well-being. Examples of this may include bruising from holding to prevent self-injury or social isolation on the pretext of protecting from others.

Often the perpetrator is a caretaker, family member or acquaintance who is able to continue to mistreat, as the person with a disability may not be able or willing to report the abuse.

Since underreporting in these at-risk populations remains a concern, it is important that the trauma team members maintain a high index of suspicion for identifying interpersonal violence in this population. Identification is the first step toward advocacy.[13]

Types of Interpersonal Violence
Abuse and neglect are the two most commonly identified types of interpersonal violence each with distinguishing characteristics.

Abuse
Abuse has many forms, including:[12]
- Physical abuse (hitting, slapping, punching)
- Emotional abuse (belittling, accusing, threatening)
- Financial abuse (controlling all of a person's money)
- Sexual abuse (forcing unwanted sexual acts)
- Spiritual abuse (denying or belittling spiritual beliefs)

In the context of trauma this chapter will primarily focus on patients experiencing physical, emotional, or sexual violence. Appendix 20-A provides additional definitions for types of abuse and neglect.

Physical Abuse
Injuries from physical abuse may be the result of a single or multiple incidents and can range from minor bruising to death. Abuse injuries include:[12]
- Bruises (in various states of healing, located in one part of the body or on both upper arms)
- Patterned scarring or burn marks
- Human bite marks
- Bruising or swelling that may indicate use of ligatures or restraints (around the ankles, wrists, throat, or penis)
- Dislocated joints
- Spiral, repeated, multiple, or untreated fractures
- Ear and eye injuries (blood behind the eardrum, black eyes, or retinal hemorrhage)
- Bleeding from the ears, nose, or mouth
- Dental injuries or injuries to the mouth
- Patterned injuries (marks shaped like fingers, thumbs, hands, belts, sticks, or other identifiable objects)

- Spotty balding (from pulled hair)
- Sprains
- Abrasions or scrapes
- Vaginal or rectal pain
- Vaginal infections
- Abrasions, bleeding, or bruising in the genital area

Any act of physical violence resulting in any physical injury or pain is physical abuse, so it is important that the trauma nurse maintain an index of suspicion regarding physical abuse patterns of injury, especially when injuries are inconsistent with the history.

Emotional Abuse

Emotional abuse is the deliberate attempt to destroy or impair a person's self-esteem or competence.[9,14] This includes verbal and nonverbal insults, humiliation, or isolation. Other forms of abuse frequently include some level of emotional abuse.[9] Any persistent or unexplained change in a patient's behavior may be the result of possible emotional abuse.

Neglect

Neglect is the failure to provide basic needs, including food, shelter, clothing, education, and medical care[15] and is one of the most common forms of pediatric and elder maltreatment. Emotional neglect may be suspected, but it is very difficult to substantiate. Physical signs may be nonspecific and healthcare providers can only rely on behavioral indicators to identify a possible abusive situation.

Physical Neglect

Physical neglect is the failure to prevent harm to a person or to provide basic needs, such as healthcare, food, shelter, and supervision.[15] This can be to a child or adult who is unable to care for himself or herself and is left unattended. It may also include the lack of providing proper nutrition, seasonally appropriate clothing, or failure to follow up with necessary medical or dental care. If there is an expectation of care and that care is not provided by a caregiver or facility, it is neglect.

Emotional Neglect

Unlike emotional abuse, emotional neglect occurs when caregivers withhold love and nurturing, failing to meet emotional and developmental needs, including psychological care. This is particularly seen in children. Fear and passivity can accompany this type of neglect and require careful listening and sensitive probing to uncover. This type of abuse can lead to feelings of depression, hopelessness, and helplessness in

individuals. Additionally, caregivers may fail to seek necessary care for an individual with emotional or behavioral problems.[15]

Intimate Partner Violence

Intimate partner violence occurs when a current or former intimate partner exhibits abusive behaviors. Women are most often the victims of this type of violence: 85% are women and 15% are men.[6] Intimate partner violence is reported in both heterosexual and same-sex relationships. It can be found across economic, racial, religious, educational, and age lines.[16]

While healthcare providers are taught to recognize the signs of intimate partner violence, not all jurisdictions require mandatory reporting. In cases of interpersonal violence, contusions, minor cuts and lacerations, and bite marks are common to the face, breasts, genitalia, or abdomen, but injuries can be anywhere and all levels of severity. While it is difficult to determine exact numbers, over the past two decades, there has been better education, screening, identification, and social programs directed toward intimate partner violence.

Sexual Violence

According to the National Institute of Justice, *sexual violence* is used in reference to "a constellation of crimes including sexual harassment, sexual assault, and rape."[17] Some estimates put incidence at as high as 30% of women experiencing rape at some point in their lives.[18] It is important for the trauma nurse to offer a medical examination and forensic evaluation if the trauma patient has disclosed or is suspected of having been sexually assaulted. Keep in mind that the unconscious patient may also have experienced sexual violence. Care is always used to assure there is informed consent for a forensic evaluation. It is also important to the care of these patients who have experienced a loss of control to provide them with choices regarding their care in the ED. Sexual assault nurse examiners (SANEs), forensic nurse examiners (FNEs), and victim advocates can help to provide expert care, evidence collection and documentation, and community advocacy for sexual assault and rape victims.[19, 20]

Drug-facilitated Sexual Violence

Drug-facilitated sexual violence is associated with alcohol or medications such as flunitrazepam and gamma-hydroxybutyrate. These substances can go undetected if added to any drink, food, or substance. The effects of these drugs are sedation and amnesia, and victims often cannot resist the assault or may not be aware that a sexual act has occurred.[21] Other substances such as marijuana, benzodiazepines, cocaine, heroin, and amphetamines can also be associated with sexual violence.

Initial Assessment for Interpersonal Violence

See Chapter 5, Initial Assessment for the systematic approach to the nursing care of the trauma patient. The following considerations are for specific interpersonal violence patient populations. Acute care and treatment, expert crisis intervention, evidence collection, detailed documentation, and appropriate referrals and counseling are considered for each patient.

Preparation
Safe Practice

Every person is entitled to feel and be safe. Part of being safe is having an environment where an individual can attend work or school, eat, sleep, or relax and not experience abuse or neglect. This safe environment can be a home, hospital, residential care facility, school, or institution. Trauma nurses can take action to provide the patient a safe environment while in the ED and work with the patient and available resources to ensure the patient has a safe environment to go to following discharge. An important consideration when caring for this patient population is to develop a safety plan.

Trauma nurses are also entitled to feel and be safe in their work environment. See Chapter 21, Psychosocial Aspects of Trauma Care, for additional information on workplace violence.

Safe Care

Safe care includes education and preparation to better care for the specific patient population. One study of nurses in a Level II trauma center showed that nurses demonstrate a willingness to incorporate forensic principles into their practice and consider forensic protocols important to their practice.[22] Although the majority (58%) had received some education in forensics, nurses felt that additional education would help them to more effectively deal with forensic issues.[22] Several national nursing organizations—The American Association of Colleges of Nursing (AACN), American Nurses Association (ANA), Emergency Nurses Association (ENA), and The Joint Commission (TJC)—suggested specific roles

for healthcare professionals related to the detection and management of forensic cases. Table 20-1 outlines recommendations for healthcare organizations regarding forensic cases.[22]

Trauma Team Considerations

Due to the prevalence of interpersonal violence in the trauma patient population, trauma team members are faced with caring for increasing numbers of these patients. Identifying and addressing any gaps in knowledge and skills regarding the care of this patient population help the team provide care in a skilled and efficient manner. Healthcare providers can find abuse or injury to vulnerable patient populations extremely difficult to manage both professionally and personally. In these circumstances, a professional approach may be in conflict with the emotions the trauma nurse may be feeling. The trauma nurse and team members can identify and evaluate their personal emotions, beliefs, values, and past experiences to determine how these perceptions may affect their attitude toward these patient situations. Based on the cases and situations involved, debriefings and counseling may be indicated for all involved. See Chapter 21, Psychosocial Aspects of Trauma Care, for more information.

Specific Considerations for the Care of Patients with Physical Abuse
H–History

The history of a patient who has been physically abused may include:

- History inconsistent with developmental milestone achievements or abilities

- No explanation for the injury, discrepancy between the caregiver's and patient's accounts, or explanation inconsistent with identified injuries

- Vague, unclear, or changing account of how the injury occurred

- Inappropriate reaction to injury (failure to cry with pain)

- Unreasonable delay in seeking medical attention

- Unrealistic expectations of the patient's developmental abilities by the caregiver

- History of previous ED visits or hospitalization for an injury or a medical condition that might have been prevented with appropriate care

Another consideration is safety of children in the care of the patient who may have experienced interpersonal violence. Ask if the children are safe, and if they are not or unsure, follow jurisdictional policies in ensuring their safety.

Table 20-1. Forensic Recommendations for Healthcare Organizations

Procedures
• Develop procedures for documenting suspected abuse and neglect
• Develop procedures for safeguarding of evidence
• Develop procedures for photo documentation
• Develop procedures for collection of forensic specimens
• Develop chain-of-custody procedures
• Establish reporting and/or referral processes
• Collaborate with emergency physicians, social services, and law enforcement personnel to develop forensic guidelines in the emergency setting
• Provide education related to testifying in legal proceedings
• Provide education related to legal and ethical issues in treating and reporting
• Advocate for the addition of forensic education classes to undergraduate and graduate nursing programs

From Eldredge.[22]

H–Head-to-toe Assessment

When assessing the patient with suspected physical abuse, inconsistencies between injury history and the injuries sustained should alert the trauma team to recognize the possibility of abuse as the cause. Examples of the injuries are discussed below.

Head Injuries

Certain types of head injuries can indicate interpersonal violence. For example, skull fractures, intra- or extracranial bleeds, a retinal hemorrhage, or other eye injuries such as a dislocated lens, or corneal laceration, are unusual in children. Abusive head trauma is a serious form of child maltreatment that occurs when the child has sustained sudden shaking or other impact injuries.[9] A head injury in an adult that is inconsistent with the history may also be suspect.

Bruises

Bruises are often seen in cases of interpersonal violence. Those intentionally inflicted injuries have distinguishing characteristics that can raise the index of suspicion for maltreatment. These include:

- Unexplained bruises or welts
- Multiple or symmetric bruises or marks
- Bruises and welts to the face, mouth, neck, chest, abdomen, back, flank, thighs, or genitalia
- Bruises and welts with patterns descriptive of an object such as a looped cord, belt buckle, shoe or boot tread, wire hanger, chain, wooden spoon, hair brush, hand or pinch marks
- Bruises in various stages of healing

Burns

Correlation of the severity and pattern of the burn injury with the history provides a basis for the identification of inflicted burns. See Chapter 15, Surface and Burn Trauma, for more information. As with bruises, inflicted burns have distinguishing characteristics including:[15]

- Burns to the lips or tongue, especially if surrounded by bruising: This may indicate forcing hot liquids
- Burns to the rectum or perineum
- Bilateral burns: A stocking- or glove-type burn, with sharp lines of demarcation, indicates being held down in hot liquid, as opposed to an accidental burn, which usually has irregular borders and splash burns as the extremity is rapidly removed from the liquid
- Sharp lines of demarcation, limited injury to the protected area, and uniform burn depth
- Burns in the shape of an object such as a cigar or cigarette, iron, heating grate, or stove

Bite Injuries

Ovoid patterns of bruising, abrasions, or lacerations may be indicative of a bite mark, triggering the need for the patient to be screened and evaluated for interpersonal violence. A canine tooth mark will commonly be the most prominent or deepest parts of the bite. If the distance is greater than 3 cm, the bite is most likely the result of an adult human, since the average space between adult human canine teeth is 2.5 to 4.0 cm.[23]

Clenched-fist injuries, resulting from a clenched fist striking the teeth of another person are treated as bites. Due to the site of injury (the knuckles) and the velocity, there is a higher risk of injury to bone, joint, tendon, or cartilage.[24] With an open wound, there may be increased risk for transmission of infection through blood and body fluids.

Skeletal Injuries

Fractures resulting from abuse may be single or multiple fractures, recent or old, or a combination. Fractures can also be found in one or more sites. One of the more commonly injured bones from abuse is the metaphysis of the humerus from the victim being grasped by the arm, pulled, swung, or jerked. In this injury, a piece of the bone is broken from the growth plate by shearing forces.[25] Other types of suspicious fractures include bilateral or symmetric fractures, transverse, oblique and spiral shaft fractures, rib fractures, scapular or sternal fractures, multiple fractures in various bones, and fractures in different stages of healing.[9]

Abdominal Injuries

Abdominal indications of interpersonal violence in children include intestinal perforation, hemorrhage, and laceration, contusion, or hematoma to the organs of the abdomen, including liver, spleen, and kidney, due to blunt force trauma. Concurrent findings such as abdominal distention, vomiting and abdominal pain, bruising, fever, hematuria, and shock (septic and hypovolemic) may also be signs of abuse.[9]

In adults, abdominal injuries are more commonly seen in the pregnant population and/or related to sexual violence around the genitalia and rectal area.

Psychosocial Impact

Victims of interpersonal violence can experience a range of emotions, from anger and rage to terror and withdrawal. As these may develop following the ED visit, refer patients to appropriate follow-up counseling.

Diagnostic Procedures

- Evidence collection: Collaborate with local law enforcement, regional chapters of the International Association of Forensic Nurses (IAFN), and experts within the facility to assure proper protocols are in place for collection of evidence. See "Evidence Collection" for general considerations.

- Imaging studies: Full-body radiographic films are used to determine if there is evidence of previously healed fractures as well as any missed injuries. If fractures

are suspected or confirmed, document with at least two views. Computed tomography (CT) is used for the detection of any intra- or extracranial injuries such as skull fractures, hemorrhage, or hematoma. CT scans can also document solid and hollow abdominal organ injuries.

- Laboratory studies: Laboratory studies include a toxicology screen if there is a suspicion of ingestion or exposure to toxic substances, use of alcohol, or overmedication. Blood and urine are best for collection, as the substance used may have been metabolized and is only present in the urine. If excessive bruising is discovered, complete blood count, platelet count, and coagulation studies can rule out bleeding disorders.

Specific Considerations for the Care of Patients with Neglect and Emotional Abuse

H–History

A thorough history, a high index of suspicion, and keen assessment skills are essential to identify the subtle cues of neglect and emotional abuse. Indications in a patient's history include:

- Delay in seeking healthcare for an injury or illness or poor healthcare, lack of follow-up or compliance with medications, and history of missed appointments

- History of previous injuries, ingestions, or exposures to toxic substances

- Excessive absenteeism from school or other social events or programs; isolation from friends and other family members

- Substance abuse

- Delinquency or repeated encounters with law enforcement

- History of being left alone, abandoned, or inadequate supervision

H–Head-to-toe Assessment

Possible indications of neglect include:

- Malnourishment, chronic dehydration, or nonorganic failure to thrive (weight below the fifth percentile)

- Inactivity or extreme passiveness

- Poor hygiene and/or inappropriate attire

- Untreated dental caries and periodontal disease that can lead to pain, infection, and loss of function, and affect learning, communication, nutrition, and other activities

- Deficits or delays in emotional and intellectual development, especially language

- Self-soothing behaviors such as finger sucking, biting, scratching, or rocking

Diagnostic Procedures

Diagnostic procedures commonly performed in patients with suspected neglect include:

- Radiographic studies to determine if there is evidence of previous or undiagnosed fractures

- Toxicology screen if an ingestion or exposure to toxic substances or overmedication is suspected

Specific Considerations for the Care of Patients Who Have Experienced Sexual Violence

Preparation and Triage

Preparation considerations include:

- Use a safe, private room for the primary patient consultation and initial law enforcement interviews

- Offer a waiting area for family members and friends and provide childcare if possible

- Assess and respond to safety concerns, such as threats to the patient or staff

- Follow facility and jurisdictional procedures, while respecting patients and maximizing evidence preservation

Triage considerations include:

- Due to the time-sensitive nature of the situation, treatment required, and recognizing that every minute patients spend waiting to be examined may cause loss of evidence and undue trauma, patients who present following sexual assault are assigned a triage category of Emergency Severity Index 2, or its equivalent in other triage systems, and they are considered a priority[19]

- Make all efforts to bring the patient immediately to a private room

- Notify specially trained examiners[19]

Specially Trained Examiners

The use of specially trained examiners to conduct the examination is a growing trend in the U.S.[26] These personnel include the following:

- SANEs are registered nurses with specialized education to fulfill clinical requirements and perform these examinations

  - Some nurses have been certified as SANE–Adult and Adolescent (SANE–A) and SANE–Pediatric (SANE-P) through the IAFN

- Others fulfill clinical requirements as FNEs, enabling them to collect forensic evidence in a variety of situations

- The terms "sexual assault forensic examiner" (SAFE) and "sexual assault examiner" (SAE) can be used more broadly to describe a healthcare provider (a physician, physician assistant, nurse, or nurse practitioner) with special education and demonstrated clinical expertise to perform this examination

Initial Assessment

If life-threatening injuries are present, assessment proceeds as described in Chapter 5, Initial Assessment. Care of non–life-threatening injuries may wait until after evidence collection has been completed.[19]

History

History includes the following:[19]

- A detailed description of the incident, if appropriate, based on facility policy and guidelines. Some facilities recommend delaying description to perform the interview one time, including nursing, medicine, social services, and law enforcement, to minimize emotional trauma with repeated description of the event. This also produces a single document of the patient's stated recollection, eliminating contradictory reports. This record includes the following:

  - Date, time, and place of the incident

  - Events surrounding the incident

    - Document everything the patient remembers about the incident

    - Be as detailed as possible

    - Be objective and use direct quotes

  - Information regarding all acts committed by the perpetrator, including verbal and physical threats, weapons or restraints used, sites of penetration or ejaculation, and the use of a condom

  - Injuries associated with the incident

  - Activities by the victim following the incident, such as bathing or showering, wound care, drinking, eating, urination and defecation, or changing clothes

- Additional obstetric and gynecologic history for female patients

  - Gravida and para status

  - Date of last menstrual period

  - Current method of birth control and compliance with the method

  - Time of last consensual intercourse (oral, vaginal, anal)

    - Note routine and recent condom use

- In any suspected drug-facilitated sexual violence, the history may include:

- The patient may have awakened in strange surroundings with disheveled clothing, unclear memory, or a feeling of being sexually violated
- If some memory of the event remains, the victim may describe feeling paralyzed, powerless, or a disassociation of mind and body
- Symptoms may be similar to alcohol intoxication, although the severity may not match the amount consumed

The patient may describe the sudden onset of symptoms after consuming a drink (15–20 minutes after ingestion), such as drowsiness, lack of coordination, confusion, or impaired memory to coma.[27]

Evidence Collection

Evidence protection and collection can be an essential aspect of the care provided to the patient who has experienced interpersonal violence. Consideration is given to the patient's potential life-threatening injuries, emotional response, as well as the consideration of the patient's rights. Complete the forensic examination only after the patient's immediate life threats are treated and the patient is stabilized. Consider the following when collecting evidence:[28]

- Patients are cautioned not to wash, change clothes, urinate, defecate, smoke, drink, or eat until initially evaluated by examiners, unless necessary for treating acute medical needs
- Clothing:
  - When cutting to remove the patient's clothing, avoid any areas that appear to be cut or torn by a weapon or projectile, are stained or have debris, such as gunshot residue[28]
  - Dry and store each item of patient clothing in a separate paper bag. Plastic bags are not recommended for evidence since moisture can cause fungal growth and evidence can be rendered useless.[28]
- Carefully assess all skin surfaces and ask the patient about areas that hurt or were injured
- In case of gunshot wounds, bagging the hands for forensic evaluation for residue may protect important evidence
- Use body diagrams to identify and describe each injury in detail, using correct terminology
  - As direct quotes are an important aspect of clear and complete documentation, certain terms used by the patient may not reflect medical terminology
  - Documentation includes explanation of the mutually agreed-upon terminology for clarification

- Forensic photography of injuries:
  - Many jurisdictions have policies on who is qualified to take forensic photographs. Please follow organizational guidelines for forensic photography.
  - Obtain photographs whenever possible before medical treatment[29]
    - Obtain consent
    - Use good lighting
    - Include a patient identifier (date of birth, medical record label) in the photograph
    - Take a distance shot of the whole body; take a picture at midrange and a close-up of the injury
    - Include a measuring device, such as a ruler or scale (the American Board of Forensic Odontology scale is recommend)
    - Photograph bite marks for dental forensic analysis
- Specimen collection:[30]
  - Swabs
    - Moisten swab with sterile water
    - Swab the following:
      ◇ Potential areas of retained body fluids, including sites of kissing or licking
      ◇ Bite marks
      ◇ Vagina and external and vaginal vault
      ◇ Penis
      ◇ Anus
    - Label all swabs for the specific site, including date, patient's name, and name of collector
    - Allow the swab to dry completely
  - Scrape under the fingernails
    - In some jurisdictions, swabbing may be preferred
  - Comb the patient's hair, both head hair and pubic hair. This step can help investigators differentiate between strands of the patient's hair and that of the perpetrator.

Forensic Evidence Chain of Custody

Securing the evidence or maintaining the chain of custody is as important as the process of collection. Use evidence tape to seal and sign or initial each receptacle once sealed. Place all evidence in a locked cabinet or area with a log of who holds the key, when and by whom it was accessed, and when and to whom it was given. Include name, badge number, and agency of the officer receiving the evidence.[19,26,30]

Interventions

Following evidence collection, the trauma nurse addresses any non–life-threatening injuries. Additional considerations for the patient presenting to the ED following sexual violence include the following:

- Provide emotional support
- Contact a victim advocate to provide services to the patient, if not already done
- Follow jurisdictional and organizational policies regarding reporting
- Complete documentation to include body maps, and diagrams
- Provide emergency contraceptive prophylaxis
- Provide sexually transmitted infection prophylaxis, including human immunodeficiency virus (HIV) prophylaxis
  - Adhere to current Centers for Disease Control and Prevention (CDC) guidelines and refer to the hospital's protocols
- Arrange for follow-up care to address any new infections, monitor side effects, and counseling or other treatments

Mandated Reporting

A *mandated reporter* is someone who is required by law to report suspected maltreatment. This designation may be applied to many professionals, including law enforcement, teachers, clergy, and others. Nurses are mandated reporters in most jurisdictions and as such are responsible for raising the question, assessing and reporting the suspicion to social services or law enforcement. Traditionally, mandated reporting has been required for suspected child maltreatment, but many states have adopted legislation to require reporting for suspected abuse of adults.[9,10,15,31] Procedures for reporting also vary by facility, so refer to the hospital's policies and procedures.

Prevention

In 2012, the U.S. Preventative Services Task Force (USPSTF) recommended the use of screening instruments designed for healthcare settings which can accurately identify women experiencing intimate partner violence.[32] This report updated previous studies that found evidence supporting screening was lacking. USPSTF noted that screening women for intimate partner violence can increase reporting, reduce incidence, and improve health outcomes depending on the population screened and outcome measured.[32] However, effectiveness trials have been noted to have important limitations.

Identification of this patient population is fundamental to the provision of care and improved health outcomes in this patient population and screening remains a recommendation of several nursing and physician organizations.[16] Considerable resources are available to trauma team members for use in the care of patients who have experienced interpersonal violence. Topics range from prevention resources, and care guidelines to screening tools, questionnaires, safety plans, and other helpful documentation tools. The CDC offers several resources as outlined in Box 20-1.

ENA and IAFN have developed a joint position statement that provides suggestions for nurses regarding interpersonal violence prevention and documention.[33] The organizations recommend the following:[33]

Box 20-1. CDC Online Resources for Interpersonal Violence Prevention

Organization	Website
Preventing Intimate Partner and Sexual Violence: Program Activities Guide	www.cdc.gov/violenceprevention/pub/ipv_sv_guide.html
CDC Facebook Page on Violence Prevention	www.facebook.com/vetoviolence
National Domestic Violence Hotline: 1-800-799-SAFE (7233), 1-800-787-3224 TTY	www.ndvh.org
National Coalition Against Domestic Violence	www.ncadv.org
National Sexual Violence Resource Center	www.nsvrc.org
Futures Without Violence	www.futureswithoutviolence.org (formerly Family Violence Prevention Fund)

- Increasing the awareness and understanding of trauma and forensic nurses in order to become more knowledgeable of family violence and intimate partner violence and to show a demonstrated commitment to assimilating the skills of identification, assessment, intervention, prevention, documentation, and reporting into their practice

- Incorporating education regarding the issues of family and intimate partner violence is important to enriching nursing curricula, and supporting mandatory continuing education is essential to developing the skills of healthcare professionals to care for this patient population

- Collaboration with other professions or disciplines to develop and implement strategies, protocols, and education for improved identification, reporting, protection, and care of all individuals and families at risk for family and intimate partner violence, maltreatment, and neglect

Additional interventions trauma team members may use in the prevention of interpersonal violence include:

- Providing educational material regarding interpersonal violence and intimate partner violence

- Making flyers and booklets with prevention measures available in the ED waiting room, treatment areas, restrooms

- Being knowledgeable regarding surrounding community services, self-help groups, shelters, legal aid services, and educational in-services from victim advocate groups

- Making appropriate referrals and follow-up appointments

- Providing comprehensive, yet specific discharge instructions

  ○ Sexual abuse prevention is more than teaching an individual to say "no"

  ○ It also attempts to teach safety in terms of potential risky situations and to notify an adult or authority figure no matter what the other person says or does

- Developing a safety plan for patients who may choose to return to a potentially unsafe environment

Summary

Trauma patients who have experienced interpersonal violence require special considerations in addition to trauma team care. Trauma team members can assure optimal delivery of trauma care to these at-risk patients by:

- Identifying and addressing any trauma team member knowledge gaps regarding the care of this patient population

- Identifying and evaluating personal emotions, beliefs, values, and past experiences to determine how these perceptions may affect their attitude toward these patient situations

- Providing safe, non-judgmental, knowledgeable and professional care

- Collaborating with FNEs, SANEs, and other care providers to assure optimal approach to serving the needs of this patient population

- Being aware of the resources in their community for this patient population

Appendix 20-A. Classification of Neglect and Abuse

Term	Definition
Physical abuse	• Any act of physical violence resulting in any physical injury or pain, usually by either a caregiver or by an intimate partner
Emotional abuse	• The deliberate attempt to destroy or impair a person's self-esteem or competence • Can include telling another that they are worthless, flawed, unloved, or unwanted • Involved in all forms of abuse • Any persistent and unexplained change in the patient's behavior is important due to possible emotional abuse
Neglect	• One of the most common forms of abuse • Characterized by the failure to provide the person's basic needs • Can be physical, emotional, or educational
Physical neglect	• The refusal of or delay in seeking healthcare, abandonment, expulsion from the home, and/or inadequate supervision
Emotional neglect	• Inattention to a person's basic needs for affection or refusal or failure to provide needed psychological care • Physical signs are often nonspecific • Behavioral indicators such as depression can identify a possible abusive situation
Educational neglect	• Includes the allowance of chronic absenteeism, failure to enroll a child of mandatory school age in school, and failure to attend to a special educational need
Sexual abuse	• The engaging of a person in sexual activities that they either cannot comprehend, are developmentally unprepared for, cannot give informed consent for, or that violate the social and legal norms of society • Includes but not limited to digital manipulation, fondling, actual or attempted oral, vaginal or anal intercourse, exhibitionism, human trafficking, and pornography
Financial exploitation	• The deliberate misuse of a vulnerable individual's personal or government funds for reasons other than their care • Usually done by a third party who has been granted oversight authority to care for the individual • Includes the deliberate withholding of funds and needs (food, clothing, medical care, etc.) so that an individual's funds are not used

Data from Cohen,[15] Cohen,[16] and Weintraub.[19]

References

1. Begle, A. M., Hanson, R. F., Danielson, C. K., McCart, M. R., Ruggiero, K. J., Amstadter, A. B., ... & Kilpatrick, D. G. (2011). Longitudinal pathways of victimization, substance use, and delinquency: Findings from the National Survey of Adolescents. *Addictive Behaviors, 36*(7), 682–689.

2. Symes, L. (2011). Abuse across the lifespan: Prevalence, risk, and protective factors. *Nursing Clinics of North America, 46*, 391–411.

3. Bradford, J. M. (2008). Violence and mental disorders. *Canadian Journal of Psychiatry, 53*(10), 635–636.

4. Rhodes, K. V., Houry, D., Cerulli, C., Straus, H., Kaslow, N. J., & McNutt, L. A. (2009). Intimate partner violence and comorbid mental health conditions among urban male patients. *Annals of Family Medicine, 7*, 47–55.

5. White, N., & Lauritsen, J. L. (2012, December). *Violent crime against youth, 1994–2010.* Retrieved from http://www.bjs.gov/content/pub/pdf/vcay9410.pdf

6. Catalano, S. (2012). *Intimate partner violence, 1993–2010.* Retrieved from http://bjs.ojp.usdoj.gov/index.cfm?ty=pbdetail&iid=4536

7. Focht-New, F., Barol, B., Clements, P. T., & Milliken, T. F. (2008). Persons with developmental disability exposed to interpersonal violence and crime: Approaches for intervention. *Perspectives in Psychiatric Care, 44*(2), 89–98.

8. Harrell, E. (2012). *Crime against persons with disabilities, 2009–2011 – Statistical tables.* Retrieved from http://bjs.ojp.usdoj.gov/index.cfm?ty=pbdetail&iid=4574

9. Black, A. (2012). Child maltreatment. In Emergency Nurses Association, *Emergency nursing pediatric course* (4th ed., pp. 343–358). Des Plaines, IL: Author.

10. Quinn, K. M., & Benson, W. F. (2012). The states' elder abuse victim services: a system still in search of support. *Generations: Journal of the American Society on Aging, 36*(3), 66–72.

11. Thomas, K. A., Sorenson, S. B., & Joshi, M. (2010). Police-documented incidents of intimate partner violence among young women. *Journal of Women's Health, 19*(6), 1079–1087.

12. State of Florida Agency for Persons with Disabilities. (n.d.). *Common signs and symptoms of abuse.* Retrieved from apd.myflorida.com/zero-tolerance/common-signs/

13. Family Violence Prevention Fund. (2004). Part II: Guidelines for responding to intimate partner violence victimization in health settings. In *National consensus guidelines on identifying and responding to domestic violence victimization in healthcare settings* (pp. 11–20). San Francisco, CA: Author. Retrieved from http://www.futureswithoutviolence.org/userfiles/file/Consensus.pdf

14. Sellas, M. I., & Krouse, L. H. (2011, June 8). *Elder abuse.* Retrieved from http://emedicine.medscape.com/article/805727-overview

15. Cohen, S. (2013). Abuse and neglect. In Emergency Nurses Association, *Sheehy's manual of emergency care* (7th ed., pp. 521–530). St. Louis, MO: Mosby Elsevier.

16. Cohen, S. (2013). Intimate partner violence. In Emergency Nurses Association, *Sheehy's manual of emergency care* (7th ed., pp. 531–536). St. Louis, MO: Mosby Elsevier.

17. National Institute of Justice. (2010, October 26). *Rape and sexual violence.* Retrieved from http://nij.gov/topics/crime/rape-sexual-violence/welcome.htm

18. Wadsworth, P., & van Order P. (2012). Care of the sexually assaulted woman. *The Journal for Nurse Practitioners, 8*(6), 433–440.

19. Weintraub, B. (2013). Sexual assault. In Emergency Nurses Association, *Sheehy's manual of emergency care* (7th ed., pp. 537–546). St. Louis, MO: Mosby Elsevier.

20. International Association of Forensic Nurses. (n.d.). *What is forensic nursing.* Retrieved at http://www.iafn.org/displaycommon.cfm?an=1&subarticlenbr=137

21. Kaufman, M., & Committee on Adolescence. (2008). Care of the adolescent sexual assault victim. *Pediatrics, 122*, 462–470.

22. Eldredge, K. (2010). Forensics in the trauma setting. *On the Edge.* Retrieved from http://iafn.org/displaycommon.cfm?an=1&subarticlenbr=436

23. American Academy of Pediatrics; American Academy of Pediatric Dentistry. (1999). Oral and dental aspects of child abuse and neglect. *Pediatrics, 104*(2), 348–350.

24. Wheeless, C. R. (2012). Clenched fist injury. In *Textbook of orthopaedics.* Retrieved from http://www.wheelessonline.com/ortho/clenched_fist_injury

25. Baz, B., Wang, N.E. (2012). Physical abuse of children: Identification, evaluation, and management in the ED setting. *Pediatric Emergency Medicine Reports, 17*(7), 77-91.

26. Henry, T. (Ed.). (2013). *Atlas of sexual violence.* St. Louis, MO: Elsevier Mosby

27. Madea, B. and Musshoff, F. (2009). Knock-out drugs: Their prevalence, modes of action, and means of detection. *Deutsches Aerzteblatt International, 106*(20), 341-347.

28. Eisert, P. J., Eldredge, K., Hartlaub, T., Huggins, E., Keirn, G., O'Brien, P., ... March K. S. (2010). CSI: New @ York: Development of forensic evidence collection guidelines for the emergency department. *Critical Care Nursing Quarterly, 33*(2), 190–199.

29. Blue Cross Blue Shield Blue Care Network of Michigan. (2007). *Reach out: Intervening in domestic violence and abuse. The healthcare provider's reference guide to partner & elder abuse.* Detroit, MI: Author. Retrieved at http://www.bcbsm.com/pdf/DV_ReferenceGuide.pdf

30. Jenny, C. (Ed.). (2010). *Child abuse and neglect: Diagnosis, treatment, and evidence.* St Louis, MO: Elsevier/Saunders.

31. Anetzberger, G. J. (2012). An update on the nature and scope of elder abuse. *Generations: Journal of the American Society on Aging, 36*(3), 12–20.

32. Nelson, H. Bougatsos, C., & Blazina, I. (2012, May). *Screening women for intimate partner violence: A systematic review to update the 2004 U.S. Preventive Services Task Force recommendation.* Retrieved from http://www.uspreventiveservicestaskforce.org/uspstf12/ipvelder/ipvelderart.htm

33. Emergency Nurses Association; International Association of Forensic Nurses. (2013). *Joint position statement on intimate partner violence.* Retrieved from http://www.ena.org/about/position/Pages/Default.aspx

Chapter 21 • Psychosocial Aspects of Trauma Care

Mary Margaret Healy, MA, BSN, CEN, CPEN
Diane Gurney, MS, RN, CEN, FAEN

Objectives

Upon completion of this chapter, the learner will be able to:

1. Describe causes and characteristics of psychological distress in the trauma patient, family, and trauma nurse immediately after a major trauma incident.

2. Evaluate the effectiveness of appropriate psychosocial interventions for the trauma patient, family, and trauma nurse.

3. Indicate interventions related to psychosocial aspects of the trauma patient, family, and trauma nurse.

4. Discuss ethical issues that affect the care of the trauma patient, family, and trauma nurse.

Introduction

Patients who experience a traumatic injury are at risk for suffering long-term physical effects of those injuries. Additionally, many patients and their families experience psychological, emotional, and spiritual effects as a result of trauma.

Evidence suggests that continued exposure to traumatic situations can affect trauma nurses as well. Nurses who routinely work with severely injured and traumatized patients may be affected physically, psychologically, emotionally, and behaviorally.[1]

Focusing on the psychological aspects of trauma patient care, completing a thoughtful assessment, and planning and implementation of psychosocial interventions can significantly affect recovery.[2]

Understanding the human response to injury and disability can provide the nurse with the tools to enhance patient care and increase self-awareness of how repeated exposure to these events may negatively affect one's well-being.

Human Response to Trauma

Traumatic events can be characterized as dangerous, frightening, unpredictable, or uncontrollable threats to life. Although responses to traumatic events vary, support and guidance are needed for patients and their families as they work through the process of coping with trauma.

Various characteristics are common to this human response:[3]
- Emotional reactions to difficult events
- Loss of ability to function
- Feelings of being overwhelmed[4]
- Exceeding coping resources[5]

The following factors can affect the level of distress experienced by the patient and his or her family:[4]
- The nature of the injury or traumatic event, including:
  ◦ Intensity
  ◦ Inescapability
  ◦ Uncontrollability
  ◦ Unexpectedness
- Characteristics of the individual exposed to the event, including:
  ◦ Previous exposure to trauma
  ◦ Support systems
  ◦ Cultural norms
- The reaction or response, including:
  ◦ Coping mechanisms
  ◦ Defense mechanisms

These factors influence the experience of injury, loss, and difficult news in the emergency care setting and can range from stoic acceptance to tearful response, anger, or even violent outbursts.

Psychosocial Nursing Care of the Trauma Patient

The psychosocial assessment begins after life-threatening injuries have been identified and stabilized. See Chapter 5, Initial Assessment, for the systematic approach to care of the trauma patient.

Secondary Survey

H–History

Complete a psychosocial history assessment in order to:

- Determine the patient's recollection of the event

- Monitor the patient's description of and reaction to the incident

- Provide a baseline for ongoing reevaluation of status

- Plan for additional resources that may be needed to cope with the effects of the event

H–Head-to-toe Assessment

Complete all necessary assessments to rule out a physiologic cause for behavioral signs and symptoms. Many signs can have either physiologic or emotional causes that can be difficult to differentiate. These signs may vary depending upon the physical, cognitive, or emotional reactions to the event, including:[6]

- Physical: Heart palpitations, tachypnea, hyperventilation, headache, nausea, vomiting, diaphoresis, muscle pain, shaking, feeling jittery, or being easily startled

- Cognitive: Repetitive questioning, forgetfulness, numbness or a blunted affect, intrusive thoughts or repetitive description of events, hyper-alertness, silence, or difficulty with concentration

- Emotional: Silence, generalized fearfulness, tearfulness, anger, disbelief, vulnerability, or fear of being alone or desire to be left alone

Interventions

Repeated reassessments can guide interventions that may help to lessen symptoms. For example, if the patient repeatedly questions events leading to injury, continue to orient the patient to place, time, and location and provide assurance that he or she is safe. Present a calm and soothing demeanor to facilitate coping.

The RESPOND mnemonic provides an outline for interventions for both the patient and family after a traumatic event:

- **R**eassure the patient and family that they are safe and well-cared for

- **E**stablish rapport with the patient and family; introduce yourself and the trauma team. Create a connection between the patient and key trauma team members.

- **S**upport the patient through the initial aftermath of the trauma. Help the patient contact family or friends. Assign a primary support person from the trauma team. Involve the hospital chaplain or bereavement team if available and the patient agrees to this support.

  ○ Patients or family members may prefer to have a social worker, a trusted friend, or advisor from the community fill the role of support

  ○ Some patients prefer to be alone or to involve others only when the extent of injury is known or admission is likely. It is important to consider the patient's wishes.

- **P**lan care; manage **p**ain.

  ○ Explain the plan of care with the patient and family succinctly, clearly, and in simple language

  ○ Explain the need for diagnostic procedures in order to evaluate the extent of injury

  ○ Include the patient and family in the planning of care when possible

  ○ Keep the patient or family apprised of what to expect next in the plan of care

  ○ Explain the pain assessment tool upon patient arrival and regularly reassess pain, the response to medication, or need for additional analgesia (see Chapter 8, Pain, for more information)

- **O**ffer hope.

  ○ While one should not offer false hope regarding the extent of injury or likelihood of survival, it is essential to provide reassurance and support to the patient and family with open, compassionate communication

  ○ With the patient's consent, update family members at regular intervals and as changes occur

- **N**ever deliver news of death or disability alone to the patient or the family

  ○ Patients and family members or friends can exhibit various reactions to news of a traumatic event, ranging from withdrawal to outbursts of anger

  ○ Rely upon colleague support when approaching the patient and family with difficult news. For example, conference or three-way calling by the physician and the trauma team is a great option when news of severe disability or death of a patient must be delivered via telephone to family.

- **D**etermine the patient's needs
  - Encourage the patient and family to express his or her feelings and needs following a traumatic event
  - Support patient involvement in the planning of care
  - Allow the opportunity to express fear, anger, and vulnerability in response to the event

Selected Psychosocial Trauma Reactions

Stress Reaction
Stress reaction is caused by an unusual event—usually an experience that elicits a feeling of dread, fear, helplessness, or threat to life or safety.[6] Stress reactions are normal responses and usually short term.

Crisis
Crisis occurs following an extraordinary or traumatic event. Usual coping mechanisms no longer work, and the patient is unable to function normally due to distress.[7] Patients become anxious and disorganized and may panic, or try to escape. They may also revert to less functional behaviors such as violence, substance abuse, and depression.[8]

The trauma nurse can apply basic principles of crisis assessment and intervention to these situations (Table 21-1).[8] The goal of the trauma team is to support the patient in his or her progress toward independent functioning and recovery.[8]

Fear and Anxiety
After experiencing a traumatic event, patients can be fearful and anxious with variable degrees of uneasiness, distress, and worry. The trauma nurse helps the patient to manage and mitigate the negative effects of these emotions (Table 21-1). Overall, the provision of clear information delivered in a thoughtful, consistent manner to patients and families can increase perception of control, diminishing fear and anxiety.[7]

Grief, Bereavement, and Mourning
Grief, bereavement, and mourning are not static events. Rather, they are processes that are influenced by personality, family, culture, religion, circumstances involving loss, manner of death, and relationship to the deceased person.[9] While the terms bereavement, mourning, and grief are sometimes used interchangeably, they are unique concepts:[9]
- Grief is the personal response to loss
- Bereavement is the period of grief and mourning
- Mourning is the individual expression of grief and loss

The most basic descriptions of grief involve individual response to loss, from such significant events as the loss of a child, to the loss of a home or the loss of feeling of security after a natural disaster.[6] Patients suffer varying dimensions of loss. Some of those include:[10]

Table 21-1. Assessment and Intervention for Patients in Crisis

Assessment	Intervention
• Assess for the patient's perception of what happened • Assess mental status and risk for harm to self or others	• Assure patient safety • Provide reassurance and support • Provide information throughout the ED stay
• Determine past and present medical history including medications	• Use a calm and empathetic manner
• Assess for family and social issues	• Establish rapport and trust • Allow for expression of feelings
• Ask about previous, successful coping mechanisms • Inquire about existing support systems	• Focus on problem solving • Offer simple basic choices to promote decision making • Facilitate patient involvement in plan of care

Adapted from Vogel.[8]

- Material: Loss of home, vehicle, or other physical objects that have meaning to a person. These can also be items of sentimental value, such as heirlooms or keepsakes.

- Relationship: The loss of ability to share experiences and have the physical presence of a person. Whether patients and family members are young or old, they may express the loss of a loved one or of a vital friendship.

- Intrapsychic or spiritual: Loss of an aspect of one's self-image or focusing on possibilities of what might have been. For example, the death of a child may lead to feeling of the loss of the experience of raising a child or the death of spouse may lead to feelings of the loss of growing old with that person.

- Functional: Feelings of grief that follow the loss of function of a limb or use of arms, legs, and the body, such as in the case of quadriplegia

- Role: Feelings of loss of a specific role within one's social network. At times, functional loss affects the ability to perform a particular role. For example, the loss of the use of a hand or arm can affect a person's ability to work in a particular profession.

Table 21-2. Human Responses Following Grief

Dimension of Grief	Behaviors
Somatic expression	• Physical complaints, such as pain, nausea, headache • Loss of appetite • Overeating or weight gain • Sleep disturbances, fatigue
Cognitive expression	• Preoccupation with the loss • Low self-esteem • Unable to concentrate or remember • Helplessness and hopelessness • Situations seem unreal
Affective expression	• Anxiety • Guilt, resentment, and aggression • Depression and despair • Loneliness • Defensiveness or self-blame
Behavioral expression	• Agitation • Fatigue • Crying • Social withdrawal

Adapted from Ramachandran, V. S. (2012). *Encyclopedia of human behavior* (2nd ed.). London, United Kingdom: Academic Press.

Grief Assessment

The experience of grief has physical, emotional, cognitive, behavioral, and spiritual dimensions.[9] While grief may be considered a universal human emotion, not all patients or family members experience grief in the same way. Just as the physiologic response to trauma varies from patient to patient, individual grief responses vary. Observation of these reactions can guide the trauma nurse in planning and intervention on behalf of the patient and family (Table 21-2).

Cultural Considerations of Grief

In addition to the individual responses to grief, ethnic and cultural variations exist in response to loss and death. Therefore, providing culturally congruent care is essential. Leininger and McFarland described culturally congruent care as "being sensitive to the patient's cultural background, beliefs, values, and practices."[11] A cultural assessment can be helpful in caring for families dealing with grief and loss.

Grief Interventions

Many of the interventions for patients experiencing stress, fear, worry, and crisis are applicable to the patient experiencing grief. Additionally, it is important that trauma team members provide spiritually sensitive interventions appropriate to each individual's unique responses to grief. Questions include:

- Are there preferred rites or rituals?

- Is there a spiritual or family leader to be contacted?

- Can these needs be met or addressed within the emergency setting?

- Is there a support person to be with them?

Support can also be provided as the patient or family prepares to the leave the emergency department (ED). Put together a grief discharge package to include pamphlets and phone numbers of local support groups. A follow-up phone call the next day can identify needs that arise after discharge.

Additional Psychosocial Care Considerations

Providing referrals for resources for the continued support of patients who have experienced injury is a fundamental step in the process of recovery. Clear policies and procedures serve to support patients and their families and to address the following needs:

- Communication and provision of interpreter services
- Family-centered care
- Opportunity for family presence during resuscitation and invasive procedures

Communication and Use of Interpreter Services

When language barriers exist, the use of interpretive services assures accuracy of medical information communicated to patients and families. In the United States (U.S.), the Office of Minority Health issues standards for culturally and linguistically appropriate care. These standards state that healthcare organizations are required to provide interpreters in a timely manner to all patients that need language assistance during all hours of operation.[12]

Communication interventions include the following:

- Determine the patient's preferred language for communication
- Identify family or friends designated to receive important medical information if the patient cannot speak for her or himself
- Speak slowly and clearly to patients and families and allow time for questions when delivering clinical findings or sharing the plan of care
- Use a professional interpreter
  - Friends and family may omit embarrassing, sensitive, or difficult information
  - Friends and family may answer for the patient in an attempt to protect him or her instead of simply translating
  - However, if the patient requests a friend or family member to act as interpreter, the patient's wishes are considered[12]
  - Follow organizational policy regarding the use of interpreters

Family-centered Care

Family-centered care and patient involvement in care are essential components of appropriate, safe, and timely healthcare in the trauma setting. The Institute of Medicine (IOM) recommends patient and family involvement in healthcare-related decisions.[13] The Institute for Patient-and Family-Centered Care suggests that hospitals review and revise organizational visitor policies with several key concepts in mind:[14]

- Reconsider the use of the term *visitor* with respect to family members in the language used in hospital policies. Family members and key friends may offer pivotal support in provision of care and should be respected as part of the care team.
- Modify the definition of *family* to include those who the patient considers to be family members
- Assure patients have the support needed for recovery and the support of palliative care or a hospice

Family Presence During Resuscitation and Invasive Procedures

Family presence during resuscitation and invasive procedures in high-acuity settings such as the ED or the intensive care unit (ICU) are more likely to succeed when facilities have sound policies and procedures in place that support such practice.[15,16]

Facilitation of family presence is most successful when clear policies are in place, when patient care teams are educated regarding expectations and parameters of such policies, and when a dedicated staff support person is assigned to family members during resuscitative events and throughout invasive procedures.[14]

If there is no clear policy in place to support family presence during resuscitative events, the trauma nurse can work with administration to develop policies in order to support patients, families, and staff in their preferences regarding family presence. In developing policies for family presence, include consideration of patient and staff safety and infection control measures.[15]

Psychosocial Aspects of Caring for Agitated Patients and Families

Each ED is a microcosm of the community it serves, and trauma nurses are exposed to difficult or even violent behavior. This may be from patients or family members under the influence of drugs or alcohol, with psychiatric disorders, and ineffective communication patterns. The ED often serves as a primary entry to the hospital with public access 24 hours a day. Trauma patients and families experiencing stress may exhibit escalating behaviors such as agitation, inappropriate communication, hostility, and physical violence. Education regarding the approach to patients and families, de-escalation techniques, and care of the psychiatric or agitated patient can help the trauma nurse control difficult situations.

It is also important to implement a safety response for situations that may become out of control.

Preventing Escalation

Some techniques for preventing escalation include:

- Minimize the chaos
  - Have one point-of-contact person for message clarity
  - Talk to families in a designated, quiet, private room
  - Limit environmental stimuli
- Promote clear communication with support
  - Assess the need for and try to provide personal space
  - Sit and talk on the same level
  - Avoid healthcare jargon and terminology
  - Promote and assist with contacting other family members or support persons
  - Assess need for spiritual support
  - Make multidisciplinary referrals for support
- Provide comfort measures (drink, food, phone, quiet room)
- Observe verbal and nonverbal cues as they may indicate family member needs

De-escalation

If the tension and frustration leads to behavioral escalation:

- Notify security to stand by
- Remain calm and nonjudgmental
- Speak in a calm, quiet voice
- Listen actively and observe their body language
- Maintain an exit route; place yourself between the patient or family and the door
- Set realistic limits and offer choices if possible

Mitigating Violence

Clinical and safety considerations in the management of violent behavior may include the following:

- Minimize stimulation in the environment
- Use a low voice and speak calmly and slowly to the patient and family
- Facilitate a safe environment for patients, families, and staff
- For a patient who is violent, consider the following:
  - Assess for physiologic cause for behavior
    - Obtain a point-of-care glucose level to assess for hypoglycemia
    - Assess for oxygen desaturation and other signs and symptoms that suggest hypoxia

- Anticipate a head computed tomography (CT) scan to rule out neurologic injury
- Obtain a toxicology screen to rule out substance abuse
  - Administer medications as ordered with support from other staff as necessary
  - If restraints are necessary, apply and follow care according to organizational policy
- If assaulted, after assuring your safety and treatment, report the incident, following your organization's procedures and seek counseling

The presence of policies and protocols together with education can optimize the trauma nurse's competence and ability to handle these difficult situations.

Ethical Considerations in Trauma

According to the ENA Scope and Standards of Practice, "[t]he emergency nurse delivers care in a manner that preserves and protects healthcare consumer autonomy, dignity, rights, values, and beliefs."[2] This standard of practice describes the nurse's role as an advocate for all patients and families despite any personal beliefs or values.

Advance Directives

Advance directives may be unavailable when the trauma patient arrives in the ED. If the patient is alert, ask about any particular wishes related to care. If not alert, the family or legal guardian can be asked to provide a copy. If there is no advanced directive and the patient is not alert, follow organizational policy for care. If information is not initially accessible, the trauma team follows the patient's wishes for care once information becomes available.[17]

Advance directives include living wills and healthcare power of attorney or proxy. They can include such directives as:[18]

- Do not intubate
- Do not resuscitate
- Do not defibrillate
- Do not hospitalize
- Comfort care only

Documents and forms can vary, so it is important for the nurse to become familiar with the documents used in his or her organization and jurisdiction, and understand the implications of each directive.[18]

Advance directives are often signed in context of a medical illness, and the patient or proxy may wish them revoked in the event of a traumatic injury. Clear explanations, when possible, will help the patient or proxy decide if the original criteria surrounding these directives are still relevant in the current situation.[17] Consider the following examples of the patient's right to choose and the patient's right to be informed.

Patient's Right to Choose

An 80 year old female is hit by a motor vehicle and sustains a fractured femur. She has a history of hypertension and heart failure and the family brought a signed do not resuscitate (DNR) order from a past hospitalization. The patient is currently living independently in her own home. What is the responsibility of the trauma team in this situation?

Discussion

The trauma nurse examines hospital policy regarding the use of DNR orders and the circumstances in which they are legal and binding. An order from another facility or an order from a previous hospitalization may not be binding during this hospitalization. In this case, the trauma team educates the patient regarding the meaning of an advanced directive and assures the patient understands the implications of an advanced directive are within the context of the injury and surgery. With the patient's health history, extubation following surgery may be difficult and carry some risk. It is important to discuss what will be involved during recovery and rehabilitation and that chances for recovery may be very good. The patient and family need to consider all risks and benefits to make decisions for care with this hospitalization.[19]

Right to Be Fully Informed

An 89 year old woman arrives to the ED following a slip and fall. The options for treatment include a surgical repair or conservative treatment. The patient's daughter states that she wishes for the conservative treatment and requests the staff not discuss it with the patient because it will "just upset her." The patient presents alert and oriented. How should the trauma team manage this situation?

Discussion

Unless there is documentation giving the daughter healthcare power of attorney AND the mother is unable to make decisions for herself, the daughter is not legally able to make decisions for her mother. In this instance, the patient is alert and oriented. Therefore, she has the right to know all the treatment options and may include her daughter in the decision-making process if she wishes, but the patient must be fully informed.

Organ and Tissue Donation

When death is inevitable, some families may receive comfort from the ability to donate their loved one's organs or tissue. Sensitivity and respect is vital when approaching families for this request. Federal law mandates that all U.S. transplant centers and organ procurement organizations (OPOs) be members of the National Organ Procurement and Transplantation Network in order to meet eligibility requirements for Medicare funding and reimbursement.[20]

The OPO determines if the patient meets qualifications as a potential donor and if the patient is medically suitable for donation. Declaration of death, medical examiner approval, notification of the OPO, and consent from next of kin are all prerequisites before organ procurement can take place.[20] The process of organ donation and recovery is a collaborative team effort between the OPO and the patient care team. Increased awareness to that process can help the trauma nurse meet the needs of the donor and his or her family.

Psychosocial Care of the Trauma Team

Caring is at the heart of nursing practice. The nature of trauma care exposes the trauma nurse to suffering. Repeated exposure to suffering or trauma can lead to compassion fatigue (CF) or secondary traumatic stress (STS).[1] Both CF and STS can impact the trauma nurse's ability to deliver quality, empathetic care.[19,21,22]

Compassion Fatigue

CF is a combination of STS and burnout and can be a predictable outcome from repeated exposure to suffering. It is important to remember that with increased awareness and understanding it can be prevented or its effects can be mitigated.[23] Table 21-3 describes symptoms associated with CF.[24]

Secondary Traumatic Stress[1]

STS is a component of CF and occurs with direct exposure to a stressor in the work environment (workplace violence). STS can also occur in response to caring for people who have experienced traumatic events and injuries. In one study, symptoms were reported to occur in three categories: intrusive, avoidance, and arousal (Table 21-4). Although the study was small, they reported a high incidence of STS in trauma nurses.[1] In a literature review of seven studies of nurses in the emergency department and other similar high-stress locations (hospice and pediatric critical care), STS was prevalent.[25]

Burnout

Burnout is another element of CF. It occurs over time, with a gradual onset, building to a stress response.[1] However, one can experience burnout and not have CF. Burnout encompasses three elements:

- Emotional exhaustion

- Depersonalization or distancing oneself from their work and others

- Decreased sense of accomplishment

Table 21-3. Symptoms of Compassion Fatigue

Work-related
• Avoidance or dread of working with certain patients or patient types
• Reduced ability to feel empathy towards patients or families
• Frequent use of sick days

Physical
• Headaches
• Digestive problems: diarrhea, constipation, upset stomach
• Muscle tension
• Sleep disturbances: inability to sleep, insomnia, too much sleep
• Fatigue
• Cardiac symptoms: chest pain/pressure, palpitations, tachycardia

Emotional
• Mood swings
• Lack of joyfulness
• Restlessness
• Irritability
• Oversensitivity
• Anxiety
• Excessive use of substances (nicotine, alcohol, illicit drugs)
• Depression
• Anger and resentment
• Loss of objectivity
• Memory issues
• Poor concentration, focus, and judgment

Reprinted with permission from Lombardo & Eyre.[24]

Burnout is also associated with difficulties in dealing with the stress of work or feelings of helplessness and professional inadequacy. Table 21-5 describes additional symptoms associated with burnout. A nurse experiencing the effects of burnout may be judgmental of patients or may be easily irritated by patients and colleagues.[1,25] The nurse with burnout can be easily overwhelmed by routine or ordinary work conditions. Burnout can lead to indifference, disengagement, and withdrawal from patients and the work environment.[19] Ultimately, burnout impacts job satisfaction, productivity and performance and may contribute to absenteeism and turnover.[26]

Workplace Violence

Workplace violence in the ED is highly prevalent.[27] In one study, 25% of respondents said they had experienced physical violence more than 20 times in the past 3 years, and other studies have found that 30% to 80% of hospital staff members were physically assaulted at least once during their careers.[27,28] These stressful conditions can have an impact on the trauma nurse, especially with repeated exposure. A potential consequence of

Table 21-4. Secondary Traumatic Stress Symptoms

Category	Symptoms
Intrusion	• Recurring thoughts about patients • Dreams about work and patients • Sense of reliving the disturbing events over and over
Avoidance	• Avoiding certain patients • Staying away from people and crowded places • Inability to remember patient information • Emotionless • Disconnected from others • Inactive
Arousal	• Sleep disturbances • Irritability • Inability to focus • Nervousness and agitation

Adapted from Dominguez-Gomez and Rutledge.[1]

practicing in a high-stress and potentially dangerous environment is the effect on the health of the trauma nurse psychologically, emotionally, and physically.

Critical Incidents

A critical incident (CI) is a traumatic event that elicits unusually strong emotional reactions or responses to the event by healthcare team members, which in turn, may adversely affect workplace morale. Care for children and adults who have been injured as a result of interpersonal violence, pediatric resuscitation, and care for a dying colleague may be considered CIs. Additional stressors may be acute, chronic, or cumulative in effect, resulting in changes that are both personal and professional. Table 21-6 lists common reactions to a traumatic event such as a CI.[29]

Table 21-5. Burnout Symptoms

Burnout Component	Symptoms
Emotional exhaustion	• Headache • Fatigue • Gastrointestinal complaints • Muscle strain and tightness • Increased blood pressure • Respiratory symptoms • Sleep disorders
Depersonalization	• Anxiety • Irritability • Sadness and despair • Hopelessness
Personal accomplishment	• Absenteeism • Frustration • Thinking about quitting • Inefficiency on the job • Decreased satisfaction with the job • Lack of dedication to the job

Adapted from Poghosyan et al.[30] *and* Maslach & Leiter.[31]

Approach to the Care of the Trauma Team

Assessment Tools
The Professional Quality of Life Tool
The Professional Quality of Life: Compassion Satisfaction and Fatigue Version 5 (ProQOL) is a 30-item instrument used to score responses regarding the phenomena of CF, burnout, and compassion satisfaction (Appendix 21-A).[23] It has been useful in identifying the nurse's response to traumatic events, ability to cope,

Table 21-6. Common Responses to a Traumatic Event

Cognitive	Emotional
• Poor concentration • Confusion • Disorientation • Indecisiveness • Shortened attention span • Memory loss • Unwanted memories • Difficulty making decisions	• Shock • Numbness • Feeling overwhelmed • Depression • Feeling lost • Fear of harm to self and/or loved ones • Feeling nothing • Feeling abandoned • Uncertainty of feelings • Volatile emotions

Physical	Behavioral
• Nausea • Lightheadedness • Dizziness • Gastrointestinal problems • Rapid heart rate • Tremors • Headaches • Grinding of teeth • Fatigue • Poor sleep • Pain • Hyperarousal • Jumpiness	• Suspicion • Irritability • Arguments with friends and loved ones • Withdrawal • Increased substance use or abuse • Excessive silence • Inappropriate humor • Increased/decreased eating • Change in sexual desire or functioning • Increased smoking

Adapted from Woods.[28]

and the possible need for intervention. Nurse leaders can administer this tool to determine interventions, support, and programs that may be needed to promote recovery from the effects of traumatic events for the individual nurse and the entire department.

Maslach Burnout Inventory
The Maslach Burnout Inventory (MBI) is most often used to measure a person's level of burnout.[30,31] In this tool, elements of burnout are divided into six categories:

- Workload: Addressing both quality and quantity
- Control: Having autonomy at work and influence over one's own practice
- Reward: Both being recognized by others and having internal job satisfaction
- Sense of community: Being engaged at work and having a supportive work environment
- Fairness: Feeling that decisions are made equitably and fairly
- Values: Having purpose and enthusiasm for the work

An analysis of these factors determined that shorter patient length of stays with more work for nurses in fewer hours with a constant turnover of patients in the ED setting was often overwhelming.[30]

The results from this tool can be used to develop strategies for preventing the emotional exhaustion, depersonalization, and lack of a sense of accomplishment. More research is needed to identify specific strategies for treating nurse burnout, and to evaluate the effectiveness of existing interventions.

Support and Strategies for the Trauma Team

Developing Resilience
Resilience represents a unique set of attributes or protective behaviors that may buffer an individual from the effects of acute and chronic stress.[32] The literature emphasizes that development of personal and professional resilience allows one to cope with the effects of stress and achieve a positive work experience.[33]

Examples of the attributes that contribute to resilience include:[33]

- Hardiness
- Coping skills
- Self-efficacy
- Optimism
- Patience
- Tolerance
- Faith
- Adaptability
- Self-esteem
- Sense of humor

The American Psychological Association (APA) outlines additional factors associated with a resilient response, based upon learned behaviors:[34]

- The power to make realistic plans and take steps to carry them out
- A positive self-view and confidence in one's strengths and abilities
- Learned communication skills and problem solving
- The self-control to manage strong feelings and impulses

Table 21-7 describes ten ways to build resilience.

Promoting Self Awareness
Awareness of loss of caring and negative attitude can prevent the development of CF and burnout, including the potentially negative mental, emotional and physical effects of these conditions.[32] ED leaders can support the trauma team with the following interventions:

- Help the trauma nurse develop a personal plan of care
  - Institute policies that promote a healthy work and personal life balance
  - Encourage the nurse to develop a self-care plan as part of the annual evaluation process[24]
- Establish informal follow-up
- Check in with team members following a traumatic event or a period of continued high stress
  - A brief conversation, e-mail, or card can be a quick way to remind the trauma nurse of the importance of self-care
- Provide private counseling services for the trauma nurse
  - Most hospitals offer employee assistance programs that support employees in work-related issues[24]
  - Counseling may provide a venue for self-reflection, identification of stressors, or identification of the need for referral to more comprehensive psychosocial services

- Develop mentorship support
  - Mentorship can be useful for the novice and the experienced nurse
  - A formal mentorship program within the department or referral to a program through a professional organization is a way to provide this support
  - Perspective and support from others can offer valuable insight to challenges common to trauma nursing practice

- Provide care for the team
  - Explore other internal resources, including social work, pastoral care, and chaplaincy
  - Provide departmental, organizational, and community defusing and debriefing resources. Establish routines for formal debriefing and informal defusing to promote a positive attitude to psychosocial care for the trauma team.

Table 21-7. 10 Ways to Build Resilience

Resilience
• **Make connections.** Good relationships with close family members, friends or others are important. Accepting help and support from those who care about you and will listen to you strengthens resilience. Some people find that being active in civic groups, faith-based organizations, or other local groups provides social support and can help with reclaiming hope. Assisting others in their time of need also can benefit the helper.
• **Avoid seeing crises as insurmountable problems.** You can't change the fact that highly stressful events happen, but you can change how you interpret and respond to these events. Try looking beyond the present to how future circumstances may be a little better. Note any subtle ways in which you might already feel somewhat better as you deal with difficult situations.
• **Accept that change is a part of living.** Certain goals may no longer be attainable as a result of adverse situations. Accepting circumstances that cannot be changed can help you focus on circumstances that you can alter.
• **Move toward your goals.** Develop some realistic goals. Do something regularly — even if it seems like a small accomplishment — that enables you to move toward your goals. Instead of focusing on tasks that seem unachievable, ask yourself, "What's one thing I know I can accomplish today that helps me move in the direction I want to go?"
• **Take decisive actions.** Act on adverse situations as much as you can. Take decisive actions, rather than detaching completely from problems and stresses and wishing they would just go away.
• **Look for opportunities for self-discovery.** People often learn something about themselves and may find that they have grown in some respect as a result of their struggle with loss. Many people who have experienced tragedies and hardship have reported better relationships, greater sense of strength even while feeling vulnerable, increased sense of self-worth, a more developed spirituality and heightened appreciation for life.
• **Nurture a positive view of yourself.** Developing confidence in your ability to solve problems and trusting your instincts helps build resilience.
• **Keep things in perspective.** Even when facing very painful events, try to consider the stressful situation in a broader context and keep a long-term perspective. Avoid blowing the event out of proportion.
• **Maintain a hopeful outlook.** An optimistic outlook enables you to expect that good things will happen in your life. Try visualizing what you want, rather than worrying about what you fear.
• **Take care of yourself.** Pay attention to your own needs and feelings. Engage in activities that you enjoy and find relaxing. Exercise regularly. Taking care of yourself helps to keep your mind and body primed to deal with situations that require resilience.

Reprinted with permission from the American Psychological Association.[34]

Critical Incident Stress Management

Critical incident stress management (CISM) is reported to mitigate the impact of traumatic events and restores adaptive functioning to those exposed to a particular incident.[26]

- *Debriefings* offer a structured response to CIs
  - A formal debriefing is open to voluntary participants within 24 to 72 hours of the CI[26]
  - It is not meant to be a venue for airing concerns about technical management; it is meant to offer a review of events throughout a given CI and sharing of individual responses[26]
- *Defusings* are more spontaneous or unstructured and are carried out informally within several hours of a traumatic event[26]

Overall, support following a CI or other traumatic event is not one-size-fits-all. Those affected by the event are invited, not forced, to receive support, and resources are made available to all members of the healthcare team on a consistent, transparent basis.

Summary

Provision of competent, safe, and compassionate psychosocial nursing care to those suffering sudden, unexpected injury or death remains a cornerstone of emergency and trauma nursing.[2] Understanding the human response to trauma can be key in offering support and guidance to patients and families and plays an important role in the development of assessment skills for the trauma nurse to use not only with patients and families, but among colleagues and oneself.

Trauma nurses work in a highly stressful environment that often includes exposure to severely injured and dying patients, emotionally laden situations, or violence. STS and burnout can be a natural consequence of that exposure, and it is essential that trauma nurses are aware of and recognize the potential consequences. It is important to realize that CF is a predictable, treatable, and preventable consequence of working with suffering people.[32] Information, education, and selected interventions can be used by the trauma nurse to ameliorate the symptoms and limit maladaptive consequences of acute, chronic, and continual exposure.

PROFESSIONAL QUALITY OF LIFE SCALE (PROQOL)

Compassion Satisfaction and Fatigue
(ProQOL) Version 5 (2009)

When you [help] people you have direct contact with their lives. As you may have found, your compassion for those you [help] can affect you in positive and negative ways. Below are some questions about your experiences, both positive and negative, as a [helper]. Consider each of the following questions about you and your current work situation. Select the number that honestly reflects how frequently you experienced these things in the _last 30 days_.

1=Never	2=Rarely	3=Sometimes	4=Often	5=Very Often

_____ 1.   I am happy.

_____ 2.   I am preoccupied with more than one person I [help].

_____ 3.   I get satisfaction from being able to [help] people.

_____ 4.   I feel connected to others.

_____ 5.   I jump or am startled by unexpected sounds.

_____ 6.   I feel invigorated after working with those I [help].

_____ 7.   I find it difficult to separate my personal life from my life as a [helper].

_____ 8.   I am not as productive at work because I am losing sleep over traumatic experiences of a person I [help].

_____ 9.   I think that I might have been affected by the traumatic stress of those I [help].

_____ 10. I feel trapped by my job as a [helper].

_____ 11.   Because of my [helping], I have felt "on edge" about various things.

_____ 12. I like my work as a [helper].

_____ 13. I feel depressed because of the traumatic experiences of the people I [help].

_____ 14. I feel as though I am experiencing the trauma of someone I have [helped].

_____ 15. I have beliefs that sustain me.

_____ 16. I am pleased with how I am able to keep up with [helping] techniques and protocols.

_____ 17. I am the person I always wanted to be.

_____ 18. My work makes me feel satisfied.

_____ 19. I feel worn out because of my work as a [helper].

_____ 20. I have happy thoughts and feelings about those I [help] and how I could help them.

_____ 21. I feel overwhelmed because my case [work] load seems endless.

_____ 22. I believe I can make a difference through my work.

_____ 23. I avoid certain activities or situations because they remind me of frightening experiences of the people I [help].

_____ 24. I am proud of what I can do to [help].

_____ 25. As a result of my [helping], I have intrusive, frightening thoughts.

_____ 26. I feel "bogged down" by the system.

_____ 27. I have thoughts that I am a "success" as a [helper].

_____ 28. I can't recall important parts of my work with trauma victims.

_____ 29. I am a very caring person.

_____ 30. I am happy that I chose to do this work.

What is my score and what does it mean?

In this section, you will score your test and then you can compare your score to the interpretation below.

Scoring
1. Be certain you respond to all items.
2. Go to items 1, 4, 15, 17 and 29 and reverse your score. For example, if you scored the item 1, write a 5 beside it. We ask you to reverse these scores because we have learned that the test works better if you reverse these scores.

You Wrote	Change to
1	5
2	4
3	3
4	2
5	1

To find your score on **Compassion Satisfaction**, add your scores on questions 3, 6, 12, 16, 18, 20, 22, 24, 27, 30.

The sum of my Compassion Satisfaction questions was	So My Score Equals	My Level of Compassion Satisfaction
22 or less	43 or less	Low
Between 23 and 41	Around 50	Average
42 or more	57 or more	High

To find your score on **Burnout**, add your scores on questions 1, 4, 8, 10, 15, 17, 19, 21, 26 and 29. Find your score on the table below.

The sum of my Burnout questions	So My Score Equals	My Level of Burnout
22 or less	43 or less	Low
Between 23 and 41	Around 50	Average
42 or more	57 or more	High

To find your score on **Secondary Traumatic Stress**, add your scores on questions 2, 5, 7, 9, 11, 13, 14, 23, 25, 28. Find your score on the table below.

The sum of my Secondary Traumatic Stress questions	So My Score Equals	My Level of Secondary Traumatic Stress
22 or less	43 or less	Low
Between 23 and 41	Around 50	Average
42 or more	57 or more	High

Appendix 21-A. The Professional Quality of Life Scale (Continued)

YOUR SCORES ON THE PROQOL: PROFESSIONAL QUALITY OF LIFE SCREENING

Based on your responses, your personal scores are below. If you have any concerns, you should discuss them with a physical or mental health care professional.

Compassion Satisfaction _____

Compassion satisfaction is about the pleasure you derive from being able to do your work well. For example, you may feel like it is a pleasure to help others through your work. You may feel positively about your colleagues or your ability to contribute to the work setting or even the greater good of society. Higher scores on this scale represent a greater satisfaction related to your ability to be an effective caregiver in your job.

The average score is 50 (SD 10; alpha scale reliability .88). About 25% of people score higher than 57 and about 25% of people score below 43. If you are in the higher range, you probably derive a good deal of professional satisfaction from your position. If your scores are below 40, you may either find problems with your job, or there may be some other reason—for example, you might derive your satisfaction from activities other than your job.

Burnout _____

Most people have an intuitive idea of what burnout is. From the research perspective, burnout is one of the elements of compassion fatigue. It is associated with feelings of hopelessness and difficulties in dealing with work or in doing your job effectively. These negative feelings usually have a gradual onset. They can reflect the feeling that your efforts make no difference, or they can be associated with a very high workload or a non-supportive work environment. Higher scores on this scale mean that you are at higher risk for burnout.

The average score on the burnout scale is 50 (SD 10; alpha scale reliability .75). About 25% of people score above 57 and about 25% of people score below 43. If your score is below 18, this probably reflects positive feelings about your ability to be effective in your work. If you score above 57 you may wish to think about what at work makes you feel like you are not effective in your position. Your score may reflect your mood; perhaps you were having a "bad day" or are in need of some time off. If the high score persists or if it is reflective of other worries, it may be a cause for concern.

Secondary Traumatic Stress _____

The second component of Compassion Fatigue (CF) is secondary traumatic stress (STS). It is about your work-related, secondary exposure to extremely or traumatically stressful events. Developing problems due to exposure to other's trauma is somewhat rare but does happen to many people who care for those who have experienced extremely or traumatically stressful events. For example, you may repeatedly hear stories about the traumatic things that happen to other people, commonly called Vicarious Traumatization. You may see or provide treatment to people who have experienced horrific events. If your work puts you directly in the path of danger, due to your work as a soldier or civilian working in military medicine personnel, this is not secondary exposure; your exposure is primary. However, if you are exposed to others' traumatic events as a result of your work, such as providing care to casualties or for those in a military medical rehabilitation facility, this is secondary exposure. The symptoms of STS are usually rapid in onset and associated with a particular event. They may include being afraid, having difficulty sleeping, having images of the upsetting event pop into your mind, or avoiding things that remind you of the event.

The average score on this scale is 50 (SD 10; alpha scale reliability .81). About 25% of people score below 43 and about 25% of people score above 57. If your score is above 57, you may want to take some time to think about what at work may be frightening to you or if there is some other reason for the elevated score. While higher scores do not mean that you do have a problem, they are an indication that you may want to examine how you feel about your work and your work environment. You may wish to discuss this with your supervisor, a colleague, or a health care professional.

References

1. Dominguez-Gomez, E., & Rutledge, D. (2009). Prevalence of secondary traumatic stress among emergency nurses. *Journal of Emergency Nursing, 35*(3), 199–204.

2. Emergency Nurses Association. (2011). *Emergency nursing scope and standards of practice* (2011 ed.). Des Plaines, IL: Author.

3. American Psychological Association. (2012, August). *Managing traumatic stress: Tips for recovering from disasters and other traumatic events.* Retrieved from http://www.apa.org/topics/trauma/index.aspx

4. Follette, V., & Vijay, A. (2009). Mindfulness for trauma and posttraumatic stress disorder. In F. Didonna (Ed.), *Clinical handbook of mindfulness* (pp. 299–318). New York, NY: Springer.

5. Shalev, A. (2012, February 14). *Treating survivors in the acute aftermath of traumatic events.* Retrieved from http://www.ptsd.va.gov/professional/pages/survivors-aftermath-trauma.asp

6. Holland, D. (2011). *The essential guide to grief and grieving: An understanding guide to coping with loss and finding hope and meaning beyond.* New York, NY: Penguin.

7. Wagley, L. K., & Newton, S. E. (2010). Emergency nurses' use of psychosocial nursing interventions for management of ED patient fear and anxiety. *Journal of Emergency Nursing, 36*(5), 415–419.

8. Vogel, C. (n.d.). *Crisis intervention: Helping patients regain safety and control.* Retrieved from http://ce.nurse.com/ce582/crisis-intervention/coursepage/

9. Buglass, E. (2010). Grief and bereavement theories. *Nursing Standard, 24*(41), 44–47.

10. Grover, R., & Fowler, S. G. (2011). *Helping those experiencing loss: A guide to grieving resources.* Santa Barbara, CA: Libraries Unlimited.

11. Leininger, M. & McFarland, M. (2006). *Culture care diversity and universality: A worldwide nursing theory* (2nd ed.). Sudbury, MA: Jones and Bartlett.

12. Lipson, J., & Dibble, S. (2009). *Culture & clinical care.* San Francisco, CA: UCSF Nursing Press.

13. Institute of Medicine. (2012, September). *Best care at lower cost: The path to continuously learning healthcare in America.* Retrieved from http://www.iom.edu/~/media/Files/Report%20Files/2012/Best-Care/BestCareReportBrief.pdf

14. Institute for Patient and Family-Centered Care. (2012). *Changing hospital "visiting" policies and practices: Supporting family presence and participation executive summary.* Retrieved from http://www.ipfcc.org/visiting.pdf

15. Kingsnorth-Hinrichs, J. (2010). Family presence during resuscitation. In P. K. Howard & R. A. Steinmann (Eds.), *Sheehy's emergency nursing: Principles and practice* (6th ed., pp. 148–154). St. Louis, MO: Mosby Elsevier.

16. Kingsnorth, J., O'Connell, K., Guzetta, C. E., Eden, J. C., Atabaki, S., Mecherikunnel, A., & Brown, K. (2010). Family presence during trauma activations and medical resuscitations in pediatric emergency department: An evidence-based practice project. *Journal of Emergency Nursing, 36*(2), 115–121.

17. Heilicser, B. (2013). Ethical dilemmas in emergency nursing. In Emergency Nurses Association, *Sheehy's manual of emergency care* (7th ed., pp. 43–48). St. Louis, MO: Mosby Elsevier.

18. Somes, J., & Donatelli, N. (2012). Do not intubate/do not resuscitate: Treating the severely ill or injured geriatric patient in the emergency department. *Journal of Emergency Nursing, 38*(3), 283–286.

19. Cole, J. B. (2011, July 27). Compassion fatigue. *Advance for Nurses.* Retrieved from http://nursing.advanceweb.com/ny-nj-ct-ma-me-ri-vt-nh-free-magazine/Regional-Content/Articles/Compassion-Fatigue.aspx

20. Bonalumi, N. (2010). Organ and tissue donation. In P. K. Howard & R. A. Steinmann (Eds.), *Sheehy's emergency nursing: Principles and practice* (6th ed., pp. 155–163). St. Louis, MO: Mosby Elsevier.

21. Landro, L. (2012, January 3). When nurses catch compassion fatigue, patients suffer. *Wall Street Journal.* Retrieved from http://online.wsj.com/article/SB10001424052970204720204577128882104188856.html?KEYWORDS=when+nurses+catch+compassion+fatigue

22. Yoder, E. A. (2010).Compassion fatigue in nurses. *Applied Nursing Research, 23*(4), 191–197.

23. Stamm, B. H. (2009, September 2). *The Professional Quality of Life Scale.* Retrieved from http://www.isu.edu/~bhstamm/

24. Lombardo, B., & Eyre, C. (2012). Compassion fatigue: A nurse's primer. *OJIN: The Online Journal of Issues in Nursing, 16*(1), 3. Retrieved from http://www.nursingworld.org/MainMenuCategories/ANAMarketplace/ANAPeriodicals/OJIN/TableofContents/Vol-16-2011/No1-Jan-2011/Compassion-Fatigue-A-Nurses-Primer.html

25. Beck, C. T. (2011). Secondary traumatic stress in nurses: A systematic review. *Archives of Psychiatric Nursing, 25*(1), 1–10.

26. Maloney, C. (2012). Critical incident stress debriefing and pediatric nurses: An approach to support the work environment and mitigate negative consequences. *Pediatric Nursing, 38*(2), 110–113.

27. Gacki-Smith, J., Juarez, A. M., Boyett, L., Homeyer, C., Robinson, L., & MacLean, S. L. (2009). Violence against nurses working in US emergency departments. *Journal of Nursing Administration, 39(7–8),* 340–349.

28. Woods, A. D. (2010, August 11). *Workplace violence in the emergency room: Are nurses safe?* Retrieved from http://www.nursingcenter.com/Blog/post/2010/08/11/Workplace-violence-in-the-emergency-room-are-nurses-safe.aspx

29. Centers for Disease Control and Prevention. (2013, February 1). *Coping with a traumatic event.* Retrieved from http://www.emergency.cdc.gov/masscasualties/copingpro.asp

30. Poghosyan, L., Aiken, L. H., & Sloane, D. M. (2009). Factor structure of the Maslach burnout inventory: An analysis of data from large scale cross-sectional surveys of nurses from eight countries. *International Journal of Nursing Studies, 46*(7), 894–902.

31. Maslach, D., & Leiter, M. P. (2007). Burnout. In G. Fink (Ed.), *Encyclopedia of stress* (2nd ed., pp. 368–371). London, United Kingdom: Academic Press.

32. Hooper, C., Craig, J., Janvrin, D. R., Westel, M. A., & Reimels, E. (2010). Compassion satisfaction, burnout, and compassion fatigue among emergency nurses compared with nurses in other selected inpatient specialties. *Journal of Emergency Nursing, 36*(5), 420–427.

33. Grafton, E., Gillespie, B., & Henderson, S. (2010). Resilience: The power within. *Oncology Nursing Forum, 37*(6), 698–705.

34. American Psychological Association. (n.d.). *The road to resilience.* Retrieved from http://www.apa.org/helpcenter/road-resilience.aspx

Chapter 22 • Disaster Management

Pamela A. Assid, MSN, RN, NEA-BC, CEN, CNS, CPEN

Objectives

Upon completion of this chapter, the learner will be able to:

1. Compare conventional triage to mass casualty triage.

2. Describe selected types of illnesses or injuries associated with disaster.

3. Discuss methods of preplanning, hazard identification, training, and implementation of the all-hazards approach to emergency preparedness.

4. Discuss nursing roles and responsibilities related to the all-hazards approach to emergency preparedness.

Introduction

On May 22, 2011, an Enhanced Fujita Scale (EF)-5 tornado with winds exceeding 200 mph was predicted to impact the area in and around Joplin, Missouri.[1] The tornado path hit Mercy St. John's Hospital directly and caused some damage to Freeman Hospital.[1] The time from initial tornado warning to impact was 19 minutes.[2]

Mercy St. John's sustained such severe structural damage that the hospital shifted off its foundation.[1] The heating, ventilation, and air conditioning (HVAC) system went down; generators were destroyed; communication systems failed; the main oxygen tank was severely damaged, discharging liquid oxygen; and the gas, sprinkler, and sewage lines broke open, creating 3 to 6 inches of standing water throughout the building.[1]

Through dark, flooded corridors littered with debris, staff managed to evacuate 183 patients. They also completed a surgical case that had been in progress when the tornado hit.[1] With no access to any internal communication, nurses began moving patients. Emergency and critical care patients, several mother–baby couplets, and many other inpatients were evacuated within a few hours.[1] Reports from the after-action critique meeting revealed that everything was done to safely evacuate patients, and the success was attributed to practice during disaster drills.[1]

Over half of the emergency response vehicles were damaged, thousands of homes were destroyed, and families were displaced. Injuries sustained throughout the community added to the challenges of patient care.[3]

Epidemiology

What Is a Disaster?

Disaster has many definitions. The United Nations Management Training Programme defines a disaster as a "serious disruption of the functions of a society, causing widespread human, material, or environmental losses which exceed the ability of the affected society to cope using only its own resources."[4] The World Health Organization (WHO) defines a disaster as a "situation or event, which overwhelms local capacity, necessitating a request to national or international level for external assistance."[5] Both definitions describe disaster as rapidly exhausting normal available resources. Resources include supplies, personnel, equipment, utilities, and facilities.

Disasters can be natural or manmade in origin. Although most disasters are natural (earthquakes, floods), manmade disasters are the focus of many coordinated response efforts and asset integration.[6]

An all-hazards approach to disaster preparedness means that one should prepare for not just a specific type of disaster or hazard but anticipate and increase preparedness for any type of hazard or disaster.[7]

The four phases of emergency management are mitigation (prevention), preparedness, response, and recovery.

Mitigation

Mitigation provides a foundation to reduce loss of life and property from natural or manmade disasters by limiting or avoiding potential impact and incorporating lessons learned from previous events.[8] A hazard vulnerability analysis (HVA) is developed, identifying the vulnerabilities most likely to put the facility at risk. The next step is to determine what actions could be taken to prevent or lessen the impact of the negative effects caused by those vulnerabilities.

For example, an HVA could identify a weather-related vulnerability such as flooding that would likely result in water leaks, electrical outages, and waterborne diseases. Mitigating those effects could consist of having maintenance personnel thoroughly inspect for leak-prone areas throughout the facility, simulating electrical outages to identify any potential generator problems, and having a defined process for identification and treatment of likely waterborne diseases with all key players (pharmacy, nursing, laboratory, and physicians) going through an exercise to test all aspects of that process.

Preparedness

Incident Command Structure

The United States (U.S.) Homeland Security Presidential Directive 5, "Management of Domestic Incidents," led to the development of the National Incident Management System (NIMS).[8] Under NIMS, the incident command system (ICS) was standardized across the country. NIMS and ICS provide many components to standardize incident organizational structure for the management of all types of disaster response.[8] Components of ICS include the following:[8]

- **Common terminology:** During a disaster, communication has been shown to be the largest vulnerability. When all first-responder agencies use different terminology, it can create confusion, cause miscommunication, and result in a failed mission. ICS builds common terminology into its structure so all first-responder agencies are describing the same situation and can achieve the same level of understanding about the objectives of the mission.

- **Modular organization:** Not every disaster requires every component of ICS to be activated. The system was designed to activate the components necessary to address each disaster without wasting resources.

- **Integrated communication:** In most disasters, typical methods of communication become inefficient or go offline. Cell towers are overwhelmed; network capabilities freeze or shut down entirely. Therefore, it is critical to not only consider high-tech options but also low-tech options (ham radio operators, runners) to augment communications planning so operations can continue uninterrupted.

- **Unity of command:** There is one person designated to be in charge of disaster operations. Each agency may have its own incident commander (IC), but all ICs work under the direction of the highest level IC. This will help to ensure adequate utilization of resources, prevent competition for scarce resources, and allow for better interagency cooperation.

- **Unified command structure:** Despite different legal, geographic, and functional responsibilities, all agencies coordinate and collaborate with a single set of objectives for the event

- **Consolidated incident action plan:** This is the master operations plan detailing the objectives of the mission. All agencies use this master plan to create their response and align their objectives.

- **Manageable span of control:** For management of an incident, having a focused and manageable span of control is essential. It is recommended that supervisors are responsible for three to seven subordinates, with five being ideal to allow for adequate supervision and timely communication.

- **Designated incident facilities:** The IC identifies and locates operational support facilities within the vicinity of the incident in order to accomplish various activities and purposes (shelters, food banks, or morgues)

- **Resource management:** Having a staging area for resources and accurate and up-to-date knowledge of available resources (supplies, people, equipment, and facilities) is necessary to ensure not only that everything is accounted for but that they are deployed to locations where they are needed and then reallocated as those needs and objectives change

Hospitals have implemented a structure similar to ICS called Hospital Incident Command System (HICS).[9] Although HICS is built upon ICS principles, it is designed as an emergency management system to be used within hospitals with core principles that include the following:[10]

- Manageable scope of supervision for all personnel

- A flexible system that can be expanded or scaled down depending on the demands of the situation

- A job action sheet (JAS), or position description for each role, that prioritizes emergency actions to be taken and serves as a reminder for personnel to adhere to established reporting chains

  ○ JASs and other forms provide documentation of details and responses to the situation critical for the recovery phase. This allows for recouping expenses and reducing liability and helps to identify key items for the focus of mitigation in future similar situations.

Hospital Disaster Preparedness Plans

HICS is one aspect of overall hospital disaster preparedness. It is critical for hospitals to develop comprehensive disaster preparedness plans that address all potential hazards. Healthcare agencies are required to have a hospital emergency management program that encompasses the disaster cycle of mitigation, preparedness, response, and recovery.[8] Table 22-1 includes elements of a hospital disaster preparedness plan.

The HVA is accessible for use by all staff and guides a facility's internal and external disaster response plan. It is typically coordinated within the community all the way to the state level so resources can be better managed in a disaster.[11]

Response

The Trauma Nurse's Role in a Disaster

An emergency management plan, HICS structure and role identification, and strategic planning are important during a disaster for successful outcomes. Trauma nurses who have an understanding of that overall plan and how their roles integrate with the system will be able to provide the best patient care possible in the face of complex, extreme events. Awareness of events surrounding the incident is essential. In the case of a flood, patients may present with submersion injuries; if the event is a wildfire, be prepared for multiple patients with burns and respiratory compromise.

Additionally, the "worried well" may arrive in large numbers wishing to be evaluated, thinking they may have been affected by the event but are asymptomatic. Family members will arrive or call, wanting information about their injured or affected loved ones. A good emergency management plan will accommodate them. When possible, this step can be managed outside of the hospital or emergency department (ED) so that personnel and equipment are available to manage the truly ill and injured.

Disaster Triage

Triage is a fundamental function in a disaster. The goal of disaster triage is to do "the greatest good for the greatest number."[6] It is important for facilities to determine ahead of time what type of disaster triage system to use, including clinical documentation and patient tracking tools. Other

Table 22-1. Elements of a Hospital Disaster Preparedness Plan

Element	Description
Emergency manager	• The primary point of contact • Develops, improves, exercises, and executes the emergency management plan
Emergency management (emergency operations) plan	• Identifies the hospital's response to internal and external disasters • Helps to proactively create plans that do not force action under pressure
Executive leadership	• Ensures commitment to emergency management preparedness from the highest organizational level • Engenders support among staff • Enforces expectations throughout the organization
Strategic planning	• Provides blueprint for the hospital's strategic plan
Emergency management committee	• Works together to integrate and prepare for disaster response • Consists of people throughout the hospital
Hazard vulnerability analysis (HVA)	• Prioritizes vulnerability to internal, external, natural, or manmade disasters based on probability, impact, and cost • Should integrate with community, state, and regional HVAs
Staff training exercises and continuous improvement	• The Joint Commission requires two per year • More frequent testing to allow the best opportunity to discover areas for improvement

key elements of disaster triage include who will be assigned to each role, locations where groups of patients will be treated, and dissemination of adequate resources to defined areas.[6]

Simple Triage And Rapid Treatment (START) is one common disaster triage system (Fig. 22-1A) and consists of four color-coded groups of patients sorted according to the level of care required: red (immediate care required), yellow (urgent care required), green (minimal care required), and black (end-of-life care required).[6] START has been adapted for use with pediatric patients (JumpSTART) (Fig. 22-1B).

Decontamination

Other considerations during many types of disasters include the potential risk of contamination and the associated danger to the hospital and staff. Whether a natural disaster, industrial incident, or manmade event, recognizing the need for adequate decontamination is crucial to ensuring the safety of emergency personnel and minimizing any cross-contamination to other people.[12]

Many mass casualty incidents have shown that most victims do not wait for emergency response personnel in order to receive field decontamination, transporting themselves to the hospital via privately owned vehicles (POVs).[12] Therefore, hospitals anticipating this group, will include decontamination plans, procedures, personnel, and equipment ready to handle the expected influx of patients arriving by POV who may require decontamination.

Up to 95% of hazardous material can be decontaminated by removing the patient's clothing and immediately washing the skin.[12,13] In order to minimize any potential adverse effects due to decontamination delays, only basic lifesaving measures are completed in the triage zone of a decontamination area.[11] If any patient contamination is suspected, ensuring the triage area is downwind and downhill from the clean treatment area is key for an optimal decontamination process.[13] An example of a typical decontamination design is seen in Figure 22-2.[12]

Evacuation

When the ED or hospital are part of the disaster event, evacuation needs to be considered. Therefore, it is vital that trauma nurses understand and prepare for possibilities such as loss of emergency power, patient evacuation, establishing alternate care facilities, and use of other facilities' mutual aid agreements. Once a situation escalates to threaten the health or safety of a facility's patients, visitors, and staff, evacuation may be necessary.[14] Some key considerations include the following:[14]

- Identification of transportation resources: Both within and outside the facility, it is necessary to identify the order of evacuation (ambulatory before stretcher patients) and the methods of evacuation (stair chairs or blanket carries).

- Tracking of patients: This allows staff to record which patients went to other areas within the facility or community, and their locations. This facilitates not only continuity of patient care, but the ability to inform families and visitors of the current patient location.

Figure 22-2. Sample Decontamination Design

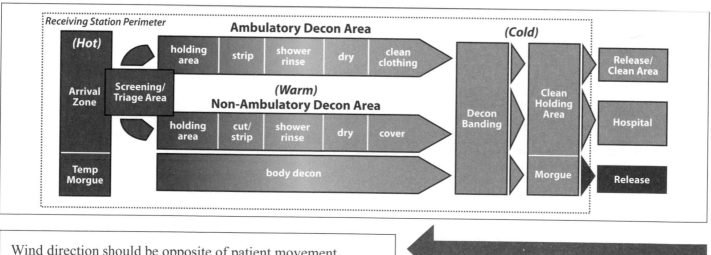

Wind direction should be opposite of patient movement.

Establishing a decontamination area requires thought regarding the various zones (hot, warm, and cold) and patient flow through them. Only basic lifesaving measures should be performed in the hot zone.
Adapted from Vogt & Sorenson.[12]

Figure 22-1A. START Adult Triage

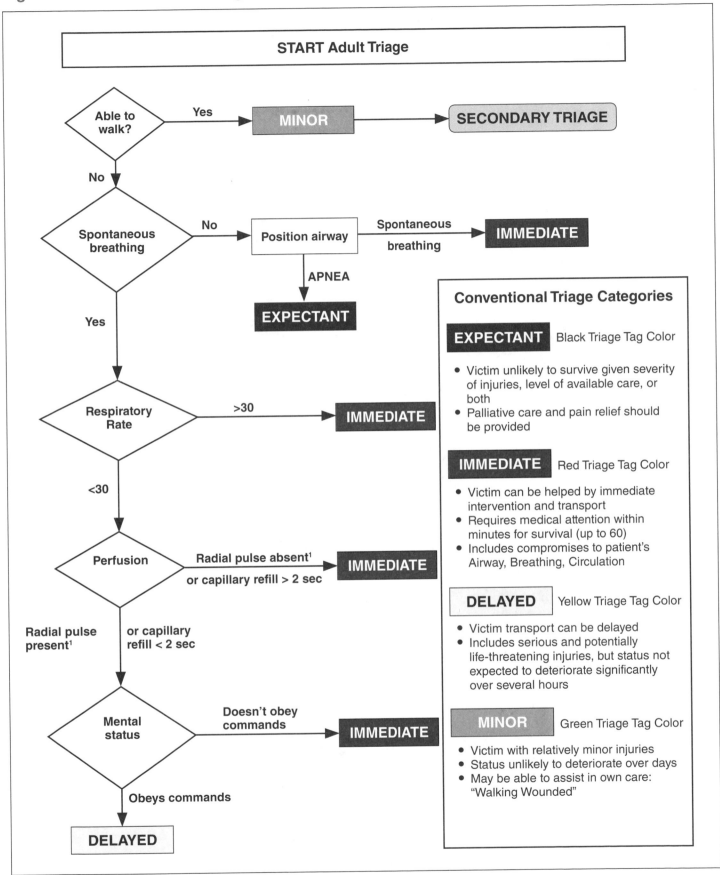

From U.S. Department of Health & Human Services. (2013, February 22). *START adult triage algorithm*. Retrieved from http://chemm.nlm.nih.gov/startadult.htm

Figure 22-1B. JumpSTART Pediatric MCI Triage

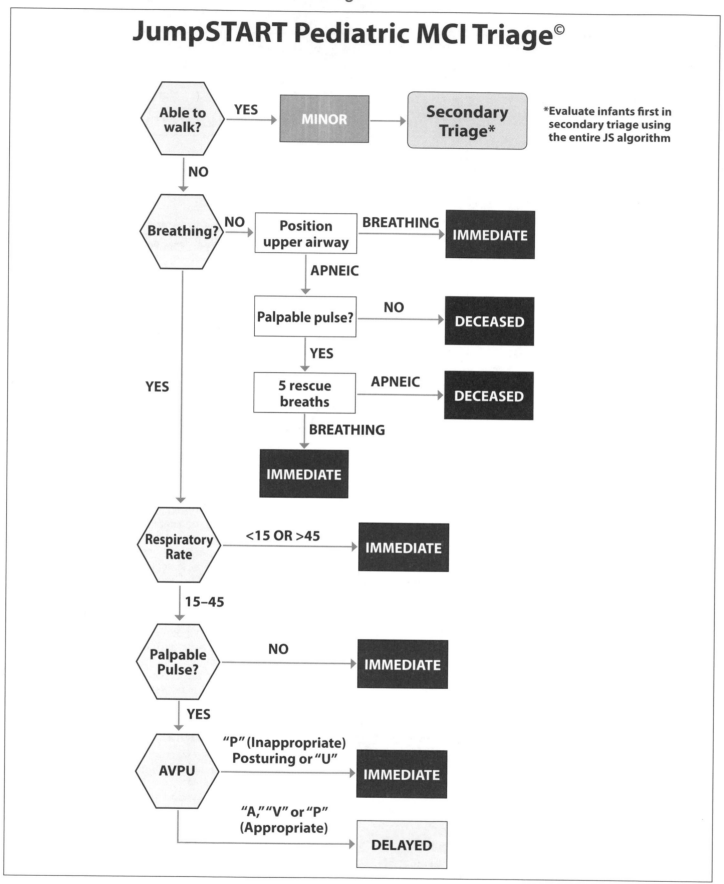

JumpSTART Pediatric MCI Triage©

Able to walk? → YES → MINOR → Secondary Triage*

*Evaluate infants first in secondary triage using the entire JS algorithm

↓ NO

Breathing? → NO → Position upper airway → BREATHING → IMMEDIATE

↓ APNEIC

Palpable pulse? → NO → DECEASED

↓ YES

5 rescue breaths → APNEIC → DECEASED

↓ BREATHING

IMMEDIATE

(Breathing? → YES) ↓

Respiratory Rate → <15 OR >45 → IMMEDIATE

↓ 15–45

Palpable Pulse? → NO → IMMEDIATE

↓ YES

AVPU → "P" (Inappropriate) Posturing or "U" → IMMEDIATE

→ "A," "V" or "P" (Appropriate) → DELAYED

From Romig, L. E. (2012, May 29). *JumpSTART home page.* Retrieved from http://www.jumpstarttriage.com/

- Transport of supplies, records, and medications: Knowing which supplies, medications, and records need to go with the patient is essential. This process includes protocols and processes for transfer of controlled substances to other care providers and ensuring privacy of patient records.
- Alternate care sites: Part of the HVA includes the identification of alternate care facilities in case the current facility proves to be unsafe or unhealthy for patients, staff, and visitors. Memoranda of Understanding (MOU) are developed ahead of time to address considerations such as facility proximity and the resources to provide the healthcare needs of patients based on various care priorities and acuity.

Types of Disasters

Natural and Manmade Disasters

Floods, hurricanes, wildfires, severe winter weather, and earthquakes are all classified as natural disasters.[15] As part of hospital disaster preparedness, facilities maintain an awareness of the potential for high-risk natural disasters in their surrounding communities and make appropriate preparations. For example, coastal regions have a higher tendency for hurricanes and flooding, whereas mountainous regions may have a tendency for severe winter weather.

Manmade disasters occur suddenly, and their impact is more difficult to predict, which requires a heightened sense of awareness. Regardless of type, if there is an agent involved, immediate identification of the agent is not as important as the immediate recognition of and response to any unusual symptoms presenting across various age groups and populations. It is also critical that trauma nurses ensure their own protection before assisting others, which is contrary to the nurse's natural inclination to assist others first. This protection extends to the emergency treatment area as well. **The overarching principle is this: The nurse cannot help anyone if he or she is affected by the exposure and becomes a patient as well.**

The Department of Homeland Security reports that reliable chemical, biologic, radiologic, nuclear, and explosive (CBRNE) countermeasures can be used to "protect life, health, property, and commerce."[16] An overview of each of the CBRNE components is important to gain an understanding of potential disaster risk, complete the hazard vulnerability assessment, and create emergency operations plans for events that are most likely to occur in a specific area.

Chemical Agents

Historically, chemical agents have been used in warfare. However, most chemical-related incidents in the U.S. have been the result of industrial accidents.[17]

Table 22-2 lists common chemical agents and their known signs and symptoms. Trauma nurses who are aware of these agents and their presenting symptoms and are able to recognize similar patient presentations in a timely manner may be able to detect a possible hazardous event, intervene to begin lifesaving measures, and help to prevent further exposures.

Biologic Agents

According to the Centers for Disease Control and Prevention (CDC), education is recommended for healthcare providers regarding any illness patterns and diagnostic clues that signal an unusual infectious disease outbreak associated with the release of biologic agent.[18] The impact of these agents may not be immediate because of the delay between exposure to the agent and illness onset. Additionally, outbreaks associated with intentional releases can closely resemble those which occur naturally. Indications of intentional release of a biologic agent include (1) an unusual temporal or geographic clustering of illness, and (2) an unusual age distribution for common diseases.[18]

The CDC defines three concepts to consider with threats for biologic agents that have potential to be used as weapons, based on ease of dissemination or transmission: (1) potential for major public health impact (high mortality); (2) potential for public panic and social disruption; and (3) requirements for public health preparedness.[19] Different potential biologic agents are listed in Table 22-3.[19]

Radiologic/Nuclear Events

For radiologic or nuclear events, three basic elements are important to keep in mind regarding exposure: time, distance, and shielding (Fig. 22-3). The risk of acute radiation illness is minimized by a shorter duration of exposure, a greater distance from the nucleus of the explosion, and a greater amount of shielding between the person and the explosion (Fig. 22-4).[20] Table 22-4 describes acute radiation syndromes.

Explosives

Explosions have the greatest likelihood of occurring in any community. They can be intentional (a bomb or improvised explosive device) or unintentional (an industrial incident or car fire). An explosive blast is an intense exothermic reaction created by a chemical rapidly converting from a solid or liquid into a gas.[21] See Chapter 4, Biomechanics, Kinematics, and Mechanisms of Injury, for information on injuries related to explosions and blasts.

Table 22-2. Chemical Agents

Agent	Signs and Symptoms	Decontamination
Nerve agents		
• **Tabun (GA)** • **Sarin (GB)** • **Soman (GD)** • **V Agents (VX)**	SLUDGE: • Salivation • Lacrimation • Urination • Defecation • Gastric disturbances • Emesis	• Remove contaminated clothing • Flush with a soap and water solution for patients • Flush with large amounts of a 5% bleach and water solution for objects
Vesicants (Blister agents)		
• **Sulfur mustard (H)** • **Distilled mustard (HD)** • **Nitrogen mustard (HN-1,3)** • **Mustargen (HN2)**	• Acts first as a cellular irritant, then as a cellular poison • Conjunctivitis, reddened skin, blisters, nasal irritation, inflammation of throat and lungs	• Remove contaminated clothing • Flush with soap and water solution for patients • Flush with large amounts of a 5% bleach and water solution for objects
• **Lewisite (L)**	• Immediate pain with blisters later	
Pulmonary agents		
Phosgene oxime (CX)	• Immediate pain with blisters later • Necrosis equivalent to full and partial thickness burns	• Leave area of exposure and get to fresh air • Remove clothing and double bag in plastic bags • Copious irrigation and skin cleansing with soap and water
Chlorine	• Coughing, chest tightness, burning sensation to nose/throat/eyes, watery eyes, blurry vision, nausea and vomiting, shortness of breath/ difficulty breathing, burning pain/ redness/blisters on skin	
Chemical asphyxiants (Blood agents)		
• **Hydrogen cyanide (AC)** • **Cyanogen chloride (CK)** • **Arsine (SA)**	• Cherry red skin or ~ 30% cyanosis • May appear to be gasping for air • Seizures prior to death • Effect is similar to asphyxiation but is more sudden	• Remove contaminated clothing • Flush with a soap and water solution for patients • Flush with large amounts of 5% bleach and water solution for objects

From Edgewood Chemical Biological Center.[19]

Table 22-3. Biologic Agents

Agent	Incubation	Symptoms	Transmission	Precautions	Treatment
Anthrax (Bacillus anthracis)	Usually <7 days but can occur up to 60 days post-exposure	• Cutaneous: Raised itchy bump initially; progresses to ulcerated blister with necrotic center • Inhalation: Initially, nonspecific flu-like illness characterized by fever, myalgia, headache, nonproductive cough, and mild chest discomfort; followed by marked high fever, dyspnea, stridor, cyanosis, and shock	Person-to-person spread extremely unlikely	Standard precautions	Multiple antibiotics including doxycycline, fluroquinolones and others effective for both types
Botulism (Clostridium botulinum)	Usually 12–36 hours (range of 6 h–2 wks)	Double vision, blurred vision, drooping eyelids, slurred speech, difficulty swallowing, and dry mouth	Not spread person-to-person	Standard precautions	Antitoxin effective if diagnosed early; supportive care
Plague (Yersinia pestis)	2–4 days	Fever, chills, headache, severe debilitation, rapidly developing shortness of breath, and chest pain	Person-to-person	Airborne, droplet, and contact precautions recommended	• Early treatment crucial • Streptomycin, gentamicin when streptomycin not available • Other antibiotics also effective
Smallpox (Variola major)	7–17 days	Initially, high fever, fatigue, headache, and backaches; rash usually develops 2 to 3 days after onset of symptoms. Rash appears first on the mouth, face, and forearms, then spreads inward to trunk of the body.	Person-to-person	Airborne and droplet precautions recommended	Supportive therapy; antibiotics to treat secondary infections
Tularemia (Francisella tularensis)	Usually 3–5 days (range of 1–14 days)	• Insect bite: Slow-healing sore and swollen lymph nodes • Inhalation: High fever, chills, headache, fatigue, cough, and chest pain • Ingestion: Sore throat, abdominal pain, diarrhea, and vomiting	Not spread person-to-person		Streptomycin; gentamicin also effective

From Edgewood Chemical Biological Center.[19]

Table 22-3. Biologic Agents (Continued)

Agent	Incubation	Symptoms	Transmission	Precautions	Treatment
Viral Hemorrhagic Fevers (VHF)	Usually < 2 weeks (range of 4–21 days)	• Symptoms are fever, fatigue, dizziness, muscle aches, loss of strength, and exhaustion • Severe cases often show signs of bleeding under the skin, in internal organs, or from body orifices • Severely ill patients may also experience shock, nervous system malfunction, coma, delirium, and seizures • Some types of VHF are associated with renal failure	Person-to-person	Airborne and droplet precautions recommended	Supportive care; some types responsive to antiviral medication

From Edgewood Chemical Biological Center.[19]

Table 22-4. Acute Radiation Syndromes[25]

Syndrome	Dose*	Prodromal Stage	Latent Stage	Manifest Illness Stage	Recovery
Hematopoietic (bone marrow)	> 0.7 Gy (> 70 rads) (*mild symptoms may occur from exposure as low as 0.3 Gy or 30 rads*)	• Symptoms are anorexia, nausea and vomiting • Onset occurs 1 hour–2 days after exposure • Stage lasts for minutes to days	• Stem cells in bone marrow are dying, although patient may appear and feel well • Stage lasts 1–6 weeks	• Symptoms are anorexia, fever, and malaise • Drop in all blood cell counts occurs for several weeks • Primary cause of death is infection and hemorrhage • Survival decreases with increasing dose • Most deaths occur within a few months after exposure	• In most cases, bone marrow cells will begin to repopulate the marrow • There should be full recovery for a large percentage of patients from a few weeks up to two years after exposure • Death may occur for some patients at 1.2 Gy (120 rads) • The LD50/60† is about 2.5–5 Gy (250–500 rads)
Gastrointestinal (GI)	> 10 Gy (> 1000 rads) (*some symptoms may occur from exposure as low as 6 Gy or 600 rads*)	• Symptoms are anorexia, severe nausea, vomiting, cramps, and diarrhea • Onset occurs within a few hours after exposure • Stage lasts about 2 days	• Stem cells in bone marrow and cells lining GI tract are dying, although patient may appear and feel well • Stage lasts less than 1 week	• Symptoms are malaise, anorexia, severe diarrhea, fever, dehydration, and electrolyte imbalance • Death is due to infection, dehydration, and electrolyte imbalance • Death occurs within 2 weeks of exposure	• The LD100‡ is about 10 Gy (1,000 rads)

*The absorbed doses quoted here are "gamma equivalent" values. Neutrons or protons generally produce the same effects as gamma, beta, or radiographs but at lower doses. If the patient has been exposed to neutrons or protons, consult radiation experts on how to interpret the dose.

†The LD50/60 is the dose that can kill 50% of the exposed population in 60 days.

‡The LD100 is the dose that can kill 100% of the exposed population.

Note: LD indicates lethal dose.

From Centers for Disease Control and Prevention.[25]

Table 22-4. Acute Radiation Syndromes[25] (Continued)

Syndrome	Dose*	Prodromal Stage	Latent Stage	Manifest Illness Stage	Recovery
Cardiovascular (CV)/Central nervous system (CNS)	> 50 Gy (5000 rads) *(some symptoms may occur from exposure as low as 20 Gy or 2000 rads)*	• Symptoms are extreme nervousness and confusion; severe nausea, vomiting, and watery diarrhea; loss of consciousness; and burning sensations of the skin • Onset occurs within minutes of exposure • Stage lasts for minutes to hours	• Patient may return to partial functionality • Stage may last for hours but often is shorter	• Symptoms include return of watery diarrhea, convulsions, and coma • Onset occurs 5 to 6 hours after exposure • Death occurs within 3 days of exposure	• No recovery is expected

*The absorbed doses quoted here are "gamma equivalent" values. Neutrons or protons generally produce the same effects as gamma, beta, or radiographs but at lower doses. If the patient has been exposed to neutrons or protons, consult radiation experts on how to interpret the dose.
†The LD50/60 is the dose that can kill 50% of the exposed population in 60 days.
‡The LD100 is the dose that can kill 100% of the exposed population.
Note: LD indicates lethal dose.
From Centers for Disease Control and Prevention.[25]

Figure 22-3. Radiation Exposure Reduction Techniques

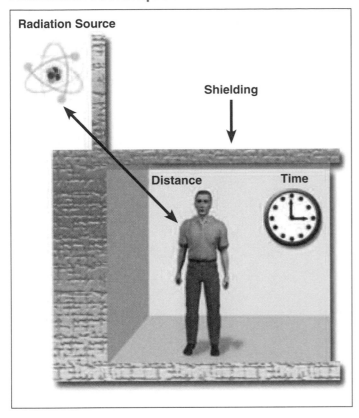

The three most important elements related to protection from radiation exposure are time, distance, and shielding. To minimize the adverse effects of radiation, the goal is to minimize the amount of exposure (time), be as far away as possible from ground zero (distance), and have as many barriers between you and ground zero as possible (shielding).
From Federal Emergency Management Agency.[23]

Figure 22-4. Penetrating Abilities of Various Types of Radiation

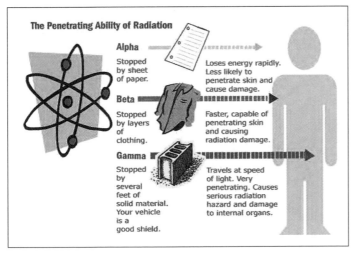

Alpha and beta particles are more easily stopped by barriers such as clothing or shielding, while gamma rays are very penetrating and are the leading cause of acute radiation sickness.
From Conference of Radiation Control Program Directors.[24]

Recovery

Long after patients have been treated for physical injuries related to a disaster, the psychological effects may continue, both for patients and healthcare professionals. If trauma nurses are aware of and can recognize the normal responses to traumatic events such as disasters, they will be in a position to help not only any traumatized patients, but also any colleagues that were affected.[22] See Chapter 21, Psychosocial Aspects of Trauma Care, for additional information.

Other considerations for recovery include:[14]

- Restoration of patient care and management activities: Within the ED operational ability in the aftermath of a disaster, it is important to assess repair of damage or disruption to the facility, restocking of supplies, restoration of services, and accounting of any equipment damaged or lost during the disaster process. This is important not just to restart clinical operations but also for logistical and financial accounting. This also means addressing staff and staffing needs. Were any staff members lost or injured in the incident, or do any need psychological recovery time? How will those deficits be managed to restore the facility's normal day-to-day function?

- Repatriation of patients: Establishing a protocol for how to safely transport patients back to the facility, when appropriate, is necessary for reestablishing patient care operations and alleviating the burden on any alternate care facilities or extra staff used during the disaster. Reunite families as soon as possible. It is common for family members to be transferred to different facilities, and effective communication will facilitate this repatriation process.

Summary

Disasters can occur anywhere at any time. Although most disasters are natural, it is important for trauma nurses to be aware of and familiar with manmade disasters. As was evident during the aftermath of the Joplin tornado, understanding the basic foundation of a hospital's disaster response program and engaging in the development of that program will help to ensure that nurses and their departments are prepared to handle any type of disaster while ensuring patients and the community are being provided with the best care possible.

References

1. South Dakota Department of Health. (2011, August 2). *Medical response to the Joplin tornado, May 22, 2011.* Retrieved from http://doh.sd.gov/ Prepare/Hospital/Documents/Joplin.pdf

2. National Weather Service. (2012, May 21). *Joplin tornado event summary: May 22, 2011.* Retrieved from http://www.crh.noaa.gov/ sgf/?n=event_2011may22_summary

3. Associated Press. (2012, May 19). *Records: Joplin twister was costliest since 1950.* Retrieved from http://www.foxnews.com/us/2012/05/19/ records-joplin-twister-was-costliest-since-150/

4. Disaster Management Training Programme. (1994). *Disaster management (2nd ed.).* Retrieved from http://iaemeuropa.terapad.com/resources/8959/ assets/documents/UN%20DMTP%20-%20Disaster%20Preparedness.pdf

5. World Health Organization. (n.d.). *Definitions: Emergencies.* Retrieved from http://www.who.int/hac/about/definitions/en/index.html

6. Reisner, A. (2006). Triage. In G. Cittone (Ed.), Disaster medicine (pp. 283–290). Philadelphia, PA: Mosby.

7. Centers for Disease Control and Prevention. (2012, November 16). *Preparedness for all hazards.* Retrieved from http://emergency.cdc.gov/ hazards-all.asp

8. Federal Emergency Management Agency. (2008, December 2). *National Incident Management System.* Retrieved from http://www.fema.gov/pdf/ emergency/nims/NIMS_core.pdf

9. California Emergency Medical Services Authority. (2006, August). *Hospital incident command structure guidebook.* Retrieved from http:// www.emsa.ca.gov/HICS/files/Guidebook_Glossary.pdf

10. Sutingo, N. (2006). The incident command system. In G. Cittone (Ed.), *Disaster medicine* (pp. 208–214). Philadelphia, PA: Mosby.

11. Chaffee, M. W. & Oster, N. S. (2006). The role of hospitals in disasters. In G. Cittone (Ed.), *Disaster medicine* (pp. 34–42). Philadelphia, PA: Mosby.

12. Vogt, B., & Sorenson, J. (2006). Chemical decontamination. In G. Cittone (Ed.), *Disaster medicine* (pp. 459–464). Philadelphia, PA: Mosby.

13. Alexander, G.A. (2006). Radiation decontamination. In G. Cittone (Ed.), *Disaster medicine* (pp. 465–472). Philadelphia, PA: Mosby.

14. American College of Emergency Physicians. (2011). *Hospital evacuation: Principles and practices.* Retrieved from http://tinyurl.com/ hospitalevacuation

15. Centers for Disease Control and Prevention. (n.d.). *National disasters & severe weather.* Retrieved from http://emergency.cdc.gov/disasters/

16. U.S. Department of Homeland Security. (n.d.). *National strategy for chemical, biological, radiological, nuclear, and explosives standards.* Retrieved from http://www.dhs.gov/national-strategy-chemical-biological- radiological-nuclear-and-explosives-cbrne-standards

17. Marcozzi, D. (2006). Introduction to chemical disasters. In G. Cittone (Ed.), *Disaster medicine* (pp. 548–555). Philadelphia, PA: Mosby.

18. Centers for Disease Control and Prevention. (2011). *Criminal and epidemiological investigation handbook.* Retrieved from http://www.cdc. gov/phlp/docs/CrimEpiHandbook2011.pdf

19. Edgewood Chemical Biological Center. (n.d.). *Biological and chemical agent quick reference tables.* Retrieved from https://www.ecbc.army.mil/ hld/ip/bca_qr.htm

20. Mole, D. (2006). Introduction to nuclear/radiological disasters. In G. Cittone (Ed.), *Disaster medicine* (pp. 517–523). Philadelphia, PA: Mosby.

21. Greenberg, M. I., & Ntaba, D.W. (2006) Introduction of explosions and blasts. In G. Cittone (Ed.), *Disaster medicine* (pp. 736–744). Philadelphia, PA: Mosby.

22. Centers for Disease Control and Prevention. (2005, July 26). *Coping with a traumatic event.* Retrieved from http://www.emergency.cdc.gov/ masscasualties/copingpro.asp

23. Federal Emergency Management Agency. (2011). *Radiological emergency management.* Retrieved from http://emilms.fema.gov/IS3/FEMA_IS/is03/ assets/REM02-06-010.jpg

24. Conference of Radiation Control Program Directors, Inc. (2006). *Handbook for responding to a radiologic dispersal device [PDF document].* Retrieved from http://www.crcpd.org/rdd_handbook/rdd- handbook-forweb.pdf

25. Centers for Disease Control and Prevention. (2006, May 10). *Acute radiation syndrome: A fact sheet for physicians.* Retrieved from http:// www.bt.cdc.gov/radiation/arsphysicianfactsheet.asp

Chapter 23 • Transition of Care for the Trauma Patient

Robin S. Powers-Jarvis, MS, RNC, CCRN, CEN
B. Alex Markwell, MSN, MHA, MBA, CEN

Objectives

Upon completion of this chapter, the learner will be able to:

1. Describe trauma patient characteristics that may require specialized or a higher level of care.

2. Recognize national, state, and/or provincial laws and regulations in place to protect patients and to facilitate the improvement of outcomes and transport for trauma patients with complex injuries.

3. Examine the risks and benefits of both intrafacility and interfacility trauma transport.

4. Discuss transport modes and qualifications of transport team members.

5. Identify concepts that promote communication for intrafacility and interfacility transport.

Introduction

Patients who experience traumatic injury require rapid assessment and stabilization of life-threatening injuries and transport to a facility capable of providing definitive care. The American College of Surgeons (ACS) recommends that certain injured patients be transported to a verified trauma center with sufficient number and types of resources.[1] Time to treatment has also been identified as crucial to optimal patient outcome, particularly the time from injury to definitive care.[1] Timely and definitive care has been related to decreased morbidity and mortality from traumatic injury.[1]

As the patient moves through the trauma care continuum, multiple transfers and hand-offs occur. These may take place within the hospital (intrafacility) or to a different facility (interfacility). It is essential for each trauma care provider to assure safe transport and provide essential information regarding the care of the patient to the next care provider. This requires the trauma nurse to be aware of the resources available at their facility as well as local and regional policies, procedures, and laws, in particular those regarding transport.

Trauma Systems and Classification of Trauma Centers

Trauma care provided in the emergency setting is only one phase of the trauma care continuum. The trauma care continuum begins with injury prevention and involves each phase of the patient's progress from the point of injury through rehabilitation and reintegration into the community. Although trauma systems vary from jurisdiction to jurisdiction, the guidelines and standards published by the ACS incorporating injury prevention, acute care, and rehabilitation are widely used.

Since trauma nurses are involved in trauma patient transport, whether it is to send or receive the injured patient, it is beneficial to understand the trauma system and the methods used to define and classify trauma centers. The American College of Surgeons-Committee on Trauma (ACS-COT) describes capabilities and resources for four levels of trauma centers.[2] Hospitals may apply to the ACS to participate in a rigorous on-site survey and review process to achieve verification and be designated by the ACS as a trauma center. The partial description of each trauma center level is outlined in Table 23-1.

Initial Care and the Emergency Medical Treatment and Active Labor Act

In the United States (U.S.), the federal Emergency Medical Treatment and Active Labor Act (EMTALA) requires that all patients who present to an emergency department receive a medical screening examination and resuscitation and stabilization of any identified emergency condition. If the patient warrants treatment beyond the capabilities and resources of the initial facility and needs to be transferred, EMTALA requires that the following conditions be met prior to transfer:[3]

- Medical screening examination and necessary stabilizing interventions (within the capacity of the facility)
- Informed consent
- Accepting physician at the receiving facility

Table 23-1. ACS-COT Levels of Trauma Centers

Trauma Center Level	Description of Trauma Center
Level I	• A regional trauma center is a tertiary care facility • Capable of providing leadership and total care for every aspect of injury from prevention to rehabilitation • Commonly is a university-based teaching hospital with residency and postgraduate programs • Research and prevention programs are essential components
Level II	• Provides trauma resuscitation and initial definitive trauma care, regardless of severity of injury • Capabilities do not include comprehensive services and specialty care that is provided by Level I trauma centers • In many areas without access to a Level I facility, the Level II trauma center will take accountability to provide education, prevention, and community outreach
Level III	• Provides the trauma patient with prompt assessment, resuscitation, stabilization, and emergency surgery as necessary • Uses accepted trauma triage criteria and ACS transfer guidelines for definitive care of the trauma patient • Generally do not accept incoming trauma transfers
Level IV	• Provides initial assessment, interventions and resuscitation of the patient with advanced trauma life support, initial assessment, and intervention • Exists in a remote area and may be a clinic without a physician in-house • Provides 24-hour emergency coverage by a physician • Provides care under the direction of a Level I or II trauma center • Provides advanced trauma life support until patients can be transferred to a higher level of trauma care • Uses ACS trauma triage and transport criteria • Generally do not accept incoming transfers

Data from American College of Surgeons Committee on Trauma.[2]

- Available bed and resources to deliver appropriate care at the receiving facility
- Patient report provided to the receiving facility
- All available medical records, laboratory, radiographic, and other related information or copies provided to receiving facility or transferred with the patient
- Appropriate transfer personnel

Although these requirements are only pertinent to those U.S. facilities that receive government funding, they are widely considered the standard of care.

Characteristics of Trauma Patients Who Require Transport

When the patient's care needs exceed available resources at the initial facility, transport to a facility that can provide the necessary specialized or higher level of care is recommended. In an organized trauma system, severely injured trauma patients are transferred to the closest facility with appropriate resources; preferably a verified trauma center. The ACS-COT has established guidelines to help identify those patients most at risk who would benefit by being transported to a trauma center (Table 23-2).

Decision to Transport

The decision to transport a patient to a specialized or higher level of care rests solely with the physician responsible for the patient's care at the initial receiving facility. Directly after the primary survey, a reevaluation decision point emphasizes early consideration for patient transfer. At the end of the secondary survey, there is another reevaluation point when all patient assessment findings can be summarized and a determination made of the need for transfer. Timeliness is key. Factors for transfer consideration include:

- Knowledge of facility resources, capabilities and limitations to provide the necessary care for that trauma patient
- Availability of specialty or higher level of trauma centers to provide definitive care (Level I trauma center, burn centers, pediatric trauma centers, acute brain and spinal cord injury referral centers, re-implantation centers, high-risk obstetrical centers)

- Available transportation services (ground, air, etc.)
- Team configuration and type of equipment required to accomplish the transport
- Risks and benefits to the patient (the patient's reaction to transport and/or the mode of transport selected)
- Policies, procedures, protocols, and transfer agreements in place

Once the decision to transport the patient to another facility is made and the patient is accepted by the receiving facility, transportation arrangements are determined, and the sending and receiving physicians collaborate to choose the most appropriate mode of transport. Considerations include the availability of equipment, workspace needs, qualifications of the transport personnel, weather and road conditions or other environmental factors, as well as the patient's or family's preference. Familiarity with existing procedures, protocols, and interfacility transfer agreements as well as

Table 23-2. American College of Surgeons' Criteria for Consideration of Transfer

A. Critical Injuries to Level I or Highest Regional Trauma Center
• Carotid or vertebral arterial injury
• Torn thoracic aorta or great vessel
• Cardiac rupture
• Bilateral pulmonary contusion with PaO_2:FiO_2 ratio < 200mm Hg
• Major abdominal vascular injury
• Grade IV or V liver injuries requiring > 6 units RBC transfusion in 6 hrs
• Unstable pelvic fracture requiring > 6 units RBC transfusion in 6 hrs
• Fracture or dislocation with loss of distal pulses
B. Life-threatening Injuries to Level I or Level II Trauma Center
• Penetrating injury or open fracture of the skull
• GCS score < 14 or lateralizing neurologic signs
• Spinal fracture or spinal cord deficit
• > 2 unilateral rib fractures or bilateral rib fractures with pulmonary contusion
• Open long bone fracture
• Significant torso injury with advanced comorbid disease (coronary artery disease, chronic obstructive pulmonary disease, type 1 diabetes mellitus, or immunosuppression)

Note: GCS indicates Glasgow Coma Scale; RBC, red blood cells.
Note: It may be appropriate for an injured patient to undergo operative control of ongoing hemorrhage before transfer if a qualified surgeon and operating room resources are promptly available at the referring hospital.
Reprinted from American College of Surgeons Committee on Trauma.[2]

the regulatory requirements pertinent to the jurisdiction, help to guide the interfacility transfer process.

Modes of Transport

The most frequently used interfacility modes of transport are described in Table 23-3.

Transport Team Composition

Intrafacility

Intrafacility transport may involve multiple transfers, to various departments: radiology, special procedures, angiography, surgery, inpatient unit, rehabilitation, or other areas within the hospital. Typically, the trauma nurse prepares, coordinates, and carries out these intrafacility transports. Respiratory therapists, additional nurses, and other personnel may assist. Adequate numbers of personnel with appropriate skills to accomplish the transport is essential.[4,5]

Interfacility

The sending physician is responsible for the care of the patient until arrival at the receiving facility and makes decisions regarding appropriate level of care and method of transport.

The composition of the transport team used during interfacility transport is determined based on the patient's condition and required level of care.[6] Depending on the nature and severity of the injuries, personnel trained in critical care or specialized teams may be required.[7]

- If ground transportation is used, the transferring facility may send personnel and equipment with the patient
  - This usually requires a nurse who is experienced in the care of trauma patients, as well as other qualified transport team members[7]
  - In some instances, specialty trauma centers may send ground transport with their own specially trained personnel

Table 23-3. Modes of Patient Transportation

Mode of Transport	Benefits	Drawbacks
Ground	• Readily available • May have space for family members • Weather less of a factor • Less restriction on weight of the team, patient, and equipment	• Longer travel time • Traffic and road conditions • Risk of collision
Helicopter	• Rapid transport within short distances • Improved survival rates • Usually a dedicated team with advanced skills • Improves access to Level I and II trauma centers for those in rural areas	• Restricted use in certain weather conditions • Expensive • Risk of crash • Noise and vibration • Physiologic changes from altitude • Space and weight restrictions • Not all hospitals are equipped with helipad
Fixed-wing aircraft	• Able to handle longer distances than helicopter • May be pressurized	• Prolonged transport times with transition to and from hospital to airfield

Data from Emergency Nurses Association. (2012). *Emergency nursing pediatric course provider manual* (4th ed.). Des Plaines, IL: Author; Galvagno, S. M., Haut, E. R., Zafar, S. N., Millin, M. G., Efron, D. T., … Haider, A. H. (2012). Association between helicopter vs ground emergency medical services and survival for adults with major trauma. *Journal of the American Medical Association, 307*(15), 1602–1610; Holleran, R. S. (Ed.). (2010). Transport physiology. In *Patient transport: Principles and practice* (4th ed., pp. 39–61). St. Louis, MO: Mosby Elsevier; Isakov, A. (2009). Urgent air-medical transport: Right patient, place and time. *Canadian Medical Association Journal, 181*(9), 569–570; McVey, J., Petrie, D. A., & Tallon, J. M. (2010). Air versus ground transport of the major trauma patient: A natural experiment. *Prehospital Emergency Care, 14*(1), 45–50; Sullivent, E. E., Faul, M., & Wald, M. M. (2011). Reduced mortality in injured adults transported by helicopter emergency medical services. *Prehospital Emergency Care, 15*(3), 295–302.

- It is important to have facility policies in place before the actual transfer becomes necessary

- Air transportation usually involves a critical care team

  - Air-medical transport teams usually include two clinical care providers in various combinations of roles, plus the pilot

    - Nurse and paramedic is a common combination

    - At times, it may include a physician, respiratory therapist, or some combination of these[7]

  - Air transport teams are trained for and qualified to monitor and respond to altitude-related hazards in addition to caring for traditional trauma conditions and complications[7]

Risks of Transport

Any transport of trauma patients regardless if inter- or intrafacility, involves risk. It is the responsibility of the team caring for the patient to ensure that the transport is accomplished in a manner that is efficient, yet safe for both the patient and the transport team. The trauma nurse anticipates the potential for, and prepares to manage the following risks of transport:

- Loss of airway patency

- Displaced or obstructed tubes, lines, or catheters

- Dislodged splinting devices

- Need to replace or reinforce dressings

- Deterioration in patient status; change in vital signs or level of consciousness

- Injury to patient and/or team members

Nursing Considerations for Transport

Multiple factors can affect the outcome of patient transport. Planning is essential. Nursing considerations include assisting with the medical screening examination and required resuscitation and/or stabilizing interventions, within the capabilities of the sending facility. Other considerations include:

- Patient consent

  - Assist with and support the process to assure that the patient and/or family are aware of the need for, as well as the risks and benefits of transport, so they can make an informed decision regarding transport and sign the consent for transfer

- Sending facility

  - Ensure that the sending physician has received acceptance from the receiving hospital for transfer

  - Arrange for the transport team

  - Provide a patient report to the receiving nurse

  - Send copies of all available medical records, laboratory, radiographic, and other related reports[3]

- Patient care

  - Ensure definitive airway control

  - Suction the airway and endotracheal tube as needed

  - Maintain breathing and provide assisted ventilations

  - Ensure patency and flow rate of intravenous (IV) infusions

  - Continually reassess the patient's neurologic status

  - Secure all monitoring devices and equipment, such as chest tubes

- Family and patient preparation

  - Explain the logistics of the transport to the patient, family, and assistive staff

  - Ensure the family has information regarding where the patient is being taken and directions to that location

  - Ensure the family has seen the patient prior to departure, if possible

- Transport team

  - Give report to the transporting personnel as necessary

  - Provide the team with copies of documentation as needed

- Follow-up

  - Call the receiving facility to notify them of the patient's departure time and estimated time of arrival (ETA)

  - Fax or send electronically any additional laboratory or radiographic reports that have returned after the patient has departed

Equipment for Transport

The trauma nurse caring for the patient is responsible to ensure the availability of proper equipment needed during transport. Depending on the status of the patient, equipment may include:

- Airway equipment

  - Suction devices

  - Oral airways

  - Endotracheal tubes

  - Laryngoscope blades and handles

  - Supplies to secure the endotracheal tube

  - Failed airway equipment such as a supraglottic device

  - Bag-mask device

- Medications
  - Pain medications
  - Sedation agents
  - Vasoactive medications
  - Resuscitation medications
- Intravenous access supplies
- Intravenous fluids
- Cardiac monitor/defibrillator
- Equipment to monitor vital signs including oxygen saturation and capnography
- Restraints

Emergency Department Boarding

Once initial assessment and stabilization of the trauma patient has been completed and the decision to transfer the patient to another facility or to admit has been made, it is essential that the patient be moved from the ED to an inpatient unit as quickly as possible for the next phase in the continuum of care.[8–10] If an inpatient bed is not readily available, post resuscitation care of the trauma patient may be provided in the ED. ED staff may be required to perform inpatient care or alternative staff may be assigned by nursing management. It is important that EDs have policies and procedures in place related to the nursing care of the critically ill trauma patient while he or she is being held (boarded) in the ED. It is essential that the patient receive the same standard of care that would be provided on the assigned inpatient unit.

Summary

A majority of trauma patients who present to the ED will require transport or patient hand-off during their care—whether intrafacility to another department such as radiology or the inpatient unit, or interfacility to a trauma or specialized center of care. The trauma nurse ensures safe and appropriate transition of care regardless of how and where the patient is being transported. There are institutional, regional, and federal laws, guidelines, policies, and procedures regarding patient transportation. The goal of the trauma team at both the sending and receiving facilities is to provide quality care, continuing the same level of care during transition, safe care for the patient, protecting them from further injury, and safe practice for the trauma team.

References

1. American College of Surgeons. (2012). *Advanced trauma life support student course manual* (9th ed.). Chicago, IL: Author.

2. American College of Surgeons Committee on Trauma. (2006). *Resources for optimal care of the injured patient.* Chicago, IL: Author.

3. Center for Medicare & Medical Service (2009, May 29). *Revision to Appendix V, "Emergency Medical Treatment & Active Labor Act (EMTALA) interpretive guidelines."* Retrieved from http://www.cms.gov/Regulations-and-Guidance/Guidance/Transmittals/downloads/R46SOMA.pdf

4. Beachley, M. (2009). Evolution of the trauma cycle. In K. A. McQuillan, M. B. Flynn Makic, & E. Whalen (Eds.), *Trauma nursing from resuscitation through rehabilitation* (4th ed., pp. 1–18). St. Louis, MO: Saunders Elsevier.

5. Fitzpatrick, M.K., & McMaster, J., (2009). Performance improvement and patient safety in trauma care. In K. A. McQuillan, M. B. Flynn Makic, & E. Whalen (Eds.), *Trauma nursing from resuscitation through rehabilitation* (4th ed., pp. 29–43). St. Louis, MO: Saunders Elsevier.

6. Von Rueden, K.T. (2009). Nursing practice through the cycle of trauma. In K. A. McQuillan, M. B. Flynn Makic, & E. Whalen (Eds.), *Trauma nursing from resuscitation through rehabilitation* (4th ed., pp. 136–160). St. Louis, MO: Saunders Elsevier.

7. Commission of Accreditation of Medical Transport Systems. (2012, August 20). *Approved 9th edition accreditation standards.* Retrieved from http://www.camts.org/Stds_Approved_EditedLL8-30-12.pdf

8. Mowery, N. T., Dougherty, S. D., Hildreth, A. N., Holmes, J. H., Chang, M. C., Martin, R. S., ... Miller, P. R. (2011). Emergency department length of stay in an independent predictor of hospital mortality in trauma activation patients. *The Journal of Trauma, 70*(6), 1317–1325.

9. Intas, G., Stergiannis, P., Chalari, E., Tsoumakas, K., & Fildissis, G. (2012). The impact of ED boarding time, severity of illness, and discharge destination on outcomes of critically ill ED patients. *Advanced Emergency Nursing Journal, 34*(2), 164–169.

10. American College of Emergency Physicians. (2012). *Boarding of admitted and intensive care patients in the emergency department.* Retrieved from http://www.acep.org/Content.aspx?id=29132

Chapter 24 • Post Resuscitation Care in the Emergency Department

Judy Stevenson, MS, RN-BC, CCRN, CEN, CPEN, CSRN

Objectives

Upon completion of this chapter, the learner will be able to:

1. Recognize potential and actual patient outcomes as a result of injuries and resuscitation efforts.

2. Discuss assessment modalities for the trauma patient during post resuscitative care.

3. Identify potential complications by predicting the pathophysiologic changes for the trauma patient during post resuscitative care.

4. Plan appropriate interventions for the trauma patient during post resuscitative care.

5. Evaluate the effectiveness of nursing interventions for the trauma patient during post resuscitative care.

Introduction

With disease processes there is often predictability regarding the course of the disease. In trauma, predictability exists in the progression of pathophysiologic responses based on the patient's mechanism of injury (MOI) and associated injuries. The trauma nurse caring for the patient in this post resuscitation phase considers the MOI, the progression of events, the trauma team's interventions, the patient's response to those interventions, and potential sequelae associated with specific injuries. Putting these pieces together guides the trauma nurse in assessment, intervention, anticipation of problems, and prevention of complications.

Trauma happens quickly, yet the consequences of injury can take hours, months, or years to overcome. The continuum of care for the trauma patient does not end with the initial resuscitation. The goal of trauma care is to return the patient to his or her full potential within the community, and trauma care continues until that potential is reached.

Mechanism of Injury

All injures may not have been immediately identified, making the mechanism of injury (MOI) a pertinent consideration as the patient moves through the continuum of trauma care. Signs of injury—such as inflammation, edema, and contusions— may appear days later, revealing delayed or missed injuries (Table 24-1).

Post Resuscitation Care

Post resuscitation care takes place in many environments. It may begin in the ED or prehospital environment, but continues in the intensive care unit (ICU), operating room, medical or surgical unit, rehabilitation unit, and the patient's home after discharge. Multiple clinicians are involved in every step of the process of trauma care, making coordination of care and communication critical.

Post resuscitation care reflects the same organized and systematic approach as the initial resuscitation. The trauma nurse begins by reevaluating the airway, breathing, circulation, disability, and environmental parameters to note any change from the initial assessment and subsequent stabilization. Additional considerations include developing acidosis and coagulopathy.

Airway

Airway management continues to be the priority in trauma patients during post resuscitation care. If the patient does not have a definitive airway, continuous monitoring and reassessments alert the trauma nurse to potential compromise and identify the need for a definitive airway. See Chapter 6, Airway and Ventilation, for additional information.

Tube Displacement or Obstruction

Endotracheal tubes (ETT) can easily become displaced or obstructed. This requires diligent observation to assure the tube remains properly placed and patent. Use of the DOPE mnemonic can help the trauma nurse to resolve these issues. See Chapter 6, Airway and Ventilation, for more information. Additional considerations include the following:

Table 24-1. Delayed Injuries and Responses and Commonly Missed Injuries

System	Delayed Injuries and Responses	Commonly Missed Injuries
Respiratory	• Pneumothorax/Hemothorax • Flail chest • Pulmonary contusion • Diaphragmatic laceration • ARDS/ALI • Fat or pulmonary embolism	• Pneumothorax/Hemothorax • Pneumomediastinum
Cardiovascular	• Shock • Splenic rupture • Rhabdomyolysis • Sepsis • Burn wound	
Neurologic/Spinal	• Intracranial hematoma • Secondary brain injury • Alcohol withdrawal	• Spinal dislocations • Spinal cord syndromes
Abdominal	• Hollow viscus injury • Intestinal rupture • Compartment syndrome	• Liver injuries • Intestinal injuries • Renal injuries
Musculoskeletal	Compartment syndrome	Fractures of the: • Face • Extremities • Clavicle/scapula • Tibial plateau • Ribs

Data from Buduhan, & McRitchie[76] and Montamany et al.[78]

- If the patient has a definitive airway, meticulous monitoring assures correct tube placement, adequate oxygenation, and ventilation
- Informing other providers that an airway was difficult to place can prevent early extubation and allow for proper planning and preparation for extubation
  ◦ Use of a difficult airway identifier, such as an armband, or sticker on the endotracheal tube, a chart sticker, or progress note can communicate this information

Breathing and Ventilation
Patients with multiple injuries benefit from the administration and titration of oxygen (see Chapter 6, Airway and Ventilation, for more information). Oxygen concentration and delivery is guided by monitoring arterial blood gases (ABGs), end-tidal carbon dioxide ($ETCO_2$), and pulse oximetry (SpO_2) and frequent reassessment of the quality of the patient's respiratory rate and effort, changes in breathing patterns, lung sounds, and overall appearance. Trauma patients may exhibit several presentations with regard to their ventilation status:
- Patients with no respiratory effort, including those with the following:

- Central nervous system (CNS) depression
- Cervical cord transection above C3 or C4

- Patients with difficult, fast, or shallow respirations, including those with the following:
  - Thoracic injuries
  - Under deep sedation
  - Prescribed analgesia

Circulation
Fluid Management
Control of blood loss with adequate volume resuscitation can preserve end-organ function and prevent death from hemorrhagic shock.[1] After definitive control of hemorrhage, the goal of resuscitation shifts to restoration of normal tissue perfusion.[2]

Rapid administration of isotonic crystalloids used in the treatment of hypovolemic shock can result in fluid overload, capillary leak syndrome, and fluid shifts to the interstitial space. Because of this phenomenon, alternatives to large volume administration of isotonic fluid have been instituted, including massive transfusion protocols (see Chapter 7, Shock, for more information).

Use of Hypertonic Solutions
Theoretically beneficial for use as an intravascular volume expander, hypertonic solutions (3% sodium chloride) have higher osmotic pressures and draw water out of the interstitial space into the intravascular space, increasing intravascular volume. The benefit of hypertonic saline to treat hypovolemic shock is that it increases mean arterial pressure (MAP) by refilling the intravascular volume without worsening cerebral edema. This can mean optimized cerebral perfusion without increasing intracranial pressure (ICP).[3] At this point, research reports conflicting evidence in the effectiveness of hypertonic saline as a volume expander in producing improved outcomes. Its most useful role may be as a component in resuscitation of those with severe head injury and massive blood loss.[4–8]

Disability (Neurologic Status)
Diffuse brain injuries range from mild traumatic brain injuries (mTBIs) to severe hypoxic ischemic encephalopathy. The computed tomography (CT) scan may initially appear normal. As the inflammatory process unfolds, later CT scans may show diffuse swelling and a loss of normal gray-white differentiation.[5] Cerebral edema can easily develop in the trauma patient with brain injury. Elapsed time and fluid resuscitation can exacerbate cerebral edema unless steps are taken to stabilize and treat increased ICP.

Subdural hematomas may develop over time and are most common in the older adult or patient who chronically uses alcohol.[10] In these patients, brain atrophy produces a larger space between the dura mater and the skull where blood has space to accumulate before symptoms occur. Observe the patient over time for subtle neurologic changes that may identify increasing ICP or developing subdural hematoma.[10]

Exposure and Environmental Control
Hypothermia
Temperature monitoring is important not only in the immediate resuscitation period, but remains a concern throughout the care of the trauma patient. Continue to maintain a warm ambient temperature in the trauma room, use warming interventions as needed, and monitor the patient's temperature to avoid overheating. Prepare for heat loss during transport to other departments with warmed blankets or other techniques. Hypothermia has been associated with the following:[11]

- Development of coagulopathy
- Delayed wound healing
- Increased surgical site infections
- Prolonged hospitalization
- Increased myocardial complications
- Increased blood loss and need for blood transfusion
- Delayed recovery from anesthesia and increase in postoperative discomfort

One of the most serious complications of trauma is the deadly triad of hypothermia, acidosis, and coagulopathy. Because of this complication, prevention of hypothermia is vital to the hypovolemic trauma patient.[12]

There is some evidence that therapeutic hypothermia in patients with severe brain injury may result in a reduction in both morbidity and mortality.[13] This is begun, when indicated, only after hypovolemic shock is treated and acid–base balance is achieved. See Chapter 9, Brain, Cranial, and Maxillofacial Trauma, for more information.

Hyperthermia
Trauma patients can be at risk of hyperthermia due to the nature of their injuries. Hyperthermia syndromes are rare in the initial phase of severe trauma care, but temperature elevation from systemic inflammatory response may begin early.

Once the trauma patient is successfully resuscitated, his or her temperature and metabolic rate may increase.[14] This increase is a natural result of stimulation of the immune system, wound healing, tissue remodeling, and functional recovery.[15] While some degree of temperature elevation may be expected, the cause of the hyperthermia is vigorously investigated as additional treatment may be necessary.

Acidosis

Acidosis is a common complication of multiple traumatic injuries. An acidic environment can affect all body systems as it changes cellular function. Specifically, in the bloodstream, acidosis can affect oxygenation, making it more difficult for hemoglobin to bind with oxygen, decreasing oxygen saturation. Acidosis in combination with hypothermia intensifies the adverse effects on coagulation and worsens clotting times.[16] Acidosis can occur via two separate routes: respiratory or metabolic.[17]

Respiratory Acidosis

- Respiratory acidosis occurs as a result of inadequate ventilation

- Hypoventilation in patients with pain, a change in mental status, patients with signs of a developing pneumothorax, weakening chest muscles, or those receiving analgesia or sedation may result in respiratory acidosis

- Treatment includes improving ventilation by assisting with a bag-mask device or making adjustments to ventilator settings to increase respiratory rate

Metabolic Acidosis

- A byproduct of tissue hypoperfusion, metabolic acidosis is associated with hemorrhagic shock in the trauma patient

- When tissue is oxygen-deficient, cells shift to anaerobic metabolism which produces lactic acid with a resulting acidosis

- Kidney hypoperfusion leads to the development of acute renal failure (ARF), and the kidney loses its ability to excrete hydrogen ions, resulting in acidosis

- Acidosis can result in vasodilatation and hypotension. A pH less than 7.2 impairs coagulation.[18]

- Restoration of tissue perfusion is needed to correct metabolic acidosis. Hypoperfusion may be prevented by aggressive resuscitation with intravenous (IV) fluids, blood administration, and hemorrhage control.

Monitoring

Acidosis, from either source, can be detected by monitoring arterial blood gases (ABGs), serum lactate levels and base deficit.[19] See Chapter 7, Shock, for more information.

Coagulopathy

Hemorrhage is one of the primary causes of death following trauma. Over 80% of deaths in the operating room and approximately 50% of deaths occurring within the first 24 hours after injury are associated with hemorrhage.[20] Coagulopathy exacerbates bleeding, and increases risk of multiple system organ dysfunction, mortality, and morbidity.[20] Many patients have some evidence of trauma-associated coagulopathy upon arrival to the ED. Fibrinolysis, an early manifestation of coagulopathy, occurs after injury or ischemia when tissue plasminogen activator (TPA) is released from the endothelium.[1] The administration of crystalloid fluids dilutes clotting factors and the oxygen-carrying capacity of the red blood cells. The increased blood pressure from fluid resuscitation prior to hemorrhage control may actually "pop the clot."[21] Shock and tissue hypoperfusion can lead to decreased hepatic flow and prolonged clotting. As a result, bleeding patients continue to bleed. Use of massive transfusion protocols can promote hemostasis and decreasing mortality. See Chapter 7, Shock, for more information.

Post Resuscitation Care of Selected Injuries

Rib Fractures

Rib fractures are one of the most frequent and painful injuries from chest trauma, and as many as 54% are missed on regular chest radiographs.[22] Rib injury associated with pulmonary contusion is an independent risk factor for the development of pneumonia and increased mortality. Multiple rib fractures predispose patients to ineffective ventilation and pulmonary insufficiency, and pain from these injuries leads to splinting of the thorax, impaired ventilation, and oxygenation and ineffective coughing.[9] Aggressive pain management for trauma patients with rib fractures is recommended in order to prevent atelectasis and improve functional residual and vital capacity. Effective pain management also promotes mobility, deep breathing, productive coughing, and the ability to clear secretions.[23] Over time, patients with rib fractures are more reluctant to take deep breaths and cough. Incentive spirometry and deep breathing, if started early, can be beneficial in preventing pneumonia.[23]

Flail Chest

Patients with flail chest can be at risk for the development of pneumonia and sepsis.[22] Mechanical ventilation may be indicated as a prophylactic treatment to minimize this risk. Open reduction and internal fixation of the rib fractures has also been included as a treatment for flail chest.[24] See Chapter 11, Thoracic and Neck Trauma, for more information.

Pulmonary Contusion

Pulmonary contusions often occur concomitantly with rib fractures[21] and are associated with respiratory failure that develops over time, rather than immediately following the chest injury. Clinical symptoms—such as respiratory distress with hypoxemia and hypercarbia—peak 72 hours after injury.[25] Management of a pulmonary contusion may change over time as the patient's condition worsens and fluid shifts into the contused area. Significant hypoxia on room air is an indication for elective intubation and ventilation. The presence of a pulmonary contusion is considered an accurate predictor of the development of acute respiratory distress syndrome (ARDS) and pneumonia.[25] Treatment includes alveolar recruitment, a technique of managing pulmonary injuries. This is a dynamic process of opening previously collapsed alveoli by increasing positive end expiratory pressure (PEEP) on the ventilator.[25] Early application of recruitment maneuvers produces the best outcomes and significantly improves oxygenation.[25]

Pneumothorax

Insertion of a chest tube is indicated in many patients with a pneumothorax. If the patient subsequently requires positive pressure mechanical ventilation, a small pneumothorax can become larger. A simple pneumothorax can develop into a life-threatening tension pneumothorax with positive pressure ventilation.[9,26] Patients with pneumothoraces of any size require decompression prior to air transport as altitude will expand the gas, increasing the size and significance of the pneumothorax.[26]

Hemothorax

A hemothorax is usually characterized by decreased or absent lung sounds and hypotension. The initial treatment is aimed at restoration of systemic intravascular blood volume and drainage of blood within the chest cavity. Continual blood loss associated with a need to transfuse blood may be an indication for a thoracotomy.

Myocardial Contusion

Myocardial injury after blunt chest trauma can be a challenge to diagnose. Patients with a myocardial contusion will complain of chest discomfort, and this might be attributed to a rib fracture or chest wall contusion. An electrocardiogram (ECG) is performed on any patient suspected of a cardiac injury, and complete serial ECGs over a period of 4 to 6 hours can help to detect changes in rhythm and conduction or reveal myocardial infarction (MI).[9,27] Premature ventricular contractions (PVCs) are most common dysrhythmias in blunt cardiac trauma.[28] The leading cause of death for patients with a myocardial contusion is related

to the development of ventricular fibrillation (VF).[27] Management of the patient with a suspected myocardial contusion starts with monitoring for hemodynamic changes. Patients with preexisting cardiac risk factors, multiple chest injuries, and abnormal ECG findings are commonly admitted and observed on continuous cardiac monitoring for at least the first 24 hours.

Cardiac Tamponade

The assessment findings of tamponade due to an atrial rupture may be slow to develop and may not be evident until after the initial trauma survey and resuscitation.[9] Cardiac tamponade can occur slowly without complaint of symptoms or suddenly with an exaggerated inspiratory decrease in systolic blood pressure, shortness of breath, chest tightness, and dizziness. Diagnosis for cardiac tamponade can be made with focused assessment with sonography for trauma (FAST).

Ruptured Diaphragm

Traumatic diaphragmatic injuries are frequently missed during the initial evaluation of trauma patients. Generally, injuries to the diaphragm are difficult to evaluate with a CT scan and may require surgical intervention for definitive identification of diaphragmatic rupture.[25,29] Diaphragmatic ruptures or tears are more commonly diagnosed when they occur on the left side due to the potential for the liver to conceal or protect the defect on the right. Evidence of an elevated diaphragm on a chest radiograph can indicate a possible diaphragmatic injury and warrants investigation.[9]

Deep Vein Thrombosis

The risk of developing deep vein thrombosis (DVT) is 50% higher among trauma patients than other hospitalized patients.[30] When considering DVT, there is a classic triad leading to venous thrombosis including:[31]

- Stasis

- Endothelial damage

- Hypercoagulability

Numerous risk factors can influence the development of DVT in the trauma patient, including altered hemodynamics (hypotension), increasing age, obesity, prolonged immobility, existing malignancy, pregnancy, and certain medications.[32] Once the risk is identified, the goal is to limit clot development and prevent pulmonary embolism (PE). Low-molecular weight heparin, such as enoxaparin, compression stockings and intermittent pneumatic compression devices are also useful in the prevention of DVT.[32]

Pulmonary Embolism

PE is the third leading cause of death in trauma patients who survive the first 24 hours following initial injury and do not receive DVT prophylaxis.[32] Research has shown that as many as 24% of PEs occur within the first 4 days after injury and may even occur on day one.[33] Therefore, prevention of venous stasis and early evaluation for signs of a DVT are critical. An acute PE occurs abruptly, and the symptoms exhibited depend on the size of the embolism. Additional considerations indicate the following:

- Anxiety
- PEs can develop early or late; assess the patient who presents even days after the injury for signs of PE[33]
- Massive PE will cause hemodynamic instability such as hypotension[34]
- Pulmonary infarction and ischemia may result from complete disruption of blood flow
- Massive PE may cause right ventricular failure and death shortly after onset of symptoms[34]

Assessment findings of a PE include:
- Abrupt onset of pleuritic chest pain
- Dyspnea
- Hypoxemia
- Hemoptysis
- Cough
- Orthopnea
- Adventitious lung sounds, including
  - Wheezing
  - Crackles
- Decreased lung sounds
- Jugular vein distension
- Hypotension

A serum D-dimer test measures cross-linked fibrin associated with clot formation. However, this may not be definitively diagnostic so further studies are warranted.[34] Studies to confirm or exclude a PE include a ventilation-perfusion (VQ) lung scan or helical CT, magnetic resonance imaging (MRI) or pulmonary angiography.[34]

Fat Embolism

During manipulation of long bones for fracture fixation, embolic marrow, including lipid microemboli, can become dislodged, resulting in a fat embolism.[35] Nearly all orthopedic patients who have multiple fractures experience intravasation of bone marrow fat.[36] A fat embolism can travel to the pulmonary vasculature, causing obstruction and subsequent ischemia. Most instances of fat embolism are asymptomatic, but in symptomatic patients there is a classic triad presentation:[37]

- Decreased mental status; starting with restlessness and agitation
- Respiratory distress; including dyspnea and hypoxia
- Petechial rash on head, neck, anterior thorax, conjunctivae, buccal mucous membranes, and axillae[37,38]

Presentation can occur as early as 12 hours following injury or as late as 2 weeks after a precipitating event; however, most fat emboli occur within 24 to 72 hours after long bone fractures.[39] A helical thoracic CT scan and chest radiographs are the most beneficial for diagnosis. Patchy pulmonary infiltrates may be seen on the chest radiograph.[39] ABGs assist in the evaluation and guide treatment of problems with ventilation, acid–base balance and hypoxia. Fat emboli can contribute to the development of ARDS.[36] In as many as 5% to 15% of patients, fat emboli are fatal.[39] Treatment is supportive with oxygenation and ventilation and promoting hemodynamic stability.[38]

Acute Lung Injury/Acute Respiratory Distress Syndrome

Acute lung injury (ALI) is a syndrome resulting in alveolar damage or collapse and pulmonary edema that is not attributable to a cardiovascular origin.[40,41] ALI develops at 24 to 48 hours after injury or onset of illness, with the stimulation of the inflammatory process.[40–42] In the trauma patient, ALI can be associated with fluid shifts from the intravascular space to the interstitial space and into the alveoli. ARDS, the most severe form of ALI, was originally known as *shock lung* because of the effect of massive fluid resuscitation with subsequent fluid shift on the lungs.[40–42] Diagnostic criteria for ALI/ARDS include:[42]

- PaO_2/FiO_2 ratio of less than 200 mm Hg (ARDS) or less than 300 mm Hg (ALI)
- Pulmonary artery occlusion pressure of 18 mm Hg
- No clinical evidence of left atrial or ventricular dysfunction

Risk factors for ALI/ARDS include:[42]
- Aspiration
- Pulmonary contusion or other thoracic trauma
- Fat embolism
- Pulmonary embolism
- Near-drowning
- Inhalation injury

- Non-thoracic trauma
- Massive transfusion
- Oxygen toxicity
- Disseminated intravascular coagulopathy (DIC)
- Shock
- Pneumonia or sepsis

Treatment for ALI/ARDS includes supportive care and ventilation strategies meant to recruit atelectatic alveoli. Positive end expiratory pressure (PEEP) ventilation with lower tidal volumes has been shown to reduce airway pressure and barotrauma.[41]

- PEEP decreases intrapulmonary shunting and increases lung compliance
- At high levels PEEP can also cause barotrauma, decrease cardiac output and increase intrathoracic pressure
- Optimal PEEP is between 10 and 15 mm Hg[43]
- More advanced strategies are generally deferred to after admission in the critical care unit and include prone positioning, high-frequency ventilation, and extracorporeal membrane oxygenation[40–43]

Pneumonia and Aspiration

Pneumonia occurs in up to 25% of mechanically ventilated patients.[44] Ventilator-associated pneumonia (VAP) develops more than 48 hours after mechanical ventilation has started.[45] One of the most critical risk factors for VAP is colonization of the oral cavity by respiratory pathogens.[46] Patients with poor dental hygiene are at higher risk of distinctive oral bacteria, and it is suggested that when patients develop VAP, the bacteria in their lung secretions originated from oral bacteria.[41] Secretions that adhere to the endotracheal tube provide a direct route for bacteria to migrate into the lower airways. Sinus and gastric colonization can also lead to VAP. Although the patient may not develop pneumonia for 48 hours, oral care provided early after intubation, even in the ED, may impact the development of pneumonia. Risk factors that can impact the development of pneumonia include the following:[44,46]

- Aspiration
- Depressed protective reflexes (gag reflex)
- Elevated gastric pH levels
- Preexisting pulmonary disease
- Immunosuppression
- Malnutrition

VAP prevention includes:[46]
- Elevating the head of the bed to 45 degrees
  - This limits the risk of aspiration. Early in the trauma process this may be difficult if the patient is on a backboard or hypotensive. Facilitate timely removal or employ a reverse Trendelenburg position as tolerated.
- Chlorhexidine oral care to decontaminate the mouth[44–46]
  - Intubated patients can benefit from early chlorhexidine oral care once ETT placement is verified, even in the ED[44]
- Subglottic suctioning
  - Oral secretions pool above the ETT cuff, allowing for contaminated fluid leakage down into the lower airway[44]
  - Biofilm forms on the surface of an ETT when bacteria adhere to the tube surface allowing for aspiration of bacteria into the lungs
- Endotracheal suctioning
  - Using an in-line, closed system suction device to prevent opening the ETT to contamination is also beneficial

Begin treatment with a broad spectrum antibiotic as soon as possible until an antibiotic can be prescribed that will match the microorganism. Timely antibiotic administration can make a difference in overall mortality. Early diagnosis and treatment is important because VAP leads to ALI and ARDS and carries a high rate of mortality.[45]

Abdominal Trauma

Hemorrhage is the second most common cause of death following trauma and is the leading cause of preventable injury death.[47] Missed abdominal injuries are often the cause of late mortality in patients who survived the early post-injury period.[47] Even a serious abdominal injury may not display obvious assessment findings, especially in blunt trauma.[48] Evaluating the abdomen can be difficult for a variety of reasons. In the patient with a decreased level of consciousness, the clinical examination can be unreliable, and some injuries may be missed. Seatbelt sign in the lower abdomen can develop slowly and may be overlooked in light of more pressing injuries. Cullen sign and Grey Turner sign may indicate retroperitoneal hemorrhage, but the signs may not appear for hours or days.[49] Awareness of these signs in the patient who seeks care days after the traumatic event or continued, serial assessments can help to identify subtle changes as they develop. See Chapter 12, Abdominal and Pelvic Trauma, for more information.

Splenic Injury

Management for patients with a splenic injury has evolved towards non-operative management with good success.[50] Initial bleeding from the spleen may or may not be identified on the FAST examination. Patients with assessment findings of splenic injury who are deemed appropriate candidates for nonoperative management are generally admitted for observation with serial laboratory evaluation of hemoglobin and hematocrit levels to identify ongoing or worsening bleeding and clinical abdominal assessments for change in tenderness, pain or rigidity.[50]

Hepatic Injury

Delayed hemorrhage, hepatic abscess, and hemobilia are complications associated with hepatic trauma that may develop following initial resuscitation. Additional laboratory studies include liver enzymes and coagulation studies.

Pancreatic Injury

Because of its position, the pancreas can be compressed against the spine with a direct blow. As a result, pancreatic injuries may result in assessment findings similar to those found with retroperitoneal hemorrhage, including abdominal pain, nausea and vomiting, diminished or absent bowel sounds, Cullen sign, and Grey Turner sign. Other diagnostic studies include abdominal CT scan, follow-up ultrasonography, and serial lipase and amylase levels.[51]

Bowel Injuries

Bowel injuries occur immediately or over time with resulting contusions, edema, rupture, or infarction. Continued abdominal assessment is valuable in early recognition of delayed or occult complications of abdominal trauma. It is important for the nurse to reevaluate all patients with abdominal trauma when nonoperative management is chosen and to take action when signs of deterioration begin to occur.

Shock

Specific assessments and interventions in the post resuscitation period are unique to each of the four types of shock.

Obstructive Shock

- Trending the patient's cardiopulmonary status can identify subtle changes that may indicate slowly accumulating pericardial fluid or pneumothoraces

- FAST can be useful to identify excess cardiac tamponade or a pneumothorax

- Both may be present initially or develop slowly over time with a delayed presentation

Cardiogenic Shock

- Patients with blunt chest trauma or myocardial infarction (MI) can experience cardiogenic shock

- This type of shock may not be evident at the time of trauma resuscitation and can develop following volume replacement when contractility is inadequate to handle the preload

- Early reperfusion therapy is the goal of treatment. Percutaneous coronary intervention in the cardiac catheterization laboratory is definitive. Inotropic support may be useful until bleeding is controlled.[52]

Distributive (Neurogenic) Shock

- Onset of neurogenic shock can occur soon after the injury or as late as 1 to 2 days later[53]

- Neurogenic shock is generally associated with injuries at T6 and above[53]

- Treatment of hypovolemia is usually the first step, but medications, including vasopressors and atropine, aimed at reestablishing vascular tone and heart rate, are more appropriate for use to restore organ perfusion[54]

Anaphylactic Shock

- The risk of anaphylactic shock as a result of an allergic reaction to a medication may be higher in the trauma patient if allergy information is unavailable upon arrival. As soon as possible, seek out records or sources of possible allergies.

- Signs of anaphylactic shock include hives or an urticarial rash, respiratory distress and stridor, angioedema and signs of shock[55]

- Treatment includes intramuscular epinephrine bronchodilators or racemic epinephrine, IV crystalloids, histamine blockers, and steroids[56]

Septic Shock

- Septic shock due to infection immediately after a traumatic injury is uncommon; its onset is usually delayed

- Septic patients can be clinically difficult to distinguish from those in hypovolemic shock since both groups have tachycardia, peripheral vasoconstriction, decreased urinary output, and decreased blood pressure with a narrowed pulse pressure[9]

- An elevated temperature is often associated with septic patients; however, trauma patients may be febrile due to the inflammatory response to injury

- Prophylactic antibiotic therapy may be indicated with open or contaminated injuries

Disseminated Intravascular Coagulopathy

DIC begins when the body's clotting system is overwhelmed, such as in cases of multiple trauma. In the patient with multiple trauma, platelets, plasma, and other vital components of the clotting cascade are lost to hemorrhage and dilution, and clotting factors become depleted through diffuse microvascular clot formation as a result of inflammatory response to injury.[57] Hypothermia may directly interfere with slowing the activity of coagulation and fibrinogen synthesis.[57] Acidosis as a result of tissue hypoperfusion and hypoxia accelerates fibrinolysis contributing to the development of DIC.[57] Table 24-2 describes the laboratory findings in DIC. Treatment is aimed at the cause, and DIC is best treated by prevention. Administration of platelets and fresh frozen plasma can help control bleeding in the trauma patient and may limit the severity of DIC.[57] While DIC is not present upon trauma presentation, the treatments and interventions completed during the initial assessment can have a dramatic effect on the development of DIC.

Abdominal Compartment Syndrome

Abdominal compartment syndrome (ACS) is a potentially lethal complication that results from intra-abdominal hypertension (IAH). ACS is reported to be seen in up to 50% of the critically ill population and is also an independent risk factor for death.[30]

Abdominal pressure is 0 to 5 mm Hg in healthy patients and varies inversely with intrathoracic pressure in normal breathing.[30] The risk for IAH is greater in patients who are morbidly obese, have chronic ascites, or are pregnant. Abdominal perfusion pressure (APP) is measured by subtracting the intra-abdominal pressure (IAP) from the mean arterial pressure (MAP). Excessive IAP is greater than 12 mm Hg.[30] Abdominal compartment syndrome is defined as a sustained IAP greater than 20 mm Hg and/or an APP less than 60 mm Hg associated with organ dysfunction.[30] IAH can affect nearly all major body systems.[30]

Abdominal Effects

- Intra-abdominal bleeding from the spleen, liver, or mesentery is the most common cause of primary IAH. The distended abdomen acts like a tourniquet compressing the organs within its compartment. Secondary IAH can occur with massive blood loss from extra-abdominal sites, followed by resuscitation with a large volume crystalloid solution, with fluid shifts and peritoneal edema.[30,58–62]

- As blood volume increases, so does IAP, compressing abdominal structures and organs. This compression results in diminished perfusion and ischemia, acidosis, leaking capillaries, intestinal swelling, and splanchnic translocation.[30,58–62]

Table 24-2. Laboratory Trends in DIC

Trends
• Decreased platelet count
• Decreased fibrinogen
• Elevated fibrin degradation product (FDP)
• Elevated D-dimer
• Prolonged prothrombin time (PT)
• Prolonged partial thromboplastin time (PTT)

Data from Gando et al.[57]

- Decreased blood flow leads to poor healing. Hepatic hypoperfusion impairs liver function, glucose metabolism and lactate clearance.[30,58–62]

Cardiovascular Effects[30,58,60–62]

- The cardiovascular system is affected as increased IAP pushes up on the diaphragm and increased intrathoracic pressures compress the heart and major vessels
  - Measurement of central venous pressure may be falsely elevated due to increased intrathoracic pressure
  - The patient may appear well hydrated or even fluid overloaded in the presence of volume depletion

- The increased intrathoracic pressure can cause a decrease in venous return resulting in a decreased preload and loss of cardiac output

- Rising intrathoracic pressure increases pulmonary vascular resistance and right ventricular afterload, which in turn increases the workload of the right ventricle and decreases left ventricular preload. Greater myocardial oxygen demand results in increased work of the heart.

- The femoral veins are compressed causing venous stasis and increasing the risk of DVT

Respiratory Effects[30,58,60–62]

- Increased thoracic pressure also affects the pulmonary system

- One of the first signs of abdominal compartment syndrome is pulmonary dysfunction[30]
  - Decreased lung expansion, limited respiratory excursion, and decreased tidal volume are all a result of increased intrathoracic pressure
  - The result is hypoxemia and hypercarbia with respiratory acidosis

- Atelectasis, Acute Lung Injury (ALI), or ARDS may develop[30]

Neurologic Effects[30,58,60–62]
- Increased intrathoracic pressure causes pressure on the jugular veins which decreases the drainage of cerebrospinal fluid and blood from the head, increasing ICP

Assessment findings for IAH and ACS include:[30,58,60,62]
- IAP Measurement
  - One indirect method of monitoring IAP is measurement of urinary bladder pressure. A partially filled bladder accurately reflects IAP. Methods used to monitor urinary bladder pressure include the following:[30,60,62]
    - A transducer technique includes attaching a pressurized transducer and tubing to the urine specimen port of a urinary catheter
    - A bladder scanner is a noninvasive alternative to confirm adequate urine volume prior to pressure measurement
      - This limits the risk of contamination with backflow into the bladder
      - Position the patient supine and zero is leveled at the symphysis pubis
    - In addition to bladder pressure, abdominal girth may be beneficial as a trending device, although increased girth is not necessarily present with IAH[30]
- Low urinary output and hypotensive shock unresponsive to fluid resuscitation
- Tense, rigid, abdomen (distension may or may not be present)
- Increased peak airway pressures without thoracic injury
- Increased ICP without head injury[63]
- Increased IAP (treatment recommended when IAP exceeds 30 mm Hg and the patient is symptomatic)[63]

Rhabdomyolysis

Rhabdomyolysis is most commonly seen in patients with crush injuries or burns. Damaged tissues result in cellular destruction that releases myoglobin into the circulation. An intracellular protein, myoglobin obstructs renal perfusion and glomerular filtration. Sloughing of the renal tubular epithelium, myoglobin cast formation, and myoglobin in the urine produces the distinctive dark red or brown colored urine. Acute kidney injury (AKI), or acute renal failure, results from obstruction and decreases in renal blood flow and glomerular filtration and occurs in 24% of patients with rhabdomyolysis.[64]

Hyperkalemia is a life-threatening complication of rhabdomyolysis.[64–67] This occurs with cell destruction that releases intracellular potassium into the extracellular space, causing serum potassium levels to rise dramatically. Potassium levels generally peak in the first 12 to 36 hours and then will steadily decrease.[68]

Treatment
Treatment for possible rhabdomyolysis begins with intravenous (IV) hydration. Fluid volume increases renal perfusion, prevents cast formation, and prevents additional ischemic kidney damage.[69] Volume aids in correction of acidosis as a result of hypoperfusion.
- Begin with aggressive fluid management to produce urine output of 100 to 300 mL per hour in adults[66–68]
- Alkalization of the urine (urine pH > 8.0), with the use of bicarbonate and osmotic diuretics, has been used, although evidence of the benefits has not been clearly established[64–67]
- Patients who develop renal failure may require hemodialysis, peritoneal dialysis, or renal replacement therapy. See Chapter 14, Musculoskeletal Trauma, for more information.
- Severe hyperkalemia should be treated with calcium gluconate, insulin, glucose, or nebulized beta-agonist[69]
  - Substances that shift potassium from extracellular to intracellular spaces are only temporarily effective[65]
  - Calcium does not affect potassium levels, but protects against cardiotoxic effects
  - Other interventions may be necessary for definitive treatment. These include:[65]
    - Diuresis
    - Intestinal potassium binders, such as sodium polystyrene sulfonate
    - Dialysis

Systemic Inflammatory Response Syndrome

Systemic inflammatory response syndrome (SIRS) is a generalized response to injury or illness that occurs as a result of an infection, trauma, or ischemia. If two or more of the following assessment findings are present, the patient meets the criteria for SIRS:[70]
- Fever greater than 38°C (100.4°F) or less than 36°C (96.8°F)
- Heart rate greater than 90 beats/min
- Respiratory rate greater than 20 breaths/min or $PaCO_2$ less than 32 mm Hg

- WBC greater than 12,000 cells/mcL or less than 4,000 cells/mcL or if there are greater than 10% band forms

The only difference between SIRS and sepsis is that sepsis has an identified source of infection and SIRS does not.[70]

Sepsis

In addition to the normal inflammatory process caused by trauma, trauma patients can be at risk for developing an infection or sepsis. Sepsis is the presence of a systemic response, rather than a localized reaction or isolated infection.[70] Patients with a variety of presenting issues may be at risk for developing infection and sepsis, including:

- Patients with penetrating injuries, or open, or contaminated wounds
- Those with blunt abdominal trauma, or contamination of the peritoneal cavity by intestinal contents (bowel perforation or splanchnic translocation)
- Those experiencing surface or burn trauma with loss of the skin's protective barrier

Sepsis can produce widespread vascular damage, which includes:

- Endotoxin release leads to capillary leakage, shifting of fluid into the interstitial space, and edema
- Increased viscosity of blood, leading to clotting in the microcirculation and the development of coagulopathy
- Tissue hypoxia that can affect every organ and if untreated or extreme, may cause multiple organ dysfunction to develop

Early recognition allows for goal-directed therapy, including timely initiation of antibiotic therapy, and improved patient outcomes.

Increased Intracranial Pressure

Cervical collars and flat, supine positioning may exacerbate ICP in the patient with head injuries.[71] Methods for decreasing ICP include:

- Remove cervical collar once cervical spine is clear
- Elevate the head of bed
- Maintain the head in a neutral, midline position
- Treat the patient for pain or anxiety
- Promote diuresis, if any shock state has been controlled
- Maintain normocarbia
- Maintain normothermia
- Reduce external stimuli by dimming lights, limiting noise, and clustering interventions

Alcohol Withdrawal

Between 30% and 50% of trauma patients report having ingested some form of intoxicant prior to injury.[72] Studies have shown that an estimated one in four to five patients admitted to the hospital has some degree of alcohol abuse or dependence.[73] It is not always easy to identify which patients are at risk for or experiencing alcohol withdrawal. Symptoms of withdrawal can appear within 6 hours after the last drink or may take days.[72,74] Since alcohol is a central nervous system (CNS) depressant, findings related to withdrawal usually show CNS stimulation. The first clinical assessment findings of alcohol withdrawal include:

- Autonomic hyperactivity
- Hand tremors
- Nausea or vomiting
- Psychomotor agitation
- Anxiety or restlessness

Additional assessment findings include:

- Insomnia
- Transient hallucinations
- Generalized tonic-clonic seizure

Treatment of alcohol withdrawal is individualized. Interventions include fluid and electrolyte replacement, supplemental thiamine, glucose, and multiple vitamins. Benzodiazepines to prevent delirium tremens may be prescribed to blunt the effects of withdrawal on the central nervous system.

Musculoskeletal Trauma

Despite careful assessment, specific fractures that may remain undiagnosed after the initial assessment include:[75]

- Femoral neck fractures
- Facial fractures
- Radial head fractures
- Fractures of the scaphoid
- C7 vertebral fractures
- Nondisplaced fractures of the pelvis
- Fractures of the odontoid process

Complications related to fractures can occur immediately, early, or late. Bones are highly vascular and prone to bleeding. Sharp bone ends can damage surrounding muscle or blood vessels. A broken rib may result in a pneumothorax or lacerated liver. Early complications related to fractures include:

- Infection
- Pneumonia

- DVT/PE
- Compartment syndrome (see Chapter 14, Musculoskeletal Trauma)
- Fat embolism
- Pressure ulcers

Missed and Delayed Injuries

Missed Injuries

Evaluating a trauma patient with multiple injuries is a challenge even for the most experienced healthcare provider. Multiple factors contribute to missed injuries including equivocal radiologic results, inadequate or incomplete studies, simultaneous presentation of multiple patients, complicated patient presentation, or clinically inexperienced staff.[76] The presence of comorbid conditions can also contribute to a challenging injury assessment. Diseases such as hypertension and diabetes create pathophysiologic factors that may not be evident early in the course of trauma.[77] Diabetes may alter the sensation of an injury due to neuropathy.

Missed injuries can be defined as any injury that was not discovered or suspected prior to or at arrival of the patient to the intensive care unit (ICU).[76] They may become clinically significant when an injury contributes to morbidity or mortality and results in a delay in treatment. Patients with missed injuries experience higher injury severity scores and longer hospital and ICU stays.[76]

The use of a tertiary survey has been shown to reduce missed injuries by 35%.[78] This consists of a complete examination performed following the primary and secondary surveys and within 24 hours after trauma to identify any injuries missed during the initial assessment.[76] The tertiary survey includes a review of initial radiology studies, any additional indicated studies, standardized reevaluation of laboratory studies, and clinical assessment for the effective detection of hidden injuries.

Delayed Injuries

There is a distinct difference in missed injuries and delayed effects of injury. Missed injuries are present upon arrival to the ED, but not identified. Delayed effects of injury may not be present upon arrival, but develop over time as a result of the initial injury. It is absolutely essential that trauma patients are continually reevaluated to note new findings and identify deterioration in previous findings.

Monitoring Adjuncts

Mechanical Ventilators

Mechanical ventilators have advanced in recent years with a variety of new modes and strategies designed to prevent barotrauma and syndromes such as post-ventilation emphysema. Closed loop mechanical ventilation regularly monitors respiratory parameters including the patient's intrinsic rate, tidal volume, pulmonary resistance and compliance, and oxygen saturation.[79,80] With this information, the ventilator is able to adjust the need for added or reduced pressure support or oxygen.[79,80] This promotes optimal settings and timely weaning and extubation.[79,80] This technology is used more often in the ICU, but it is useful for the trauma nurse to be aware of fluctuation in ventilator settings to evaluate the status of the mechanically ventilated patient.

Capnography

$ETCO_2$ measures the level of exhaled carbon dioxide (CO_2), which can be a marker of metabolic acidosis, dehydration, or tissue perfusion.[81] Post resuscitation, monitoring the $ETCO_2$ level can be helpful in patients who are receiving sedation and analgesia or mechanical ventilation as it is a valuable marker of hypoventilation and apnea.[81] There are three components to interpretation of capnography; the numeric value, the waveform, and the gradient.[81–83]

- Numeric value
  - The partial pressure of end-tidal carbon dioxide ($PETCO_2$) reveals some information regarding ventilation
  - Changes in $PETCO_2$ identify ventilatory issues before pulse oximetry (Table 24-3)
- Waveform
  - The waveform is divided into three phases of the respiratory cycle. Each phase reveals different information.
    - Phase I: During the beginning of expiration, reflecting exhalation of air in the anatomic dead space where there should be no CO_2
    - Phase II: As CO_2 is exhaled, the waveform rises sharply
    - Phase III: This is the majority of the expiratory cycle, where the waveform plateaus. The end of this phase is where the $ETCO_2$ is measured.
  - The waveform can reveal a great deal of information to those who know how to interpret it
    - Loss of waveform indicates a misplaced or occluded endotracheal tube or a disconnected circuit

- A positive waveform with each compression shows effective cardiopulmonary resuscitation (CPR)
- A change in the shape of the waveform may be an indication of bronchospasm, obstruction, or ventilation/perfusion (V/Q) mismatch
- $PETCO_2$–$PaCO_2$ gradient
  - A changing gradient can mean hemodynamic instability, or decreasing lung compliance

Central Venous Pressure

Measuring central venous pressure has been traditionally used to evaluate volume status in patients with hypovolemia; however, central venous pressure changes minimally in early shock and is a poor identifier of adequate resuscitation.[84]

Summary

Trauma care does not end with the initial assessment. Ongoing monitoring and observation are vital aspects to care of the trauma patient after resuscitation and stabilization. Many complications develop early on in the post resuscitative period and the prepared trauma nurse anticipates them, intervening proactively. Even if the initial assessment is inconclusive, a high degree of suspicion will help the trauma nurse identify subtle changes based on predicted injuries and mechanism of injury. Assessment and reassessment are important not only of identified injuries but potential and worsening injuries. The above conditions and complications may not manifest while the trauma patient remains in the ED, but knowledge of potential outcomes can be valuable factors in the critical thinking and decision making of the trauma nurse. Review of admission orders and knowledge of care pathways will promote early treatment and limit the risk of complications, making the transition to definitive care smooth and efficient.

Table 24-3. Conditions Associated with Changes in $PETCO_2$

Causes of Abnormal $PETCO_2$	Increase in $PETCO_2$	Decrease in $PETCO_2$
Metabolic	• Malignant hyperthermia	• Hypothermia
	• Thyroid storm	• Metabolic acidosis
	• Severe sepsis	
Circulatory	• Carbon dioxide rebreathing	• Pulmonary embolism
	• Treatment of acidosis	• Profound hypovolemia/shock
		• Cardiogenic shock
Respiratory	• Hypoventilation	• Hyperventilation
	• Chronic obstructive pulmonary disease	• Intrapulmonary shunt
	• Asthma	• Pulmonary edema
Technical	• Exhausted carbon dioxide absorber	• Disconnection
	• Contamination of the monitor	• Blockage in tubing

Data from Eipe & Dherty,[81] Kodali,[82] and Ortega et al.[83]

References

1. Moore, K. (2011). Managing hemorrhagic shock in trauma: Are we still drowning patients in the field? *Journal of Emergency Nursing, 37*(6), 594–596.

2. Dutton, R. (2006). Fluid Management for trauma: Where are we now? *Continuing Education in Anaesthesia, Critical Care, & Pain, 6*(4), 144–147.

3. Johnson, A. L., & Criddle, L. A. (2004). Pass the salt: Indications for and implications of using hypertonic saline. *Critical Care Nurse, 24*(5), 36–38.

4. Patanwala, A. E., Amini, A., & Erstad, B. L. (2010). Use of hypertonic saline injection in trauma. *American Journal of Health-System Pharmacy, 67*(22), 1920–1928.

5. Kirkpatrick, A.W., Ball, C. G., D'Amours, S. K., & Zygun, D. (2008). Acute resuscitation of the unstable adult trauma patient: Bedside diagnosis and therapy. *Canadian Journal of Surgery, 51*(1), 57–69.

6. Galvagno, S. M., & Mackenzie, C. F. (2013). New and future resuscitation fluids for trauma patients using hemoglobin and hypertonic saline. *Anesthesiology Clinics, 31*(1), 1–19.

7. Duchesne, J. C., Simms, E., Guidry, C., Duke, M., Beeson, E., Mcswain, N. E., & Cotton, B. (2012). Damage control immunoregulation: Is there a role for low-volume hypertonic saline resuscitation in patient managed with damage control surgery? *The American Surgeon, 78*(9), 962–968.

8. Dubose, J. J., Kobayashi, L., Lozornio, A., Teixeira, P., Inaba, K., Lam, L., … Rhee, P. (2010). Clinical experience using 5% hypertonic saline as a safe alternative fluid for use in trauma. *Journal of Trauma, 68*(5), 1172–1177.

9. American College of Surgeons (2012). *Advanced trauma life support student manual* (9th ed.). Chicago, IL: Author.

10. Marsh, J. D., & Banasik, J. L. (2013) Acute disorders of brain function. In L. E. Copstead & J. L. Banasik (Eds.), *Pathophysiology* (5th ed., pp. 898–921). St. Louis, MO: Elsevier Saunders.

11. Qadan, M., Gardner, S. A., Vitale, D. S., Lominadze, D., Joshua, I. G., & Polk, H. (2009). Hypothermia and surgery: Immunologic mechanisms for current practice. *Annals of Surgery, 250*, 134–140.

12. Martini, W. Z. (2009). Coagulopathy by hypothermia and acidosis: Mechanisms of thrombin generation and fibrinogen availability. *Journal of Trauma, 67*(1), 202–208.

13. Brain Trauma Foundation. (2007). *Guidelines for the management of severe traumatic brain injury* (3rd ed.). New York, NY: Mary Anne Liebert, Inc.

14. McIlvoy, L. (2012). Fever management in patients with brain injury. *AACN Advanced Critical Care, 23*, 204–211.

15. Mizushima, Y., Ueno, M., Idoguchi, K., Ishikawa, K., & Matsuoka, T. (2009). Fever in trauma patients: Friend or foe? *The Journal of Trauma, 67*(5), 1062–1065.

16. Jansen, J. O., Thomas, R., Loudon, M., & Brooks, A. (2009). Damage control resuscitation for patients with major trauma. *British Medical Journal, 338*, b1778.

17. Felver, L. (2013). Acid-base homeostasis and imbalances. In L. E. Copstead & J. L. Banasik (Eds.), *Pathophysiology* (5th ed., pp. 539–548). St. Louis, MO: Elsevier Saunders.

18. Lier, H., Bottiger, B. W., Hinkelbein, J., Krep, H., & Bernhard, M. (2011). Coagulation management in multiple trauma: A systematic review. *Intensive Care Medicine, 37*, 572–582.

19. Moore, K. M. (2011). The four horsemen of the apocalypse of trauma. *Journal of Emergency Nursing, 37*(3), 294–295.

20. Nunez, T. C., Young, P. P., Holcomb, J. B., & Cotton, B. A. (2010). Creation, implementation, and maturation of a massive transfusion protocol for the exsanguinating trauma patient. *Journal of Trauma, 68*, 1–16.

21. Nelson, R. (2010). Advances in trauma care. *American Journal of Nursing, 111*, 19–20.

22. Lafferty, P. M., Anavian, J., Will, R. E., & Cole, P. A. (2011). Operative treatment of chest wall injuries: Indications, technique, and outcomes. *Journal of Bone and Joint Surgery, 93*(1), 97–110.

23. Keel, M., & Meier, C. (2007). Chest injuries – What is new? *Current Opinion Critical Care, 13*, 674–679.

24. Athausen, P. L., Shannon, S., Watts, C., Thomas, K., Bain, M. A., Coll, D., … Bray, T. (2011). Early surgical stabilization of flail chest with locked plate fixation. *Journal of Orthopedic Trauma, 25*, 641–648.

25. Stein, D. M., York, G. B., Boswell, S., Shanmuganathan, K., Hanna, J. M., & Scalea, T. M. (2007). Accuracy of computed tomography (CT) scan in the detection of penetrating diaphragm injury. *The Journal of Trauma, 63*(3), 538–543.

26. Waydhas, C., & Sauerland, S. (2007). Pre-hospital pleural decompression and chest tube placement after blunt trauma: A Systematic review. *Resuscitation, 72*, 11–25.

27. Mullins, J., & Harrahill, M. (2010). Blunt cardiac trauma. *Journal of Emergency Nursing, 36*(6), 597–598.

28. Wall, M. J., Tsai, P., & Mattox, K. L. (2013). Heart and thoracic vascular injuries. In K. L. Mattox, E. E. Moore, & D. V. Feliciano (Eds.), *Trauma* (7th ed., pp. 395–413). New York, NY: McGraw-Hill.

29. Lopez, P. P., Arango, J., Gallup, T. M., Cohn, S. M., Myers, J., Corneille, M., … Dent, D. L. (2010). Diaphragmatic injuries: What has changed over a 20-year period? *The American Surgeon, 76*(5), 512-516.

30. Lee, R. K. (2012). Intra-abdominal hypertension and abdominal compartment syndrome: A comprehensive overview. *Critical Care Nurse, 32*(1), 19–31.

31. Mackman, N. (2012). New insights into the mechanisms of venous thrombosis. *Journal of Clinical Investigation, 122*, 2331–2336.

32. Gay, S. E. (2010). An inside view of venous thromboembolism. *The Nurse Practitioner, 35*, 32–39.

33. Menaker, J., Stein, D. M., & Scalea, T. M. (2007). Incidence of early pulmonary embolism after injury. *The Journal of Trauma, 63*, 620–624.

34. Headley, C. M., & Melander, S. (2011). When it may be a pulmonary embolism. *Nephrology Nursing Journal, 38*, 127–137, 152.

35. Whelan, D. B., Byrick, R. J., Mazer, C. D., Kay, C., Richards, R. R., Zdero, R., & Schemitsch, E. (2010). Posttraumatic lung injury after pulmonary contusion and fat embolism: Factors determining abnormal gas exchange. *The Journal of Trauma, 69*, 512–518.

36. Blankstein, M., Byrick, R. J., Richards, R. R., Mullen, J. B. Zdero, R., & Schemitsch, E. H. (2010). Pathophysiology of fat embolism: A rabbit model. *Journal of Orthopaedic Trauma, 25*, 674–680.

37. Sara, S., Kenyhertz, G., Herbert, T., & Lundeen, G. A. (2011). Fat emboli syndrome in a nondisplaced tibia fracture. *Journal of Orthopaedic Trauma, 25*, e27–e29.

38. Tzioupis, C. C., & Giannoudis, P. V. (2011). Fat embolism syndromes: What have we learned over the years? *Trauma, 13*(4), 259–281.

39. Carlson, D. S., & Pfadt, E. (2011). Fat embolism syndrome. *Nursing, 41*(4), 72.

40. Benson, A. B., & Moss, M. (2009). Trauma and acute respiratory distress syndrome: Weighing the risks and benefits of blood transfusions. *Anesthesiology, 110*(2), 216–217.

41. Maxwell, R. A., Green, J. M., Waldrop, J., Dart, B. W., Smith, P. W., Brooks, D., Barker, D. (2010). A randomized prospective trial of airway pressure release ventilation and low tidal volume ventilation in adult trauma patients with acute respiratory failure. *The Journal of Trauma, 69*, 501–511.

42. Dechert, R. E., Haas, C. F., & Ostwani, W. (2012). Current knowledge of acute lung injury and acute respiratory distress syndrome. *Critical Care Nursing, 24*, 377–401.

43. Stacy, K. M. (2011). Pulmonary disorders. In L. D. Urden, K. M. Stacy, & M. E. Lough, (Eds.), *Priorities in critical care nursing* (6th ed., pp. 283–311). St. Louis, MO: Mosby.

44. Grap, M., Munro, C. L., Hamilton, V. A., Elswick, R. K., Sessler, C. N., & Ward, K. R. (2011). Early, single chlorhexidine application reduces ventilator-assisted pneumonia in trauma patients. *Heart and Lung, 40*(5), e115–e122.

45. Tseng, C. C., Liu, S. F., Wang, C. C., Tu, M. L., Chung, Y. H., Lin, M. C., & Fang, W. F. (2012). Impact of clinical severity index, infective pathogens, and initial empiric antibiotic use on hospital mortality in patients with ventilator-assisted pneumonia. *American Journal of Infection Control, 40,* 648–652.

46. O'Grady, N. P., Murray, P. R., & Ames, N. (2012). Preventing ventilator-associated pneumonia. *Journal of the American Medical Association, 307,* 2534–2539.

47. Jansen, J., Yule, S., & Loudon, M. (2008). Investigation of blunt abdominal trauma, *British Medical Journal, 336, 938–942.*

48. Blank-Reid, C. (2013). Abdominal trauma: Dealing with the damage. *Nursing2013, 4–11.*

49. Schroeppel, T., & Croce, M. A. (2007). Diagnosis and management of blunt abdominal solid organ injury. *Current Opinion in Critical Care, 13,* 399–404.

50. Wisner, D. H. (2013). Injury to the spleen. In K. L. Mattox, E. E. Moore, & D. V. Feliciano (Eds.), *Trauma* (7th ed., pp. 561–580). New York, NY: McGraw-Hill.

51. Tsai, M. T., Sun, J. T., Tsai, K. C., Lien, W. C. (2010). Isolated traumatic pancreatic rupture. *American Journal of Emergency Medicine, 28,* 745. e3–745.e4

52. Reynolds, H. R., & Hochman, J. S. (2008). Cardiogenic shock: Current concepts and improving outcomes. *Circulation, 117,* 686–697.

53. Mallek, J. T., Inaba, K., Branco, B. C., Ives, C., Lam, L., & Talving, P., … Demetriades, D. (2012). The incidence of neurogenic shock after spinal cord injury in patients admitted to a high-volume level I trauma center. *American Surgeon, 78*(5), 623–626.

54. Calder, S. (2012). Shock. In Emergency Nurses Association, *Sheehy's manual of emergency care* (7th ed., pp. 213–221). St. Louis, MO: Mosby Elsevier.

55. The Mayo Clinic. (2013, January 16). *Anaphylaxis.* Retrieved from http://www.mayoclinic.com/health/anaphylaxis/DS00009

56. Wilmont, L. (2010). Shock: Early recognition and management. *Journal of Emergency Nursing, 36,* 134–139.

57. Gando, S., Sawamura, A., & Hayakawaa, M. (2011). Trauma, shock, and disseminated intravascular coagulation: Lessons from the classical literature. *Annals of Surgery, 254*(1), 10–19.

58. Balogh, Z., Bendinelli, C., Politt, T., Kozar, R. A., & Moore, F. A. (2008). Postinjury primary abdominal compartment syndrome. E*uropean Journal of Trauma and Emergency Surgery, 34*(4), 369–377.

59. Gonzalez, E. A., & Moore, F. A. (2010). Resuscitation beyond the abdominal compartment syndrome. *Current Opinion in Critical Care, 16*(6), 570–574.

60. Malbrain, M. L., & De Laet, I. E. (2012). Intra-abdominal hypertension: Evolving concepts. *Critical Care Nursing Clinics of North America, 24*(2), 275–309.

61. Rizoli, S., Mamtani, A., Scarpellini, S., & Kirkpatrick, A.W. (2010). Abdominal compartment syndrome in trauma resuscitation. *Current Opinion in Anesthesiology, 23*(2), 251–257.

62. Searle, R. D., Wenham, T. N., & Garner, J. P. (2009). Abdominal compartment syndrome: The new killer. *Trauma, 11*(2), 111–121.

63. Walker, J., & Criddle, L. M. (2003). Pathophysiology and management of abdominal compartment syndrome. *American Journal of Critical Care, 12,* 367–371.

64. Elsayed, E. F., & Reilly, R. F. (2010). Rhabdomyolysis: A review, with emphasis on the pediatric population. *Pediatric Nephrology, 25, 7–18.*

65. Bosch, X., Poch, E., & Grau, J. M. (2009). Rhabdomyolysis and acute kidney injury. *New England Journal of Medicine, 361,* 62–72.

66. de Wolff, J.F. (2012). Rhabdomyolysis. *British Journal of Hospital Medicine, 73*(2), C30–C32.

67. Cervellin, G., Comelli, I., & Lippi, G. (2010). Rhabdomyolysis: Historical background, clinical, diagnostic, and therapeutic features. *Clinical Chemistry and Laboratory Medicine 48*(6), 749–756.

68. American College of Surgeons. (2012). Musculoskeletal trauma. In *Advanced trauma life support student course manual* (9th ed., pp. 206-229). Chicago, IL: Author

69. Luck, R. P. & Verbin, S. (2008). Rhabdomyolysis: A review of clinical presentation, etiology, diagnosis, and management. *Pediatric Emergency Care, 24,* 262–268.

70. Burdette, S. D., Parilo, M. A., & Kaplan, L. J. (2012, April 11). *Systemic inflammatory response syndrome.* Retrieved from http://emedicine.medscape.com/article/168943-overview

71. Schouten, R., Albert, T., & Kwon, B. (2012). The spine-injured patient: Initial assessment and emergency treatment. *Journal of the American Academy of Orthopaedic Surgeons, 20,* 336–346.

72. Eastes, L. E. (2010). Alcohol withdrawal syndrome in trauma patients: A review. *Journal of Emergency Nursing, 36,* 507–509.

73. Elliott, D. Y., Geyer, C., Lionetti, T., & Doty, L. (2012). Managing alcohol withdrawal in hospitalized patients. *Nursing,* 22–30.

74. Desy, P., Howard, P. K., Perhats, C., & Li, S. (2010). Alcohol screening, brief intervention, and referral to treatment conducted by emergency nurses: An impact evaluation. *Journal of Emergency Nursing, 36*(6), 538–545.

75. Whiteing, N. (2008) Fractures: Pathophysiology, treatment and nursing care. *Nursing Standard, 23,* 49–57.

76. Buduhan, G., & McRitchie, D. I. (2000). Missed injuries in patients with multiple trauma. *The Journal of Trauma, 49,* 600–605.

77. Weber, J., Jablonski, R., & Penrod, J. (2009). Missed opportunities: Under-detection of trauma in elderly adults involved in motor vehicle crashes. *Journal of Emergency Nursing, 36,* 6–9.

78. Montmany, S., Navarro, S., Rebassa, P., Hermoso, J., Hidalgo, M., & Canovas, G. (2007). A prospective study on the incidence of missed injuries in trauma patients. *Cirugía Española 84,* 32–36.

79. Lellouche, F., Bojmehrani, A., & Burns, K. (2012). Mechanical ventilation with advanced closed-loop systems. *European Respiratory Monograph, 55,* 217–218.

80. Chatburn, R. L., & Mireles-Cabodevila, E. (2011). Closed-loop control of mechanical ventilation: Description and classification of targeting schemes. *Respiratory Care, 56*(1), 85–102.

81. Eipe, N., & Dherty, D.R. (2010). A review of pediatric capnography. *Journal of Clinical Monitoring and Computing, 24,* 261–268.

82. Kodali, B. S. (2013). Capnography outside the operating rooms. *Anesthesiology, 118*(1), 192–201.

83. Ortega, R., Connor, C., Kim, S., Djang, R., & Patel, K. (2012). Monitoring ventilation with capnography. *New England Journal of Medicine, 367*(19), e27–e34.

84. Marik, P. (2007). Noninvasive hemodynamic monitoring in the intensive care unit. *Critical Care Clinics, 23,* 383–400.

Overview of Skill Stations

Objectives

The learner will have the opportunity for interactive, hands-on practice. These three separate skill stations include:

1. The trauma nursing process (TNP) skill station will guide the learner through the initial assessment, including all the process points, the A-I mnemonic, all interventions, and evaluations. This is the only tested station.

2. The airway and ventilation skill station focuses on the assessments and interventions to open and maintain a patent airway and promote adequate ventilation.

3. The trauma interventions skill station provides the learner the opportunity to discuss, observe, and demonstrate the use of a variety of skills associated with other steps in the TNP.

Introduction

The psychomotor skills associated with trauma care are divided into three stations:
1. Trauma Nursing Process (TNP)
2. Airway and Ventilation
3. Trauma Interventions

Each of these stations gives the learner the opportunity to discuss trauma concepts and observe and practice trauma skills in a simulated, case-based, learning environment.

This portion of the TNCC is intended to promote active and collaborative learning. Each learner is expected to contribute to the discussion and demonstrate and describe assessments and interventions as indicated within the case or selected skill.

During actual patient care, all personnel with direct contact with the patient or the patient's bodily fluids wear personal protective equipment (PPE). In the skill stations, care is simulated and the use of PPE is optional. Any mention of a certain brand of equipment or supply does not constitute endorsement of that product. It is recommended that each learner and instructor is familiar with brands and products used in their own institutions.

The centerpiece of the TNCC is the TNP skill station. This is an active performance of a scenario-driven initial assessment of a simulated trauma patient, while integrating chapter content, lecture information, and critical thinking. Throughout the scenario, the learner demonstrates the appropriate assessment techniques of inspection, auscultation, and palpation.

The *trauma nursing process behaviors* are the foundation for the steps outlined in the skill station. They include:
- Assessment
- Outcomes/Planning
- Implementation
- Evaluation

Overarching the nursing process steps are the **operational process points,** used by the trauma team for the systematic and standardized approach to the care of the trauma patient. These include:
- Preparation and triage
- Primary survey (ABCDE) with resuscitation adjuncts (FG)
- Reevaluation (consideration of transfer)
- Secondary survey (HI) with reevaluation adjuncts
- Reevaluation and post resuscitation care
- Definitive care or transfer

General Principles

During the TNP skill stations, the learners in each group will be presented with specific case scenarios.
- There are six scenarios based on specific learning objectives, and five of those focus on one of the special populations presented in the Provider Manual

- Each scenario also includes a list of discussion points. These points are unique to each scenario and are intended for small group discussion and additional learning. It is expected that all learners will contribute to the discussion.

- The instructor will guide the learner through the scenario, answer questions, help the learner to perfect their skills, and will provide additional information as requested by the learner

- During the primary and secondary survey, the learner is expected to evaluate the effectiveness of interventions that are likely to have an immediate effect on the patient (auscultation of breath sounds after intubation)

TNP Testing Principles

For the TNP testing station, evaluation will follow these principles:

- Each learner will be evaluated individually at one TNP testing station. The learner is cautioned about attempting to memorize any specific teaching scenario as a new scenario is used.

- Any starred criteria must be performed for successful completion of the skill station

- The double-starred criteria (**) are performed within the priority element. This means that double-starred criteria (**) are completed in order before moving to the next step.

  - These criteria usually represent a critical assessment step or an intervention as a response to a life-threat identified within the primary assessment

  - If at the end of the primary survey, any double-starred criteria (**) have been missed, the instructor will end the evaluation, review the process, and refer the learner to the course director for further instruction and retesting, if applicable.

- The single-starred criteria (*) are essential skill steps and are expected to be performed during the skill station demonstration but their sequence is not critical

- For successful completion, all double-starred criteria (**) must be demonstrated in order, all single-starred criteria (*) must be completed, and demonstration of 70% of total points/steps is required

- During evaluation, the instructor will answer specific questions and provide assessment data but is not allowed to provide prompts

- The learner is expected to state and/or demonstrate both criteria if two criteria are listed with an **AND** (auscultates breath sounds **AND** heart tones; inspects **AND** palpates the head **AND** face)

- The learner is expected to demonstrate appropriate assessment techniques (auscultation and palpation)

  - It is not acceptable for the learner to state, "I would palpate the abdomen," without actually touching the model

  - The correct method to auscultate breath sounds is dependent on whether the patient is intubated or not

    - If the patient is not intubated, lung fields are immediately auscultated

    - If the patient is intubated, watch for rise and fall of the chest while listening over the epigastrium and auscultate the lung fields

- During the teaching scenarios, if a step asks for a specific number of required elements, once the learner has assessed for the required number, all the response information will be given by the instructor

  - However, during testing, only information requested and assessed will be provided

  - If the learner does not state the required number of elements, the instructor may not prompt the learner to provide the additional number or required steps

Trauma Nursing Process Skill Station

Prehospital Report

The teaching station begins with the scenario or prehospital report provided using the **MIST** mnemonic:

- **M**echanism of injury

- **I**njuries sustained

- **S**igns and symptoms in the field

- **T**reatment in the field

Across-the-room Observation

The across-the-room observation is the first look as the patient arrives in the trauma room. Uncontrolled hemorrhage is a major preventable cause of death in the trauma patient, and this is the first of several identified steps to evaluate for that hemorrhage. This step allows immediate assessment for uncontrolled external bleeding and the opportunity to decide if this patient requires reprioritizing to <C>ABC.

Primary Survey

The goal of the primary survey is to identify life-threatening situations and rapidly intervene. The elements assessed during the primary survey include:

- Airway and alertness with simultaneous cervical spinal stabilization

- Breathing and ventilation

- Circulation and Control of hemorrhage

- Disability (neurologic status)

- Exposure and Environmental Control

These elements are critical in nature, and any deviations from baseline require immediate intervention. The severity of the patient's condition may require simultaneous assessment and intervention. The process is prioritized and systematic; therefore, any life-threatening situations need to be completed in the current element before moving on to the next (B is not assessed until A is addressed, and so on).

Resuscitation Adjuncts to the Primary Survey (FG)

These adjuncts are assessments and diagnostics to assure that all life threats are identified and a baseline is established for trending and ongoing reassessment.

- Full set of vital signs and family presence

- Get resuscitation adjuncts

  ○ Laboratory studies to include, but not limited to arterial blood gases and a specimen for blood type and crossmatch

  ○ Monitor for continuous cardiac rate and rhythm assessment

  ○ Naso- or orogastric tube consideration

  ○ Oxygenation and ventilation assessment, including pulse oximetry and capnography, if indicated

  ○ Pain assessment and management, including the use of an appropriate, validated pain scale with nonpharmacologic and pharmacologic interventions combined for optimal management of traumatic pain. For patients who have been intubated using rapid sequence intubation (RSI), pain response will be indeterminate. Pain is assumed to be present based on mechanism of injury and is treated accordingly.

  ○ Note: The placement of a urinary catheter is not included here as in previous editions. With the risk of catheter-associated urinary tract infections, the insertion of a urinary catheter has been deprioritized and, if indicated, is addressed in the perineum and pelvis section of the head-to-toe assessment.

Reevaluation

This step of reevaluation is included to determine if any findings from the primary survey raise suspicion for uncontrolled internal hemorrhage, the need for emergency surgical intervention, or transport to a trauma center. If so, the arrangements can begin. Additionally, with the suspicion of uncontrolled internal hemorrhage, a portable radiograph of the pelvis or a focused assessment with sonography for trauma (FAST) may be performed at this time in order to expedite additional interventions aimed at the control of internal hemorrhage.

Secondary Survey (HI)

The goal of the secondary survey is to identify all injuries in order to determine priorities for the planning/outcomes and implementation phases of the nursing process.

- History: This can be additional information from prehospital providers, information generated by the patient or family regarding the traumatic event, and/or past medical history.

- Head-to-toe assessment: Once the primary assessment is complete and immediately life-threatening conditions have been identified and treated, the head-to-toe assessment is an organized, detailed review of systems, using the assessment concepts of inspection, auscultation, and palpation. Priority is also given to any injuries found in the secondary survey that have the potential to compromise the airway, breathing, circulation, disability (neurologic status), or exposure/environmental control.

Reevaluation Adjuncts to the Secondary Survey

Reevaluation adjuncts are diagnostic studies and interventions that supplement the clinical assessment in the secondary survey, confirm findings, or rule out other possible injuries in preparation for the reevaluation phase. Additionally, important nursing interventions for stabilization and planning for post resuscitation care are included at this point.

Reevaluation and Post Resuscitation Care

At this point, the patient is evaluated for response to and the effectiveness of interventions. Identification of outcomes, planning, and implementation continue, and reevaluation of the primary survey, vital signs, pain, and all injuries is ongoing. Post resuscitation care is continued until disposition of the patient to definitive care.

Definitive Care or Transfer

Consideration is given to all assessment criteria, identified injuries, response to interventions, and standardized transfer criteria as the decision is made for definitive care and/or transfer.

Overview of Skill Station Video Demonstration

Objectives

1. Identify indications for intubation in the trauma patient.
2. Perform assessment of the head and neck, identifying potential injuries.

Prehospital MIST Report

- An ambulance is en route with a 22 year old unhelmeted motorcyclist who struck an automobile at 45 mph (72.4 kph)
- The patient is arousable, but confused
- Blood pressure of 112/60 mm Hg, pulse of 72 beats/min, and she has spontaneous respirations of 14 breaths/min
- She is in full cervical spinal immobilization on a spine board
- She has one large-caliber intravenous catheter with isotonic crystalloid solution infusing, and oxygen is being administered via a nonrebreather mask

The patient has just arrived in the trauma room. Please begin your initial assessment.

Skill Steps	Instructor Responses	Demonstrated Yes	No
Preparation and Triage			
1. States the need to activate the trauma team	*"The trauma team is activated."*	_____	_____
2. States the need to prepare the trauma room • Rapid infuser • Chest trauma equipment	*"Preparation is complete."*	_____	_____
3. States the need to don personal protective equipment (PPE)	*"PPE has been donned by the team."*	_____	_____
Across-the-room Observation			
4. Assesses for obvious uncontrolled external hemorrhage	*"There is no uncontrolled external hemorrhage and no need to consider reprioritizing to <C>ABC."*	_____	_____

Skill Steps	Instructor Responses	Demonstrated	
		Yes	**No**
Primary Survey			
Airway and Alertness with Simultaneous Cervical Spinal Stabilization			
5. Assess level of consciousness using AVPU	*"The patient responds to verbal stimuli by opening eyes but is unable to follow commands."*	** _____	_____
6. States the need for a second person to provide manual cervical spinal stabilization **AND** demonstrates manual opening of the airway using the jaw-thrust maneuver	*"Manual cervical spinal stabilization is being provided. Please demonstrate your opening of the airway."*	** _____	_____
7. Demonstrates and describes techniques for determining the patency and protection of the airway, using inspection, auscultation, and palpation (identifies at least **FOUR**): • Is the tongue obstructing? • Are there any loose or missing teeth? • Are there any foreign objects? • Is there any blood, vomitus, or other secretions? • Is there any edema? • Is there any snoring, gurgling, or stridor?	• *"There is no tongue obstruction."* • *"There are no loose or missing teeth."* • *"No foreign objects are noted."* • *"There is no bleeding, vomitus, or other secretions."* • *"There is no edema."* • *"Snoring is heard when the jaw-thrust is released.* • *No gurgling or stridor is heard."*	** _____	_____
8. States the need for oropharyngeal airway (OPA)	*"The OPA has been placed."*	** _____	_____
9. States the need for a definitive airway	*"The team is gathering equipment to begin intubation. Please continue your assessment."*	_____	_____
10. Reassesses the airway after insertion of OPA	*"No snoring is heard. The airway is now patent."*	_____	_____

The double starred (**) criteria are performed within the priority element. This means that double starred (**) criteria are completed in order before moving to the next step. The single starred criteria (*) are essential skill steps and are expected to be performed during the skill station demonstration but their sequence is not critical.

Skill Steps	Instructor Responses	Demonstrated	
		Yes	No
Breathing and Ventilation			
11. Demonstrates and describes techniques for determining breathing effectiveness, using components of inspection, auscultation, and palpation (identifies at least **FOUR**): • Is there spontaneous breathing? • Is there symmetrical chest rise? • What are the depth, pattern, and rate of respirations? • Is there increased work of breathing? • What is the skin color? • Are there open wounds or deformities? Is there subcutaneous emphysema? • Is there any tracheal deviation or jugular venous distention? • Are breath sounds present and equal?	• *"Breathing is spontaneous."* • *"Chest rise is symmetrical and shallow."* • *"Respirations are very slow and shallow."* • *"There are no signs of increased work of breathing."* • *"The skin is pale."* • *"No open wounds are noted. There is no subcutaneous emphysema. The chest wall is intact."* • *"There is no tracheal deviation or jugular venous distention."* • *"Breath sounds are diminished."*	****** _____	_____
12. States the need for assisted ventilation with bag-valve mask device	*"Ventilations are being assisted."* **NOTE: If the learner has stated the need for assisted ventilation with placement of the OPA it is not considered out of order.**	****** _____	_____
The patient has just been intubated using rapid sequence intubation. What is your next step?			

The double starred (**) criteria are performed within the priority element. This means that double starred (**) criteria are completed in order before moving to the next step. The single starred criteria (*) are essential skill steps and are expected to be performed during the skill station demonstration but their sequence is not critical.

Skill Steps	Instructor Responses	Demonstrated	
		Yes	**No**
13. Assesses endotracheal tube placement (uses correct sequence below): • Attaches a carbon dioxide (CO_2) detector • Observes for rise and fall of the chest. Auscultates over the epigastrium **AND** then bilateral breath sounds. • After 5 or 6 breaths, observes the CO_2 detector for evidence of CO_2 in exhaled air • Assesses for improvement in skin color	• *"A CO_2 detector is attached."* • *"Chest rises and falls with ventilation. No gurgling is heard over the epigastrium. Breath sounds are equal bilaterally."* • *"After 5 or 6 breaths, there is positive evidence for CO_2 indicating the tube is correctly in the trachea."* • *"The skin color improves."* **NOTE: If the learner chooses a capnography sensor, give credit for this in Oxygenation and capnography in Get Resuscitation Adjuncts.** **NOTE: If the learner states the need to insert a gastric tube, it can be done here without penalty for order. Give credit in resuscitation adjuncts.**	** _____	_____
14. States the need to assess endotracheal tube (ETT) position by noting the number at the teeth **AND** secures the ETT; identifying the method used	*"The ETT is secure; the number at the teeth is documented."*		
15. States the need to begin mechanical ventilation or continues assisted ventilation	*"Ventilations continue."*		

The double starred (**) criteria are performed within the priority element. This means that double starred (**) criteria are completed in order before moving to the next step. The single starred criteria (*) are essential skill steps and are expected to be performed during the skill station demonstration but their sequence is not critical.

Skill Steps	Instructor Responses	Demonstrated	
		Yes	No
Circulation and Control of Hemorrhage			
16. Demonstrates and describes techniques for determining the adequacy of circulation, using components of inspection, auscultation, and palpation (identifies **ALL THREE**) • Inspects for any uncontrolled hemorrhage • Palpates a central pulse • Inspects and palpates the skin for color, temperature, and moisture	• *"There is no uncontrolled external bleeding."* • *"The central pulse is present and strong."* • *"Skin is normal colored, warm and dry."*	** _____	_____
17. Assesses the patency of prehospital intravenous line	*"The prehospital IV line is patent."*	_____	_____
18. States the need to place an additional large-caliber IV catheter	*"An additional catheter is placed."* **NOTE: If the learner elects to obtain blood samples for typing, credit is given in reevaluation adjuncts.**	** _____	_____
19. States the need for administration of warmed, isotonic crystalloid with blood tubing **AND** at a **CONTROLLED RATE**	*"Warmed, isotonic crystalloid solution is infusing via blood tubing at a controlled rate."*	_____	_____
Disability (Neurologic Status)			
20. Describes the assessment for the Glasgow Coma Scale (GCS) score • What is the best eye opening? • Best verbal response? • Best motor response?	• *"There is no eye opening." (1)* • *"There is no verbal response." (1)* • *"The patient localizes to painful stimuli." (5)* • *"GCS score is 7."*	** _____	_____
21. Assesses pupils	*"Pupils are equal, round, and sluggishly reactive to light."*	_____	_____
22. States the need for computed tomography (CT) of the head and cervical spine	*"CT scan has been ordered, and radiology has been notified to expect the patient."*	** _____	_____

The double starred (**) criteria are performed within the priority element. This means that double starred (**) criteria are completed in order before moving to the next step. The single starred criteria (*) are essential skill steps and are expected to be performed during the skill station demonstration but their sequence is not critical.

Skill Steps	Instructor Responses	Demonstrated	
		Yes	No
Exposure and Environmental Control			
23. States the need to remove all clothing **AND** inspect for uncontrolled bleeding or obvious injuries	*"Clothing is removed. Multiple abrasions and contusions are noted on the face."*	** _____	_____
24. States the need to keep the patient warm by (identifies at least **ONE**): • Blankets • Warming lights • Increased room temperature • Warmed fluids • Warmed oxygen	*"A warming method has been applied."*	_____	_____

NOTE: If learner did not intervene to correct life-threatening findings in the primary survey and/or did not complete all double-starred criteria, stop the station, review purpose of the primary survey and notify the course coordinator.

Skill Steps	Instructor Responses	Demonstrated	
Resuscitation Adjuncts			
Full Set of Vital Signs			
25. Obtain a full set of vital signs	• BP: 110/60 mm Hg • HR: 84 beats/min • RR: assisted at 12 breaths/min • T: 98°F (36.8°C)	_____	_____
Facilitate Family Presence			
26. States the need to facilitate family presence	*"The family has just arrived and the family presence liaison is preparing to bring them in."*	_____	_____
Get Resuscitation Adjuncts (LMNOP)			
27. States the need for **laboratory** analysis (blood typing, blood gases, and lactate)	*"Blood samples are sent to the laboratory for blood typing and arterial blood gases."*	_____	_____
28. Attaches patient to cardiac **monitor**	*"Electrocardiogram (ECG) shows normal sinus rhythm with no ectopy."*	_____	_____

The double starred (**) criteria are performed within the priority element. This means that double starred (**) criteria are completed in order before moving to the next step. The single starred criteria (*) are essential skill steps and are expected to be performed during the skill station demonstration but their sequence is not critical.

Skill Steps	Instructor Responses	Demonstrated	
		Yes	No
Get Resuscitation Adjuncts (LMNOP) Continued			
29. States the need to consider insertion of a **naso- or orogastric tube**	*"Nasogastric tube may be contraindicated given the possible head injury; an orogastric tube is inserted."*	_____	_____
30. Attaches patient to pulse **oximetry AND capnography**	• *"SpO$_2$: 98%"* • *"Capnography value within normal limits."*	_____	_____
31. States the need to assess **pain** using an appropriate pain scale	*"The patient's pain is indeterminate due to RSI. Assume pain is present based on MOI and identified injuries."*	*_____	_____
32. Gives appropriate nonpharmacologic comfort measure (identifies at least **ONE**): • Apply ice to swollen areas • Repositioning • Padding over bony prominences • Other, as appropriate	*"Nonpharmacologic interventions have been instituted."*	_____	_____
33. States the need to consider obtaining order for analgesic medication	*"An appropriate dose of analgesia has been ordered and administered."*	_____	_____
Secondary Survey			
History			
34. States the pertinent history to be obtained (identifies at least **ONE**): • MIST • Past medical history	• *"No additional information is obtained from prehospital providers."* • *"Family states she has no relevant medical history."*	_____	_____

The double starred (**) criteria are performed within the priority element. This means that double starred (**) criteria are completed in order before moving to the next step. The single starred criteria (*) are essential skill steps and are expected to be performed during the skill station demonstration but their sequence is not critical.

Skill Steps	Instructor Responses	Demonstrated	
		Yes	No
Head-to-toe Assessment			
NOTE: Learner describes and demonstrates the head-to-toe assessment by describing appropriate inspection techniques and demonstrating appropriate auscultation and palpation techniques.			
35. Inspects **AND** palpates head **AND** face for injuries	*"Multiple abrasions and contusions to face are noted. No other abnormalities are noted."*	_____	_____
36. Inspects **AND** palpates neck for injuries; demonstrating removal **AND** replacement of cervical collar for assessment	*"I will maintain cervical spinal stabilization while you perform your assessment."* *"There is a step-off deformity and crepitus is palpated at C4–C6."*	_____	_____
37. Inspects **AND** palpates chest for injuries	*"No abnormalities are noted."*	_____	_____
38. Auscultates breath sounds **AND** heart sounds	*"Breath sounds are clear and equal bilaterally, and heart sounds are normal."*	_____	_____
39. Inspects the abdomen **AND** flanks for injuries	*"No abnormalities are noted."*	_____	_____
40. Auscultates bowel sounds	*"Bowel sounds are present in all four quadrants."*	_____	_____
41. Palpates all four quadrants of the abdomen for injuries	*"No abnormalities are noted."*	_____	_____
42. Inspects the pelvis **AND** perineum for injuries	*"No abnormalities are noted."*	_____	_____
43. Applies gentle pressure over iliac crests downward and medially	*"There is no instability noted."*	_____	_____
44. Applies gentle pressure on the symphysis pubis	*"There is no instability noted."*	_____	_____
45. States the need to assess for indications and contraindications for placement of a urinary catheter	*"A urinary catheter is indicated for intake and output. There are no contraindications. A catheter is placed with clear, yellow urine obtained."*	_____	_____
46. Inspects **AND** palpates all four extremities for neurovascular status and injuries	• *"Assessment of sensation and motor function is deferred after RSI."* • *"Pulses are strong in all four extremities. Color, temperature and warmth are normal in all four extremities."*	_____	_____

The double starred (**) criteria are performed within the priority element. This means that double starred (**) criteria are completed in order before moving to the next step. The single starred criteria (*) are essential skill steps and are expected to be performed during the skill station demonstration but their sequence is not critical.

Skill Steps	Instructor Responses	Demonstrated	
		Yes	No
Posterior Surfaces			
47. States the need to maintain manual cervical and spinal stabilization to turn patient for posterior assessment	*"The team maintains spinal stabilization for assessment of posterior surfaces."*	*_____	_____
48. Inspects **AND** palpates posterior surfaces	*"No abnormalities are noted."*	_____	_____
49. States the need to consider removal of spine board	*"The spine board has been removed."*	_____	_____
Reevaluation Adjuncts			
NOTE: The learner summarizes injuries identified, listed below, throughout the scenario. If the learner has not already identified them all, ask for any additional noted at this time.			
50. Identify all simulated injuries	• Possible head injury • Possible cervical spinal injury (CSI) • Facial abrasions and contusions	_____	_____
"What reevaluation adjuncts will you expect for this patient?"			
51. States the need for reevaluation adjuncts (identifies at least **THREE**): • Cervical spinal CT scan or radiograph • Chest radiograph or CT scan • Abdominal CT scan • Pelvic radiograph • Revised trauma score • Clean and dress wounds • Tetanus immunization		_____	_____
"What findings will you reevaluate?"			
52. States the need to reevaluate primary assessment		_____	_____
53. States the need to reevaluate vital signs		_____	_____
54. States the need to reevaluate pain		_____	_____
55. States the need to reevaluate all identified injuries and effectiveness of interventions		_____	_____

The double starred (**) criteria are performed within the priority element. This means that double starred (**) criteria are completed in order before moving to the next step. The single starred criteria (*) are essential skill steps and are expected to be performed during the skill station demonstration but their sequence is not critical.

Skill Steps	Instructor Responses	Demonstrated	
		Yes	No
"What is the definitive care for this patient?"			
56. Considers transfer to a trauma center or admission. Depending on the result of a CT of head or cervical spine, preparation for surgery may also be considered.		_____	_____

The double starred (**) criteria are performed within the priority element. This means that double starred (**) criteria are completed in order before moving to the next step. The single starred criteria (*) are essential skill steps and are expected to be performed during the skill station demonstration but their sequence is not critical.

Addendum:
Chapter 3 • Epidemiology

Gabrielle Lomas, RN, BSc (Hons), Jill Windle, RN, MSc, FRCN

Note: Data from the United Kingdom (UK) was unavailable at the time of original publication.

Introduction

In the UK, data on morbidity and mortality is collected in various ways across the four countries. It is therefore difficult to obtain accurate national statistics on injury figures owing to the separate collection of data for Scotland, Northern Ireland, England, and Wales. The Trauma Audit and Research Network (TARN) is the independent monitor of trauma care in England and Wales,[1] while the Scottish Trauma Audit Group (STAG)[2] collates similar information from all major trauma units in Scotland.

The Trauma Audit and Research Network is committed to making a real difference in the delivery of care to the injured. The data collected are used to promote improvements in care through a national comparative clinical audit that is used to inform and improve trauma care across the UK.

Incidence in the UK

Every year across England and Wales, 12,500 people die after being injured. Trauma is the leading cause of death among children and young adults, 44 years and under. In addition, there are many thousands who are left severely disabled.[1]

The Trauma Audit and Research Network reported the following common causes of traumatic death in 2014:[1]
- Falls < 2m (56.2%)
- Falls > 2m (17.1%)
- Motor vehicle collisions (15.4%)
- Assault (2%)
- Shooting and stabbing (1.7%)
- All other traumatic events (7.6%)

All included tables are provided by TARN and cover the year 2014.

Table 3-2 shows the distribution of life-threatening injuries according to body system. Head injuries remain the leading cause of death, with over half of all trauma deaths attributed to these injuries (55.8%). Chest injuries are the next most common presentation (26.1%), followed by spinal injuries (10.2%) and abdominal injuries (4.3%).

Table 3-2. Frequency of AIS (Abbreviated Injury Scale)

Group	Total	AIS 3 + Injury N (% of total)			
		Head	Chest	Abdomen	Spine
All patients	49531	13203 (26.7%)	9453 (19.1%)	1838 (3.7%)	4622 (9.3%)
Deaths	2941	1642 (55.8%)	769 (26.1%)	127 (4.3%)	299 (10.2%)

Patients may appear in more than one category, so rows may add up to more than 100%

Human Characteristics

Age

Although the greatest number of trauma injuries occurs in ages 15 to 54, the highest death rate is for those over the age of 75. The elderly population is less likely to recover from injury, with co-morbidities playing a part in poor outcomes for many of these patients.

When analyzing deaths by age and mechanism of injury, the leading cause of death for ages 15 to 44 remains that of motor vehicle collisions. In the 75-years-plus age group, however, the most common mechanism is falls of < 2m.[1] (Table 3-3)

Gender

There are differences in male and female injury death rates depending on the cause of the injury. Overall death rate from injuries is twice as high for males as females. Exposure to the injury-producing event, the amount of risk involved, occupation, and cultural norms are possible reasons for the gender differences.

Alcohol

The number of alcohol-related deaths in England and Wales has continued to rise year on year. The number of male deaths increased from 4,439 in 2010 to 4,518 in 2011 and the number of female deaths increased from 2,230 in 2010 to 2,405 in 2011. More men than women died from each of the causes directly related to alcohol except for chronic hepatitis, where the reverse was true.[3]

2014 TARN data demonstrate that alcohol-related causes accounted for 13.1% of trauma patients and 8.6% of the deaths.[1] See Table 3-4.

Table 3-3. Death by Age Band and Mechanism

Age	Total	Mechanism N (% of total)					
		RTC	Fall≥ 2m.	Fall≤ 2m.	Shooting/ stabbing	Blow(s)	Other
<1	8	0 (0%)	0 (0%)	1 (12.5%)	0 (0%)	1 (12.5%)	6 (75%)
1-4	17	5 (29.4%)	0 (0%)	0 (0%)	0 (0%)	1 (5.9%)	11 (64.7%)
5-14	21	11 (52.4%)	1 (4.8%)	0 (0%)	1 (4.8%)	0 (0%)	8 (38.1%)
15-24	147	81 (55.1%)	10 (6.8%)	2 (1.4%)	20 (13.6%)	4 (2.7%)	30 (20.4%)
25-34	148	69 (46.6%)	19 (12.8%)	8 (5.4%)	10 (6.8%)	9 (6.1%)	33 (22.3%)
35-44	123	33 (26.8%)	27 (22%)	18 (14.6%)	6 (4.9%)	10 (8.1%)	29 (23.6%)
45-54	181	43 (23.8%)	37 (20.4%)	44 (24.3%)	4 (2.2%)	10 (5.5%)	43 (23.8%)
55-64	219	35 (16%)	66 (30.1%)	88 (40.2%)	4 (1.8%)	6 (2.7%)	20 (9.1%)
65-74	328	50 (15.2%)	89 (27.1%)	162 (49.4%)	3 (0.9%)	6 (1.8%)	18 (5.5%)
75-84	757	69 (9.1%)	137 (18.1%)	529 (69.9%)	1 (0.1%)	8 (1.1%)	13 (1.7%)
≥85	992	56 (5.6%)	118 (11.9%)	800 (80.6%)	2 (0.2%)	3 (0.3%)	13 (1.3%)
Total	2941	452 (15.4%)	504 (17.1%)	1652 (56.2%)	51 (1.7%)	58 (2%)	224 (7.6%)

RTC: Road traffic collision.

Table 3-4. Frequency of Alcohol at Point of Injury

Group	Total	Alcohol N (% of total)	
		At incident	**As PMC**
All Patients	49531	6494 (13.1%)	3495 (7.1%)
Deaths	2941	254 (8.6%)	216 (7.3%)

There are strict alcohol limits for drivers, but the limits in Scotland were reduced in 2014, resulting in non-uniform levels across the UK.[4] See Table 3-5.

Table 3-5. Level of Alcohol

Level of Alcohol	England, Wales, and Northern Ireland	Scotland
Mcg/100 mL of breath	35	22
Mg/100 mL of blood	80	50
Mg/100 mL of urine	107	67

Substance Misuse

There is growing recognition that the use of illegal substances, either with or without alcohol ingestion, is a factor related to trauma deaths. The true picture of deaths as a result of substance abuse is difficult to capture and calculate. From March 2015, police in England will be able to carry out random roadside drug testing as a routine feature of traffic policing.[4]

Suicide

The Office of National Statistics[5] shows that 6,233 suicides of people aged 15 and over were registered in the UK in 2013, representing a 4% increase from 2012 (252 more suicide deaths). The UK suicide rate was 11.9 deaths per 100,000 people in 2013. The male suicide rate was more than three times higher than the female rate, with 19.0 male deaths per 100,000 compared with 5.1 female deaths.

The male suicide rate in 2013 was the highest since 2001. The lowest male rate since the beginning of the data series was 16.6 per 100,000 in 2007. Female rates have stayed relatively constant since 2007. The highest UK suicide rate in 2013 by broad age group was 25.1 per 100,000 in men aged 45 to 59, the highest for that age group since 1981. The most common method of suicide in the UK in 2013 was reported as 'hanging, strangulation, and suffocation,' accounting for 56.1% of male suicides and 40.2% of female suicides.[5]

Violence

Violence in British society is increasing. According to TARN data, however, only 3.1% of trauma deaths are attributed to violent episodes, including penetrating trauma, knife/gunshot wound, and non-accidental injury (Table 3-6).

The increasing incidence of violence in the UK is a cause for concern for both the general public and government. The risks and predetermining factors that need to be investigated include gang culture, lack of nonviolent male role models, drug culture, and unemployment.

Table 3-6. Breakdown by Intent

Group	Total	Injury Intent N (% of total)			
		Non-intentional	**Alleged Assault, inc. NAI**	**Suspected Self-harm**	**Other, inc. Sport**
All patients	49531	42911 (86.6%)	2672 (5.4%)	883 (1.8%)	3065 (6.2%)
Deaths	2941	2570 (87.4%)	91 (3.1%)	174 (5.9%)	106 (3.6%)

Injury Prevention

Across the UK there are well established safety intervention practices to ensure cycle safety, especially for children, with courses on road safety and promotion of helmet wearing. Seat-belt wearing has been mandatory since 1983. Children must use the appropriate child restraint for their weight when travelling in the front or back seat of any car, van, or goods vehicle. 'Child restraint' means any baby seat, child seat, booster seat, or booster cushion. Children can use an adult belt when they reach 135cm or their 12th birthday, whichever comes first.[6]

Safe Drive Stay Alive

Around 1 in 4 road deaths occur among drivers aged 17–24. Young drivers are much more likely to be involved in a collision on the roads, often due to inexperience and a lack of knowledge of the risks. Since 2004, the number of people under the age of 25 killed in car collisions has fallen by nearly three quarters, but there is still more to do. The Safe Drive Stay Alive initiative is produced by a road safety partnership including police forces, hospitals, local councils, and emergency services. Each partner has been working for years to reduce the number of people dying on the roads, with over 130,000 young people having attended a Safe Drive presentation by the end of 2013. Through a combination of roads policing, road safety education, engineering measures, and speed-limit enforcement, road collision victims killed or seriously injured fell to an all-time low by the end of 2014. A disproportionate number of these remain young, inexperienced drivers. This is why The Safe Drive Stay Alive campaign focuses on reaching new and pre-drivers in an emotive and hard-hitting way, influencing behavior and attitude on the roads.[7]

Acknowledgement

The authors would like to acknowledge the Trauma Audit and Research Network (TARN) group, UK, for providing the relevant data.

References

1. Trauma Audit & Research Network (TARN). (2014). Retrieved from https://www.tarn.ac.uk

2. The Scottish Trauma Audit Group (STAG). (2005). Retrieved from http://www.stag.scot.nhs.uk/index.htm

3. Office for National Statistics.(2015). *Alcohol-related deaths in the United Kingdom, registered in 2013*. Retrieved from http://www.ons.gov.uk/ons/dcp171778_394878.pdf

4. Department for Transport. (2014). *Drink driving*. Retrieved from http://think.direct.gov.uk/drink-driving.html

5. Office for National Statistics. (2015). *Suicides in the United Kingdom, 2013 registrations*. Retrieved from http://www.ons.gov.uk/ons/rel/subnational-health4/suicides-in-the-united-kingdom/2013-registrations/index.html

6. Department for Transport. (2014). *Child car seats and safety belts*. Retrieved from http://think.direct.gov.uk/education/early-years-and-primary/parents/3-to-5s/child-car-seats-and-safety-belts/

7. Safe Drive Stay Alive campaign website. (2015). Retrieved from: http://www.safedrive.org.uk/

Index

Axis, 177, 183

Musculoskeletal injuries
    concurrent injuries, 195
    delayed and commonly missed, 332
    fractures, 195, 196–197, 244, 288
    indicating potential abuse, 288
    mechanisms, 195
    nursing care, 199–202
    pathophysiology, 196
    pediatric patients, 245
    post resuscitation care, 341–342
    selected types, 196–199
Musculoskeletal system
    anatomy and physiology review, 193–194
    effects of aging, 263
    mechanisms of injury, 195
    obesity's effects, 272, 275
    pain's effects on, 97
    pregnancy's effects on, 227
Mustard gas exposure, 318
Mustargen, 318
Myocardial contractility, 138
Myocardial infarction, 74
Myocardium, blunt injuries to, 140, 335
Myoglobinuria
    from burn trauma, 220
    from damaged muscles, 198
    interventions, 201, 220

N

N-acetylcysteine, 170
Nalbuphine, 98
Naloxone, 118
Naproxen, 98
Narcan, 118
Nasogastric tubes
    for bariatric patients, 279
    pediatric trauma patients, 241
    as resuscitation adjuncts, 47
    in skill station evaluation, 356
Nasopharyngeal airways, 43, 62
Nasopharynx anatomy, 55
Nasotracheal intubation, 63
National Acute Spinal Cord Injury Study, 188
National Council on Aging, 11
National Emergency X-Radiography Utilization Study, 188, 191, 244
National Highway Traffic Safety Administration, 11
National Incident Management System, 312
National Organ Procurement and Transplantation Network, 301
National Strategy for Injury Prevention (Canada), 17
National Trauma Registry (Canada), 18
Natural disasters, 317. *See also* Disaster management

Near-infrared spectroscopy, 201, 202
Neck anatomy, 55–57, 138–139
Neck injuries
    concurrent injuries, 140, 141
    initial assessment, 49
    nursing care, 141–143
    selected types, 143–144
Needle decompression placement, 149
Needle pericardiocentesis, 147
Needle thoracentesis, 145
Neglect, 285, 288–289
Neospinothalamic tract, 91
Nerve agents, 318
Nerve plexuses, 175–176
Nerves
    of bones, 194, 196
    cranial, 106, 124
    of larynx, 57
    spinal, 173–176
    of stomach, 152
    of upper limbs, 139, 140
Nervous system
    anatomy, 91
    delayed and commonly missed injuries, 332
    effects of aging, 263
    effects of radiation exposure, 322
Nervous tissue, 193
Netherlands, trauma epidemiology, 18–19
Neurogenic shock
    causes, 75
    hypovolemic shock versus, 186
    post resuscitation care, 338
    spinal shock versus, 180
    vascular system response, 181
Neurologic status
    assessing in older adults, 264
    assessing in shock patients, 83
    assessing with brain injuries, 110, 111, 112
    assessing with spinal cord injuries, 186
    deterioration with epidural hematoma, 114
    initial assessment and intervention, 45–46
    monitoring, 333
    pediatric trauma patients, 239
    skill station evaluation, 354
Neuromatrix theory of pain, 93
Neuromuscular blocking agents, 67, 70
Neurons, 91
Neuropathic pain, 94
Neuroplasticity theory, 93
Neutrophil accumulation, 77
Newton's Laws of Motion, 26
NEXUS criteria, 188, 191, 244
Nitrogen mustard gas, 318
Nitroglycerin, 266

S

Sacral nerves, 175
Sacral plexus, 176
Sacral sparing, 182–183, 187
Sacral vertebrae, 177
Safe care
  bariatric patients, 280
  elements of, 40
  pediatric patients, 235, 248, 253
  for victims of violence, 286
Safe practice, 39
SafeKids Worldwide, 11
Safety belts. *See* Seatbelts
Safety plans, 286
Sarin, 318
SBAR strategy, 7
SBIRT approach to intervention, 12
Scalds, 211, 212
Scalene muscles, 58
Scalp anatomy, 105
SCALP mnemonic, 105
School-aged children, 252
Sclera, 123, 128
Scrotum, 153, 165
Seatbelts
  abdominal injuries from, 159, 164
  energy distribution, 34
  forces on body tissues, 29, 30
  Swedish laws, 22
Second impact syndrome, 115
Second Law of Motion (Newton), 26
Secondary blast injuries, 33, 34
Secondary brain injury, 108
Secondary injury prevention measures, 10
Secondary spinal cord injuries, 180–181
Secondary surveys
  with abdominal injuries, 159
  bariatric patients, 279–280
  with brain injuries, 112–113
  burn trauma, 218–219
  elements of, 47–51
  eye injuries, 125
  musculoskeletal trauma, 199
  older adults, 265–267
  pediatric trauma patients, 241–244
  psychosocial assessments, 296
  skill station evaluation, 349
  with spinal cord injuries, 186–187
  surface trauma, 208
Secondary traumatic stress
  elements of, 301, 302
  evaluation tools, 308, 309
Secondary wound closure, 210

Sedation, 67, 69–70, 99–101. *See also* Medications
Seidel test, 128
Self-awareness, 304
Self-inflicted injuries, 16
Self-reports of pain, 95–96
Sensorimotor period, 250
Sensory pathways, 174–175
Sepsis, 163, 341
Septic shock, 75, 338
Serous fluid, 151
Serum D-dimer test, 336
Sesamoid bones, 194
Severe traumatic brain injuries, 115
Sexual assault nurse examiners, 285, 289
Sexual violence, 285–286, 289–291
Sexually transmitted infections, 291
Shearing strength of tissues, 27
Shock
  classification and etiology, 73–75
  current management strategies, 80–81
  defined, 73
  emerging trends in treatment, 85
  nursing care, 82–84
  pathophysiologic responses, 76–78
  post resuscitation care, 338
  reevaluations, 84–85
  with spinal cord injuries, 180, 181
  stages, 78–79
Shooting injuries. *See* Firearm injuries
Short bones, 193
Short-acting barbiturates, 70
Shotguns, 32
Simple pneumothorax, 144–145
Simple sensations, 175
Simple Triage And Rapid Treatment (START), 314, 315, 316
Sinuses, 56
Six P's of compartment syndrome, 198, 200
Skeletal muscle defined, 194
Skeletal system. *See* Bones; Musculoskeletal system
Skill stations. *See also* Interventions
  general principles, 3, 347–348
  overview of video demonstration, 350–359
  trauma nursing process behaviors evaluated, 348–349
Skin and soft-tissue trauma. *See* Burns; Integumentary system; Surface trauma
Skin color, 44, 61, 236
Skull anatomy, 56, 105
Skull fractures, 113, 114, 116. *See also* Head injuries
Skull series, 118
Sleep apnea, 270, 271, 273
Slit lamp examination, 128
Small bowel
  anatomy and physiology review, 152–153
  blunt and penetrating trauma, 160–161, 164

Notes

Notes

Notes

Notes

Notes

Notes